Grammar and Writing

TEACHER'S ANNOTATED EDITION GRADE 9

WITH TEACHER'S MANUAL

Macmillan Publishing Co., Inc.
866 Third Avenue, New York, N.Y. 10022
Collier Macmillan Publishers, London
Collier Macmillan Canada, Ltd.

Printed in the United States of America
ISBN 0-02-245890-5

Authors and Advisers

WALTER LOBAN, general adviser, has long been active in English education. He is professor of education at the University of California at Berkeley. Among Dr. Loban's scholarly publications in the area of language is *Teaching Language and Literature: Grades 7–12,* of which he is co-author. Dr. Loban's landmark study *Language Development: Kindergarten Through Grade 12* (NCTE: 1976) has provided unique and valuable information about the acquisition of syntactic elements by student writers.

DONALD C. FREEMAN, specialist in linguistics, has been professor of English and chairman of the committee on linguistics at Temple University, Philadelphia. He was formerly head of the department of linguistics at the University of Massachusetts (Amherst). His in-depth examination of student writing has made him a leader in the field of error analysis.

ROBERT W. REISING, specialist on grammar and composition, is professor of communicative arts at Pembroke State University, Pembroke, North Carolina. Dr. Reising has been involved in workshops on the teaching of advanced placement English courses, most recently at the University of North Carolina, at Charlotte.

JAMES HARKNESS, writer of "Libraries and Information," has had articles on the subject published by the *New York Times.* His fiction and essays appear in national magazines, and he is working on a book dealing with universal language.

VICKI JACOBS, contributor to the vocabulary section, has taught secondary school in Holbrook, Massachusetts, for several years. She is currently working on her doctorate at the Harvard Graduate School of Education.

ROBERT J. JONES, specialist on test taking, is chairman of the Humanities Department of College Board Programs at Educational Testing Service in Princeton, New Jersey. He has long been involved in design and development of standardized tests and writing assessment programs.

PATRICIA LAURENCE, specialist on composition, has taught basic writing, literature, and linguistics at City College of the City University of New York. Ms. Laurence's articles on writing have appeared in *Basic Writing* and *College English.*

SANDRA STOTSKY, developer of the vocabulary section, teaches at Curry College, Milton, Massachusetts, and works extensively with teachers in the Holbrook and Boston public schools. Dr. Stotsky's articles on vocabulary acquisition and sentence combining have been published in *Basic Writing* and *Research in the Teaching of English.*

Consultants

Martha Brooks, Abilene Independent School District, Abilene, Texas
Leslie MacIntyre, Homestead High School, Mequon, Wisconsin
Henry F. Mooney, Danvers Public Schools, Danvers, Massachusetts
Norman Rudnick, Miramonte High School, Orinda, California
Milton Schaeffer, Maplewood–South Orange School District, New Jersey
Mary Jo Wagner, Leland High School, San Jose, California

OVERVIEW OF THE GRAMMAR AND WRITING SERIES

Grammar and Writing provides secondary school students with (1) a firm foundation in grammar; (2) instruction, exercises, and assignments for the improvement of writing sentences, paragraphs, and complete compositions; and (3) information, instruction, and assignments in research, test taking, and editing. The contents of the student text for each grade are based on national curriculums. A teacher's edition like this one is available at each grade.

Each book in the series is designed to be both a reference handbook and a basic text. For use as a handbook, each of the sections of the text is self-contained, embracing a clearly defined area of the secondary curriculum, with rules and definitions keyed for reference. To form a basic text, the sections are presented in logical sequence and can be used in that sequence or as dictated by your student needs and your course requirements. Material within each section is arranged for sequential, developmental instruction.

There are few fundamental changes in content in these textbooks across the grades because (1) these textbooks are often used as handbooks—to which students turn seeking information that may be just as important at ninth grade as at twelfth grade; and (2) the spiral of skills and concepts in grammar and composition that is all-important in elementary grades has been completed. There are, however, differences across the grades in the extensiveness of material. Reading level and interest level are also adjusted from book to book, and you will also notice a different range of topics in the models and in exercises from grade to grade.

FEATURES OF THE TEACHER'S EDITION

Annotated full-sized student pages with

- answers in place for easy reference while teaching or correcting exercises
- annotations called "Extra's" that suggest additional exercises or activities

A Teacher's Manual that provides

- teaching strategies and methods
- different uses of the text for flexibility of content
- summaries of sections
- options for different ability groups and skill levels
- suggestions for reinforcing listening and speaking skills
- evaluation procedures and information for the teacher
- techniques for applying skills to standard forms, such as applications

CONTENTS OF TEACHER'S MANUAL

SPECIAL FEATURES OF THE TEXT

The following guide helps you to find examples of special features in this level of the student text.

FEATURE	PAGE
Grammar and Usage	
1. Drill items with controlled readability and high-interest content	4, 49
2. "Application" exercises that ask students to use parts of speech, phrases, and clauses in sentences of their own	8, 105
3. Tables, charts, and other graphic aids to clarify concepts	24, 54–55, 141
4. Additional exercises in the back of the student text for more practice	646
5. Special boxes relating grammar and writing:	
"Avoiding Errors" boxes to show students how to prevent and correct grammar and writing errors	11, 48
Punctuation boxes to introduce mechanics	91, 101
Spelling boxes to introduce spelling rules related to grammar	26
Word Study	
6. A Word List for Writers developed from the writings of professionals	281–288
7. Word pattern lists to help students build their vocabulary	271
8. List of frequently misspelled words	323–326
Sentences	
9. Hundreds of exercise items for composing sentences by using sentence-combining and sentence-completion techniques	198, 205, 207

FEATURE	PAGE

SECTION-BY-SECTION PREVIEW

GRAMMAR, USAGE, AND SENTENCES

WORD STUDY

WRITING AIDS

SPECIAL SECTION

COMPOSITION

RESOURCES

TESTS

SUMMARIES OF SECTIONS OF STUDENT TEXT

You will find the following items provided here for the sections of the student text:

- general introduction to the section, including the aims and objectives of the section
- list of special features
- points to preview (Items listed for each section will help you to present material in class.)

SECTION 1: Parts of Speech

In this ninth-grade book the purpose of Section 1 is to review or to introduce, with examples and exercises, terms and concepts of grammar called *parts of speech*. Although throughout the series examples and exercises reflect student development across the high school grades, the coverage of parts of speech remains much the same from grade to grade. One of the aims of this section in all grades is to help students to recognize parts of speech in a way that will be useful to them in discussing sentence composition (see Section 3).

All aspects of each part of speech are covered in this one section. Where points of usage are related to a part of speech, they are introduced here—again, as an aid to sentence composition.

Where we know that errors are likely to occur in applying the grammar of this section, we include cautionary examples and instruction in "Avoiding Errors" boxes. Points of spelling, punctuation, and capitalization are also included at the points where they apply to the grammar.

Secure diagnostic tests for this section appear on TM pp. 57–60.

SPECIAL FEATURES
- **"Applications"**: Although this section concentrates on re-

cognizing and differentiating the parts of speech, exercises labeled "Application" build on the need of students to put the parts of speech to work in sentences of their own.

- **"Avoiding Errors" boxes:** The "Avoiding Errors" boxes are part of a catching-classifying-and-correcting-errors system in the textbook. (See TM p. 21.) These boxes alert students to points of grammar that they have to remember if, as writers, they are going to profit from studying these parts of speech. Students will learn more rapidly to reduce the number of sentence-level errors in their writing if they view the error as a *negative* aspect of a *positive* rule or system. These errors are not, as many students must feel, arbitrary; they are failures to apply a system.

The "Avoiding Errors" boxes in Section 1 are as follows:

Avoiding Errors with Nouns (plurals, possessives), page 11

Avoiding Errors with the Present Progressive, page 28

Avoiding Errors with Verbs (General), page 36

Avoiding Errors with Adjectives for Comparison, page 48

Avoiding Errors with Personal Pronouns, pages 58–59

Avoiding Errors with Reflexive Pronouns, page 61

Avoiding Errors with Demonstrative Pronouns, page 63

Avoiding Errors with Interrogative Pronouns, page 64

Avoiding Errors with Relative Pronouns, page 67

Avoiding Errors with Adverbs, page 83

Avoiding Errors with Prepositions, page 89

Avoiding Errors with Coordinating Conjunctions, page 92

Avoiding Errors with Participles and Participial Phrases, page 102–103

- **Punctuation boxes:** The punctuation boxes that appear in appropriate positions throughout Section 1 supplement Section 7, "Capitalization and Punctuation," by providing simultaneous instruction in mechanics at the point of grammar instruction. The punctuation boxes in Section 1 are as follows:

Commas with Coordinating Conjunctions, page 91
Commas with Subordinating Conjunctions, page 97
Commas with Participles and Participial Phrases, page 101

- **Spelling boxes:** A number of common spelling rules are more closely related to grammar than most students realize: forming plurals of nouns, forming possessives of nouns, and forming tenses of verbs. Again, there are practical and theoretical advantages to introduce spelling rules at the point at which the grammar is studied. There are two spelling boxes in Section 1:

Spelling Present-Tense Verbs, page 26
Spelling Comparative and Superlative Forms of Adjectives, page 46

POINTS TO PREVIEW

- **Verbs:** Notice that modals can be studied as a kind of auxiliary, or "helping," verb, or they can be viewed separately.
- **Adjectives:** The meaning, or semantic aspect, of adjectives is introduced because of its use to a writer. In this text we want students not only to be able to recognize adjectives but also to be able to use adjectives in writing, to select them, to be aware of adjectives that are based on sense perception, and to recognize those that are value judgments.
- **Pronouns:** The chart on pages 54-55 shows all forms of all kinds of pronouns, providing an overview (and review) that puts each form in context. The chart is thus very helpful in discussing the peculiar problem of *case*.
- **Articles:** Articles are classified with determiners.
- **Determiners:** The term *determiner* is included in this section because it is a useful umbrella covering several parts of speech. The term covers *a(an)* and *the*, the indefinite and definite article, respectively, and other words that are used before nouns to "determine" (point to or limit) the noun but that are not true adjectives. Such words (*some, any, all, twenty-three, these*, and so on) cannot be considered true

adjectives for the following reasons: (1) They do not name the quality of a noun; (2) they cannot be used in the predicate as predicate adjectives (complements following *be*); (3) they cannot be used after a noun (you cannot say "Boy some drove by").

- **Verbals:** Verbals are treated in this section because, whether or not they are classified technically as parts of speech, they are a *kind* of word, and all kinds of words are a part of the writer's arsenal.

    Special attention is given to participles used as adjectives before nouns because they are an important tool to writers and are used naturally in speech by students.

SECTION 2: Parts of a Sentence

Section 2 has much the same aim as Section 1: to review or introduce for ninth-grade students concepts and terms that will be useful in discussing sentence composition. The prepositional phrase as subject complement and the object complement are not introduced until the upper grades.

Diagnostic tests for this section appear on TM pp. 60–61.

SPECIAL FEATURES

Section 2 also contains "Application" exercises, "Avoiding Errors" boxes, and punctuation boxes, as listed below. Annotated sentences show how the various parts of a sentence relate to one another and how the parts of speech introduced in Section 1 are used in parts of sentences.

- **"Applications":** While the main focus of this section is recognition of the parts of a sentence, students do get opportunities to practice manipulating sentence parts.

- **"Avoiding Errors" boxes:** The "Avoiding Errors" boxes in Section 2 are as follows:

    Avoiding Errors with Sentence Fragments, page 114
    Avoiding Errors with Subjects and Prepositional Phrases, page 121
    Avoiding Errors with Predicate Nominatives, page 146
    Avoiding Errors with Run-on Sentences, page 155

- **Punctuation boxes:** The punctuation boxes in Section 2 are as follows:

POINTS TO PREVIEW

- **Coverage of subject-verb agreement in all its variations,** pages 119–135
- **Diagraming:** Models of traditional diagraming and exercises are included on pages 172–182 as optional material.

SECTION 3: Writing Sentences

The section is essentially one of structured sentence composition. Each kind of sentence is explained, and examples are provided. Extensive exercises follow each explanation. The section can be viewed as having three parts:

1. expanding simple sentences
2. combining sentences to form complex, compound, and compound-complex sentences
3. writing clear sentences

With Sections 1 and 2 available for review and reference, Section 3 is set up for guidance and practice in the actual writing of sentences. It is not, however, necessary to use Sections 1 and 2 before moving into Section 3.

Here eight common kinds of simple sentences are used as a basis for sentence expansion. There are nine in the tenth-grade text, twelve in the eleventh-grade text, and thirteen in the twelfth-grade text.

SPECIAL FEATURES

- **"Word Banks":** Word Banks are provided for sentence-expanding assignments (e.g., page 187). The purpose of these banks is to provide students with content so that they can concentrate on *sentence structure*.

- **"Writing Clear Sentences":** A six-page feature at the end of the section includes exercises that give practice in eliminating errors that are difficult to categorize but that plague many student writers.

- **"Avoiding Errors" boxes:** There are two "Avoiding Errors" boxes in Section 3:

    Avoiding Errors When Joining Main Clauses, page 200
    Avoiding Errors with Participial Phrases, page 230

- **Punctuation boxes:** Immediate instruction on the conventional uses of punctuation is provided as students get in-depth drill in the writing of sentences. (This instruction is, of course, greatly expanded in Section 7, "Capitalization and Punctuation.") The punctuation boxes in Section 3 are as follows:

    Commas Between Main Clauses, page 195
    Punctuation with Conjunctive Adverbs, page 200
    Commas and Adverb Clauses, page 203
    Commas with Adjective Clauses, page 216

- **Sentence combining:** A methodology that has received much attention from the profession in the last twenty years has been sentence combining. Most teachers find that sentence combining can successfully be combined with other methods of presenting grammar. The way you use sentence-combining exercises depends on the needs of your students.

    Over the years a number of positive results have emerged from sentence combining that seem to hold true regardless of the format of the sentence-combining exercises. Here is a list of some of these results:

1. Students discover that they really do have some choice in the arrangement of their sentence structure.

2. They discover that one sentence can nest inside another—very often squarely between the subject and verb—and that the subject of that nested sentence can be a word like *who*, *which*, or *that*.

3. They discover that a whole sentence can function as a single word when it is moved to fill a SOMETHING slot in the main sentence.

4. They discover that a sentence ceases to be a sentence when they attach certain words to the front of it—words such as *when, after, although, who, which,* and *that.*

Most average and above-average students can work through the sequence of exercises in Section 3 as it is presented in the textbook. It is a logical sequence, sensible to all teachers and students who are used to traditional instruction in the sentence.

Bibliography on Sentence Combining

The following publications provide background and support for the use and structuring of sentence-combining exercises.

Combs, Warren E. "Further Effects of Sentence-Combining Practice on Writing Ability." *Research in the Teaching of English,* Fall 1976, pp. 137-149. [Shows that sentence-combining practice must continue for effects to be maintained.

Cooper, Charles R. "An Outline for Writing Sentence-Combining Problems," *English Journal,* January 1973, pp. 96-102 + [Suggests sequence moving from adjective problems to noun substitutions to multiple embeddings.]

Hunt, Kellogg W. *Grammatical Structures Written at Three Grade Levels.* NCTE Research Report No. 3 Champaign, Ill.: NCTE, 1965. [Report discusses sentence complexity.]

Mellon, John C. *Transformational Sentence-Combining.* NCTE Research Report No. 10. Champaign, Ill.: NCTE, 1969. [Studies the development of syntactic maturity.]

O'Hare, John Frank. *Sentence Combining.* NCTE Research Report No. 15. Champaign, Ill.: NCTE, 1973. [Replicates Mellon's study; shows syntactic growth.]

Stotsky, Sandra. "Sentence-Combining as a Curricular Activity: Its Effects on Written Language Development and Reading Comprehension." *Research in the Teaching of English,* Spring 1975, pp. 30-71. [Traces the interrelationship of reading, writing, and language development.]

Strong, William. "Sentence Combining: Back to Basics and Beyond." *English Journal,* February 1976, pp. 56+. [Sees sentence combining as adjunct to regular composition work; recommends schedule and compares kinds of exercises.]

SECTION 4: Vocabulary

This section is unusual in several specific ways and in its general aim to help students to develop their *own writing vocabularies*.

Although the basic approach to vocabulary building remains the same across the grades, certain changes in content do occur. For example, *words in context* is given special attention in this book (pages 251–254).

Diagnostic tests for this section appear on TM p. 62.

SPECIAL FEATURE

- **"Word List for Writers"**: This list, derived from the vocabulary of professional writers (discussed below), appears on pages 281–288.

POINTS TO PREVIEW

This section helps to develop vocabularies for writers in several specific ways.

- **Concentration on one part of speech at a time:** Most vocabulary-building material does not discriminate among parts of speech. Students are asked to add lists of new words to their vocabularies without regard for the class of the word, or whether it will be useful in *writing* prose for school, college, or business. This section distinguishes the parts of speech and concentrates on usefulness of words to writers. Specific attention is given to building noun, verb, adjective, and adverb vocabularies.

- **"Patterns" for derived forms:** To show students that knowing one form of a word can help them learn several related forms (and, therefore, extend their word stockpile), words that can take similar endings are grouped together. (See pages 270–279.)

- **Word list derived from professional writers in the media:** The word lists that traditionally appear in grammar and composition books are composed of words that have been selected in one way or another as reading obstacles for high school students. As such they are undoubtedly useful but not as a tool for *writing*. Of the four vocabularies that we all have—two passive (words we hear and words we read) and two active (words we speak and words we write) —the most neglected and, ironically, the most useful in your present task of teaching writing is the active writing vocabulary.

The words for the list were gathered from the following sources:

a. a representative sample of writing (25 essays) from reputable magazines (The criteria for choosing both the magazines and the essays were thorough, objective, and detailed, based on research by Margaret Ashida.)

b. tapes of national television news broadcasts. (Through a computer process, the most frequently used words were extracted from these essays and tapes. Then the words in the Harris-Jacobson Basic Elementary Reading list were subtracted on the assumption that they had become part of the student vocabulary, leaving the final "Word List for Writers" as a source for students who want to be efficient writers.)

SECTION 5: Spelling

As students enter the high school years and more demand is placed on their writing ability, their individual spelling problems are likely to become more apparent. This section is designed to assist you with student spelling problems. It analyzes the causes of spelling problems, and it is organized to support the teaching approaches suggested by these problems.

Diagnostic tests appear on TM p. 63.

SPECIAL FEATURES

Different students acquire spelling proficiency in different ways. This section offers various approaches, so that all students can benefit from it.

- **Pronunciation as a spelling aid** (page 293)
- **Spelling rules** (page 298)
- **Mnemonic device to distinguish commonly confused words** (page 312)

POINT TO PREVIEW

- **Spelling list:** The list of 400 words incorporates words with many of the problems examined in the first parts of this section. The spelling list can be used in various ways depending on the needs of your students: as source for practice (learning a certain number a week), as a self-check, as a test file.

SECTION 6: The Dictionary

By the ninth grade most students are familiar with the dictionary, but few have learned to use it as a *writer's* tool. You may want to stress 6.d. This emphasis on writing should make a review of so-called dictionary skills different enough to claim the attention of "jaded" ninth-graders.

Ninth-graders may also enjoy comparing school dictionaries with the more "mature" dictionaries they will soon be using (see page 329).

SECTION 7: Capitalization and Punctuation

For ninth-graders this section may appear long and very complete. Once your students realize that they are not going to be studying it day after day but rather using it as a handbook and reference guide (as well as for drill material, of course), they will come to appreciate its usefulness in answering many questions. It is designed chiefly for reference use, especially for use in self- and peer-editing. (Along with Section 5, "Spelling," it functions as a reference source in the error-and-editing program that grows out of the Editing Chart in Section 9, pages 443–453. The material here actually supplements the Editing Chart, which does not cover errors in mechanics.)

Many conventions of mechanics are dealt with in Sections 1, 2, and 3 at the appropriate points of grammar instruction. See preceding lists of Punctuation boxes.

A diagnostic test for this section appears on TM p. 65.

SPECIAL FEATURE

- **"Avoiding Errors" boxes**

POINTS TO PREVIEW

- **Commas:** The material on commas is broken down into four major classifications of comma use.

1. Conventional Uses

2. Items in Series

3. Clauses and Phrases

4. Extra Expressions

- **Apostrophes:** Much of this material is covered from a different perspective in 5.b.5, "Spelling Possessives." Learners need different presentations of materials at different times.

- **Parentheses:** Students should learn the value in using but not overusing these marks.

- **Quotation Marks:** You may emphasize this section in particular as your students carry out research report assignments (see Section 14).

SECTION 8: Glossary of Usage Problems

This kind of alphabetical listing of common usage errors may be new to ninth-grade students. The usage problems listed in the glossary in this section are those that might be called diction. They are distinct from the usage problems treated in Section 1 and Section 2 in one or all of the following ways:

a. They involve words more than they do sentences.

b. They often involve a distinction between oral and written language.

c. They cannot be explained by the grammar system itself and, therefore, pedagogy does not benefit from treating these problems along with the points of grammar introduced in Sections 1 and 2.

A diagnostic test for this section appears on TM p. 65.

SECTION 9: Catching, Classifying, and Correcting Errors

The idea that errors should be viewed as a part of a learning process may be new to ninth-graders. On the other hand, your students must realize that editing is needed to remove errors and that errors spoil writing by annoying readers.

This section presents a systematic method for teaching one important aspect of editing: the editing of sentences for errors in grammar and clarity, all of which are presented on an Editing Chart (pages 443–453). Errors in spelling can be traced back to Section 5. Errors in mechanics (capitalization and punctuation) can be traced back to Section 7. Certain errors in usage, most of which are based on words and expressions that grow up in spoken language and do not carry over well into written English, can be traced back to Section 8. Problems in paragraph coherence, unity, and transitions are taken up in Sections 10–11.

Whether you are going to develop a peer-editing program or ask students to learn to edit their own written material—or even if you are going to be the sole reader of student writing—you will find this section of the text especially useful.

Research in Errors and Their Classification

The foundation for the catching-classifying-and-correcting system in the textbook is multileveled. At the same time that the public became concerned about the writing abilities of young people, we examined and abstracted three basic kinds of materials that ultimately suggested our approach to errors.

1. **Studies analyzing the writing of students:** Generally, student writing in these studies were judged by teachers as *good* or *poor*. One of the seminal studies was Mina Shaughnessy's *Errors and Expectations* (Oxford University Press, 1977). There have also been studies by other writing instructors—instructors in average courses, in remedial courses, and in English as a Second Language courses. Their analyses have appeared in the *Journal of Basic Writing*, *English Journal*, *College English*, *College Communication and Composition*, *Research in the Teaching of English*, and other respected publications of the profession. Several of these reports have been written by Donald Freeman, linguistics consultant to *Grammar and Writing*, and Patricia Laurence, contributor and consultant on composition.

2. **Samples of student writing:** With the publication of *Selected Essays and Letters* by the National Assessment of Educational Progress, a wealth of material became available. The National Assessment regularly conducts writing samples in an attempt to evaluate the abilities of students. Approximately 1,700 of the essays written by 13-year-olds, 17-year-olds, and young adults were categorized as *lower*, *middle*, and *higher* and published in the last decade. They are a remarkable source for determining where young people's writing strengths and weaknesses lie.

3. **Standardized tests that require error recognition and correction:** The SAT, the TSWE, the ECT, and ACT, and the New York State Regents examination all have short-answer sections requiring error eradication. Analysis of these tests yielded another indicator of what adults expect from student writers.

These three kinds of materials determined the degree of emphasis we gave each error in "Avoiding Errors" boxes and suggested the classification system used in Section 9.

SPECIAL FEATURES

- **Comprehensiveness:** Students will see the extent of the "error problem" in writing in general.

- **Classification:** Students will see the kinds, or categories, of errors that most often arise in written English.

- **Reliable examples:** Students will see within each classification of errors on the Editing Chart *specific* errors and *specific* ways to correct them. (Examples are taken or adapted from essays written by young people tested in the National Assessment of Educational Progress.)

- **Cross references:** Students are given, on the Editing Chart, cross references to the rule or text discussion that will help them to understand the error and how best to prevent its recurrence.

- **Editing signals:** Students are shown how to edit papers.

- **Exercises:** Students are given exercises that provide practice in catching and correcting errors and in using editing signals.

With these features in mind, you may find one or more of the following procedures helpful:

1. Go over the Editing Chart with your class, explaining the purpose of each aspect of it, explaining just how the chart can be used for the purposes listed above.

2. Hold an oral warm-up session or two with your students in which you put sentences with certain errors (see Practice Errors, p.24) on the chalk board and ask individual students to find the corresponding error in the Editing Chart. Doing so will help students understand the classifications of errors on the chart. It will also help students learn how to use the cross references to find the rule covering that kind of error.

3. Assign the exercises following the Editing Chart.

4. When you have a suitable sample of written composition from your students, ask them to review their own or a classmate's paper for all grammatical errors (exclude, for this purpose, spelling and punctuation and capitalization errors) and to mark them with the signals shown on the

Editing Chart. You can use Exercise 1 (page 456) as a warm-up for this procedure.

5. Follow out the peer-editing or self-editing procedures that you prefer. Work in the Editing Chart as a means of identifying and marking papers.
(NOTE: See "Student Editing," TM p. 40, for a fuller discussion of this important aspect of writing.)

Practice Errors

1. Subject-verb agreement (singular noun as subject)
The student work very long on each composition.

2. Case (object of action verb)
The principal invited Bob and I to speak.

3. Parts of speech (past-time verbs)
Washington always show his patriotism.

SECTION 10: The Paragraph

In this section the topic sentence is used as the starting point for building strong expository paragraphs. The entire section is developed with models, but, in addition, students are asked to select, write, and judge topic sentences based on data (such as school track results and flight tables).

A substantial portion of the section is given over to models and exercises on developing paragraphs in various ways. Then *unity* and *coherence* are studied, and the section ends with the presentation of different kinds of paragraphs: (1) narrative paragraphs, (2) descriptive paragraphs, and (3) paragraphs of comparison and contrast as examples of expository paragraphs. The culminating exercise involves writing different kinds of paragraphs based on the same idea.

SPECIAL FEATURES

- Data for paragraph development as well as numerous models showing methods of development, characteristics of a good paragraph, and kinds of paragraphs
- Checklist for Revising a Paragraph (pages 501–502); Editing and Proofreading Checklist (page 502)

POINTS TO PREVIEW

- **Basis for judging topic sentences:** Notice that examples showing levels of generalizing are given.

- **Numerous models:** Models (some annotated) support all teaching points in the section and are used as the basis of exercises.

- **Data (tables and other information):** Students are given material to use for content as they practice putting sentences together into paragraphs.

- **Logical connectives to aid coherence:** The use of logical connectives to support the plan for development of paragraphs is introduced (page 490).

SECTION 11: Patterns of Thinking and Writing

This section is designed to help students to learn to think and plan a piece of writing beyond the boundaries of the paragraph using patterns of thinking and writing that are familiar to them in daily life but seldom thought of as part of composition. These are the familiar patterns: "This is what happened" (narration), "This is what it looks, sounds, smells, tastes, feels, or acts like" (description), and "This is like (or unlike) that" (comparison/contrast).

What this section does is to show, with models, the skills involved in using these patterns to develop a piece of writing. Brief "Warm-up" exercises give students a chance to develop these skills. Finally, at the end of the section, a series of longer, less close-ended exercises and composition assignments ("Pattern Practices") provide students with occasions for applying these patterns in writing. As in Section 10, "data" (tables and generally nonverbal information) are used as stimuli and takeoff points for composition.

The use of patterns of thinking as a step in the process of helping students to write is recommended by Mina P. Shaughnessy in her important book, *Errors and Expectations* (Oxford University Press, 1977). Also we are indebted to Mary S. Lawrence for significant contributions in the form of ideas and exercises which appear in Section 11.

SECTION 12: The Composition

This section is one in which all the instruction and practice of all the earlier writing sections can be focused on the preparation of a single composition. Various kinds of paragraphs and patterns can be used in the development of this single composition. The most important features of this section are that it provides the following:

(1) ideas for selecting a topic
(2) advice on determining audience and purpose
(3) instruction in developing a working and, then, formal outline
(4) aid in writing the thesis statement, introduction, and conclusion
(5) reminders about using transitions, and
(6) checklists for revising and editing.

POINT TO PREVIEW

- **Complete model composition:** Included is a complete brief research report about *The Wizard of Oz* in which the writer used all three patterns.

SECTION 13: Libraries and Information

All the information that you would expect a ninth-grader to need is easily accessible in this section: how to use a library, why to use a library, when to use different kinds of reference materials. Students need to feel comfortable with, not intimidated by or bored by, libraries.

All students should also be aware of the technology that is now available in many libraries to help meet the "information explosion" with which all of us will be dealing in the 1980s.

SPECIAL FEATURES

- **Attention to microforms**
- **Parts of a book**
- **Other sources of information** (e.g., the government; see page 572)

SECTION 14: The Research Report

While not all ninth-graders are required to write reports based on outside sources, this section is included as a gentle lead-in to a kind of writing that students will be called upon to do more and more often as they move through high school.

One of the most important points to communicate to young writers is how to move from reading someone else's thoughts to using those thoughts in a paper of their own. Naturally, plagiarism must be explained. Furthermore, students should be encouraged not simply to report what others have said but to evaluate what they read. In short, research reports in general would be more intriguing to write and more rewarding to read if young writers could see the project as an attempt to show some originality.

SPECIAL FEATURES

- **Step-by-step guidelines:** These steps are supplemented by examples of how a real student followed the process.
- **Sample footnote and bibliography entries**
- **A complete (annotated) model student paper:** The topic, "Breakthroughs in Contact Lenses," was chosen because it clearly demonstrates how research reports can be written for any subject class.
- **Research Report Checklist**

POINT TO PREVIEW

- **Outlining:** Although explained and illustrated here, more detailed instruction appears in Section 12, "The Composition," on pages 547–549.

SECTION 15: The Letter

A brief section, the instruction here centers around direct advice on how to communicate effectively and how to win respect. Exercises were developed to underscore the wide range of important business that can be carried out in writing.

POINTS TO PREVIEW

- Annotated model letters
- Advice on how to avoid sexism in letter writing

SECTION 16: Study Skills and Test Taking

The first part of this section succinctly itemizes methods, approved by educators and psychologists, for students to get the most out of their books and their time in class. The second section covers a wide range of test items that young people should become acquainted with in order to feel comfortable with both classroom and standardized tests (short answer and essay).

SPECIAL FEATURES

- **Two methods for note taking:** The standard outlining method is supplemented here with the new approach of "mapping."
- **Strategies for test taking:** Each kind of test item is prefaced by a list of specific considerations.
- **Sample questions from standardized tests**

ADDITIONAL EXERCISES

You will find Additional Exercises on pages 646–660, keyed to Section 1, "Parts of Speech," Section 2, "Parts of a Sentence," and Section 7, "Capitalization and Punctuation." All the exercises on pages 646–660 are listed in sequence on page 645.

USING THE TEXT

In the following pages you will find the following material:

Semester and Quarterly Plans (to help you divide the material according to your students' needs)

Flexibility of Content

Teaching Grammar (hints for traditional instruction)

Teaching Writing

Student Editing (more detailed information than discussed in the notes for Section 9)

Drill Sequences (a series of drill sequences and composition assignments that cut across the sections and that will offer alternative arrangements of material)

Teaching Different Ability Groups

Listening Skills (adapting text exercises)

Speaking Skills (adapting text exercises)

Evaluation (notes on testing, assigning essays, evaluating essays; diagnostic tests)

Preparing Forms and Applications

FLEXIBILITY OF CONTENT

Different teachers and different classes have different needs. You may find various ways of adapting this sixteen-section textbook for your particular students. We suggest viewing the textbook in at least the following five different ways:

1. as a course in grammar and usage
2. as a course in written composition
3. as a guide to using other source materials
4. as an aid in test taking
5. as a guide to editing

USES OF THE TEXT

	As a course in grammar	As a course in composition
Section 1 PARTS OF SPEECH and Section 2 PARTS OF A SENTENCE	Both sections give succinct definitions, clear examples, and numerous drills.	Introduces terms used in sentence composition
Section 3 WRITING SENTENCES	Introduces sentence expansion and sentence combining using various parts of speech	Provides a structured approach to composing various kinds of sentences
Section 4 VOCABULARY	Shows how parts of speech are useful in developing vocabulary	Concentrates on building vocabulary for use in writing
Section 5 SPELLING	Shows how meaning often determines spelling	Relates spelling to needs of students developing their writing ability
Section 6 THE DICTIONARY	Shows that a dictionary can be used to resolve questions about parts of speech	Shows how useful a dictionary can be to writers
Section 7 CAPITALIZATION AND PUNCTUATION	Shows relationship of syntax and punctuation	Shows conventions that readers demand of writers
Section 8 GLOSSARY OF USAGE PROBLEMS	Presents an alphabetically organized list of points of usage	Shows conventions of word choice and levels of usage

As a guide to research	As an aid in test taking	As a guide to editing
	Introduces terminology useful in analyzing test items dealing with grammar and usage	Provides instruction after errors have been identified
	Prepares students for tests involving sentence construction and analysis	Teaches students how to improve sentences
Encourages building a vocabulary useful in writing research reports	Provides a base for all test taking involving vocabulary use and analysis	Provides a base for improving word choice in sentences
	Helps students to write correctly spelled essay tests	Serves as a spelling reference guide for editors
Shows how a dictionary can be useful in research		Encourages students to "look it up" rather than misspell, especially inflections
Contains rules specific to the research report	Covers punctuation and capitalization items that appear on tests	Serves as an editor's handbook on capitalization and punctuation
	Covers diction and usage errors often tested	Alerts students to problematic pairs they may encounter in editing

USES OF THE TEXT

	As a course in grammar	As a course in composition
Section 9 CATCHING, CLASSIFYING, AND CORRECTING ERRORS	Makes cross references to positive instruction in grammar in Sections 1 and 2	Suggests how to develop a program in self-editing and peer-editing for the improvement of writing
Section 10 THE PARAGRAPH	Illustrates how parts of speech contribute to creating *coherent* paragraphs	Illustrates the elements and varieties of paragraphs
Section 11 PATTERNS OF THINKING AND WRITING	Illustrates how grammar can help to create *coherence* in narration, description, and exposition	Structured writing assignments in narration, description, exposition
Section 12 THE COMPOSITION	Shows options open to writers of compositions	Uses all preceding composition sections as input
Section 13 LIBRARIES AND INFORMATION	Lists reference works on language	Explains the basis for the research report and compositions
Section 14 THE RESEARCH REPORT		Provides a guide to composing and writing a research report
Section 15 THE LETTER		Explains the conventions used in this form of composition
Section 16 STUDY SKILLS AND TEST TAKING	Shows how to prepare for tests involving grammar	Previews requirements for writing essay tests

As a guide to research	As an aid in test taking	As a guide to editing
	Helps students to reduce sentence errors in essays	Implements all kinds of sentence-level editing
Emphasizes the importance of supporting generalizations	Provides a basis for paragraph development for essay tests	Contains Editing and Proofreading Checklist
Provides practice in thinking about data	Provides instruction in ordering ideas and writing for essay tests	
	Gives specific advice for preparing for essay tests	Contains Editing and Proofreading Checklist
Explains the library skills used in the research report		
Makes a beginning step in the use of outside sources		Contains Research Report Checklist
Helps in writing for information	Prepares students for letter writing that is included on some tests	
	Gives detailed practice in standardized-test items	

SEMESTER AND QUARTERLY PLANS

The following suggestions for using *Grammar and Writing* may be helpful to you in planning your program.

FOR A ONE-YEAR COURSE (FOUR QUARTERS)

In using the book for a one-year course, you may follow the logical presentation of the book from *Grammar, Usage,* and *Sentences* (Sections 1-3) through to *Resources* and *Study Skills and Tests* (Section 13-16). Depending upon the ability and achievement levels of your students, you may want to include or to eliminate Section 13, "Libraries and Information," and Section 14, "The Research Report."

You may, however, want to group sections in an alternate way, creating a syllabus that is geared to the needs and abilities of your students.

Plan A

FIRST QUARTER
Parts of Speech (Section 1)
Parts of a Sentence (Section 2)
Writing Sentences (Section 3)
Vocabulary (Section 4)
Study Skills and Test Taking (Section 16)

SECOND QUARTER
The Paragraph (Section 10)
Spelling (Section 5)
The Dictionary (Section 6)
Libraries and Information (Section 13)

THIRD QUARTER
Patterns of Thinking and Writing (Section 11)
The Composition (Section 12)

FOURTH QUARTER
The Research Report (Section 14)
The Letter (Section 15)

Sections 7, 8, and 9: for review throughout the year

Plan B

FIRST QUARTER
Parts of Speech (Section 1)
Parts of a Sentence (Section 2)
Writing Sentences (3.a)
Capitalization and Punctuation (7.a-7.g.16)
Spelling (5.a-5.a.2)
The Dictionary (Section 6)
The Paragraph (10.a–10.i)
Study Skills and Test Taking (16.a–16.c)

SECOND QUARTER
Writing Sentences (3.b–3.h)
Capitalization and Punctuation (7.h–7.n)
Vocabulary (Section 4)
The Paragraph (10.j–10.r)
Patterns of Thinking and Writing (11.a–11.d)

THIRD QUARTER
Patterns of Thinking and Writing (11.e–11.l)
Spelling (5.b–5.b.5)
The Composition (Section 12)

FOURTH QUARTER
Patterns of Thinking and Writing (11.m–11.n)
Spelling (5.c.–5.d)
Libraries and Information (Section 13)
The Research Report (Section 14)
The Letter (Section 15)
Study Skills and Test Taking (16.d–16.o)

Sections 8 and 9: as these sections provide general support, use them for review throughout the year

FOR A ONE–SEMESTER COURSE

Grammar and Writing may also be used for a half-year course. You may use Sections 1, 2, and 3 as one complete unit to be covered in one semester. Alternately, you may use Sections 10, 11, and 12 as a self-contained one-semester course, using other sections as necessary for reference and for exercises.

FOR SHORTER COURSES OR FOR UNITS WITHIN LONGER COURSES

Grammar and Writing may be used for quarter-year mini-courses, electives, and independent study. *Grammar and Writing* may also be introduced only at particular points during the longer courses for specific purposes, as listed below. Relevant sections are itemized.

1. As preparation for basic skills tests:
   Section 1, "Parts of Speech"
   Section 2, "Parts of a Sentence"
   Section 3, "Writing Sentences"
   Section 5, "Spelling"
   Section 6, "The Dictionary"
   Section 7, "Capitalization and Punctuation"
   Section 8, "Glossary of Usage Problems"
   Section 9, "Catching, Classifying, and Correcting Errors"
   Section 16, "Study Skills and Test Taking"

2. As a guide for using outside sources:
   Section 13, "Libraries and Information"
   Section 14, "The Research Report"

3. As preparation for academic writing:
   Section 10, "The Paragraph"
   Section 11, "Patterns of Thinking and Writing"
   Section 12, "The Composition"

TEACHING GRAMMAR

We concentrate in Sections 1 and 2 on the parts of speech, the parts of a sentence, the qualities of a good sentence, and the kinds of sentences before we ask students to write sentences extensively in Section 3. Nevertheless, there are "Applications" exercises in Sections 1 and 2 so that students always do have some immediate practice in grammar that goes beyond strict recognition. Furthermore, it is entirely feasible to move straight into Section 3, "Writing Sentences," without spending time in Sections 1 and 2 with its definitions, examples, and exercises. The amount of straight grammar instruction—its quantity and frequency—remains each teacher's or school's decision.

TEACHING WRITING

Various sections and features of *Grammar and Writing* have been designed to help you teach writing. Here you will find some additional background.

A THEORY OF WRITING

Writing is a process so related to thinking that we are tempted to say that nothing of great importance or difficulty separates the two. By the time a student reaches your classroom, the basic processes of learning the letters of the alphabet and using them to encode words will have been mastered. This does not mean, of course, that the student has learned to "write" or even to think in a way that one must in order to write.

Practice is needed in learning to select words, to arrange them in sentences, to have some purpose for putting one sentence after another into paragraphs and for putting one paragraph after another. Thinking must be incorporated into these processes. In the classroom the thinking-writing process can be practiced with units as small as single words and sentences as well as with longer units.

A DEFINITION OF WRITING

A definition of writing that is endorsed by people who write for a living is the following:

Writing is the ordering into words of experience and data.

By *data* we mean everything from a sunrise to a baseball box score. Both involve some kind of sensory perception by the writer. Sometimes experience is explicit—the sun actually sets before our eyes—and sometimes experience must be remembered, inferred, predicted, or imagined.

When confronted with some combination of data and experience, a writer undertakes to transform this data into written words. The scholar Hannah Arendt points out that to think (and, therefore, to write) a person withdraws from the sensory world and holds a silent dialogue within himself or herself, relating the data to experience. Out of this exchange—perhaps lengthy, arduous, repetitious—comes an *idea*, a way of ordering the data-experience into words, sentences, and paragraphs. In perhaps the way that an artist, painter, or sculptor, confronted with an idea looks for paint, brush, or chisel, the writer now looks for words, sentences, and paragraphs to be grouped into patterns of thought.

USING THIS BOOK TO HELP WRITERS TO WRITE

As explained under "Teaching Grammar" (TM p. 36), the creation of sentences is itself an important aspect of composition. Since, however, the common connotation of *writing* is "material of a paragraph or longer," the following discussion concentrates on teaching students to compose paragraphs, compositions, essays, and so on.

You will notice that this process of teaching writing begins with Section 10. Although we are concerned with writing in this book, we deliberately placed the sections on grammar, punctuation, etc.—the tools of the writer's trade—before those on writing itself. At the point when they begin to order their ideas, we want the writers who use this book to be familiar with these tools or at least to know where to find them.

INVENTION AND DATA–BASED COMPOSITION

Much has been published about prewriting and "invention": getting ideas for writing, identifying the purpose for writing, and identifying the audience for one's writing (see p. 39). Everyone agrees that these aspects of composition are important. The problem, from the viewpoints of practical teaching and of student time, is that most approaches to prewriting are so open-ended. Practicing prewriting in the classroom often suffers because often students have no common ground as the basis for prewriting exercises. The common ground is necessary, for how else will students be able to discuss matters together before they begin to write? How else will they see that data can be interpreted in various ways?

Data-based composition simply refers to our recurrent strategy of building in data—charts, tables, facts, and figures—as the common ground for students to use in composition assignments. An example of such data is the flight table in Section 10, page 468, from which a topic sentence is developed.

DIRECTING WRITING TO A SPECIFIC AUDIENCE

Most often in classrooms, the teacher is the audience for student writing. With our suggestions for peer editing, we hope to encourage more opportunities for students to write for their friends and fellow students.

You may wish, however, to specify audiences for composition assignments. The following chart will help you.

Assignments for Specific Audiences

Section 11	Suggested Audiences
Assignment A: Daily Time Chart, page 527	
Pattern Practice 1	diary entry
Pattern Practice 2	story for young children
Pattern Practice 3	letter to English pen pal
	letter to a grandparent or friend
Assignment B: Space Science, page 529	
Pattern Practice 4	social studies class report
	NASA bulletin
Pattern Practice 5	Astronomy club
	Interplanetary travel guide
Pattern Practice 6	essay contest entry
	science class report
Pattern Practice 7	inhabitants of Mars
	inhabitants of Earth
Assignment C: TV Programing, page 532	
Pattern Practice 8	school paper humor column
	TV column in local paper
Pattern Practice 9	pro-TV friend/anti-TV friend
Pattern Practice 10	TV rating service
	ABC (NBC, etc.) program planners
Assignment D: Science Fiction, page 537	
Pattern Practices 11–13	short-story contest entry
	Star Trek convention

STUDENT EDITING

The following discussion pertains to student editing. See TM p. 51 for a discussion of *teacher* evaluation of writing.

We believe that students benefit from reading each others' writing; many of them have excellent ideas and unique ways of expressing thoughts. Peer editing leads to good self-editing practices under conditions that do not seem tiresome and boring to students. It also helps them to develop a sense of audience, to see how their writing affects others, and to develop an awareness of their own voice.

An effective approach to student writing is to have an in-class editing program that embraces both self-editing and peer editing.

Grammar and Writing has been designed to help you develop a program of student editing. If you wish to use such a system, you will find certain parts of the book helpful. The introduction to Section 9, "Catching, Classifying, and Correcting Errors" (TM p. 21), suggests ways that this section can be used as the basis for student editing of sentence-level, grammatical errors. The more holistic concerns of paragraph development, organization, coherence, and unity can be addressed by using the Checklists for Editing on pages 502 and 556 of the student text.

THE PEER–EDITING PROCESS

In any peer-editing program, students will have to address themselves both to holistic concerns (organization, unity, coherence, etc.) and to grammatical, sentence-level errors. As teacher and administrator of a peer-editing program, you will have to give students guidelines for both levels of evaluation. Although it is best to vary your strategy somewhat on different assignments, we suggest that you always keep in mind the two strands of evaluation.

Since it is clearly impossible for students to look for all kinds of errors in each paper, they should be directed to look for specific problem areas. In fact, you might provide students with a different checklist for each assignment. The first questions, aimed at holistic concerns, should probably remain fairly constant. They might include questions such as:

1. What is the best section of the composition? What makes it good?
2. Which passages need improvement?
3. Are there any questions the writer has left unanswered?
4. What are one or two ways in which the writer can improve his or her next piece of writing?

Other holistic concerns that might vary from assignment to assignment can include treatment of topic sentences, paragraph development, unity, coherence, etc.

Finally, with regard to grammatical errors, the students might be directed to look for observance of or errors in the grammatical points then being taught in class.

PROCEDURES FOR IMPLEMENTING PEER–EDITING PROGRAMS

Specific procedures will vary with the teacher. Two model processes follow.

A Model Oral Process

1. The teacher assigns a topic (of a specified length, scope, and pattern) to the whole class. (The teacher may develop a checklist for each different kind of assignment so that students will have some criteria for both writing and criticizing the assignment.)
2. Each student writes a paragraph (or more) on the topic. (It is helpful if the teacher also does the assignment.)
3. The students gather in a circle and read aloud their compositions.
4. Students then comment on the papers. At the early stages of this process, students may respond on a voluntary basis. (To establish an atmosphere of trust the teacher should emphasize the positive aspects of criticism.)
5. The teacher helps the class to focus on specific areas of concern by asking questions. For example, *Is there anything more the reader needs to know? Has the writer left questions unanswered?*
6. Students then revise their papers, using class comments as a basis for revision.

7. At the next class session, students may have questions about their own work to ask the class. (The teacher may have worked individually with students beforehand to help them formulate questions that will elicit helpful responses from the class.)

8. The teacher grades the final draft and discusses the papers with students individually, pointing out only a limited number of areas that the student should give careful attention to on the next paper.

A Model Written Process

1. Students bring to class a paragraph (or more) on a topic assigned earlier.

2. The teacher divides the class into groups of four or five students each and asks them to exchange papers and to examine them.

3. Each student comments on all the other papers in the group. (Each student should use a different colored pen to identify the writer to be arranged ahead of time.) The easiest way to follow this process is to have students simply mark possible errors or awkward phrasing using the signals shown in Section 9 (the Editing Chart) of the student textbook.

4. At this point, members of the group may need to discuss with each other some of the comments or suggestions. The teacher circulates among the groups, intervening only if necessary.

5. Then, the papers are rewritten and handed in to the teacher with the first draft.

PEER-EVALUATION FORM

You may reproduce or modify in any way the form that appears on the facing page. In general, the form may be used in one of two of the following ways:

1. The student editor can fill it out and attach it to the piece of writing being returned.

2. The student writer can fill it out himself or herself based on an examination of the editor's marks.

PEER–EVALUATION FORM

Name _____

Course/Project _____

Editor _____

Assignment _____

Date _____

Strengths and Weaknesses of Paper _____

1. Introduction _____

_____

2. Topic Sentences; Thesis Statement _____

_____

3. Paragraph Structure and Unity; Supporting Statements _____

_____

4. Transitions; Logical Connectives _____

_____

5. Conclusion _____

_____

6. Mechanics (Spelling, Capitalization, Punctuation) _____

_____

7. Word Choice _____

_____

8. Style (Sentence Variety, etc.) _____

_____

9. General Comments (Use back of sheet if necessary) _____

_____

_____

_____

DRILL SEQUENCES: Relating Grammar and Writing

In the following pages, you will find eleven drill sequences in grammar and composition. Each sequence groups exercises from several different sections because they are related to each other by a single pedagogical aim. For example, although most work is done on parts of speech in Section 1, there are exercises in other sections that focus on parts of speech, albeit from different angles. It may well be that you would not ordinarily assign exercises from different sections in close sequence if you were taking one section at a time. The sequences here give you and your students a cross-section view of grammar and writing skills and permit a certain variety of assignment.

TEACHING DIFFERENT ABILITY GROUPS

Above-average Students

Above-average ninth-grade students are generally proficient in identifying parts of speech and parts of the sentence. These same students, however, often lack skill in identifying participles and participial phrases, gerunds and gerund phrases, and infinitives and infinitive phrases. These students may also demonstrate a lack of skill in identifying and using noun clauses, adjective clauses, and adverb clauses. What they need in the ninth grade is more adeptness with verbals, clauses, and kinds of sentences. To help students achieve these skills refer to Sections 1–3.

Because ninth-grade students are young and inexperienced, they generally have difficulty in generating ideas for writing as well as in structuring and connecting paragraphs. To help them achieve these skills, see Section 10, "The Paragraph," and Section 11, "Patterns of Thinking and Writing." In conjunction with their writing, ninth-grade students should review Section 7, "Capitalization and Punctuation."

Above-average students should be given an opportunity to develop skills in original research and in writing a brief research report. Section 14, "The Research Report," and the related Section 13, "Libraries and Information," will be useful in this respect. To further challenge these above-average students, have them suggest and carry out an original research design in the physical or biological sciences, the social studies, or literature. It is important for students to learn to write "across the curriculum."

Because of the number of papers generated by such assignments and the limitations of your time, you may want to introduce peer editing as one strategy for managing the work load. See Section 9, "Catching, Classifying, and Correcting Errors." This section of the text will help you to provide a checkpoint for sentence errors dealing with grammar and clarity and give you guides for setting up an editing program.

Lower-ability Students

Entering the last year of junior high school or the first year of high school may be anxiety producing for lower-ability students because they are aware of their academic limitations. To help these students overcome their skills deficiencies, the following sections of the text will be most helpful. These sections provide students with opportunities for concrete mastery of subject matter:

Section 1, "Parts of Speech"
Section 2, "Parts of a Sentence"
Section 3, "Writing Sentences"
Section 5, "Spelling"
Section 7, "Capitalization and Punctuation"

After practice in the fundamentals and in sentence writing and sentence combining, lower-ability students should move into writing paragraphs and compositions in which their ideas are developed into several paragraphs.

The following sections of the text will be valuable in giving students ideas to write about, models and suggestions for writing good paragraphs, and opportunities for developing their thinking.

Section 10, "The Paragraph"

Section 11, "Patterns of Thinking and Writing"

LISTENING SKILLS

Getting your students to listen more attentively may seem a hopeless task at times. For example, how many of them might not be able to answer this old chestnut correctly: *What was the color of George Washington's white horse?*

Listening is an important skill to practice. In the classroom students must listen to directions and listen to and participate in student-teacher discussions. It is vital that they learn to listen well. Below are sample listening exercises, adapted from material in the student textbook.

See also the discussions on note taking (both outlining and mapping) in Section 16, "Study Skills and Test Taking." These strategies can be applied to taking notes from oral sources.

General directions: You will use exercise items from the student textbook, but you must ignore the writing directions at the beginning of the exercises since they do not apply here. Before you begin reading the items in each exercise, explain to your students exactly what they will be expected to do (e.g., answer questions) and how you will proceed (e.g., read each statement once).

Listening Skills in Understanding Content

1. Section 1, Exercise 10 (page 15): Tell students that they will have to answer specific questions about the content. Read Sentences 1–10 aloud once. Then ask students to write the answers to the following questions: *How do octopuses*

conceal their escape? *How do bees protect themselves? How does the chameleon camouflage itself?*

2. Section 1, Exercise 39 (page 78): Tell students that they will have to answer specific questions about the content. Read Sentences 1–10 aloud once. Then ask students to write the answers to the following questions: *Where are pearls produced? In what kind of creature are pearls found? How are the very finest pearls shaped?*

SPEAKING SKILLS

If you would like to have your class develop their speaking skills, the following guidelines may be helpful. In the classroom, speaking skills usually fall into two general categories: (1) taking part in group discussions and (2) giving informal talks or formal speeches to the group.

Skills for Group Discussions

1. Read and think about the subject beforehand and take notes.
2. Be ready to participate.
3. Listen carefully to what others say.
4. Take notes as you participate.
5. Politely listen to the views of others even if you disagree.
6. State your views neutrally; do not get emotional.
7. Support your views with facts and examples.

Skills for Informal Talks or Formal Speeches

1. Try to choose a suitable, lively, and interesting topic.
2. Be sure that your talk or speech has a clearly defined beginning, middle, and end.
3. Support your ideas with examples or incidents, facts or statistics, and concrete details.
4. Whether you are giving an informal talk using notes or a formal speech using a manuscript, speak in complete, correct, and varied sentences.

5. To get the group's full attention, try to start with an interesting fact or anecdote.

6. If you are reading from a written speech, practice reading it aloud beforehand.

Have your students use some of the longer models in Sections 10–11 as the basis for giving a speech from a prepared paper. Encourage your students to follow Section 14, "The Research Report," step by step with an eye toward presenting their report orally as well as in writing.

Using the above guidelines, students can set up individual skill charts on which they can record their progress.

EVALUATION

We offer within this section suggestions for creating essay questions that are clear and that will give students opportunities to be successful. The other side of evaluation involves assessing specific skills and prior mastery of grammar, usage, spelling, vocabulary, and mechanics. To this end, you will find here a series of diagnostic tests that you may reproduce for in-class testing.

GUIDELINES FOR DEVELOPING AND EVALUATING ESSAY QUESTIONS

Developing Essay Tests

The following suggestions may help in the development of questions for classroom essay tests. (Many of these suggestions apply to all essay questions whether for test purposes or not.)

1. The essay questions should be as brief as words will allow and as clear as it can be written.

2. A test situation is different from the situation that allows time for the developed outline and paper. Students usually have no dictionaries, notes, or texts and bibliographies to use in writing essay examinations. Therefore, the question should contain all the direction that the student needs in order to do well.

3. Students should be told directly that *how* they write is an important factor in the score or grade given to their answer. That is, quantity of prose is not the same as quality of writing.

4. Every essay question should include some suggestion for organizing the response. That is, no question should simply ask students just to "discuss" or to "tell" or to "analyze" an idea or statement. An organizing principle should be given the student: *Compare and contrast . . ., Agree or disagree with . . . .*

5. A good test of the usefulness and quality of an essay question is for the teacher to write an answer to the question. This experience will immediately reveal to the teacher any weakness, vagueness, or ambiguity of the question.

The essay question below is an obvious example of a weak, diffuse question, one that almost invites the students to wander off in many directions and to discover too late that their essays lack point and structure:

Weak Essay Question (20 minutes). Discuss the importance of the boys' and girls' sports programs in your school.

The next question is a good example of a directed exercise that permits students to focus immediately on the problem presented and to think in terms of a structured response before they start writing.

Good Essay Question (20 minutes). Write a composition that compares the boys' sports program with the girls' sports program in your school. For example, do both programs have equal opportunity to use the gym, the athletic facilities, and the athletic faculty? Be specific and give facts and examples from your personal experience. Finally, end your essay with suggestions about ways to improve both sports programs.

Evaluating Essay Tests

The essay test presents problems in measurement that can seriously weaken its effectiveness. Unlike the objective or multiple-choice test, which offers students as many opportunities to demonstrate their knowledge as there are questions in the test, the essay test allows usually only one or two opportunities to demonstrate that knowledge or skill. Obviously, a sample of 100 questions is fairer than a sample of one or two questions. In addition, there is the problem of scoring. So far, no machine or computer has done a satisfactory job of scoring essays in spite of many research studies aimed at computerized scoring. It is a fact that scoring by humans can be unreliable because subjective judgment plays so large a part. Yet much can be done to improve the measurement qualities of the essay.

Sentence-level Errors

Major areas of concern in evaluating essay tests are (1) sentence errors and (2) overall performance. Even though the aim of an exam may have been to assess students' ability to *support a topic sentence with facts*, you will not want to ignore the sentence-level errors in grammar, usage, punctuation, and clarity that creep into the student sentences. You can use the Editing Signals on the Editing Chart (pages 443–453) to mark an essay test, and you may penalize or credit students for ability to write effective sentences.

Holistic Evaluation

The total composition should be looked at as a whole—holistically, as it were. In other words, although students commit various errors, their work must be reacted to for its overall strengths and its overall weaknesses.

Holistic evaluation is most often applied in large-scale testing situations when many essays must be read within a relatively short period of time. The evaluation is almost always performed by several readers.

In the classroom the basic philosophy of holistic scoring can counterbalance too much attention to sentence-level errors, distracting though they may be. (For a detailed discussion, see Charles R. Cooper, "Holistic Evaluation of Writing," in *Evaluating Writing*, edited by Charles R. Cooper and Lee Odell, published by NCTE in 1977.)

Two composition evaluation forms are reprinted on pages 54 and 55. You may reproduce the forms. You should, of course, adjust the forms, especially those with weighted ratings, to reflect the emphases that you stress.

Composition Evaluation Form #1

	Yes	No	
I. Content			
	_____	_____	1. Insightful or original ideas
	_____	_____	2. Clearly expressed ideas
II. Organization			
	_____	_____	3. An obvious thesis
	_____	_____	4. Order of thesis idea followed throughout essay
	_____	_____	5. Adequately developed thesis
	_____	_____	6. Every paragraph relevant to thesis
	_____	_____	7. Controlling idea in every paragraph
	_____	_____	8. Each paragraph developed with relevant details
	_____	_____	9. Well-ordered details
III. Grammar, Usage, Mechanics			
	_____	_____	10. Many misspellings
	_____	_____	11. Serious or excessive punctuation errors
	_____	_____	12. Errors in the use of verbs
	_____	_____	13. Errors in the use of pronouns
	_____	_____	14. Errors in the use of modifiers
	_____	_____	15. Errors in word usage
	_____	_____	16. Awkward sentences

Adapted from Arthur M. Cohen, "Assessing College Students' Ability to Write Compositions," *Research in the Teaching of English*, No. 5, 1971, pp. 24–36.

Composition Evaluation Form #2

	Low	Middle	High	
General Impression				
Ideas	2	4 6 8	10	
Organization	2	4 6 8	10	
Word choice	1	2 3 4	5	
Tone	1	2 3 4	5	_____
Specifics				
Grammar and usage	1	2 3 4	5	
Punctuation, cap	1	2 3 4	5	
Spelling	1	2 3 4	5	
Handwriting	1	2 3 4	5	_____
			Total	_____

Adapted from Paul B. Diederich, *Measuring Growth in Writing* (Urbana, Ill.: • NCTE, 1974).

DIAGNOSTIC TESTS

You will find here diagnostic tests for the sections of the student text listed below. Test may be reproduced without permission of the publisher.

> Section 1, "Parts of Speech"
> Section 2, "Parts of a Sentence"
> Section 4, "Vocabulary"
> Section 5, "Spelling"
> Section 7, "Capitalization and Punctuation"
> Section 8, "Glossary of Usage Problems"

These are the sections for which diagnostic testing measures are available and useful at the secondary level.

Not tested are sections and parts of sections that fall into the following two categories:

a. *Material for which diagnostic measurement devices are not available:* No one, for example, has devised a means of testing diagnostically the ability of students to write a research report. This same situation exists with respect to other forms of original composition.

b. *Material that, although useful, lies beyond the context of knowledge that we can expect most secondary students to have readily available, without some review:* For example, it may be useful for students to realize that certain "helping," or as we call them *auxiliary*, verbs have special characteristics and can, therefore, be studied separately under a label of their own (*modals*), but it would be unfair and time-wasting for you to try to discover in advance how well your class knows modals.

Validity of the Diagnostic Tests

The testing techniques employed in preparing the tests that follow have been devised or approved by test authorities. You will undoubtedly recognize techniques used by the Educational Testing Service. These tests measure the ability of a group or class. If you were trying to test the ability of an individual student, other tests would have to be used.

Uses of the Diagnostic Tests

You will find these tests most useful in helping you to decide whether to use a particular section as (1) review, (2) reference, (3) drill material, (4) part of an editing and error-correcting program, or (5) the basis of a classroom unit of instruction. If, for example, the tests for Sections 1 and 2 reveal that most of your students are familiar with the terms for the major parts of speech and can recognize them in sentences but that many of your students have difficulty in recognizing and distinguishing between a subject and a predicate, you can treat Section 1 as review or reference material but give concentrated classroom instruction in the portions of Section 2 that deal with subject and predicate.

Evaluating Diagnostic Tests

The tests are diagnostic tests, which, as the name implies, are devised to help you to diagnose the strengths and weaknesses of your class in the fundamentals of grammar, usage, spelling, vocabulary, and mechanics. These tests are presented simply to assist you in planning your use of the student text. Whatever the results, no alarm or special efforts, or, on the other hand, complacency is called for. If, for example, *all* of your class perform faultlessly on *all* of the tests, these results simply mean that you can use the six related sections of the book for review, reference, drill exercises, and as part of your peer-editing and error-correction program. You will be able to invest most of your instruction time on the second part of the book, Sections 10–16.

Distinguishing Among Nouns, Verbs, Adjectives, and Adverbs

Decide if each underlined word is a noun, a verb, an adjective, or an adverb. In the space that corresponds to the number under the word, write the letter *n* if the word is a noun; write *v* if it is a verb; write *adj* if it is an adjective; write *adv* if it is an adverb.

Americans use an <u>enormous</u> amount of

certain products <u>yearly</u>. For example,

each <u>person</u> in this country <u>uses</u> 40

pounds of household soaps and <u>indus-</u>

<u>trial</u> cleaners every year, and each adult

uses about 553 pounds of <u>paper</u>. Ameri-

cans <u>often</u> talk by telephone, too; they

<u>make</u> 188 billion telephone <u>calls</u> a year.

Finally, Americans <u>drink</u> coffee <u>thirstily,</u>

consuming more than one billion pounds

of it during a <u>single</u> year.

adj	adv
1	2
n	v
3	4
adj	n
5	6
adv	v
7	8
n	v
9	10
adv	adj
11	12

Identifying Common Nouns

Decide if each underlined word is a common noun. If it is, write the letter n in the numbered space that corresponds to the number under the word. If the word is not a common noun, leave the numbered space blank.

There is a huge <u>potential</u> for muscular control in the human body. In <u>itself</u>, the act of walking is a <u>remarkable</u> feat. The <u>margin</u> for error in walking is fairly large; after all, a <u>person</u> will often take a misstep and not fall. It is the mobility of the hands and <u>face</u> that is truly incredible. When a person <u>smiles</u>, thirteen or more <u>tiny</u> muscles must move, and if that person <u>frowns</u>, fifty or more <u>muscles</u> are required.

n	
1	2
	n
3	4
n	n
5	6
7	8
	n
9	10

Identifying Action Verbs

Decide if each underlined word is an action verb or not. If it is an action verb, write the letter v in the space at the right with a number corresponding to the number under the word. If it is not an action verb, leave the space blank.

Halley's Comet <u>appears</u> again in our
                 1
skies in May of 1986, and scientists <u>plan</u>
                                           2
to send a spacecraft out to it <u>when</u> it
                                  3
does. Their plans <u>include</u> tests to find
                      4
out what the <u>tail</u> is composed of. As of
                5
now, instruments <u>gather</u> only small bits
                     6
of <u>information</u> about comets. Scientists
      7
<u>know</u> much less about comets <u>than</u> they
  8   9
would like to, and they <u>hope</u> to learn
                            10
<u>from</u> Halley's Comet <u>something</u> about
  11   12
how the solar system was formed.

v	v
1	2
v	v
3	4
	v
5	6
	v
7	8
	v
9	10
11	12

Possessive, Plural, and Plural-Possessive Nouns

Choose the form of the noun that correctly
completes each sentence. Write the letter
of your answer in the space at the right.

1. Some people do not seem to realize   <u>d</u>
   how dangerous ____ can be.
   a. bear's   b. bear
   c. bears'   d. bears
2. Park ____ jobs are complicated by   <u>a</u>
   bears.
   a. rangers'   b. ranger's
   c. ranger   d. rangers
3. A ____ instincts are those of a wild   <u>b</u>
   animal.
   a. bears   b. bear's
   c. bears'   d. bear

4. What seems to you a normal move-   <u>d</u>
ment may seem an attack movement
in many _____ perceptions.
  a. animal   b. animal's
  c. animals   d. animals'

5. Thus bears may be threatened by a   <u>c</u>
_____ small movement.
  a. person   b. persons'
  c. person's   d. persons

6. I once saw a group of _____ around   <u>c</u>
a bear in a park.
  a. adult's   b. adult
  c. adults   d. adults'

7. A woman was taking her _____ pic-   <u>a</u>
ture, and he had his arm around the
bear's neck.
  a. husband's   b. husbands'
  c. husbands   d. husband

8. The bear stared curiously at the ___   <u>b</u>
camera.
  a. wives   b. wife's
  c. wives'   d. wife

9. They were lucky that those _____ did   <u>b</u>
not show a bear attacking a man.
  a. picture   b. pictures
  c. picture's   d. pictures'

Recognizing Subjects and Predicates

Decide if the underlined words in each
sentence are the subject or the predicate
of the sentence. In the space at the right,
write *s* if the words are the subject and *p*
if they are the predicate.

Scuba diving gear <u>allows people to</u>

<u>swim under water for as long as two</u>   <u>p</u>
    1   1

hours. In the past <u>people who wanted to</u>
2

<u>dive</u> had only two choices. They <u>could</u>
3

<u>descend under water in a container that</u>
3

<u>was linked with the surface air</u>. Also,

they <u>could learn to fill their lungs very</u>
4

<u>full of air</u>. <u>The first of these two choices</u>
5

allowed people to stay under water for

a long time but did not allow mobility.

<u>The second choice, which did allow</u>
6

<u>mobility</u>, limited severely the length of

time spent under water.

s
2
p
3
p
4
s
5
s
6

Main vs. Subordinate Clauses

Decide if each numbered clause is a main
clause or a subordinate clause. In the
space at the right, write *m* if the clause is
a main clause; write *s* if it is a subordinate clause. The spaces at the right are
numbered to correspond with the numbers below the clauses.

<u>(1) Musical tastes have changed over the
centuries.</u> Many composers <u>(2) who are
considered great today</u> were not accepted in their lifetimes. <u>(3) This
situation was true in the early part of
this century</u> <u>(4) when composers began
using notes</u> <u>(5) that were dissonant.</u>
<u>(6) Today many of their compositions are</u>

1. <u>m</u>
2. <u>s</u>
3. <u>m</u>
4. <u>s</u>
5. <u>s</u>
6. <u>m</u>

well-loved. (7) Musical tastes do not only change from generation to generation, however. (8) Whatever kind of music a person likes as a young adult may not be the same kind (9) that he or she enjoys later in life. (10) Thus someone may love folk music for some years; (11) later, he or she may enjoy rock, country-western, or classical music. (12) What you enjoy listening to today may sound dull to you next year.

7. __m__
8. __s__
9. __s__
10. __m__
11. __m__
12. __s__

Vocabulary: Synonyms from Writer's List

In the spaces at the right, write synonyms for the underlined words. The spaces are numbered to correspond with the numbers under the words.

Many inventors of the past are unknown today; only their clever inventions remain known to us. Such inventions are quite varied in function. They range from the wheel to the candle. Most of them are things we depend on daily, things which help people enjoy life more. It is difficult to judge exactly how much we owe those unknown people. We can only admit that we owe them much

1. __anonymous__
2. __ingenious__
3. __diverse__
4. __rely__
5. __savor__
6. __assess__
7. __concede__

and <u>praise</u> their efforts as we use the
       8

8. _____ commend _____

results of their labors.

Spelling: Commonly Confused Words

Choose the correct spelling of each word
to complete each sentence. Write the letters of your answer choices in the spaces
at the right.

1. There are many ____ bushes near
   my house.
   a. berry   b. bury
   c. barey   d. beary

1. __a__

2. Most of them grow down near the
   ____.
   a. creak   b. creep
   c. crease   d. creek

2. __d__

3. We could fill up a ____ with fruit
   easily.
   a. pail   b. pale
   c. pall   d. pile

3. __a__

4. Let me know when you have ____
   the bushes as we are walking.
   a. scene   b. seine
   c. seen   d. sewn

4. __c__

5. We want to be sure we have not
   ____ them.
   a. past   b. passed
   c. paste   d. placed

5. __b__

6. Be careful not to hurt your ____ on a
   thorn while we are picking the fruit.
   a. he'll   b. heal
   c. hall   d. heel

6. __d__

Frequently Misspelled Words

Choose the correct spelling for each
word to complete each sentence. Write

the letters of your answer choices in the
spaces at the right.

1. I saw my history ____ in the store today.
   a. proffessor   b. professor
   c. profesor   d. proffesor

1. <u>b</u>

2. He was with his ____ son, looking at garden tools.
   a. adolecent   b. adolesent
   c. adolescent   d. adollescent

2. <u>c</u>

3. I decided not to ____ them.
   a. interrupt   b. interupt
   c. interrup   d. innterupt

3. <u>a</u>

4. They were having an ____ about which saw to buy.
   a. arguement   b. aregument
   c. arrgument   d. argument

4. <u>d</u>

5. I did not want to ____ them by intruding.
   a. embarrass   b. embarass
   c. embarras   d. embaras

5. <u>a</u>

6. Each of them had a ____ opinion about which saw was the better one.
   a. deafinite   b. definate
   c. definite   d. definit

6. <u>c</u>

7. They discussed the ____ good and bad points of the saws at great length.
   a. varous   b. various
   c. varyous   d. varrious

7. <u>b</u>

8. It was quite ____ to me that it would take some time for them to agree.
   a. aparent   b. apparrent
   c. apparent   d. apparant

8. <u>c</u>

9. Both of them had a lot of ____ about the subject.
   a. knoledge   b. knowlege
   c. knolledge   d. knowledge

9. <u>d</u>

10. As I left, I hoped that they would
_____ a solution that would satisfy
both of them.

a. achieve   b. acheive
c. acheeve   d. acheve

10. ___a___

Capitalization and Punctuation

Many of the words in the paragraph below should be capitalized, and much of
the punctuation has been left out. Circle
the words that should be capitalized and
insert punctuation where it is needed.

Antarctica has been explored by people from many different
nations. Charles Wilkes of the United States first discovered
that Antarctica was a continent in 1840. In 1895 Leonard
Kristensen, a Norwegian captain, landed a party on the
Antarctic coast. The first group to stay through the winter
was led by a member of that first landing party, C. E.
Borchgrevink. Another Norwegian, Roald Amundsen, became the first person to reach the South Pole on December
14, 1911. The American explorer Richard E. Byrd established
an Antarctic base in 1929; that base has been used by
explorers ever since. The International Geophysical Year,
from July 1957 through December 1958, gave scientists the
opportunity to do research in Antarctica. Scientists from the
following countries, among others, continue the research
today: the United States, Japan, the Soviet Union, France,
and Australia.

Glossary of Usage Problems

Choose the correct word from each pair at
the left to complete each sentence. Write
your answers in the spaces at the right.

emigrate/ immigrate	1. Many families decide each year to ___ to other countries.	emigrate
amount/ number	2. The ___ of such families is constantly increasing.	number
bring/take	3. When they leave their old homes, they ___ with them their personal treasures.	take
between/ among	4. People who move to other countries can choose ___ many possible new homelands.	among
than/then	5. For various reasons, one country may suit them better ___ another.	than
affect/ effect	6. Wherever they decide to move, the decision will ___ their lives deeply.	affect

PREPARING FORMS AND APPLICATIONS

Filling out various forms and applications is a very practical writing skill for many students. Whether your students complete high school or whether their formal or full-time education ends before graduating from high school, for most of their adult lives they will fill out forms and applications ranging from simple bank deposit slips to more complex federal income-tax forms. They may complete applications for college or for jobs as well as applications for social security, automobile insurance, and a driver's license. They may also fill out forms for insurance claims, automobile accident reports, mail orders, applications for marriage, and, finally, medicare and medicaid.

To help your students develop the necessary writing skills, design your lessons to focus on jobs and practical life skills.

JOBS

1. Applying for a social security number
2. Investigating sources for jobs
   a. want ads
   b. private employment agencies
   c. government employment agencies
   d. personnel departments
   e. civil service
3. Writing letters of request for job applicaion forms
4. Filling out forms

You may obtain a job application form from a local business that may permit you to duplicate it for your students' practice.

LIFE SKILLS

Money

1. Opening a savings account
2. Making a savings account deposit
3. Opening a checking account
4. Making a checking account deposit
5. Writing checks
6. Preparing a state income-tax form
7. Preparing a federal income-tax form

Automobile

Design your lessons to include some of the following:

1. Appling for a driver's license
2. Applying for a car loan
3. Appling for automobile insurance
4. Applying for gasoline company charge cards

HELPFUL HINTS

1. Various forms may be obtained from government agencies and local businesses.
2. Because of the terminology used in some forms, you may

want to design a team-teaching lesson with a business or mathematics teacher.

3. One successful method for interested students is to use community resource people, such as a local insurance agent, an automobile dealer, a bank representative, and an armed services recruiter.

4. Because of the number of forms generated by your classes, you may want to use peer-editing as a strategy for sharpening your student's skills as well as making your own workload manageable.

5. Points you may want to stress with students:
   a. Always read and examine entire form *before* you begin to respond.
   b. Print clearly, or type your responses.
   c. Answer all questions where applicable and to the best of your knowledge.

ADDITIONAL ANSWERS FOR TEXT EXERCISES

In general, answers to exercises are in place in this Teacher's Edition. Answers too lengthy for placement on the text page are given here.

1.

Lions | roar

aviators | remember | biplanes
Old-time | still

farms | have expanded
Many | in
years
recent

movies | are | funny
Home | often

2.

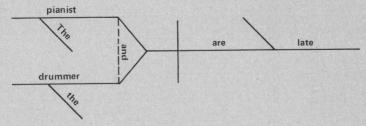

3. Answers will vary. The first example of a compound sentence on page 153 is diagramed below.

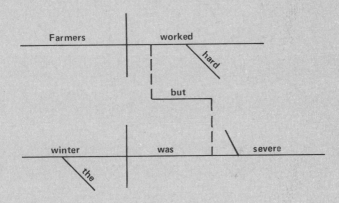

4. Answers will vary. The first example sentence on page 172 is diagramed below.

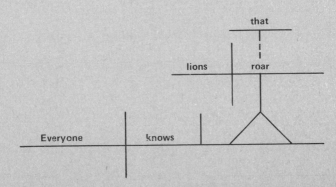

5.

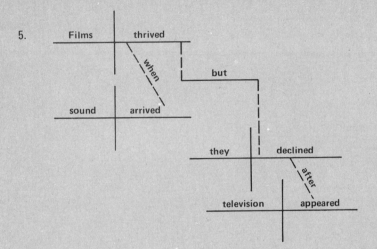

Section 6, Exercise 3 (page 334)
1. (sān) a large fishing net
2. (i͞ d'l) a short poem or prose work
3. (ik strap´ ə lāt´) to arrive at a conclusion by observing
4. (ri sind´) to abolish or cancel
5. (vō sif´ ər əs) loud, noisy
6. (no͞o) large African antelope
7. (nän´ ə ji ner´ ē ən) a person ninety to ninety-nine years old
8. (rə vänsh´ iz´m) revenge (especially of a defeated country demanding territory back)
9. (il´ ē əm) Latin name for Troy
10. (dā no͞o´ män) the outcome of a plot

Section 6, Exercise 4 (page 335)
1. (frē´ kwənt), adj. ; (frē kwent´), v.
2. (rē´ jekt), n. ; (ri jekt´), v.
3. (kän´ trakt), n.; (kən trakt´), v.
4. (mäd´ ər it), adj.; (mäd ə rāt´), v.
5. (dez´ ig nāt), v.; (dez´ ig nit), adj.
6. (präj´ ekt), n.; (prə jekt´), v.
7. (pur´ fikt), adj.; (pər fekt´), v.
8. (ek´ spərt), n.; (ik spurt´), adj.
9. (di lib´ ər it), adj.; (di lib´ ər āt), v.
10. (äb´ jikt), n.; (əb jekt´), v.

Section 6, Exercise 5 (page 337)
1. from Old French finer, "to settle an account"
2. from Latin armatus, "armored"
3. from Algonquian (Native American) ärä̆kun, "snatcher"
4. from Latin opinari, "to think"
5. from Greek deinos, "terrible," and sauros, "lizard"
6. from Sanskrit pitár (from baby talk)
7. after John L. McAdam (1756-1836), Scottish engineer who invented the process of mixing broken stone and asphalt
8. from Latin conglomeratus, "to gather into a ball"
9. from Latin pedalis, "foot"
10. from Latin inimicus, "not a friend"

Section 6, Exercise 10 (page 341)
1. British dialect: a companion or comrade
2. Slang: attractive
3. Golf: to hit from the tee

4. Tennis: an error in serve
5. Colloquial: a weak-willed person
6. Tennis: a stroke in which the ball is sent high in the air, usually into the opponent's back court
7. Slang: desirable because important ("a fat role")
8. Poetic: before in time
9. Archaic: feeling or causing sorrow
10. Architecture: a style of English Gothic

Section 12, Exercise 5 (page 549)

I.   Discover geography of city
    A. Walking up and down steep streets
    B. Wandering through evening fog
    C. Sailing on San Francisco Bay

II. Ride cable cars up famous hills
    A. Nob Hill
        1. Victorian mansions
        2. Famous hotels
    B. Russian Hill and Crookedest Street in the World
    C. Telegraph Hill
        1. Tour of Bohemian area
        2. View of city from Coit Tower
        3. One of many cafés to eat in

III. Visit Chinatown
    A. Shopping at vegetable stands and fish markets
    B. Having lunch at a tearoom

IV. Drive or bicycle across Golden Gate Bridge
    A. Marin County
    B. Spectacular view of San Francisco

Section 15, Exercise 1 (page 607)

1. The Buyer's Guide
    1500 Manin Street
    Manin, Illinois 61224

    Dear Sir or Madam:

2. James Morrison
    Five Star Music Company
    101 Tremont Avenue
    Jasper, Missouri 64755

    Dear Mr. Morrison:

3. President
   Daygrow Seed Company
   659 Grand Street
   Wilmington, Vermont 05360
   Dear Sir or Madam:
4. Ms. Louise Hilton
   Editor-in-Chief
   Grand Publishing Company
   82 East 40th Street
   New York, New York 10043
   Dear Ms. Hilton:
5. Professor R. Mark Mizner
   English Department
   Colby College
   Waterville, Maine 04890
   Dear Professor Mizner:

Section 15, Exercise 2 (page 609)
1. Joyce Keating, Director
   Hillcrest Photo Studios
   162 Del Paso Boulevard
   Sacramento, California 95815
   Dear Ms. Keating:
   Sincerely yours,
2. The Seacraft Company
   8500 Long Beach Road
   Darien, Connecticut 06845
   Dear Sir or Madam:
   Very truly yours,
3. Patrick Larch, Director
   All-Stars Soccer Camp
   P.O. Box 660
   Manchester, New Hampshire 03106
   Dear Patrick Larch:
   Cordially,
4. Manager
   Cheyenne Sports Arena
   Cheyenne, Wyoming 82002
   Dear Sir or Madam:
   Respectfully yours,
5. Answers will vary.

Section 16, Exercise 1 (page 619)

I. Weaknesses in electoral-college system

   A. A candidate with more citizen votes may still lose election.
   B. Electors in the electoral college may vote for anyone.
   C. A President may have to be elected by the House of Representatives.

II. An advantage in electoral-college system: All states with same number of senators

   A. Less populated states have a better ratio of votes.
   B. Large states have great power to swing an election.

Section 16, Exercise 2 (page 621)

NOTES

NOTES

NOTES

NOTES

TM80

Grammar and Writing

AUTHORS AND ADVISERS

Walter Loban
General Adviser
Professor of Education
University of California
at Berkeley

Donald C. Freeman
Specialist, Linguistics
Temple University
Philadelphia, Pennsylvania

Robert W. Reising
Specialist, Grammar and
Composition
Pembroke State University
Pembroke, North Carolina

James Harkness
Specialist, Libraries and
Information
State University of New York
Albany, New York

Patricia Laurence
Specialist, Composition
The City College, C.U.N.Y.
New York, New York

Sandra Stotsky
Specialist, Vocabulary
Curry College
Milton, Massachusetts

Vicki Jacobs
Specialist, Vocabulary
Holbrook Public Schools
Holbrook, Massachusetts

Robert J. Jones
Specialist, Test Taking
Educational Testing Service
Princeton, New Jersey

CONSULTANTS

Martha Brooks, Abilene Independent School District, Abilene, Texas
Leslie MacIntyre, Homestead High School, Mequon, Wisconsin
Henry F. Mooney, Danvers Public Schools, Danvers, Massachusetts
Norman Rudnick, Miramonte High School, Orinda, California
Milton Schaeffer, Maplewood–South Orange School District, New Jersey
Mary Jo Wagner, Leland High School, San Jose, California

Grammar and Writing

Macmillan Publishing Co., Inc.
New York
Collier Macmillan Publishers
London

WALTER LOBAN, General Adviser, has been active in English education for many years. Among his scholarly publications in the area of language is *Teaching Language and Literature: Grades 7–12*, of which he is co-author. Dr. Loban's landmark study *Language Development: Kindergarten Through Grade 12* (NCTE: 1976) has provided unique and valuable information about the acquisition of syntactic elements by student writers.

DONALD C. FREEMAN, who is special adviser on grammar, is professor of English and chairman of the committee on linguistics at Temple University, Philadelphia. His examination of student writing has made him a leader in error analysis.

ROBERT W. REISING, who is adviser on grammar and composition, is professor of communicative arts at Pembroke State University, Pembroke, North Carolina. He has led workshops in English, most recently at the University of North Carolina, at Charlotte.

PATRICIA LAURENCE, who is adviser on composition, teaches basic writing, literature, and linguistics at The City College of the City University of New York.

SANDRA STOTSKY, who developed the vocabulary section, is associated with Curry College, Milton, Massachusetts, and Harvard University. She works extensively with teachers in the Holbrook and the Boston public schools.

Macmillan Publishing Co., Inc.
866 Third Avenue, New York, New York 10022
Collier Macmillan Canada, Ltd.

Printed in the United States of America

Student Edition ISBN 0-02-245880-8
Teacher's Edition ISBN 0-02-245890-5
987654321

ACKNOWLEDGMENTS

Grateful acknowledgment is given authors and publishers for permission to reprint the following material:

We are indebted to Mary S. Lawrence for significant contributions in the form of ideas and exercises that appear in Section 11 of this text. This material is from *Writing As a Thinking Process* by Mary S. Lawrence, published by the University of Michigan Press, copyright © by The University of Michigan 1972.

HM Study Skills Program, Level II. Copyright © 1979, by NASSP, 1904 Association Dr., Reston, Va. 22091. All Rights Reserved. Selections reprinted by permission of the publisher.

Information Please Almanac 1979. Copyright © 1976, 1978, Information Please Publications, Inc. Reprinted by permission of Simon & Schuster, a Division of Gulf & Western Corporation.

Macmillan Dictionary, William D. Halsey, Editorial Director. Copyright © 1977, 1973 Macmillan Publishing Co., Inc. Selections reprinted by permission of the publisher.

"The MacNeil/Lehrer Approach," by John Grossmann, *American Way*, November 1979. Reprinted by permission of the publisher.

Readers' Guide to Periodical Literature. Copyright © 1979 by the H. W. Wilson Company. Selections reproduced by permission of the publisher.

Webster's New World Dictionary, Second College Edition. Copyright © 1978 by William Collins + World Publishing Co., Inc. Selections reprinted by permission of the publisher.

"Who Are You?" reprinted excerpt, from *Cricket*, Vol. 4, No. 5, Jan. 1977. Copyright © 1977 by permission of Susan Schoon Eberly.

CONTENTS

Grammar, Usage, and Sentences

Word Study

1

PARTS OF SPEECH

Parts of Speech

See summary of section in Teacher's Manual. See also Additional Exercises 1-8 (pages 646-653), which provide additional drill on parts of speech and verbals.

The term *parts of speech* may be quite familiar to you by now. It may, however, be one of those terms that you have heard for years but have never really stopped to think about. What does *parts of speech* actually mean?

The English language has hundreds of thousands of words. Fortunately, though, these words can all be grouped into a few different categories. Once you group them, you can more easily learn their characteristics. You can learn what makes the words in one group different from the words in another group. You can learn which group (or subgroup) gives you trouble when you write or speak. You can learn how the words in one group can connect with words in another group.

The parts of speech, then, are no more than the groups into which the hundreds of thousands of words are placed. Some of the groups (such as *nouns*) are themselves huge and can grow. Other groups (such as *conjunctions*) are much smaller and, generally speaking, do not grow. You will study all the groups in this section.

Section Review Exercises on pages 109-110 can be used as diagnostic tests at the beginning or as a brief mastery tests at the end of Section 1.

1.a NOUNS

EXTRA: Elicit from students nouns that have come into our language in the past five years.

A **noun** is a word that names a person, place, thing, or idea.

Examples of nouns naming a person are *woman* and *student*. Examples of nouns naming a thing are *pen* and *party*. Nouns also name animals, objects, places, groups, actions, times, events, ideas, and qualities.

EXAMPLES

PERSON: boy, girl, woman, man, baby, uncle, grand-mother, singer, artist

ANIMAL: butterfly, ant, chicken, dinosaur, horse, dog, fish, clam, seagull, zebra

OBJECT: coat, comb, mirror, picture, wallet, bicycle, wheel, wall, tree, bud, newspaper

PLACE: attic, state, farm, garden, village, neighbor-hood, airport, island

GROUP: army, team, club, flock, herd, audience, pack, troop, society, band

ACTION: laughter, a somersault, a spin, a race, a touch, a sneeze, a hug, a fall

TIME: midnight, morning, minute, hour, day, month, year, century, second

EVENT: party, test, graduation, wedding, trip, date, meeting, ceremony, funeral

IDEA OR QUALITY: democracy, justice, truth, beauty, warmth, fear, loneliness

A noun that names a group is called a **collective noun.** *Army, club,* and *audience* are collective nouns. (For more information about collective nouns, see 1.a.4.)

EXERCISE 1. Tell what each of the numbered nouns names. Give one of the letters on the right to each of the numbered nouns on the left. You may repeat letters.

1. the *planet* d
2. the *bone* c
3. the *cousin* a
4. the *prom* g
5. the *afternoon* f
6. the *orchestra* e
7. the *coolness* h
8. the *kangaroo* b
9. the *beach* d
10. the *contest* g

a. person
b. animal
c. object
d. place
e. group
f. time
g. event
h. idea or quality

APPLICATION. To see how nouns can become part of your own writing, compose one sentence for each of five of the nouns from Exercise 1. *Answers will vary; an example is "I wore a blue gown to the junior prom."*

1.a.1 Proper nouns and common nouns

Nouns can be divided into two groups: common nouns and proper nouns. A **common noun** is the *general* name for something — dog, uncle, lake. A **proper noun,** on the other hand, is the *specific* name for a particular thing — Snoopy, Uncle Lou, Lake Michigan. Your own name is a proper noun because it names a specific person. Proper nouns are capitalized; common nouns are not capitalized. (For the rules of capitalization of proper nouns, see 7.a.)

PROPER NOUNS
PERSON: Margaret Mead, George Washington Carver
PLACE: Jupiter, France, Salt Lake City, California
ANIMAL: Bugs Bunny, Jaws, Sounder
OBJECT: *Air Force One,* the *Mona Lisa*
GROUP: the Red Cross, the Miami Orchestra
TIME: Friday, November, Washington's Birthday
EVENT: the Olympics, the World Series, World War II
IDEA: Judaism, Marxism, Lutheranism

EXERCISE 2. Tell whether each of the italicized nouns in the sentences below is a proper noun or a common noun.

1. The earliest skates were made of *bone* and wood. *common*
2. Iron *skates* were found to be stronger. *common*
3. Ice skating is a traditional means of travel in *Holland,* where there are many canals that freeze in winter. *proper*
4. Skating is both a means of travel and a *sport.* *common*
5. Skating is a popular sport in the United States and *Canada.* *proper*
6. Montreal and *Toronto* are well-known for their ice skating events. *proper*
7. Figure skating is an important event in the *Olympics.*
proper

8. An American named *Jackson Haines* invented figure skating in the 1860s. *proper*

9. The *National Ice Skating Hall of Fame* is in Newburgh, New York. *proper*

10. The *hall* has outstanding exhibits. *common*

1.a.2 Compound nouns

Compound nouns are nouns that are made up of more than one word. In some compound nouns the words are separate: *high school.* In others the words are combined: *wheelchair.* In still other compound nouns the words are separated by hyphens: *great-grandmother.*

EXAMPLES

hairdresser	french fries	sister-in-law
mailbox	gas station	actor-director

EXERCISE 3. For each category below, list four common nouns and one proper noun.

EXAMPLE nouns that are in a house — for example, *plate*

ANSWER common nouns: *door, television, chair, stove*
proper noun: *Spot*

1. nouns that you can ride in — for example, *car* subway, *Orient Express*

2. nouns that you can read — for example, *novel* poem, *Moby Dick*

3. nouns that you can belong to — for example, *club* team, the Y.M.C.A.

4. nouns that you can hear or listen to — for example, *radio* lecturer, the Chicago Symphony Orchestra

5. nouns that you can swim in — for example, *lake* pool, the Atlantic Ocean

6. nouns that you can play — for example, *chess*

7. nouns that you can learn in school — for example, *algebra* ice hockey, French violin, Monopoly

8. nouns that you can attend — for example, *parade* lecture, Mummers' Parade

9. nouns that you can eat — for example, *crackers* ice cream, Gouda

10. nouns that you can give as gifts — for example, *bracelet* tie, *The Oxford Companion to Film*

APPLICATION. Look again at the four common nouns and the one proper noun that you listed for *one* of the items in Exercise 3. Write *one* sentence that uses all five nouns.

> EXAMPLE **Spot** *left the warm spot in front of the* **stove,** *dashed through the* **door** *to the living room, and jumped onto the* **chair** *to watch the dog-food commercial on* **television.**

1.a.3 Singular nouns and plural nouns

Most nouns can have both singular and plural forms. The word *singular* means "one." A **singular noun** names one person or one thing. The word *plural* means "more than one." A **plural noun** names more than one person or thing.

EXAMPLES

Singular nouns	Plural nouns
car	cars
game	games
cousin	cousins
cat	cats
morning	mornings

The following chart summarizes the rules for changing a singular noun into a plural noun. (See Section 5 for more information about spelling plurals.)

FORMING PLURAL NOUNS

For most nouns, add s.	For nouns ending in s, x, z, sh, ch, add es.	For nouns ending in y preceded by a consonant, change the y to i and add es.
table, tables parrot, parrots month, months	bus, buses box, boxes waltz, waltzes wish, wishes lunch, lunches	colony, colonies country, countries lullaby, lullabies

For nouns ending in y preceded by a vowel, add s.	For most nouns ending in f or fe, add s.	For some nouns ending in f or fe, change the f or fe to v and add es.
monkey, monkeys boy, boys day, days	roof, roofs safe, safes	leaf, lea**ves** life, li**ves**
For most nouns ending in o preceded by a consonant, add es.	**For nouns ending in o preceded by a vowel, add s.**	**For some irregular nouns, learn the special forms.**
tomato, tomato**es** veto, veto**es**	radio, radio**s** cameo, cameo**s**	child, **children** tooth, **teeth** woman, **women** man, **men** ox, **oxen**
For some nouns, the plural form is the same as the singular.	**For compound nouns, follow the preceding rules. If the compound is hyphenated or written as separate words, make the most important part of the compound plural.**	**For most proper nouns, add s. Add es to proper nouns that end in s, x, z, sh, ch.**

deer, deer
sheep, sheep
series, series
species, species
	boxful, boxful**s**
	mother-in-law,
	   mother**s**-in-law
	city-state, city-state**s**
	ice cream, ice cream**s**
	attorney general,
	   attorney**s** general
		Long, the Long**s**
		Quincy, the Quincy**s**
		Harris, the Harris**es**
		Bendix, the Bendix**es**
		Velez, the Velez**es**
		Rush, the Rush**es**
		March, the March**es**

Some singular nouns look and sound like plural nouns because they end in *s* or *es*. Because they name only one thing, however, they are singular.

SINGULAR NOUNS THAT END IN *S*

mathematics	mumps
physics	measles
news	electronics
rabies	dominoes [the game]

EXERCISE 4. Write the plural form of each of the following singular nouns. Check your answers in a dictionary to be sure of the correct spelling.

1. curtain   *curtains*
2. moss   *mosses*
3. sky   *skies*
4. giraffe   *giraffes*
5. life   *lives*
6. potato   *potatoes*
7. radio   *radios*
8. halo   *halos, haloes*
9. deer   *deer*
10. father-in-law   *fathers-in-law*
11. passer-by   *passers-by*
12. battery   *batteries*
13. tax   *taxes*
14. baby   *babies*
15. shelf   *shelves*
16. orange   *oranges*
17. station wagon   *station wagons*
18. mouthful   *mouthfuls*
19. delay   *delays*
20. gas   *gases*

APPLICATION. Select five nouns from Exercise 4. For each noun write *one* sentence that uses *both* the singular and the plural forms of the noun.   *Answers will vary.*

> EXAMPLE   *The gold* **curtain** *parted to reveal three muslin* **curtains** *behind it.*

1.a.4 Collective nouns

A **collective noun** names a group. It may name a group of people — *army* — or a group of things — *flock*.

EXAMPLES

the public	the pack (of dogs)
the staff	the litter (of young animals)
the group	the herd

Collective nouns can be either singular or plural depending on the meaning intended. If you mean the group as a whole, the collective noun has a singular meaning.

HINT: Most collective nouns are used as singular nouns. A good test to see whether a collective noun is singular is to substitute the word *it* for the collective noun in your sentence. If you can substitute *it* for the collective noun, the collective noun is singular.

SINGULAR COLLECTIVE NOUNS

The **committee** meets in the office.
[**It** meets in the office.]

The **jury** has reached a verdict.
[**It** has reached a verdict.]

Plural collective nouns refer to the individual members of the group.

HINT: If you can substitute the word *they* or *them* for the collective noun, the collective noun is plural.

PLURAL COLLECTIVE NOUNS

The **committee** argued among themselves.
[**They** argued among themselves.]

The **jury** were unable to agree.
[**They** were unable to agree.]

EXERCISE 5. Tell whether the italicized collective noun in each sentence below is singular or plural. Remember that collective nouns are singular or plural according to how they are used. Read each sentence carefully.

1. The German *army* moved its troops into Italy and France during World War II. *sing.*

2. The *army* prepared for battle by cleaning equipment and turning in early. *pl.*

3. A *litter* of newborn hamsters is delightful to watch. *sing.*

4. The *litter* blindly crawl about, scenting food with their keen noses. *pl.*

5. A famous South American rock *group* is Santana. *sing.*

6. The *group* compose songs that appeal to almost everyone. *pl.*

7. The Navajo *tribe* is located in the Southwest. *sing.*

8. The *tribe* have developed special talents in making turquoise jewelry and rugs. *pl.*

9. The *public* usually think of their own interests first. *pl.*
10. The United States *public* has a strong voice in the country. *sing.*

1.a.5 The possessive form of nouns

Use the **possessive form** of a noun to show possession, ownership, or the relationship between two nouns. The following chart summarizes the rules for making the possessive forms of nouns. (See also 5.b.5 and 7.k.)

POSSESSIVE FORMS OF NOUNS

For singular nouns that do not end in s, add 's.	*For singular nouns of one syllable that end in s, add 's.*	*For singular nouns of more than one syllable that end in s, add '.*
the cat**'s** paw Helen**'s** friend	the kiss**'s** meaning Charles**'s** shirt	the witness' story Carlos' bicycle
For plural nouns that do not end in s, add 's.	*For plural nouns that end in s, add '.*	*For compound nouns, follow the preceding rules in making the last part of the compound possessive.*
the women**'s** group the sheep**'s** wool	the girls' skates the zebras' stripes the Dodgers' record	hairdresser**'s** shop ice cream**'s** flavor mothers-in-law**'s** letters

EXERCISE 6. Reword each of the following expressions by using a possessive form of the noun.

EXAMPLE an opinion that the woman has
ANSWER *the woman's opinion*

1. the ideas that my brother has *my brother's ideas*
2. an opinion that the sisters have *the sisters' opinion*
3. the testimony of the witness *the witness' testimony*
4. the beauty of the glass *the glass's beauty*
5. the mittens of the children *the children's mittens*

6. the gallop of the horse   *the horse's gallop*
7. the job that my sister-in-law has   *my sister-in-law's job*
8. the power of the committees   *the committees' power*
9. a car that belongs to Dr. Andros   *Dr. Andros' car*
10. a house that belongs to the Charleses   *the Charleses' house*

EXTRA: Ask students to use five of their reworded expressions from Exercise 6 in sentences.

AVOIDING ERRORS WITH NOUNS

1. Remember to change a singular noun to its plural form when you mean "more than one."

   NOT   two ~~rose~~   many ~~rose~~
   BUT   two rose**s**   many rose**s**

2. Do not confuse the possessive form (*'s*) with the plural form (*s, es*). Do not use an apostrophe with a noun when you mean "more than one."

   NOT   The boy has fifty ~~record's~~ in his collection.
   BUT   The boy has fifty record**s** in his collection.

REVIEW EXERCISE A. In each of the sentences below, tell whether the italicized noun is a common noun or a proper noun. Then tell whether it is singular or plural.

   EXAMPLE Snakes have skin made of *scales..*
   ANSWER   *scales — common noun, plural*

1. A snake sheds its *skin* several times a year.   *common noun, sing.*
2. The *mouth* of a snake can open very wide.   *common noun, sing.*
3. Snakes have no *ears*, and their eyelids do not open and shut.   *common noun, pl.*
4. The ancient *Egyptians* worshiped snakes.   *proper noun, pl.*
5. Scientists think that snakes originally descended from *lizards*.   *common noun, pl.*

6. Some snakes inject a *poison* into their prey. *common noun, sing.*

7. A poisonous snake bite can even cause death to *humans.* *common noun, pl.*

8. Most snakes lay *eggs.* *common noun, pl.*

9. There are no snakes in New Zealand or *Ireland.* *proper noun, sing.*

10. *St. Patrick* is said to have driven the snakes out of Ireland. *proper noun, sing.*

EXTRA: Ask students to identify common and proper nouns not italicized in Review Exercise A.

1.b VERBS

A **verb** is a word that expresses action or that helps to make a statement.

Verbs are the life of language. Without verbs sentences do not really have meaning. There are two main kinds of verbs: action verbs and linking verbs.

Action verbs tell what someone or something *does.* Look at the action verbs below, and see how each one can be used in a sentence.

play   We **play** baseball.
watch   Fans **watch** the game.
hit   All the players **hit** well.

Linking verbs tell that someone or something *is*, not what someone or something *does.*

ACTION VERBS	LINKING VERBS
Fish **swim.**	Fish **are** cold-blooded.
Whales **dive.**	Whales **look** huge.
Dolphins **play.**	Dolphins **seem** happy.

EXERCISE 7. Identify the action verb in each of the following sentences. Remember than an action verb tells what someone or something *does.*

1. Many Americans eat Chinese food.

2. Americans often cook Chinese food at home.

3. Chinese chefs mix vegetables, meats, and spices.

4. Those chefs <u>choose</u> the freshest vegetables possible.

5. Chinese chefs <u>cut</u> food into bite-sized pieces.

6. Some Americans <u>use</u> chopsticks in Chinese restaurants.

7. Restaurants usually <u>serve</u> rice, tea, and soy sauce with Chinese dinners.

8. Some people <u>add</u> spicy mustard to Chinese food.

9. People of the Szechuan region <u>prepare</u> food differently from those of the Hunan region.

10. People of both regions <u>enjoy</u> hot, spicy dishes.

EXERCISE 8. Tell which of the following words can be action verbs by deciding which make sense in the following blank: *They _____ it.* Remember also that an action verb tells what someone or something *does.*

1. like √	8. add √	15. play √
2. around	9. eat √	16. prepare √
3. kick √	10. desk	17. study √
4. about	11. cook √	18. happy
5. use √	12. very	19. watch √
6. see √	13. when	20. nobody
7. slowly	14. sing √	

APPLICATION. Select five of the action verbs that you identified in Exercise 8. Use each one in a sentence.

Answers will vary; an example is
"Some people <u>like</u> opera."

1.b.1 Action verbs: physical and mental

Some action verbs express physical action, and some express mental action.

EXAMPLES
Athletes **run.** [physical action]
Coaches **draw** diagrams. [physical action]
Players **dream** of victory. [mental action]

1.b.2 Transitive and intransitive verbs

Sometimes an action verb is followed by a word that answers the question *what?* or *whom?* A word that answers the question *what?* or *whom?* after an action verb is a direct object (see 2.k). An action verb that has, or "takes," a direct object is called a **transitive verb.**

TRANSITIVE VERBS
Space shuttles **fly** passengers. [action verb + word that answers the question *fly whom?*]
Astronauts **train** recruits. [action verb + word that answers the question *train whom?*]

An action verb that does not take a direct object is called an **intransitive verb.** An intransitive verb may be followed by a word that tells *how* or *when* the action takes place, but an intransitive verb is not followed by words that answer the questions *what?* or *whom?*

INTRANSITIVE VERBS
Space shuttles **fly.** [action verb alone]
Astronauts **train** hard. [action verb + word that tells *how*]

Most action verbs, like *fly* and *train* in the examples above, can be used as either transitive or intransitive verbs. If they take a direct object, they are transitive; if not, they are intransitive.

EXAMPLES
Astronauts **study** the moon. [The verb *study* takes the direct object *moon;* therefore, it is transitive.]
Astronauts **study** carefully. [*Study* has no direct object; therefore, it is intransitive.]

EXERCISE 9. Find the transitive verb and its direct object in each of the following sentences. The direct object of a verb never follows a preposition.

1. Americans plan vacations early.
      t.v. *d.o.*

2. Many people *enjoy* the *sun* at the beach. _(t.v. / d.o.)_
3. Stores *sell* *sunscreen* to people afraid of sunburn. _(t.v. / d.o.)_
4. At ocean beaches surfers *ride* *waves*. _(t.v. / d.o.)_
5. Athletic people *play* *softball* in the summer. _(t.v. / d.o.)_
6. Many families *organize* *picnics* with their neighbors. _(t.v. / d.o.)_
7. Millions of Americans *drink* *lemonade*. _(t.v. / d.o.)_
8. Gardeners *raise* *vegetables* in their back yards. _(t.v. / d.o.)_
9. Other people *make* *ice cream* in home freezers. _(t.v. / d.o.)_
10. Children *build* *castles* in the sand. _(t.v. / d.o.)_

EXERCISE 10. Find the action verb in each of the following sentences. Tell whether each action verb is a transitive verb or an intransitive verb. One of the sentences contains two action verbs.

1. Animals <u>react</u> in many different ways to danger. *i.*
2. Lions and tigers <u>fight</u> with their claws and teeth. *i.*
3. Bees, wasps, and jellyfish <u>sting</u> attackers. *t.*
4. Ostriches as well as horses <u>kick</u> enemies. *t.*
5. Opossums simply <u>lie</u> on the ground as if dead. *i.*
6. The chameleon and other lizards <u>change</u> colors. *t.*
7. Skunks <u>release</u> an odor when in danger. *t.*
8. People sometimes <u>die</u> from poisonous snakebites. *i.*
9. Some octopuses <u>squirt</u> "ink" around themselves and <u>conceal</u> their escape. *t., t.*
10. Rabbits, with no other means of protection, <u>run</u> as fast as possible. *i.*

APPLICATION. Select five of the action verbs that you identified in Exercise 10. Use each in an original sentence.

Answers will vary; an example is "People usually <u>change</u> a great deal as they grow older."

1.b.3 *Be:* a linking verb

Linking verbs tell that someone or something *is.* They link, or join, one word with another word that adds a description or identification. Linking verbs are always followed by words that answer the question *what?*, *who?*, or *where?*

The most common linking verbs are forms of *be*. Forms of *be* include *am, is, are, was, were, be, being, been.*

EXAMPLES

Squash **is** an indoor sport.
Squash and tennis **are** fast games.
They **were** hockey fans.
I **was** too slow.

1.b.4 Other linking verbs

In addition to *be*, English has other linking verbs. Some of these other linking verbs are listed below.

EXAMPLES

APPEAR: Energy and fuel conservation **appear** necessary. [*Appear* links *conservation* with a word of description, *necessary.*]

BECOME: Impractical ideas often **become** practical eventually. [*Become* links *ideas* with a word of description, *practical.*]

FEEL: Families **feel** nervous about fuel prices.

GROW: Building costs **grow** higher each year.

LOOK: New houses **look** different from old houses.

REMAIN: New sources of energy **remain** expensive.

SEEM: Solar energy **seems** unlimited.

SOUND: Many ideas for new energy sources **sound** impractical.

STAY: Insulated houses **stay** warm or cool better than houses without insulation.

EXERCISE 11. Identify the linking verb in each of the following sentences.

1. Many clothing fads become outdated.
2. Other fashions stay popular for a long time.

3. The styles of earlier generations often <u>appear</u> ridiculous today.
4. In the 1980s blue jeans <u>seem</u> as popular as ever.
5. Conservative blue and gray suits <u>remain</u> the standard dress for many business people.
6. Natural fabrics like cotton and wool <u>grow</u> popular.
7. Cotton clothes <u>feel</u> soft next to the skin.
8. Synthetic fabrics <u>stay</u> pressed better than cotton and wool.
9. Certain styles <u>look</u> odd on people of the wrong age.
10. Shorter people wearing vertical stripes <u>appear</u> taller.

1.b.5 Linking verbs or action verbs?

Except for *be* and *seem*, all verbs that are used as linking verbs can also be used as action verbs. The following pairs of sentences show the same word used first as a linking verb and then as an action verb.

EXAMPLES
LINKING: Solar heaters on roofs **look** strange at first.
ACTION: Scientists **look** for new energy sources.
LINKING: Taxpayers often **grow** angry about taxes.
ACTION: Californians **grow** avocados.

One way of telling if the verb in a sentence is a linking verb or an action verb is to substitute a form of *seem* for the verb. If the sentence still makes sense, the verb is probably a linking verb.

EXAMPLES
That milk **tastes** sour.
That milk **seems** sour. [Sentence makes sense; *taste* is a linking verb.]
I **taste** the milk.
I ~~**seem**~~ the milk. [Sentence does not make sense; *taste* is an action verb.]

EXERCISE 12. Find the verb in each sentence in each pair. Indicate if it is a linking verb or an action verb.

1. a. National parks <u>remain</u> popular with tourists. *l.v.*
   b. In Yellowstone National Park people <u>remain</u> in their cars while on tours of the park. *a.v.*
2. a. Bears sometimes <u>appear</u> in campsites. *a.v.*
   b. Bears sometimes <u>appear</u> friendly. *l.v.*
3. a. A guard should <u>sound</u> the alarm in case of trouble. *a.v.*
   b. Not all pianos <u>sound</u> alike. *l.v.*
4. a. Fresh raspberries <u>taste</u> wonderful. *l.v.*
   b. Many people <u>taste</u> liver reluctantly. *a.v.*
5. a. Children seldom <u>stay</u> quiet for long. *l.v.*
   b. You <u>stay</u> here. *a.v.*
6. a. I <u>smell</u> smoke. *a.v.*
   b. Cinnamon and nutmeg <u>smell</u> different from each other. *l.v.*

1.b.6 Agreement in number

A verb, action or linking, must **agree in number** with the person or thing that it is talking about (its **subject**).

With every verb except *be,* you have to worry about this rule only in the present tense and only with a singular third-person subject. In the present tense with a **singular** third-person subject, add -*s* or -*es* to the basic form of the verb. With a plural third-person subject do not add -*s* or -*es* to the verb.

HINT: The best way to remember when to add the -*s* (or-*es*)for present-tense verbs is to think about the following rule: In general, an *s* appears on the noun *or* on the verb — but not on both.

The top spin**s**.	The top**s** spin.
The dolphin splashe**s**.	The dolphin**s** splash.
The cat grin**s**.	The cat**s** grin.
The clown laugh**s**.	The clown**s** laugh.

EXERCISE 13. Ten words in the following paragraph end in *s*. Some of them are plural nouns (review 1.a.3). Some are present-tense verbs that agree in number with third-person singular nouns. Copy the passage. Write *n* above each noun that ends in *s*. Write *v* above each verb that ends in *s*.

¹Rhododendron leaves help to tell the temperature. ²The broad-leaved plants ordinarily decorate thousands of suburban yards. ³When the temperature drops below freezing, however, those broad leaves change shape. ⁴A person who knows that a rhododendron plant adjusts to temperature can look through a window and estimate the temperature. ⁵The colder and dryer the air becomes, the more the leaves roll up.

1.b.7 Principal parts of verbs

All verbs have four forms, called **principal parts.** The principal parts are used by themselves or in combination with other words to form the different tenses and to form verb phrases. The principal parts of some common verbs are listed below.

PRINCIPAL PARTS OF VERBS

Basic verb	Present participle	Past tense	Past participle
work	working	worked	worked
sing	singing	sang	sung
build	building	built	built
be	being	was/were	been
live	living	lived	lived

1.b.8 Regular verbs

Verbs can be divided into two groups, regular verbs and irregular verbs, on the basis of the way they form their past tense and past participle. Most verbs are **regular**

verbs, which means that both the past tense and the past participle are formed by adding -*d* or -*ed* to the basic verb.

REGULAR VERBS

Basic verb	Past tense	Past participle
talk	talk**ed**	talk**ed**
answer	answer**ed**	answer**ed**

1.b.9 Irregular verbs

Many of the most common verbs are irregular verbs. An **irregular verb** forms its past tense and past participle in some other way than by adding -*d* or -*ed* to the basic verb. There are many different ways to form the past tense and past participle of irregular verbs. Sometimes the two parts are different (*sang* and *sung*), sometimes they are the same (*caught* and *caught*), and sometimes they are the same as the basic form of the verb (*put* and *put*).

COMMON IRREGULAR VERBS

Basic verb	Past tense	Past participle
become	became	become
begin	began	begun
bite	bit	bitten
bring	brought	brought
catch	caught	caught
come	came	come
do	did	done
draw	drew	drawn
drink	drank	drunk
drive	drove	driven
eat	ate	eaten
fall	fell	fallen
fly	flew	flown
freeze	froze	frozen
give	gave	given
go	went	gone

Basic verb	Past tense	Past participle
grow	grew	grown
have	had	had
know	knew	known
lose	lost	lost
ride	rode	ridden
ring	rang	rung
run	ran	run
see	saw	seen
sing	sang	sung
speak	spoke	spoken
steal	stole	stolen
sting	stung	stung
swim	swam	swum
take	took	taken
think	thought	thought
throw	threw	thrown
win	won	won
wear	wore	worn
write	wrote	written

EXERCISE 14. In order to practice using the principal parts of both regular and irregular verbs, use the appropriate form of each of ten basic verbs in the following sentence.

I am ____ where you ____ and where your brother
present participle   past tense

has ____ for years.
past participle

EXAMPLE: basic verb: write

ANSWER: *I am writing where you wrote and where your brother has written for years.*

1. work	5. drive	8. swim
2. draw	6. ride	9. build
3. sing	7. run	10. speak
4. live		

5. *driving, drove, driven*
6. *riding, rode, ridden*
7. *running, ran, run*
8. *swimming, swam, swum*
9. *building, built, built*
10. *speaking, spoke, spoken*

1. *working, worked, worked*
2. *drawing, drew, drawn*
3. *singing, sang, sung*
4. *living, lived, lived*

1.b.10 Auxiliary verbs

Auxiliary verbs are also called helping verbs. The forms of *be* and *have* are the only auxiliary, or helping, verbs. You add auxiliary verbs to the present participle or to the past participle of verbs to show continuing action and to form certain tenses (see 1.b.12). An auxiliary verb and a participle together form a **verb phrase.**

EXAMPLES
I **am** studying.   I **have** studied.
I **was** studying.   I **had** studied.
I **have been** studying.
I **had been** studying.

Remember to make the auxiliary *have* and the auxiliary *be* agree in number with the person or thing that you are talking about.

Singular	Plural
Night **has** fallen.	The stars **have** come out.
Earth **is** rotating.	All planets **are** rotating.

1.b.11 Modals

Modals act like auxiliary verbs. They are used to form questions, to help make an expression negative, and to show emphasis, possibility, obligation, and condition. Except for *do*, every modal can be used either (1) before a basic verb or (2) before the auxiliary verb *have* or *be.* Together the modal, the auxiliary, and the basic verb form a **verb phrase.** A list of the modals follows.

MODALS
do, does, did
   To form a question: **Do** they dance?
   To make an expression negative: He **does** not dance.
   To show emphasis: Once he **did** actually dance.

can, could	She **can** skate.
may, might	She **may/might** skate again.
must	You **must** sing to me.
will, shall	She **will** go tomorrow.
would	They **would** appreciate the help.
should, ought to	She **should/ought to** skate more.

You can use every modal except *do, does,* and *did* with the auxiliaries *be* and *have* in addition to the basic verb. For example, you can say *She may have skated.* You can also say *She may be skating.* You can also say *She may have been skating.*

EXERCISE 15. Point out the verb phrase in each of the following sentences. Remember that a verb phrase is made up of an auxiliary verb or modal plus a form of an action verb or linking verb.

1. The development of airplanes <u>has led</u> to the development of parachutes.
2. Researchers <u>are performing</u> many experiments on parachute design.
3. Parachutes <u>should be</u> in a small and lightweight package.
4. Unfortunately, a badly packed parachute <u>could cause</u> a fatal accident.
5. The parachute <u>ought to open</u> like an umbrella.
6. The harness <u>must detach</u> easily on the ground.
7. An aircraft <u>may carry</u> parachutes as safety devices for its passengers.
8. Passengers <u>would use</u> the parachutes in an emergency on the plane.
9. A person with a parachute <u>will fall</u> to earth at the rate of eighteen feet per second.
10. Not everyone <u>can jump</u> out of an airplane, even with a parachute.

1.b.12 Time and tense

The **tenses** of a verb are forms that help to show time.

In addition to telling us *what* happens, verbs also help to tell us *when* things happen. They can tell us that things happen *now, tomorrow, always, later, until now,* and at many other times. Basically, however, they tell whether something happens in the past, the present, or the future.

EXAMPLES

	When	Tense
We **listened**	yesterday.	past
We **listen**	today.	present

The chart below reviews the various ways to show the time of a verb. These will be explained in this section.

▰▰▰▰▰▰▰ TIMES OF VERBS ▰▰▰▰▰▰▰

Present time	Past time	Future time
present tense	past tense	*will* or *shall* + verb
present progressive	past progressive	*going to* or *about to* +verb
	present perfect tense	future perfect
	present perfect progressive	present or present progressive with adverb or prepositional phrase
	past perfect tense	
	past perfect progressive	

1.b.13 Present time: the present tense

The **present tense** expresses "now" time: *We listen* (now). The present tense of an action verb tells that something *happens now.* The present tense of a linking verb tells that someone or something *exists now.*

EXAMPLES

Action verb
The dog **barks.**
The engines **race.**

Linking verb
The dog **is** a collie.
The engines **sound** noisy.

The time expressed by the present tense may not be limited to "right now." The present tense is also used to express the idea of habitual, or "ongoing," truth and of general truth, such as scientific fact.

EXAMPLES
I always **wear** green on St. Patrick's Day. [something that happens every year]
Jupiter **is** the largest planet in the solar system. [a scientific fact]

Except for *be*, all verbs have two forms in the present tense. One form, which is just like the basic verb, is used to talk about *I, you,* or more than one person or thing. The other form, which is used to talk about one person or thing, is usually made up of the basic verb plus the ending *-s*.

PRESENT TENSE OF VERB

	Singular	Plural
1ST PERSON:	I sing.	We sing.
2ND PERSON:	You sing.	You sing.
3RD PERSON:	He sing**s**.	They sing.
	She sing**s**.	
	It sing**s**.	
	A bird sing**s**.	Birds sing.

Be has three forms in the present tense: *am, is,* and *are.* Use the form that agrees in number with the person or thing you are talking or writing about.

PRESENT TENSE OF *BE*

	Singular	Plural
1ST PERSON:	I **am** hopeful.	We **are** hopeful.
2ND PERSON:	You **are** hopeful.	You **are** hopeful
3RD PERSON:	He **is** hopeful.	They **are** hopeful.
	She **is** hopeful.	The parents **are** hopeful.
	It **is** hopeful.	
	The mood **is** hopeful.	

SPELLING PRESENT–TENSE VERBS

1. When you write about the third- person singular, generally add -s to the basic verb.

   I walk.   He walk**s.**

2. If the verb ends in *s, o, x, z, ch,* or *sh,* add *-es.*

   They miss her.   He miss**es** her.
   They go.   He go**es.**
   They wax the car.   He wax**es** the car.
   Soft drinks fizz.   Ginger ale fizz**es.**
   They watch.   He watch**es.**
   They blush.   He blush**es.**

3. If the verb ends in a consonant + *y,* change the *y* to *i* and add *-es.*

   I worry.   He worr**ies.**

4. The verb *have* becomes *has.*

   I **have** a headache.   He **has** a headache.

EXERCISE 16. For each of the following sentences, write the correct present-tense form of the verb in parentheses.

EXAMPLE Mexico City _____(be)_____ the capital of Mexico.
ANSWER   *Mexico City _____is_____ the capital of Mexico.*

1. Mexico __(border)__ the United States on the north and Guatemala and Belize on the south. *borders*
2. Mexico __(contain)__ thirty-one states and the Federal District, which includes Mexico City. *contains*
3. Mexico City _____(be)_____ one of the largest cities in the Western Hemisphere. *is*
4. Guadalajara and Monterrey also _____(be)_____ very large cities. *are*

5. Mexico __(have)__ only one major political party in the country. *has*
6. The government ___(own)___ some of the basic industries and methods of transportation. *owns*
7. Mexico's rich artistic tradition ___(go)___ back to Aztec, Mayan, and Toltec civilizations. *goes*
8. The typical Mexican ___(be)___ of mixed native and Spanish descent. *is*
9. Every Mexican school __(teach)__ Spanish as the country's official language. *teaches*
10. The Spanish influence in Mexico __(remain)__ strong. *remains*

APPLICATION. Write five original sentences. Each sentence should use a present-tense verb that says something interesting about Mexico. Begin each sentence with *Mexico* ____ .

Answers will vary; an example is "Mexico lies south of the United States."

1.b.14 Present time: the present progressive

The **present progressive** emphasizes that an action or state of being is continuing in the present. You can often use the present progressive rather than the present tense to express present time. Instead of saying *She watches television now* (present tense), you would probably say *She is watching television now* (present progressive).

Form the present progressive in the following way:

Present tense of *be*	+	Present participle of verb
am		reading
are		writing
is		playing

EXAMPLES
I **am reading** a magazine.
She **is writing** a report.
They **are playing** chess.

EXERCISE 17. Rewrite each of the following sentences,
using the correct present-progressive form of the verb in
parentheses. Remember that the present progressive
consists of a form of *be* and the present participle of the
verb.

1. Rapid transit systems ___(gain)___ in popularity in
   American cities. *are gaining*
2. The energy shortage ___(force)___ people to look at new
   ways of moving around. *is forcing*
3. Their efficiency ___(make)___ rapid transit systems
   attractive today. *is making*
4. Researchers ___(test)___ many new forms of rapid
   transit. *are testing*
5. Los Angeles ___(plan)___ to build a "people mover"
   in its downtown area. *is planning*
6. Some airports and amusement parks already
   ___(use)___ "people movers." *are using*
7. Several large cities ___(build)___ subways. *are building*
8. Other cities ___(revive)___ their abandoned streetcar
   systems. *are reviving*
9. Computers ___(help)___ to run some of the newer
   rapid transit systems. *are helping*
10. The growth of rapid transit systems does not nec-
    essarily mean that the automobile ___(lose)___ its
    popularity. *is losing*

1.b.15 Past time: the past tense

The **past tense** expresses an action or a state of being that happened or existed in the past.

Except for *be*, all verbs have only one form in the past tense. For most verbs, the past tense ends in *-ed*; these are called regular verbs (see 1.b.8). A verb with a past tense that does not end in *-ed* is an irregular verb (see 1.b.9).

EXAMPLES

She **worked** in a downtown office. [regular verb in past tense]

She **rode** the bus to her job. [irregular verb in past tense]

Be has two forms in the past tense: *was* and *were*. Use the form that agrees in number with the person or thing you are talking or writing about.

PAST TENSE OF *BE*

	Singular	Plural
1ST PERSON:	I **was** angry.	We **were** angry.
2ND PERSON:	You **were** angry.	You **were** angry.
3RD PERSON:	He **was** angry.	They **were** angry.
	She **was** angry.	Many people
	It **was** angry.	**were** angry.
	One person **was** angry.	

EXERCISE 18. Identify which of the following verbs are in the past tense. You may use the list in 1.b.9 for help.

1. became √
2. test
3. batted √
4. lost √
5. was √
6. decided √
7. rang √
8. skipped √
9. reveals
10. preferred √
11. complete
12. stole √
13. are
14. seemed √
15. nodded √
16. pick
17. began √
18. took √
19. winked √
20. bloom

APPLICATION. Select five of the past-tense verbs from Exercise 18. Write an original sentence for each. *Answers will vary; an example is "In time, they __became__ good friends."*

EXERCISE 19. Rewrite each of the following sentences, giving the past-tense form of the verb or verbs in parentheses.

1. Primitive people __(draw)__ and __(carve)__ pictures on rocks all over the world. *drew, carved*

2. The reasons that prehistoric people __(do)__ this are not certain. *did*

3. The artists __(die)__ long ago. *died*

4. The prehistoric artists of Europe and Africa __(be)__ often highly skilled. *were*

5. In some places rock artists __(paint)__ over an older rock painting. *painted*

6. Many rock paintings __(show)__ *showed* scenes of hunting.

7. Artists __(color)__ *colored* their drawings of wild animals.

8. As agriculture __(develop)__, rock carvings and paintings __(become)__ less common. *developed, became*

9. Rock carvers __(chip)__ the stone surface with another stone. *chipped*

10. Some artists __(combine)__ painting and carving techniques. *combined*

EXERCISE 20. Rewrite each of the following sentences, giving the past-tense form of the verb in parentheses.

1. Lucretia Coffin Mott __(be)__ a reformer. *was*

2. She __(speak)__ against slavery and for the rights of women. *spoke*

3. She __(become)__ a Quaker minister in 1821. *became*

4. She __(move)__ from Boston to Philadelphia. *moved*

5. She __(help)__ runaway slaves. *helped*

6. She __(organize)__ the first women's rights convention in the United States. *organized*

7. The women's rights convention __(take)__ place in Seneca Falls, New York, in 1848. *took*

8. Not until well after her death ____(be)____ women in the United States able to vote. *were*

9. Lucretia Coffin Mott ____(see)____ slavery abolished in her lifetime. *saw*

10. James Mott, her husband, also ____(work)____ for the rights of women. *worked*

1.b.16 Past time: the past progressive

The **past progressive** tells that an action or condition *continued* for some time in the past. For example, instead of saying She **watched** television (past tense), you can say She **was watching** television (past progressive). Obviously, there is more than one way to talk or write about past time.

Form the past progressive in the following way:

Past tense of *be*	+	Present participle of verb
was		planting
were		looking

EXAMPLES
She **was planting** tulip bulbs.
He **was weeding** the garden.
They **were looking** at the sky.
You **were planning** to arrive early.

Often you will want to tell about some action that happened while another action was going on. Then you should write a sentence that has one verb in the past tense and another verb in the past progressive.

EXAMPLES
She **was taking** a shower when the phone **rang.**
  past progressive   past tense

He **was weeding** the garden when the weather **changed.**
  past progressive   past tense

They **were looking** at the sky when the eclipse **occurred.**
  past progressive   past tense

1.b.17 Past time: the present-perfect tense

Another way to express past time is to use the **present-perfect tense.** Use the present perfect when you want to say that an action happened or a condition existed at some unstated time in the past. The present perfect also can express the idea that an action or condition began in the past and has continued up to the present.

Form the present perfect in the following way:

Auxiliary *has* or *have*	+	Past participle of verb
has		worked
have		seen

EXAMPLES

I **have seen** that film before. [an action that happened at an unstated time in the past]

She **has worked** here for three weeks. [a condition that began in the past and has continued up to the present]

Notice that you can also form the present perfect progressive in the following way:

Has been or *have been*	+	Present participle of verb
has been		thinking
have been		studying

EXAMPLES

She **has been thinking** about her paper.

I **have been studying** all day.

1.b.18 Past time: the past-perfect tense

Use the **past-perfect tense** when you want to show that one past action ended before another past action began. Form the past perfect in the following way:

Had	+	Past participle of verb
had		played
had		voted

EXAMPLES

James Brown **had played** baseball before he **became** a singer.

Jimmy Carter **had been** governor of Georgia before he **ran** for President.

Before I **arrived,** twenty people **had voted.**

Notice that you can also form the past perfect progressive in the following way:

Had been + **Present participle of verb**
had been   waiting

EXAMPLE

I **had been** waiting for two hours when the plane landed.

EXERCISE 21. Replace the blank in the following sentences with a past-progressive, a present-perfect, or a past-perfect form of the verb. The basic verb and the appropriate form to use are given in parentheses at the end of each sentence.

1. Blues music ___ *has been* popular for almost a hundred years. (present perfect of *be*)
2. Sophie Tucker ___ *was singing* the blues before that music became popular. (past progressive of *sing*)
3. Bessie Smith, "The Empress of the Blues," ___ *had traveled* with Ma Rainey and had recorded with Louis Armstrong. (past perfect of *travel*)
4. Blues singers Alberta Hunter and Ethel Waters ___ *had introduced* the American blues to European audiences. (past perfect of *introduce*)
5. Blues singer Ella Fitzgerald ___ *was performing* in Harlem when she was discovered. (past progressive of *perform*)
6. Ella Fitzgerald ___ *was conducting* Chick Webb's band at the same time that she was recording songs. (past progressive of *conduct*)
7. Many blues singers ___ *have performed* as gospel singers. (present perfect of *perform*)

8. Concerts at both Carnegie Hall and the Newport Jazz
Festival _____ gospel singer Mahalia Jackson. (present
perfect of *feature*)

have featured

9. Mahalia Jackson _____ at the inauguration of John F.
Kennedy and at the funeral of Martin Luther King, Jr.
(past perfect of *sing*)

had sung

10. Jazz singers Billie Holliday and Lena Horne _____ in
films as well. (present perfect of *act*)

have acted

1.b.19 Future time

You can show future time in several different ways.

1. Using *will* or *shall*: I **will fix** dinner.
2. Using *going to*: I **am going to fix** dinner.
3. Using *about to*: I **am about to fix** dinner.
4. Using the present tense or the present progressive
   with an adverb or a prepositional phrase that shows
   future time: I **leave tomorrow** or I **am leaving** *at five
   o'clock.*

Still another way to show that something will happen
in the future is to use the **future perfect.** The future perfect expresses the idea that a future event will be finished
before another future event begins. You form the future
perfect by adding *will have* to the past participle of an
action verb or a linking verb.

EXAMPLES
By ten o'clock I **will have done** my homework.
You **will have gone** on vacation when I see you again.
In 1990 we **will have known each other for fifteen
years.**

EXERCISE 22. Rewrite the following sentences according
to the following instructions: (1) Add to the beginning of
the sentence the element given in parentheses; (2) change
the verb from the future to the future perfect.

EXAMPLE I will eat dinner. (By the time you arrive,)

ANSWER   *By the time you arrive, I* **will have eaten** *dinner.*

1. I will win the chess tournament. (The next time you see me,) *The next time you see me, I will have won the chess tournament.*

2. My parents are going to be married fifteen years. (On July 2) *On July 2 my parents will have been married fifteen years.*

3. She will hide in the attic. (When I finish counting to twenty,) *When I finish counting to twenty, she will have hidden in the attic.*

4. I will return home. (By the time you receive this postcard,) *By the time you receive this postcard, I will have returned home.*

5. He will buy a new stereo. (Before next year) *Before next year he will have bought a new stereo.*

1.b.20 Voice: active and passive

The form of the verb that you use determines if a sentence is in the **active voice** or the **passive voice.** Notice the difference between the following two sentences.

ACTIVE VOICE: The cook burned the hamburgers.

PASSIVE VOICE: The hamburgers were burned by the cook.

In the first sentence the *cook* performs the action. The cook seems to be quite important. In the second sentence the *hamburger* gets more attention. The *cook* is merely tacked on.

You form the passive by using a form of *be* and the past participle of a verb. You may add a phrase beginning with *by* after the verb.

EXAMPLES

	Form of *be*	Past participle	by . . . (optional)
Toys	are	broken	(by them).
Dishes	were	washed	(by us).
Cars	have been	parked	(by him).

In many cases you can use either the active voice or the passive voice. The active voice is usually a stronger, more direct way of expressing what you are trying to say. Sometimes you will want to use the passive voice, however. Use the passive voice if you want to emphasize the receiver of the action, if you do not want to call attention to the performer of the action, or if you do not know who or what the performer is.

EXAMPLES

Jimmy Carter **was elected.** [You want to emphasize Carter, not the voters.]

The Corvette **was wrecked.** [You may not want to say who did it.]

The bank **was robbed.** [You may not know who did it.]

AVOIDING ERRORS WITH VERBS (GENERAL)

Unless your topic forces you to, do not shift from one verb tense to another. Unnecessary shifts confuse your readers.

NOT   The President changed his mind several times. First he ~~wants~~ voluntary controls on inflation. Then he ~~wants~~ tax cuts. Then he ~~wants~~ price controls.

BUT   The President **changed** his mind several times. First he **wanted** voluntary controls on inflation. Then he **wanted** tax cuts. Then he **wanted** price controls.

EXERCISE 23. In each of the following sentences, change the voice of the verb. Make passive verbs active, and make active verbs passive.

EXAMPLE Magic and witchcraft are included in the category of folk medicine. [passive]

ANSWER *The category of folk medicine includes magic and witchcraft.* [active]

EXAMPLE Folk medicine can also prevent disease. [active]

ANSWER *Disease can also be prevented by folk medicine.* [passive]

1. Folk medicine is not considered outdated by many people. *Many people do not consider folk medicine outdated.*

2. Herbs, animal parts, and ceremonies have apparently cured diseases. *Diseases have apparently been cured by herbs, animal parts, and ceremonies.*

3. Disease and death are blamed by some tribes on evil spirits or beings. *Some tribes blame disease and death on evil spirits or beings.*

4. Some folk cures have been found effective by medical science. *Medical science has found some folk cures effective.*

5. Sailors took castor oil as a health tonic. *Castor oil was taken by sailors as a health tonic.*

6. Modern research has discovered necessary vitamins in castor oil. *Necessary vitamins have been discovered in castor oil by modern research.*

7. In some folk cures the healing object and the diseased part of the body share something in common. *In some folk cures something is shared in common by the healing object. . .*

8. A healer may use red poppies for blood disorders. *Red poppies may be used by a healer for blood disorders.*

9. Skin diseases have been treated with spotted plants by healers. *Healers have treated skin diseases with spotted plants.*

10. Folk medicine is handed down by one generation to another through word of mouth. *One generation hands down folk medicine to another through word of mouth.*

APPLICATION. Find a short paragraph in a news story in a current newspaper. Rewrite the paragraph so that all active-voice verbs become passive-voice verbs. Compare the two versions. Which do you prefer? Why? *Answers will vary.*

REVIEW EXERCISE B. Each of the following sentences uses an incorrect form of a verb. Write the correct form of the verb in italics. *Where there are two possible answers, both are given.*

1. The game of tennis *have attracted* many talented American athletes. *has attracted, attracted*

TIME	For third-person plural and for I, you	For third-person singular
Present	Babies **smile.**	The baby **smiles.**
Present progressive	Babies **are smiling.**	The baby **is smiling.**
Past	Babies **smiled.**	The baby **smiled.**
Past progressive	Babies **were smiling.**	The baby **was smiling.**
Present perfect	Babies **have smiled.**	The baby **has smiled.**
Past perfect	The babies **had smiled** before the clown arrived.	The baby **had smiled** before the clown arrived.
Future	Babies **will smile.**	The baby **will smile.**
Future perfect	The babies **will have smiled** by the time the parade ends.	The baby **will have smiled** by the time the parade ends.

2. In the past, women tennis players *wear* long skirts, high collars, and hats. *wore*

3. In 1919 Pauline Betz was a table tennis expert; later, she also *was played* tennis well. *played, was playing*

4. Californian Helen Wills (later Helen Wills Moody) *winned* many tennis matches in the 1920s and 1930s. *won*

5. Tennis champion Alice Marble *were playing* tennis with severe health problems. *was playing, played*

6. Alice Marble's coach later *teached* American champion Maureen Connolly. *taught*

7. Althea Gibson *is* a star in the 1950s on the Caribbean circuit. *was*

8. The game of tennis still *do appeal* to many fans. *does appeal, appeals*

9. Tracy Austin *play* tennis steadily and with absolute accuracy. *plays*

10. Tracy Austin *defeat* her opponents with ease. *defeats*

TIME	For third-person plural and for I, you	For third-person singular
Present	Babies **are** cute.	The baby **is** cute.
Present progressive	The babies **are being** cute.	The baby **is being** cute.
Past	The babies **were** cute.	The baby **was** cute.
Past progressive	The babies **were being** cute for all the friends and relatives.	The baby **was being** cute for all the friends and relatives.
Present perfect	The babies **have been** cute.	The baby **has been** cute.
Past perfect	The babies **had been** cute until they became ill.	The baby **had been** cute until she became ill.
Future	Babies **will be** cute.	The baby **will be** cute.
Future perfect	The babies **will have been** ill for a while by then.	The baby **will have been** ill for a while by then.

REVIEW EXERCISE C. In each of the following sentences, tell whether the italicized verb or verb phrase is a linking verb or an action verb. If it is an action verb, tell whether it is a transitive verb or an intransitive verb.

1. Endangered species *may become* extinct as a result of human activities. *l.v.*

2. Hunting, trapping, and poisoning *have killed* mammals and birds. *a.v., t.*

3. Birds and other kinds of animals *die* from chemicals in insecticides. *a.v., i.*

4. Chemicals sometimes *seem* harmless at first but later turn out to be very harmful. *l.v.*

5. The bald eagle, the California condor, and the whooping crane *appear* endangered. *l.v.*

6. The passenger pigeon, once the most numerous bird in North America, *disappeared* long ago. *a.v., i.*

7. Pollution of breeding areas *threatens* many species. *a.v., t.*

8. The number of native habitats *decreases.* *a.v., i.*

9. Federal laws *protect* certain endangered species from hunters. *a.v., t.*

10. Nations and private groups *cooperate* in conservation activities. *a.v., i.*

REVIEW EXERCISE D. Identify the tense of the italicized verb or verb phrase in each of the following sentences.

1. Babe Didrikson *has been* a model for many American woman athletes. *present perfect*

2. Many people *consider* her the greatest athlete of the century. *present*

3. She *was* a track, baseball, and basketball star. *past*

4. In the 1932 Olympics she *won* two gold medals. *past*

5. At a national track and field championship she *had placed* first in five events and had tied for first in another. *past perfect*

6. After 1934 she *concentrated* on golf. *past*

7. Today many people *remember* her primarily as a golf star. *present*

8. By the end of 1947 she *had won* fifteen golf tournaments in one year. *past perfect*

9. She *became* the first American to win the British Open. *past*

10. Few athletes *have matched* her performance in such a variety of sports. *present perfect*

1.c ADJECTIVES

An **adjective** is a word that tells more about a noun or pronoun.

When you add the adjective *tall* to the noun *tree*, you are giving more information about the tree. Adjectives tell about size, shape, color, texture, speed, temperature, and many other qualities or conditions.

EXTRA: Not every adjective is suitable for every noun. Ask students for examples of adjectives that do not suit the nouns below — for example, *a salty road.*

SIZE
a **small** bird
a **wide** road

SPEED
a **fast** trip
a **slow** walk

SHAPE
a **round** window
a **square** table

TEMPERATURE
a **cold** nose
a **hot** griddle

COLOR
a **yellow** leaf
a **turquoise** sea

DEGREE
a **serious** mistake
a **severe** punishment

TEXTURE
a **rough** blanket
a **smooth** cheek

QUALITY
a **ripe** pear
a **romantic** story

When an adjective tells something about a noun, it is said to *modify* the noun.[1]

When you want to tell more about a noun, you often have a choice of several adjectives. If you want, for example, to describe a party, you can write *a **large** party, a **noisy** party,* or *a **dull** party.* You should always try to choose adjectives that are clear and precise.

EXAMPLES
A ***hilarious*** *film* is more precise than *a **good** film.*
A ***generous*** *boy* is more precise than *a **nice** boy.*
An ***impractical*** *plan* is more precise than *a **bad** plan.*

EXERCISE 24. Identify the adjectives in each of the following sentences. The number of adjectives in each sentence is given in parentheses after the sentence.

1. There are a <u>large</u> number of books that advise men how to dress well in business. (1)
2. You should wear <u>gray</u> or <u>blue</u> suits. (2)

---

[1]Adjectives also modify pronouns (a *happy* someone) and gerunds (*rapid* jogging). For the sake of simplicity, we talk only about nouns here.

3. Even in the <u>hot</u> summer, <u>woolen</u> fabrics are preferred for suits. (2)

4. Shirts should be <u>white</u>, <u>blue</u>, or <u>yellow</u>. (3)

5. Shirts should be of <u>natural</u> material (like cotton), not <u>synthetic</u> material (like polyester). (2)

6. A <u>bold</u> tie should match the shirt and jacket. (1)

7. Ties should be in <u>dark</u> colors and have <u>conservative</u> patterns. (2)

8. Even if you prefer <u>black</u> or <u>navy</u> coats, you should wear a <u>tan</u> topcoat. (3).

9. Do not wear <u>heavy</u> jewelry, except for a <u>gold</u> ring. (2)

10. A <u>black</u> umbrella and a <u>white</u> handkerchief complete the <u>fashionable</u> outfit. (3)

EXERCISE 25. Below is a list of twenty nouns. List five adjectives that can logically tell more about each noun.
Two examples for each are given below.

EXAMPLE thunderstorm

ANSWER *sudden, noisy, brief, dangerous, ferocious*

1. truck *big, long*
2. game *complex, tedious*
3. pool *wide, deep*
4. kitchen *hot, bright*
5. rose *red, full*
6. jeans *cotton, tight*
7. breakfast *heavy, delicious*
8. skateboard *fast, smooth*
9. mountain *grand, icy*
10. turtle *old, slow*
11. afternoon *windy, quiet*
12. lawyer *smart, tall*
13. hospital *old, modern*
14. pillow *fat, soft*
15. ketchup *thick, tasty*
16. shadow
17. room *dark, wide*
18. beach *big, round*
19. orchestra *sandy, hot*
20. kangaroo *loud, new*
    nervous, wild

APPLICATION. Select two nouns from Exercise 25. For each noun write five sentences. In each sentence use the noun and *one* of the adjectives that you listed for it. *Answers will vary; an example is "My <u>cotton jeans</u> shrunk in the wash."*

EXERCISE 26. In each of the following sentences, two adjectives appear in parentheses. Decide which adjective makes sense in the sentence.

EXAMPLE The kettledrum is a (musical/delicious) instrument.

ANSWER *musical*

1. The kettledrum has a (<u>round</u>/rare) base.
2. The kettledrum's playing surface is made of (<u>tight</u>/rapid) calfskin.
3. The kettledrum is played with (important/<u>wooden</u>) drumsticks.
4. The kettledrum has an (<u>ancient</u>/eager) history.
5. (Lucky/<u>Early</u>) players carried two kettledrums.
6. European composers later used kettledrums for (<u>joyful</u>/orange) music.
7. These drums are unusual because they can be tuned to (<u>exact</u>/angry) pitches.
8. A (happy/<u>loose</u>) surface produces a low pitch.
9. Some kettledrums have pedals for (ridiculous/<u>rapid</u>) changes in tone.
10. Modern orchestras usually have two kettledrums, each with a (<u>different</u>/dangerous) pitch.

APPLICATION. Select five of the adjectives that you did *not* choose in Exercise 26. Write one original sentence for each of the five adjectives. *Answers will vary; an example is "Bobsledding can be a <u>dangerous</u> sport."*

1.c.1 Positions of adjectives in sentences

You can use adjectives in various positions and in various ways in a sentence. Notice that in the first sentence below the adjective is before the noun. In the second sentence the adjective is after the noun and a linking verb.

EXAMPLES
The **expensive** shirt is made of silk.
The shirt is **expensive.**

Here are other examples of sentences with the adjective after the noun:

EXAMPLES
The man considered the shirt **beautiful.**
The shirts, **soft** and **expensive,** covered the counter.

1.c.2 Properties of adjectives

Most words that can be adjectives have the following important properties in common:

1. Most adjectives can follow the word *very*. (For important exceptions, see "Avoiding Errors with Adjectives for Comparison" in 1.c.4.)

   How **very handsome** you look!
   The shirt is **very attractive.**

2. Most adjectives can take comparative and superlative forms. For example, the adjective *cold* can take the comparative form **colder** and the superlative form **coldest.**

EXERCISE 27. Rewrite each of the following sentences, filling each blank with an adjective that makes sense in the sentence. Do not use *a, an,* or *the.* If you have trouble, you may use the Word Bank below for suggestions. *Answers will vary; examples are given below.*

EXAMPLE _____ supermarkets are very _____ and _____.

ANSWER *Modern supermarkets are very efficient and convenient.*

1. Supermarkets are a *recent* and *important* _____ development.

2. How *essential* _____ supermarkets have become!

3. Supermarkets, *suburban* and *urban* , dot the country from coast to coast.

4. Supermarkets in the city are sometimes *small* and *expensive* .

5. Suburban supermarkets have *long* shelves, *wide* aisles, and *bright* lights.

   WORD BANK

important	suburban	wide	bright
expensive	recent	essential	
urban	small	long	

APPLICATION. Use the ten words in the Word Bank for Exercise 27 to write a few sentences on a topic other than supermarkets. Use all ten adjectives. *Answers will vary; an example is "The bright sun created long and wide shadows."*

1.c.3 Forms of adjectives: comparison

Most adjectives have three **degrees**—the regular form, the **comparative,** and the **superlative.** An adjective that shows two things being compared is called comparative. An adjective that shows three or more things being compared is called superlative.

The basic form of the adjective tells you the basic condition or quality. The comparative degree expresses "more," and the superlative degree expresses "most."

EXAMPLES

Basic quality or condition	"More"	"Most"
green	green**er**	green**est**
late	lat**er**	lat**est**
ugly	ugli**er**	ugli**est**

As with *green, late,* and *ugly,* you can use the endings *-er* and *-est* with many adjectives to make comparisons. You can also make comparisons in other ways:

1. by using *more* and *most*

   EXAMPLES

afraid	**more** afraid	**most** afraid
comical	**more** comical	**most** comical
desperate	**more** desperate	**most** desperate

2. by using *as*

   EXAMPLE
   Ramona is **as** tall **as** Irene.
   She is just **as** tall.
   She is **as** thin **as** her brother.

3. by using *less* and *least*

   EXAMPLES
   He is **less** tired than I am.
   He is the **least** tired of the group.
   Algebra is his **least** favorite subject.

As you can see, some adjectives use -*er* and -*est* to form the comparative and superlative degrees, and some use *more* and *most*. The following chart shows that -*er* and -*est* are used for adjectives of one syllable, and *more* and *most* are used for adjectives of three syllables or more. For many two-syllable adjectives either form may be used. In those cases you should use your own judgment about which sounds or looks better.

When you add -*er* and -*est* to the basic form of the adjective, you sometimes have to make a spelling change. The following chart summarizes these spelling rules. (For more detailed rules, see 5.b.3.)

SPELLING COMPARATIVE AND SUPERLATIVE FORMS OF ADJECTIVES

1. Adjective ends in consonant + *y*.

Change the *y* to *i,* and add -*er* or -*est*.

silly — **sillier, silliest**
dry — **drier, driest**
funny — **funnier, funniest**

2. Adjective ends in silent *e*.

Drop the final *e,* and add -*er* or -*est*.

sure — **surer, surest**
blue — **bluer, bluest**
true — **truer, truest**

3. One-syllable adjective ends in single vowel + single consonant.

Double the consonant, and add -*er*, -*est*.

hot — **hotter, hottest**
big — **bigger, biggest**

-er, -est		more, most
one-syllable adjectives	*two-syllable adjectives; two syllables and prefix*	*more-than-two-syllable adjectives*
cold	*common*	*excellent*
cold**er**, cold**est**	common**er**, **more** common commonest, the **most** common	**more** excellent the **most** excellent
fine	*unhappy*	*dangerous*
fin**er**, fin**est**	unhappi**er**, **more** unhappy unhappi**est**, the **most** unhappy	**more** dangerous the **most** dangerous

1.c.4 Irregular adjectives: comparison

A few common adjectives have special forms for the comparative and superlative.

	Comparative form	Superlative form
good	better	(the) best
well (health)	better	(the) best
bad	worse	(the) worst
ill	worse	(the) worst
far (distance)	farther	farthest
far (degree)	further	furthest

EXERCISE 28. For each of the adjectives below, write the comparative and superlative forms. (Two of the adjectives take *more* and *most*.)

1. soggy *soggier, soggiest*
2. small *smaller, smallest*
3. nice *nicer, nicest*
4. slippery *more slippery, most slippery*
5. far (distance) *farther, farthest*
6. cool *cooler, coolest*
7. wise *wiser, wisest*
8. fat *fatter, fattest*
9. baggy *baggier, baggiest*
10. important *more important, most important*

EXERCISE 29. Each sentence has an adjective in parentheses. Give the superlative form of the adjective.

> EXAMPLE   Mercury is the (near) planet to the sun.
>
> ANSWER   *Mercury is the **nearest** planet to the sun.*

1. Jupiter is the (large) planet in the solar system. *largest*
2. Venus is the (close) planet to Earth. *closest*
3. The (far) planet from the sun is Pluto. *farthest*
4. The (small) planet is Mercury. *smallest*
5. Kepler was an early astronomer who gave the (good) description of the planets' motions. *best*

AVOIDING ERRORS WITH ADJECTIVES FOR COMPARISON

1. Do not make a **double comparison,** which incorrectly uses both -*er* or -*est* and *more* or *most.*

   NOT   August is more warmer than December.
   BUT   August is **warmer** than December.

2. Do not make an incomplete comparison. Use the word *other* or *else* when you compare one thing with the other members of the group to which it belongs.

   NOT   Mercury is closer to the sun than any planet.
   BUT   Mercury is closer to the sun than **any other** planet.

   NOT   The baby was more fun than anyone.
   BUT   The baby was more fun than anyone **else.**

1.c.5 Adjective or noun?

Many words can be either adjectives *or* nouns, depending on how they are used.

EXAMPLES

She acted in plays at **school.** [noun]
She acted in **school** plays. [adjective]

This **summer** was very hot. [noun]
My father wore a **summer** suit. [adjective]

Blue is my favorite color. [noun]
He painted the room **blue**. [adjective] *Blue is an object complement.*

When a combination of an adjective and a noun becomes so common that the two words are thought of as a unit, the combination is called a **compound noun** (see 1.a.2).

EXAMPLES

square dance   grand jury
high school   sweet potato

EXERCISE 30. In each of the following sentences, indicate whether the italicized word is acting as a noun or as an adjective.

1. *Bicycle* riders have been pedaling around on their machines since the 1880s. *adjective*
2. The motorized *bicycle,* or moped, was first manufactured in 1885 by a German. *noun*
3. John Boyd Dunlop, a *tire* developer, revolutionized travel on wheels. *adjective*
4. Dunlop's *tire* was made of rubber and filled with air to cushion the cyclist's ride. *noun*
5. Early *motor* bikes were messy and dangerous. *adjective*
6. The *motor* was run by gas vapor. *noun*
7. Turn-of-the-century manufacturers studied ways to motorize *pedal* bikes. *adjective*
8. In fact, nearly all early motor bikes had *pedals.* *noun*
9. As *engine* technology advanced, the moped was gradually replaced by the motorcycle of today. *adjective*
10. Only recently has the moped, with its pedals and gas-saving *engine,* become popular once again. *noun*

1.c.6 Proper adjectives

Proper adjectives are adjectives formed from proper nouns (see 1.a.1). Like proper nouns, proper adjectives are capitalized.

Sometimes proper nouns and proper adjectives share the same form.

EXAMPLES

February is the shortest month of the year.
proper noun

The trees suffered from the **February** storms.
proper adjective

New York is an exciting city.
proper noun

The Empire State Building is a **New York** landmark.
proper adjective

Most proper adjectives, however, have a different form from that of the corresponding proper noun.

EXAMPLES

Puerto Rico is famous for its beaches.
proper noun

The beaches are a **Puerto Rican** tourist attraction.
proper adjective

America needs new sources of energy.
proper noun

Do you drive an **American** car?
proper adjective

Many people enjoy reading about the adventures of
Sherlock Holmes.
proper noun

Your outfit looks like a **Holmesian** disguise.
proper adjective

Shakespeare was an English poet.
proper noun

She appreciates **Shakespearean** drama.
proper adjective

EXERCISE 31. Each of the following items has a proper noun. Give the corresponding proper *adjective*. Check your dictionary to be sure of the correct spelling.

> EXAMPLE a meal of France; a _____ meal
>
> ANSWER   *a **French** meal*

1. a kilt from Scotland; a _____ kilt *Scottish, Scotch*
2. a jig of Ireland; an _____ jig *Irish*
3. wool from England; _____ wool *English*
4. cork from Portugal; _____ cork *Portuguese*
5. a dancer of Spain; a _____ dancer *Spanish*
6. furniture from Denmark; _____ furniture *Danish*
7. the desert in Israel; the _____ desert *Israeli*
8. a safari in Africa; an _____ safari *African*
9. a car from Japan; a _____ car *Japanese*
10. a cheese from Italy; an _____ cheese *Italian*

REVIEW EXERCISE E. The following sentences are the beginning of the Declaration of Independence. Identify the nine adjectives that are used in the excerpt. Then answer the questions below the quotation.

> When in the course of <u>human</u> events, it becomes <u>necessary</u> for one people to dissolve the <u>political</u> bonds which have connected them with another and to assume among the powers of the earth the <u>separate</u> and <u>equal</u> station to which the laws of Nature and Nature's God entitle them, a <u>decent</u> respect to the opinions of mankind requires that they should declare the causes which impel them to the separation. We hold these truths to be <u>self-evident</u>, that all men are created <u>equal</u>, that they are endowed by their Creator with . . . <u>unalienable</u> rights, that among these are life, liberty, and the pursuit of happiness.

1. Which words that you identified as adjectives can be either adjectives or nouns, depending on how they are used in a sentence? *human, equal*

2. Suggest a proper adjective that completes the following sentence: *The Declaration of Independence is an* ____ *document.*   American

1.d PRONOUNS

A **pronoun** is a word that takes the place of a noun.

The English language has about seventy-five pronouns. In a sentence, you use pronouns just like you use nouns and proper nouns. In general, a pronoun takes the place of a noun or nouns. English has the following kinds of pronouns:

- personal pronouns, including possessive pronouns and reflexive pronouns
- demonstrative pronouns
- interrogative pronouns
- relative pronouns
- indefinite pronouns

1.d.1 Personal pronouns

Personal pronouns refer to specific persons and things. They refer to the *person* speaking (*I, we*), to the *person* spoken to (*you*), and to the *person* or *thing* spoken about (*he, she, it, they*).

■ Case

Except for *you*, personal pronouns take a different form, or case, depending on whether they are subjects of a sentence or objects of a verb or of a preposition. A pronoun used as the subject of a sentence is in the **subjective case** (or the **nominative case**) and is sometimes called a *subjective* (or *nominative*) *pronoun*. A pronoun used as the object of a verb or of a preposition is in the **objective case** and is sometimes called an *objective pronoun*.

EXAMPLES

Subjective case	Objective case
I sang the song. [subject of sentence]	The audience applauded **me.** [object of verb]
	The audience sang with **me.** [object of preposition]
We sang together.	The audience applauded **us.**
	The audience sang with **us.**
He played the guitar.	The audience loved **him.**
	The crowd called to **him.**
She played the piano.	The audience crowded around **her.**
They bought the tickets.	We paid **them** for the tickets.

Be careful to use the subjective case in a compound subject made up of a pronoun and a noun:

EXAMPLES
Luisa and **she** sang a duet.
The treasurer and **I** collected tickets.

Be careful to use the objective case in a compound object made up of a pronoun and a noun.

EXAMPLES
The music thrilled Mark and **me.**
The sound came clearly to Luisa and **him.**

In general, use the subjective case of a pronoun rather than the objective case after a form of *be.*

EXAMPLES
I know it was **she.**
I believe the winner will be **he.**
Could it be **they?**

In speaking, you can use *me* instead of *I* after a form of the verb *be: It's **me.*** In writing, however, use the subjective form: *It is **I.***

PERSONAL PRONOUNS

	nominative case singular	nominative case plural	objective case singular	objective case plural
first person	I	we	me	us
second person	you	you	you	you
third person	he, she, it	they	him, her, it	them

POSSESSIVE FORMS

singular	plural

	used as determiners	used alone	used as determiners	used alone
first person	my	mine	our	ours
second person	your	yours	your	yours
third person	his	his	their	theirs
	her	hers		
	its	its		

REFLEXIVE FORMS

Reflexive pronouns have no case.

singular	plural

	singular	plural
first person	myself	ourselves
second person	yourself	yourselves
third person	himself	themselves
	herself	
	itself	

RELATIVE PRONOUNS

Relative pronouns have no distinction between singular and plural.

Who is the only relative pronoun that has an objective case
and a possessive form.

people only	nonpeople	nonpeople in formal usage; people in informal
who, whom whose	which	that

INTERROGATIVE PRONOUNS

Interrogative pronouns have no distinction between singular and plural.

Who is the only interrogative pronoun that has an objective case and a possessive form.

people only	nonpeople	people and nonpeople
who? whom? whose?	what?	which?

Compounds: whoever, whomever, whatever

DEMONSTRATIVE PRONOUNS

Demonstrative pronouns have no case or person.

	singular	*plural*
near	this	these
far	that	those

INDEFINITE PRONOUNS

	universal	*"some"*	*"any"*	*negative*
always singular[1]	everybody everyone everything each either	somebody someone something somewhere another	anybody anyone anything anywhere	nobody no one nothing neither nowhere
always plural		both, few many, several		
singular or plural	all	some enough more, most such	any	none

---

[1]By "always singular" we mean that the verb will have a singular form usually adding -s to third-person present tense).

■ Number and person

Like most nouns, personal pronouns have **number** — that is, they are either singular or plural. The personal pronouns *I*, *he*, *she*, and *it* are singular and can take the forms *me*, *him*, *her*, and *it*. The personal pronouns *we* and *they* are plural and can take the forms *us* and *them*. *You* can be singular or plural.

There are three "persons" in English:

- **First person** refers to the person who is speaking or writing. The first-person pronouns are *I*, *me*, *we*, and *us*.
- **Second person** refers to the person or persons being addressed. The second-person pronoun is *you*.
- **Third person** refers to the person or persons (and to the thing or things) being spoken or written about. The third-person pronouns are *he*, *him*, *she*, *her*, *it*, *they* and *them*.

■ Gender

Pronouns have **gender.** That is, pronouns can be masculine (to refer to males), feminine (to refer to females), or neuter (to refer to things that are neither male nor female).

- **Masculine pronouns** are *he*, *him*, *his*.
- **Feminine pronouns** are *she*, *her*, *hers*.
- **Neuter pronouns** are *it* and *its*.

■ Pronoun-antecedent agreement

An **antecedent** is the noun (or other word) that a pronoun replaces. The antecedent may appear earlier in the sentence or in a preceding sentence. It may be a noun or another element that can be used as a noun — a gerund, an infinitive, a noun clause, a prepositional phrase, or another pronoun. A pronoun must have the same number (singular or plural) and the same gender (masculine, feminine, or neuter) as its antecedent.

MASCULINE ANTECEDENT AND PRONOUN
Charles washed **his** car. [singular]
The **brothers** cleaned **their** bedroom. [plural]

FEMININE ANTECEDENT AND PRONOUN
Ellen was captain of **her** team. [singular]
The **girls** won **their** tournament. [plural]

NEUTER ANTECEDENT AND PRONOUN
The **dog** wagged **its** tail. [singular]
The **trees** have lost **their** leaves. [plural]

When the gender of the antecedent is unknown, a masculine pronoun is traditionally used.

EXAMPLE
An author must capture **his** readers.

If you object to using a masculine pronoun when the antecedent *may* be female, try to rephrase your statement in the plural or to eliminate the pronoun.

EXAMPLES
Authors must capture **their** readers.
An author must capture **the** readers.

(For advice on agreement between personal pronouns and antecedents that are indefinite pronouns, see 1.d.7.)

EXERCISE 32. Decide which forms of the given personal pronoun you would use to fill in the blanks in the following sentences.

1. Select a form of the personal pronoun *I.*
   That is __*my*__ Susan B. Anthony dollar, and I think that the one next to it is __*mine*__ also.

2. Select a form of the personal pronoun *you* (singular or plural).
   The paper dollars in the collection are __*yours*__ because I saw them in __*your*__ display case yesterday.

3. Select a form of the personal pronoun *she.*

   I think that Susan Anthony would have liked __*her*__ coin and that no picture would have been more suitable than __*hers*__.

4. Select a form of the personal pronoun *he.*

   Frank Gaaparro deserves credit for __*his*__ beautiful design, for I understand that the design is __*his*__.

5. Select a form of the personal pronoun *it* and of its plural form *they.*

   The interest in this coin is in __*its*__ history, and you can be sure that the History Club will want to make it __*theirs*__.

AVOIDING ERRORS WITH PERSONAL PRONOUNS

1. Be sure to use the correct case of personal pronouns in compound elements of sentences. Always use the objective case after prepositions.

   NOT   That will be decided by you and he.
   BUT   That will be decided by you and **him.**

2. Do not use a personal pronoun that could refer to more than one antecedent. Change the sentence so that the antecedent is clear.

   NOT   The governor told the mayor that he would win by a landslide. [Who would win by a landslide?]
   BUT   The governor, who believed he would win by a landslide, told the mayor so.
   OR   The governor, who believed the mayor would win by a landslide, told him so.

1.d.2 Personal pronouns: possessive forms

Page 54 shows you the possessive forms of personal pronouns. There are two possessive forms for each personal pronoun. One form is used before nouns, as a determiner (see 1.e). The other form is used alone, like a noun.

POSSESSIVE USED AS DETERMINER
I like **your** chair.
Do you like **my** green chair?

POSSESSIVE USED ALONE
The chair you are sitting in is **yours.**
Mine is the green chair.

---

continued

3. Be careful to use the right case of the pronoun after *than* or *as.* In some sentences, the case actually determines the meaning of the sentence.

   NOT   She shoots baskets better than ~~him~~. [better than she shoots him?]
   BUT   She shoots baskets better than **he.** [better than he does]

   Notice the difference in meaning between these two sentences.

   I know you better than **him.** [I know you better than I know *him.*]
   I know you better than **he.** [I know you better than *he* knows you.]

4. Do not use an apostrophe in the possessive forms of personal pronouns.

   NOT   The dog wagged ~~it's~~ tail in greeting.
   BUT   The dog wagged **its** tail in greeting.

EXERCISE 33. In each of the following sentences, identify the antecedent noun to which the italicized pronoun refers.

1. The Greeks first held *their* Olympic games in 776 B.C. *pl.*
2. The Olympic games, which were the largest Greek festivals, were at *their* height in the fifth century B.C. *pl.*
3. Contestants were required to take an oath swearing that *they* had observed the ten-month training period. *pl.*
4. Greek games for women were introduced by Queen Hypodameia, according to legends of *her* life. *sing.*
5. The Baron De Coupertin used *his* influence to revive the Olympic games in modern times. *sing.*
6. The first modern Olympics were held in 1896 in Athens, Greece, because *it* was considered an appropriate place. *sing.*
7. In 1912 women had *their* first chance to compete in the Olympics. *pl.*
8. Olympic contests for winter sports made *their* appearance in 1924. *pl.*
9. As Americans, *we* can be proud of the world records set by Jesse Owens in 1936. *pl.*
10. Jesse Owens held *his* records in the broad jump and the two-hundred-meter race for twenty years. *sing.*

EXERCISE 34. Look again at the italicized pronouns in Exercise 33. Indicate which are singular and which are plural. *Answers are given in Exercise 33.*

1.d.3 Personal pronouns: reflexive forms

Reflexive pronouns are used to refer back to a noun or pronoun that has already been mentioned in the same sentence. The reflexive form can also be used to emphasize another word. Reflexive forms have no case. Each personal pronoun has only one reflexive form, except for *yourself/yourselves.*

EXAMPLES

I told **myself** that he was right.

She made **herself** a sandwich.

They have great confidence in **themselves.**

You do not seem **yourself** today.

The President **himself** drove the car.

We **ourselves** built the cabin.

AVOIDING ERRORS WITH REFLEXIVE PRONOUNS

Do not use *hisself* for *himself* or *theirselves* for *themselves.* Neither is a word.

NOT   He looked at hisself in the mirror.
BUT   He looked at **himself** in the mirror.

NOT   They theirselves paid the bill.
BUT   They **themselves** paid the bill.

EXERCISE 35. Identify each reflexive and possessive form of personal pronouns in each of the following sentences. Tell which of the forms is reflexive and which is possessive.

1. Not only sportscasters but also we ourselves use sports terminology in our everyday speech.
2. Ordinary words change when their meanings are applied to the sports world.
3. The word *ace* itself refers to a hole-in-one in golf.
4. You also use *ace* to refer to a serve in tennis so well placed that your opponents themselves cannot reach it.

5. In baseball a beanball is a pitch thrown so near the batter's head that his ^{poss.} head itself ^{reflex.} is in danger of being hit.

6. The pitcher himself ^{reflex.} may be removed from the game if the umpire determines that the beanball was intentional.

7. You have heard the word *eagle* applied to the animal itself ^{reflex.}.

8. You yourself ^{reflex.} may not know that the word *eagle* is used in golf to mean "two strokes under par."

9. Even love itself ^{reflex.} has taken on a new meaning in the sports world.

10. Its ^{poss.} meaning in tennis is "a score of zero."

EXERCISE 36. For each of the following sentences, supply the personal pronoun that makes sense according to the antecedent in bold type.

> EXAMPLE: On **my** birthday, ＿＿＿ went to Washington, D.C.
>
> ANSWER: *On my birthday, **I** went to Washington, D.C.*

1. **My** friends gave _me_ a pair of tickets to a show at Kennedy Center for my birthday.

2. **I** _myself_ had wanted to go to Washington for months.

3. **My** birthday was _my_ big chance to go.

4. Once I got to Washington, **my** time was _mine_ to do with as I pleased.

5. **I** went to a restaurant with one of _my_ best friends, and then we went together to the show.

6. **Our seats** were in the balcony, and _we_ had to climb a flight of stairs to reach _them_ .

7. The **actors** projected _their_ lines very clearly.

8. **We** enjoyed _ourselves_ enormously at the theater, and the play will be part of _our_ memories for a long time.

9. **My friend and I** returned to _our_ home town on a train.

10. **We** _ourselves_ were not the only people at the station when we arrived home, but I think that _ours_ had probably been the most enjoyable brief vacation.

1.d.4 Demonstrative pronouns

Demonstrative pronouns are used to "demonstrate," or point to, something. The only demonstrative pronouns are *this* and *that* and their plural forms, *these* and *those*. They may act as determiners before a noun (see 1.e) or alone in place of a noun. Demonstrative pronouns used as determiners are sometimes called **demonstrative adjectives.**

DEMONSTRATIVE PRONOUNS USED AS DETERMINERS
This book is excellent.
These people are my cousins.
Do you remember **that** game?

DEMONSTRATIVE PRONOUNS USED ALONE
This is my birthday.
Those are the lights from the satellite.

AVOIDING ERRORS WITH DEMONSTRATIVE PRONOUNS

1. Do not use *this* when you simply mean *a* or *an*.

   NOT   I had ~~this~~ wonderful teacher.
   BUT   I had **a** wonderful teacher.

2. Do not use *here* or *there* after a demonstrative pronoun.

   NOT   ~~This here~~ sandwich is stale.
   BUT   **This** sandwich is stale.

   NOT   I live in ~~that there~~ house.
   BUT   I live in **that** house.

3. Do not use *them* when you mean *those*.

   NOT   I never saw ~~them~~ keys.
   BUT   I never saw **those** keys.

1.d.5 Interrogative pronouns

Interrogative pronouns are used to form questions. There are three basic interrogative pronouns: *who, which,* and *what. Who* has the form *whom* for the objective case and the form *whose* for showing possession.

EXAMPLES
Who is the tallest in the class?
Whom do you trust?
Whose ideas are these?
Which stereo did you buy?
What is her name?

EXTRA: Ask students if questions formed with an interrogative pronoun may be answered "yes" or "no."

Although many people do not use *whom* in everyday speech because they think it sounds too stiff or formal, always use *whom* in writing when the pronoun is the object of a verb or of a preposition.

EXAMPLES
Whom did you invite?
With whom do you go to concerts?

AVOIDING ERRORS WITH INTERROGATIVE PRONOUNS

Do not confuse **whose** and **who's**. *Whose* is the possessive form of the interrogative pronoun *who*. *Who's* is the contracted form of *who is* or *who has*.

NOT ~~Whose~~ invited to your party?
BUT **Who's** invited to your party? [Who is invited?]
NOT ~~Who's~~ party are you going to?
BUT **Whose** party are you going to?

EXERCISE 37. Each of the following numbered items contains at least one mistake with demonstrative or interrogative pronouns. Correct each mistake.

1. ~~This here~~ country has excellent trails for hikers and horseback riders. *This*

2. ~~Whose~~ hiked the famous Appalachian Trail? *Who's*

3. You can hike or ride on horseback along ~~that there~~ trail, which runs along the Appalachian Mountains. *that*

4. Hiking the Appalachian Trail will give you a chance to view ~~them~~ extraordinary sights of the eastern United States, such as Great Valley in Virginia and the Pocono Mountains in Pennsylvania. *those*

5. Along the trail in Tennessee you will have ~~this~~ beautiful view of the blue and mist-covered Smoky Mountains. *a*

6. In autumn be sure to visit the Pocono Mountains, ~~who's~~ tree-covered peaks display rich and vibrant reds, oranges, and yellows. *whose*

7. The Catskill Mountains, which lie along the Appalachian Trail, are the scene of ~~that there~~ story about Rip Van Winkle. *that*

8. Along the trail in Vermont and New Hampshire you will find ~~this~~ scenic area for skiing. *a*

9. The Appalachian Trail does not run through ~~them~~ populated areas. *those*

10. If you are looking for quiet, solitude, and extraordinary natural scenery, hike or ride along ~~this here~~ trail.
this

1.d.6 Relative pronouns

Relative pronouns are used at the beginning of subordinate clauses (see 2.p) to "relate" the subordinate clause to the main clause. Three of the basic relative pronouns are *who*, *which*, and *that*. *Who* becomes *whom* in the objective case and *whose* to show possession.

■ who

Who and the forms based on it are used to refer only to people. Remember to use *whom* if the pronoun is the object of a verb or of a preposition.

The artist **who** painted this picture won an important award.

Arturo Delgado, **who** painted this picture, won an important award.

I know **who** told you the story.

The woman **whom** you saw is the principal. [*Whom* is the object of the verb *saw.*]

The woman with **whom** you spoke is the principal. [*Whom* is the object of the preposition *with.*]

The artist **whose** picture we saw in the museum was Arturo Delgado.

▣ which, that

Which and *that* are used to refer only to things, not to people. (You may hear *that* referring to people, but you should always write *who* when referring to people.)

EXAMPLES

My car, **which** I bought last month, is very small.

The car **that** I liked has been sold.

Here is some advice on choosing between *which* and *that*:

- Use *that* to begin a subordinate clause that is essential to the meaning of the sentence.
- Use *which* to begin a subordinate clause that merely adds extra information to the sentence. In such a case you will also use commas.

EXAMPLES

The book **that** we studied last fall was *Great Expectations*. [The clause *that we studied last fall* is essential to the meaning of the sentence.]

The main character of *Great Expectations*, **which** we read last fall, is named Pip. [The clause *which we read last fall* is not essential to the meaning of the sentence.]

AVOIDING ERRORS WITH RELATIVE PRONOUNS

1. In writing, do not use *that* to refer to people.

   NOT   I am the person ~~that~~ you want.
   BUT   I am the person **whom** you want.

2. Do not use *which* unless its antecedent is clear.

   NOT   The factory exploded, ~~which~~ was heard all over the city. [What was heard?]
   BUT   The noise of the factory explosion was heard all over the city.

EXERCISE 38. Identify each relative pronoun in the following sentences. Some sentences contain more than one relative pronoun.

1. The cacao tree's product, <u>which</u> we call chocolate, is used for sweets and for drinks.
2. The cocoa nibs remain after the seeds are processed, and it is their quality <u>that</u> determines the flavor of the chocolate.
3. The nibs must be heated, dried, and roasted, processes <u>that</u> also affect the quality of the chocolate.
4. A person <u>who</u> loves chocolate would admire the high standards for making it.
5. The chocolate <u>that</u> is produced should be rich and dark in color and should have a smell <u>that</u> is appealing.
6. The Aztecs of Mexico made a chocolate drink, <u>which</u> the Spanish explorers brought back to Europe around 1500.
7. Chocolate, <u>which</u> is still a major export from Switzerland, quickly became a fashionable drink in Europe.
8. The city in the United States <u>that</u> first manufactured chocolate was Milton Lower Falls, Massachusetts.

9. M. D. Peter of Switzerland was the man <u>who</u> developed milk chocolate, a flavor <u>that</u> is popular in candy, cakes, puddings, and ice creams.

10. Many people will even eat ants <u>that</u> are covered with chocolate.

1.d.7 Indefinite pronouns

As you can see from the chart on page 55, you use **indefinite pronouns** all the time. They are called "indefinite" because you often do not know the nouns to which they refer.

EXAMPLES
Everything that you say is true.
Somebody is calling me.
Anything you want to eat is fine with me.
You can invite **anyone** you like.
Nobody knows her address.
They had **nowhere** to go after school.

Indefinite pronouns can be divided into four groups:

1. the universals — *all, everything,* etc.
2. the *some* group
3. the *any* group
4. the negatives — *nobody, nothing,* etc.

■ Subject-verb agreement with indefinite pronouns

EXTRA: Give students a list of singular and plural nouns and indefinite pronouns. Have them write a sentence using each as the subject and then underline the verb.

As the chart on page 55 shows you, indefinite pronouns fall into the following groups:

- those that are always singular
- those that are always plural
- those that can be either singular or plural depending on the nouns they refer to

In some cases, the verb that you use with an indefinite pronoun shows whether it is singular or plural (see 2.d).

ALWAYS SINGULAR
Everything has its proper place.
Each of the houses **looks** different.

ALWAYS PLURAL
Few of our friends **have** cars.
Several of the houses **are** for sale.

SINGULAR OR PLURAL
SINGULAR: We can go if **some** of the money **is** raised.
PLURAL: **Some** of the cookies **were** sold.

■ Pronoun-antecedent agreement with indefinite pronouns

A personal pronoun must agree in number and gender with an indefinite pronoun that is its antecedent, just as it must agree with a noun antecedent (see 1.d.1).

EXAMPLES
1. **Each** of the boys must buy **his** own uniform.
2. **Each** of the girls must buy **her** own uniform.
3. **Each** of the band members must buy **his** own uniform.
4. **All** of the band members must buy **their** own uniforms.

When an indefinite-pronoun antecedent may be either male or female, a masculine pronoun — *he, him, his,* or *himself* — is usually used, as in Sentence 3, above. If you object to using a masculine pronoun when the indefinite pronoun *may* include females, try to rephrase your statement in the plural, as in Sentence 4. Try to avoid using two pronouns (*he or she, his or her*), which usually make a sentence sound awkward.

EXERCISE 39. Supply the missing possessive personal pronoun in each of the following sentences. The personal pronoun must agree with its indefinite pronoun antecedent.

1. Everything in the world is an element or is made up of __its__ own unique combination of chemical elements.

2. Several of the elements, such as sulfur, gold, and mercury, are ancient; __their__ discovery was made centuries ago.

3. Most of the elements are formed naturally; __their__ presence may be detected in every natural substance on earth.

4. Some of the elements are manufactured by humans; __their__ composition is always radioactive.

5. Many of the elements are metals; __their__ names include copper, nickel, iron, and tin.

6. One of the discoverers of polonium, Marie Curie, had __her__ name used for the ninety-sixth element, curium.

7. One of the most famous scientists of the modern world, Albert Einstein, lends __his__ name to the ninety-ninth element, einsteinium.

8. Each of the elements has __its__ own symbol; for instance, H is the symbol for hydrogen, and O is the symbol for oxygen.

9. Both of these unite __their__ components to form water, or H_2O.

10. All of the combinations of elements have __their__ chemical names, like H_2O.

REVIEW EXERCISE F. Reword or revise each of the following sentences to eliminate its unclear or weak pronoun. Before you start, review the following: "Avoiding Errors with Personal Pronouns" (pages 58– 59), "Avoiding Errors with Reflexive Pronouns" (page 61), and "Avoiding Errors with Relative Pronouns" (page 67).

1. Thomas Alva Edison was the person ~~that~~ made many of our modern conveniences and luxuries possible. who

2. More than one thousand mechanical devices were invented and patented by ~~he.~~ him

3. He ~~hisself~~ was proud of his work on the electric light bulb. *himself*

4. Before ~~this~~, people used firelight to light their homes and public buildings. *the invention of the electric light bulb*

5. An electric light bulb gives off light because electricity heats up ~~it's~~ coil inside and makes it glow. *its*

6. ~~This~~ is the energy which heats the light bulb's coil and makes it glow. *Electricity*

7. With his invention of the phonograph Edison earned ~~hisself~~ the title "Napoleon of Science." *himself*

8. Around the same time the automobile — "the horseless carriage" — was being developed; ~~it's~~ inventor was Henry Ford. *its*

9. Edison and ~~him~~ were great friends and camping companions. *he*

10. Henry Ford, however, was not as productive an inventor as ~~him~~. *he*

1.e DETERMINERS

A **determiner** is a word other than an adjective (or a participle used as an adjective) that can be used before a noun to identify the noun.

Determiners include the following five categories of words:

1. articles (*the*, *a*, and *an*)
2. indefinite pronouns (like *every*, *all*, and *few*)
3. possessive pronouns (like *his*, *her*, and *it*)
4. demonstrative pronouns (*this*, *that*, *these*, and *those*)
5. numbers and numerals

Determiners are different from adjectives. Determiners can be used only before a noun or an adjective-and-noun combination. Most adjectives can be used in a variety of places in a sentence.

1.e.1 Articles

The words *a*, *an*, and *the* are often called **articles.** *A* and *an* are called **indefinite articles.** *The* is the **definite article.**

The definite article, *the*, identifies a definite, or specific, person, place, thing, or idea. The indefinite articles, *a* and *an*, are used for something that has not been mentioned previously. For example, **the** *red car* means something different from **a** *red car.* The definite article, *the*, shows that you are referring to a specific car that has already been mentioned. The indefinite article, *a*, shows that you are referring to any red car or to one that has not been mentioned.

Use *a* before all words beginning with a consonant *sound*, even if the first letter is a vowel: **a** *European*, **a** *once-in-a-lifetime opportunity*, **a** *union.* Use *an* before all words beginning with a vowel *sound*, even if the first letter is an *h*: **an** *honor*, **an** *apple.* (Follow the same rules for abbreviations: **a** *UN meeting.*)

1.e.2 Indefinite pronouns as determiners

Some indefinite pronouns that can be used alone (see 1.d.7) can also be used before a noun to tell "how many." Such words as *no*, *every*, and *other* are used as determiners in the same way, although they are not categorized as pronouns.

EXAMPLES

A **few** of the runners dropped out. [The indefinite pronoun *few* is the subject of the sentence.]

Few runners dropped out. [Here the indefinite pronoun *few* is a determiner before the noun *runners*, which is the subject of the sentence.]

Some runners dropped out.

Many runners dropped out.

No runners dropped out.

1.e.3 Possessive pronouns as determiners

The possessive pronouns *my, your, his, her, its, our,* and *their* are used as determiners. Some of the indefinite pronouns also have possessive forms that are used as determiners.

EXAMPLES
His brother won the prize.
My car gets good mileage.
Everyone's bills are going up.

1.e.4 Demonstrative pronouns as determiners

The demonstrative pronouns *this* and *that* are used as determiners before singular nouns. *These* and *those* are used as determiners before plural nouns.

EXAMPLES
This dog growls.   **These** dogs howl.
That dog is friendly.   **Those** dogs were quiet.

1.e.5 Numbers and numerals as determiners

Numbers and numerals can act as determiners. They are sometimes considered adjectives.

EXAMPLES
The golfer won **two** tournaments.
The dancer won **third** prize.
She was **sixteen** years old today.

EXERCISE 40. Identify the determiners in each of the following sentences. Remember that a determiner can be an article, a number, or a form of a pronoun. The number in parentheses after each sentence tells you how many determiners are in that sentence.

1. No animal is more familiar to humans than the trusty dog. (2)
2. The dog is an unusual animal for two reasons. (3)
3. The first unusual characteristic is its range. (3)
4. Dogs live in all parts of the world, from the tropics to the Arctic Circle. (4)
5. Another unusual feature of dogs is the variation in their size. (3)
6. Some dogs are forty inches high at the shoulder. (3)
7. Other dogs are only six inches high. (2)
8. For many centuries people have bred dogs for an assortment of special tasks. (2)
9. The Eskimos breed dogs to pull their sleds through the snow. (3)
10. Some dogs have been bred to be hunters. (1)
11. These sporting dogs hunt by detecting scents in the air. (2)
12. Several breeds (for example, pointers, retrievers, setters, and spaniels) are classified as sporting dogs. (1)
13. Those dogs classified as hounds track their prey by the scent it leaves on the ground. (4)
14. Many scientists think that the dog was the first animal to live peacefully with humans. (4)
15. The dog is probably descended from a wolflike ancestor. (2)
16. The first domestic dogs probably looked like the present-day dingo, or wild dog, of Australia. (3)
17. Dogs have existed in many areas throughout recorded history. (1)
18. Few breeds are as old as the basenji from central Africa. (2)
19. Several breeds of dog were kept by the ancient Egyptians. (2)
20. Everyone's dog seems special. (1)

1.f ADVERBS

An **adverb** is a word that tells more about a verb, an adjective, or another adverb.

Adverbs are words that tell *when, where, how,* or *to what degree.* In the examples below, the arrows show you which words the adverbs modify.

EXAMPLES

Bright red trucks **quickly** drove **there yesterday.**
degree   how   where   when

My **very** dirty sneakers **now** are drying **slowly outside.**
degree   when   how   where

1.f.1 Kinds of adverbs

There are five basic kinds of adverbs: adverbs of time, adverbs of place, adverbs of degree, adverbs of manner, and sentence adverbs.

■ Adverbs of time

Adverbs of time tell *when.* Some adverbs of time tell "at what time" (*now, tomorrow*), some tell "how long" (*slowly, instantly*), and some tell "how often" (*seldom*).

EXAMPLES
I saw you **yesterday.**
I **immediately** waved at you.
I waved at you **twice.**

COMMON ADVERBS OF TIME

afterward	first	once	today
again	forever	rarely	tomorrow
always	late	seldom	usually
before	never	soon	weekly
eventually	now	then	yearly
finally	often		

■ Adverbs of place

Adverbs of place tell *where*. Some adverbs of place tell about position (*locally*), some tell about direction (*left, upward*), and most can tell about either position or direction (*there, anywhere*).

EXAMPLES
She turned **left** at the corner.
It was hot **everywhere** yesterday.

■ Adverbs of degree

Adverbs of degree tell *to what degree* or *to what extent*. When they are used with adjectives or other adverbs, they are sometimes called **intensifiers.**

EXAMPLES
Rachel is running **very** fast.
I **definitely** think she will win.
She is **really** graceful.

The words in bold type in the following expressions are other common adverbs of degree:

absolutely lovely	**otherwise** happy
almost never	**partly** done
certainly charming	**rather** silly
greatly improved	**scarcely** tired
hardly ever	**simply** ridiculous
however quickly	**so** ugly
sad **indeed**	**somewhat** thirsty
only two	**too** expensive

■ Adverbs of manner

Adverbs of manner tell *how* an action is done (*move* **unwillingly**) or the *means by which* an action is done (*heated* **electrically**). Adverbs of manner can also give information about adjectives (***tragically*** *short career*).
Here are some examples of adverbs of manner:

"HOW"	"BY WHAT MEANS"
treated **badly**	treated **surgically**
cooked **professionally**	cooked **automatically**
carefully polished	**mechanically** polished

Most adverbs of manner end in *-ly* and come from an adjective. For example, if you add *-ly* to the adjectives *warm* and *mechanical*, you form the adverbs *warmly* and *mechanically*. Not all adverbs of manner end in *-ly*, however. For example, the adverb of manner *together* in *they skied **together*** does not end in *-ly*. Furthermore, some words that end in *-ly* are not adverbs, but adjectives (*friendly*, *lovely*).

■ Sentence adverbs

Sentence adverbs tell something about the entire sentence rather than about only a word in the sentence.

EXTRA: Ask students to use the following sentence adverbs in sentences: <u>undoubtedly</u>, <u>surprisingly</u>, <u>fortunately</u>.

EXAMPLES

Happily, the snow has melted.
The roof leaks, **unfortunately.**
Specifically, what is bothering him?

EXERCISE 41. Identify the adverb in each of the following sentences.

1. Bessie Smith is <u>often</u> considered the world's greatest blues singer.
2. She grew up in an <u>extremely</u> poor family.
3. By the age of fourteen, Bessie Smith was <u>often</u> touring with Ma Rainey and her Rabbit Foot Minstrels.
4. Bessie Smith sang <u>dramatically</u>, and her sound was more sophisticated than Ma Rainey's.
5. Some critics have said that Bessie Smith was <u>rhythmically</u> adventurous.
6. Record companies considered her <u>unpleasantly</u> "rough" for a long time.
7. In 1923 she produced two <u>commercially</u> successful records for Columbia Records.

8. Probably, her best period was between 1925 and 1927.

9. *Nobody's Blues but Mine,* which covers 1925 to 1927, is a record still popular today.

10. Bessie Smith died tragically in a car accident in 1938.

APPLICATION. Select five of the adverbs that you identified for Exercise 41. Write one original sentence for each adverb. *Answers will vary; an example is "Architects must be extremely precise in their measurements."*

EXERCISE 42. Identify each italicized adverb in the following sentences as (a) an adverb of time, (b) an adverb of place, (c) an adverb of degree, (d) an adverb of manner, or (e) a sentence adverb.

1. Pearls are unusual gems because they are produced *underwater.* *b*

2. *Actually* , although people value pearls as gems, the animals that produce them do not need them. *e*

3. When a mollusk's body is irritated by something like a grain of sand, it *automatically* produces a layer of pearl around the irritant. *d*

4. Pearls are built up *slowly* and *laboriously* in layers of material. *d, d*

5. The very best pearls are round. The *next* best pearls are pear-shaped. *c*

6. The Persian Gulf *supposedly* produces the finest saltwater pearls. *e*

7. The Red Sea was *formerly* an important source of pearls. *a*

8. *Today,* the Japanese are known for their *highly* sophisticated methods of producing pearls. *a, c*

9. Pearls are "planted" by opening a mollusk's shell *slightly* and putting a small mother-of-pearl bead *inside.* *c, b*

10. Black pearls are *so* rare that they are *almost always* valuable. *c, c, a*

APPLICATION. Select five of the adverbs used in Exercise 42. Write one original sentence for each. *Answers will vary; an example is "Bridge is a highly complex card game."*

1.f.2 Negative words as adverbs

The word *not* and the contraction *n't* are adverbs. Other negative words can also act as adverbs.

EXAMPLES
The pearl is **not** in the oyster.
The pearl is **nowhere** in sight.
The pearl is **hardly** round.

1.f.3 Forms of adverbs: comparison

Most adverbs have three **degrees** — the regular form, the **comparative,** and the **superlative.**

The regular form is the basic form. The **comparative degree** is used to compare two people or things. The **superlative degree** is used to compare more than two.

You can express comparison with adverbs in several different ways:

1. by using *-er* and *-est* or *more* and *most*
2. by using *as*
3. by using *less* and *least*

In general, use *more* and *most* for adverbs that end in *-ly* and *-er* and *-est* for other adverbs.

1.f.4 Irregular adverbs: comparison

A few adverbs have special forms.

	Comparative adverb	Superlative adverb
badly, ill	worse	(the) worst
well	better	(the) best
far	farther, further	(the) farthest, (the) furthest
little	less	(the) least

EXERCISE 43. Complete each of the following sentences by supplying the correct form of the adverb, as indicated in parentheses.

1. Your eyes react _more quickly_ ____ to color and light than does most photographic film. (comparative of *quickly*)
2. Certain black-and-white films react _more quickly_ ____ to light than others. (comparative of *quickly*)
3. Color film reacts _more slowly_ ____ to light than most black-and-white films. (comparative of *slowly*)
4. A part of your eye distinguishes black and white _more accurately_ ____ than color. (comparative of *accurately*)
5. Your eyes distinguish most colors _more clearly_ ____ in sunlight. (comparative of *clearly*)
6. Green, however, is a color that you perceive _most keenly_ ____ in dim light. (superlative of *keenly*)
7. Our eyes see black and white _best_ ____ in dim light. (superlative of *well*)
8. Cats and most rodents see _most effectively_ ____ in dim light. (superlative of *effectively*)
9. The pupils of your eyes dilate _most rapidly_ ____ in bright light. (superlative of *rapidly*)
10. You can see _farthest_ ____ when you squint your eyes. (superlative of *far*)

1.f.5 Adjective or adverb?

Some words can be either adjectives or adverbs, depending on how they are used in a sentence. You can tell whether a word is an adjective or an adverb by looking at the word it tells about, or modifies. Adjectives tell about nouns (see 1.c). Adverbs tell about verbs, adjectives, and other adverbs.

EXAMPLES

The train arrived **early.** [Here, *early* is an adverb that tells *when* the train arrived.]

The train was **early.** [Here, *early* is an adjective.]

Hard, long, late, and *low* are other words that can be either adverbs or adjectives. In general, when they follow action verbs, they are adverbs. When they precede nouns or follow linking verbs, they are adjectives.

1.f.6 *Good* vs. *well; bad* vs. *badly*

Good and *bad* are always adjectives. *Badly* is always an adverb. *Well* can be either an adverb or an adjective (meaning "in good health"). The following chart shows how each form is used.

GOOD vs. WELL; BAD vs. BADLY

	good	well
adjective (after linking verb)	I feel **good.** [healthy; happy] You look **good** in that. [well-dressed]	I feel **well.** [healthy] You look **well.** [healthy]
adverb (after action verb)	DO NOT USE WITH ACTION VERB.	I drive **well.** [how I drive]

	bad	badly
adjective (after linking verb)	I feel **bad.** [ill, sad] You look **bad.** [ill]	DO NOT USE WITH LINKING VERB.
adverb (after action verb)	DO NOT USE WITH ACTION VERB.	I drive **badly.** [how I drive]

1.f.7 Noun or adverb?

Some words can be either nouns or adverbs of time or place. *Yesterday, today,* and *tomorrow* are examples of words that can be either nouns or adverbs of time. *Home, downtown,* and *upstairs* are examples of words that can be either nouns or adverbs of place.

EXAMPLES

Yesterday was rainy.
    noun

I went jogging **yesterday.**
           adverb of time

Today is his birthday.

He is going to a party **today.**
         adverb of time

Home was a welcome sight.
    noun

Do you want to go **home?**
        adverb of place

Downtown is covered with smog.
    noun

She drives **downtown** every day.
      adverb of place

EXERCISE 44. In each of the following sentences, decide if the italicized word is correct. If it is incorrect, give the correct form.

1. Ted Williams is *widely* considered one of the greatest baseball players. *correct*
2. He started out *good* at the age of seventeen with the San Diego Padres of the Pacific Coast League. *well*
3. By 1939 he was *well* enough to start with the Boston Red Sox as a regular outfielder. *good*
4. Williams played *continuous* for the Red Sox from 1939 until 1960, except during World War II and the Korean War. *continuously*
5. He felt *badly* at having to leave the Red Sox during the war years. *bad*
6. But Williams felt *good* to be serving his country. *correct*
7. Williams hit *hard*, and he was one of baseball's all-time great hitters. *correct*
8. He hit especially *good* in 1941, when he had a .406 batting average. *well*

9. Williams did not do *bad* in 1942, either. *badly*

10. In both 1941 and 1942, his performance was so *good* that he led the league in home runs. *correct*

AVOIDING ERRORS WITH ADVERBS

1. Ordinarily, do not use two negative words (a **double negative**) in the same clause. Use only one negative word to express a negative idea.

   NOT I never saw nobody in the hall.
   BUT I **never** saw **anybody** in the hall.

   NOT She does not have no money.
   BUT She does **not** have **any** money.
   OR   She has **no** money.

   Sometimes two negative words are used together to express a positive idea. The first negative word in effect denies the second.

   I am **never not** at home on Monday nights. [I am always at home on Monday nights.]
   Nobody does**n't** like cheesecake. [Everybody likes cheesecake.]

2. Place adverbs of degree as close as possible to the words they modify. Misplaced adverbs make a sentence confusing.

   NOT He has almost finished all the assignments. [Has he not completely finished any of them?]
   BUT He has finished **almost** all the assignments. [He has finished most of them.]

REVIEW EXERCISE G. Identify the adverbs in the following sentences. Some of the sentences contain more than one adverb.

1. Hurricanes are very severe storms with winds that blow wildly.
2. Specifically, hurricanes are storms that occur in the northern Atlantic Ocean.
3. Oddly, the same kind of storm in the western Pacific Ocean is called a typhoon.
4. The very same storm in the Indian Ocean is called a cyclone.
5. A hurricane is officially defined as a storm with winds of at least seventy-five miles per hour.
6. Hurricanes usually start in the North Atlantic and move westward.
7. Sometimes hurricanes move northeastward from the Mexican coast.
8. Hurricanes start moving at about ten miles per hour and gradually speed up.
9. About 3.5 storms in the North Atlantic annually turn into hurricanes.
10. Hurricanes and typhoons ordinarily mature during the summer or the fall.
11. Actually, scientists do not yet completely understand all the factors that produce hurricanes.
12. A fully mature hurricane is nearly circular.
13. A hurricane's range can extend outward for five hundred miles.
14. The very inmost center of the hurricane is called the eye.
15. Air pressure in the eye of a hurricane can be extremely low.
16. In the eye the air barely moves, the atmosphere seems calm, and the sky often looks blue.
17. Clouds that swirl rapidly outside the eye, however, bring deadly winds and rains.
18. Hurricanes live only one to thirty days.
19. When hurricanes strike thickly settled areas, they can take thousands of victims.

20. Fortunately, forecasters now can <u>frequently</u> predict <u>the path of</u> a hurricane in time for people to take precautions.

1.g PREPOSITIONS

A **preposition** is a word that shows the relationship of a noun or pronoun to some other word in the sentence.

Prepositions never stand alone. They always appear in a phrase.

Some prepositions show space relationships.

EXAMPLES
The cookie fell **on** the floor.
I brought cookies **from** the supermarket.
The cookie jar broke **inside** the cupboard.

Some prepositions show time relationships.

EXAMPLES
Can you help me clean up **after** the party?
He forgot his lines **during** the performance.
I have lived here **since** June.

Some prepositions show other kinds of relationships.

EXAMPLES
You enter **among** friends here.
For whom is that gift?
She grinned, **beside** herself with joy.

There are many prepositions, but you probably know them all.

COMMON PREPOSITIONS

about	against	around
above	along	as
across	amid	at
after	among	before

behind	from	respecting
below	in	since
beneath	inside	through
beside	into	throughout
besides	like	to
between	of	toward
beyond	off	under
by	on	underneath
concerning	onto	until
despite	out	unto
down	outside	up
during	over	upon
except	past	with
excepting	pending	within
for	regarding	without

Some prepositions, called **compound prepositions,** are made up of more than one word.

COMMON COMPOUND PREPOSITIONS

according to	in addition to
apart from	in spite of
aside from	instead of
as to	on account of
because of	on top of
by way of	out of

EXERCISE 45. Identify the prepositions in each of the following sentences. The number of prepositions in each sentence is given in parentheses at the end of the sentence.

1. Sonny Rollins, a great jazz musician, was born <u>in</u> New York <u>in</u> 1930. (2)

2. He came <u>from</u> a musical family, and he chose the tenor saxophone <u>as</u> his instrument. (2)

3. Most <u>of</u> his work <u>before</u> 1954 is flawed. (2)

4. His early work has been called daring, but it could not compare <u>with</u> his later work. (1)

5. Rollins often improvised <u>on</u> themes <u>within</u> the music. (2)

6. <u>In</u> 1954 his album *Moving Out* put him <u>at</u> the top <u>of</u> his profession. (3)

7. His work was notable <u>for</u> its great energy. (1)

8. <u>By</u> 1959 Rollins was known <u>as</u> a jazz master. (2)

9. Rollins continued experiments <u>with</u> his music <u>throughout</u> the 1960s. (2)

10. One <u>of</u> his experiments was making the sound <u>from</u> his saxophone bounce <u>off</u> walls and ceilings. (3)

EXERCISE 46. Identify the compound preposition in each of the following sentences. One of the sentences contains two compound prepositions.

1. Sonny Rollins sometimes played his saxophone outdoors <u>instead of</u> indoors in the 1960s.

2. He wanted to take music <u>out of</u> its usual locations.

3. <u>In addition to</u> his experimental work, Rollins played the music for the movie *Alfie* during the 1960s.

4. <u>According to</u> Rollins, he did commercial work in this period <u>because of</u> his heavy dental bills.

5. <u>In spite of</u> his brilliance, Rollins has "retired" temporarily at several times during his career.

1.g.1 Prepositional phrases; objects of prepositions

A **prepositional phrase** is a group of words that begins with a preposition and usually ends with a noun or pronoun.

The **object of a preposition** is usually a noun or pronoun that follows the preposition.

A preposition never stands alone. It is always part of a prepositional phrase. Objects of prepositions can be nouns, proper nouns, pronouns, gerunds (see 1.n), other prepositional phrases, or noun clauses (see 2.u).

EXAMPLES

The plums sit **in bowls.** [noun as object of preposition]

The class went **to Washington, D.C.** [proper noun as object]

The letter was sent **to me.** [pronoun as object]

Balance is important **in skiing.** [gerund as object]

We were surprised **by what he told us.** [clause as object]

Adjectives or determiners often come between the preposition and its object.

EXAMPLES

The plums are sitting **in** her new glass **bowls.**

The class went **to** lovely but humid **Washington, D.C.**

EXERCISE 47. Identify each prepositional phrase in each of the following sentences. Remember that some prepositions are made up of more than one word. Each sentence contains one prepositional phrase.

1. Weaving a tapestry on a hand loom is a unique hobby.
2. First, wrap heavy string vertically around a wooden frame (this is called the warp).
3. Then, weave colored thread or wool horizontally between the warp strings (this is called the weft).
4. Alternately weave two light-colored strands and two dark-colored strands for a wavy design.
5. Alternating one dark strand with one light strand creates vertical stripes.
6. You can also weave grasses, twigs, or flowers into your tapestry.
7. Tying knots in the weft threads creates a rough and nubby effect.
8. When you have finished your tapestry, tie all loose threads at the back.
9. Cut a fringe at the bottom.
10. Attach a stick on top of your finished tapestry, and hang the tapestry.

1.g.2 Prepositions followed by personal pronouns

A preposition generally takes a pronoun in the objective case.

Occasionally, a preposition takes a possessive pronoun, but you should never use a nominative pronoun as the object of a preposition.

EXAMPLES

Give your coat to **me.** [objective pronoun]
You can stand in front of **him.** [objective pronoun]
His chair is behind **hers.** [possessive pronoun]

In writing, remember to use *whom*, not *who*, as the object of a preposition.

EXAMPLES

Whom are you speaking to?
I know **whom** she was looking for.

AVOIDING ERRORS WITH PREPOSITIONS

Use prepositions consistently in a series.

NOT   I collected class dues ~~from~~ the freshmen, the sophomores, and ~~from~~ the juniors. [Two items in the series have prepositions; one does not.]

BUT   I collected class dues **from** the freshmen, the sophomores, and the juniors. [one preposition for the series]

OR   I collected class dues **from** the freshmen, **from** the sophomores, and **from** the juniors. [a preposition for each item]

For more advice about specific prepositions, refer to the Glossary of Usage Problems, Section 8.

1.h CONJUNCTIONS

A **conjunction** is a word that joins other words or groups of words.

Conjunctions can connect nouns, pronouns, adjectives, verbs, adverbs, prepositions, other conjunctions, phrases, or clauses. There are four kinds of conjunctions:

1. coordinating conjunctions
2. correlative conjunctions
3. conjunctive adverbs
4. subordinating conjunctions

1.h.1 Coordinating conjunctions

Coordinating conjunctions are single words used to connect parts of a sentence that are grammatically equal: for example, words, phrases, or clauses. *And* , *but* , and *or* are the three most common coordinating conjunctions. *For* and *nor* are also sometimes used as coordinating conjunctions.

■ and

Use *and* to mean "also" (*He went to the movies **and** to a restaurant*), to mean "plus" (*Two **and** two are four*), and to mean "as a result" (*She did not study, **and** she failed the test*). Do not overuse *and*.

■ but

Use *but* to show a contrast (*I forgot your birthday, **but** he remembered it*) and to mean "yet" (*I do not agree with her plan, **but** I will not oppose it*).

■ or

Use *or* to show a choice or alternative (*Do you prefer vanilla **or** chocolate?*) and to mean "otherwise" (*Hurry, **or** we will be late*).

■ for

Use *for* as a conjunction to mean "because" or "seeing that" (*The pioneers were sad,* **for** *they were leaving their families and friends*).

■ nor

Nor is sometimes used as a coordinating conjunction after a negative statement to make the following statement negative (*I have not seen her,* **nor** *do I know where she is*).

COMMAS WITH COORDINATING CONJUNCTIONS

1. Use a comma before a coordinating conjunction that joins two main clauses (see 2.n).

   I wanted to go on the trip, **but** I had no money.

2. Do not use a comma before the coordinating conjunction that joins the two parts of a compound verb.

   NOT   We played basketball and went swimming.
   BUT   We played basketball and went swimming.

EXERCISE 48. Identify the coordinating conjunction in each of the following sentences.

1. Ross Macdonald is his pen name, but Kenneth Millar is his real name.

2. Ross Macdonald was born and still lives in California.

3. He is a famous writer of mysteries, for his books give unique descriptions of life in southern California.

4. Macdonald went to school in Canada and in the United States.

5. The main character in his mysteries is Lew Archer, a tough but understanding private detective.

6. Do you think you would prefer a Macdonald novel <u>or</u> a movie based on one?

7. Macdonald's mystery novels often deal with how someone's past affects the present <u>or</u> how the loss of a father affects a family.

8. Macdonald's books describe a society that is shallow <u>but</u> evil.

9. Macdonald <u>and</u> his wife, Margaret Millar, are both novelists.

10. Both write mysteries, <u>but</u> their styles differ.

AVOIDING ERRORS WITH COORDINATING CONJUNCTIONS

1. Do not forget to use a coordinating conjunction (or a semicolon) between two main clauses (see 2.n). If you forget the conjunction, you will have a **run-on sentence.**

   NOT She bought a red sweater̸ I bought a green one.

   BUT She bought a red sweater, **and** I bought a green one.

2. Do not use *so* as a coordinating conjunction in writing. Use *and so,* or reword your sentence.

   NOT They had spent all their money, s̸o they went home.

   BUT They had spent all their money, **and so** they went home.

   OR **Because** they had spent all their money, they went home.

EXERCISE 49. For each of the following sentences, supply the coordinating conjunction (*and, or, but,* or *for*) that makes the best sense in the blank. Do not write in this book.

1. Many Americans take a vacation in Jamaica _or_ one of the other islands in the Caribbean Sea.

2. Jamaica's capital is Kingston, _and_ its other important cities are Spanish Town and Montego Bay.

3. Most tourists visit the northern coast, _for_ it has lovely beaches.

4. Jamaica's main export crops are coffee _and_ sugar-cane.

5. These crops are grown on large plantations, _but_ Jamaica also has smaller farms.

6. The smaller farms export some items, _but_ they mostly produce food for local use.

7. Jamaica has large bauxite deposits, _and_ it is one of the world's leading bauxite producers.

8. Tourism is important to the island's economy, _for_ it brings in foreign currency.

9. The government provides many jobs, _or_ Jamaica's high unemployment rate would be even higher.

10. Most Jamaicans are descendants of Africans, _but_ some immigrants came from Lebanon, Syria, China and India.

1.h.2 Correlative conjunctions

The **correlative conjunctions** are the following pairs of words:

both . . . and	neither . . . nor
either . . . or	not only . . . but also
just as . . . so	whether . . . or

Correlative conjunctions connect words and groups of words that are grammatically equal, just as coordinating conjunctions do. They make the relationship between these words or groups of words stronger and clearer than coordinating conjunctions can. The first part of the correlative conjunction is used before the first word or group of words and the second part before the related word or group of words.

EXAMPLES

Coordinating conjunctions

You **and** she are invited.

You **or** she will be elected.

You **and** she will not be elected.

She was nominated **and** elected.

Correlative conjunctions

Both you **and** she are invited.

Either you **or** she will be elected.

Neither you **nor** she will be elected.

She was **not only** nominated **but also** elected.

EXERCISE 50. Each of the following sentences contains one correlative conjunction. Identify both parts of each correlative conjunction.

1. Just as people like to know the weather forecast today, so people thousands of years ago tried to predict weather conditions.

2. Not only have methods of predicting weather grown more complicated, but also they have grown more accurate.

3. Both modern and ancient cultures have looked to the sky for weather signs.

4. Whether their predictions were correct or incorrect, the ancients used very different methods from those of today.

5. Neither the thermometer nor the barometer was invented until a few hundred years ago.

6. Both the telegraph and the satellite made it possible to exchange weather information more rapidly.

7. Satellites can provide early warnings not only of hurricanes but also of cyclones and typhoons.

8. Just as advances in mathematics helped weather scientists, so did high-speed computers.

9. The National Oceanic and Atmospheric Administration is responsible for both studying and forecasting the weather.

10. Weather forecasting is done not only by government agencies but also by private companies.

1.h.3 Conjunctive adverbs

Conjunctive adverbs are used to join closely related main clauses in a compound sentence (see 2.o). They show the relationship between the clauses in a stronger and more precise way than coordinating conjunctions. A semicolon must be used between clauses connected by a conjunctive adverb.

EXAMPLES

The summer has ended, **but** the weather is still warm. [coordinating conjunction]
The summer has ended; **however,** the weather is still warm. [conjunctive adverb]

She has played the piano for five years, **and** she is now taking voice lessons. [coordinating conjunction]
She has played the piano for five years; **furthermore,** she is now taking voice lessons. [conjunctive adverb]

Conjunctive adverbs have several uses:

1. to replace *and* or to reinforce: *also, besides, furthermore, moreover*
2. to replace *but: however, nevertheless, still, though, yet*
3. to state a result: *consequently, therefore, thus*
4. to state equality: *equally, likewise, similarly*

EXERCISE 51. In each of the following sentences, replace the italicized word or words with a conjunctive adverb that means the same thing. In some sentences you will have to change a comma to a semicolon. *Answers will vary, possibilities are given below.*

1. The Toltec civilization of ancient Mexico was advanced in arts and architecture, ~~and~~ it was very skilled in stonework. *; moreover,*

2. The Toltec religion at one time centered around Quetzalcoatl; ~~as a result,~~ this sacred beast appeared in many legends. *consequently,*

3. Quetzalcoatl was the name of a deity, ~~and~~ it was the name of a legendary ruler. *;also*

4. Quetzalcoatl was the god of civilization; ~~in consequence,~~ he was the force of good. *thus,*

5. Quetzalcoatl was identified with the wind, ~~and~~ he was identified with the planet Venus. *;furthermore,*

1.h.4 Subordinating conjunctions

Subordinating conjunctions are words or groups of words that join subordinate clauses to main clauses in sentences (see 2.p). A subordinating conjunction shows the relationship in meaning between a subordinate clause and a main clause.

EXAMPLES

We raked the leaves **because** *we needed some exercise.* [The subordinate clause tells *why* the action of the main clause took place.]

We raked the leaves **before** *we had lunch.* [The subordinate clause tells *when* the action of the main clause took place.]

Wherever *the leaves had fallen,* we raked them into piles. [The subordinate clause tells *where* the action of the main clause took place.]

COMMON SUBORDINATING CONJUNCTIONS

after	since	whenever
although	than	where
as	though	whereas
because	unless	wherever
before	until	while
if	when	

Notice that some of the above words can also be used as other parts of speech. For example, *after, before, since,* and *until* can be prepositions, and *before* can be an adverb.

Compound subordinating conjunctions are made up of more than one word.

COMPOUND SUBORDINATING CONJUNCTIONS

as far as	for fear that	seeing (that)
as long as	inasmuch as	so long as
as soon as	in order that	so that
as though	in the hope that	supposing that
considering (that)	provided (that)	to the end that

COMMAS WITH SUBORDINATING CONJUNCTIONS

If a sentence begins with a subordinating conjunction (and a subordinate clause), use a comma after the subordinate clause.

Unless you eat it quickly, your ice cream cone will drip.
So long as there are hot summer days and cold ice cream, cones will drip.

EXERCISE 52. Identify the subordinating conjunction in each of the following sentences. Remember that some subordinating conjunctions are made up of more than one word.

1. As far as most people are concerned, Timbuktu is an imaginary place.
2. Whenever people want to express the idea of a faraway place, they call it Timbuktu.
3. Although many people do not know it, Timbuktu really exists.
4. Although Timbuktu is not large, about ten thousand people live there.

5. It is a trading center <u>because</u> it lies at the crossroads of North Africa and West Africa.

6. Nomadic peoples of the Sahara go there <u>when</u> they need to trade.

7. The Tuareg people founded Timbuktu in the eleventh century <u>so that</u> they would have a seasonal camp.

8. By the fourteenth century, Timbuktu had become known in Europe, <u>as</u> it had a thriving gold trade.

9. <u>While</u> it was part of the Songhoi empire from 1469 to 1591, Timbuktu was a center for education and Muslim culture.

10. Timbuktu declined gradually for three hundred years <u>until</u> it was occupied by the French in 1893 and 1894.

REVIEW EXERCISE H. Find each conjunction in the following sentences, and tell whether it is (a) a coordinating conjunction, (b) a correlative conjunction, (c) a conjunctive adverb, or (d) a subordinating conjunction.

1. <u>Before</u> he was sixteen years old, Jesse James had joined a Confederate guerilla band. *d*

2. James fought with the band in Kansas <u>and</u> in Missouri during the Civil War. *a*

3. By 1866 <u>both</u> Jesse <u>and</u> his brother Frank were leading a gang of outlaws. *b*

4. The gang began by robbing only banks; <u>however</u>, they went on to rob trains. *c*

5. <u>Not only</u> did the James gang steal money, <u>but also</u> they stole horses. *b*

6. In 1876 most of the gang were captured <u>or</u> had escaped. *a*

7. The James brothers escaped <u>and</u> hid for a few years. *a*

8. <u>After</u> they robbed a train in 1879, the governor of Missouri offered a reward for their capture. *d*

9. An outlaw joined the gang <u>so that</u> he could capture Jesse. *d*

10. Frank James gave himself up <u>but</u> was acquitted. *a*

1.i INTERJECTIONS

An **interjection** is a word or phrase that expresses emotion or exclamation. An interjection has no grammatical connection to any other words.

An interjection can be part of a sentence, or it can stand alone.

EXAMPLES
Oh, I didn't realize that.
My goodness!
Ouch! That hurts.

1.j VERBALS

Verbals are formed from verbs and, therefore, carry the idea of action.

Verbals can be used as nouns, adjectives, and adverbs. Because they have some of the characteristics of verbs and some of the characteristics of these other parts of speech, it is helpful to think of verbals as separate parts of speech themselves. There are three kinds of verbals: participles, which are used as adjectives; gerunds, which are used as nouns; and infinitives, which are used as nouns, adjectives, or adverbs. Each kind of verbal is discussed in more detail on the following pages.

1.k PARTICIPLES AS ADJECTIVES

The present-participle form and the past-participle form of a verb can be used as adjectives.

EXAMPLES

Verb	Present participle	Past participle
burn	burning	burned
fall	falling	fallen

The **burning** building collapsed with a crash.
No one would eat the **burned** toast.
We were warned to watch out for **falling** rocks.
The **fallen** tree blocked the road.

Remember that present participles always end in -*ing*.

EXERCISE 53. The following sentences contain participles used as adjectives. Find each participle, and tell whether it is a present participle or a past participle. Some of the sentences contain more than one participle.

1. State and county fairs are <u>established</u> events across the country. *past part.*

2. Judges taste <u>baked</u> and <u>canned</u> goods and make their decisions. *past part., past part.*

3. <u>Winning</u> entries receive blue ribbons. *pres. part.*

4. In games of chance and skill people win <u>stuffed</u> animals. *past part.*

5. Booths attract passers-by with <u>tempting</u> smells. *pres. part.*

6. <u>Competing</u> politicians shake hands with voters. *pres. part.*

7. Large stables contain <u>mooing</u> cows, <u>neighing</u> horses, and <u>oinking</u> pigs. *pres. part, pres. part., pres. part.*

8. Barkers advertise shows with <u>talking</u> dogs and <u>tattooed</u> ladies. *pres. part., past part.*

9. Companies demonstrate their newly <u>patented</u> products. *past part.*

10. <u>Screaming</u> passengers enjoy roller coasters and other <u>thrilling</u> rides. *pres. part., pres. part.*

APPLICATION. Select five of the participles that you identified for Exercise 53. Use each one as an adjective in a sentence of your own. *Answers will vary; an example is "Both water skiing and snow skiing can be <u>thrilling</u> sports."*

1.1 PARTICIPIAL PHRASES

A **participial phrase** contains a participle and other words that describe, or modify, the participle.

Participial phrases may contain either a present participle or a past participle. They can be used in various positions in a sentence.

EXAMPLES

We watched the teams **playing the World Series.** [a present participle plus its object]

The first batter stepped up to the plate, **smiling confidently.** [a present participle plus an adverb]

Looking into the sun, the centerfielder dropped a fly ball. [a present participle plus a prepositional phrase]

Defeated in the last inning, the home team retired. [a past participle plus a prepositional phrase]

The winning team, **very excited by their narrow victory,** jumped and cheered. [an adverb plus a past participle plus a prepositional phrase]

COMMAS WITH PARTICIPLES AND PARTICIPIAL PHRASES

1. Use commas to set off participles or participial phrases that add extra information to a sentence.

   The spectators**,** **cheering wildly,** slowly left.
   The pitcher**,** **carried by her teammates,** waved.

2. Do not set off a participle or participial phrase that is essential to the meaning of the sentence.

   The player **standing between second base and third base** is the shortstop.
   A player **blinded by the sun** may drop the ball.

3. Always use a comma after a participial phrase that begins a sentence.

   Dancing with glee, the winning pitcher ran off.

EXERCISE 54. Identify the participial phrase in each of the following sentences.

1. The Northwest Coast of North America, <u>extending from southern Alaska to northern California</u>, was the home of many native tribes.
2. The dense forests <u>inhabited by these tribes</u> have a temperate climate with plentiful rainfall.
3. Salmon <u>caught in streams and rivers</u> provided an important source of food.
4. <u>Knowing the woodlands well,</u> the tribes gathered berries and wild fruit to eat.
5. The Northwest tribes ordinarily had houses <u>built of wood</u>.
6. <u>Dressed for battle</u>, they wore armor and helmets.
7. Some of the tribes had totem poles <u>decorated with carvings</u>.
8. <u>Displaying great artistic skill</u>, the Northwest tribes produced baskets, rattles, and masks.
9. The Northwest tribes had a distinctive culture, <u>not affected by Europeans for a long time</u>.
10. Europeans <u>seeking furs and natural resources</u> finally came to the area in the late 1700s.

AVOIDING ERRORS WITH PARTICIPLES AND PARTICIPIAL PHRASES

1. Do not make a participle or participial phrase refer to the wrong part of your sentence or to a word that is not in the sentence but only in your mind. This error is called a **dangling modifier** or **dangling participial phrase.**

   NOT   Walking out of the theater, the glare blinded her.
   BUT   Walking out of the theater, she was blinded by the glare.

---

continued

NOT   Sleeping too late, the ~~train~~ had already left.

BUT   I slept too late, and the train had already left.

In the first example, *walking out of the theater* sounds as if it referred to *glare* rather than *her.* In the second example, *sleeping too late* sounds as if it referred to *train.* Actually it refers to *I,* a word that is not in the sentence. Check sentences with participial phrases to be sure that they make sense. Be sure that the participial phrase clearly modifies the right word.

HINT: A participial phrase that begins a sentence must be followed by the word it modifies.

2. Do not make a participle or participial phrase modify the wrong noun or pronoun in the sentence. This error is called a **misplaced modifier.**

NOT   The secretary ~~ignored the telephone~~ being too ~~busy.~~ [Was the telephone busy?]

BUT   **Being too busy,** the secretary ignored the telephone.

NOT   Her ~~father did not hear~~ the alarm ~~clock~~ snoring soundly. [Was the alarm clock snoring soundly?]

BUT   **Her father, snoring soundly,** did not hear the alarm clock.

3. Do not treat participial phrases as if they were sentences. They are not sentences. A sentence must have a real action verb or linking verb, not just a participle (see 2.b).

NOT   The dog ~~howling at the moon, keeping everyone awake.~~ [not a sentence]

BUT   The dog **was howling** at the moon, keeping everyone awake.

EXERCISE 55. In each of the following sentences, reword the sentences to correct the "dangling" participial phrases or the misplaced modifier. *Answers will vary; possibilities are given below.*

1. Driving very slowly, the tree suddenly appeared in the road. *Driving very slowly, we saw a tree on the road.*

2. Flying out of Chicago, I saw the plane crash in Lake Michigan. *I saw the plane that was flying out of Chicago crash in Lake Michigan.*

3. We ran to the door laughing loudly. *Laughing loudly, we ran to the door.*

4. Crying loudly, she picked up the baby. *The baby was crying loudly as she picked her up.*

5. Falling out of the crystal vase, I rearranged the spring flowers. *I rearranged the spring flowers that were falling out of the crystal vase.*

6. Raining cats and dogs, we ran into a doorway for shelter. *It was raining cats and dogs; we ran into a doorway for shelter.*

7. Howling at the moon, we saw the dog in the alley. *We saw the dog in the alley howling at the moon.*

8. She picked the daisies gaily dressed in a sunsuit. *Gaily dressed in a sunsuit, she picked the daisies.*

9. Smiling into the mirror, his clothes looked wonderful. *He smiled into the mirror, seeing that his clothes looked wonderful.*

10. He took a cab being late for the meeting of parents and teachers. *Already late for the meeting of parents and teachers, he took a cab.*

1.m GERUNDS

A **gerund** is a verb form that ends in *-ing* and that is used in the same ways a noun is used.

The difference between a present participle and a gerund is that a present participle is used as part of a verb or as an adjective. A gerund is used as a noun.

GERUNDS	NOUNS
I enjoy **skating.**	I enjoy **soccer.**
Skiing is another winter sport.	**Hockey** is another team sport.
You might prefer **swimming** or **jogging.**	You might prefer **baseball** or **basketball.**

Do not be confused by the sense of action that gerunds may have because they are formed from verbs. Gerunds act as nouns.

EXERCISE 56. Identify each gerund in each of the following sentences. Some of the sentences contain more than one gerund.

1. In the late 1970s roller skating suddenly became a national craze.
2. New plastic wheels made riding quieter than it used to be on metal wheels.
3. In city parks skating sometimes seemed to crowd out jogging and bicycling.
4. Skaters also tried dancing.
5. Of course, rolling can be hazardous for the beginner.
6. Balancing is often difficult at first.
7. Another problem is stopping, which for many beginners means falling.
8. Downhill skating requires particular skill as well as good balance.
9. The possibility of crashing does not discourage skaters.
10. They find that coasting gives them a thrill that walking or running does not.

APPLICATION. Select five of the gerunds from Exercise 56. Write one original sentence for each. Make sure that you use the -*ing* word as a gerund, not as a present participle.

Answers will vary; an example is "Moderate jogging is a form of exercise."

1.n GERUND PHRASES

A **gerund phrase** contains a gerund and other words that describe, or modify, the gerund.

A gerund phrase can be quite short or rather long, depending on how the gerund is expanded.

EXAMPLES

Disco dancing became a craze in the 1970s. [a gerund preceded by an adjective]

Exciting dancing can be seen in every city. [a gerund preceded by a participle]

The dinner was followed by **dancing to live music.** [a gerund followed by a prepositional phrase]

Fred Astaire's dancing in the movies still excites his fans. [a gerund preceded by a possessive noun and followed by a prepositional phrase]

Dancing the tango is not as easy as it looks. [a gerund followed by its object]

Dancing gracefully is the goal of every ballet dancer. [a gerund followed by an adverb]

EXERCISE 57. Identify the gerund phrases in each of the following sentences. Each sentence contains two gerund phrases.

1. Deep-sea fishing is one of the best ways of enjoying the crystal clear waters of the Caribbean.

2. Relaxing in the sun and doing nothing are ideal vacation pastimes for some people.

3. For the more athletic, the Caribbean offers year-round swimming and scuba diving among the reefs.

4. Using special scuba gear makes underwater breathing possible.

5. Searching for treasure and observing a school of fish are among the pleasures of underwater exploration with scuba gear.

1.0 INFINITIVES

An **infinitive** is a verb form, usually preceded by the word *to,* that is used as a noun, an adjective, or an adverb.

When the word *to* is used before a verb, the *to* is not a preposition.

EXAMPLES

to + walk = **to walk**
to + be = **to be**

You can use infinitives in the same ways that you use nouns, adjectives, and adverbs.

INFINITIVES	NOUNS
To walk is fun.	A **car** is fun.
I want **to walk**.	I want a **car**.
Our goal is **to walk**.	Our goal is a **car**.

INFINITIVES	ADJECTIVES
She had the idea **to walk**.	She had the **best** idea.

INFINITIVES	ADVERBS
He was eager **to walk**.	He was **very** eager.
They plan **to walk**.	They plan **carefully**.

1.p INFINITIVE PHRASES

An **infinitive phrase** contains an infinitive and other words that describe, or modify, the infinitive.

EXAMPLES

They want **to walk there slowly later.** [an infinitive followed by three adverbs]

They want **to walk through the park at night.** [an infinitive followed by two prepositional phrases]

To walk as far as they can is their plan. [an infinitive followed by a clause; see 2.p]

They plan **to walk to improve their endurance.** [Adding another infinitive to the first infinitive creates an infinitive phrase.]

In general, do not split an infinitive. A **split infinitive** has an adverb between *to* and the basic verb. It is almost always better to place the adverb somewhere else in the sentence.

NOT   She wants to ~~tastefully~~ decorate her apartment.

BUT   She wants to decorate her apartment **taste-fully.**

EXERCISE 58. Point out the infinitive phrase in each of the following sentences.

1. The United States launched two spacecraft to explore the solar system.
2. *Voyager 1* and *Voyager 2* were designed to fly past Jupiter and Saturn and possibly even Uranus.
3. It took the craft, weighing 1,800 pounds each, nearly two years to reach Jupiter.
4. Each craft was equipped to take thousands of photographs of Jupiter and its moons.
5. Large antennae made it possible to send radio messages more than 570 million miles across space.
6. Scientists expected to find that Jupiter's moons were dead, dry, silent places.
7. *Voyager 1* was able to discover volcanic eruptions on one of Jupiter's moons, Io.
8. When *Voyager 2* was scheduled to pass Jupiter's moons, the scientists were prepared.
9. They instructed it to look for evidence of volcanic activity on Europa, Jupiter's largest moon.
10. They were very surprised to see instead an ice-covered surface as smooth as a billiard ball.

REVIEW EXERCISE I. Identify the verbal phrase in each of the following sentences as a participial phrase, a gerund phrase, or an infinitive phrase. (One sentence has two phrases.)

1. Elephants have the distinction of being the largest land mammals. *participial phrase*
2. Living in the tropical regions of Asia and Africa, they may reach a height of thirteen feet. *participial phrase*

Section Review Exercises I-IV may be given at the beginning as diagnostic tests.
They also may be given after completion of Section 1 as brief mastery tests. See
also secure diagnostic test in the Teacher's Manual.

3. Their tusks, <u>weighing up to two hundred pounds each</u>, can be more than ten feet long. *participial phrase*

4. Their ears are huge, <u>measuring up to forty-two inches in diameter</u>. *participial phrase*

5. They use their fingerlike trunks <u>to pick up objects.</u> *infinitive phrase*

6. Elephants browse all day, <u>feeding on leaves, shoots, and tall grasses</u>. *participial phrase*

7. Elephants can learn <u>to carry logs</u> and <u>to perform in circuses</u>. *infinitive phrase, infinitive phrase*

8. <u>Training young elephants</u> takes great skill. *gerund phrase*

9. It can be difficult <u>to handle them</u>, too. *infinitive phrase*

10. <u>Hunted for food and for ivory</u>, elephants now must struggle for their survival. *participial phrase*

SECTION REVIEW EXERCISE I. Identify the nouns, pronouns, and adjectives in each of the following sentences. Do not count articles as adjectives. (If you have trouble, review 1.a, 1.d, and 1.c.)

1. *prep.* <u>In</u> *n.* <u>New England</u> *prep.* <u>in</u> the *n.* summer, ox-pulls are *v.* still a *adv.* *adj.* popular *n.* event.

2. Oxen *n.* are *v.p.* harnessed together *adv.* <u>with</u> *prep.* a wooden *adj.* <u>yoke</u> *n.*.

3. Teams *n.* <u>of oxen</u> *prep. n.* then struggle *adv. v.* to pull *inf.* loads.

4. Usually, *adv.* a flat, *adj.* wheelless *adj.* platform, *n.* or *conj.* sleigh, *n.* is loaded *v.p.* <u>with</u> *prep.* bales *n.* <u>of straw</u> *prep. n.*.

5. Teams *n.* compete *v.* to determine *inf.* the one that *pron.* can pull *pron. v.p.* the heaviest *adj.* sleigh.

6. Ox pullers, *n.* as *conj.* they *pron.* are called, *v.p.* spend *v.* time *n.* and *conj.* effort *n.* and *conj.* money *n.* to develop *inf.* a team *n.*.

7. Just as *conj.* hockey, *n.* baseball, *n.* and *conj.* football *n.* have *v.* a season, *n.* so ox-pulls *n.* are *v.* particularly *adv.* popular *adj.* <u>at</u> *prep.* a certain *adj.* time *n.* <u>of year</u> *prep. n.*.

8. The summer *n.* is *v.* the season *n.* <u>for ox-pulls</u> *prep. n.* <u>at</u> *prep.* the fairs *n.* that *pron.* are *v.* so common *adv. adj.* <u>in</u> *prep.* New England *n.*.

9. Teams *n.* go *v.* <u>from fair</u> *prep. n.* <u>to fair</u> *prep. n.* seeking *part.* fame *n.* and *conj.* glory, *n.* attempting *part.* <u>by the end</u> *prep. n.* <u>of the season</u> *prep. n.* to become *inf.* the best *adj.* team *n.* <u>in the land</u> *prep. n.*.

10. Horse-pulls are an equally popular event at fairs.
   n. ~ *v.* ~ *adv.* ~ *adj.* ~ *n.* ~ *prep.* *n.*

11. Ox-pulls have a longer history than horse-pulls.
   n. ~ *v.* ~ *adj.* ~ *n.* ~ *conj.* ~ *n.*

12. In New Hampshire oxen were used for work around the farms before horses were introduced.
   prep. *n.* ~ *v.p.* ~ *prep.* *n.* *prep.* *n.* *conj.* *n.* *v.p.*

13. In colonial times cattle served important purposes.
   prep. *adj.* *n.* ~ *n.* *v.* *adj.* *n.*

14. Cattle provided food, milk, and meat and helped with the heavy work of the farm.
   n. *v.* *n.* *n.* *conj.* *n.* *conj.* *v.* *prep.* *adj.* *n.* *prep.* *n.*

15. Since horses never have served as a steady and popular source of food in America, they did not work on farms in colonial times.
   conj. *n.* *adv.* *v.p.* *prep.* *adj.* *conj.* *adj.* *n.* *prep.* *n.* *prep.* *n.* *pron.* *v.p.* *adv.* *v.p.* *prep.* *n.* *prep.* *adj.* *n.*

16. Oxen also created power for lumberjacks.
   n. *adv.* *v.* *n.* *prep.* *n.*

17. Gradually, the horse, then steam, and finally petroleum replaced oxen as a source of power.
   adv. *n.* *adv.* *n.* *conj.* *adv.* *n.* *v.* *n.* *prep.* *n.* *prep.* *n.*

18. In New Hampshire especially, farmers continued to keep oxen, finding them most useful for tasks around a farm.
   prep. *n.* *adv.* *n.* *v.* *inf.* *inf.* *n.* *part.* *pron.* *adj.* *prep.* *n.* *prep.* *n.*

19. Today, oxen are superior in power and appearance.
   adv. *n.* *v.* *adj.* *prep.* *n.* *conj.* *n.*

20. To get oxen to work together in a yoke is truly possible but requires patience.
   inf. *n.* *inf.* *adv.* *prep.* *n.* *v.* *adv.* *adj.* *conj.* *v.* *n.*

SECTION REVIEW EXERCISE II. Identify the verbs and verb phrases and adverbs in the sentences in Section Review Exercise I. Do not identify verbals as verbs. (If you have trouble, review 1.b and 1.f.) *Answers are given in Section Review Exercise I.*

SECTION REVIEW EXERCISE III. Identify the prepositions and prepositional phrases and conjunctions in the sentences in Section Review Exercise I. (If you have trouble, review 1.g and 1.h.) *Prepositional phrases are underlined; answers are given in Section Review Exercise I.*

SECTION REVIEW EXERCISE IV. Identify the participles and infinitives in the sentences in Section Review Exercise I. (If you have trouble, review 1.j, 1.k, and 1.o.) *Answers are given in Section Review Exercise I.*

PARTS OF A SENTENCE

2 Parts of a Sentence

See summary of section in Teacher's Manual. See also Additional Exercises 9-13 (pages 653-658), which provide additional drill on the parts of a sentence.

You have been studying sentences for many years. You know that there are all different kinds of sentences — long, short, simple, complicated. All sentences, however, have two parts in common, namely a *subject* and a *predicate*. Some sentences also have other parts, such as *direct objects* or *indirect objects*.

In this section you will learn about the different parts of a sentence. Why should you study these parts? There are two main reasons. First, one of the biggest problems young writers have is in writing nonsentences. Learning to recognize parts of the sentence and to understand how they work together may help you to avoid this problem. Second, knowing the parts of the sentence can help you to understand all the different ways you can use the nouns, the pronouns, the adjectives, and the other parts of speech that are covered in Section 1.

See the Teacher's Manual for diagnostic tests for Section 2.

2.a THE SENTENCE

A **sentence** is a group of words that expresses a complete thought.

EXAMPLES
Lions roar.
Old-time aviators still remember biplanes.
Many farms have expanded in recent years.
Home movies are often funny.

2.b SUBJECT AND PREDICATE

Every sentence can be divided into two parts: the **subject** and the **predicate.** The **subject** is the part about which you are speaking or writing. The **predicate** is the part that discusses the subject.

SUBJECT	PREDICATE
Lions	roar.

In the above example the subject is *lions*, and the predicate is *roar*.

In a command sentence the subject is omitted but "understood." See 2.d.3 for a complete discussion of command sentences.

EXAMPLES
Roar!
Prepare for takeoff.

A word or a group of words is a predicate only if it includes an action verb or a linking verb. The predicate tells what the subject does or is. The predicate can be a verb alone or a verb plus other words. The verb itself is sometimes called a **simple predicate.** The verb plus other words is called the **complete predicate.** Remember that a predicate must always contain a *verb* — not just a participle or an infinitive. The following sentences show different kinds of complete predicates:

SUBJECTS	PREDICATES
Lions	**roar.**
Lions	**roar ferociously.**
Lions	**will roar.**
Lions	**roared in the circus yesterday.**
Lions	**are large cats.**
Lions	**are large.**

The subject answers the question *who?* or *what?* about the predicate. (See 2.c for information about *simple subjects.*) The following sentences show a variety of subjects:

SUBJECTS	PREDICATES
Lions	roar.
All angry lions	roar.
Lions in the forest	roar.

A group of words that begins with a capital letter and finishes with a period but that does not have both a subject *and* a predicate is a **sentence fragment.** Although some professional writers use sentence fragments for special effect, you should not use them in your writing.

AVOIDING ERRORS WITH SENTENCE FRAGMENTS

One way to avoid writing sentence fragments is to be sure that you do not use just a participle or an infinitive instead of a real verb (see 1.j). Your predicate must contain a real verb — either an action verb or a linking verb. Remember that a participle or an infinitive alone is not enough.

NOT Lions ~~roaring~~.
BUT Lions **are roaring.**

NOT Lions ~~to roar~~.
BUT Lions **love** to roar.

EXERCISE 1. Indicate whether each of the following numbered items is a complete sentence or a sentence fragment.

1. Many American suburbs are being invaded by raccoons. *sentence*
2. Homeowners are inventing all kinds of raccoon traps.
   sentence

3. Heavy rocks atop garbage cans, sprays, and "raccoon-proof" clamps. *fragment*
4. Most raccoons are too smart for these traps. *sentence*
5. Generally said to be animals of high intelligence. *fragment*
6. Raccoons like to eat berries, birds, corn, moles, and most forms of garbage. *sentence*
7. Seem to eat almost anything but tomatoes. *fragment*
8. Normally friendly, if messy, creatures. *fragment*
9. Tame raccoons will purr like kittens. *sentence*
10. Although sometimes hissing like geese, growling like dogs, or screeching like owls. *fragment*

APPLICATION. Make each of the sentence fragments from Exercise 1 a complete sentence by adding a subject or a real verb. *Answers will vary; an example is "Raccoons are generally said to be animals of high intelligence."*

EXERCISE 2. Identify where the subject ends and the predicate begins in each of the following sentences. Remember that the predicate tells what the subject does or is.

1. Many present American roads/were old pioneer trails.
2. Some pioneer trails/run through the American West.
3. Pioneer trails/are scenic and historic.
4. Buffaloes, ghost towns, and Native American museums/are found along pioneer trails.
5. Pioneers/traveled slowly.
6. The pioneer trails in the Rocky Mountains/were steep, rocky, and icy.
7. The first pioneers/explored bravely.
8. The trail through Death Valley/was a sun-baked road.
9. The Pecos Trail in Texas/now winds among oil fields.
10. The Cheyenne-Deadwood Trail/had led to gold fields.

APPLICATION. For each of the sentences in Exercise 2, keep the subject but write a new predicate, *or* keep the predicate but create a new subject. (Indicate whether you have added a new subject or a new predicate.) *Answers will vary; an example is "Some pioneer trails are now historic landmarks."*

2.b.1 Finding the subject and the predicate

In general, you can find the subject of a sentence by first finding the predicate. To find the predicate, look for the action verb or linking verb. Then ask *who?* or *what?* before that verb. In the following sentence the action verb is *danced.* Who danced? *The lion* danced. *The lion,* therefore, is the subject.

SUBJECT | PREDICATE

The lion | danced in the circus.

Sometimes, as below, the subject follows the predicate. In the first sentence the action verb is *lived.* Who lived? The answer, *the lion,* is the subject. In the second sentence the linking verb is *were.* Who were? *Hungry lions* were; therefore, *hungry lions* is the subject. (See 2.c for information about *simple subjects.*)

PREDICATES | SUBJECTS

In the jungle lived | the lion.
Everywhere on the plains were | hungry lions.

Here, then, are the steps for finding the subject:

1. Find the action verb or the linking verb (the real verb, not just a participle or infinitive).
2. Ask *who?* or *what?* before the verb.

2.b.2 Finding the subject and the predicate in sentences beginning with *there* and *it*

Many sentences begin with the expletives *there* and *it.* **Expletives** are words that have no real meaning of their own but that are often used to start a sentence. In sentences with expletives, the subject usually follows the predicate.

PREDICATES	SUBJECTS
There are	many kinds of lions.
It is dangerous	to pet a lion.

You can identify the subjects in the above sentences by omitting the expletives — *there* and *it* — and then asking *who?* or *what?* before the verbs. The subject of the first sentence is *many kinds of lions.* The subject of the second sentence is *to pet a lion.*

Remember that the first step in finding the subject is to find the predicate. Be aware also that the subject of a sentence is not always a noun. (See 2.d for a discussion of the different kinds of subjects.)

EXERCISE 3. Identify the complete predicate in each of the following sentences. Remember that sometimes the predicate comes before the subject.

> EXAMPLE Ours is a right-handed world.
>
> ANSWER   predicate: *is a right-handed world*

1. Life can be difficult for left-handed people.
2. Doorknobs are always hard to reach.
3. American children were once forced to write with the right hand.
4. Some countries even have taboos against eating with the left hand.
5. It is necessary to use special scissors.
6. It is messy to write with fountain pens.
7. There is a store for left-handed people.
8. It sells a bumper sticker with the slogan LEFT ON!
9. There are many famous left-handed people.
10. Leonardo da Vinci, Charlie Chaplin, Paul McCartney, Judy Garland, and Babe Ruth are all "lefties."

2.c **THE SIMPLE SUBJECT**

The **simple subject** is the principal word or words in the subject.

The subject of a sentence can be made up of one word or a *group* of words. When the subject is a group of words, it is called the **complete subject.** There is usually a key term, called the **simple subject,** within the complete subject. The simple subject is what remains when you remove all determiners, adjectives, and prepositional phrases from the complete subject.

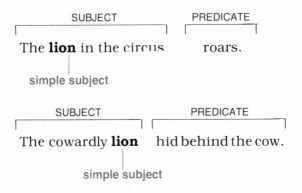

In the first example above, the complete subject contains the prepositional phrase *in the circus.* The simple subject can *never* be within a prepositional phrase. A prepositional phrase often contains a noun. Do not mistake this noun for the simple subject of the sentence. You can avoid confusion by remembering that the simple subject can never be within a prepositional phrase and by asking *who?* or *what?* before the verb. (See 1.g and 2.i.)

The simple subject by itself can answer the question *who?* or *what?* before the action verb or the linking verb. In the first sentence above, the simple subject is *lion,* not *circus.* The sentence does not say that the circus roars; it says that the lion in the circus roars.

HINT: Cross out all prepositional phrases when you are looking for the simple subject.

2.d SUBJECT – VERB AGREEMENT

You must be able to recognize the simple subject in order to make the action verb or linking verb agree in number with it. If the simple subject is third-person singular, you must use one form of a present-tense verb. If the simple subject is third-person plural, you must use another form of the verb. (Remember that the present-tense action verb that agrees in number with a third-person singular subject generally ends in *-s*. (See 1.b.6.) The following chart shows some different kinds of simple subjects. Study this chart for help in recognizing simple subjects even when they have other words around them.

KINDS OF SIMPLE SUBJECTS

	SUBJECT	PREDICATE
COMMON NOUNS		
3rd-person singular	The lion in the cage	roar**s**.
3rd-person plural	The lion**s** in the cage	roar.
PROPER NOUNS		
3rd-person singular	Leo Smith next door	sing**s**.
3rd-person plural	The Smith**s** next door	sing.
COMPOUND NOUNS		
3rd-person singular	The mother-in-law	speak**s**.
3rd-person plural	The mother**s**-in-law	speak.
PERSONAL PRONOUNS		
3rd-person singular	He	scream**s**.
	She	scream**s**.
	It	scream**s**.
3rd-person plural	They	scream.

SUBJECT	PREDICATE

INDEFINITE PRONOUNS

3rd-person singular	Another of the people	works.
	Anybody in town	works.
	Anyone in town	works.
	Anything from that store	works.
	Each of the boys	works.
	Either of the boys	works.
	Everybody in town	works.
	Everyone in town	works.
	Everything from that store	works.
	Neither of the boys	works.
	Nobody in town	works.
	No one in town	works.
	Nothing on the shelf	works.
	One of the boys	works.
	Somebody in town	works.
	Someone in town	works.
	Something on that shelf	works.
3rd-person plural	Both of the boys	work.
	Few of the boys	work.
	Many of the boys	work.
	Several of the boys	work.

Singular or Plural

The indefinite pronouns below can be considered singular or plural, depending on what they refer to.

all	S: All of the water	evaporates.
	P: All of the lions	roar.
any	S: Any of the trouble	upsets me.
	P: Any of the lions	roar.
more	S: More of the plant life	grows there.
	P: More of the lions	roar.
most	S: Most of the plant life	dies there.
	P: Most of the lions	roar.
none	S: None of the plant life	grows there.
	P: None of the lions	roar.
some	S: Some of the plant life	dies.
	P: Some of the lions	roar.

INFINITIVES AND GERUNDS

Singular	To skate	is fun.
	Skating on ponds	is fun.

AVOIDING ERRORS WITH SUBJECTS AND PREPOSITIONAL PHRASES

Remember that the simple subject can never fall within a prepositional phrase. Make sure that the action verb or linking verb agrees with the simple subject of the sentence, *not* with the object of the preposition.

NOT   Her **collection** of gold coins impress me.

BUT   Her **collection** of gold coins impress**es** me. [The simple subject is singular.]

NOT   The **plans** for the cookout is ambitious.

BUT   The **plans** for the cookout **are** ambitious. [The simple subject is plural.]

EXERCISE 4. In each of the following sentences, identify first the complete subject and then the simple subject.

EXAMPLE   A simple form of English for talking to foreigners is called pidgin English.

ANSWER   complete subject: *A simple form of English for talking to foreigners* /simple subject: *form*

1. One of the newest versions of pidgin English is spoken on the Pacific island New Guinea.
2. The name of this language comes from slurring the words *business English.*
3. Words in pidgin English come from English, Portuguese, and several other languages.
4. Many of the words are quite interesting to speakers of English.
5. Some of them seem especially unusual.
6. The phrase in pidgin for *butter* is "cow oil."
7. The word for *hair* translates as "grass belongs head."
8. The term for *envelope* is "pants belong letter."

9. Adding the word *finish* indicates the past tense.
10. The pidgin word for the future tense is *bimeby.*

2.d.1 Subject-verb agreement in *there* sentences

In a sentence that begins with *there* or *here*, you must identify the simple subject before you can choose the verb. The action verb or the linking verb must agree in number with the simple subject.

EXAMPLES

There **is** a lion here. [The simple subject, *lion*, is singular; the linking verb agrees.]

There **are** lions here. [The simple subject, *lions*, is plural; the linking verb agrees.]

Here **comes** the lion. [The simple subject, *lion*, is singular; the action verb agrees.]

Here **come** the lions. [The simple subject, *lions*, is plural; the action verb agrees.]

EXERCISE 5. In each of the following sentences, first identify the complete subject, and then identify the simple subject. Notice that in some of the sentences the predicate comes before the subject.

EXAMPLE   Everyone at the festival learns about wool making.

ANSWER   complete subject: *Everyone at the festival/* simple subject: *Everyone*

1. There are many interesting crafts fairs.
2. One of the most unusual fairs is the Sheep-to-Shawl Festival.
3. This interesting festival is held on the grounds of the Van Cortlandt Manor near New York City.
4. There are many talented people.
5. These creative people include shearers, spinners, and weavers.

6. There are even <u>some baaing sheep</u>.

7. <u>Many of the artisans</u> work with antique spinning wheels and looms.

8. <u>Everybody at the fair</u> dresses in colorful colonial style.

9. The <u>technique of making cloth</u> is demonstrated.

10. <u>All of the sheep</u> are first shorn of their wool.

11. <u>Few of the animals</u> resist the shearing.

12. <u>Most of them</u> are actually glad to get rid of the hot wool.

13. <u>Spinners with wooden spinning wheels</u> then turn the wool into yarn.

14. <u>Large pots of dye</u> bubble over wood fires.

15. <u>All of the dyes</u> are plant and vegetable dyes.

16. There is <u>no synthetic cloth</u>.

17. <u>Some of the yarn</u> then simmers in the dye.

18. <u>To make the cloth</u> is the task of weavers.

19. <u>Weavers of this kind</u> are rare in today's industrial world.

20. <u>Many of their patterns</u> are similar to those used by American colonists.

EXTRA: *Ask students to identify the complete predicate in each sentence of Exercise 5.*

EXERCISE 6. In each of the following sentences, choose the appropriate form of the action verb or the linking verb in parentheses. Remember that the verb must agree in number with the simple subject of the sentence.

1. Many old horror films (is shown/<u>are shown</u>) each night on television.

2. There (<u>is</u>/are) renewed interest in these films today.

3. Even young children (clamors/<u>clamor</u>) to see *Frankenstein.*

4. Watching *The Creature from the Black Lagoon* (<u>is</u>/are) always frightening.

5. Many in the audience always (feels/<u>feel</u>) sorry for the creature at the end.

6. Something about these films (<u>appeals</u>/appeal) to many different people.

7. Everyone (enjoys/enjoy) being frightened by giant ants and terrible monsters.

8. To scream in fear and horror (is/are) sometimes great fun.

9. All of the first horror movies (was produced/were produced) in Germany.

10. There (is/are) some horror stories by well-known authors.

11. *Frankenstein* (was written/were written) by Mary Shelley.

12. Vampires on screen (is/are) always popular.

13. One of the most famous vampires (is/are) the subject of a Broadway play.

14. Dracula with his cape and coffin (seems/seem) to be almost immortal.

15. Few (is/are) able to resist his charms.

16. Many new horror films from Hollywood (reflects/reflect) the modern space age.

17. The day of blobs and zombies (is/are) past.

18. Ghosts of all kinds (remains/remain) popular, however.

19. Many of today's horror films (is/are) humorous.

20. Some of them actually (makes/make) fun of older horror films.

EXTRA: Ask students to find the simple subject and to identify it as singular or plural in the sentences in Exercise 6.

2.d.2 Subject-verb agreement with special subjects

Certain subjects need special attention when you select an action verb or a linking verb to go with them. For example, some nouns (such as *staff*) can be singular *or* plural, depending on how you think of them. Most of these special subjects, however, are third-person singular. Therefore, the verb that agrees with them in the present tense will usually be either a form of the linking verb *is* or of an action verb that ends in -*s*. See the following chart.

collective nouns

When the noun refers to a group as a whole, it has a singular meaning. When the noun refers to individual members of a group, it has a plural meaning. (See 1.a.4 for examples of collective nouns.)

	SUBJECT	PREDICATE
singular	The staff	get**s** in at nine sharp.
	The Detroit Tigers	**is** a fine team.
plural	The staff	get different raises.

special nouns

Even though some nouns that end in *s* or *es* look plural, they are singular because they refer to one thing only.

	SUBJECT	PREDICATE
singular	Mumps	**is** a common disease.
	Physics	**is** interesting.

nouns of amount

When the noun refers to one thing or idea, it is singular. When the noun refers to a number of separate things or ideas, it is plural.

	SUBJECT	PREDICATE
singular	Seven dollars	**is** the price.
plural	Seven dollars	are on the counter.

titles

The title of a book or a work of art is always considered singular, even if a noun in the title is plural.

	SUBJECT	PREDICATE
singular	*The Grapes of Wrath*	**is** a popular book.

the number, a number

singular	The number of errors **is** frustrating.
plural	A number of errors are particularly serious.

EXERCISE 7. Choose the appropriate form of the action verb or the linking verb in parentheses in each of the following sentences. Remember that the verb must agree in number with the simple subject.

1. Many animals (is trained/<u>are trained</u>) to help people.
2. A large number of dogs (is trained/<u>are trained</u>) especially to work for human beings.
3. Each kind of dog (<u>was developed</u>/were developed) for certain tasks.
4. One group (<u>is called</u>/are called) working dogs.
5. German shepherds (works/<u>work</u>) for the police.
6. *True Stories of German Shepherds at Work with the Law* (<u>tells</u>/tell) about police dogs.
7. Years ago, a pack of dogs (<u>was</u>/were) important for hunting.
8. Sheep dogs (controls/<u>control</u>) herds.
9. For hundreds of years, this group of dogs (<u>has helped</u>/have helped) farmers.
10. Seeing Eye dogs (performs/<u>perform</u>) an important job.
11. A Seeing Eye dog (<u>is</u>/are) the eyes for a blind person.
12. Unfortunately, the expense of owning a Seeing Eye dog (<u>is</u>/are) great.
13. A Seeing Eye dog's litter (<u>brings</u>/bring) a high price.
14. Several thousand dollars (<u>is</u>/are) the general cost of training a Seeing Eye dog.
15. "Hearing ear" dogs (helps/<u>help</u>) deaf people to hear sirens and doorbells.
16. A number of other animals (has aided/<u>have aided</u>) people.
17. *All About Guard Dogs* (<u>describes</u>/describe) the different kinds of watchdogs.
18. A number of watchdogs (growls/<u>growl</u>) fiercely.
19. Cats (helps/<u>help</u>) people too.
20. Many cats (has alerted/<u>have alerted</u>) their sleeping owners to fire.

2.d.3 Subject-verb agreement in commands and questions

A **statement sentence,** or declarative sentence, must have a subject and an action verb or a linking verb. The subject generally comes before the verb. When the sentence has a third-person subject and a present-tense verb, you must make the subject and the verb agree.

STATEMENT SENTENCES

SUBJECTS

Lions roar.
The lion roars.

action verbs

A **command sentence** is also known as an **imperative sentence.** In the command sentence the subject is "understood" to be *you.* You use the same verb form whether you are talking to one subject or to more than one.

COMMAND SENTENCE

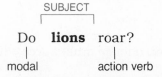

UNDERSTOOD SUBJECT

(**You,**) Help!

action verb

A **question sentence,** or **interrogative sentence,** is one that asks a question. In a question sentence the subject generally *follows* a modal, a linking verb, or an auxiliary. The modal *do* (see 1.b.11), the linking verb, or the auxiliary must agree with the subject.

QUESTION SENTENCES

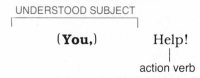

SUBJECT

Do **lions** roar?

modal   action verb

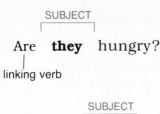

SUBJECT

Are **they** hungry?

linking verb

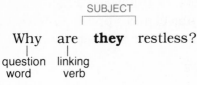

SUBJECT

Why are **they** restless?

question word | linking verb

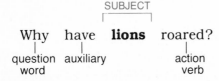

SUBJECT

Why have **lions** roared?

question word | auxiliary | action verb

EXERCISE 8. Choose the appropriate form of the auxiliary, modal, or linking verb in parentheses in each of the following questions. The form you choose must agree with the simple subject.

1. (<u>Does</u>/Do) money grow on trees?
2. (<u>Is</u>/Are) silence golden?
3. (Has/<u>Have</u>) you ever wished upon a star?
4. (Does/<u>Do</u>) cats have nine lives?
5. Why (<u>does</u>/do) a rabbit's foot bring good fortune?
6. (<u>Has</u>/Have) a broken mirror ever brought you bad luck?
7. (<u>Does</u>/Do) the early bird catch the worm?
8. (Is/<u>Are</u>) four-leaf clovers good signs?
9. Why (<u>does</u>/do) walking under a ladder bring bad luck?
10. (<u>Is</u>/Are) the moon made of cheese?

EXERCISE 9. Choose the appropriate form of the auxiliary, modal, or linking verb in parentheses in each of the following questions. The form you choose must agree with the simple subject.

1. (<u>Does</u>/Do) a smile use fewer muscles than a frown?
2. (<u>Is</u>/Are) raw steak the best cure for a black eye?
3. (<u>Does</u>/Do) hair grow faster in the summer?
4. (<u>Does</u>/Do) spinach put hair on anyone's chest?
5. (<u>Is</u>/Are) fish brain food?
6. (<u>Does</u> /Do) an apple a day keep the doctor away?
7. (<u>Has</u>/Have) chicken soup ever cured a cold?
8. (<u>Does</u>/Do) bread crust make hair curly?
9. (Is/<u>Are</u>) carrots good for vision?
10. (<u>Does</u>/Do) a wishbone really bring good luck and a wish come true?

APPLICATION. Make up ten questions like those in Exercise 8 or Exercise 9. Five of them should have plural nouns for subjects. Five of them should have singular nouns for subjects. *Answers will vary; an example is "Are dogs really a person's best friend?*

2.e COMPOUND SUBJECTS

A **compound subject** is made up of two or more subjects that are joined by a conjunction and that have the same verb.

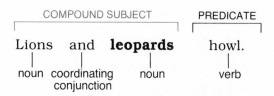

COMPOUND SUBJECT			PREDICATE
Lions	and	**leopards**	howl.
noun	coordinating conjunction	noun	verb

Compound means "made of two or more parts." Usually, the parts of a compound subject are joined by a coordinating conjunction (*and* or *or*). A compound subject can also be formed with correlative conjunctions — for example, *either . . . or* or *neither . . . nor*. The following sentences show examples of various kinds of compound subjects.

	SUBJECT	PREDICATE
common nouns	**Lions, leopards,** and **tigers**	are howling.
proper nouns	**Leo** and **Leonardo**	are howling at the trainer.
	Betty or **Veronica**	is planning the picnic.
personal pronouns	**He** and **she**	are howling triumphantly.
demonstrative pronouns	**This** and **that**	are important.
indefinite pronouns	**All** of the lions and **all** of the tigers	are howling.
infinitives and gerunds	**To howl** and **to growl**	are natural.
	Howling and **growling**	are natural.

COMMAS WITH COMPOUND SUBJECTS

With compound subjects of three or more words, use a comma after each word except the last.

Lions, leopards, and tigers roar.
Skating, swimming, and skiing take energy.

Do not use commas if you use the word *and* or *or* between each part of the compound subject. (See also 7.g.6.)

Lions and leopards and tigers roar.

EXERCISE 10. Identify the compound subject in each of the following sentences. The compound subject may be made up of nouns, pronouns, gerunds, or infinitives.

> EXAMPLE John Updike and Denise Levertov live in the Boston area.
>
> ANSWER *John Updike (and) Denise Levertov*

1. The lives (and) the works of many American writers are associated with the city of Boston.
2. Henry David Thoreau (and) E. E. Cummings are among Boston's most well-known writers.
3. Henry Wadsworth Longfellow (and) Nathaniel Hawthorne also lived in the Boston area.
4. The city of Boston (and) several nearby towns are important in American literary history.
5. Cambridge, Concord, (and) Salem all gave America talented writers.
6. Emerson, Thoreau, (and) Hawthorne are buried in Concord's Sleepy Hollow Cemetery.
7. *The Scarlet Letter* (and) *The House of the Seven Gables* were both set in Salem.
8. The Customs House (and) the house with seven gables are still standing in Salem today.
9. Ralph Waldo Emerson, from Concord, (and) James Russell Lowell, of Cambridge, played important roles in American literature in the 1800s.
10. Emerson's *Nature* (and) Thoreau's *Walden* both show back-to-nature ideas.
11. To visit Walden Pond (and) to see Thoreau's cabin help one to understand *Walden*.
12. Boston's Beacon Hill (and) Back Bay have been the homes of many American writers.
13. William Dean Howells (and) Louisa May Alcott both lived in Louisburg Square on Beacon Hill.
14. Some of Alcott's novels (and) many of her stories were written in a Boston apartment.

15. <u>Jo</u>, <u>Beth</u>, <u>Amy</u>, (and) <u>Meg</u> may have been based on actual Bostonians.

16. <u>Culture</u> (and) <u>refinement</u> have always been important in certain parts of Boston.

17. <u>Mark Twain</u> (and) several other <u>Westerners</u> thought the good manners silly.

18. The <u>tales</u> (and) <u>rhymes</u> of Mother Goose supposedly were written by a Bostonian.

19. <u>T. S. Eliot</u> (and) <u>Elizabeth Bishop</u> have both taught at universities in the Boston area.

20. <u>He</u> (and) <u>she</u> both taught literature courses.

2.f SUBJECT–VERB AGREEMENT WITH COMPOUND SUBJECTS

In a sentence with a compound subject, you must notice the conjunction joining the parts of the subject and the meaning of the subject. Then you will know what form of the action verb or linking verb to use with that subject. Study the following chart for examples of subject-verb agreement with compound subjects.

AGREEMENT OF VERBS AND COMPOUND SUBJECTS

AND

When the parts of a compound subject are joined by *and*, the subject is generally considered plural. The compound subject is considered singular, however, when its parts are actually parts of one unit, or when they refer to the same person or thing.

	SUBJECT	PREDICATE
plural	The lion **and** the tiger	roar.
	Studying **and** exercising	are important.
singular	Steak **and** potatoes [Steak and potatoes is seen as one dish.]	is today's special.
	His friend **and** lawyer [One person is both the friend and the lawyer.]	advise**s**.

OR, NOR

When the parts of a compound subject are joined by *or* or *nor*, always look at the subject nearer the verb. The verb must agree in number with that subject.

	SUBJECT	PREDICATE
plural	The lion **or** the tigers	roar.
	Neither the lion **nor** the tigers	roar.
singular	The lion **or** the tiger	roar**s**.
	Neither the lion **nor** the tiger	roar**s**.
	The lions **or** the tiger	roar**s**.

EXERCISE 11. Choose the appropriate form of the action verb or linking verb in parentheses in each of the following sentences.

1. Physical fitness and physical injuries sometimes (goes/<u>go</u>) hand in hand.
2. Bone injuries and muscle damage (is/<u>are</u>) common.
3. Roller-skating and skate-boarding (causes/<u>cause</u>) many bruised knees.
4. Feet and legs (suffers/<u>suffer</u>) most in running sports.
5. Traffic and air pollution (is/<u>are</u>) troublesome for runners.
6. Joggers and runners (has/<u>have</u>) to be careful of cars.
7. Friends and spouses often (jogs/<u>jog</u>) together just in case of injury.
8. A friend and partner (<u>makes</u>/make) jogging more pleasant.
9. Auto traffic and pollution (causes/<u>cause</u>) problems for cyclists, too.
10. Neither potholes nor a bumpy road (<u>stops</u>/stop) a dedicated cyclist, however.
11. The baseball player and the tennis player (dreads/<u>dread</u>) a sprained back muscle.
12. Neither Ron Guidry nor Billie Jean King (<u>is</u>/are) immune to injury.

13. The tennis player or the football player (<u>suffers</u>/suffer) from broken bones, sprains, and bruises.

14. Knees, legs, or the whole body (<u>is</u>/are) easily hurt in football.

15. Both the fans and the other players (causes/<u>cause</u>) danger in soccer.

16. All tobogganers or any honest skier (<u>fears</u>/fear) a bad spill.

17. An athlete's skills or physical condition (<u>affects</u>/affect) performance.

18. The weekend player or the armchair athlete (<u>strains</u>/strain) a muscle badly now and then.

19. Ill-fitting sports equipment or poor health (<u>leads</u>/lead) to danger in any sport.

20. Even so, both young people and old people (benefits/<u>benefit</u>) from sports activity.

2.g SUBJECT–VERB AGREEMENT WITH INTERVENING EXPRESSIONS

Words that are joined by the "intervening" expressions listed below are not considered compound subjects. These expressions can be considered interrupters, and they do not affect the number of the subject.

EXPRESSIONS NOT AFFECTING NUMBER OF SUBJECT

along with	plus
as well as	together with
in addition to	

Study the following examples. The first sentence contains a conjunction. A conjunction, remember, creates a compound subject. The second sentence contains an interrupter. Interrupters do not create compound subjects. Pay special attention to the verb, in a singular or plural form, that follows each subject.

EXAMPLES

The pianist **and** the drummer **are** late. [Conjunction forms compound subject that is plural.]

The pianist **as well as** the drummer **is** late. [interrupter]

A compound subject is considered singular when it is preceded by the expressions *many a* or *every.*

EXAMPLES

Many a cardinal, blue jay, and pigeon **eats** at the feeder.

Every rabbit and squirrel **knows** that old man.

EXERCISE 12. Choose the appropriate form of the action verb or linking verb in parentheses in each of the following sentences.

1. Fabric remnants and scraps (makes/make) nice patchwork quilts.
2. Many a cover or blanket (has been created/have been created) with small pieces of cloth.
3. Calico or brocade (works/work) well in patchwork.
4. First, the bits and pieces of cloth (is cut/are cut) into geometric shapes.
5. Then, the little squares, triangles, and rectangles (is sewed/are sewed) together.
6. The patchwork top plus batting and backing (is quilted/are quilted) on a large frame.
7. Traditional patterns and some modern patterns (has/have) a name.
8. The ninepatch, the grandma's flower garden, and the log cabin (is/are) popular patterns.
9. Many a pillowcase and blanket (is/are) pretty enough to frame.
10. A quilting party or other similar gatherings (was/were) very common many years ago.
11. Every bride and bridegroom (was given/were given) at least one quilted coverlet.

12. Today, quilting exhibits or even an occasional quilting bee (<u>is</u>/are) once again popular with church groups.

13. The sewing and the quilting (goes/<u>go</u>) quickly with a group of friends.

14. Friendship together with much enthusiasm (<u>makes</u>/make) the quilting go quickly.

15. Good eyesight, in addition to great patience, (<u>is</u>/are) essential for quilters.

16. A sense of design plus some sewing skills (<u>helps</u>/help) produce a fine quilt.

17. Many a man and woman (<u>possesses</u>/possess) quilts.

18. An antique quilt along with other handmade coverlets (<u>brings</u>/bring) high prices today.

19. New York's Museum of Modern Art together with many regional museums (<u>has</u>/have) shows featuring antique quilts.

20. Today, a man as well as a woman (<u>sews</u>/sew) quilts.

<u>EXTRA:</u> *Have students identify the simple subject in each sentence of Exercise 12.*

2.h COMPOUND VERBS

A **compound verb** is made up of two or more verbs that are joined by a conjunction and that have the same subject.

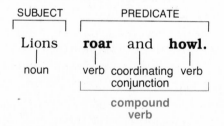

EXAMPLES

The batter **stood** at the plate and **glared** at the pitcher.
The fans **had yelled** and **had screamed**.
The pitcher **got** his sign, **rocked** back, and **threw**.
The fans **will remember** and **talk** about that pitch.

Two or more linking verbs can also be used in a predicate.

EXAMPLES
San Francisco **has been, is,** and probably always **will be** popular with tourists.
Terry **is** and **will be** terribly busy for some time.
Lorraine **is** out now but **will be** back shortly.

EXERCISE 13. Identify the compound verb in each of the following sentences.

1. Volcanoes <u>are</u> (and) always <u>will be</u> a source of fear to humans.
2. For hundreds of years, volcanoes <u>have erupted</u> (and) <u>have spilled</u> lava over many lands.
3. The earth's crust <u>moves</u> (and) <u>shifts</u> during many eruptions.
4. Unseen forces within the earth <u>build</u>, <u>expand</u>, (and) <u>explode</u> through the volcano's vent, or opening.
5. An early eruption of the volcano Mt. Vesuvius <u>overwhelmed</u> (and) <u>buried</u> two cities in A.D. 79.
6. Some eruptions either <u>are accompanied</u> by earthquakes (or) <u>are followed</u> by darkness.
7. Millions of years ago volcanoes <u>erupted</u> in North America (and) <u>formed</u> the western mountains from Canada to Mexico.
8. Crater Lake, Oregon, <u>occupies</u> the site of an old volcano (but) <u>is</u> not active.
9. The Hawaiian Islands <u>were created</u> by volcanic activity (and) still <u>contain</u> several active volcanoes.
10. Volcanoes <u>have created</u> islands, <u>destroyed</u> cities, (and) <u>built</u> mountains.

EXERCISE 14. In each of the following sentences, indicate whether the subject is *compound* or *not compound.* Indicate also whether the verb is *compound* or *not compound.* Four sentences do not have any compounds.
Compounds are indicated.

1. A group of Confederate patriots moved to Brazil at the end of the Civil War.
2. The Emperor of Brazil granted them citizenship, sold them land, and paid for transportation costs. *compound verb*
3. The group called their settlement Americana, Brazil.
4. Their four hundred descendants are still living and are growing cotton in Brazil. *compound verb*
5. The settlers established their own cemeteries and often changed their names. *compound verb*
6. The original pioneers and succeeding generations communicated in English and Portuguese. *compound subje*
7. Speaking or writing Portuguese does not affect the descendants' southern drawl. *compound subject*
8. The climate and geography of the South and of Brazil are similar in many ways. *compound subject*
9. To visit relations in the United States was difficult for some descendants.
10. On the whole, however, the descendants have no desire to return to the United States.

2.i PREPOSITIONAL PHRASES

A **prepositional phrase** is a group of words that begins with a preposition and usually ends with a noun or pronoun.

A prepositional phrase can be used anywhere in a sentence — in a subject or in a predicate — and can perform several functions. Like an adjective, a prepositional phrase can tell more about a noun. Like an adverb, it can tell *where, when,* or *how* an action takes place, or *where* or *when* a condition exists. It is even possible for an entire prepositional phrase to be the subject of a sentence. It is *not* possible, however, for the subject to occur *within* a prepositional phrase. Look at the first sentence on the next page, for example. The simple subject, *lions,* is not within the prepositional phrase *on the mountain.* Instead, the prepositional phrase is in the complete subject.

REVIEW EXERCISE A. Answer the questions in parentheses at the end of each of the following sentences.

1. A visit to Colonial Williamsburg in Virginia. (How can you make this sentence fragment a complete sentence? Suggest at least two ways.) *Answers will vary.*

2. Visitors to Williamsburg <u>form a clear picture of life in America during the 1800s.</u> (What is the complete predicate of this sentence? What is the simple predicate, or verb?)

3. <u>Women musicians in Williamsburg</u> played only the harpsichord or guitar. (What is the complete subject? The simple subject?)

4. The <u>violin</u> (and) the <u>flute</u> were considered unladylike. (What is the compound subject of this sentence?)

5. Important men in Williamsburg <u>wore</u> bigger wigs (and) <u>put</u> the word *bigwig* into the English language. (What is the compound verb in this sentence?)

6. "Mob caps" <u>were worn</u> at first only by Colonial servants ("the mob") (but) then <u>were adopted</u> by "women of quality" such as Martha Washington. (What is the compound verb in this sentence?)

7. Visitors <u>to this small town</u> often (<u>stay</u>/stays) <u>in houses</u> resembling those <u>of the original Colonists.</u> (Select the form of the action verb that agrees with the subject. What are the three prepositional phrases in this sentence?)

8. The famous <u>speech</u> by Patrick Henry (or) the <u>ghost</u> of Thomas Jefferson (<u>seems</u>/seem) real in the restored town of Williamsburg. (What is the compound subject of this sentence? Select the linking verb that agrees with the subject.)

9. It is probably fascinating <u>to eat southern foods in the restaurants of Colonial Williamsburg.</u> (What is the subject of this sentence, which begins with the expletive *it*?)

10. Peanut soup, barbecued ribs, Smithfield ham, pecan pie, and white hominy grits are only five <u>of the offerings</u> <u>in the restaurants</u> of Williamsburg. (What are the three prepositional phrases in the predicate of this sentence?)

2.j OTHER PARTS OF THE PREDICATE

You know that a predicate has to contain an action verb or a linking verb. You have probably noticed, however, that in many sentences the predicate includes more than just a single or a compound verb. What other elements can a predicate contain? The following subsections (2.k – 2.m) will explain the other parts of the predicate. Some of the parts follow action verbs. Some of the parts follow linking verbs.

2.k DIRECT OBJECTS

The **direct object** answers the question *what?* or *whom?* after a subject and an action verb.

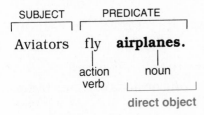

SUBJECT   PREDICATE

Aviators   fly   **airplanes.**

action   noun
verb
direct object

In the above example the noun *aviators* is the subject of the sentence, and *fly* is the verb. The noun *airplanes* is the direct object of the sentence: It tells *what* the aviators fly. The following sentences give additional examples of the various kinds of words that can serve as direct objects.

EXAMPLES

Aviators fly   **biplanes.**

noun

Aviators do   **stunts.**

noun

Aviators fly   **jets** in the air show.

noun

Aviators love   **to fly.**

infinitive

Aviators love   **gliding** over open fields.

gerund

direct objects

It is also possible to have compound direct objects, as the following examples show.

Aviators fly **biplanes** and **triplanes.**
Aviators love **to dip** and **to plunge.**

EXERCISE 15. Identify the direct object in each of the following sentences.

1. Scuba divers seek <u>adventure</u> in the ocean.
2. To stay under water for long periods of time, divers use special <u>equipment</u>.
3. Besides masks and fins they wear air-filled <u>tanks</u>.
4. Scuba divers sometimes find spectacular <u>corals</u>.
5. In some areas, divers discover lost <u>treasure</u>.
6. Many scuba divers observe tropical <u>fish</u>, such as parrot fish, yellow-tail snappers, and sea anemones.
7. Other divers like <u>to study the ocean</u>.
8. Jacques Cousteau conducts <u>studies</u> in the ocean.
9. Some professional scuba divers repair <u>bridges</u>.
10. Divers also inspect <u>dams</u>(and)<u>pipelines</u>.

APPLICATION. Rewrite each of the sentences in Exercise 15, but make up a new direct object for each. *Answers will vary.*

    EXAMPLE   1. *Scuba divers seek* **treasure** *in the ocean.*

2.I INDIRECT OBJECTS

An **indirect object** answers the question *to whom?* or *for whom?* or *to what?* or *for what?* after an action verb.

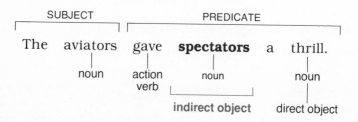

In the previous example the noun *aviators* is the subject of the sentence, and the noun *thrill* is the direct object of the verb *gave*. The noun *spectators* is the indirect object: It tells *to whom* the aviators gave a thrill. An indirect object, then, is the person or thing indirectly affected by the action of the verb.

You will notice that a sentence can have an indirect object only if it has a direct object and that the indirect object always comes before the direct object. The following sentences show different kinds of indirect objects.

EXAMPLES

The aviators gave **spectators** a scare.

The aviators gave **them** a thrill.

The spectators gave **flying** their attention.

A sentence may have more than one direct object.

EXAMPLE

The spectators gave the short **pilot** and the tall **copilot** a hand.

An indirect object can never occur in a prepositional phrase. Notice that after the words *to* or *for* a word is part of a prepositional phrase, not an indirect object.

The crowd gave an ovation to the aviators.
           | |
        direct   object of
        object   preposition

The crowd gave the aviators an ovation.
               | |
           indirect   direct
           object   object

EXERCISE 16. Identify all the direct objects and indirect objects in each of the following sentences. Some sentences have only direct objects.

1. Professional sports offer young <u>people</u> *i.o.* many interesting <u>careers.</u> *d.o.*

2. Television or radio sportscasters broadcast sporting <u>events</u>. *d.o.*
3. A good sports announcer gives <u>fans</u> *i.o.* play-by-play <u>descriptions</u>. *d.o.*
4. The announcer tells sports <u>fans</u> *i.o.* interesting <u>statistics</u> *d.o.* (and) <u>anecdotes</u>. *d.o.*
5. Writers and photographers also cover athletic <u>competitions</u>. *d.o.*
6. Newspapers in particular give <u>sports</u> *i.o.* much <u>coverage</u>. *d.o.*
7. Teaching a sport may give a <u>person</u> *i.o.* much <u>satisfaction</u>. *d.o.*
8. Managers, coaches, and trainers all help bring <u>teams</u> *i.o.* <u>success</u>. *d.o.*
9. Sports also give <u>referees</u>, *i.o.* <u>umpires</u>, *i.o.* and <u>doctors</u> *i.o.* <u>jobs</u>. *d.o.*
10. Athletic events even give hot dog and peanut <u>vendors</u> *i.o.* <u>work</u>. *d.o.*

<u>EXTRA:</u> *Ask students to write five original sentences containing both a direct object and an indirect object.*

2.m SUBJECT COMPLEMENTS[1]

A **subject complement,** or completer, follows a subject and a linking verb and identifies or describes the subject.

A linking verb is almost always followed by one or more words in the predicate. After all, the linking verb *links* the subject to something else.

There are three kinds of subject complements: predicate nominatives (2.m.1), predicate adjectives (2.m.2), and predicate adverbs (2.m.3).

2.m.1 Predicate nominatives

A **predicate nominative** is a noun or pronoun that follows a linking verb and that points back to the subject and further identifies it.

---

[1]Some grammarians use the term *complement* to include not only predicate adjectives, predicate nominatives, and predicate adverbs, as here, but also direct objects and indirect objects. This book labels sentence parts as (1) direct and indirect objects and (2) subject complements.

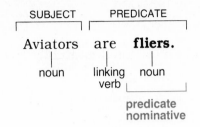

In the above example the noun *aviators* is the subject, and *are* is the linking verb. The noun *fliers* is the predicate nominative: It identifies the subject *aviators* as fliers. You might say that the predicate nominative gives another name to the subject. A predicate nominative is usually a noun or a pronoun, but it can also be a gerund or an infinitive.

EXAMPLES

Aviators are   **fliers.**
                      |
                  noun

Aviators are   **pilots.**
                      |
                  noun

The jet pilot is   **she.**
                      |
              pronoun

predicate
nominatives

You usually find predicate nominatives (as well as predicate adjectives and predicate adverbs) in sentences having forms of the linking verb *be*. Such sentences often label or classify things. Several other linking verbs — for example, *become* — can also be followed by a predicate nominative. Notice how the predicate nominatives on the next page point back to the subjects.

EXAMPLES

Aviators are **fliers.**

Fenway Park has become a Boston **landmark.**

Humphrey Bogart remains a **legend.**

The train station became a **restaurant.**

O'Hare is the nation's busiest **airport.**

Iris is a **friend** of mine.

AVOIDING ERRORS WITH PREDICATE NOMINATIVES

1. Do *not* make a linking verb agree with a predicate nominative. The linking verb must always agree with its *subject.*

   NOT   The award ~~were~~ fifty dollars and a trophy.
   BUT   The award **was** fifty dollars and a trophy.

2. Do *not* use the objective case for a pronoun that is a predicate nominative. A predicate pronoun is usually in the nominative case. If a sentence sounds awkward to you, you can rewrite it as in the third sentence below. (The exception is *me;* see below.)

   NOT   The winner was ~~him.~~
   BUT   The winner was **he.**
   OR   He was the **winner.**

   NOT   I am ~~him.~~
   BUT   I am **he.**

   The one exception is *me.* In speaking, it is acceptable to use either *me* or *I* after forms of *be.* In writing, however, *I* is still preferred.

   NOT   It was ~~me.~~
   BUT   It was **I.**

EXERCISE 17. Identify the predicate nominative in each of the following sentences.

1. Jim Thorpe was a famous American <u>athlete</u>.
2. Jim Thorpe was a <u>Native American</u>.
3. Thorpe became an all-around <u>player</u> in school.
4. He was a <u>star</u> in football, track, and baseball.
5. Thorpe became a world <u>champion</u> in 1912.
6. That year he was a <u>competitor</u> at the Olympics.
7. Thorpe was a gold-medal <u>winner</u>.
8. He became an American <u>hero</u> by winning both the decathlon and the pentathlon competitions.
9. His achievements were an <u>inspiration</u> to all sports enthusiasts.
10. Jim Thorpe remains <u>one</u> of our finest athletes.

APPLICATION. As in Exercise 17, write ten sentences that describe an American hero. Include at least one predicate nominative in each sentence. *Answers will vary; an example is "Tracy Austin is an American tennis pro."*

2.m.2 Predicate adjectives

A **predicate adjective** follows a linking verb and points back to the subject and further describes it.

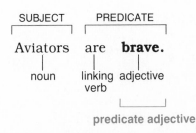

In the above example the noun *aviators* is the subject of the sentence, and *are* is the linking verb. The adjective *brave* is the predicate adjective: It describes *aviators*. The sentences on the next page also show examples of predicate adjectives.

Aviators are **brave.**
| adjective

Aviators are **daring.**
| present participle

predicate adjectives

Predicate adjectives can follow any linking verb.

EXAMPLES
The candidate had become very **cautious.**
Gabriela seemed **rested** and **happy.**
The performance will be **exciting.**
The aviator grew **doubtful.**
The class looks **ready** for the demonstration.
He feels **good.** [in spirit]
She feels **well.** [healthy]
The team remained **cheerful** all week.

EXERCISE 18. Identify the predicate adjective in each of the following sentences. One sentence has more than one predicate adjective.

1. The air has become <u>hot.</u>
2. Lift-off time is <u>close.</u>
3. The balloon is <u>ready</u> for the flight.
4. Soon it will be <u>airborne.</u>
5. The crew is <u>alert</u> (and) <u>brave.</u>
6. Fortunately, the weather seems <u>clear.</u>
7. The clouds are <u>lovely.</u>
8. The cars look <u>toylike</u> on the highway below.
9. The wind remains <u>calm.</u>
10. The flight is <u>successful.</u>

APPLICATION. As in Exercise 18, write ten sentences that tell about a sporting event. Include at least one predicate adjective in each sentence. *Answers will vary; an example is "The ice skaters felt tense."*

2.m.3 Predicate adverbs: adverbs of place

A **predicate adverb** follows a linking verb and points back to the subject and states its condition.

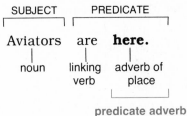

SUBJECT   PREDICATE

Aviators   are   **here.**

noun   linking verb   adverb of place

predicate adverb

In the example above, the noun *aviators* is the subject of the sentence, and *are* is the linking verb. The adverb *here* is the predicate adverb: It tells *where* the aviators are.

EXERCISE 19. Identify the predicate adverb in each of the following sentences.

1. Descendants of Polish settlers are here.
2. German settlers are everywhere.
3. Japanese people remained there.
4. Chinese immigrants stayed there, too.
5. Native Americans have always been here.

EXERCISE 20. Identify the subject complement in each of the following sentences. The subject complement may be a predicate adjective, a predicate nominative, or a predicate adverb.

1. The history of the modern tomato is colorful.
2. According to scientists, the tomato is actually a fruit.
3. Probably, it is foreign to North America.
4. The wild tomato is a kind of cherry tomato.
5. Wild tomatoes were common in Mexico before Columbus' time.
6. Soon they became an international favorite.

7. The tomato became a <u>curiosity</u> in Europe sometime in the 1500s.
8. The tomato was <u>unpopular</u> there at first.
9. Americans were at first <u>distrustful</u> of the unknown red fruit.
10. Tomatoes were <u>poisonous</u>, Europeans and Americans thought.
11. Thomas Jefferson was a <u>fan</u> of tomatoes.
12. The tomato became a <u>crop</u> at his farm.
13. It remained a <u>novelty</u> in America until the 1860s.
14. Today the tomato has become a common <u>food</u>.
15. Beefsteak tomatoes are <u>large</u>.
16. Plum tomatoes are <u>medium-sized</u>.
17. Some new tomatoes are <u>orange (or) yellow</u>.
18. The little cherry tomatoes are still <u>here</u>, also.
19. The original tomato remains <u>tasty</u>.
20. Tomatoes are <u>rich</u> in vitamin C.

REVIEW EXERCISE B. Answer the questions in parentheses at the end of each of the following sentences.

1. Davenport, Iowa, was the <u>home</u> of jazz musician Leon Bix Beiderbecke (1903–1931). (What is the predicate nominative of this sentence?)
2. Mississippi riverboats floating past Davenport gave <u>Bix Beiderbecke</u> the opportunity to hear jazz music. (What is the indirect object of this sentence?)
3. Bix Beiderbecke played the <u>cornet</u> (and) the <u>piano</u>. (What are the direct objects of this sentence?)
4. Unlike the trumpet's sound, the cornet's sound was <u>mellow</u> (and) <u>rich</u>. (What are the predicate adjectives of this sentence?)
5. Bix Beiderbecke carried his <u>cornet</u> in a brown paper bag. (What is the direct object of this sentence?)
6. Louis Armstrong once met young <u>Bix</u> on a Mississippi riverboat. (What is the direct object of this sentence?)

7. Bix Beiderbecke's parents were conservative, wealthy <u>Midwesterners.</u> (What is the predicate nominative of this sentence?)

8. His parents did not give <u>Bix</u> any financial <u>assistance.</u> (What is the direct object of this sentence? What is the indirect object?)

i.o. ... d.o.

9. Beiderbecke's musical compositions were <u>semiclassi- cal.</u> (What is the predicate adjective of this sentence?)

10. The Bix Festival is Davenport's major <u>event</u> in July. (What is the predicate nominative of this sentence?)

2.n THE CLAUSE

A **clause** is a group of words that has a subject and a predicate and that is used as part of a sentence.

A sentence may have one or more than one clause. The following example has two clauses.

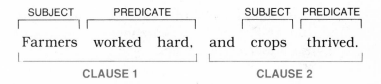

| SUBJECT | PREDICATE | | SUBJECT | PREDICATE |

Farmers worked hard, and crops thrived.

CLAUSE 1 — CLAUSE 2

There are two kinds of clauses:

1. *main clauses,* also called independent clauses
2. *subordinate clauses,* also called dependent clauses

If the clause can stand alone as a sentence, it is a **main clause.** A sentence, as you know, must have a subject and a predicate. A sentence, in other words, must have at least one *main* clause.

If the clause cannot stand alone as a sentence, it is a **subordinate clause.** Remember that *subordinate* means "lower in rank" or "of less importance." A subordinate clause does not make sense by itself and needs a main clause to complete its meaning.

In the sentence below, Clause 1 and Clause 2 both make sense on their own as complete sentences: *Farms prospered. And the economy grew.* Therefore, they are both main clauses.

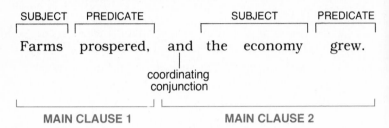

Notice that a clause that follows a coordinating conjunction (*and, but, or, for*) is still considered a main clause.

In the next example the first clause expresses a complete thought and can stand on its own as a sentence: *The economy grew.* It is a main clause. The second clause, *when farms prospered,* does not express a complete thought even though it contains a subject and a predicate. It cannot stand on its own as a sentence because it is introduced by the subordinator *when*.

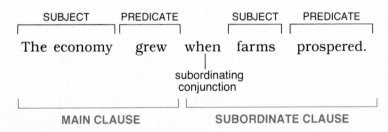

Notice that without the word *when* the subordinate clause would be a complete sentence: *Farms prospered.* Subordinate clauses often begin with words such as *when, if,* or *because.* These words make the clauses subordinate. They announce a subordinate clause and let you know that the sentence needs a main clause to be complete.

2.0 SIMPLE SENTENCES, COMPOUND SENTENCES

A sentence with only one main clause is called a **simple sentence.** The subject can be a compound subject, and the predicate can have a compound verb. Both the subject and the verb can be expanded in any number of ways. For example, with adjectives, adverbs, infinitives, participles, and prepositional phrases.

EXAMPLES

Farmers worked hard. [simple sentence]

Farmers and ranchers worked hard. [simple sentence with compound subject]

Farmers worked hard and lived well. [simple sentence with compound verb]

Farmers in the San Joaquin Valley have prospered in recent years. [simple sentence expanded]

A sentence that contains two or more main clauses is known as a **compound sentence.** The clauses in a compound sentence can be joined by a comma and a coordinating conjunction (*and, but, or, for*)[1] or by a semicolon.

EXAMPLES

Farmers worked hard, **but** the winter was severe.

Farmers worked hard, the winter was mild, **and** food prices dropped.

The drought struck; crops were destroyed.

Be aware that a sentence with two or more verbs but only one subject is *not* a compound sentence. Such a sentence has a compound verb, but it is still a simple sentence because it has only one main clause. The examples on the next page illustrate the difference between a simple sentence and a compound sentence.

---

[1]See 1.h for a more detailed explanation of conjunctions.

SIMPLE SENTENCE

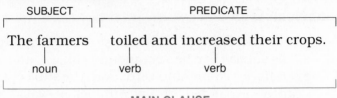

COMPOUND SENTENCE

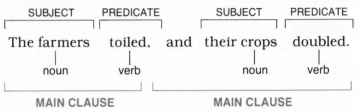

PUNCTUATION: COMPOUND SENTENCES

1. If a compound sentence has two main clauses joined by a coordinating conjunction, put a comma between the clauses.

   Cotton farms use mechanical harvesters, but fruit farms still use hand pickers.

   You can also use a semicolon between the main clauses.

   Cotton farms use mechanical harvesters; fruit farms still use hand pickers.

2. If a compound sentence has three or more main clauses, use a comma after each clause except the last.

   Farms began to grow, the region prospered, and land values rose.

   Farms began to grow, the region prospered, but land values remained stable.

AVOIDING ERRORS WITH RUN-ON SENTENCES

In a sentence with two main clauses, do not use *only* a comma to separate the clauses. You must also use a coordinating conjunction along with the comma. If you use only commas, you will have a **run-on sentence** (one main clause simply running on into the next main clause).

NOT   Vegetable farms have become quite specialized,/most grow only one kind of vegetable.

BUT   Vegetable farms have become quite specialized, **and** most grow only one kind of vegetable.

OR   Vegetable farms have become quite specialized. Most grow only one kind of vegetable.

OR   Vegetable farms have become quite specialized; most grow only one kind of vegetable.

EXERCISE 21. Each of the following sentences has more than one main clause. Identify each main clause.

1. Loch Ness is one of Scotland's most famous and interesting lakes, for it may be the home of a much talked about giant sea monster.
2. The monster has the cute name Nessie, but she is probably not cute.
3. Nessie was first reported 1,500 years ago, and since then she has been spotted often enough to keep the legend alive.
4. In the 1930s several people took photographs of her, / and one person even took a movie of the elusive sea monster.
5. A number of people talk about Nessie, but everyone describes her differently.

6. <u>Some describe her as a large snake</u>, <u>but others see her as more like a dinosaur.</u>
7. <u>Most people have seen her rising above the lake</u>, <u>but one couple claimed to see her on the road.</u>
8. <u>Scientific experts have searched for Nessie</u>, <u>but no one has yet proven her existence.</u>
9. <u>She may be a leftover from prehistoric times</u>, <u>or she may be a kind of reptile.</u>
10. <u>A very large creature really lives in Loch Ness</u>, <u>or many people have been seeing things.</u>

EXERCISE 22. Decide whether there are one or two main clauses in each of the following sentences.

1. Loch Ness is famous for its monster, but many other lakes may also have large sea creatures. *two*
2. People have reported seeing similar animals in eight other Scottish lochs. *one*
3. Almost all sightings occur in deep freshwater lakes. *on*
4. Huge snakelike creatures have been observed and studied in several Canadian lakes. *one*
5. Ancient Native American legends tell of water snakes, and the creatures were greatly feared. *two*
6. Some experts think similar creatures exist elsewhere, and many people travel in search of sea monsters. *two*
7. There are old stories of a large water animal in Lake Champlain. *one*
8. There must be some truth to these tales, for they are supported by some photographic evidence. *two*
9. The sea monsters may actually be giant eels, or perhaps they are a kind of reptile. *two*
10. Perhaps they are nothing at all; who knows? *two*

2.p SUBORDINATE CLAUSES

Like a main clause, a subordinate clause contains a subject and predicate. A subordinate clause is different from a main clause, however, because it begins with a word called a subordinator. A *subordinator* can also be called an *introductory word.*

Two kinds of subordinators are subordinating conjunctions (for example, *because* or *since*) and relative pronouns (for example, *that* or *who*). The point to remember is that a subordinator makes the subject and predicate a nonsentence. Any clause that begins with a subordinator, or introductory word, is a subordinate clause. A subordinate clause can be part of a sentence, but it cannot be a sentence in its own right.

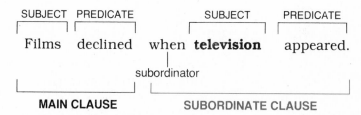

SUBJECT PREDICATE   SUBJECT   PREDICATE

Films   declined   when **television**   appeared.

subordinator

MAIN CLAUSE   SUBORDINATE CLAUSE

Sometimes the subordinator and the subject are actually one and the same word. In the following sentence, for example, *who* is both the subordinator and the subject of the subordinate clause.

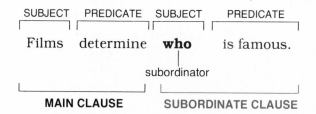

SUBJECT PREDICATE SUBJECT   PREDICATE

Films   determine   **who**   is famous.

subordinator

MAIN CLAUSE   SUBORDINATE CLAUSE

2.q COMPLEX SENTENCES, COMPOUND–COMPLEX SENTENCES

A simple sentence with one or more subordinate clauses added becomes a **complex sentence.** A compound sentence with one or more subordinate clauses added becomes a **compound-complex sentence.**

COMPLEX SENTENCE

Films changed | when sound arrived.
MAIN CLAUSE | SUBORDINATE CLAUSE

COMPOUND-COMPLEX SENTENCE

Films thrived | when sound arrived, | but they declined
MAIN CLAUSE | SUBORDINATE CLAUSE | MAIN CLAUSE

after television appeared.
SUBORDINATE CLAUSE

2.r SUBORDINATORS

Following is a list of most of the common subordinators used to introduce subordinate clauses, which will be studied in more detail in 2.s–2.v.

COMMON SUBORDINATORS

Subordinating conjunctions

after	even though	unless
although	how	until
as	if	when
as if	in order that	whenever
as long as	provided (that)	where
as soon as	since	whereas
as though	so that	wherever
because	than	whether
before	though	while

Relative pronouns
that
what, whatever
which, whichever (in which, for which, of which)
who, whoever
whom, whomever (in whom, for whom, of whom)
whose (in whose)

2.s ADVERB CLAUSES

An **adverb clause** is a subordinate clause that tells more about a verb, an adjective, or an adverb. It tells *when, where, how, why,* or *under what conditions.*

EXAMPLES

He was happy. [main clause]

Whenever we saw him, he was happy. [Adverb clause tells *when.*]

Wherever he went, he was happy. [Adverb clause tells *where.*]

He laughed **as though he had never heard a joke.** [Adverb clause tells *how.*]

Because guests were coming, they brushed the dog. [Adverb clause tells *why.*]

Even though they were terribly busy, they brushed the dog. [Adverb clause states conditions.]

In general, the subordinators that introduce adverb clauses are subordinating conjunctions. They can be grouped according to meaning.

SUBORDINATORS FOR ADVERB CLAUSES

SUBORDINATORS THAT TELL WHEN: after, as, as long as, as soon as, before, since, until, when, whenever, while

SUBORDINATORS THAT TELL WHERE: where, wherever

SUBORDINATORS THAT TELL HOW: as if, although, than

SUBORDINATORS THAT TELL WHY: as, because, in order that, since, so that

SUBORDINATORS THAT STATE CONDITIONS: although, as long as, even though, if, provided (that), though, unless, whereas, whether, while

Notice that some of the above subordinators are included in more than one category. These subordinators can have more than one meaning, depending on how they are used.

COMMAS AND ADVERB CLAUSES

Use a comma after an introductory adverb clause, even a very short one.

When the conductor appeared, the audience applauded.

In general, do not use a comma before an adverb clause that ends a sentence. Such a clause usually adds essential information; it should not be set off by a comma.

The audience applauded when the conductor appeared.

An adverb clause from which some words have been omitted is called an **incomplete adverb clause.** The omitted words are understood, however, and can easily be supplied.

EXAMPLES
I run faster **than you** [run].
I ran faster today **than** [I ran] **yesterday.**
Although [I was] **tired,** I did not stop to rest.

Sometimes you have to recognize an incomplete clause and be able to supply the omitted words in order to know which form of a pronoun to use in the sentence. Use the form of the pronoun that you would use if the clause were complete.

EXAMPLES
Sonia likes Armando better than **she.** [The incomplete clause is *than* **she** because the complete clause would be *than* **she** *likes Armando.*]
Sonia likes Armando better than **her.** [The incomplete clause is *than* **her** because the complete clause would be *than Sonia likes* **her.**]

EXERCISE 23. Identify each adverb clause in the following sentences.

1. Hurricanes have been known <u>since people recorded weather.</u>

2. <u>Whenever a hurricane came</u>, tribes of the Caribbean somehow were prepared.

3. <u>While Columbus was on his final voyage in 1503</u>, he ran into a hurricane.

4. <u>As summer passes,</u> hurricanes develop over the open water of the ocean.

5. <u>Although hurricanes begin as simple low-pressure areas</u>, they can quickly become full-fledged storms.

6. The humidity, or moisture, in the air must be high enough <u>before a hurricane can develop</u>.

7. <u>When conditions are right</u>, the air mass begins to spin in a circular pattern.

8. <u>As the air mass spins around its center</u>, the whole unit begins to move forward.

9. The circular wind speed within a hurricane must reach seventy-four miles per hour <u>before a storm can be called a hurricane</u>.

10. <u>Although most hurricanes threaten the southern states</u>, New England has also been badly hit.

11. <u>As September of 1938 drew to a close</u>, the New England coast was hit by a hurricane.

12. <u>After "The Long Island Express" had struck,</u> six hundred people were dead.

13. <u>Where the storm tides struck the coast</u>, they were twenty-five feet high.

14. <u>Wherever a strong hurricane hits,</u> destruction is widespread.

15. <u>Although forecasting now allows scientists to track hurricanes effectively</u>, they cannot prevent the storms.

16. <u>Because the average hurricane may possess the power of many atomic bombs</u>, destruction can be enormous.

17. <u>When a hurricane is coming,</u> oldtimers in Florida often feel the signs.

EXTRA: Ask students to read their local newspaper and to find five complex sentences containing adverb clauses.

18. <u>As a hurricane arrives</u>, it sounds like several express trains coming at once.

19. <u>When its "eye" passes over</u>, the storm calms down.

20. The power of the wind and rain during the height of a hurricane is frightening <u>even though it dies at last</u>.

APPLICATION. Select ten of the adverb clauses that you identified in Exercise 23. Use each in a sentence of your own. That is, make up a new main clause for each adverb clause.   *Answers will vary; an example is "As a hurricane arrives, animals become panicky."*

EXERCISE 24. Choose the appropriate form of the pronoun in parentheses in each of the following sentences.

1. The U.S.S.R. has had more world champions in chess than (<u>we</u>/us).

2. We, however, have had more tennis champions than (<u>they</u>/them).

3. The Russian Anatoly Karpov and the American Bobby Fischer play chess better than (<u>we</u>/us).

4. Chris Evert Lloyd and Tracy Austin play tennis better than (<u>we</u>/us).

5. Chris Evert Lloyd has won more championships than (<u>she</u>/her).

2.† ADJECTIVE CLAUSES

An **adjective clause** is a subordinate clause that, like an adjective, gives more information about a noun, a pronoun, or a gerund in the main clause.

An adjective clause can be placed in various positions within a sentence. In the following examples, the arrow points to the word that the adjective clause describes.

EXAMPLES

The Woody Allen film is at the theater. [main clause]

The Woody Allen film **that I want to see** is at the theater.

The Woody Allen film is at the theater **that we pass every day on the way to school.**

The director **whom we admire most** won the award.

We never go to films **that are violent.**

The following subordinators are used to begin adjective clauses.

SUBORDINATORS FOR ADJECTIVE CLAUSES
who[1]
whom (in whom, for whom, of whom, by whom)
whose (in whose)
which (in which, for which, of which, by which)
that
where
when

Sometimes an adjective clause is essential to the meaning of the sentence. Without the adjective clause, the reader would not be able to recognize the noun, or the sentence would not make sense.

EXAMPLE
Notorious is the only film **that I have seen for a long time.**

Without the adjective clause the above example does not make sense. *Notorious* is certainly not the only film. An adjective clause that is necessary (or essential) to make the meaning clear or to avoid an absurd sentence is called a **restrictive clause,** or an **essential clause.**

In some sentences, like the one below, the adjective clause is not essential. It simply adds *more* information.

EXAMPLE
Notorious, **which is one of Alfred Hitchcock's best films,** is frequently shown on television.

---

[1]In adjective clauses, *who, whom, whose, which,* and *that* are sometimes called *relative pronouns* (see 1.d.6)

The previous sentence would be perfectly clear without the adjective clause. This kind of adjective clause — one that is not absolutely needed — is called a **nonrestrictive clause,** or a **nonessential clause.** (It is also known as an **extra clause.**)

Notice the way that you can use the subordinators *that* and *which* with essential and extra clauses. You can use both words with essential clauses, although *that* is preferred. With extra clauses, however, you should use only *which* — never *that.*

EXAMPLES

Star Wars is known for its special effects**, which** are indeed impressive.

Star Wars is the only film **that** I really enjoyed.

ADJECTIVE CLAUSES AND COMMAS

1. With an *extra* (or nonrestrictive) clause, use *extra* commas. If the clause comes at the end of a sentence, put a comma before it. If the clause comes within the sentence, use a comma on either side of it. The important word to remember is *extra*: Clauses containing extra information require extra commas.

   The Marx Brothers' greatest film was *A Night at the Opera,* **which pokes fun at opera.**

   A Night at the Opera, **which was the Marx Brothers' greatest film,** pokes fun at opera.

2. With an essential, or restrictive, clause, do not use commas. The key word to remember is *essential*: The information in an essential clause actually gives the meaning of the sentence. It is *not* extra information and does *not* take extra commas.

   Sounder was the film **that I saw last night.**
   The film **that I saw last night** was *Sounder.*

EXERCISE 25. Identify each adjective clause in the following sentences.

1. Extrasensory perception, <u>which is abbreviated as ESP</u>, interests many people.
2. Certain people, <u>who are called psychics,</u> claim to be able to foretell future events.
3. They claim to feel and see forces <u>that other people cannot sense.</u>
4. Such people seem to have psychic abilities <u>that stun experts.</u>
5. Sometimes police are aided by psychics <u>who claim to have "visions."</u>
6. One woman, <u>who received her information from a dream</u>, was able to lead police to a kidnapped child.
7. Dreams <u>that foretell an event</u> are common.
8. There are some astonishing psychic stories <u>that have never been explained.</u>
9. Scientists <u>who study such people and happenings</u> have done research at Duke University in North Carolina.
10. Many people are still doubtful about ESP, <u>which they find baffling or even unbelievable.</u>

EXERCISE 26. Select a relative pronoun (*who, that,* or *which*) for each of the following sentences. Remember that you should not use *that* when you use commas.

1. Many people ___*who*___ are afraid of snakes do not realize that snakes ___*that/which*___ eat rats and mice perform a very useful service.
2. Snakes' skin, ___*which*___ most people think of as slimy and damp, is really a body covering ___*that/which*___ is smooth, dry, and often beautiful.
3. A snake can swallow an object ___*that/which*___ is many times larger than its own head.
4. Many ribs and a long backbone, ___*which*___ are the bulk of a snake, give the snake an appearance ___*that/which*___ is certainly distinctive.

5. Some pythons have pieces of bone _____ *that/which* some think may be parts of legs _____ the snakes had.
that/which

EXTRA: Ask students to read their local newspaper and to find five complex sentences containing adjective clauses.

2.u NOUN CLAUSES

A **noun clause** is a subordinate clause used as a noun.

You can use a noun in many parts of a sentence. Similarly, you can use a noun clause in different parts of a sentence, as shown below.

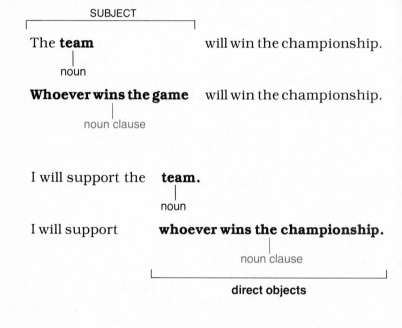

SUBJECT

The **team** will win the championship.
|
noun

Whoever wins the game will win the championship.
|
noun clause

I will support the **team.**
|
noun

I will support **whoever wins the championship.**
|
noun clause

direct objects

The referees believe in fair **play.**
|
noun

The referees believe in **what is fair.**
|
noun clause

objects of prepositions

The quarterback is a **hero.**
|
noun

The quarterback is **who saved the team.**
|
noun clause

predicate
nominatives

Following is a list of some of the subordinators that can be used to introduce noun clauses.

SUBORDINATORS FOR NOUN CLAUSES

how	whichever
that	who
what	whoever
whatever	whom (in whom, for whom,
when	by whom)
where	whose
which	why

Here are additional examples of noun clauses with some of the above subordinators.

EXAMPLES
Everyone knows for **whom you played.**
Do you care **what we do?**
Whatever you want is fine.
His book tells **how the team won the championship.**
Do you know **where the team plays tomorrow?**

EXERCISE 27. Identify the noun clause in each of the following sentences.

1. <u>That some twins lead unusual lives</u> is well known.
2. <u>Whatever twins do</u> is usually noticed.
3. <u>Whoever is born first</u> is considered the older.
4. Many parents admit <u>that their identical twins fool even them.</u>

5. People often have to think twice about <u>which twin is which</u>.

6. Some twins say <u>that they dislike being a twin</u>.

7. "<u>Whoever is a twin is lucky</u>," said one girl.

8. Years ago, <u>whoever had twins</u> always dressed them alike.

9. Now, parents know <u>that it is better to dress identical twins differently.</u>

10. Parents now encourage <u>whatever each twin tries to do</u>.

REVIEW EXERCISE C. Identify each subordinate clause in the following sentences. Tell whether the subordinate clause is an adverb clause, an adjective clause, or a noun clause, and tell why.

adj. 1. Plants <u>that eat insects</u> make unusual pets. *tells about noun*

adj. 2. The most common plant of this kind is the Venus' flytrap, <u>which grows wild only in a swampy area of North Carolina.</u> *tells about noun*

adv. 3. People are amazed <u>when the flytrap's leaves open to receive food</u>. *tells about verb*

adv. 4. <u>After they get the food</u>, the leaves again close. *tells about ve*

adj. 5. Sundews and pitcher plants, <u>which also trap insects</u>, are other natives of America. *tells about noun*

adj. 6. A sticky substance <u>that is secreted by the sundew plant</u> captures insects. *tells about noun*

n. 7. <u>Whatever falls into the straight-sided tube of the pitcher plant</u> cannot get out. *subject of sentence*

adj. 8. The prey then undergo digestion, <u>which is a leisurely process</u>. *tells about noun*

adj. 9. The Venus' flytrap has many leaves, <u>which work like traps.</u> *tells about noun*

adv. 10. An open leaf is triggered to close <u>whenever an insect lands on it</u>. *tells about verb*

n. 11. Tiny guard hairs sense <u>where the insect lands</u>. *direct obje*

n. 12. The hairs tell the plant <u>that it has made a catch</u>.
direct object

*adj.*13. The trap has a hinge in the middle, <u>which then snaps shut on the insect.</u> *tells about noun*

*adv.*14. <u>After the trap has closed,</u> it bathes the insect in a fluid. *tells about verb*

*adj.*15. The fluid, <u>which slowly dissolves the insect's soft parts,</u> also nourishes the plant. *tells about noun*

*adv.*16. <u>When the trap later opens,</u> it reveals fragments of the insect. *tells about verb*

*adv.*17. <u>After the remnants are washed away,</u> the plant's traps are ready for new prey. *tells about adjective*

*adj.*18. The insects <u>that struggle the most in the grip of the Venus' flytrap</u> are large flies. *tells about noun*

*adv.*19. The plant wins <u>even though the fly buzzes fiercely.</u> *tells about verb*

*adj.*20. All insect-eating plants need an environment <u>that is both moist and acid.</u> *tells about noun*

REVIEW EXERCISE D. Answer the questions in parentheses at the end of each of the following sentences.

1. <u>Whoever likes ragtime or blues</u> will love jazz music. (What is the noun clause in this sentence?)

2. Jazz music originated and flourished in New Orleans, Louisiana. (How many main clauses are there in this sentence?) *one*

3. <u>Whoever played the cornet, trumpet, or clarinet</u> could lead a jazz band. (What is the noun clause in this sentence?)

4. The cornet, <u>which is the most popular lead instrument in a jazz band,</u> has a mellower sound than does a trumpet or clarinet. (What is the adjective clause in this sentence?)

5. <u>Jazz was first popular in New Orleans and Chicago,</u>/<u>and then St. Louis and New York City became jazz centers.</u> (What are the two main clauses in this sentence?)

6. Jazz music became popular in New York City <u>because the recording industry was there.</u> (What is the adverb clause in this sentence?)

7. Detroit and Kansas City were also major jazz centers. (How many main clauses are there in this sentence?) *one*

8. George Gershwin, (<u>who</u>/which/that) wrote *Porgy and Bess* and *Rhapsody in Blue,* was greatly influenced by jazz music. (Complete this sentence by supplying the appropriate relative pronoun.)

9. The music <u>that Charlie Parker writes and performs</u> is called modern jazz. (What is the adjective clause in this sentence?)

10. Chicago, (<u>which</u>/that) is a modern rock group, imitates modern and traditional jazz. (Complete this sentence by supplying the appropriate relative pronoun.)

2.v *WHO* VS. *WHOM* IN SUBORDINATE CLAUSES

The case, or form, of the subordinator depends on how it is used within the subordinate clause.

Decide whether the subordinator is the subject of the subordinate clause, the direct object of the subordinate clause, the object of a preposition in the clause, or the predicate nominative of the clause. Do not pay attention to any other words in the sentence outside of the subordinate clause. Then follow these rules:

1. Use *who* if you have the subject of a clause or the predicate nominative of a clause.

2. Use *whom* if you have the direct object of a verb or the object of a preposition.

Try to follow the solutions in each of the following examples.

EXAMPLES

The director (who/whom) you admire won the Oscar. [The subordinator is the direct object of the verb *admire.* The correct choice is *whom.*]

The Oscar was given to (whoever/whomever) deserved it. [The subordinator is the subject of the verb *deserved.* The correct choice is *who*ever.]

EXERCISE 28. Select the appropriate word from the parentheses in each item below.

1. Newspapers tell about adults (<u>who</u>/whom) have the best of both worlds.
2. Some adults, (who/<u>whom</u>) the papers describe, work one week and stay home one week.
3. Two people, (<u>who</u>/whom) must treat each other with respect, share one job.
4. Some people (who/<u>whom</u>) the plan works for are women with young children.
5. One worker generally knows (<u>who</u>/whom) her replacement is on alternate weeks.

2.w A REVIEW OF SENTENCES: SIMPLE, COMPOUND, COMPLEX, COMPOUND–COMPLEX

There are four kinds of sentences:

1. **Simple sentence:** A simple sentence has one main clause and no subordinate clauses. A simple sentence, therefore, has one subject (single or compound) and one predicate (a single or compound verb plus optional parts such as objects and complements).

   EXAMPLES
   Lions roar.
   Aviators fly antique planes and test experimental jets.

2. **Compound sentence:** A compound sentence has two or more main clauses and no subordinate clauses. Each of the main clauses in a compound sentence can function as a simple sentence, described above.

   EXAMPLES
   Lions roar, and tigers growl.
   Some films become classics, but many are quickly forgotten.

3. **Complex sentence:** A simple sentence to which at least one subordinate clause has been added becomes a complex sentence. A complex sentence, therefore, has one main clause and one or more subordinate clauses.

EXAMPLES

Everyone knows that lions roar.

The aviator, who always wears goggles and a leather cap, has appeared on the covers of magazines.

After they planted the seed but before they irrigated the soil, the farmers had bad luck with the weather.

4. **Compound-complex sentence:** A compound sentence to which at least one subordinate clause has been added becomes a compound-complex sentence. A compound-complex sentence, therefore, has at least two main clauses and at least one subordinate clause.

EXAMPLE

Alfred Hitchcock's films, which are my favorites, are suspenseful, but they are not as frightening as some people assume.

DIAGRAMING SENTENCES

Diagraming is a method of showing the relationship of various words and parts of a sentence to the sentence as a whole. You can check your understanding of how subjects, predicates, phrases, and clauses work together by using diagrams. On the following pages you will see how a simple two-part diagram grows as you add more parts to a sentence and, therefore, more lines to the diagram. In this book the new element on each diagram will always be in red.

You begin a sentence diagram by putting down a horizontal line and then dividing it into two parts, one for the subject and one for the verb, as shown in Diagram 1.

Diagram 1: Subject, verb

Divide the horizontal line into two parts, one for the subject, one for the verb. Make sure the vertical appears above and below the horizontal. This is the major division of a diagram.

SENTENCE: Athletes work.

Diagram 2: Understood subject

Place *you* in parentheses on the subject line.

SENTENCE: (you) Work.

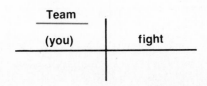

Diagram 3: Direct address

Place the noun or proper noun of direct address on a horizontal line above the understood subject.

SENTENCE: Team, fight!

Diagram 4: Sentence beginning with *there*, *it*

Place *there* or *it* on a separate line.

SENTENCE: There are athletes.

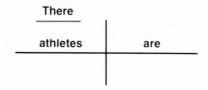

Diagram 5: Compound subject, compound verbs

Place the parts of a compound element on a "fork." Then place them at the appropriate point on the diagram. Notice how to write in a conjunction.

SENTENCE: Athletes and coaches both plan and practice.

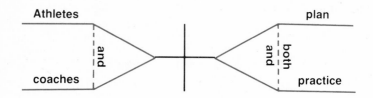

Diagram 6: Adjectives, adverbs, determiners

Place all modifiers on slanted lines below the noun or verb that they modify.

SENTENCE: Good athletes practice hard and thoroughly.

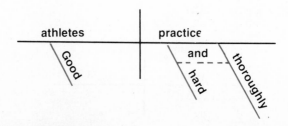

Diagram 7: Adverbs that modify adjectives or adverbs

You can place an adverb on one slanted line that grows out of another.

SENTENCE: Very good athletes practice extremely hard.

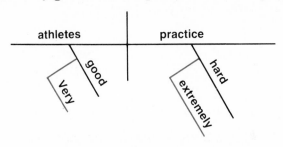

Diagram 8: Predicate nominatives

Place a predicate nominative along the horizontal line of the predicate. Separate it from the linking verb by using a slanted line.

SENTENCE: Athletes are favorite heroes.

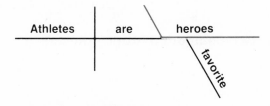

Diagram 9: Predicate adjectives

Place a predicate adjective the same way that you place a predicate nominative. Notice the "fork" for a compound element.

SENTENCE: Our athletes are strong and brave.

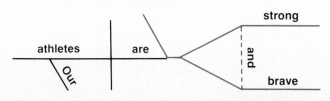

Diagram 10: Direct objects

Place a direct object along the horizontal line of the predicate. Separate it from the action verb by using a vertical line (which does *not* cut through the horizontal).

SENTENCE: Athletes win scholarships.

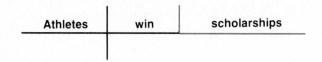

Diagram 11: Indirect objects

Draw a slanted line below the verb and then a horizontal line off the slanted line.

SENTENCE: Athletes give schools spirit.

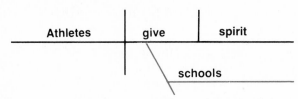

Diagram 12: Compound direct objects and indirect objects

Notice the "forks."

SENTENCE: Athletes bring parents and friends excitement and pride.

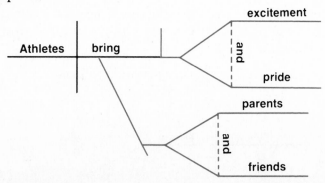

Diagram 13: Prepositional phrases

Place the preposition on a slanted line that comes down from the word modified by the prepositional phrase. Then draw a horizontal line off the slanted line. Place the object of the preposition on the horizontal.

SENTENCE: Athletes of today set new records at every opportunity during a season.

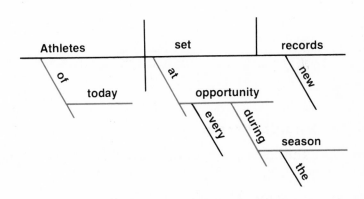

Diagram 14: Participles and participial phrases

Curve the participle as shown below.

SENTENCE: Recovering his balance, the quarterback completed the pass.

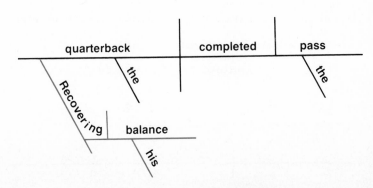

Diagram 15: Gerunds and gerund phrases

Place the gerund on a step as shown below. The phrase in the subject position is placed on a "stilt."

SENTENCE: Winning every game is one way of gaining confidence.

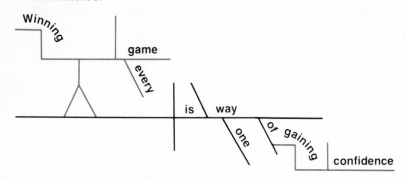

Diagram 16: Infinitives and infinitive phrases

These infinitives are diagramed like prepositional phrases (see Diagram 13).

SENTENCE: Athletes are going to travel far.

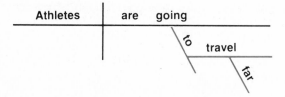

Diagram 17: Infinitives and infinitive phrases as nouns

Here, you have to use "stilts" again.

SENTENCE: To be a champion is to taste glory.

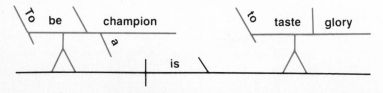

Diagram 18: Appositives

Place the appositive in parentheses.

SENTENCE: The coach, a graduate of the school, teaches us team spirit, an important ingredient.

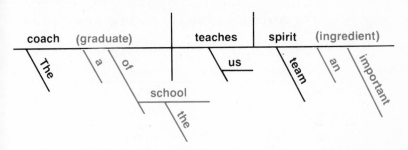

Diagram 19: Compound sentences

Place each main clause on a diagram of its own. If the main clauses are connected by a semicolon, use a dotted line to connect the verbs of each main clause. If the main clauses are connected by a conjunction, place it on a solid horizontal line.

SENTENCE: Athletes like to win, but we must learn to lose.

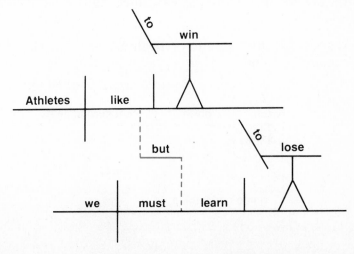

Diagram 20: Adjective clauses

Place the main clause in one diagram and the subordinate clause in another diagram. Use a dotted line to connect the subordinator of the subordinate clause to the word it modifies.

SENTENCE: The coach whom you like won games that were close.

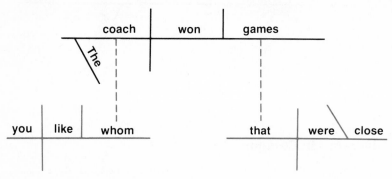

Diagram 21: Adverb clauses

Place the main clause in one diagram and the subordinate clause in another diagram. Place the subordinating conjunction on a dotted line connecting the verb of each clause.

SENTENCE: Before a game begins, the coach gives encouragement.

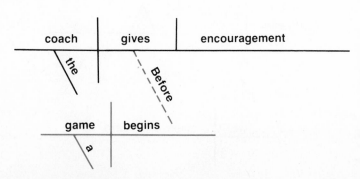

Diagram 22: Noun clauses as subject

Use a "stilt" growing out of the subject position for the noun clause. Place the subordinator as subject, object, or predicate nominative of the noun clause itself.

SENTENCE: What the coach says is important.

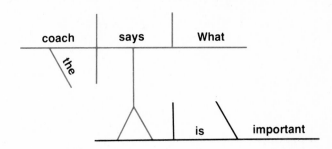

Diagram 23: Noun clauses as object

Use a "stilt" growing out of the object position. If the subordinator merely introduces the noun clause, simply place it on a line of its own.

SENTENCE: The coach knows that the rival may win.

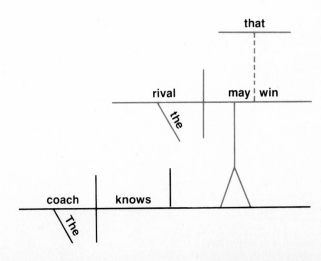

DIAGRAMING EXERCISE. Use the preceding models of diagraming to diagram the sentences specified below.

See answers at the back of the Teacher's Manual.

1. The four example sentences in 2.a (p. 112).

2. The first example sentence in 2.g (p. 135).

3. An example of a compound sentence in 2.o (p. 153).

4. An example of a complex sentence in 2.w (p. 172).

5. The compound-complex sentence on p. 158.

3

WRITING SENTENCES

3 Writing Sentences

See summary of section in Teacher's Manual. [Included in the summary is a discussion of sentence combining as treated in Section 3. Sentence-combining exercises are asterisked.]

You know that an English sentence must have both a subject and a predicate. If, however, every sentence has *only* a subject and a verb, your readers may soon become bored and perhaps stop reading what you have written. Your thoughts, your ideas, your sentences will stop there and will never "get through" to anyone.

It is therefore important to learn to write different *kinds* of sentences. Remember that there is usually more than one way to say what you want to say.

In this section you will practice writing all kinds of sentences. Then, when you sit down to write a whole paragraph (see Section 10) or a series of paragraphs (see Sections 11, 12, and 14), you will be able to put together a rich variety of sentences that will capture and hold your reader.

WRITING SIMPLE SENTENCES

3.a SIMPLE SENTENCES

A **simple sentence** has only one subject (single or compound) and one predicate.

There are at least eight kinds of simple sentences that you should practice. The basic element that makes the eight sentences different from one another is the predicate — the *kind* of verb and the parts that follow the verb. You do not have to memorize these eight basic simple sentences, but you should be aware that they form the basis of all your writing. Later, you will see how you can build up and expand each of these eight kinds of sentences, but for the moment simply turn your attention to them as presented below.

■ Kinds of simple sentences

1. Music **entertains.**
   subject + action verb

2. Music **entertains students.**
   subject + action verb + direct object

3. Music **gives students pleasure.**
   subject + action verb + indirect object + direct object

4. Music **is life.**
   subject + linking verb + predicate nominative

5. Music **is important.**
   subject + linking verb + predicate adjective

6. Music **is everywhere.**
   subject + linking verb + predicate adverb

7. Music **is appreciated by everyone.**
   passive-voice sentence

8. **There is** music.
   subject + linking verb in inverted order

■ Expanding simple sentences

Each of the eight basic simple sentences listed in 3.a is made up of at least one noun and one verb. You can, of course, tell more about each noun and verb by adding words or phrases. Notice that even if you add words or phrases these sentences can remain simple sentences. In other words, you can write better, more descriptive sentences that will still be considered simple sentences.

On the next page you will see several ways to expand one of the eight basic simple sentences. You can make similar additions to the basic simple sentences in 3.a.

■ Expanding a simple sentence to tell more about nouns

BASIC SIMPLE SENTENCE
Music entertains students.

ADD ADJECTIVE.
Popular music entertains students.
Music entertains **modern** students.

ADD PARTICIPLE OR PARTICIPIAL PHRASE USED AS ADJECTIVE.
Music entertains **finger-snapping** students.
Creating lively moods, music entertains students.

ADD POSSESSIVE.
Today's music entertains students.

ADD PREPOSITIONAL PHRASE USED AS ADJECTIVE.
Music **from everywhere** entertains students **of today.**

ADD INFINITIVE (OR INFINITIVE PHRASE) AS ADJECTIVE.
Music **to play loudly** entertains students.

■ Expanding a simple sentence to tell more about verbs

BASIC SIMPLE SENTENCE
Music entertains students.

ADD ADVERB OF MANNER.
Music **increasingly** entertains students.

ADD PREPOSITIONAL PHRASE AS ADVERB.
Music entertains students **in many ways.**

ADD INFINITIVE (OR INFINITIVE PHRASE) AS ADVERB.
To help them relax, music entertains students.

Exercises 1 – 10 and Review Exercises A – C will give you practice writing sentences that have more than just plain subjects and verbs.

EXERCISE 1: Using adjectives and participles to expand simple sentences.   Expand each of the five simple sentences below by placing the most appropriate word from the Word Bank in front of the italicized word. Use each Word Bank item only once.

1. Early Eskimos ate *meat.* c
2. Many *groups* sought seals. d
3. Their harpoons had *points.* e
4. Some hunters paddled *kayaks.* b
5. Eskimo hunters wore *parkas* made of fur. a

> **WORD BANK**
> a. long-sleeved
> b. canoelike
> c. raw
> d. hunting
> e. sharp

EXTRA: Ask for other examples of adjectives or participles used as adjectives that can be used in sentences in Exercise 1.

EXERCISE 2: Using adjectives and participles to expand simple sentences.   Expand each of the five simple sentences below by placing the most appropriate word from the Word Bank in front of the italicized word. Use each Word Bank item only once.

1. Plains tribes ate *buffalo.* e
2. The *hides* provided shelter. c
3. The *tepees* were portable. b
4. Some *rituals* involved the buffalo. a
5. Buffaloes roamed the *plains.* d

> **WORD BANK**
> a. religious
> b. tall
> c. leather
> d. dusty
> e. roasted

EXTRA: Ask for other examples of adjectives or participles used as adjectives that can be used in sentences in Exercise 2.

EXERCISE 3: Using prepositional phrases as adjectives to expand simple sentences. Expand each of the five simple sentences below by placing the most appropriate phrase from the Word Bank after the italicized word. Use each Word Bank item only once.

1. Some *tribes* smoked foods. *d*
2. They also picked *berries.* *e*
3. The ocean provided *fish.* *b*
4. *Animals* were another food source. *a*
5. Many tribes dried *food.* *c*

WORD BANK

a. like deer
b. like halibut and cod
c. in the sun
d. of the Pacific Northwest
e. from bushes

EXTRA: Ask for other examples of prepositional phrases as adjectives that can be used in sentences in Exercise 3.

EXERCISE 4: Using infinitives as adjectives to expand simple sentences. Expand each of the five simple sentences below by placing the most appropriate item from the Word Bank after the italicized word. Use each Word Bank item only once.

1. The Southwest presented many *problems.* *d*
2. Tribes found little *game.* *e*
3. Farming supplied the *food.* *a*
4. There was much dry *land*, however. *c*
5. Cotton or sheep provided *clothing.* *b*

WORD BANK

a. to eat
b. to wear
c. to irrigate
d. to solve
e. to hunt

EXERCISE 5: Using infinitive phrases as adjectives to expand simple sentences. Expand each of the following five simple sentences by placing the most appropriate phrase from the Word Bank after the italicized word. Use each Word Bank item only once.

1. The *rainfall* was heavier in early days. *b*
2. The Southwest had lush *plant life*. *c*
3. *Animals* were plentiful. *d*
4. Climate changes created a dry *desert*. *e*
5. Agricultural *methods* were developed by the Cochise tribe. *a*

WORD BANK
a. to cultivate the dry land
b. to support plant growth
c. to feed mammoths and other plant-eating animals
d. to hunt for food
e. to make life difficult for the southwestern tribes

EXTRA: Ask for other examples of infinitive phrases as adjectives that can be used in sentences in Exercise 5.

EXERCISE 6: Using participial phrases to expand simple sentences. Expand each of the five simple sentences below by placing the most appropriate phrase from the Word Bank after the italicized word. Use each Word Bank item only once.

1. Eastern *tribes* sought deer and other animals. *c*
2. Sometimes they gathered *berries*. *e*
3. Groups near water collected *shellfish*. *b*
4. New England *tribes* got maple syrup. *a*
5. *Mound Builders* raised corn, squash, and beans. *d*

WORD BANK
a. tapping the maple trees
b. found in the many lakes and streams
c. hunting in the forests
d. using farming methods of southwestern tribes
e. growing on wild plants

EXERCISE 7: Using adverbs to expand simple sentences. Expand each of the following five simple sentences by placing the most appropriate word from the Word Bank in front of the italicized word. Use each Word Bank item once.

1. The earliest western tribes *stalked* large game. *d*
2. Over the centuries the game *died out.* *e*
3. The tribes *depended* on wild plants. *a*
4. Farming methods were *unknown.* *c*
5. Tribes *stored* food for the winter months. *b*

WORD BANK

a. increasingly

b. wisely

c. completely

d. bravely

e. slowly

EXERCISE 8: Using prepositional phrases as adverbs to expand simple sentences. Expand each of the five simple sentences below by using the most appropriate phrase from the Word Bank. Use each Word Bank item only once.

1. Most Native Americans traveled˰on waterways. *a*
2. They walked˰along rocky trails. *e*
3. Eskimos used dogsleds˰. *c*
4. Many groups traded goods˰. *b*
5. Shells and furs were used˰sometimes. *d*

WORD BANK

a. in canoes

b. with one another

d. as money

e. with backpacks

c. on snowy lands *EXTRA: Ask for other examples of prepositional phrases as adverbs that can be used in sentences in Exercise 8.*

EXERCISE 9: Using infinitive phrases as adverbs to expand simple sentences. Expand each of the five simple sentences below by using the most appropriate phrase from the Word Bank.

1. Most Native Americans built simple, portable homes˰. *c*
2. Plains hunters moved their tepees often˰. *e*
3. Eskimos constructed igloos in winter˰. *b*
4. Navajos lived in hard-to-spot underground hogans˰. *a*
5. Pueblo tribes constructed sturdy adobe villages˰. *d*

WORD BANK

a. to hide from enemies

b. to suit the cold climate

c. to live in

d. to provide more permanent shelter

e. to follow the game

EXERCISE 10. Go back to the sentences that you wrote in Exercises 7, 8, and 9. See if you can rewrite each sentence by changing the position of the adverb or adverb phrase.
Answers will vary; an example is Ex. 8 #3: On snowy lands Eskimos used dogsleds.

REVIEW EXERCISE A: Expanding sentences with all structures. Rewrite each of the following basic simple sentences twice. First add Item *a* to the original sentence, creating a new sentence. Then add Item *b* to the original sentence, creating another new sentence. *Answers will vary; possibilities are given below.*

1. The polka is a˄folk dance˄. *b, a*
   a. of Central Europe
   b. lively

2. ˄Immigrants brought the polka˄to the United States. *b, a*
   a. from their homelands
   b. Slavic

3. Dancers often wear˄costumes˄. *b, a*
   a. at polka festivals
   b. colorful

4. The National Polka Festival˄draws˄crowds. *a, b*
   a. in Hunter, New York
   b. enthusiastic

5. Small bands˄play music˄. *a, b*
   a. of accordionists
   b. with a fast polka beat

6. The˄atmosphere˄makes everyone merry. *b, a*
   a. immediately
   b. cheerful

7. There are˄contests and dancing lessons˄. *b, a*
   a. to instruct beginners
   b. special

8. Puppet shows∧delight the∧children. *a, b*
   a. of Slavic folk dancers
   b. young
9. Artists∧exhibit∧craft work. *b, a*
   a. their
   b. proudly
10. ∧Ukrainian eggs are on display∧. *a, b*
    a. decorated
    b. here

REVIEW EXERCISE B: Expanding sentences in a variety of ways.   Rewrite each of the following sentences by adding items from the Word Bank. The italicized letters at the end of each sentence indicate which lettered list in the Word Bank contains the appropriate item.

> EXAMPLE   Young people work. *C, D*
> ANSWER   *Young people* **on vacation sometimes** *work.*
> **C**   **D**

1. Students find∧jobs∧. *A, E 2, 2*
2. Restaurants∧hire students∧. *C, E 3, 3*
3. Lakes and pools require∧lifeguards∧. *B, E 4, 1*
4. ∧Typists∧give students their jobs. *B, D 1, 3*
5. ∧Camp counselors∧lead hikes. *C, D 6, 5*
6. ∧Actors are paid by∧theaters. *B, A 6,1*
7. Organizations∧sponsor∧programs. *C, B 2, 2*
8. ∧Students take classes∧. *A, E 5,4*
9. Youths∧can travel∧. *C, D 4, 4*
10. The National Music Camp attracts∧students. *B, A 5, 3*

WORD BANK

A. Adjectives
1 small
2 part-time
3 orchestral
4 purple
5 serious

B. Participles
1 vacationing   *4* swimming
2 training   *5* gifted
3 mowing   *6* unknown

C. Prepositional phrases as adjectives

1 in national parks
2 like the National Science Foundation
3 in resort areas
4 ~~on vacation~~
5 on surfboards
6 in youth hostel programs

D. Adverbs

1 helplessly
2 enthusiastically
3 temporarily
4 abroad
5 ~~sometimes~~

E. Infinitive phrases as adverbs

1 to watch people in the water
2 to earn extra money
3 to wait on tables
4 to further their education
5 to exterminate insects

REVIEW EXERCISE C. Rewrite each of the following sentences twice by making each of the specified additions. When the instructions call for an added phrase, add words as necessary to complete the phrase. There is more than one possible answer to each item. *Answers will vary; possibilities are given below.*

EXAMPLE   Matthew Henson and Admiral Peary sought the North Pole.
Use a form of *dare*
a. in a participial phrase
b. as an adverb

ANSWER   a. **Daring to brave the frozen Arctic,** *Matthew Henson and Admiral Peary sought the North Pole.*
b. *Matthew Henson and Admiral Peary* **daringly** *sought the North Pole.*

1. The⸏Arctic waters covered Henson⸏. *a, b*
   Use a form of *ice*
   a. as an adjective *icy*
   b. in a prepositional phrase as adverb *with ice*

2. A⸏sled carried the admiral back⸏. *a, b*
   Use a form of *shake*
   a. as an adjective *shaky*
   b. as a participle *shaking*

3. ₄They met many hardships₄ along the way. *a, b*
   Use a form of *discourage*
   a. as a participle *discouraged*   *to discourage*
   b. in an infinitive phrase as adjective   *them*
4. Henson₄ spoke the language of the Eskimos₄. *a, b*
   Use a form of *fluent*
   a. as an adverb *fluently*
   b. in a prepositional phrase as adverb *with fluency*
5. They₄ reached the North Pole on April 6, 1909₄. *a, b*
   Use a form of *final*
   a. as an adverb *finally*
   b. in a participial phrase *finally attaining their goal*

WRITING COMPOUND SENTENCES

3.b JOINING MAIN CLAUSES

A **compound sentence** consists of two or more main clauses.

A simple sentence, as you know, is made up of one main clause — one subject + one predicate. Sometimes, instead of writing only simple sentences, you may want to join a few main clauses together to form a compound sentence.

3.b.1 Joining main clauses with coordinating conjunctions

You know that main clauses can be joined with the word *and.* You should make an effort, however, not to overuse *and* in joining main clauses. Learn to use the **coordinating conjunctions** *and, but, or,* and *for* to form compound sentences. Each of these words will give your sentence a slightly different meaning. You should be careful to make your meaning as clear as possible by using the right coordinating conjunction.

COMMAS BETWEEN MAIN CLAUSES

Use a comma before the coordinating conjunction in compound sentences. The comma is necessary to avoid possible confusion, as in Sentence 1 below.

1. The cat hissed at the bird and the dog growled.
2. The cat hissed at the bird, and the dog growled.

Do you see how the comma in Sentence 2 prevents confusion or misreading? A reader might accidentally read Sentence 1 as *The cat hissed at the bird and the dog.*

▥ The coordinating conjunctions and their uses

AND

1. Music entertains Americans, **and** sports challenge them.
2. The concert was late in getting started, **and** people became impatient.

Sentence 1 shows that you can use *and* to balance two main clauses that are equally important in the sentence. Sentence 2 shows that you can use *and* to set up a time relationship. First one thing happens, *and* then another thing happens.

BUT

3. The concert started late, **but** the performances were first-rate.

Sentence 3 shows how you should use *but* — to join contrasting ideas. *But* emphasizes that the second clause is unexpected in view of the first or even contrary to the first. If you had used *and* in Sentence 3, your reader would have been left wondering what the two main clauses had to do with each other.

OR

4. You will enjoy the rock concert, **or** you will decide to listen to only classical music in the future.

Sentence 4 shows that you can use *or* to introduce an alternative.

FOR

5. The Beatles brought new ideas to rock music, **for** they studied other cultures and other instruments.

Sentence 5 shows that you can use *for* to join two clauses when the second clause gives a reason for the statement in the first clause.

EXERCISE 11. Rewrite the following sentences, adding the appropriate coordinating conjunctions (*and, but, or,* and *for*).

1. Philippe Petit walks the line, _and_ his walks take place two hundred feet above ground.
2. Philippe Petit walks the line, _for_ he is a high-wire artist.
3. Petit performed between the two 110-story towers of the World Trade Center, _and_ thousands of workers were spellbound.
4. Petit performed between the two 110-story towers of the World Trade Center, _but_ New York's police were not amused.
5. Was the fellow mad, _or_ was it a publicity stunt?
6. Was the fellow mad, _and_ how did he get up there?
7. Petit had practiced for years, _and_ the World Trade Center escapade came off smoothly.
8. Petit had practiced for years, _for_ he was passionate about his technique.
9. The artist was arrested, _for_ surely he had broken some law.
10. The artist was arrested, _but_ he did not receive an ordinary sentence.

11. Petit was ordered to entertain in Central Park, _but_ he did not consider this "punishment."

12. Petit was ordered to entertain in Central Park, _and_ he delighted thousands of New Yorkers.

13. Petit once crossed Sydney Harbor Bridge, _but_ he did not pay the toll.

14. Petit once crossed Sydney Harbor Bridge, _and_ he has also walked between the spires of Notre Dame.

15. Ringling Brothers Barnum & Bailey Circus offered him center ring, _for_ he would draw crowds.

16. Ringling Brothers Barnum & Bailey Circus offered him center ring, _and_ he toured America.

17. Once, Petit had a serious accident during a rehearsal, _and_ he went to Puerto Rico to recover.

18. Once, Petit had a serious accident during a rehearsal, _but_ he was performing again in four months.

19. Petit's style is simple, _for_ he uses no glitter or trickery.

20. Petit's style is simple, _or_ at least it seems simple.

EXERCISE 12. Use the clauses below to compose five compound sentences. Match each main clause in Column I with a main clause in Column II. You must use each clause from each column.

Column I	Column II
1. People should conserve natural resources, _c_	a. or adventurous homeowners can try solar energy.
2. My family insulated the basement, _b_	b. for good insulation cuts heating costs.
3. My sister collects old newspapers, _e_	c. and conservation begins in the home.
4. People can switch to gas heat, _a_	d. but Americans keep buying it.
5. Gasoline costs more and more, _d_	e. and my brother brings them to school.

EXERCISE 13. Use the clauses below to compose five compound sentences. Match each main clause in Column I with a main clause in Column II. You must use each clause from each column.

Column I	Column II
1. Elephant seals were almost extinct, *d*	a. or they were stuffed for collections.
2. The seals were killed for their oil, *a*	b. and the United States passed similar laws.
3. Mexico outlawed seal hunting, *b*	c. and they are reproducing at an alarming rate.
4. Elephant seals were saved, *e*	d. for hunters were killing them in large numbers.
5. Today's seals have no natural enemies, *c*	e. but now there may be too many.

EXERCISE 14. Compose a main clause to go with the given clause and coordinating conjunction in each of the following sentence frames. *Answers will vary.*

1. Some people have seen unidentified flying objects, but _____ .

2. _____ , or they see saucers flying through the skies.

3. _____ , but the "spaceships" were only oddly shaped cloud formations.

4. The space visitors usually appear at night, and _____ .

5. _____ , and science-fiction movies may encourage these visions.

6. Most UFO sightings have had earthbound explanations, but _____ .

7. _____ , and the airplane pilots seemed very reliable.

8. One day the earth may have space visitors, for _____ .

9. Nothing is impossible, or _____ .

10. _____ , for scientists have not found positive proof.

3.b.2 Joining main clauses with conjunctive adverbs

If you want your writing to be more formal, you can use a semicolon and conjunctive adverb to join two main clauses. Notice how the second sentence in each pair below sounds more formal than the first even though the two sentences in each pair say basically the same thing.

EXAMPLES

Music is valued in most places, but it is treated almost like poetry in Brazil.

Music is valued in most places; **however,** it is treated almost like poetry in Brazil.

Many Brazilians are of African descent, and so samba music contains rhythms of African origin.

Many Brazilians are of African descent; **as a result,** samba music contains rhythms of African origin.

Here are conjunctive adverbs and other expressions that you can use at the beginning of the second main clause when joining two main clauses. They are grouped according to meaning.

CONJUNCTIVE ADVERBS AND SIMILAR EXPRESSIONS

instead, however, nevertheless, still, yet

also, besides, furthermore, in addition, moreover, similarly

as a result, consequently, therefore, hence, thus

for example, for instance, that is

PUNCTUATION WITH CONJUNCTIVE ADVERBS

You must use punctuation marks to set off most conjunctive adverbs. Unless they appear as the first word in a sentence, conjunctive adverbs should usually have some punctuation on either side.

Christmas carols are international favorites; **therefore,** most people know the words to "Deck the Halls."

Christmas carols are international favorites; most people, **therefore,** know the words to "Deck the Halls."

Christmas carols are international favorites; most people know the words to "Deck the Halls," **therefore.**

AVOIDING ERRORS WHEN JOINING MAIN CLAUSES

Do not join two main clauses with just a comma. Use either (1) a coordinating conjunction and a comma or (2) a semicolon and a conjunctive adverb. Remember also that you can always begin a new sentence.

NOT   The audience cheered with great enthusiasm the group sang another encore.

BUT   The audience cheered with great enthusiasm, **and** the group sang another encore.

OR   The audience cheered with great enthusiasm; **therefore,** the group sang another encore.

OR   The audience cheered with great enthusiasm. The group sang another encore.

EXERCISE 15. Compose a main clause that will logically complete the sentence in each of the following items. If necessary, check the Idea Bank below for topics to use in the main clauses. *Answers will vary.*

1. Many families feel the pinch of high food costs; in addition, ——————— .
2. Many families feel the pinch of high food costs; as a result, ——————— .
3. More and more people are growing their own food; consequently, ——————— .
4. More and more people are growing their own food; for example, ——————— .
5. A vegetable garden must be well planned; moreover, ——————— .
6. A vegetable garden must be well planned; nevertheless, ——————— .
7. Some vegetables require a lot of space; for example, ——————— .
8. Some vegetables require a lot of space; however, ——————— .
9. Soil quality and sunlight are important factors; therefore, ——————— .
10. Soil quality and sunlight are important factors; for instance, ——————— .

IDEA BANK
vegetable gardens now very common
Corn and pumpkins need a large area.
five hours of sunlight daily minimum
raise tomatoes and other vegetables
Poor soil may need fertilizer.
People are seeking ways to save.
high prices for other necessities
care and attention required
Many vegetables need little space.
planning not difficult
fresh air and sunshine

WRITING COMPLEX SENTENCES

A **complex sentence** has one main clause and one or more subordinate clauses.

You can add variety to your writing (1) by using different kinds of simple sentences, (2) by expanding the basic simple sentences, and (3) by combining simple sentences to form compound sentences. Even so, writing that contains only simple sentences may begin to sound monotonous. To make your writing more interesting you should work in some complex sentences. The first kind of complex sentence that you will practice here will have one main clause and one adverb clause.

3.c WRITING SENTENCES WITH ADVERB CLAUSES

An **adverb clause** is made up of a subordinating conjunction + a subject + a predicate. An adverb clause cannot stand alone. It must be added to a main clause to make sense. An adverb clause can tell *when, where, how, why,* or can *state conditions.* The following examples show how you can use a sentence with an adverb clause as an alternative to a compound sentence.

TELLING "WHEN"

The Beatles visited America in 1964, and Americans loved them. [compound sentence]

After the Beatles visited America in 1964, Americans loved them. [sentence with adverb clause]

TELLING "WHERE"

Popular musicians tour, and fans mob them everywhere. [compound sentence]

Wherever popular musicians tour, fans mob them. [sentence with adverb clause]

TELLING "HOW"

Maria Callas sang beautifully, and few sopranos sing as well. [compound sentence]

Few sopranos sing **as Callas sang.** [sentence with adverb clause]

TELLING "WHY"

Many kinds of dancing have become popular again, and record and tape sales have boomed. [compound sentence]

Record and tape sales have boomed **because many kinds of dancing have become popular again.** [sentence with adverb clause]

STATING CONDITIONS

Disc jockeys play certain records over and over, and those records become popular. [compound sentence]

Certain records become popular **if disc jockeys play them over and over.** [sentence with one adverb clause]

COMMAS AND ADVERB CLAUSES

1. Use a comma after an adverb clause (even a very short one) that comes *before* a main clause. See 7.g.10.

   When you travel, you should learn about local food, clothes, and music.

2. In general, do not use a comma before an adverb clause that comes *after* a main clause. See also 7.g.10.

   You should learn about local food, clothes, and music when you travel.

3.c.1 Writing adverb clauses that tell "when"

You can write an adverb clause before or after a main clause to give information about "when."

EXAMPLES
Drums have been important **since civilization began.**
Before the telephone was invented, drums carried messages.

Any of the following subordinating conjunctions can be used to begin an adverb clause that tells "when."

SUBORDINATORS THAT TELL "WHEN"

after	before	when
as	since	whenever
as long as	until	while
as soon as		

EXERCISE 16. Compose five sentences. Match each main clause in Column I with the appropriate clause in Column II. You must use each clause from each column.

Column I

1. Paul Newman was a film star *b*
2. Diana Nyad swam *d*
3. Diana Ross recorded on her own *e*
4. Reggie Jackson hit the home run *a*
5. Margaret Mitchell has been well known *c*

Column II

a. when there were two outs.
b. before he was a director.
c. since *Gone with the Wind* was published.
d. until she reached the shore.
e. after she left the Supremes.

EXERCISE 17. Complete each of the following sentences by adding an adverb clause that tells "when." *Answers will vary.*

1. Some workers retire from their jobs as soon as
   _____ .

2. Other people work as long as _____ .

3. Most people eligible for retirement have been working
   since _____ .

4. As _____ , others join the work force.

5. While _____ , people usually work.

*EXERCISE 18: **Sentence Combining.** Combine each of the following pairs of sentences into one complex sentence. Begin each sentence by moving the expression in parentheses to the front of the sentence on that line, as the example shows.

> EXAMPLE People think of Leslie Uggams. (**WHEN**)
>   They think of *Roots*.
>
> ANSWER *When people think of Leslie Uggams, they think of* Roots.

Until 1. Leslie Uggams starred as Kizzy in *Roots*., (**UNTIL**)
many ~~Many~~ people thought of her only as a singer.

While 2. Uggams was a child., (**WHILE**)
she ~~She~~ studied acting under Stella Adler.

When 3. Uggams was six years old, (**WHEN**)
she ~~She~~ was in the television show *Beulah*.

When 4. Uggams won $25,000 on *Name That Tune*., (**WHEN**)
she ~~She~~ was fourteen years old.

As soon as 5. Leslie Uggams sang with Mitch Miller., (**AS SOON AS**)
she ~~She~~ became a nationwide celebrity.

Before 6. Uggams sang on Mitch Miller's show., (**BEFORE**)
she ~~She~~ had played the Apollo Theater in Harlem.

After 7. *Sing Along with Mitch* went off the air., (**AFTER**)
Leslie Uggams appeared in nightclubs.

As long as 8. Uggams continued to star as a singer., (**AS LONG AS**)
people ~~People~~ did not recognize her as a dramatic actress.

As 9. Uggams starred in Broadway musicals., (**AS**)
her ~~Her~~ acting abilities became more widely known.

Whenever people 10. ~~People~~ recognize Leslie Uggams today., (**WHENEVER**)
they ~~They~~ remember her dramatic role in *Roots*.

* # EXERCISE 19: Sentence Combining.

Combine each of the following pairs of sentences into one complex sentence. Move the expression in parentheses to the front of the sentence on that line, as the example shows.

EXAMPLE   Paul Cadwell was an attorney.
           He retired to play the banjo. (**BEFORE**)

ANSWER   *Paul Cadwell was an attorney before he retired to play the banjo.*

1. Cadwell has been a talented banjo player, *since*
   he ~~He~~ began playing at age ten. (~~**SINCE**~~)

2. He took banjo lessons from master player Fred Van Eps, *when*
   he ~~He~~ was attending elementary school. (~~**WHEN**~~)

3. Cadwell performed with a guitarist and a fiddler, *until*
   he ~~He~~ graduated from high school. (~~**UNTIL**~~)

4. Cadwell made his public debut, *before*
   he ~~He~~ began college at Princeton. (~~**BEFORE**~~)

5. Cadwell went to Harvard Law School, *after*
   he ~~He~~ graduated from Princeton in 1910. (~~**AFTER**~~)

6. Cadwell was a soloist with the Harvard Banjo Club, *while*
   he ~~He~~ was studying at Harvard. (~~**WHILE**~~)

7. Audiences enjoyed Cadwell's superb playing, *whenever*
   he ~~He~~ gave performances. (~~**WHENEVER**~~)

8. Paul Cadwell was honored at the Philadelphia Folk Festival, *when he*
   ~~He~~ was ninety years old. (~~**WHEN**~~)

9. He played "The Princeton Varsity Jig," *after*
   the ~~The~~ audience applauded enthusiastically. (~~**AFTER**~~)

10. Classical banjo playing will flourish, *as long as*
    there ~~There~~ are players like Paul Cadwell. (~~**AS LONG AS**~~)

* # EXERCISE 20: Sentence Combining.

Combine each of the following pairs of sentences into one complex sentence. First select a subordinator that tells "when" from the list in 3.c.1. Begin each complex sentence by placing the subordinator at the beginning of the sentence on the top line, as the example shows. Try to use as many different subordinators as you can. *Answers will vary; possibilities are given in the exercise.*

EXAMPLE   People get behind schedule.
           They begin to rush.

ANSWER   *When people get behind schedule, they begin
           to rush.*

When people
1. ~~People~~ are in a hurry, *, they*
   ~~They~~ seem to forget something.

As
2. I rushed to the laundry yesterday, *,*
   I forgot the keys to the apartment.

While
3. I raced to the washing machine, *,*
   I thought about the baseball game.

Before the
4. ~~The~~ Red Sox lost the previous day, *, they*
   ~~They~~ had been first in the division.

Since the
5. ~~The~~ Yankees were in town, *, the*
   ~~The~~ fans were restless.

As soon as
6. I finished my laundry, *,*
   I scrambled home.

While
7. I was up the stairs, *,*
   I was searching for the keys.

When
8. I reached the door, *,*
   I began pounding frantically.

Before my
9. ~~My~~ sister opened the door, *,*
   I had lost all hope of entering.

After
10. I finally arrived at the ball park, *,*
    I had forgotten the tickets.

* **EXERCISE 21: Sentence Combining.**   Combine each of
the following pairs of sentences into one complex sentence. First select a subordinator that tells "when" from
the list in 3.c.1. Place this subordinator at the beginning
of the sentence on the second line, as the example shows.
Try to use several different subordinators.   *Answers will vary;
possibilities are given in the exercise.*

EXAMPLE   People have been style conscious.
           They began wearing clothing.

ANSWER   *People have been style conscious since they
           began wearing clothing.*

1. People will continue to buy unnecessary clothes, *as long as*
fashion ~~Fashion~~ dictates wardrobes.

2. Miniskirts became unpopular, *as soon as*
maxiskirts ~~Maxiskirts~~ came into fashion.

3. Some women rushed to buy new wardrobes, *after*
they ~~They~~ saw the required skirt length.

4. Three-button suits had been fashionable, *until*
men ~~Men~~ wore two-button suits.

5. Double-breasted suits were in mothballs, *as soon as*
they ~~They~~ were out of style.

6. Anklets had not been popular, *since*
they ~~They~~ went out of fashion in the sixties.

7. Few women would dare to wear anklets, *until*
fashion ~~Fashion~~ designers finally reintroduced them.

8. New fashions are slow to catch on, *when*
times ~~Times~~ are bad.

9. Interest in new fashions goes down, *as unemployment*
~~Unemployment~~ goes up.

10. Old suspenders might seem perfectly stylish, *whenever*
people ~~People~~ are tightening their belts.

3.c.2 Writing adverb clauses that tell "where"

You can add an adverb clause to a main clause to give information about "where."

EXAMPLES
Calypso music began **where people sang the news.**
Songs and melodies develop **wherever people get together.**

There are two important subordinators that begin adverb clauses of place: *where* and *wherever.*

EXERCISE 22. Compose five sentences. Match each main clause in Column I with a suitable clause in Column II. Begin each sentence with the main clause. Use each clause from each column.

Column I	Column II
1. There are valleys *e*	a. where the coastline forms harbors.
2. Deserts are found *d*	b. where forests abound.
3. Seaports grow *a*	c. where soil is rich.
4. Crops flourish *c*	d. where rainfall is rare.
5. Lumber is an important product *b*	e. wherever there are mountains.

3.c.3 Writing adverb clauses that tell "how"

You can add an adverb clause to a main clause to tell "how" the action of the main clause takes place. Begin the adverb clause with *as, as if,* or *as though.*

EXAMPLE

Music comes naturally to many children, **as if they were born with a sixth sense.**

EXERCISE 23. Compose five sentences. Match each main clause in Column I with a suitable clause in Column II. Begin each sentence with the main clause. Use each clause from each column.

Column I	Column II
1. Bessie Smith sang the blues *c*	a. as if "comedy" were her middle name.
2. Carol Burnett sparks laughter *a*	b. as most ballerinas glide on a stage.
3. Willie Mays played baseball *d*	c. as if the world's troubles were her own.
4. John Wayne made westerns *e*	d. as if the sport had been invented for him.
5. Peggy Fleming glides over ice *b*	e. as though he had been born on a horse.

*EXERCISE 24: Sentence Combining.** Combine each of the following pairs of sentences into a complex sentence by adding the subordinator *as if, as though, where,* or *wherever* before either the first or the second sentence. For each pair you must decide whether the first or the second clause should be the adverb clause. *Answers will vary; possibilities are given below.*

EXAMPLE Our family gets together.
There is always good food.

ANSWER *Wherever our family gets together, there is always good food.*

1. I eat and eat, *,as if my*
~~My~~ stomach has no bottom.

2. Grandma cooks marvelously, *,as though she*
~~She~~ learned from the finest Spanish chefs.

Where we
3. ~~We~~ gather in the living room, *,cousin*
~~Cousin~~ Maria plays the guitar.

4. We sing energetically, *,as if our*
~~Our~~ voices improve with volume.

Wherever there
5. ~~There~~ is music playing, *,some*
~~Some~~ of us dance.

6. We always dance, *where there*
~~There~~ is enough room.

As if the
7. ~~The~~ latest steps are part of his daily routine,
Dad dances up a storm.

8. Everyone enjoys the family album, *,where we*
~~We~~ see pictures of our former selves.

9. There is so much good feeling, *wherever we*
~~We~~ all enjoy ourselves.

As if
10. Thanksgiving falls more than once a year, *,our*
~~Our~~ family is always thankful to be together.

3.c.4 Writing adverb clauses that tell "why"

You can add an adverb clause to a main clause to tell "why" — that is, to explain why the action of the main clause takes place. Begin an adverb clause with one of the following subordinating conjunctions: *as, because, since, in order that,* and *so that.*

EXAMPLES
Countries have national songs **because all people are proud.**
Since Americans have roots in many cultures, we have songs in many languages.

EXERCISE 25. Compose five sentences. Match each main clause in Column I with a suitable clause that tells "why" in Column II. Begin each sentence with the main clause. Use each clause from each column.

Column I	Column II
1. Some American consumers use credit cards *c*	a. as they do not want the additional expense and paper work.
2. Many department stores issue free "charge cards" *d*	b. since payment is postponed but never eliminated.
3. Smaller shops do not usually accept credit cards *a*	c. because they do not want to carry cash.
4. Some shoppers still prefer cash *e*	d. so that shopping there is easy.
5. Credit cards save time but not money *b*	e. because they do not like receiving large monthly bills.

3.c.5 Writing adverb clauses that state conditions

You often have to add an adverb clause to a main clause to state the conditions under which the main clause is true. For example, it is not necessarily true that "everyone will pass the math test." You might, however, be able to say, **If everyone studies and understands the problems,** *everyone will pass the math test.* Here are a few other examples of adverb clauses that state conditions.

EXAMPLES
You will ruin your records **unless you replace the needle.**
As long as you play your stereo at top volume, your neighbors are bound to complain.

You can use any of the following conjunctions to begin an adverb clause that states conditions.

SUBORDINATORS THAT STATE CONDITIONS

although	though	whether (or not)
as long as	unless	while
if	whereas	

EXERCISE 26. Compose five sentences. Match each main clause in Column I with a suitable adverb clause in Column II.

Column I	Column II
1. You cannot make an omelet *b*	a. if the water is boiling.
2. You can make spaghetti sauce *d*	b. unless you break the eggs.
3. You can brew tea *a*	c. although fresh vegetables have more vitamins.
4. You may like low-fat cottage cheese *e*	d. as long as you have tomatoes.
5. You can cook frozen vegetables *c*	e. whether or not you are on a diet.

*__EXERCISE 27: Sentence Combining.__ Combine each of the following pairs of sentences into a complex sentence by adding a subordinator that tells "why" (*as, because,*

since, in order that, so that) or a subordinator that states a condition (although, as long as, if, though, unless, whereas, whether or not, while). Decide whether the adverb clause should come first or last. *Answers will vary; possibilities are given below.*

EXAMPLE We took up tap-dancing.
It was the latest fad.

ANSWER *We took up tap-dancing because it was the latest fad.*

1. ~~Fads~~ come and go. ,*the* *Although fads*
~~The~~ average fad rarely returns.

2. Hula hoops were popular in the fifties. ,*though they*
~~They~~ disappeared in the sixties.

3. ~~Hula~~ hoops required a great deal of swiveling. ,*they* *Since hula*
~~They~~ provided good exercise.

4. Hula hoops led to the twist. ,*so that some*
~~Some~~ people see a similarity.

5. The twist did not require a hoop. ,*though it*
~~It~~ involved gyrations similar to hula-hooping.

6. Limbo dancers needed strong knees. ,*so that they*
~~They~~ could pass under a low horizontal stick.

7. ~~The~~ twist and the limbo did not last long. ,*they* *Since the*
~~They~~ might be called dance fads.

8. ~~The~~ late sixties saw the advent of Frisbees. ,*that* *Whereas the*
~~That~~ fad has remained popular longer than most.

9. ~~Every~~ decade has its dance fads. ,*the* *Since every*
~~The~~ seventies was no exception.

10. Seventies dancers frequented discos. *as long as they*
~~They~~ knew the complex dances.

11. ~~You~~ knew disco dances like the hustle. ,*you* *Unless you*
~~You~~ probably avoided discos.

12. Roller-skating has always been popular in rural America. ,*so that it*
~~It~~ may not qualify as a fad.

13. Roller-skating can be termed a fad. ,*since it*
~~It~~ certainly was very popular in the late seventies.

14. Roller-skating became big in discos. ,*though it*
~~It~~ also was popular on city streets.

15. Bicycles seemed faddish at first. *, though bicycle*
~~Bicycle~~ riding has remained popular.

16. Bicycles cannot be called fads. *, as they*
~~They~~ are here to stay.

If you
17. ~~You~~ sat on a flagpole in the twenties. *, you*
~~You~~ would not have been considered so unusual.

Although sitting
18. ~~Sitting~~ on flagpoles and squeezing into phone booths were certainly fads. *, these*
~~These~~ pastimes are rare today.

Unless you
19. ~~You~~ attended college during the twenties. *, you*
~~You~~ have probably never swallowed a goldfish.

If you
20. ~~You~~ want to learn about other outdated fads. *, ask*
~~Ask~~ your parents or grandparents.

---

* **REVIEW EXERCISE D: Sentence Combining.** Combine each of the following pairs of sentences into a complex sentence. Move the expression in parentheses to the front of the sentence.

EXAMPLE You have probably heard of Hale and Revere. (**THOUGH**)

Do you know the stories of other spies of the American Revolution?

ANSWER *Though you have probably heard of Hale and Revere, do you know the stories of other spies of the American Revolution?*

until
1. Lydia Darragh was a Philadelphia homemaker.
events ~~Events~~ made her an American spy. (**UNTIL**)

Whereas the
2. ~~The~~ Darraghs lived on the west side of Second Street. (**WHEREAS**)
the ~~The~~ British headquarters was located on the east side.

Whenever the
3. ~~The~~ family had information helpful to the American cause. (**WHENEVER**)
they ~~They~~ would write it in shorthand on small slips of paper.

4. Mrs. Darragh would sew the paper under the cloth of her son's coat buttons. *so that the*
~~The~~ boy could take the information to George Washington's encampment nearby. (**SO THAT**)

Since the
5. ~~The~~ Darraghs' older son was a lieutenant stationed in Washington's camp~~.~~ (**SINCE**)

he
~~He~~ delivered the messages to his brother Charles.

After
6. Charles Darragh decoded the shorthand~~.~~ (**AFTER**)

he
~~He~~ took the information to General Washington.

As the
7. ~~The~~ war continued~~.~~ (**AS**)

the
~~The~~ Darraghs' messages became more important.

When the
8. ~~The~~ time for a British attack arrived~~.~~ (**WHEN**)

the
~~The~~ British army played into Lydia Darragh's hands.

Whether or not you
9. ~~You~~ know the Quartering Act~~.~~ (**WHETHER OR NOT**)

you ~~You~~ will recall the laws imposed on the colonists.

10. The Quartering Act allowed the British army to use colonists' homes~~.~~ *when they*
    ~~They~~ needed lodgings for their troops. (**WHEN**)

11. The officers moved into the Darraghs' home~~.~~ *, although the*
    ~~The~~ Darraghs were allowed to remain in some rooms. (**ALTHOUGH**)

12. One night the British officers held a conference~~.~~ *while the*
    ~~The~~ Darraghs were supposedly asleep. (**WHILE**)

13. Lydia Darragh slipped into a closet~~.~~ *, where she*
    ~~She~~ could hear the British discussing final plans for a surprise attack. (**WHERE**)

Unless she
14. ~~She~~ informed Washington~~.~~ (**UNLESS**)

the ~~The~~ unprepared American forces would be defeated!

15. She discarded the button-message method~~.~~ *, as speed*
    ~~Speed~~ was essential. (**AS**)

If she
16. ~~She~~ carried the message herself~~.~~ (**IF**)

no ~~No~~ one was likely to be suspicious.

17. She left the house with a flour bag~~.~~ *, as if she*
    ~~She~~ needed flour from the mill outside town. (**AS IF**)

Wherever she
18. ~~She~~ walked in the British area~~.~~ (**WHEREVER**)

unsuspecting
~~Unsuspecting~~ soldiers let her pass.

As soon as she
19. ~~She~~ reached an American outpost~~.~~ (**AS SOON AS**)

she ~~She~~ related her information.

Because the
20. ~~The~~ "surprise attack" came as no surprise to General Washington~~.~~ (**BECAUSE**)

the ~~The~~ British were forced to retreat.

3.d WRITING ADJECTIVE CLAUSES

You can add an **adjective clause** to tell more about a noun in the same way that you might add an adjective to tell more about a noun. Adding an adjective clause to a main clause creates a complex sentence.

MAIN CLAUSE
She likes the tune.

MAIN CLAUSE WITH ADJECTIVE
She likes the **Mexican** tune.

MAIN CLAUSE AND ADJECTIVE CLAUSE
She likes the tune **that she heard in Mexico.**

MAIN CLAUSE
The tune is well-known.

MAIN CLAUSE WITH ADJECTIVE
The **old** tune is well-known.

MAIN CLAUSE AND ADJECTIVE CLAUSE
The tune, **which she learned from her grandfather,** is well-known.

COMMAS WITH ADJECTIVE CLAUSES

Remember that there are two kinds of adjective clauses: (1) essential, or restrictive, and (2) nonessential, or nonrestrictive. You should not use commas to set off an essential clause. After all, if the information in the clause is essential, you do not want to separate it from the noun it is talking about.

Carousel is the one musical that I really enjoy.

A nonessential clause (or nonrestrictive clause) is also called an extra clause. You should use *extra* commas to set off an *extra* clause.

Carousel, which I saw recently, has lovely music.

EXERCISE 30. Compose five complex sentences with an adjective clause beginning with *where* or *when*. Match each subordinate clause in Column II with the appropriate main clause in Column I. You must use each clause from each column.

Column I	Column II
1. Philadelphia has many historic sites. *e*	a. where the Tea Party occurred
2. Boston also looms large in American history. *a*	b. when Americans celebrated the Centennial
3. New York City was the nation's first capital. *c*	c. where the Statue of Liberty is located
4. The year 1876 marked one hundred years of American independence. *b*	d. when Americans marked two hundred years of freedom
5. The Bicentennial took place in 1976. *d*	e. where the Continental Congress met

*EXERCISE 31: **Sentence Combining.** Combine each of the following pairs of simple sentences into one complex sentence. Replace the underlined word with the word in parentheses. The word in parentheses then becomes the first word (subordinator) in the new subordinate clause.

EXAMPLE Printing is an industry.
Technology is always improving there. (**WHERE**)

ANSWER *Printing is an industry where technology is always improving.*

EXAMPLE Improvements have especially changed the typesetting business.
These improvements have occurred in recent years. (**THAT**)

ANSWER *Improvements that have occurred in recent years have especially changed the typesetting business.*

1. One such improvement is a new method of typesetting, *th*
   This typesetting is done by computer. (**THAT**)

2. Computer typesetting uses special disks, *that*
   These disks contain alphabet letters. (**THAT**)

3. Most companies work with modern languages only.
   that These companies set type. (**THAT**)

4. People cannot always find the right typesetter.
   who These people need type set in ancient languages. (**WHO**)

5. Nachum Kornfeld and Abraham Walzer are typesetters, *w*
   These typesetters can set several languages. (**WHO**)

6. The two men run a typesetting business, *where ancient*
   Ancient languages are set electronically there. (**WHERE**)

7. The flourishing business is located in a Brooklyn neighborhood. *where many*
   Many people speak ancient languages in this neighborhood. (**WHERE**)

8. People use their service for special occasions. *when*
   Greek, Hebrew, Aramaic, or Akkadian material is required on these occasions. (**WHEN**)

9. Kornfeld and Walzer set type for publishers, *whose*
   The publishers' books are written in one of those languages. (**WHOSE**)

10. Rabbis often use their service.
    whose These rabbis' documents are in Hebrew. (**WHOSE**)

* **EXERCISE 32: Sentence Combining.** Combine each of the following pairs of simple sentences into one complex sentence. Replace the underlined words with the word in parentheses. The word in parentheses then becomes the first word in the new subordinate clause. Notice that all of the subordinate clauses are nonessential and so must be set off with commas.

EXAMPLE   Windmills are actually practical structures.
          Windmills bring to mind the impractical Don Quixote. (**WHICH**)

ANSWER   *Windmills, which bring to mind the impractical Don Quixote, are actually practical structures.*

1. The seventh century gave birth to the windmill.
, *when* ~~Europe~~ was in the Dark Ages, ~~then~~. (**WHEN**)

2. Windmills were invented by the Persians.
, *which* ~~Windmills~~ harness wind power. (**WHICH**)

3. Windmills reached Europe with returning Crusaders.
, *which* ~~Windmills~~ were taken to China. (**WHICH**)

4. Americans are now trying windmills.
, *who* ~~Americans~~ seek new ways to generate electricity. (~~**WHO**~~)

5. One Navajo reservation uses a windmill to provide its electric power.
, *where fifteen* ~~Fifteen~~ hundred people live, ~~there~~. (**WHERE**)

6. The reservation did not have electricity before.
, *which* ~~The reservation~~ is in a remote part of the state of Arizona. (**WHICH**)

7. Kansas has many windmills.
, *where winds* ~~Winds~~ are steady, ~~there~~. (**WHERE**)

8. Researchers point out the need for steady winds.
, *whose* ~~Researchers~~' enthusiasm for windmills is lukewarm. (**WHOSE**)

9. Windmills will not be mass produced for some years.
, *which* ~~Windmills~~ are now expensive. (**WHICH**)

10. Future users will pay less for windmills.
, *whom officials* ~~Officials~~ estimate ~~these users~~ may someday include 10 percent of the population. (**WHOM**)

3.e WRITING SENTENCES WITH APPOSITIVES

An **appositive** is a noun or pronoun (sometimes with modifiers) that is placed next to another noun or pronoun to identify it or to give additional information about it.

You can sometimes shorten an adjective clause so that it becomes just a word or phrase but still tells more about a noun. Such a word or phrase is called an appositive. Look at the examples on the following page, which illustrate how an appositive and an adjective clause differ.

ADJECTIVE CLAUSE	APPOSITIVE
The triangle, **which is a percussion instrument,** is her favorite.	The triangle, **a percussion instrument,** is her favorite.
She visited Symphony Hall, **which is the home of the Boston Symphony.**	She visited Symphony Hall, **the home of the Boston Symphony.**

* **EXERCISE 33:** **Sentence Combining.**   Combine the following pairs of sentences by forming an appositive phrase out of the second sentence in each pair. Remove all unnecessary or repeated words in the second sentence. Remember to set off the appositive phrase with commas.

EXAMPLE   San Francisco is a fascinating city.
San Francisco is famous for its cable cars.

ANSWER   *San Francisco, famous for its cable cars, is a fascinating city.*

1. "I Left My Heart in San Francisco," describes "little cable cars."
   "~~I Left My Heart in San Francisco" is~~ the well-known song,

2. The cable car, was invented by Andrew Hallidie in 1873.
   ~~The cable car is,~~ pulled by a steel cable,,

3. Cable cars, transport many San Franciscans to work.
   ~~Cable cars are,~~ a fast way to travel up steep hills/,

4. San Francisco, depends on its cable cars.
   ~~San Francisco is,~~ a city of steep hills,,

5. Cable cars, have become a symbol of that city.
   ~~Cable cars are,~~ a prime tourist attraction,,

6. Unfortunately, the cars, require a great deal of maintenance.
   ~~The cars are,~~ nineteenth-century vehicles,,

7. The Municipal Railway, requires much funding.
   ~~The Municipal Railway is,~~ the operator of the system,,

8. In the 1950s city officials tried to close the cable cars.
   ~~The city officials were~~ practical administrators. ,

9. The public voted to keep the cable cars running forever.
   ~~The public was~~ a more emotional group. ,

10. The cable cars were declared a national monument.
    ~~The cable cars are~~ the only ones in the nation. ,

EXERCISE 34: Sentence Combining. Combine the following pairs of sentences by forming an appositive phrase out of the second sentence in each pair. Remove all unnecessary or repeated words in the second sentence. Remember to set off the appositive phrase with a comma.

> EXAMPLE   The Tucson area offers a fascinating museum. The museum is the Arizona Sonora Desert Museum.
>
> ANSWER   *The Tucson area offers a fascinating museum, the Arizona Sonora Desert Museum.*

1. Visitors enjoy the museum.
   ~~The museum is~~ an informative display of desert life.

2. The exhibits cover Arizona and Sonora, Mexico.
   ~~Arizona and Sonora, Mexico, are~~ two areas with extensive desert land.

3. The exhibits also cover Baja California.
   ~~Baja California is~~ a peninsula in Mexico.

4. Parts of the museum resemble a botanical garden.
   ~~A botanical garden is~~ an exhibition of plantlife.

5. Other parts resemble a zoological garden.
   ~~A zoological garden is~~ a collection of animals.

6. The amphibian room includes toads and salamanders.
   ~~Toads and salamanders are~~ two types of desert animals.

7. An underground section houses nocturnal creatures.
   ~~Nocturnal creatures are~~ animals active at night.

8. An aquarium contains multicolored fish.
   ~~The multicolored fish are~~ unlikely to be desert inhabitants.

9. These fish inhabit desert streams,∧
   ~~The desert streams are~~,saltwater rivers in Sonora.
10. The aquarium also displays invertebrates,∧
    ~~Invertebrates are~~,creatures without backbones.

3.f WRITING NOUN CLAUSES

A noun clause can be used in all the ways that a noun or pronoun can be used. Compare the following sentences.

SIMPLE SENTENCES	SENTENCES WITH NOUN CLAUSES
Dancing is good exercise. This fact is well-known.	**That dancing is good exercise** is well-known.
You suggest some music. We will listen to it.	We will listen to **whatever you suggest.**
You choose a movie. We will watch it.	We will watch **what you choose.**

Use the subordinators below to begin noun clauses.

SUBORDINATORS FOR NOUN CLAUSES

that	who	whom
what	whoever	whomever
whatever		

*EXERCISE 35: **Sentence Combining.** Combine the following pairs of sentences to create a sentence with a noun clause *as a subject*. Place the word in parentheses in the beginning of the sentence on that line. Eliminate any underlined word in that sentence. Substitute the newly formed noun clause for the word SOMEONE or SOMETHING in the first sentence.

EXAMPLE   SOMEONE knows self-defense.
          Someone knows karate. (**WHOEVER**)
ANSWER   *Whoever knows karate knows self-defense.*

1. *Whatever* ~~SOMETHING~~ is done with grace and polish.
   ~~Something~~ karate experts do. (**WHATEVER**)

2. *What* ~~SOMETHING~~ is speed as well as strength.
   ~~Something~~ is required. (**WHAT**)

3. *What* ~~SOMETHING~~ is concentration.
   ~~Something~~ is most important. (**WHAT**)

4. *Whoever* ~~SOMEONE~~ must study for years.
   ~~Someone~~ wants to master the art. (**WHOEVER**)

5. *Whoever* ~~SOMEONE~~ is a karate expert.
   ~~Someone~~ holds a black belt. (**WHOEVER**)

* **EXERCISE 36: Sentence Combining.** Combine the following sentences to create a sentence with a noun clause *as object.* Put the word in parentheses in the beginning of the sentence on that line. Eliminate any underlined word. Substitute the newly formed noun clause for the word SOMETHING or SOMEONE in the first sentence.

1. The duties of airport police include ~~SOMETHING~~. *whatever*
   ~~Something~~ is a problem at an air terminal. (**WHATEVER**)

2. They help ~~SOMEONE~~. *whomever*
   they ~~They~~ can assist ~~someone~~ in some way. (**WHOMEVER**)

3. An arriving passenger has ~~SOMETHING~~. *what*
   ~~Something~~ seems to be a language problem. (**WHAT**)

4. A traveler screams ~~SOMETHING~~. *that*
   his ~~His~~ baggage is missing. (**THAT**)

5. An arriving passenger cannot find ~~SOMEONE~~. *whoever*
   ~~Someone~~ is supposed to meet him. (**WHOEVER**)

6. A visiting diplomat says ~~SOMETHING~~. *that*
   she ~~She~~ needs an escort. (**THAT**)

7. The commanding officer sends ~~SOMEONE~~. *whoever*
   ~~Someone~~ is available. (**WHOEVER**)

8. Airport-police calls indicate ~~SOMETHING~~. *what*
   ~~Something~~ must be done in emergencies. (**WHAT**)

9. A "32" means ~~SOMETHING~~. *that firefighting*
   ~~Firefighting~~ equipment must be ready. (~~THAT~~)

10. A "25" indicates ~~SOMETHING~~. *that*
    a ~~A~~ hijacking is taking place. (~~THAT~~)

EXERCISE 37. Use the word in parentheses to form a noun clause. Use the noun clause to complete Sentences *a* and *b*.

> EXAMPLE   A "hot line" exists between Washington and Moscow. (**THAT**)
>   a. Most Americans know _____ .
>   b. _____ shows a desire for world peace.
>
> ANSWER   a. *Most Americans know that a "hot line" exists between Washington and Moscow.*
>   b. *That a "hot line" exists between Washington and Moscow shows a desire for world peace.*

what
1. Americans call the "hot line." (**WHAT**)
   a. Frederick, Maryland, houses _____ .
that the   b. _____ is actually a computer teleprinter.

2. ~~The~~ "hot line" is a red telephone. (**THAT**)
   a. Many people think _____ .
that monitoring   b. _____ is a misconception.

3. ~~Monitoring~~ the "hot line" is a boring job. (**THAT**)
   a. _____ seems ironic.
that the   b. Most people do not realize _____ .

4. ~~The~~ "hot line" is operating properly. (**THAT**)
   a. Every six hours technicians determine _____ .
that security   b. _____ is important.

5. ~~Security~~ is tight at "hot line" headquarters. (**THAT**)
   a. _____ is not surprising.
   b. Most people assume _____ .

WRITING COMPOUND — COMPLEX SENTENCES

A **compound-complex sentence** consists of two or more main clauses and one or more subordinate clauses.

You can add subordinate clauses to compound sentences in the same way that you can add subordinate clauses to simple sentences. Adding one or more subordinate clauses to a compound sentence creates a compound-complex sentence.

3.g ADDING SUBORDINATE CLAUSES TO COMPOUND SENTENCES

Once you can write compound-complex sentences, your writing will have more variety. Compound-complex sentences are often quite long, however, and should not be overused.

COMPOUND SENTENCE
"Hard rock" has a driving beat, but "soft rock" is quite different.

COMPOUND-COMPLEX SENTENCE
"Hard rock," **which is one form of popular music,** has a driving beat, but "soft rock" is quite different, **as the name suggests.**

EXERCISE 38. Expand each of the following compound sentences into two compound-complex sentences by adding, where the carets (∧) indicate, each of the subordinate clauses. Be sure to punctuate properly.

EXAMPLE The United States has many myths and legends ∧, but few of these tales have ever been proved true.
    a. which are fabulous stories
    b. which are popular stories from the past

ANSWER   a. *The United States has many myths and legends,* **which are fabulous stories,** *but few of these tales have ever been proved true.*

      b. *The United States has many myths and legends,* **which are popular stories from the past,** *but few of these tales have ever been proved true.*

1. The nineteenth century ∧ gave birth to many legends, and one such legend was about the notorious Deadwood Dick.
   a., when America moved west ,
   b., when the West was wild ,

2. Deadwood Dick ∧ was a fictional creation, but many real people claimed to be he.
   a., who was the hero of popular dime novels ,
   b., who was known as the black rider of the Black Hills ,

3. Was Nat Love really Deadwood Dick, or was the claim ∧ only a publicity stunt?
   a., which Love made in his autobiography ,
   b., which others had made before Love ,

4. Nat Love ∧ was a cattle driver and a sharpshooter, and he did once live in the town of Deadwood.
   a., who was born a slave in Tennessee ,
   b., whom some people recognize as the real-life Deadwood Dick ,

5. His autobiography ∧ was full of adventure, but his claim to be Deadwood Dick has never been proved.
   a., which was published in 1907 ,
   b., which described a glorious life on the range ,

EXERCISE 39. Expand each of the following compound sentences into two compound-complex sentences by adding, where the carets (∧) indicate, each of the subordinate clauses. Be sure to punctuate the new sentences properly. Follow the example in Exercise 38 as a model.

1. Thornton Biggs worked on Ora Haley's Two Bar Ranch ∧ , and he was reputedly the best bronco buster in Colorado.
   a. when the ranch was one of the best in Colorado
   b. before he moved to Cheyenne, Wyoming

2. ∧ Wyoming became the center of the cattle business, *Although* and Cheyenne was booming.
   a. ~~although~~ Colorado remained important cattle-
   Because raising territory ,
   b. ~~because~~ Colorado had less land suitable for grazing ,

3. ∧B. M. Ford was a prominent citizen, for he owned
   Since Cheyenne's finest hotel.
   a. ~~since~~ many people headed for Cheyenne ,
   b. ~~while~~ Cheyenne prospered ,

4. Cheyenne is famous for its colorful history, and the
   city also fostered racial and religious tolerance ∧.
   a. before the rest of America was ready to give up its
      prejudices
   b. , as if its new prosperity went hand in hand with new
      ideas

5. ∧Cheyenne's blacks and whites worked and studied
   together; Protestants, Catholics, and Jews were all
   Whereas active citizens.
   a. ~~whereas~~ racial discrimination was widespread
      Because elsewhere ,
   b. ~~because~~ townspeople had mutual interests ,

WRITING SENTENCES WITH PARTICIPIAL PHRASES

3.h SENTENCES WITH PARTICIPIAL PHRASES

A **participial phrase** is a group of words that contains a
participle and other words that describe or clarify that
participle. You can use a participial phrase in many of the
same ways that you might use a clause. Using participial
phrases is another way to add variety to your writing.

SENTENCE WITH SUBORDINATE CLAUSE	SENTENCE WITH PARTICIPIAL PHRASE
As new groups become known, they give more concerts.	**Becoming known,** new groups give more concerts.
She submitted her song, **of which she felt proud.**	She submitted her song, **feeling proud of it.**

AVOIDING ERRORS WITH PARTICIPIAL PHRASES

Be careful to put a participial phrase at the proper point in the sentence. The phrase must clearly relate to a specific noun or pronoun. Otherwise it will be a **dangling** or **misplaced modifier.**

NOT ~~Playing a march, we heard a band go by.~~

BUT Playing a march, **a band** went by.

---

*EXERCISE 40. **Sentence Combining and Reducing.** Combine each of the following pairs of sentences into one new sentence. Make the first sentence of each pair into a participial phrase.

EXAMPLE   Trini Alvarado saw Shirley Temple on television. Trini Alvarado decided to be a dancer.

ANSWER   ***Seeing Shirley Temple on television,*** *Trini Alvarado decided to be a dancer.*

1. ~~Trini Alvarado performed~~ with her father. ,   *Performing* Trini Alvarado entertained at Spanish festivals.

2. ~~Her father accompanied~~ himself on the guitar. ,   *Accompanying* her ~~Her~~ father sang Spanish songs.

3. ~~Trini performed~~ in a small New York play. ,   *Performing* Trini was "discovered" by a Broadway producer looking for new dancers.

4. ~~The producer encouraged~~ her. ,   *Encouraging* the ~~The~~ producer persuaded Trini to audition for a Broadway musical.

5. ~~She won~~ the part. ,   *Winning* she ~~She~~ gave a widely acclaimed performance.

6. ~~Trini sang~~ a number from the show. ,   *Singing* Trini appeared on the Tony Awards telecast.

7. ~~She signed~~ for a movie. ,   *Signing* she ~~She~~ was not yet twelve.

8. ~~She made~~ her film debut , *she* ~~She~~ won praise from critics. *Making*

9. ~~She acted~~ in the film *Rich Kids* , *she* ~~She~~ gave a realistic performance. *Acting*

10. ~~Trini works~~ hard , Trini also attends school full time. *Working*

REVIEW EXERCISE E: **Expanding sentences in a variety of ways.** There are many structures that can be used when adding information to sentences. In this section you have practiced the following seven structures.

METHODS OF EXPANDING SENTENCES

1. adjectives or participles used as adjectives
2. adverbs
3. prepositional phrases
4. adverb clauses
5. adjective clauses
6. appositives
7. participial phrases

Expand each of the numbered sentences below by adding the information that is given at its right. Expand each numbered sentence in two different ways. Be sure to use each of the seven methods of expansion at least once.

Answers will vary; possibilities are given below.

Additional information

1. Anna decided to give a party. *7*

   Anna wanted to celebrate her birthday.

2. Her birthday was Friday, October 13. *4*

   Anna threw a "Friday the Thirteenth Birthday Party."

3. Guests were told to bring charms. *3*

   The charms were for good luck.

4. Cindy brought a rabbit's foot. *6*

   Cindy was Anna's best friend.

5. Luis wore lucky shoes. *5*

   He always wears them for math tests.

6. Raymond brought a penny. *4*

   He had found the penny in the schoolyard.

	Additional information
7. Greta brought a shamrock. *6*	A shamrock is a lucky clover from Ireland.
8. The guests tossed lucky horseshoes. *2*	They played "Pin the Tail on the Black Cat."
9. The party was a huge success. *1*	Everyone had a wonderful time.
10. Anna felt lucky. *4*	She had so many friends.

WRITING CLEAR SENTENCES

If you use all the kinds of sentences examined and drilled in this section, your writing will be varied and interesting. In addition to checking for variety, you should be careful about clarity in your sentences. The following three pieces of advice can help you to write sentences that are both clear and strong:

1. Do not bury the subject of the sentence. Try to make the subject of the sentence crystal clear.
2. Do not use unnecessary words. Eliminate words that do not serve a purpose. If a word can be taken out without hurting a sentence, take it out.
3. Use the active voice unless you have a good reason for using the passive voice.

3.i MAKING THE SUBJECT CLEAR

In each sentence let your reader know as soon as possible what you are talking about. In other words, make the subject of your sentence clear.

In general, it is best to leave yourself out of the sentence. After all, if you are writing the sentence, you do not have to begin by saying *I feel* or *I think* or *I believe*. Compare the following sentences. Notice how the second sentence makes the most important idea the subject of the sentence.

EXAMPLES

I feel *that practicing the piano helps me.* [important idea as object of verb]

Practicing the piano helps me. [important idea as subject of sentence]

Certainly, at times it may be appropriate to include yourself in a sentence. Be aware, however, of what happens to your main ideas when too many sentences begin with expressions such as *I think.*

EXERCISE 41. Rewrite the following sentences, eliminating all expressions such as *I think* or *I believe.*

> EXAMPLE I think that Los Angeles is one of the great American cities.
>
> ANSWER *Los Angeles is one of the great American cities.*

1. ~~It is my opinion that the~~ _The_ outdoor life style in Los Angeles is ideal.
2. ~~I feel that living~~ _Living_ between golden beaches and snow-capped mountains is really living.
3. ~~I think that there~~ _There_ is a certain excitement to the motion-picture and television industries.
4. ~~I think that the~~ _The_ Los Angeles Dodgers is a consistently fine team.
5. ~~In general, I believe that tourists~~ _Tourists_ are enchanted by the City of Angels.

3.j BEING CONCISE

Give your reader enough information, but do not say the same thing over and over again. Reading the same information again and again is repetitious and, therefore, boring. Examine the three groups of sentences on the next page. Either of the first two sentences in each group would be all right by itself. The third sentence in each group, however, contains words that are repetitive and, therefore, unnecessary.

EXAMPLES

ALL RIGHT: She had the courage to go.

ALL RIGHT: She did not fear anything.

REPETITIVE: She had the courage to go and did not fear anything. [Saying that she had courage and that she did not fear anything is saying the same thing twice. The sentence is repetitious.]

ALL RIGHT: The concert hall would greatly improve the town.

ALL RIGHT: The concert hall would change the town for the better.

REPETITIVE: The concert hall would greatly improve the town for the better.

ALL RIGHT: He worked for many months to regain the use of his arm.

ALL RIGHT: He worked for many months to gain the use of his arm once more.

REPETITIVE: He worked for many months to regain the use of his arm once more.

Reread each of the sentences you write to eliminate any words that merely repeat what other words have already said. Sometimes you will even find one word that can take the place of many words.

EXERCISE 42. Rewrite the following sentences, eliminating any repetitious information. Notice from the example that there is sometimes more than one way to rewrite the sentences. You have to do only one.

EXAMPLE Ms. Schlichtmann had a strong desire to succeed and wanted very much to be a success.

ANSWER a. *Ms. Schlichtmann had a strong desire to succeed.*

ANSWER b. *Ms. Schlichtmann wanted very much to be a success.*

1. Alumni attend homecoming events to relive ~~again the memories of past~~ school days.

2. That candidate seems to have the essential experience and education ~~required for the job~~.

3. Too much time in the ~~clothes~~ dryer caused the purple sweater to shrink ~~and become smaller~~.

4. Margot is extremely self-confident ~~and never seems to doubt herself~~.

5. Everyone thought Mr. Hayes was improving, but his condition suddenly took a ~~bad~~ turn for the worse.

3.k USING THE ACTIVE VOICE

It is not wrong to use the passive voice — to say, for example, *His courage was shown during the crisis.* In fact, at times you have to use the passive voice because you do not really know who performed a particular action (see 1.b.20). When you reread your compositions, however, you should check to make sure that you are not overusing the passive voice. If you begin to wonder who is doing all these things, you had better change some sentences to the active voice. You may say, for example, *He showed his courage during the crisis.*

EXAMPLES
Poor: performer not clear
His talent was shown in the concerts he gave at
  school.

Better: clear performer and action
He showed his talent in the concerts he gave at
  school.

EXERCISE 43. Rewrite each of the following sentences, changing all verbs that are in the passive voice into the active voice.

EXAMPLE Alexandra Tolstoy's life was spent trying to carry
  out her father's philosophies.

ANSWER *Alexandra Tolstoy spent her life trying to carry
  out her father's philosophies.*

1. *A Life of My Father,* an account of Leo Tolstoy, was published by her in 1953. *She published...*

2. Many of Tolstoy's later manuscripts were transcribed and published by her. *She transcribed and published...*

3. She emigrated from Russia to the United States in 1931, where her time was spent lecturing about her father. *... where she spent her time...*

4. The Tolstoy Foundation was founded by her to aid other Russian refugees. *She founded...*

5. Many Russian exiles have been helped to get started in the United States by the Tolstoy Foundation. *The Tolstoy Foundation has helped...*

REVIEW EXERCISE F: Writing clear sentences. Each of the sentences below suffers from one or more of the faults, listed below, which are discussed in the preceding pages:

　　1. Weak or unclear subject
　　2. Wordiness
　　3. Dependence on the passive voice

Rewrite each sentence to eliminate these problems.

1. ~~It is an opinion that~~ Memphis, Tennessee, has become a fascinating city to visit.

2. History ~~of past times~~ stands out everywhere ~~in all places~~ in Memphis, especially on Beale Street, where W. C. Handy gave birth to the blues.

3. *Many know* ~~The famous Memphis riverfront is known by many, especially for~~ DeSoto Park, the site from which the Mississippi was first viewed by the Spanish explorer in 1541.

4. ~~It is believed that good~~ *Good* food also makes Memphis a place worth visiting.

5. Many barbeque restaurants offer rice and beans, and people revisit ~~again those barbeque places that have made favorable impressions on them~~. *the places they favor.*

6. Of course, some people going south like grits, red-eye gravy, biscuits, and Tennessee ham, ~~and these foods can be~~ found at many Memphis restaurants.

Southern

7. It is my opinion that southern cooking is an essential ~~to~~
   ~~part of~~ American cuisine.

un
by 8. One famous sightseeing spot is the Memphis Pink Palace, an unfinished mansion that Clarence Saunders, a
   supermarket builder, never completed.

9. The palace contains a miniature five-ring circus, an
   insect zoo, and a turn-of-the-century soda fountain.
   from the 1900s.

10. You can also take a day trip to Shiloh National Military
    Park, or William Faulkner's home in Oxford can be
    visited.

VOCABULARY

4 Vocabulary

See summary of section in Teacher's Manual.

Learning how to increase the number of words that you recognize and use is one of the most important skills you will need in school and in life. With a strong vocabulary you will understand more of what you hear and read. You will express better what you want to say and write. This section will teach you various ways to learn the vocabulary that good writers find useful. The bigger your vocabulary of nouns, verbs, adjectives, and adverbs, the easier it will be for you to find the right word to express your meaning. Furthermore, you will learn words that can replace longer expressions. Those words will make your writing easier to read and more interesting. For example, you can use the word *nostalgia* instead of the expression *longing for the past.*

There are many ways to expand your vocabulary for writing:

- You can use a reference book such as a dictionary or a thesaurus to help you discover new words (see 6.d.5).
- You can keep a notebook of words that you wish to learn and use in your own writing. These words may come from your reading or conversations with friends and teachers.
- You can expand your vocabulary by one part of speech at a time.
- You can learn to add word elements to words that you already know in order to create new words.

EXPANDING YOUR VOCABULARY: PARTS OF SPEECH

It is easy to extend your vocabulary if you think in terms of separate parts of speech: nouns, verbs, adjectives, and adverbs.

4.a ADDING TO YOUR NOUN VOCABULARY

You can find a noun to name almost every *thing* in the universe. Nouns name things such as people, animals, places, objects, and abstract ideas. Nouns can name groups of things (for instance, *crowd, collection, pack*) as well as parts of things (for instance, *wrist, hand, finger*).

Nouns that name a specific, particular thing — not just some thing — are called **proper nouns.** Nouns that are the general names of things or ideas are called **common nouns.**

EXAMPLES

Proper nouns	Common nouns
Billie Jean King	woman
Black Beauty	horse
Grand Canyon	landmark
U.S. Constitution	document
Wyoming	state

A good way to add to your noun vocabulary is to make a list of proper nouns and to find two or three common nouns that correspond to each proper noun. For example, the common nouns *woman, athlete,* and *celebrity* correspond to the proper noun *Billie Jean King.* Similarly, the common nouns *horse, animal,* and *book* correspond to the proper noun *Black Beauty.*

A noun that names an idea or quality (for instance, *happiness*, *beauty*, *travel*, *space*) is called an **abstract noun.** A noun that names a physical object is called a **concrete noun.**

EXAMPLES

Abstract nouns	Concrete nouns
patriotism	Germany
greed	baby
love	Virginia
mathematics	wristwatch

Another way of adding to your noun vocabulary is to take an object, such as an automobile, and to try to find abstract and concrete nouns that are related to that object. First think of abstract nouns related to the automobile, such as *travel* or *speed.* Then think of concrete nouns, such as *vehicle* or *Ford.* A good way to find concrete nouns is to think of different *parts* of the object.

You can also add to your noun vocabulary by adding suffixes to nouns, to verbs, and to adjectives that you already know. For example, you can add the suffix **-ness** to the adjective *happy* to form the noun *happi**ness.*** You can add the suffix **-hood** to the noun *child* to form the noun *child**hood.***

Adding suffixes to nouns, verbs, and adjectives to form nouns can help you to make your writing more *concise* — that is, to express your ideas in fewer words. For instance, it is more concise to add the suffix -*hood* to the noun *child* and to use the noun *childhood* than it is to use the expression *the time of life when one is a child.* See 4.i for more information about adding to your noun vocabulary by using noun-forming suffixes.

EXERCISE 1. For each of the following proper nouns, give at least two common nouns that correspond to it.
Answers will vary; examples are given in exercise.
EXAMPLE *Mona Lisa*

ANSWER *portrait, painting, artwork, picture*

1. General Motors   *car, truck*
2. New York   *city, state*
3. Jimmy Carter   *man, person*
4. Golden Gate Bridge   *bridge, steel*
5. Aretha Franklin   *singer, woman*
6. Gettysburg   *town, battle*
7. Walter Cronkite   *newscaster, human*
8. the Fourth of July   *holiday, day*
9. San Diego Padres   *baseball, team*
10. Snoopy   *dog, comics*

EXERCISE 2. Match each abstract noun in the left-hand column below with three of the concrete nouns on the right. The crossed-out words are used in the example.

EXAMPLE   abstract noun: education
ANSWER   concrete nouns: *teacher, notebook, homework*

Abstract nouns

a music
b transportation
education

Concrete nouns

a drums   notebook
a stereo   *a* piano
b bus   *b* airplane
b bicycle   homework
teacher

EXERCISE 3. Replace the italicized expressions in the sentences with nouns from the Word Bank on the next page. Notice that the nouns in the Word Bank are formed by adding suffixes to nouns, verbs, and adjectives.

1. One of the rights guaranteed by the Constitution is the right to *the state of being private.*   *privacy*
2. The *action of the reversing* of a negative can produce an unusual photograph.   *reversal*
3. *A geographer's work* involves geology and ecology.   *geography*
4. Too many animals within a small feeding area can result in *the act of starving.*   *starvation*
5. Dew consists of *small drops* of water.   *droplets*
6. The *tiny seeds*, or sprouts, of the soybean plant make a delicious salad.   *seedlings*
7. *The condition of being free* is one of the most important American ideals.   *freedom*
8. *Those who work in an art* often have difficulty making a living from their work.   *artists*

9. The American colonies' *act of resisting* led to the Revolutionary War. *resistance*

10. Guiomar Novaēs, the *person who plays the piano*, is famous for playing Chopin. *pianist*

WORD BANK

starvation	freedom
droplets	seedlings
pianist	resistance
reversal	privacy
artists	geography

4.b ADDING TO YOUR VERB VOCABULARY

You can find a verb to express almost any process or action. A strong verb vocabulary is very important because using the right verb adds movement and meaning — and life — to your writing. For example, it will help your writing if you know the many precise verbs that can take the place of the general verb *walk: march, hike, stroll, saunter, plod,* and so on. A good way to add to your verb vocabulary is to take a general verb and to think of more specific and precise verbs that express the same process or action. When you learn a new verb, try to use it in your own writing.

You can also add to your verb vocabulary by adding suffixes to nouns and adjectives that you already know. For example, you can add the suffix *-en* to the noun *length* to form the verb *lengthen.* You can add the suffix *-ize* to the adjective *central* to form the verb *centralize,* meaning "to make central."

Adding suffixes to form verbs can help make your writing more concise. For instance, it is more concise to use the verb *lengthen* than it is to use the expression *increase in length.* See 4.i for more information about adding to your verb vocabulary by using verb-forming suffixes.

EXERCISE 4. For each of the following general verbs think of at least two more specific and precise verbs that have a similar meaning. *Answers will vary; examples are given below.*

EXAMPLE drink
ANSWER   *gulp, sip, quaff*

1. eat   *devour, consume*   4. sleep   *nap, doze*
2. run   *race, speed*   5. speak   *talk, communicate*
3. think   *ponder, meditate*

EXERCISE 5. Match the italicized expressions in Column I with the corresponding verb in Column II. Notice that the verbs in Column II are formed by adding suffixes to nouns and adjectives.

Column I
1. *give a vaccine* against cholera *d*
2. *cause terror in* young children *a*
3. *make* a government *central* *e*
4. *cause* a highway *to become wide* *b*
5. *coordinate the decor of* a room *c*

Column II
a. terrify
b. widen
c. decorate
d. vaccinate
e. centralize

APPLICATION. Write five sentences, each of which uses a different verb from Column II. *Answers will vary; an example is "The children were vaccinated against cholera."*

4.c ADDING TO YOUR ADJECTIVE VOCABULARY

Finding the right adjective to express your meaning is not as easy as finding the right noun or the right verb. You may be tempted to fall back on general, "catchall" adjectives such as *old, new, good, bad, big, little, beautiful, ugly, nice,* or *fine.* Using more precise adjectives, however, will make your writing more interesting and effective. For instance, the expression *the repetitive essay* is more interesting and effective than *the bad essay.* The adjective *repetitive* specifically describes the "bad" quality of the essay. The adjective *bad* could mean almost anything.

Here is one way of adding to your adjective vocabulary: Make a list of "catchall" adjectives. Then think of more precise adjectives that can substitute for each.

EXAMPLES

"Catchall" adjectives	More precise adjectives
old	ancient, antique, archaic, outworn
bad	dull, sinister, corrupt, unpleasant
big	immense, massive, extensive, vast
beautiful	handsome, exquisite, lovely, attractive

Your verb vocabulary will also help you to add to your adjective vocabulary. **Participles** are forms of verbs that act as adjectives. There are two kinds of participles, present participles and past participles (see 1.b.7). Most verbs form their present participle by adding *-ing* and their past participle by adding *-ed*. For instance, the verb *embarrass* can be made into the present participle *embarrassing: My embarrassing remarks made her angry. Embarrass* can also be made into the past participle *embarrassed: The embarrassed mother apologized for her child's conduct.*

A good way of adding to your adjective vocabulary is to write down a list of verbs and to determine whether they can be used as present participles, as past participles, or as both.

EXAMPLES

Verb	Participle forms used as adjectives	
disturb	a *disturbing* noise	a *disturbed* dog
finish	a *finishing* rinse	a *finished* product
tire	a *tiring* day	a *tired* runner

You can also add to your adjective vocabulary by adding suffixes to nouns, adjectives, and verbs that you already know. For example, you can add the suffix *-able* to the noun *reason* to form the adjective *reasonable.* You can add the suffix *-ive* to the verb *attract* to form the adjective *attractive.*

Adding suffixes to form adjectives can help to make your writing more concise. For instance, it is more concise to add the suffix *-ive* to the verb *attract* and to use the adjective *attractive* than it is to use the expression *having the ability to attract.* See 4.i for more information about adding to your adjective vocabulary by using adjective-forming suffixes.

EXERCISE 6. Replace the "catchall" adjectives in each of the following items with two more precise adjectives or participles. Do not repeat adjectives or participles. *Answers will vary; examples are given below.*

EXAMPLE   a) fine pianist   b) fine pitcher

ANSWER   a) **talented** *pianist*   b) **strong** *pitcher*

1. a) ugly living room   b) ugly portrait   *dingy, unflattering*
2. a) new book   b) new idea   *recent, modern*
3. a) little person   b) little trip   *short, brief*
4. a) good record   b) good stereo   *interesting, superb*
5. a) nice day   b) nice dinner   *sparkling, delicious*

EXERCISE 7. Choose two highly descriptive and specific adjectives to describe each of the following nouns. One of the adjectives that you choose should be a past participle or a present participle. *Answers will vary; one example is given for each.*

EXAMPLE   star

ANSWERS   *a* **tiny** *star; a* **glittering** *star*

1. story   *boring*   5. stereo   *broken*   8. crime   *minor*
2. idea   *overworked*   6. automobile   *old*   9. tree   *budding*
3. diamond   *fake*   7. purpose   *evil*   10. city   *bustling*
4. question   *silly*

EXERCISE 8. Change the verb at the end of each of the following sentences into either a present participle or a past participle. Add -ing to form a present participle; add -ed to form a past participle.

1. A *relaxed* atmosphere in a job interview is productive for both the interviewer and the job applicant. (relax)
2. Yoga is a very *relaxing* form of exercise. (relax)
3. *Peeled* apples contain less fiber than apples with their peels. (peel)
4. *Peeling* paint should be scraped off before a wall is re-painted. (peel)
5. Spiders weave very *interesting* designs in their webs. (interest)
6. An *interested* child is easier to teach than one who is bored. (interest)
7. Knock on a *closed* door before entering. (close)
8. The *closing* words of a speech should be powerful. (close)
9. The *dating* couple treated each other as equals. (date)
10. A *dated* style will eventually become popular again. (date)

EXERCISE 9. Replace the italicized expression in each of the following sentences with one of the adjectives from the Word Bank. Notice that adjectives in the Word Bank are formed by adding suffixes to nouns, verbs, and adjectives.

1. Many wool clothes have to be dry-cleaned because they are not *able to be washed.* washable
2. A large spot on the surface of Jupiter looks *like the color red.* reddish
3. Children's literature is often *full of fancy.* fanciful
4. Changes that are *characteristic of the seasons* do not occur at the poles and the equator. seasonal
5. Brass, which looks *like gold,* is much less valuable than gold. golden
6. Insects preserved in amber look alive and real, but they are completely *without life.* lifeless

7. An injury may produce a paralysis that is *characteristic of death*.   *deathly*

8. In the area of the United States called the Dust Bowl, the earth is very dry and *like dust*.   *dusty*

9. Many words in the English language have an origin that is *of the Germans*.   *Germanic*

10. The bite of a poisonous snake is *full of venom*.   *venomous*

WORD BANK

fanciful	dusty	deathly
seasonal	reddish	golden
lifeless	washable	venomous
Germanic		

4.d ADDING TO YOUR VOCABULARY WITH ADVERBS OF MANNER

Adverbs of manner add meaning to verbs by telling *how* someone acts (*grins* **cheerfully**) or the *means by which* something or someone acts (**legally** *adopts* — that is, by legal means).

You can use your adjective vocabulary to form adverbs of manner. Adverbs of manner can be formed by adding *-ly* to most adjectives. For instance, the adjective *quick* can be made into the adverb of manner *quickly*. If the adjective ends in *y*, the *y* is usually changed to *i* before the *-ly* is added. For instance, the adjective *happy* can be made into the adverb of manner *happily*.

ADJECTIVE	ADVERB OF MANNER
a respectful man	behaves respectfully
a purposeful person	acts purposefully
a brave soldier	fights bravely
a graceful dancer	performs gracefully

EXERCISE 10. Complete the sentences on the next page by adding *-ly* to the italicized adjective to form an adverb of manner.

1. An *absent-minded* professor lectures _absent-mindedly_
2. A *quick* student answers _quickly_ .
3. A *grumpy* customer complains _grumpily_ .
4. A *messy* child gobbles _messily_ .
5. A *furious* umpire gestures _furiously_
6. A self-*important* politician struts _importantly_
7. An *impatient* reporter questions _impatiently_ .
8. A *stylish* model dresses _stylishly_
9. An *angry* boss speaks _angrily_ .
10. A *spiteful* busybody gossips _spitefully_

4.e SYNONYMS

Synonyms are words that mean almost the same thing as one another. Every synonym, however, has a slightly different meaning from the other words that it is like. Choosing a synonym with exactly the right shade of meaning is one of your most important decisions as a writer. For instance, the following verbs all mean "walk," but each verb has a slightly different shade of meaning. Which one of the following verbs would you use to describe the action of an old horse? Of a soldier? Of a nervous lecturer?

SYNONYMS OF *WALK*
amble   march
pace   stroll

A good way to find synonyms is to look in the dictionary. A dictionary often defines a word by using other words that mean about the same thing — that is, by using synonyms. In addition, a list of synonyms may appear at the end of the entry. See Section 6 for more information on using the dictionary.

Another way to find synonyms is to look in a thesaurus, which is a book that lists synonyms. *Roget's Thesaurus* and *Webster's Collegiate Thesaurus* are two books that you should find helpful.

EXERCISE 11. Using a dictionary or a thesaurus, find two synonyms for each of the following words. *Answers will vary.*
One example is given for each.

1. choose *pick*   6. fly (noun) *insect*
2. wealthy *rich*   7. steal *pilfer*
3. freedom *liberty* 8. angry *furious*
4. mystery *puzzle*   9. boss (noun) *employer*
5. funny *hilarious* 10. child *offspring*

EXPANDING YOUR VOCABULARY: CONTEXT

If, as a reader, you pay attention to all the words in a passage, you will often be able to figure out the meaning of problem words. Then, as a writer, you will learn to take care in making sure that your readers will not have trouble with any unfamiliar words that you use.

4.f MEANING FROM CONTEXT

The **context** of a word consists of the other words around it (either in the same sentence or elsewhere in the paragraph). Sometimes the context of a word is the situation itself.

There are two important ways in which context — the other words around a problem word — can help:

1. Often a word has more than one meaning. The rest of the sentence will help a reader to decide on which meaning is intended.

   EXAMPLE
   The **ruler** was hailed by his subjects. [This *ruler* is a person, perhaps a king.]
   The **ruler** was marked off in centimeters. [This *ruler* measures lengths.]

2. The context can help a reader figure out the meaning of an unfamiliar word.

EXAMPLE
How could he be so charming and helpful but then run out on us? It's a **paradox.** [*Paradox* must have something to do with a contradiction.]

■ Context clues

The writer needs to make the context clear enough so that all the words are understandable. There are a number of methods and signals that a writer can use to make the meaning clear. These are often called *context clues.* Each kind is discussed and illustrated here.

GIVING A DEFINITION
Shin splints is pain in the shin area, often caused by running on hard surfaces.
What **aerobic means,** literally, is "promoting the supply and use of oxygen."
The condition known as hardening of arteries **is referred to as atherosclerosis.**

GIVING EXAMPLES
Condiments make food more interesting; **for example,** garlic and oregano add zest to sauces.
A **permeable substance, such as** gravel or sandstone, was recommended by the architect.

RESTATING IN DIFFERENT WORDS
Carcinogens — **that is,** materials that cause cancers — seem to be everywhere.
Many exercises are **anaerobic. In other words,** they do nothing to help you to use oxygen.

EXERCISE 12. Each of the following words has at least two meanings (given in parentheses). Write two sentences for each word, one for each meaning. The context of each sentence must make the word's meaning clear. *Answers will vary; an example is "There are ten houses on my block."*

1. block (piece of wood; a city street)

2. bore (to drill; to weary by being dull)

3. coach (a vehicle; a sports instructor)

4. file (a tool; a cabinet)

5. handle (knob; nickname)

6. bar (candy; soap)

7. justice (fairness; a judge)

8. game (play; wild animals)

9. cord (amount of wood; thick string)

10. fan (admirer; cooling instrument)

11. course (subject in school; path)

12. court (palace; playing area)

13. organ (part of body; musical instrument)

14. plot (evil plan; story)

15. sole (part of foot; fish)

16. spring (season; elastic device)

17. fall (season; moving down)

18. graduate (to finish school; to divide)

19. bolt (to lock; to move quickly)

20. watch (clock; time on duty)

EXERCISE 13. Write a sentence or two using each of the following words. Use a context clue to make the meaning of each word clear to your readers. Use a dictionary where necessary, but do *not* copy the definition. *Answers will vary; an example is given below.*

1. trampoline	6. huggermugger
2. patriarch	7. devil's advocate
3. googolplex	8. dew point
4. missive	9. bugaboo
5. howitzer	10. lazy susan

My grandfather is a bearded patriarch.

11. jamboree	16. whetstone
12. hackamore	17. tricolor
13. gossamer	18. nesselrode
14. glucose	19. octogenarian
15. whipper-snapper	20. ocelot

EXPANDING YOUR VOCABULARY: WORD BUILDING

A limited number of words and word elements are put together in many different ways to produce the tremendous vocabulary of the English language. The word elements that are used to build English words are word roots and base words (see 4.g), prefixes (see 4.h), and suffixes (see 4.i).

4.g WORD ROOTS AND BASE WORDS

A **word root** is the main part of a word, but it is not a complete word in itself.

A word root (or, simply, root) becomes a word only when another element is added to it at the beginning or at the end. For example, the root -rupt-, which means "break," cannot stand on its own as an independent word. The root must have another element before it, after it, or both before and after it in order to become a complete English word. You can have **dis**rupt, **inter**rupt**ion,** or rupt**ure,** for example.

A **base word** is an element that can be used to build words but that is also a complete word in itself.

For example, the base words happy, credit, hope, dread, and kind can stand on their own as independent words, but they can also have word elements added to them, as in **un**happy, **dis**credit, hope**less,** dread**ful,** and *kind**ness.*** Word roots come to English from other languages. Base words are already English words.

Below, you will find other examples of roots, base words, and added elements.

EXAMPLES

Root		With other elements
-rupt-	("break")	interruption, rupture
-duc-	("lead")	conductor, introduce
-fin-	("end")	finish, finality
-port-	("carry")	export, portable

Base word	
break	breakable, breakage
lead	unleaded, leader
end	endless, endlessly
carry	carrier

The elements that are added to word roots and to base words are **prefixes** and **suffixes.** In the following pages you will see how to use prefixes and suffixes to increase your writing vocabulary.

As you read through the list of common word roots, remember that the spelling of the word root may change slightly when it is used in an English word.

WORD ROOTS

Root	Meaning	Examples in English words
-am-	love	amicable, amity
-audi-	hear	auditorium, audience
-ben-	good, well	benevolent, benefit
-brev-	short	abbreviate, brevity
-cap-	head	capital, decapitate

Root	Meaning	Examples
-cid-	kill, cut	incisive, regicide
-cogn-	know	incognito, recognition
-cred-	believe	incredible, credit
-culp-	blame	culpable, culprit
-domin-	lord	domain, domineering
-duc-	lead	education, conduct
-equ-	equal	equation, unequal
-err-	stray	erroneous, error
-fac-, -fec-	do, make	manufacture, perfect
-fid-	belief, faith	confidence, fidelity
-fin-	end	define, finish
-frag-, -frac-	break	fraction, fragmentary
-fus-	pour	profuse, infusion
-jac-, -ject-	throw	adjective, inject
-jud-	judge	judicial, prejudice
-junc-, -jug-	join	conjunction, junction
-jur-	swear	conjure, jury
-loqu-	speak	eloquence, ventriloquist
-magn-	great	magnificent, magnify
-mal-	bad	malady, malicious
-man-	hand	manual, manuscript

Root	Meaning	Examples
-mit-, -miss-	send	admit, dismiss
-mor-	die	morbid, mortality
-ped-	foot	pedal, pedestrian
-port-	carry	import, porter
-prim-	first	primer, primitive
-pugn-	fight	pugnacious, repugnant
-rump-, -rupt-	break	disruption, interrupt, rupture
-sci-	know	conscience, scientist
-scrib-, -scrip-	write	inscription, scribble
-sent-, -sens-	feel	consent, sensitive
-sol-	alone	desolation, solo
-son-	sound	sonic, dissonance, unison
-spir-	breath	perspiration, spirit
-trah-, -tract-	draw, pull	abstract, tractor, contract
-ven-, -vent-	come	convention, event
-verb-	word	adverb, verb, proverb
-vert-, -vers-	turn	controversy, revert
-via-	way	deviation, viaduct
-vid-, -vis-	see	evidence, vision
-vit-	life	vital, vitamin

EXERCISE 14. Column I is a list of words made up of word roots plus prefixes or suffixes. Match each word in Column I with its meaning in Column II. You may not know the meaning of the prefix or suffix, but the meaning of the word root will help you to figure out the meaning of the entire word.

Column I

1. trans*mit* e
2. in*duce* g
3. *vit*al a
4. *aud*ible j
5. *sol*itude c
6. *magn*ification h
7. in*equ*ality i
8. *fid*elity f
9. re*verse* b
10. in*scribe* d

Column II

a. characteristic of life
b. turn back
c. state of being alone
d. write in
e. send across
f. quality of having faith
g. lead into (persuade)
h. act of making greater or larger
i. state of being not equal
j. able to be heard

EXTRA: Ask students to choose five of the words in Column I, Exercise 14, and to write a sentence for each.

4.h PREFIXES

Prefixes are word elements that are attached to the beginnings of roots and base words.

EXAMPLES

Prefix		Word		New word
un-	+	friendly	=	**un**friendly
non-	+	stop	=	**non**stop
dis-	+	please	=	**dis**please
pre-	+	cooked	=	**pre**cooked

Using prefixed words will make your writing more concise.

In the following pairs of sentences, notice how the prefixed word makes the second sentence more concise and more direct.

EXAMPLES

Highways *between states* connect important cities in the United States.

Interstate highways connect important cities in the United States.

In *the middle of September* football season begins.
In **mid-September** football season begins.

Certain organizations *that are not run for profit* do not pay property taxes.
Certain **nonprofit** organizations do not pay property taxes.

The following lists will introduce you to six groups of prefixes and their meanings. The exercises following the groups of prefixes will show you ways to use prefixed words to *revise* your writing so that it will be smoother and more concise.

A hyphen is sometimes required between a prefix and the base word. For example, a hyphen is always used after the prefix *ex-* and before a base word that begins with a capital letter. For advice on when to use hyphens with prefixes, consult your dictionary.

PREFIXES WITH NEGATIVE MEANINGS

Prefix	Meaning	Can be used with
a-	without; not; lacking in	moral, social, historical, typical
dis-	not; opposite of	honest, agree, like, please, respectful
in-	not; without; lacking	dependent, correct, decent, convenient, curable
il-	variant of *in-*	legal, literacy, logical, legible
im-	variant of *in-*	proper, pure, personal, perfect, balance, mortal

Prefix	Meaning	Can be used with
ir-	variant of *in-*	resistible, reversible, responsible, relevant
mal-	bad; wrongful; ill	form, function, nourished, treat, nutrition
mis-	wrongly; astray	read, count, informed, pronounce
non-	not	profit, violent, stop, verbal, fiction
un-	not; opposite of	friendly, hurried, identified, pleasant, popular

PREFIXES THAT REVERSE ACTIONS

Prefix	Meaning	Can be used with
de-	to reverse an action; to deprive of; to remove	code, populate, throne, value
dis-	to reverse an action; to take away; to remove	advantage, allow, appear, arrange, mount, approve
un-	to reverse an action; to deprive of	button, fasten, hook, wind, bending

EXERCISE 15. In each of the following sentences, combine the prefix given in parentheses with a word in the italicized phrase or clause. Sometimes you may have to move the prefixed word to another part of the sentence.

> EXAMPLE Foreign aid *that is not military* is often called technical assistance. (non-)
>
> ANSWER **Nonmilitary** *foreign aid is often called technical assistance.*

1. Union members who are *not pleased* with their job conditions may go on strike. (dis-) *displeased*
2. Biographies and autobiographies are two kinds of writing *that are not fiction.* (non-) *nonfiction writing*
3. Reports of flying objects *that have not been identified* lead many people to believe in life on other planets. (un-) *unidentified flying objects*
4. Certain forms of cancer may be controlled, but they are still *not curable.* (in-) *incurable*
5. Many hunting injuries are caused by rifles that have *fired wrongly.* (mis-) *misfired*
6. A lack of oil in a gasoline engine will cause it to *function in the wrong way.* (mal-) *malfunction*
7. If you allow your fishing line to *reverse its wind* too much, you will not be able to feel the fish's nibble on the hook. (un-) *unwind*
8. Presidents have the right to veto legislation with which they *do not agree.* (dis-) *disagree*
9. An epidemic or war can result in the *loss of population* of a large area. (de-) *depopulation*
10. A country may *reduce the value of* its currency in order to sell more of its products to foreign customers. (de-) *devalue*

PREFIXES THAT TELL TIME OR ORDER

Prefix	Meaning	Can be used with
ex-[1]	previous; former	convict, fighter, champion, schoolteacher
post-	after	season, election, diagnostic
pre-	before	dawn, attack, packed, cooked, cut
re-	again; back	birth, introduce, think, use, learn, check

---

[1]Always hyphenate *ex-* before the base word.

EXERCISE 16. In each of the following sentences, combine the prefix given in parentheses with a word in the italicized phrase or clause. Be sure the prefixed word is placed so that your revision reads smoothly.

> EXAMPLE Sports reporters often try to obtain an interview *after a game* with the winning coach. (post-)
>
> ANSWER *Sports reporters often try to obtain a **postgame** interview with the winning coach.*

1. The first battle of the American Revolution was a skirmish *before dawn* on the Lexington Green. (pre-) *predawn skirmish*

2. After you have written something, take an hour or even a day to *think back on* your ideas before you begin revising. (re-) *rethink*

3. Legislation *that is passed after an election* should fulfill preelection promises. (post-) *Postelection legislation*

4. In the 1970s the music of the 1950s was *introduced again.* (re-) *reintroduced*

5. Many fast-food restaurants use food *that has been cooked beforehand.* (pre-) *precooked food*

6. Buying meat *that has been cut beforehand* is costlier than buying whole sides of beef. (pre-) *precut meat*

7. There are many organizations that help *former convicts* to find jobs. (ex-) *ex-convicts*

8. Germany's government *after World War I* was called the Weimar Republic. (post-) *post-World War I government*

9. *Former Presidents* have often acted as "elder statesmen" of their parties. (ex-) *Ex-Presidents*

10. A student whose first application to a college is rejected is often allowed to *apply again* at a later date. (re-) *reapply*

PREFIXES THAT TELL LOCATION

Prefix	Meaning	Can be used with
inter-	between; among	American, town, office, state
intra-	within	coastal, city, company

Prefix	Meaning	Can be used with
mid-	in the middle of	air, continent, day, range
sub-	under; beneath	way, soil, structure
trans-	across	shipment, Pacific, Atlantic, continental

EXERCISE 17. From the Word Bank below, select a prefixed word that can replace the italicized phrase in each of the following sentences. Then revise each sentence, placing the prefixed word *before* the noun.

> EXAMPLE To cross most boundaries *between nations,* you must have a passport.
>
> ANSWER *To cross most* **international** *boundaries,* you must have a passport.

1. In August 1967 a diesel cargo liner completed one of the fastest crossings *across the Pacific*: eight days and thirty-five minutes. *transpacific crossings*

2. Many communications *between offices* are made on an intercom system. *interoffice communications*

3. The waterway *within the coastline* from Boston to Florida Bay is 1,550 miles long. *intracoastal waterway*

4. Spruce, fir, and other evergreen trees grow in the region *below the Arctic Circle.* *subarctic region*

5. The sun *in the middle of the day* is often the hottest.

midday sun

WORD BANK

intracoastal   midday
transpacific   interoffice
~~international~~   subarctic

PREFIXES THAT TELL DEGREE

Prefix	Meaning	Can be used with
out-	going beyond; more than; better than	do, grow, shout, number, run
over-	excessive; too much	emphasize, spend, correct

Prefix	Meaning	Can be used with
sub-	lower in status than; less than	standard, commander, category, station
under-	insufficient; too little	rate, privileged, aged, estimate

PREFIXES THAT SHOW SUPPORT OR OPPOSITION

Prefix	Meaning	Can be used with
anti-	against; opposite	war, American, aircraft, freeze
co-	together with; joint	star, worker, editor
pro-	on the side of; in favor of	business, modern, American, union

EXERCISE 18. In each of the following sentences, combine the prefix given in parentheses with a word in the italicized phrase or clause. Be sure the prefixed word is placed so that your revision reads smoothly.

EXAMPLE A film *that is not rated highly enough* may not make much money. (under-)

ANSWER An **underrated** *film may not make much money.*

overcorrection

1. Research has shown that *too much correction* of their writing tends to discourage most students. (over-)

2. A technical knockout, or TKO, is an official measure of whether or not a boxer has *fought better than* an opponent. (out-) *outfought*

3. Most of the vitamin content of vegetables is lost if they are *cooked too much.* (over-) *overcooked*

4. Some cheeses that are *not aged enough* have a bland taste. (under-) *underaged cheeses*

5. An army general's *commanders who are lower in rank* are colonels, majors, captains, and lieutenants. (sub-) *subcommanders*

6. During the Civil War Mary Lincoln was suspected of being *on the Confederate side* because she had several relatives fighting for the South. (pro-)

pro-Confederate

Suffix	Meaning	Base word or word with root	New noun
-ation	action, state, result	cancel confirm	cancellation confirmation
-dom	domain	king	kingdom
-ee	one receiving action	address employ	addressee employee
-eer	one in an activity	puppet chariot	puppeteer charioteer
-er; *-or*	performer of an action	bat write elevate	batter writer elevator
-ful	amount	room	roomful
-hood	state, condition	brother adult	brotherhood adulthood
-ion	action, result, state	infect progress	infection progression
-ism	system	critic national	criticism nationalism
-ist	follower, doer	vocal ideal	vocalist idealist
-ity	state, quality	public electric	publicity electricity
-ment	action or its result	treat encourage	treatment encouragement
-ness; *-ery*	quality, state	happy blind green	happiness blindness greenery
-ship	state, condition	citizen owner	citizenship ownership

Suffix	Meaning	Base word or word with root	New noun
-tude	quality, state	serve apt	servitude aptitude
-ure	act, result, means	moist fail	moisture failure
-y	state, condition, study of	stenographer photograph	stenography photography

SUFFIXES THAT FORM ADJECTIVES

Suffix	Meaning	Base word or word with root	New adjective
-able; -ible	able to be acted upon	respect wash access permit	respectable washable accessible permissible
-al	characteristic of	herb magic music	herbal magical musical
-ary	related to	diet document	dietary documentary
-en	made of, like	wool oak	woolen oaken
-ful	full of, having	grace spite	graceful spiteful
-ic	having the nature of, characteristic of	cube acid	cubic acidic
-ish	like, characteristic of	red freak	reddish freakish

Suffix	Meaning	Base word or word with root	New adjective
-ive	tending to	possess create	possessive creative
-less	without, lacking	harm penny	harmless penniless
-like	similar	child life	childlike lifelike
-ly	like, charac-teristic of	scholar father	scholarly fatherly
-ous	full of, of the nature of	fame poison	famous poisonous
-some	apt to	adventure weary	adventuresome wearisome
-y	like, showing	mold greed	moldy greedy

SUFFIXES THAT FORM NOUNS AND ADJECTIVES

Suffix	Meaning	Base word or word with root	New noun or adjective
-an; -ian	belonging to	republic Jordan	republican Jordanian
-ese	of a style or place	official China	officialese Chinese

SUFFIXES THAT FORM VERBS

Suffix	Meaning	Base word or word with root	New verb
-ate	become, cause to become	alien valid	alienate validate

Suffix	Meaning	Base word or word with root	New verb
-en	make, cause to become	black sharp	blacken sharpen
-fy; *-ify*	cause, make	intense simple	intensify simplify
-ize	make, cause to become	capital standard	capitalize standardize

4.j DERIVATIONAL PATTERNS

The many derivational suffixes listed above (4.i) can help you to use words that you already know while building up your writing vocabulary further. You should notice that there are definite patterns to how words take suffixes. By thinking about and observing the patterns of word building, you can begin to predict the kinds of suffixes that certain words will take. For instance, if you know that the word *select* can become *selective* and *selection*, you can predict that *protect* can become *protective* and *protection* and that *elect* can become *elective* and *election.* By simply learning one pattern, you can create a whole list of words.

You will find nine patterns on the following pages. The words in each pattern take the same two derivational suffixes to form two related words.

Each pattern is followed by an exercise that will give you practice in using the various forms of words in that pattern. In doing the exercises, keep in mind that in your own writing you usually will not use two or three related forms in the same sentence. The exercises are designed to give you practice in moving quickly from one form to another.

The verbs in Patterns 1–5 can be transformed into two different kinds of nouns.

PATTERN 1: -ment, -er

Verb	Noun	Noun
achieve	achievement	achiever
adjust	adjustment	adjuster
advertise	advertisement	advertiser
argue	argument	arguer
develop	development	developer
employ	employment	employer
manage	management	manager
measure	measurement	measurer
move	movement	mover
reinforce	reinforcement	reinforcer

EXERCISE 19. Substitute the word given in parentheses or one of its derived forms for each blank. (The derived forms will end in *-er* or *-ment*.)

EXAMPLE A high school wished to _____ in a newspaper for a new gym teacher. The _____ it hired ran the _____ for two weeks. (advertise)

ANSWER *A high school wished to* **advertise** *in a newspaper for a new gym teacher. The* **advertiser** *it hired ran the* **advertisement** *for two weeks.*

1. Athlete Babe Zaharias was a high *achiever* in the sports world. Perhaps her greatest *achievement* was the winning of three gold medals in the 1932 Olympics, held in Los Angeles. (achieve)

2. To *develop* a photograph you need two different chemicals. One of them, called a *developer*, produces an image on paper and is used during the first stage of *development* (develop)

3. The earth and other planets *move* in an elliptical, or oval-shaped, orbit. The *movement* of the earth around the sun takes 365 days. (move)

4. Life in the first *settlement* in Plymouth was extremely difficult; every *settler* faced the threats of disease and starvation. (settle)

5. Many adults tried to *discourage* Tom Sawyer and Huckleberry Finn. The *discouragement*, however, only made the boys try even more daring exploits. (discourage)

PATTERN 2: *-ify, -ification, -ifier*

Verb	Noun	Noun
classify	classification	classifier
glorify	glorification	glorifier
justify	justification	justifier
modify	modification	modifier
simplify	simplification	simplifier
unify	unification	unifier
verify	verification	verifier

NOTE: *Satisfy* becomes *satisfaction.*

EXERCISE 20. Substitute the word given in parentheses or one of its derived forms for each blank. (The derived forms will end in *-ification* or *-ifier.*)

EXAMPLE   We attempted to ____ the rocks into different geologic periods. According to the geology book, our ____ was accurate. (classify)

ANSWER   *We attempted to **classify** the rocks into different geologic periods. According to the geology book, our **classification** was accurate.*

1. One *qualification* ____ of a cartoonist is the ability to draw people. Those who *qualify* ____ as talented artists, however, must also have a lively sense of humor. (qualify)

2. A common enemy is a great *unifier* ____ of people; there is strength in *unification* ____. (unify)

3. The late arrival of a softball team is grounds for *disqualification* ____ ; when the umpire decides to *disqualify* ____ a team, that team loses the game. (disqualify)

4. A *modifier* ____ is a word that is used to limit the meaning of, or *modify* ____ , another word. (modify)

5. Even when there is no *justification* ____ for their behavior, some people will always try to *justify* ____ themselves and their actions. (justify)

PATTERN 3: -ize, -ization, -izer

Verb	Noun	Noun
civilize	civilization	civilizer
pressurize	pressurization	pressurizer
rationalize	rationalization	rationalizer
reorganize	reorganization	reorganizer
tranquilize	tranquilization	tranquilizer
vaporize	vaporization	vaporizer

EXERCISE 21. Substitute the word given in parentheses or one of its derived forms for each blank. (The derived forms will end in *-ization* or *-izer.*)

EXAMPLE To ____ workers into a union, a large labor ____ employs an official called an ____ . (organize)

ANSWER *To **organize** workers into a union, a large labor **organization** employs an official called an **organizer.***

1. Anthropologist Margaret Mead left Western ____ *civilization* to live in several Pacific Island cultures. Mead was a student, not a ____ *civilizer*, of these cultures. (civilize)

2. Alexander Hamilton wished to ____ *centralize* the American government. His rival, Thomas Jefferson, argued against the ____ *centralization* of government. (centralize)

3. Many countries have chosen to ____ *nationalize* the operation of railroads and power companies. Early in its history the United States decided upon the ____ *nationalization* of the postal service. (nationalize)

4. In order to ____ *tranquilize* a patient before an operation, a doctor often prescribes a ____ *tranquilizer* . (tranquilize)

5. The ____ *reorganization* of ideas in a paper may be difficult once you have written a second draft. Learn to ____ *reorganize* your ideas in the formal outline. (reorganize)

PATTERN 4: -ate, -ation, -ator

Verb	Noun	Noun
accelerate	acceleration	accelerator
calculate	calculation	calculator

Verb	Noun	Noun
complicate	complication	complicator
create	creation	creator
cultivate	cultivation	cultivator
decorate	decoration	decorator
dictate	dictation	dictator

NOTE: Both -*er* and -*or* have the same meaning: "one who does." The suffix -*or* is used to form a noun from verbs that end in -*ate*.

EXERCISE 22. Substitute the word given in parentheses or one of its derived forms for each blank. (The derived forms will end in -*ation* or -*ator*.)

EXAMPLE   An interior _____ coordinates rugs, drapes, furniture, and other forms of _____ in houses and office buildings. (decorate)

ANSWER   *An interior **decorator** coordinates rugs, drapes, furniture, and other forms of **decoration** in houses and office buildings.*

1. Many high school students use a _____ *calculator* for even the simplest mathematical *calculation* _____. (calculate)

2. The best-known *creation* _____ of Walt Disney, the *creator* _____ of famous animals for cartoons and motion pictures, is probably Mickey Mouse. (create)

3. To *accelerate* _____ a car the driver steadily presses down the *accelerator* _____ . (accelerate)

4. Farmers use a *cultivator* _____ to destroy weeds on land that is under *cultivation* _____. (cultivate)

5. Many mineral waters have natural *carbonation* _____ ; you can artificially *carbonate* _____ a liquid with carbon dioxide. (carbonate)

PATTERN 5: -*ation, -er*

Verb	Noun	Noun
adapt	adaptation	adapter
fix	fixation	fixer
form	formation	former
import	importation	importer

Verb	Noun	Noun
inform	information	informer
relax	relaxation	relaxer
transport	transportation	transporter

EXERCISE 23. Substitute the word given in parentheses or one of its derived forms for each blank. (The derived forms will end in *-ation* or *-er.*)

EXAMPLE The simplest cure for sleeplessness is ＿＿＿ . An effective way to ＿＿＿ is to drink warm milk and honey. (relax)

ANSWER *The simplest cure for sleeplessness is **relaxation.** An effective way to **relax** is to drink warm milk and honey.*

1. The third step in developing photographs is to _fix_ an image permanently on the paper. The solution used in this stage is called a _fixer_ . (fix)

2. The _reformer_ Martin Luther and others who wanted to _reform_ the Roman Catholic Church eventually left the church in the period known as the Protestant _Reformation_ (reform)

3. The United States is an _exporter_ of grain. The _exportation_ of corn, soybeans, and wheat eliminates much of the country's grain surplus. (export)

4. A potter can _form_ a vase by hand or on a wheel. The method of _formation_ will affect the shape and design of the vase. (form)

5. Railroads were once the major _transporter_ of goods in the United States. Now trucks are the major form of commercial _transportation_ . (transport)

The verbs in Patterns 6–8 can be transformed into nouns *and* adjectives.

PATTERN 6: *-ion, -ive*

Verb	Noun	Adjective
affect	affection	affective
aggress	aggression	aggressive

Verb	Noun	Adjective
attract	attraction	attractive
construct	construction	constructive
correct	correction	corrective
express	expression	expressive
impress	impression	impressive
select	selection	selective

EXERCISE 24. Substitute the word given in parentheses or one of its derived forms for each blank. (The derived forms will end in *-ion* or *-ive*.)

EXAMPLE A conjunction is a _____ word. For example, the word *therefore* can be used to show a _____ between two clauses. (connect)

ANSWER *A conjunction is a **connective** word. For example, the word* therefore *can be used to show a **connection** between two clauses.*

1. In order to __construct__ a skyscraper, workers often must work at great heights on the __construction__ (construct)

2. A good fisher tries to __attract__ a fish with the bait particularly __attractive__ to that kind of fish. (attract)

3. During their conventions the Democratic and Republican parties each __select__ a candidate. The __selection__ of one of the parties will be the next President. (select)

4. People wear __corrective__ lenses to __correct__ faulty vision. (correct)

5. A weather forecast should accurately __predict__ bad weather. Unfortunately, tornadoes often escape __prediction__. (predict)

PATTERN 7: *-ion, -ive*

The verbs in Pattern 7 undergo almost the same kinds of changes as the words in Pattern 6 above. Notice, however, the spelling changes as the word moves from verb to noun.

Verb	Noun	Adjective
consume	consumption	consumptive
deceive	deception	deceptive

Verb	Noun	Adjective
decide	decision	decisive
divide	division	divisive
include	inclusion	inclusive
perceive	perception	perceptive
permit	permission	permissive
produce	production	productive
submit	submission	submissive

EXERCISE 25. Substitute the word given in parentheses or one of its derived forms for each blank. (The derived forms will end in *-ion* or *-ive.*)

EXAMPLE   Students learn how to _____ a large number by a smaller number in long _____ . (divide)

ANSWER   *Students learn how to **divide** a large number by a smaller number in long **division.***

1. Psychologists have found that children who were raised by _____ *permissive* parents give their own children _____ *permission* to act independently. (permit)

2. Some _____ *exclusive* restaurants _____ *exclude* men who are not wearing ties and jackets. (exclude)

3. The assembly line makes the mass _____ *production* of goods possible. Companies are willing to spend a great deal of money to make their factories more _____ *productive* . (produce)

4. Because cars _____ *consume* so much petroleum, the government is trying to reduce fuel _____ *consumption* in new car models. (consume)

5. A device that can _____ *transmit* electric signals through the air is used in the _____ *transmission* of radio and television programs. (transmit)

PATTERN 8: *-ence, -ent*

Verb	Noun	Adjective
adhere	adherence	adherent
persist	persistence	persistent
depend	dependence	dependent
differ	difference	different

Verb	Noun	Adjective
excel	excellence	excellent
exist	existence	existent
refer	reference	referent

EXERCISE 26. Substitute the word given in parentheses or one of its derived forms for each blank. (The derived forms will end in *-ence* or *-ent*.)

EXAMPLE French chefs are famous for their _____ sauces. In fact, French cooking sets the standard of _____ for all of Europe. (excel)

ANSWER *French chefs are famous for their **excellent** sauces. In fact, French cooking sets the standard of **excellence** for all of Europe.*

1. Human children are totally *dependent* _____ on their parents for several years. This period of *dependence* lasts longer than in any other species. (depend)

2. *Coherent* _____ writing follows a logical pattern of thought. Making an outline will help you to give a paper *coherence* _____. (cohere)

3. American English began to *diverge* _____ from British English at an early date; however, the *divergence* _____ is not wide enough to prevent understanding. (diverge)

4. Some species of insects *differ* _____ so little from one another in color and size that only an expert can tell the *difference* _____. (differ)

5. Thomas Edison was *persistent* _____ in his search for a workable electric light. His *persistence* _____ was finally rewarded in 1879. (persist)

PATTERN 9: *-ism, -ist, -istic*

Adjective or noun	Noun	Adjective
capital	capitalism, capitalist	capitalistic
expression	expressionism, expressionist	expressionistic

Adjective or noun	Noun	Adjective
human	humanism, humanist	humanistic
ideal	idealism, idealist	idealistic
modern	modernism, modernist	modernistic
natural	naturalism, naturalist	naturalistic
optimist	optimism	optimistic
real	realism, realist	realistic

EXERCISE 27. Substitute the word given in parentheses or one of its derived forms for each blank. (The derived forms will end in -*ism*, -*ist*, or -*istic*.)

EXAMPLE A truly _____ person will rarely feel disappointment, because _____ leads one to expect the worst. (pessimist)

ANSWER *A truly **pessimistic** person will rarely feel disappointment, because **pessimism** leads one to expect the worst.*

1. An _____ *optimistic* person feels that life will be better in the future than it is now. An _____ *optimist* will often try to change the way things are. (optimist)

2. A government encourages _____ *capitalism* by supporting private businesses. A _____ *capitalist* is a person who invests _____ *capital* in a privately owned business. (capital)

3. _____ *Humanism* is a system of thought in which _____ *human* interests, values, and standards are of most importance. (human)

4. An _____ *individualistic* person refuses to conform to the standards of other people and relies upon _____ *individual* values and morals. (individual)

5. _____ *Expressionism* is a style of painting that attempts the _____ *expression* of emotions. (expression)

WORD LIST FOR WRITERS

The following list contains words that you can use in your writing. These words were taken from highly respected magazine articles and television news broadcasts. Therefore, they have already proved useful to professional writers.

Most of the words on the list are given in several different related forms so that you can explore all of the possible meanings and uses of one basic word.

Keep the following points in mind as you study the list:

1. As many as six forms of a single word can be found on the list: noun, verb, adjective, present participle used as adjective, past participle used as adjective, and adverb of manner. Only those adverbs of manner that are commonly used in writing are listed, although other forms may exist. Sometimes, if more than one noun or adjective exists for a word, both are given (see page 281).

2. In order to show how participles can be used as adjectives before a noun, each participle is followed by a noun in parentheses.

3. The most familiar form of the word is the form that is defined on the list.

4. Words that have difficult meanings are followed by a sentence that demonstrates their use.

You must do more than recognize these words and know what they mean. You should feel confident about using them in your sentences and about spelling them correctly (check a dictionary whenever necessary).

Do not try to learn this list all at one time. Try learning a few words at a time, and begin with the most familiar form of the word (the form that is defined). Write a sentence using this form of the word. Then write other sentences using other forms of the word as they appear on the list.

VERB	NOUN	▲ ADJECTIVE
		● PARTICIPLES
		■ ADVERB

abolish	abolition	▲ - - -
do away with		● abolished (law)
		■ - - -

The Thirteenth Amendment *abolished* slavery in the United States.

absorb	absorption	▲ absorbent
take, drink in;	absorbent	● absorbing (story)
take all the time		● absorbed (listener)
or attention of		■ - - -

She was so *absorbed* in her work that she forgot the time.

abstain	abstinence	▲ abstinent
voluntarily	abstention	● abstaining (voter)
do without	abstainer	■ abstinently

Many of the members *abstained* from voting on the controversial proposal.

accord	accord	▲ accordant
agree;	accordance	● - - -
give, grant	*agreement*	■ accordingly

What she did was not in *accordance* with our plans.
The city *accorded* the astronaut a hero's welcome.

aggress	aggression	▲ aggressive
	aggressor	*inclined to attack*
		● - - -
		■ aggressively

alienate	alien	▲ alien
make	alienation	*strange, foreign*
unfriendly		● alienated (friend)
		■ - - -

Her bad temper often *alienated* people she met.

VERB	NOUN	▲ ADJECTIVE ● PARTICIPLES ■ ADVERB
align *bring into line;* *ally with others*	alignment	▲ - - - ● aligned (wheels) ■ - - -

In an outline, headings of the same level should be *aligned.*
Small nations often *align* themselves with larger nations for
  protection.

amend *improve;* *change*	amendment	▲ amendatory ▲ amendable ● amending (legislation) ● amended (proposal) ■ - - -

- - -	anonymity	▲ anonymous *nameless, unknown* ● - - - ■ anonymously

The person who donated the money wishes to remain
  anonymous.

assess *set the value of;* *judge*	assessment assessor	▲ - - - ● assessed (property) ■ - - -

It was hard to *assess* the effect of that issue on the campaign.

commend *entrust; recom-* *mend; praise*	commendation	▲ commendatory ▲ commendable ● commended (actor) ■ commendably

The owner of the wallet *commended* her for returning it.

compel *force*	compulsion	▲ compulsive ▲ compulsory ● compelling (reason) ■ compulsively ■ compellingly

His honesty *compelled* him to admit his mistake.

VERB	NOUN	▲ ADJECTIVE ● PARTICIPLES ■ ADVERB
concede *admit; grant*	concession	▲ - - - ● conceded (loss) ■ - - -

She was forced to *concede* that she had been wrong in her opinion of him.

conform *make or become* *the same*	conformity conformist	▲ conformable ● conforming (behavior) ■ - - -

She refused to *conform* to other people's expectations and stubbornly held her ground.

congest	congestion *overcrowding*	▲ congestive ● congested (streets) ● congesting (traffic) ■ - - -

detect *discover*	detection detective detector	▲ detectable ● detected (crime) ■ - - -

devastate *ruin, destroy*	devastation	▲ - - - ● devastating (remark) ● devastated (town) ■ devastatingly

diversify	diversity	▲ diverse *different, varied* ● diversified (business) ■ diversely

Thomas Jefferson was a man of *diverse* talents.

emerge *come out,* *develop*	emergence	▲ emergent ● emerging (beauty) ■ - - -

The bear *emerged* after months of hibernation.

VERB	NOUN	▲ ADJECTIVE ● PARTICIPLES ■ ADVERB
entice *attract*	enticement	▲ - - - ● enticing (display) ● enticed (victim) ■ enticingly

A famous poem tells how a spider *entices* a fly into its parlor.

exceed *go or be beyond; outdo*	excess	▲ excessive *too much* ● exceeding (joy) ● exceeded (goal) ■ exceedingly ■ excessively
- - -	fervor *intense emotion*	▲ fervent ● - - - ■ fervently

The candidate was always surrounded by *fervent* supporters.

- - -	flexibility	▲ flexible *easily bent or persuaded* ● - - - ■ flexibly
- - -	grandeur *splendor, nobility*	▲ grand ● - - - ■ grandly
identify *recognize to be the same*	identification	▲ identifiable ● identifying (mark) ● identified (criminal) ■ identifiably
implement *put into effect*	implement *tool, instrument* implementation	▲ implemental ● implemented (reform) ■ - - -

The executive branch of the government *implements* laws passed by Congress.

VERB	NOUN	▲ ADJECTIVE ● PARTICIPLES ■ ADVERB
inflame *excite; increase* *the intensity of*	inflammation *redness, pain, and* *swelling in a body* *part*	▲ inflammatory ● inflaming (speech) ● inflamed (mob) ■ - - -

The *inflammatory* editorial made the tense situation worse.

	ingeniousness ingenuity	▲ ingenious *clever, original* ● - - - ■ ingeniously
- - -		

His suggestion was very *ingenious*, but it did not work.

intensify	intensity	▲ intense *strong, extreme* ● intensifying (storm) ● intensified (pressure) ■ intensely

- - -	intrepidity	▲ intrepid *brave* ● - - - ■ intrepidly

The *intrepid* explorers finally reached their goal.

menace *threaten*	menace	▲ - - - ● menacing (army) ■ menacingly

- - -	nomad *wanderer*	▲ nomadic ● - - - ■ nomadically

- - -	orthodoxy	▲ orthodox *conforming to* *doctrine* ● - - - ■ - - -

The candidate held *orthodox* Republican views.

VERB	NOUN	▲ ADJECTIVE ● PARTICIPLES ■ ADVERB
parallel	parallel parallelism	▲ parallel *closely similar* ● - - - ■ - - -

The two authors reached the same conclusion by *parallel* arguments.

VERB	NOUN	▲ ADJECTIVE ● PARTICIPLES ■ ADVERB
penalize	penalty *punishment*	▲ penal ● penalized (player) ■ - - -
perpetuate	perpetuity perpetuation perpetuator	▲ perpetual *eternal, constant* ● perpetuated (rumor) ■ perpetually
reconcile *bring into* *agreement*	reconciliation	▲ reconciliatory ▲ reconcilable ● reconciling (gesture) ● reconciled (friends) ■ - - -

It was difficult to *reconcile* the two versions of the story.

VERB	NOUN	▲ ADJECTIVE ● PARTICIPLES ■ ADVERB
rely *depend, trust*	reliance	▲ reliable ● - - - ■ reliably
repute *regard*	reputation	▲ reputable *well regarded* ● reputed (wealth) ■ reputably ■ reputedly
resolve *decide, find an* *answer to*	resolve *determination* resolution	▲ resolute *determined* ● resolved (problem) ■ resolutely

The long meeting failed to *resolve* the issue.

VERB	NOUN	▲ ADJECTIVE ● PARTICIPLES ■ ADVERB
respond *answer*	response	▲ responsive *reacting easily* ● responding (letter) ■ responsively

The *responsive* audience applauded the speaker frequently.

- - -	rogue *rascal, mischiev-* *ous person*	▲ roguish ● - - - ■ roguishly

salvage *rescue*	salvage salvager	▲ salvageable ● salvaging (crew) ● salvaged (cargo) ■ - - -

We were unable to *salvage* anything from the wreckage.

savor *taste or smell;* *enjoy*	savor	▲ savory *appetizing* ● savored (aroma) ■ - - -

The team *savored* its victory for days.

- - -	solitude	▲ solitary *alone, single* ● - - - ■ solitarily

taboo *forbid*	taboo *social restriction*	▲ taboo *forbidden* ● tabooed (subject) ■ - - -

Blue jeans were *taboo* at the expensive restaurant.

tense	tension tenseness	▲ tense *stretched tightly;* *strained* ● - - - ■ tensely

VERB	NOUN	▲ ADJECTIVE ● PARTICIPLES ■ ADVERB
texture	texture *structure,* *character*	▲ textural ● - - - ■ - - -

Silk clothing has a very soft *texture.*

▬▬▬ OTHER WORDS THAT CAN HELP YOU IN WRITING ▬▬▬

The following list has been divided into nouns, verbs, and adjectives. From each of these groups, select five words at a time and use each in a sentence. Look up words that you are unfamiliar with and keep a special list of them.

VERBS

abandon
accelerate
accumulate
accuse
admire
advocate
agitate
analyze
antagonize
appall
assemble
assert
attain
attract

baffle
balk

collaborate
compare

compensate
comprehend
conceal
conclude
confront

denounce
deny
detach
detest
deviate
dismiss
disparage
distort
distract

elude
emphasize
enable
enact
enhance

enlighten
enrich
enroll
entangle
evaluate
exaggerate
exile

fascinate

illustrate
immerse
immobilize
impair
infiltrate
infuriate
insist
intend
inundate
involve
irritate

justify

lament

mock

overpower

overshadow

overwhelm

precede

ransack
refute
resent

shirk
shun
stimulate

thwart
transform

underestimate

NOUNS

afterthought
ancestor
array
audacity
awareness

beverage
bias

caricature
catastrophe
ceremony
clique
column
comment
component
composure
concept
conjecture

deluge
delusion
discrepancy

dismay
duty

embargo
enthusiasm
episode
era

facade
fantasy
flattery

headway
homage

impartiality
incentive
inequality
infection

jeopardy

mire

panacea

predecessor

regime
residence
routine
rubble

scholarship
situation
skirmish
stamina
stature
stigma
symbol

tactic
transition
trifle
triumph
turmoil
tycoon

zest

ADJECTIVES

absolute
absurd
academic
adverse

ambivalent
arbitrary
artificial
austere

boisterous

callous
candid

cantankerous
ceaseless
compatible
complacent
congenial
cordial
crucial

deliberate
discreet
dormant
drab
durable
dynamic

eccentric
erratic
eventual
evident
explicit
extravagant

festive
flawless
forcible
fruitful

glum

habitual
hectic
hideous

idealistic
immature
impeccable
imperfect
impractical
indestructible

ineffective
insufficient
invariable
inverse
involuntary
irresistible

jovial

melancholy

negligible
noble

objective
oblivious
outmoded

partisan
perfunctory
peripheral
pessimistic
petty
pious
plaintive
plausible
profound

quaint

relevant
reluctant
reminiscent
reticent
robust

sensitive
sentimental
shabby

shrewd
simultaneous
sizable
skeptical
slack
slovenly
sluggish
solitary
spacious
spontaneous
sporadic
strenuous
subjective
subservient
succinct
superstitious
susceptible

tangible
tentative
therapeutic
timid

unbearable
uncanny
unconcerned
unconditional
uncooperative
uneasy
unforeseen
unimaginative
unpredictable
unquestionable

verbal

wholesome

5

SPELLING

5 Spelling

See summary of section in Teacher's Manual.

You may have heard people complain about the problems of spelling English words. You may have heard people brag about how bad their spelling is. You may have heard the tired, old lines about famous people who were poor spellers. No matter what you have heard, you must face the fact that letters on paper (or on a computer display screen) are a common, basic, and important way of communicating. If those letters do not form meaningful words, they are useless. There is no getting away from the truth: Spelling is important. You must learn how to spell well.

Why do people have trouble spelling? What can you do to improve your spelling? Here are some suggestions:

1. *Pronounce* words carefully. If you have trouble with writing a word, you may not be *saying* it correctly. (See 5.a.)

2. Take advantage of *spelling rules.* Yes, every rule has exceptions, but it is easier to learn a basic rule and its exceptions than to treat every word as a new problem. (See 5.b.)

3. Be on the lookout for words and pairs of words that most people mix up (for example, *there* and *their*). Make a point of keeping them straight (not *strait*). (See 5.c.)

4. Use a dictionary to help you spell a word that you *almost* know but are not quite sure of. Learn how a dictionary can help you with all the forms of a word, such as its plural form or its past-tense form. (See Section 6.)

5. Always check over your answers or writing of any kind (a friendly letter, a composition, a test). Too many times a misspelling that will give your readers trouble is nothing more than carelessness. You may have been writing quickly, and you may have written *e* instead of *y*, for example, but your reader will lose time figuring out that *be* should really be *by*. In other words, *proofread.*

EXERCISE 1. Proofread the following letter written by an adult. Correct the ten misspelled words. Each error may have come about because the writer worked too quickly and did not proofread carefully.

Dear Commissioner Stroud:
    I am writting in regard to your plans concerning the expresway between Market Beach and the capital. We should approve the expresway because it would possible bring new industry to the area. I fell the expressway will give are town a chace to grow.
    Think you for letting me give by opinion on the matter.

                    Sincerly yours,
                    [name]

5.a PRONUNCIATION AND SPELLING

Letters, of course, represent sounds. Make sure that you know what a word sounds like so that you will be able to put it down on paper. If you want to write about the device that keeps rain off you, make sure that you know there are three syllables in *umbrella* (um·brel·la). Some people say the word as if it had four syllables, and as a result these people spell it wrong (umberella).

As good as your pronunciation is, however, some kinds of sounds may give you problems in writing. Here, you will study certain sounds and practice spelling words with those sounds.

5.a.1 Variant spellings of some consonant sounds

Several consonant sounds in English have more than one spelling and, as a result, may cause you difficulties as a speller. The /k/ sound, for example, can be spelled *k*, *c*, and *ck*, as in *kite*, *coach*, and *attack*. There are certain patterns, however, that can help you to know when to use *k*, *c*, or *ck*. Study the following patterns for the /f/ sound, the /j/ sound, and the /k/ sound. Learning these patterns can take much of the guesswork out of spelling consonant sounds.

SPELLING SOUNDS

1. *f, ff, gh,* or *ph*?

In general, use *ff* at the end of a one-syllable word or at the end of a syllable with a short vowel sound.

dif·fer	staff
of·fer	stiff

Use *gh* after *au* or *ou* at the end of a word or a syllable.

enough	laugh·ter
laugh	tough

Use *ph* in a few words that have come to English from Greek.

biography	graph
emphasis	photo

Use *f* in all other instances.

fifteen	prefer
from	soft

2. The /j/ sound: *j, g, ge,* or *dge*?

Initial /j/ sound
Use *j* generally at the beginning of a word or of a syllable.

jam	re·ject
joke	un·just

Use *g* for the initial /j/ sound only before *e* or *i*.

general	giant
genius	gibberish
geology	ginger

Final /j/ sound
Use *dge* after a short vowel sound.

dredge	ridge
fudge	trudge

Use *ge* generally after a long vowel sound.

huge	siege
rage	stage

---

3. The /k/ sound: *c, k,* or *ck*?

Initial /k/ sound
Use *k* before *i* or *e*.

ketchup	king

Use *c* before *a, o,* or *u*.

call	cure

Final /k/ sound
Use *ck* at the end of a one-syllable word with a short vowel sound.

back	tuck

Use *ck* at the end of a stressed syllable.

crack'·er	un·lock'

Use *c* at the end of a word with an unstressed final syllable.

a·rith'me·tic	ton'ic
met'·ric	traf'fic

EXERCISE 2. The italicized words in each of the following sentences are misspelled. Correct each misspelled word.

1. *Huf* and *puf* and blow the house down!   *huff, puff*
2. It is not *enuf* to *laff.*   *enough, laugh*
3. Do you want the star's *foto* or her *autograf*?   *photo,*
4. It is *kool* in *kamp.*   *cool, camp*   *autograph*
5. *Pik* a *pek* of *pikles.*   *Pick, peck, pickles*

5.a.2 Spelling words with silent consonants

Many English words are spelled with consonants that are not sounded, such as the *p* in *psychology,* the *k* in *know,* and the *g* in *sign.* Most of these words came to English from other languages in which these consonants were pronounced. For example, *pseudo* is pronounced as *p'se·ō̄o·dō* in Greek. As English developed, the pronunciation of these words changed, but the spelling did not.

Learning to spell words with silent consonants can sometimes be a problem. One solution is to study lists of these words until you can easily *visualize,* or picture, the correct spelling of each. Write each troublesome word several times until you can spell it automatically. You might also mentally pronounce the silent consonant so that it makes a strong impression in your mind. Study the following lists of common words. The silent consonant is in dark type.

WORDS WITH SILENT CONSONANTS

SILENT *b*: bom**b**, com**b**, de**b**t, dou**b**t, dum**b**, thum**b**
SILENT *g*: **g**nat, **g**naw, campai**g**n, rei**g**n
SILENT *gh*: dau**gh**ter, li**gh**t, mi**gh**t, thou**gh**, thou**gh**t
SILENT *h*: **c**hristen, g**h**ost, r**h**etoric, r**h**ythm, silhou-ette, ve**h**icle
SILENT INITIAL *k*: **k**nack, **k**neel, **k**night, **k**nob, **k**not, **k**nowledge
SILENT *n*: autum**n**, colum**n**, condem**n**, hym**n**, solem**n**
SILENT *p*: **p**neumonia, **p**salm, **p**sychology, rasp**b**erry
SILENT *t*: bus**t**le, Chris**t**mas, glis**t**en, hus**t**le, of**t**en, sof**t**en, wres**t**le
SILENT *w*: **w**rap, **w**reck, **w**ring, **w**rite, **w**rong, ans**w**er

EXERCISE 3. Write the following phrases and sentences, correcting any misspelled words.

1. a silouette   *silhouette*
2. a campain speech   *campaign*
3. autum leaves   *autumn*
4. Rite me.   *Write*
5. rasberry ice   *raspberry*
6. nowledge   *knowledge*
7. an old hym   *hymn*
8. mity smart   *mighty*
9. sychology   *psychology*
10. Anser!   *Answer*
11. my dauter   *daughter*
12. pumkin pie   *pumpkin*

13. a well-known salm *psalm*
14. It is doutful. *doubtful*
15. She thout so. *thought*
16. a Chrismas song *Christmas*

17. Boms away! *Bombs*
18. Colum right! *Column*
19. neumonia *pneumonia*
20. rythm *rhythm*

5.a.3 The schwa: spelling vowels in unstressed syllables

Pronounce the following words: *hun'ger, mur'mur, per'il, a·bout'*, and *ma'nor*. Each word has two syllables, one that is stressed and another that is not. The stressed syllable is the one that is pronounced with more emphasis. The unstressed syllable is given less emphasis. Each of the unstressed syllables is spelled with a different vowel. Notice, however, that all five unstressed syllables have the same sound. We call this sound **schwa** and represent it with the symbol **ə.**

There are no rules or tricks to help you to spell words containing the schwa sound. Study the following lists. If a word with a schwa sound gives you particular difficulty, try making up a mnemonic device, a trick for remembering. For example, remember that rip**en** comes from rip**e**. Write a problem word over and over again until you can spell it automatically, almost without thinking. Whenever you are in doubt, check a dictionary.

COMMON SPELLINGS OF THE SCHWA SOUND
a: **a**bove, equ**a**l, gorill**a**, leg**a**l, wom**a**n
e: ben**e**fit, cat**e**gory, **e**stablish, rip**e**n
i: def**i**nite, med**i**cine, opt**i**mism, or**i**gin, pol**i**tics
o: clam**o**r, c**o**mpose, fav**o**r, mel**o**drama, mem**o**ry
u: lux**u**ry, murm**u**r, sub**u**rb, sulf**u**r

EXERCISE 4. Write the following words, filling in the blanks with *a, e, i, o,* or *u.*

1. ben _e_ fit
2. med _i_ cine

3. cat _e_ gory
4. opt _i_ mism

5. mem _o_ ry
6. rip _e_ n
7. wom _a_ n [singular]
8. def _i_ nite
9. orig _i_ n
10. _o_ ccur
11. lux _u_ ry
12. sub _u_ rb

13. pol _i_ tics
14. c _o_ mpose
15. gorill _a_
16. _a_ bove
17. leg _a_ l
18. clam _o_ r
19. murm _u_ r
20. sulf _u_ r

5.b SPELLING RULES

A spelling rule is based on a generalization. You form a generalization when you look at many examples and see that they all have something in common. You would be able to figure out some spelling generalizations if you took the time to look at a great many words. Examine the following pages to see how other people have generalized about English spelling. They have stated their generalizations in the form of rules. You will find rules about the following:

- whether to put *i* before *e* or *e* before *i*
- adding prefixes
- adding suffixes
- spelling noun plurals
- spelling possessives

5.b.1 *IE* or *EI*?

The following rule will help you to decide when to write *ie* and when to write *ei*.

Write *i* before *e*
except after *c*
or when sounded like *a*
as in *neighbor* and *weigh*.

EXAMPLES

i before *e*	except after *c*	or when sounded like *a* as in *neighbor* and *weigh*
br**ie**f	c**ei**ling	b**ei**ge
front**ie**r	conc**ei**ted	**ei**ght
p**ie**ce	dec**ei**ve	n**ei**ghbor
rel**ie**f	rec**ei**ve	v**ei**n
shr**ie**k		w**ei**ght

EXCEPTIONS

either
l**ei**sure
n**ei**ther
w**ei**rd

EXERCISE 5. Write the following phrases, filling in the blanks with *ie* or *ei*. Check any spellings you are unsure of in the dictionary.

1. a sales rec _ei_ pt
2. the grass f _ie_ ld
3. her n _ie_ ce
4. a br _ie_ f note
5. my best fr _ie_ nd
6. a gain in w _ei_ ght
7. the cracked c _ei_ ling
8. What a rel _ie_ f!
9. a long s _ie_ ge
10. n _ei_ ther you nor I
11. terribly conc _ei_ ted
12. tug at the r _ei_ n
13. a b _ei_ ge dress
14. a black v _ei_ l
15. very w _ei_ rd
16. two dollars ap _ie_ ce
17. a loud shr _ie_ k
18. a bright chandel _ie_ r
19. a quick repr _ie_ ve
20. the western front _ie_ r

5.b.2 Adding prefixes

The spelling of a word remains the same when a prefix is added to it.

A prefix is a syllable or group of syllables that, when placed before a word, changes the meaning of that word.

The word *inexact*, for example, contains the prefix *in-*, which means "not." *Inexact*, therefore, means "not exact." When a prefix is added to a word, the spelling of the word itself does not change. Do not leave out any letters of the original word. Many words with prefixes contain double letters — one from the prefix and one from the original word. Two examples are *illiterate* and *overrule*.

EXAMPLES
in- + correct = incorrect
re- + do = redo
mis- + spell = misspell
im- + possible = impossible
dis- + satisfied = dissatisfied
un- + natural = unnatural

For a more detailed discussion of prefixes, see 4.g.

EXERCISE 6. Write the following phrases or sentences, combining the prefix in parentheses with the italicized word.

1. the *reasonable* price (un-) *unreasonable*
2. rather *social* (anti-) *antisocial*
3. *Pay* the loan. (re-) *repay*
4. totally *legal* (il-) *illegal*
5. a child of *school* age (pre-) *preschool*
6. *spelled* two words (mis-) *misspelled*
7. threatened to *appear* (dis-) *disappear*
8. the *exact* measurement (in-) *inexact*
9. a strong *action* (re-) *reaction*
10. the *possible* explanation (im-) *impossible*

11. the *necessary* comment (un-) *unnecessary*
12. highly *regular* (ir-) *irregular*
13. a *satisfied* client (dis-) *dissatisfied*
14. *legible* penmanship (il-) *illegible*
15. the *modest* dwelling (im-) *immodest*
16. the *happy* day (un-) *unhappy*
17. tastes *cooked* to me (under-) *undercooked*
18. a *historic* exhibit (pre-) *prehistoric*
19. *Heat* the coffee. (re-) *reheat*
20. *adequate* warning (in-) *inadequate*

5.b.3 Adding suffixes

A suffix is a letter, a syllable, or a group of syllables added to the end of a word. The addition either changes the function of the word or actually creates a new word.

EXAMPLES

Word	Suffix		Result
walk	+ -ed	=	walked

[The suffix *-ed* changes the function of the verb by making it a *past-tense* verb.]

annoy	+ -ance	=	annoyance

[The suffix *-ance* creates a new word from *annoy*.]

You must follow certain spelling rules when you add suffixes to words.

■ Words ending in *y*

When adding a suffix to a word that ends in a consonant + *y*, change the *y* to *i*.

EXAMPLES
pity + -ful = pitiful
silly + -ness = silliness

EXCEPTIONS
With suffixes beginning in i: **babyish, trying**
With words formed from certain one-syllable words: **dryness, shyly**

When adding a suffix to a word that ends in a vowel + *y*, generally keep the *y*.

EXAMPLES
boy + -hood = boyhood
play + -ful = playful
relay + -ing = relaying

EXCEPTIONS
day: daily
lay: laid
say: said

EXERCISE 7. Combine the following words and suffixes. Write the new words.

1. beauty + -ful *beautiful*
2. happy + -ly *happily*
3. try + -ing *trying*
4. lovely + -er *lovelier*
5. pity + -ful *pitiful*
6. easy + -ly *easily*
7. stay + -ing *staying*
8. shy + -ly *shyly*
9. study + -ous *studious*
10. buy + -er *buyer*
11. angry + -est *angriest*
12. annoy + -ance *annoyance*
13. pretty + -er *prettier*
14. dry + -ness *dryness*
15. clumsy + -ly *clumsily*
16. boy + -ish *boyish*
17. duty + -ful *dutiful*
18. play + -er *player*
19. day + -ly *daily*
20. empty + -ness *emptiness*

EXERCISE 8. Add the suffix *-ed* to the following words. Write the new words.

1. delay *delayed*
2. hurry *hurried*
3. empty *emptied*
4. carry *carried*
5. study *studied*
6. betray *betrayed*
7. cry *cried*
8. dignify *dignified*
9. worry *worried*
10. employ *employed*

■ Words ending in silent e

When adding a suffix that begins with a consonant to a word that ends in a silent *e*, generally keep the *e*.

EXAMPLES
amuse + -ment = amus**e**ment
bare + -ly = bar**e**ly
care + -less = car**e**less
move + -ment = mov**e**ment
use + -less = us**e**less

It is important to keep the *e* before each suffix in the above words in order to maintain the vowel sound of the original word and to prevent confusion with another word. Look at the word *careless*, for instance. If the final *e* in *care* were dropped, the new word would be *carless* — a word with a different sound and a different meaning.

argue + -ment = argument
awe + -ful = awful
judge + -ment = judgment
nine + -th = ninth
true + -ly = truly

When adding *y* or a suffix that begins with a vowel to a word that ends in a silent *e,* generally drop the *e.*

EXAMPLES
arrive + -al = arrival
bite + -ing = biting
hope + -ing = hoping
like + -able = likable
noise + -y = noisy
use + -able = usable

You can drop the silent *e* in *biting* because the long *i* sound remains when the vowel suffix is added. Notice, however, what happens when you add a suffix beginning with a consonant to *bite:* You must retain the silent *e* or the word becomes *bitful* instead of *biteful.*

EXCEPTIONS
In words ending in *ce* or *ge,* keep the *e* before an *a* or *o* to retain the soft *c* or *g* sound.

notice + -able = notic**e**able
advantage + -ous = advantag**e**ous

In one-syllable words ending in *ie,* change *-ie* to *y* before adding *-ing.*

lie + -ing = l**y**ing
tie + -ing = t**y**ing

EXERCISE 9. Combine the following words and suffixes. Write the new words.

1. notice + -able   *noticeable*
2. care + -less   *careless*
3. love + -able   *lovable*
4. die + -ing   *dying*
5. excite + -ment
              excitement
6. use + -ing   *using*
7. true + -ly   *truly*
8. use + -less   *useless*
9. believe + -able   *believable*
10. move + -ment   *movement*
11. hope + -ing   *hoping*
12. bare + -ly   *barely*
13. taste + -less   *tasteless*
14. live + -able   *livable*
15. awe + -ful   *awful*

16. entire + -ly   *entirely*
17. pure + -ly   *purely*
18. amuse + -ment   *amusement*
19. adore + -able   *adorable*
20. hope + -less   *hopeless*

Loveable and *liveable* are also acceptable.

■ Doubling the final consonant

Double the final consonant before a suffix beginning with a vowel (1) if the word ends in one vowel + one consonant and (2) if the word is only one syllable or is accented on the final syllable.

ONE-SYLLABLE WORD

$$\text{RUN} \quad + \quad \text{-ER} \quad = \quad \text{RU\textbf{NN}ER}$$

ends in one vowel   suffix beginning
+ one consonant   with a vowel

EXAMPLES
drip: dri**pp**ed, dri**pp**ing
hop: ho**pp**ed, ho**pp**ing
plan: pla**nn**er, pla**nn**ing
tap: ta**pp**ed, ta**pp**ing

The consonant is doubled to keep the preceding vowel sound short. *Hop,* for example, becomes *hopped* to retain the short *o* sound. If the *p* is not doubled, the word becomes *hoped,* which has a different sound and a different meaning.

EXAMPLES

tap + -ing = ta**pp**ing   *but*   tape + -ing = taping
plan + -ed = pla**nn**ed   *but*   plane + -ed = planed

TWO-SYLLABLE WORD

RE·GRET′   +   -ED   =   REGRE**TT**ED

ends in one   stress on   suffix beginning
vowel + one   final syllable   with a vowel
consonant

EXAMPLES

be·gin′: begi**nn**er, begi**nn**ing
con·trol′: contro**ll**er, contro**ll**ed, contro**ll**ing
for·get′: forge**tt**ing

Never double the final consonant if the stress does not fall on the last syllable.

EXAMPLES

co′ver: covered, covering
o′pen: opened, opener, opening

Never double a final consonant before a suffix beginning with a consonant.

EXAMPLES

commit + -ment = commitment   *but*   committed, committing, committee

win + -less = winless   *but*   winner, winning

EXERCISE 10. On your paper write these two headings: *Accent on last syllable* and *Accent on first syllable.* Write each of the following words under the proper heading. Then add -*ing* to the item, and spell the resulting word.

1 = *first syllable*   2 = *second syllable*

2	1. upset	*upsetting*	11. impel	2 *impelling*
1	2. summon	*summoning*	12. confer	2 *conferring*
1	3. shower	*showering*	13. offer	1 *offering*
1	4. ballot	*balloting*	14. equip	2 *equipping*
2	5. deter	*deterring*	15. regret	2 *regretting*
1	6. sharpen	*sharpening*	16. refer	2 *referring*
1	7. order	*ordering*	17. acquit	2 *acquitting*
1	8. profit	*profiting*	18. submit	2 *submitting*
2	9. propel	*propelling*	19. hover	1 *hovering*
2	10. allot	*allotting*	20. commit	2 *committing*

EXERCISE 11. Combine the following words and suffixes. Write the new words.

1. tan + -er   *tanner*
2. omit + -ed   *omitted*
3. differ + -ence   *difference*
4. red + -est   *reddest*
5. hum + -ing   *humming*
6. begin + -er   *beginner*
7. prefer + -ed   *preferred*
8. occur + -ence   *occurrence*
9. hit + -less   *hitless*
10. tap + -ed   *tapped*
11. happen + -ing   *happening*
12. cover + -ed   *covered*
13. forget + -ful   *forgetful*
14. forget + -ing   *forgetting*
15. admit + -ed   *admitted*
16. suffer + -ing   *suffering*
17. grip + -ing   *gripping*
18. flop + -ed   *flopped*
19. flavor + -ing   *flavoring*
20. skim + -ed   *skimmed*

EXERCISE 12. Write the following sentences, choosing the correctly spelled word from the parentheses in each one.

1. On the way out of the theater, Lynne (humed/ <u>hummed</u>) the musical theme from the show.
2. Andy tried three (beginings/<u>beginnings</u>) for his essay.
3. The rookie second baseman (commited/<u>committed</u>) two errors.

4. The students (suffered/sufferred) through exams.
5. Very few commercial planes are still driven by (propelers/propellers).

5.b.4 Spelling noun plurals

Plural simply means "more than one." In English, when you talk or write about "more than one" person, place, thing, or idea, you generally have to make a change in the ending of the noun. Usually, you just add an s to the end of the word, but there are various other spelling changes that are necessary for certain kinds of nouns. These are explained on the following chart.

SPELLING NOUN PLURALS

1. To form the plural of most singular nouns and proper nouns, add s.

    chair, chair**s**   Roth, Roth**s**
    hand, hand**s**

---

2. To form the plural of nouns ending in s, sh, ch, x, and z, add es.

    mess, mess**es**   tax, tax**es**
    bush, bush**es**   buzz, buzz**es**
    church, church**es**

---

3. To form the plural of nouns ending in a consonant + *y*, change the *y* to *i* and add *es*.

    city, cit**ies**   rally, rall**ies**

One exception is proper names:

    Kelly, Kelly**s**   Koblensky, Koblensky**s**

To form the plural of nouns ending in a vowel + *y*, add s.

    day, day**s**   toy, toy**s**
    monkey, monkey**s**   turkey, turkey**s**

---

4. To form the plural of most nouns ending in a vowel + *o*, add s.

    cameo, cameo**s**   rodeo, rodeo**s**
    ratio, ratio**s**   studio, studio**s**

To form the plural of most nouns ending in a consonant + *o*, generally add *s*, but sometimes add *es*.

cello, cello**s**	hero, her**oes**
halo, halo**s**	tomato, tomat**oes**
piano, piano**s**	veto, vet**oes**

5. To form the plural of most nouns ending in *f* and all nouns ending in *ff*, add *s*.

belief, belief**s**	huff, huff**s**
gulf, gulf**s**	staff, staff**s**

To form the plural of some nouns ending in *f* or *fe* and many nouns ending in *lf*, change the *f* to *v* and add *es*.

leaf, lea**ves**	half, hal**ves**
life, li**ves**	self, sel**ves**

6. Some nouns have irregular plural forms. They do not follow any one spelling rule. Learn the most common irregular plurals.

basis, bas**es**	man, m**e**n
crisis, cris**es**	tooth, t**ee**th
foot, f**ee**t	mouse, mic**e**
goose, g**ee**se	woman, wom**e**n

7. Some nouns have the same form in both the singular and plural.

corps, corps	series, series
deer, deer	sheep, sheep

8. To form the plural of compound nouns written as one word, add *s* or *es*.

hairbrush, hairbrush**es**	icebox, icebox**es**
handful, handful**s**	schoolbook, schoolbook**s**

To form the plural of compound words that are hyphenated or written as more than one word, make the most important part of the word plural.

editor in chief, editor**s** in chief
father-in-law, father**s**-in-law
music box, music box**es**

9. To form the plural of numerals, words, signs, and letters treated as words, add *'s*.

5**'s**	three *R***'s**
&**'s**	Mind your *p***'s** and *q***'s**

EXERCISE 13. Make the following nouns plural. You can refer to the chart on pages 307–308.

1. plant *plants*
2. fox *foxes*
3. batch *batches*
4. sofa *sofas*
5. rodeo *rodeos*
6. lunch *lunches*
7. chimney *chimneys*
8. gulf *gulfs*
9. self *selves*
10. city *cities*
11. half *halves*
12. goose *geese*
13. activity *activities*
14. tomato *tomatoes*
15. daisy *daisies*
16. commander in chief *commanders in chief*
17. loaf *loaves*
18. deer *deer*
19. cello *cellos*
20. basis *bases*
21. woman *women*
22. book *books*
23. McCloud *McClouds*
24. cameo *cameos*
25. series *series*
26. golf club *golf clubs*
27. spoonful *spoonfuls*
28. tray *trays*
29. key *keys*
30. Wisneski *Wisneskis*
31. Morris *Morrises*
32. sister-in-law *sisters-in-law*
33. trench *trenches*

EXERCISE 14. Write the following phrases, choosing the correct plural form from the parentheses in each one.

1. all my (notebooks, notesbook)
2. dangerous (reefs, reeves)
3. a flock of (sheep, sheeps)
4. visited several (countrys, countries)
5. many strong (allys, allies)
6. fried (potatoes, potatos)
7. two (mother-in-laws, mothers-in-law)
8. white clapboard (churches, churchs)
9. in the recording (studios, studioes)
10. many (activitys, activities)

EXERCISE 15. Write the following phrases and sentences, correcting any incorrectly formed plurals.

1. three grand ~~pianoes~~ *pianos*
2. the cloudy skies
3. high taxes
4. two English series
5. several ~~loafs~~ of bread *loaves*
6. many ~~crisises~~ *crises*
7. four brave ~~womans~~ *women*
8. a herd of ~~deers~~ *deer*
9. three ~~daughter-in-laws~~
10. two ~~halfs~~ *daughters-in-law halves*
11. the Greek ~~heros~~ *heroes*
12. ~~radioes~~ for sale *radios*
13. the deep valleys
14. sang many solos
15. a bunch of keys
16. the zoo's ~~monkies~~ *monkey*
17. the two armies
18. handfuls of sand
19. their attorneys
20. those bowling alleys

5.b.5 Spelling possessives

There are a few rules to follow when showing that one person or thing owns or is related to another person or thing.

Add **'s** to form the possessive of singular and plural nouns that do not end in *s*.

EXAMPLES
the woman**'s** magazine
the women**'s** magazine
Tania**'s** nieces
Bill**'s** apartment

Add an apostrophe alone—without *s*—to form the possessive of singular nouns of more than one syllable that end in *s* and of all plural nouns that end in *s*.

NOTE: It is also correct to use *'s* to form the possessive of singular nouns of more than one syllable ending in *s*: *Doris'* or *Doris's*.

EXAMPLES
Esther Williams' backstroke
the witness' memory
the girls' gymnasium
the Yankees' ace reliever

Add **'s** to form the possessive of singular nouns of one syllable ending in *s*.

EXAMPLES
Chris**'s** favorite team
the class**'s** leader

Add **'s** to form the possessive of indefinite pronouns such as *somebody* or *anyone*.

EXAMPLES
anybody**'s** guess
someone**'s** responsibility

Write personal pronouns without any apostrophes.

EXAMPLES
This is his bicycle.
This bicycle is yours.
The books are hers.

EXERCISE 16. Write the following phrases, making each italicized word possessive.

1. *Los Angeles*'roads
2. *Bette Davis*'most famous role
3. the *catcher*'s throw
4. the *Beatles*'hits
5. the *teachers*'lounge
6. *women*'s club
7. *doctor*'s fees
8. *doctors*'fees

9. *everyone*'s favorite
10. the *senator*'s staff
11. *Luis Tiant*'s fast ball
12. *others*'wishes
13. *Roy Rogers*'horse
14. the *actresses*'roles
15. my *mother-in-law*'s business
16. the *swimmers*'victories

Items 1, 2, and 13 can also take 's.

17. the *bookstore* sale
18. *James* sister
19. the *dresses* prices
20. her *boss* office
21. the *children* visit
22. *sons-in-law* business
23. a *nurse* training

Items 27 and 28 can also take 's.

24. the *catchers* records
25. the *man* promises
26. the *men* promises
27. the *actress* roles
28. the *witness* story
29. the *witnesses* stories
30. the *Davises* memories

5.c SPELLING COMMONLY CONFUSED WORDS

Homophones are words that sound alike and may cause spelling problems.

English has many pairs of words that sound exactly alike but have different meanings and different spellings. Words such as these are called homophones. For example, *hear* and *here* sound alike, but, obviously, one word has to do with ears, and one has to do with a place. Just remembering that you "use an *ear* to *hear*" may be a clue to keeping the two spellings straight. (A clue of this kind is called a mnemonic, or memory, device.)

Other pairs of words do not sound *exactly* alike but are so close in sound or spelling that they, too, may cause you problems. An example of such a pair is *quiet* and *quite*.

The following list may help you keep pairs of problem words clear in your mind. As you read through the list or use it to look up an item, complete each sample sentence. That way, you will be sure that you understand the explanations.

accept   to agree to take; to assume
except   but

    a) I gladly (accept/except) your job offer.
    b) No one (accept/except) me was qualified.

affect   to influence
effect   a result of some action

a) Scientists are studying the long-term (affect/<u>effect</u>) of exposure to microwaves.
b) Events in Washington, D.C., can (<u>affect</u>/effect) our lives in many ways.

all ways   every way
always   at all times; continually

a) The Rachal family (all ways/<u>always</u>) watches the six o'clock news.
b) Locked out, we tried (<u>all ways</u>/always) to remove the bolt from the door.

berry   a fruit
bury   to put into the earth; to cover up

a) The Castles' dog Nutmeg ran off to (berry/<u>bury</u>) her bone.
b) Those birds did not leave a single (<u>berry</u>/bury) on the bush!

capital   a city that is the seat of government
capitol   a building in which a legislature meets

a) Each day hundreds of tourists visit Washington, D.C., the nation's (<u>capital</u>/capitol).
b) The dome of the (capital/<u>capitol</u>) in our city can be seen for miles.

choose   to select
chose   the past tense of *choose*

a) Helen (<u>chose</u>/choose) a seat near the door.
b) Why do you (chose/<u>choose</u>) to sit there?

clothes [klō*th*z]   garments
cloths [klô*th*z, klôths]   fabrics

a) It used to be said that (<u>clothes</u>/cloths) make the man (and the woman!).
b) He wiped the floor with damp (clothes/<u>cloths</u>).

council   a group of advisers
counsel   advice; to give advice

    a) Our school activities are planned by a student (council/counsel).

    b) The defendant rejected his lawyer's (council/counsel) and pleaded not guilty.

creak   to make squeaking sounds; a squeaking sound
creek   a small stream

    a) Spring rains turned the (creak/creek) into a flowing stream.

    b) With each motion, the old rocking chair gave a pathetic (creak/creek).

desert [di·zurt′]   to abandon
desert [dez′ərt]   a dry, barren region
dessert [di·zurt′]   the last course of a meal

    a) The Mojave (Desert/Dessert) is in southeastern California.

    b) For (desert/dessert) we all ordered apple pie.

    c) A sentinel must never (desert/dessert) his post.

EXERCISE 17.   Write twenty brief sentences. In each sentence use correctly *one* of the commonly confused words that falls between the *accept/except* pair and the *desert/desert/dessert* group.   *Answers will vary.*

dew   light moisture in small drops
do   to act or perform
due   owed; payable; expected to arrive

    a) Terry is (dew/do/due) to arrive any minute.

    b) What are you going to (dew/do/due) on Thanksgiving?

    c) The sun glistened on the morning (dew/do/due).

for   a preposition with many meanings, including *with the purpose of*, *in favor of*, and *in place of*
fore   in front; a prominent position; in golf, a warning meaning "look out!"

four   the number between *three* and *five*

   a) The day shift at the factory ends at (for/fore/<u>four</u>) o'clock.

   b) A vote for Scaramella is a vote (<u>for</u>/fore/four) progress!

   c) The unemployment issue came to the (for/<u>fore</u>/four) early in the campaign.

formally   politely; according to custom or rule
formerly   previously (Notice the *formal* in *formally* and the *former* in *formerly*.)

   a) The new department head was (<u>formally</u>/formerly) presented to the staff at a party.

   b) She (formally/<u>formerly</u>) worked for a company in Boston, Massachusetts.

forth   forward; onward; out into view
fourth   the ordinal number between *third* (notice the *four* in *fourth*) and *fifth*

   a) This is only the (forth/<u>fourth</u>) time Kate has been skiing.

   b) Suddenly the sun burst (<u>forth</u>/fourth) from behind the clouds.

heal   to get well; to cure
heel   the rear part of the foot; the part of a shoe that is under the foot's heel
he'll   contraction of *he will*

   a) Sonia twisted her ankle when the (heal/<u>heel</u>/he'll) of her shoe caught in a grating.

   b) The doctor said her ankle would (<u>heal</u>/heel/he'll) in a week or so.

   c) (<u>He'll</u>/Heal/Heel) know more after seeing the X-rays.

hear   to be aware of sounds; to listen (Notice the *ear* in *hear*.)
here   in this place

   a) Did you (<u>hear</u>/here) *Porgy and Bess* last night on the radio?

   b) (Hear/<u>Here</u>) is my driver's license, officer.

hole   a hollow place in something solid; an opening
whole   complete

    a) Joan will be away for the (hole/<u>whole</u>) summer.
    b) Neil dropped his key down a (<u>hole</u>/whole) in the pavement.

its   belonging to *it*
it's   contraction of *it is* or *it has*

    a) (Its/<u>It's</u>) about time spring arrived!
    b) The robin flew back to (<u>its</u>/it's) nest with a worm in (<u>its</u>/it's) beak.

know   to be aware of; to be acquainted with
no   not so; the opposite of *yes;* not any

    a) Do you (<u>know</u>/no) what time we will arrive in San Antonio?
    b) Before 1973 that road had (know/<u>no</u>) speed limit.

EXERCISE 18. Write twenty brief sentences. In each sentence use correctly *one* of the commonly confused words that falls between the *dew/do/due* group and the *know/no* pair. *Answers will vary.*

later   the comparative form of *late*; after some time
latter   the second of two mentioned

    a) George should arrive (<u>later</u>/latter) in the morning.
    b) If McCann and Schwann run against each other, be sure to vote for the (later/<u>latter</u>).

loose   free; not confined; not snug
lose   to have a loss

    a) The baby's front tooth was knocked (<u>loose</u>/lose).
    b) No one expected Ruiz to (loose/<u>lose</u>) in her own district.

mail   letters and packages handled by post
male   relating to men and boys; masculine

    a) (Mail/<u>Male</u>) birds are often more colorful than female birds.
    b) Our neighbor's phone bill came in today's (<u>mail</u>/male).

moral [môr′əl]   virtuous; ethical; the lesson of a fable
morale [mə·ral′]   spirit; mental condition

a) In spite of three consecutive losses, the team's (moral/morale) remained high.
b) Mr. Burrows believes he has a (moral/morale) as well as a legal right to property.

pail   a round, open container
pale   having little light or color

a) With a (pail/pale), a towel, and a mystery novel, Rhoda set off for the beach.
b) It was her first day in the sun, and she was (pail/pale) compared to the other sunbathers.

passed   past tense and past participle of the verb *pass* (Notice the *pass* in *passed*.)
past   ended; just gone by; the time before the present

a) A great sense of relief (passed/past) over the class when the exam was postponed.
b) In the (passed/past) all students studied Latin.

peace   a period of no war; calmness
piece   a portion or part of a whole

a) An important (peace/piece) of the tape was erased.
b) The treaty of (peace/piece) was ratified by the Senate.

personal [pur′s'n·əl]   individual; private
personnel [pur·sə·nel′]   the people employed at any place of work

a) The (personal/personnel) of an orchestra changes from year to year.
b) Some players leave for (personal/personnel) reasons.

plain   simple, not fancy; a flat expanse of ground
plane   a flat surface; an airplane

a) A (plain/plane) leaves for Chicago every hour.
b) When traveling, Leo normally wears a (plane/plain) pair of slacks and a sport shirt.

principal the head of a school; greatest or first
principle a basic truth; a rule of conduct; integrity

   a) The (principal/principle) speaker was an award-winning film director.
   b) A person of (principal/principle) would never have accepted such a gift from a client.

EXERCISE 19. Write twenty brief sentences. In each sentence use correctly *one* of the commonly confused words that falls between the *later/latter* pair and the *principal/principle* pair. *Answers will vary.*

quiet making little or no noise
quite completely; very; rather

   a) All Aunt Ruth wants is a little peace and (quiet/quite).
   b) That's (quiet/quite) a lot to ask of a five-year-old nephew.

right correct; suitable; proper; opposite of left; a privilege
rite a ceremonial act or procedure
write to form letters, words, symbols on a surface

   a) Do whatever you think is (right/rite/write).
   b) Will you have time to (right/rite/write) to Louisa this evening?
   c) The marriage ceremony is a common (right/rite/write) in most cultures.

scene the place where an event occurs: a setting
seen past participle of the verb *see* (Notice the *see* in *seen.*)

   a) A crowd always gathers at the (scene/seen) of an accident.
   b) The Monet exhibit was (scene/seen) by hundreds of people.

stair one step of a stairway
stare to look intently

   a) A portrait of the ballerina hung on the wall at the top of the (stairs/stares).
   b) It is not polite to (stair/stare) at a stranger.

stationary   fixed; unmoving
stationery   writing paper and envelopes

a) My grandmother gave me monogrammed (stationary/<u>stationery</u>) for my birthday.
b) The hummingbird remained (<u>stationary</u>/stationery) in the air for a moment and then flew off.

than   in comparison with
then   at that time; next

a) Willie is two years older (<u>than</u>/then) Marie.
b) Life seemed simpler (than/<u>then</u>).

their   belonging to them
there   in that place
they're   contraction of *they are* (Notice the *heir* in *their*, both words relating to possession. See also the *here* in *there*, two words about location.)

a) (Their/<u>There</u>/They're) they are, just across the street.
b) (Their/There/<u>They're</u>) waiting for us.
c) I hope they remembered to bring (<u>their</u>/there/they're) lunch.

threw   the past tense of *throw*
through   in one side and out the other; from beginning to end; finished

a) Guidry (<u>threw</u>/through) a blazing fast ball for a third strike.
b) The ball went (threw/<u>through</u>) the infield for a base hit that drove in a run.

to   in the direction of; also used as the first word of the infinitive form of a verb
too   also; more than enough
two   the number between *one* and *three*

a) They bought (to/too/<u>two</u>) seats for the ballet.
b) She has a ticket for this performance, (to/<u>too</u>/two).
c) The three of them will go (<u>to</u>/too/two) the ballet together.

weak   not strong
week   a period of seven days

   a) The tennis tournament started on Monday and ran for the rest of the (weak/<u>week</u>).
   b) In spite of a (<u>weak</u>/week) backhand, Peg won in straight sets.

which   what one or ones; that
witch   a woman who practices magic

   a) Dorothy's house landed on the Wicked (Which/<u>Witch</u>) of the East.
   b) The (which's/<u>witch's</u>) death, (<u>which</u>/witch) made the Munchkins rejoice, was quick.

who's   contraction of *who is* or *who has*
whose   possessive case of *who*

   a) (Who's/<u>Whose</u>) sweater is missing?
   b) (<u>Who's</u>/Whose) the person who lost her sweater?

your   belonging to you
you're   contraction of *you are*

   a) (Your/<u>You're</u>) right on time.
   b) May I borrow (<u>your</u>/you're) cassette player?

EXERCISE 20. Write twenty-five brief sentences. In each sentence use correctly *one* of the commonly confused words that falls between the *quiet/quite* pair and the *your/you're* pair. Answers will vary.

REVIEW EXERCISE. Select the correctly spelled item in each pair below.

   1. a) <u>argument</u>   b) arguement
   2. a) campain   b) <u>campaign</u>
   3. a) <u>capital city</u>   b) capitol city
   4. a) <u>commitment</u>   b) committment
   5. a) <u>compose</u>   b) cumpose
   6. a) condem   b) <u>condemn</u>

7. a) kope   b) cope
8. a) daily   b) dayly
9. a) dessert island   b) desert island
10. a) disatisfied   b) dissatisfied
11. a) excitment   b) excitement
12. a) entrys   b) entries
13. a) fathers-in-law   b) father-in-laws
14. a) freind   b) friend
15. a) gentle   b) jentle
16. a) halves   b) halfs
17. a) happyness   b) happiness
18. a) It's late.   b) Its late.
19. a) It was hers.   b) It was her's.
20. a) Jame's shoes   b) James's shoes
21. a) journies   b) journeys
22. a) ladies   b) ladys
23. a) leafs   b) leaves
24. a) leisure   b) liesure
25. a) loose ends   b) lose ends
26. a) manageable   b) managable
27. a) mispell   b) misspell
28. a) offering   b) offerring
29. a) outwitted   b) outwited
30. a) oxes   b) oxen
31. a) photograph   b) fotograph
32. a) peace of pie   b) piece of pie
33. a) the plain truth   b) the plane truth
34. a) pledge   b) plege
35. a) potatos   b) potatoes
36. a) the principal reason   b) the principle reason
37. a) pumpkin   b) pumkin
38. a) recieve   b) receive
39. a) referring   b) refering

40. a) rhythm   b) rythm
41. a) rodeoes   b) rodeos
42. a) shriek   b) shreik
43. a) sipping   b) siping
44. a) sister-in-laws   b) sisters-in-law
45. a) the Smith's house   b) the Smiths' house
46. a) solos   b) soloes
47. a) theif   b) thief
48. a) vallies   b) valleys
49. a) weight   b) wieght
50. a) wisdom   b) wisedom

5.d FREQUENTLY MISSPELLED WORDS

Some English words are misspelled so often that they have come to be known as *spelling demons.* You can deal with some of these words by using pronunciation clues or spelling rules. Many, however, seem to defy any logic or rule, and simply must be memorized. You can try to make up your own *mnemonic*, or memory, devices to help you remember the spellings of many words that give you trouble.

The following list contains four hundred spelling demons. Study them ten or twenty at a time to find out which ones cause you difficulty. (Perhaps someone can say them aloud for you to spell.) Keep a list of those words that you misspell. Study them individually to fix them in your mind, your eye, and your hand.

Try to determine which part of the word gives you trouble. Say each word syllable by syllable. Make up memory devices for words that present special problems. If you sometimes forget the first *e* in *loneliness*, for example, remember that it contains the word *lone*. Become aware of your own personal spelling demons, and make an effort to learn them. Above all, know when to reach for the dictionary.

absence
accidentally
accommodate
accompany
accomplish
accuracy
accustomed
ache
achieve
acquaint
acquired
across
actually
address
adolescent
advertise
affectionate
afraid
again
aggravated
aggressive
aisle
all right
almost
alphabet
already
altogether
aluminum
always
amateur
ambassador
analysis
analyze
anonymous
answer
apology

apparent
appearance
approach
appreciate
arctic
argument
arrangement
ascend
assassinate
assistance
athletic
attendance
attitude
authority
autumn
awkward

bachelor
balloon
basically
basis
battalion
beggar
beginning
behavior
believe
benefited
boulevard
boundary
bruise
budget
build
built
business

calendar
campaign

canister
capital
capitol
cellophane
cemetery
changeable
characteristic
chief
civilization
colonel
column
comfortable
commissioner
committee
compel
competent
competition
conceive
condemn
confidential
conscience
conscious
consistent
constitution
cooperate
corporation
corps
correspond
cough
could
counterfeit
country
coupon
courtesy
criticize
cylinder

debtor
deceit
defendant
defense
deficient
definite
deny
dependent
descendant
desirable
despair
desperate
dictionary
difference
dilemma
disappearance
disappointment
disastrous
discipline
discuss
disease
disgusted
dissatisfied
distinction

eighth
elaborate
eligible
embarrass
emergency
emphasize
endeavor
environment
equipped
equivalent
essential

exaggerate
exceed
excellent
excess
excitement
exercise
exhibit
exhilarate
existence
extraordinary
extravagant

familiarize
fascinating
fatal
fatigue
favorable
February
fictitious
fiend
financier
flourish
forehead
foreign
forfeit
forty
fourteen
friend
fulfill

gaiety
gauge
gorgeous
government
gracious
grammar

grief
guarantee
guess
guidance
gymnasium
gypsy

handicapped
handkerchief
happiness
height
heroes
humorous
hygiene
hypocrite

icy
ignorance
immediate
immense
impossible
incidentally
inconsistent
incredible
inevitable
innocent
inquire
insistence
install
installment
intellectual
intelligent
interfere
interpret
interrupt
irresistible

jewelry
judgment

kerosene
knew
know
knowledge

laboratory
leisure
library
license
lieutenant
lightning
likelihood
literature
livelihood
liveliness
loneliness
lovable
luxurious

magnificent
maintain
maneuver
marriage
mathematics
meant
millionaire
miniature
minute
minimum
miscellaneous
missile
misspell
modern
mortgage

mosquitoes
muscle

narrative
necessary
neighbor
neither
nickel
niece
ninety
ninth
noticeable
noticing
nuclear
nuisance

occasionally
occur
occurred
occurrence
offense
official
often
omission
omitted
once
opponent
opportunity
orchestra

pamphlet
parallel
paralyze
parliament
pastime
peasant
peculiar

penicillin
perceive
perform
permanent
permissible
persistent
personal
perspiration
persuade
phenomenon
picnic
picnicking
pleasant
pneumonia
pollution
Portuguese
possession
possible
practice
precede
precedent
preference
preferred
pressure
primitive
privilege
proceed
process
professor
pronunciation
propeller
proportion
psalm
psychology

questionnaire
quiet

quite

realize
receipt
receive
recognize
recommend
reference
referred
regrettable
reign
relevant
remembrance
reminisce
repentance
repetition
representative
resistance
responsibility
restaurant
rhyme
rhythm
roommate

satellite
scene
schedule
scheme
scissors
secretary
seize

senate
separate
sergeant
several
shepherd
sheriff
shriek
siege
significance
silhouette
similar
solemn
specimen
sponsor
subtle
succeed
successful
sufficient
sugar
summary
superstitious
suppress
sure
syllable

technique
tendency
thorough
though
through
tomorrow

tonight
tortoise
tough
tournament
traffic
transferred
trespass
trouble
truly
twelfth

unanimous
uncontrollable
unnecessary
usage
useful
using

vacuum
various
vehicle
veteran
villain

Wednesday
weird
whole
women

yacht

zinc

EXTRA: As a diagnostic dictation exercise, read aloud the following
sentences, which contain a number of frequently misspelled words:
"Correct spelling is definitely important, for the occurrence of any
quantity of familiar words spelled incorrectly is truly noticeable.
One hopes that you have benefited from this diagnostic quiz. Now,
correct the misspelled words."

THE DICTIONARY

6 The Dictionary

See summary of section in Teacher's Manual.

Using the dictionary will help you to read, speak, and write more effectively. In the dictionary you will find information about spelling, punctuation, meaning, and usage. You can also use the dictionary as a research tool for quick reference to general information. This section will tell you the most efficient ways to use the dictionary when you read, speak, write, and do research.

There are three basic kinds of dictionaries: the unabridged dictionary, the college dictionary, and the school dictionary. This section discusses the school dictionary in detail because you will probably use the school dictionary most at this stage of your education.

The unabridged dictionary is the largest of the three basic kinds of dictionaries. Because people constantly create new words, no dictionary can list every word in the English language; however, the unabridged dictionary contains most of the words now in use — 450,000 of them. The word *unabridged* means "complete; not shortened." There are several unabridged dictionaries that may be available in your school or township library. Two of the most popular unabridged dictionaries are *Webster's New International Dictionary* and the *Random House Dictionary of the English Language: Unabridged Edition.*

A college dictionary, which contains about 150,000 words, is an abridged, or shortened, dictionary. A college dictionary contains less detailed information than an unabridged dictionary.

School dictionaries are similar to college dictionaries. The school dictionary, however, is directed to your needs as students. The school dictionary has fewer entries, and the definitions reflect your own ideas and experiences.

Compare the following entries for the same word taken from each of the three different kinds of dictionaries.

entry word pronunciation

stu·dent (stŏod′ənt, stūd′-) *n.* **1.** person enrolled in or attending a school, college, or university. **2.** one devoted to study or investigation of a particular subject: *a student of language.* [Latin *studēns,* present participle of *studēre* to be eager or diligent, apply oneself to learning.] }definitions }word origin

School Dictionary: *Macmillan Dictionary*

pronunciation

entry word — **stu·dent** (stŏod′'nt, styŏod′-) *n.* [ME. *studiante, studente* < OFr. & L.: OFr. *estudiant* < L. *studens,* prp. of *studere,* to STUDY] **1.** a person who studies, or investigates *[a student* of human behavior*]* **2.** a person who is enrolled for study at a school, college, etc. —*SYN.* see PUPIL[1] }word origin }definitions

synonym information

College Dictionary: *Webster's New World Dictionary of the American Language*

pronunciation

entry word — **stu·dent** \'st(y)üd²nt\ *n* -s *often attrib* [ME, fr. L *student-, studens,* fr. *student-, studens,* pres. part. of *studēre* to be eager, be diligent, study — more at STUDY] **1 :** a person engaged in study **:** one devoted to learning: as **a :** one enrolled in a class or course in a school, college, or university **:** PUPIL **b :** one who independently carries on a systematic study or detailed observation of a subject ⟨a ~ of human nature⟩ ⟨to ~*s* of ships and the sea, the Museum offers a valuable library —Dana Burnet⟩ **2** *often cap* **:** a member of a university foundation (as at Christ Church, Oxford) }word origin

definitions —

example of word in use

Unabridged Dictionary: *Webster's Third New International Dictionary*

By permission. From *Webster's Third New International Dictionary*© 1976 by G.&C. Merriam Co., publishers of the Merriam-Webster dictionaries.

The entries become more detailed as you move from a school to a college to an unabridged dictionary.

6.a INFORMATION FOR READERS: DEFINITIONS

As a reader, you will use the dictionary to look up the definitions of words. Some words have only one meaning, but most words have more than one meaning. A dictionary entry lists all the definitions of a given word. After you look up a word, read through *all* the definitions. Then, decide which definition makes the most sense in the context of what you are reading.

All standard dictionaries give similar definitions, but the definitions do not always appear in the same order. Some dictionaries list the oldest definitions first and then move on to the more recent meanings of the word. Other dictionaries list definitions according to how frequently they are used, starting with the most common definition and moving on to the least common definition.

Nearly all dictionaries group together a word's definitions by part of speech. The definitions of one word used as a noun are grouped together; the definitions of the same word used as a verb are grouped together; and so on. Following is a list of the parts of speech and their abbreviations that may be used in a dictionary entry.

noun	n.
transitive verb	v. t. *or* vt.
intransitive verb	v. i. *or* vi.
adjective	adj.
adverb	adv.
pronoun	pron.
preposition	prep.
conjunction	conj.
interjection	interj.

Look at the entry for *pop*[1] on page 331. The definitions are grouped according to part of speech. Then, within each group, they are listed from most common meaning to least common meaning.

entry word——— **pop¹** (pop) **popped, pop·ping.** *v.i.* **1.** to make a short, sharp, explosive sound: *The champagne cork| popped when the bottle was opened.*
2. to burst open or explode with such a sound: *The corn popped quickly.*
definitions of **3.** to move, go, appear, or come quickly, suddenly, or unexpectedly: *to*
pop used as *pop out of bed. She popped in to see us yesterday.* **4.** (of the eyes) to open
intransitive verb wide, esp. suddenly, so as to protrude or start from the sockets: *Their eyes popped when they heard the news.* **5.** to shoot a firearm. **6.** *Baseball.* to hit a pop fly (often with *out* or *up*). —*v.t.* **1.** to cause to burst with a short, sharp, explosive sound. **2.** to put or thrust quickly, suddenly,
definitions of or unexpectedly: *She popped the bread into the oven. He popped his head*
pop used as *out the window.* **3.** *Baseball.* to hit (the ball) high into the air into or
transitive verb near the infield, in such a manner that an opposing player can catch it before it touches the ground. **4. to pop the question.** *Informal.* to propose marriage, esp. suddenly or unexpectedly. —*n.* **1.** short, sharp, explosive sound. **2.** flavored, nonalcoholic, carbonated beverage; soda.
definitions of——— —*adv.* **1.** with a pop. **2.** suddenly; unexpectedly. [Imitative.]
pop used **pop²** (pop) *adj. Informal.* of, relating to, or designating popular music:
as adverb *a pop singer, a pop concert.* [Short for POPULAR.]

—*Macmillan Dictionary*

Homographs are words that are spelled the same way but that have different origins and different meanings. English has a large number of homographs. In a dictionary homographs appear as separate entries with superscripts, or raised numbers. In the above entry *pop¹* and *pop²* are homographs. *EXTRA: Ask students to look up in a dictionary and write two sentences showing the meanings of the following homographs:*

■ **Alphabetical order** *invalid, bow, desert, present, stern.*

The words in a dictionary are listed in alphabetical order. In addition to whole words you will find commonly used abbreviations, such as *U.S.A.* and *lb.* When you look up an abbreviation in the dictionary, consider the letters of the abbreviation as letters in a word. For instance, *ft.* follows *f stop* and comes before both *FTC* and *fuchsia.*

f stop, any of the settings for the f number of a camera.
ft. **1.** feet; foot. **2.** fort. **3.** fortification.
FTC, Federal Trade Commission.
fuch·sia (fū′shə) *n.* **1.** any shrub or small tree, genus *Fuchsia,* of the evening primrose family, native to tropical America, bearing pink, red, or purple clusters of funnel-shaped, usually drooping flowers. **2.** bright purplish-pink color. [Modern Latin *Fuchsia,* from Leonhard *Fuchs,* 1501–66, a German botanist.]

—*Macmillan Dictionary*

EXTRA: Ask students to look up in a dictionary the abbreviations listed in 7.a.8 and to write them with the dictionary entries that precede and follow them.

In addition to such abbreviations as *ft.* and *FTC,* the dictionary lists scientific and mathematical abbreviations, such as *Mg* (magnesium) and *cos* (cosine).

EXERCISE 1. Look up the word *house* in a dictionary. Copy from your dictionary the definition of *house* that best fits the use of the word in each sentence below.

1. There was a full *house* for tonight's concert. *audience*
2. We will have the party at my *house.* *dwelling*
3. The Congresswoman entered the *House.* *legislative building*
4. Queen Elizabeth II is a member of the *House* of Windsor. *royal line or family*
5. The turtle carries its *house* on its back. *shelter*
6. The *House* voted on the bill yesterday. *legislative body*
7. The whole *house* came down with the flu. *household*
8. That banking *house* is one hundred years old. *place of business*
9. The administration is building another fraternity *house* on campus. *building*
10. The reptile *house* is always popular at the zoo. *shelter*

EXERCISE 2. Arrange the following words and abbreviations in alphabetical order as they would appear in the dictionary. Look up any words or abbreviations that you do not understand.

3	hockey	*4*	impulse
5	in.	*2*	festival
9	united	*10*	U.S.A.
1	Fe	*6*	iron
8	prove	*7*	Pg.

6.b INFORMATION FOR SPEAKERS: PRONUNCIATION

You cannot always tell how to pronounce a word from the way it is spelled. If you want to know how to pronounce a word, a dictionary can help. Directly following each entry word you will find its pronunciation given in symbols (either in parentheses or between slanted lines).

Spoken English is made up of approximately forty-five sounds, but written English uses only the twenty-six letters of the alphabet. Dictionaries use phonetic (sound) symbols to indicate sounds for which the English alphabet has no individual letters. Each phonetic symbol stands for only one sound. Phonetic symbols include diacritical marks and the schwa. Diacritical marks, which combine with letters to indicate various sounds, include the following:

••	as in /kär/ for *car*	¯	as in /mēt/ for *meet*
⌃	as in /lô/ for *law*	¯	as in /bīt/ for *bite*
¯	as in /dāt/ for *date*	ə	as in /ə gō/ for *ago*

The schwa (ə) represents an unaccented vowel sound that is used constantly in English. For example, the schwa stands for the following:

the *a* in *above* (ə buv′)   the *o* in *lemon* (lem′ən)
the *e* in *agent* (a′jənt)   the *u* in *circus* (sur′kəs)
the *i* in *sanity* (san′ə tē)

To complicate matters, different dictionaries use different phonetic symbols. If you look up the word *moody* in three different dictionaries, you will find the following:

mood·y (mōō′dē)   *Macmillan Dictionary*
moo dy (mü′dē)   *Thorndike Barnhart Advanced*
                              Dictionary
moody \‘müdē, di\   *Webster's Third New*
                              International Dictionary

You must check the pronunciation key in your dictionary to interpret its phonetic symbols. All dictionaries include a complete pronunciation key. You should become familiar with the phonetic symbols used in your dictionary, but you do not need to memorize them, since you can always refer to the pronunciation key.

■ Stress

A word written in phonetic symbols is usually broken into syllables. When a word has two or more syllables, one syllable is generally spoken louder, or with more *stress.* The stressed syllable is marked with a *primary accent mark.* A word that has more than one stressed syllable is shown with a primary accent and a *secondary,* or weaker, *accent mark.*

> an·ces·try (an′ses′trē)
> tol·er·ate (tol′ə rāt′)

—*Macmillan Dictionary*

■ Variant pronunciations

Sometimes a word has more than one acceptable pronunciation. Dictionaries list the most widely used pronunciation first, usually followed by the less common pronunciations, called **variants.** For example, the word *apricot* can be pronounced /ā′prə kot′/ or /ap′rə kot′/.

Many words can be used as more than one part of speech; for example, a word can be used as a noun and as a verb or as an adjective and as an adverb. Sometimes the pronunciation of a word varies depending on its part of speech. Symbols such as *n., v., adj.,* and *adv.* placed before the pronunciation of a word indicate for what part of speech the pronunciation is used.

> con·trast (*v.,* kən trast′; *n.,* kon′trast)

—*Macmillan Dictionary*

EXERCISE 3. Look up each of the following words in a dictionary. Give one definition of the word, and pronounce it correctly. *Answers are given at the back of the Teacher's Manual.*

1. seine	6. gnu
2. idyll	7. nonagenarian
3. extrapolate	8. revanchism
4. rescind	9. Ilium
5. vociferous	10. denouement

EXERCISE 4. Each of the following words has two different pronunciations, depending on its part of speech. Look up each word in a dictionary, and copy down its two different pronunciations and parts of speech. *Answers are given at the back of the Teacher's Manual.*

1. frequent
2. reject
3. contract
4. moderate
5. designate

6. project
7. perfect
8. expert
9. deliberate
10. object

6.c INFORMATION FOR RESEARCHERS

The dictionary provides a great deal of information for researchers, such as biographical information and scientific descriptions. Most dictionaries begin with essays on language, and many contain a diagram showing the history of the languages that gave birth to English.

■ Word origins (etymologies)

Words have histories, just as countries and people do. Many English words had their beginnings in French, German, Latin, ancient Greek, and other languages. Knowing the **etymology,** or history, of a word may give you a better understanding of the spelling or pronunciation of the word and may help you to remember its present meaning. In a dictionary the etymology of a word is usually printed inside brackets as part of the word's definition. The etymology gives the earliest known spelling and meaning of the word. As an example, the etymology, or word origin, for *student* is given in each entry on page 329.

If your dictionary uses abbreviations of languages in its etymologies — for example, *L.* (Latin) and *ME.* (Middle English) — you can look up their meanings in the list of abbreviations usually located at the beginning of the dictionary.

■ People

Most dictionaries include the names of famous people as well as a line or two of biographical information. Names of famous people are either included in the main alphabetical listings or listed together in a separate section. Under the person's name you will find the spelling and pronunciation of first and last names, the dates of birth and death, nationality, and the reason for fame.

■ Places

Most dictionaries list the names of countries, states, important cities, mountains, rivers, and other geographical features. Like names of famous people, places are either included in the main alphabetical listing or grouped together in a separate section. Under the place name you will find the spelling and pronunciation of the name; its abbreviations (such as *Tex.* for *Texas*); relevant data such as area, population, or height; and its historical or political significance.

■ Science

Many dictionaries give the descriptions and scientific names of plants and animals. For instance, the following dictionary entry gives a brief description of the giant panda and tells you that its scientific name is *Ailuropoda melanoleuca.*

entry word   scientific name

giant panda a large, black-and-white, bearlike mammal
description ——— (*Ailuropoda melanoleuca*) of China and
Tibet that feeds on bamboo shoots

GIANT PANDA
(4 ft. high at
shoulder)

*—Webster's New World Dictionary of the
American Language*

EXERCISE 5. Look up the etymology of each of the following words, and explain how its present meaning is related to its original meaning. *Answers are given at the back of the Teacher's Manual.*

1. finance
2. armadillo
3. raccoon
4. opinion
5. dinosaur
6. father
7. macadam
8. conglomerate
9. pedal
10. enemy

6.d INFORMATION FOR WRITERS

As a writer, you should consider the dictionary as one of your most valuable resources. Using the dictionary while writing will help you to spell and capitalize properly, to know the proper division of syllables for the purpose of hyphenation, to know the proper usages of words, and to find synonyms for words that you already know.

6.d.1 Spelling

Some words have more than one acceptable spelling. Often the British spelling of a word differs from the American spelling. The entry word in the dictionary shows the most common spelling. The alternative spellings — called **variants** — are printed next to the entry word. See the example for *ketchup,* below. If a word has variant spellings, you may use any of them as long as you spell the word the same way throughout your composition.

entry word
|

ketch·up (kĕch'əp, kăch'-) *n.* Also **catch·up** (kăch'əp, kĕch'-), **cat·sup** (kăt'səp, kăch'əp, kĕch'-). A condiment consisting of a thick, smooth-textured, spicy sauce usually made with tomatoes. [Malay *kechap,* from Chinese (Amoy) *kōetsiap, kētsiap,* brine of fish : *kōe,* minced seafood + *tsiap,* brine, sauce, juice, corresponding to Mandarin Chinese *chih³.*]

variant spellings

—The American Heritage Dictionary of the English Language

Inflected forms of a word are the forms that show *plural, time* (or *tense*), and *degree.*

plural of nouns	time (or tense) of verbs	degrees of adjectives
goal	**dash**	**low**
goals	dashed	lower
	dashing	lowest
party	**steal**	**lucky**
parties	stole	luckier
	stolen	luckiest
	stealing	

The inflected forms *goals, dashed, dashing, lower,* and *lowest* are formed regularly, simply by adding an ending to the base word. These regular forms do not appear in the dictionary.

In general, the dictionary includes any inflected forms that are irregular or that might be in doubt. The inflected forms of *party, steal,* and *lucky,* therefore, appear in the dictionary after the entry word. See the example of *lucky,* below. The inflected forms given are the comparative and superlative forms of the adjective.

entry word   inflected forms

luck·y (luk′ē) **luck·i·er, luck·i·est.** *adj.* **1.** having good luck; fortunate. **2.** occurring happily or fortunately. **3.** thought to bring good luck. —**luck′i·ness,** *n.*

—*Macmillan Dictionary*

Check your dictionary whenever you are uncertain about the spelling of inflected forms. If the dictionary does not give an irregular form of a word, then you can safely add the regular endings without any additional spelling changes.

EXERCISE 6. Look up each of the following words in a dictionary, and write down its variant spelling.

1. catalog *catalogue*
2. pedlar *peddler*
3. pell-mell *pellmell*
4. coconut *cocoanut*
5. epaulet *epaulette*

EXERCISE 7. Use a dictionary to find the correct spelling of each of the following items.

1. the comparative degree of the adjective *thin*, meaning "more thin" *thinner*
2. the past tense of the verb *burst* *burst*
3. the superlative degree of the adjective *crafty*, meaning "most crafty" *craftiest*
4. the plural of the noun *hippopotamus* *hippopotamuses,-mi*
5. the plural of the noun *ox* *oxen*

6.d.2 Syllabification

Dictionaries usually separate the syllables of the entry word with a dot, a dash, or a space. In general, if you must break a word at the end of a line of writing, break it between the syllables shown for the entry word in the dictionary.

EXERCISE 8. Show all the points at which you can hyphenate each of the following words. Use a dictionary to check your answers.

1. slumber *slum-ber*
2. goldenrod *gold-en-rod*
3. governor *gov-er-nor*
4. kangaroo *kan-ga-roo*
5. clarinet *clar-i-net*
6. spelling *spell-ing*
7. routine *rou-tine*
8. speedometer *speed-om-e-ter*
9. separate *sep-a-rate*
10. graceful *grace-ful*

6.d.3 Capitalization

The dictionary will help you to capitalize words correctly. Some words, like *Olympics*, always begin with a capital letter. Other words are capitalized only when they refer to something specific or are part of a proper noun or adjective. For example, the word *house* is not ordinarily capitalized, but when it names certain buildings or a legislative body — the *House of Representatives*, for instance — it is capitalized. Some dictionaries use the abbreviation *cap.* to indicate that a certain use of a word is capitalized. Other dictionaries simply capitalize the word within the entry, as shown below. Notice that the capitalized word *Democrat* is used as a proper noun.

entry word

dem·o·crat (dem′ə krat′) *n.* **1.** one who believes in or advocates democracy as a principle of government. **2.** one who believes in and practices political and social equality. **3. Democrat.** member of the Democratic Party.

usage
capitalized

—*Macmillan Dictionary*

Sometimes the abbreviation *not cap.* ("not capitalized") appears in a dictionary entry. *Not cap.* indicates that a word that is normally capitalized — *Cupid*, for instance — may also be written without a capital letter to signify a common noun.

EXERCISE 9. Using the dictionary, write two sentences for each of the following words. One of the sentences should contain the capitalized word. The other sentence should contain the uncapitalized word. (Do not use the word at the beginning of the sentence.) *Answers will vary; an example is given below.*

1. thanksgiving
2. derby
3. Ottoman
4. Java
5. liberal
6. pariah
7. republican
8. company
9. senate
10. Angora

We gathered for Thanksgiving dinner.
Grandmother recited a prayer of thanksgiving.

6.d.4 Special labels

Subject labels and **usage labels** are used in dictionary definitions to direct your attention to the special uses of a word. Subject labels include such topics as *Classical Mythology, Chemistry, Tennis, Music,* and *Medicine.* A meaning that follows one of these subject labels applies only to that subject. For example, within the definitions for *fall,* you will find a special meaning after the subject label *Wrestling.* In wrestling a *fall* is "the act of throwing and holding an opponent on his back with both shoulders on the mat for a specified number of seconds."

Usage labels include *Colloquial, Conversational, Informal, Slang, British,* and *Archaic* (a word or meaning that is no longer in use). Note the usage label for *pop*² on page 331.

EXERCISE 10. Look up each of the following words in a dictionary, and look for subject and usage labels among the definitions. Write down the label and the special meaning of the word. *Answers are given at the back of the Teacher's Manual.*

1. bully	6. lob
2. nifty	7. fat
3. drive	8. ere
4. fault	9. careful
5. jellyfish	10. perpendicular

6.d.5 Synonyms

Synonyms are words that have nearly the same meaning. As a writer, you use synonyms to avoid using the same words again and again. Most dictionaries provide a list of synonyms under the abbreviation *Syn.* at the end of many entry words. Some dictionaries even include short discussions that point out small differences among the meanings of the synonyms.

EXERCISE 11. Look up each of the following words in a dictionary. Write the synonyms listed for each word. *One example for each is given below.*

1. give (verb) *grant*
2. fight (noun) *struggle*
3. play (verb) *frolic*
4. kind (adjective) *benign*
5. pull (verb) *tug*
6. poor (adjective) *destitute*
7. empty (adjective) *vacant*
8. fault (noun) *foible*
9. fashion (noun) *fad*
10. mix (verb) *blend*

REVIEW EXERCISE. Use your dictionary to answer each of the following items.

1. Show the ways that you can divide the word *disintegration* at the end of a line. *dis-in-te-gra-tion*
2. What is the plural of *mosquito*? *mosquitoes, -os*
3. What is the scientific name of the whale? *Cetacea*
4. What languages contributed to the English noun *jury*? *Latin, Old French, Old Irish, Middle English, Indo-European*
5. What definition of the word *motor* has a special meaning (usage) in Great Britain? *to convey by automobile (verb)*
6. In what country is the city Hanover? *Germany*
7. What is the slang meaning for *neat*? *terrific*
8. What is a synonym for the noun *effect*? *result*
9. Write two sentences using the word *mature.* In the first use *mature* as an adjective. In the second use *mature* as a verb. *Answers will vary.*
10. Write the definition of *key* that describes a place where you might find a jellyfish. *a reef or low island*

7

CAPITALIZATION AND PUNCTUATION

7 Capitalization and Punctuation

See summary of section in Teacher's Manual. See Additional Exercises 14 and 15 (pages 658-659) for more practice in capitalization and punctuation.

Why should you and all writers of English follow certain rules? Remember, most of your writing is eventually going to be read by at least one other person. You have to do everything possible to help that person get the meaning of your writing. You have a better chance of making your meaning clear if you keep four principles in mind:

1. Write complete sentences. (See Sections 2 and 3.)
2. Spell correctly. (See Section 5.)
3. Use the correct forms of words. (See Sections 1 and 4.)
4. Punctuate your sentences carefully, and capitalize words appropriately.

This section will help you with the fourth principle. It explains and gives many examples of why and when you should use each punctuation mark and capital letters. It tells you how and when to use two punctuation marks together. It points out common errors that you should avoid.

After you finish a piece of writing, remember to check very carefully for the proper use of punctuation and capitalization. The process of checking is called *proofreading.*

7.a CAPITALIZATION

Capital letters are also called upper-case letters. Small letters are also called lower-case letters. When you started to write, you may have used *only* capital letters. By now, though, you are aware of the advantages of having the two styles — capital letters and lower-case letters — for each letter in the alphabet. Here, you can review and practice the special uses of capital letters.

7.a.1 Capitalization of sentences

Capitalize the first word of a sentence.

Baseball is often called "the national pastime."
Why did he say that?
She asked him why he said that.
We laughed when he answered.
Speak clearly.

EXERCISE 1. Rewrite the following passage, correcting all errors in capitalization. (You will find ten errors. Not every sentence has an error.)

¹In the early 1880s an insulting article entitled "What Girls Are Good For" appeared in the *Pittsburgh*
T *Dispatch.* ²the article made one teen-aged reader very
T angry. ³this reader's letter of complaint so impressed the editors of the *Pittsburgh Dispatch* that they hired her as a reporter. ⁴Writing under the false name Nellie
t Bly, The young woman soon became a famous reporter
E for the *New York World.* ⁵everyone wanted to read
I Nellie Bly's stories. ⁶in order to obtain material for her
S stories Nellie Bly took great risks. ⁷she once threw her-
t self into the Hudson River To find out how efficient the rescue team was. ⁸For other stories Nellie Bly pretended to be a mentally disturbed woman. ⁹By the age
a of twenty-three Nellie Bly was world famous, And her
M stories had brought about many changes. ¹⁰many people thought that Nellie Bly was a team of male report-
b ers, But she was Elizabeth Cochrane from Pittsburgh, Pennsylvania.

7.a.2 Capitalization of direct quotations

Capitalize the first word of a direct quotation that is a complete sentence (see 7.l.1).

Eleanor Roosevelt wrote, "**N**o one can make you feel inferior without your consent." [The quotation could stand alone as a sentence.]

Do not capitalize the first word of a direct quotation that is only part of a sentence.

President Lincoln urged his audience to heal "**t**he nation's wounds." [The quotation is part of a sentence.]

7.a.3 Capitalization of lines of poetry

Traditionally, poets and songwriters have capitalized the first word of each line. Many modern poets no longer follow this custom, however.

Full fathom five thy father lies;
Of his bones are coral made;
Those are pearls that were his eyes.

—William Shakespeare

7.a.4 Capitalization of the pronoun *I* and the interjection *O*

Capitalize the pronoun *I* and the interjection *O*.

O is used mainly in poetry and religious writing. The interjection *oh* is less formal. *Oh* is not capitalized unless it occurs at the beginning of a sentence or a line of poetry.

Because **I** was late, **I** missed the opening kickoff.

If we must die, **O** let us nobly die.   —Claude McKay

We flew over the Grand Canyon — **o**h, what a sight!

EXERCISE 2. Rewrite each of the following sentences, correcting the errors in capitalization.

1. Patrick Henry summed up the American spirit when he said, "give me liberty, or give me death." *G*

2. Newspaper editor William Allen White wrote, "liberty is the one thing you cannot have unless you are willing to give it to others." *L*

3. Gertrude Stein wrote the following comment: "in the United States there is more space where nobody is than where anybody is." *I*

4. Social critic Jessica Mitford wrote that everything is "Much faster in America." *m*

5. Writer Oriana Fallaci wrote, "America's a hard school, I know, but hard schools make excellent graduates." *I*

7.a.5 Capitalization of proper nouns

Capitalize a proper noun.

Remember that a proper noun is the name of a particular person, place, or thing (see 1.a.1). For example, the proper noun *Nigeria* is the name of a particular country in Africa. The word *country,* on the other hand, is a common noun, or the name of a general class of things.

Proper nouns	Common nouns
Virginia	**s**tate
Nancy **L**opez	**g**olfer
the **H**awaiian **I**slands	**i**slands
Lake **O**ntario	**l**ake
Agatha **C**hristie	**w**riter
Our *Town*	**p**lay

In proper nouns of more than one word, capitalize only the important words. Do not capitalize articles, conjunctions, or prepositions of fewer than five letters.

Treaty of **P**aris	**W**illiam the **C**onqueror
Secretary of **S**tate	**C**ollege of **W**illiam and **M**ary

Some of the kinds of proper nouns are listed below.

1. names of people and animals

Theodore Roosevelt	Sequoyah
Marian Anderson	Billie Jean King
Robert Frost	Lassie

2. titles of people
Capitalize titles used before a name.

Senator Hayakawa	Prime Minister Margaret
King George III	Thatcher
Governor Ella Grasso	Pope John Paul II

Do not capitalize titles used alone or used after a name unless you wish to show respect or unless the person is a high official. For example, always capitalize the word *President* when you refer to the President of the United States.

Mayor Jane Byrne	*but*	duties of the mayor
Henry Kissinger,	*but*	Linda Lee, secretary
Secretary of State		of the committee
the Vice President	*but*	the vice president
of the United States		of our bridge club

Capitalize titles of family relationships when they are used before a name or in place of a name. Do not capitalize a word of family relationship if a possessive pronoun is used before it (unless the word is considered part of a name).

What did you say, Mother?	*but*	Sarah's mother
a gift for Dad	*but*	his dad
I saw your Aunt Maria.	*but*	I saw your aunt.

3. names of nationalities, ethnic or regional groups, and languages

Italians	Native Americans
a Mexican	French
the Japanese	Swahili
a Texan	Greek

4. organizations, institutions, government bodies, political parties and their members, business firms

American Bar Association
Girl Scouts of America
University of Kansas
House of Representatives

Democratic party
a Republican
Exxon Corporation
Eastern Airlines

5. buildings, monuments, bridges, dams

White House
Independence Hall
Astrodome
Detroit Plaza Hotel

World Trade Center
Lincoln Memorial
Walt Whitman Bridge
Grand Coulee Dam

6. trade names

Pepsi
Kleenex

Rice Krispies
Chevrolet

Do not capitalize a common noun that follows a trade name.

Texaco station   Maxwell House coffee

7. documents, awards, laws

Bill of Rights
Emancipation Proclamation
Pulitzer Prize

a Grammy
Stamp Act
Fifth Amendment

EXTRA: Make up a list of ten geographical terms of your surrounding area, and dictate to students.

8. geographical terms

Capitalize the important words in the names of continents, regions, countries, states, counties, cities, parks, geographical features, and streets.

Antarctica
Middle East
France
Delaware
Seattle
Des Moines
Estes National Park

Atlantic Ocean
Potomac River
Rocky Mountains
Cape Hatteras
Staten Island
Fifth Avenue
Harbor Freeway

9. compass points

Capitalize compass points such as *west* and *north-east* when they refer to a specific area of the country or the world or when they are part of a proper name. Do not capitalize compass points if they merely indicate direction.

The **W**est is known for its spectacular scenery.
Coal is the main natural resource of **W**est **V**irginia.
Ohio is **w**est of Pennsylvania.

10. planets and other heavenly bodies

Mars	**N**orth **S**tar
Saturn	**L**ittle **D**ipper

Do not capitalize *sun* and *moon*. Do not capitalize *earth* unless it is used with the names of other planets. The word *earth* is never capitalized when it is preceded by *the*.

Only one side of the **m**oon can be seen from the **e**arth.
Mercury is smaller than **E**arth.

11. ships, planes, trains, spacecraft

Mayflower [ship]	**C**oncorde [plane]
Cannonball [train]	*Viking I* [spacecraft]

12. historical events and eras

French **R**evolution	**R**econstruction
Battle of the **B**ulge	**M**iddle **A**ges

13. days of the week, months, holidays, events

Friday	**F**ourth of **J**uly
July	**H**anuka
Labor **D**ay	the **W**orld **S**eries
Christmas	**S**enior **P**rom

His birthday is on **S**unday, **M**arch 8.

Do not capitalize the names of the seasons (*spring, summer, autumn, fall, winter*).

14. religious terms

Capitalize names of religions, denominations and their members, names of religious works, and words referring to the Deity.

Christianity	**L**utherans
Buddhism	**M**uslims
Judaism	**G**od
the **R**oman **C**atholic **C**hurch	the **L**ord
the **B**ible	the **K**oran

Do not capitalize the word *god* when it refers to the gods of mythology.

> The ancient Romans named the **g**od of the sea Neptune.

15. school courses

Capitalize school courses that are languages or that are titles of specific courses. Do not capitalize general names of subjects.

English	*but*	**g**eography
Algebra 1	*but*	**a**lgebra
History 303	*but*	**c**ivics

EXERCISE 3. Rewrite the following phrases, correcting all errors in capitalization.

1. a french course *F*
2. mother's day *M, D*
3. the west *W*
4. the senate *S*
5. exxon corporation *E, C*
6. protestant ministers *P*
7. the academy award *A, A*
8. biology 101 *B*
9. the gobi desert *G, D*
10. the chinese *C*
11. new mexico *N, M*
12. the atomic energy act *A, E, A*
13. louisiana purchase *L, P*
14. crest toothpaste *C*
15. the peace corps *P, C*
16. queen elizabeth 2 *Q, E*
17. macarthur's park *M, P*
18. the planet mars *Accept variations.*
19. the bill of rights *B, R*
20. professor miller *P, M*

EXERCISE 4. Rewrite the following phrases, correcting all errors in capitalization.

1. minneapolis *M*
2. republicans *R*
3. ohio university *O, U*
4. South of the city *s*
5. Grand canyon *C*
6. the Korean war *W*
7. April Fool's day *D*
8. geography 101 *G*
9. Chrysler building *B*
10. Kleenex Tissues *t*

11. voyager plane *V*
12. "Hi, uncle Mark." *U*
13. my Mother *m*
14. ash wednesday *A, W*
15. general Patton *G*
16. the Sun *s*
17. the Spring season *s*
18. New Year's eve *E*
19. the congress *C*
20. Mickey mouse *M*

EXERCISE 5. Rewrite each of the following sentences, adding capital letters to proper nouns. (The number of capital letters that you must add to each sentence is indicated in parentheses.)

1. In 1607 the London Company sent three ships (the *godspeed*, the *discovery*, and the *sarah constant*) to america. (5) *G, D, S, C, A*

2. Captain john smith and other English settlers disembarked from the ships at jamestown, virginia. (4)*J, S, J, V*

3. jamestown (as well as the james river) had been named after king james I. (5) *J, J, R, K, J*

4. Captain john smith, the president of the town council, stayed in jamestown for only two years. (3) *J, S, J*

5. When captain smith returned to england, he told many stories about the new land and people. (3) *C, S, E*

6. Smith's most famous story concerns pocahontas, an Algonquian princess. (1) *P*

7. Pocahontas was the daughter of powhatan. (1) *P*

8. The name pocahontas was only a nickname for the princess, whose real name was matoaka. (2) *P, M*

9. Captain smith told the english that pocahontas had saved his life in north america. (5) *S, E, P, N, A*

10. Pocahontas later became a christian and changed her name to rebecca. (2) *C, R*

11. With the blessing of her father, chief powhatan, pocahontas married john rolfe. (5) *C, P, P, J, R*

12. John rolfe had experimented with a plant from the west indies called tobacco. (3) *R, W, I*

13. Pocahontas' marriage in the spring of 1614 was followed by a period of peace between the algonquians and the English settlers. (1) *A*

14. Rolfe and pocahontas visited london, where they met king james I and queen anne. (6) *P, L, K, J, Q, A*

15. The Rolfes went to the Globe Theatre to see william shakespeare's play *The Tempest*. (2) *W, S*

16. Shakespeare had been buried a few weeks before on april 25, 1616, at a small church in stratford, england. (3) *A, S E*

17. Before she could return to her native land, pocahontas died on march 21, 1617. (2) *P, M*

18. The story of pocahontas has been retold by many American poets, such as carl sandburg and hart crane. (5) *P, C, S, H, C*

19. In later years captain smith explored what is now the northeast in the united states. (5) *C, S, N, U, S*

20. Captain smith is the person who named new england. (3) *S, N, E*

7.a.6 Capitalization of proper adjectives

Capitalize proper adjectives; do not capitalize common adjectives. Proper adjectives are adjectives formed from proper nouns.

Some words, such as *Chinese* or *Republican*, are used as both proper nouns and proper adjectives. The noun and the adjective have the same form.

Some of the kinds of proper adjectives are listed on the following page.

1. **formed from names of people**

Elizabethan	**N**apoleonic
Jacksonian	**M**arxist

2. **formed from place names and names of national and ethnic groups**

African	**P**arisian
French	**A**fro-**A**merican
Israeli	**H**ispanic

3. **formed from political and religious terms**

Republican	**R**oman **C**atholic
Democratic	**J**ewish

EXERCISE 6. Following is a list of proper nouns. Change each proper noun into a proper adjective. Check your dictionary to be sure you are spelling the proper adjective correctly.

EXAMPLE Spain
ANSWER *Spanish*

1. America *American*
2. Elizabeth *Elizabethan*
3. Sweden *Swedish*
4. Japan *Japanese*
5. Shakespeare *Shakespearean*
6. Africa *African*
7. Europe *European*
8. Israel *Israeli*
9. Italy *Italian*
10. Mexico *Mexican*
11. Victoria *Victorian*
12. Australia *Australian*
13. Korea *Korean*
14. Puerto Rico *Puerto Rican*
15. Poland *Polish*
16. Canada *Canadian*
17. China *Chinese*
18. Asia *Asian*
19. France *French*
20. Russia *Russian*

EXERCISE 7. Rewrite each of the following sentences, adding capital letters to proper nouns *and* proper adjectives. (The number of capital letters that you must add to each sentence is indicated in parentheses.)

1. After the revolution, the american capital was established first in new york city and then in philadelphia. (5) *A, N, Y, C, P*

2. The new american government faced a huge debt caused by the revolutionary war. (3) *A, R, W*

3. The secretary of the treasury, alexander hamilton, wanted the government to help settle the immense war debt. (4) *S, T, A, H*

4. Thomas jefferson, the secretary of state, did not want the government to be involved in money matters. (3) *J, S, S*

5. Many citizens in the north supported hamilton, who wanted to tax european products. (3) *N, H, E*

6. These citizens also wanted to tax american products. (1) *A*

7. The jeffersonians (supporters of jefferson) disagreed with hamilton's plans for paying the war debt. (3) *J, J, H*

8. Many of jefferson's followers in the south wanted the national capital moved to the south. (3) *J, S, S*

9. The leaders of congress approved hamilton's financial plans. (2) *C, H*

10. The congress also agreed to move the capital to washington, a city in the south. (3) *C, W, S*

11. When the french army went to war against great britain and spain in 1793, jefferson and hamilton again took opposite sides. (6) *F, G, B, S, J, H*

12. The jeffersonians wanted the united states to side with the french. (4) *J, U, S, F*

13. The hamiltonians wanted the united states to side with the british and the spanish. (5) *H, U, S, B, S*

14. President washington did not want to take sides with either the french army or the british army. (3) *W, F, B*

15. The united states signed treaties with the british government and the spanish government. (4) *U, S, B, S*

16. After washington's two terms were over, john adams became president. (4) *W, J, A, P*

17. John adams, like washington, wanted to use treaties to solve the european problems. (3) *A, W, E*

18. The disagreements between hamilton and jefferson gave rise to two american political parties. (3) *H, J, A*

19. The people in the north who supported hamilton were called federalists. (3) *N, H, F*

20. Jefferson and his supporters in the south were called democratic-republicans. (3) *S, D, R*

7.a.7 Capitalization of titles of works

Capitalize the first and last words and all important words in titles of works.

Titles of artistic works are proper nouns — the names of particular things. Capitalize the first and last words and all important words in titles of books, short stories, poems, plays, television series, movies, newspapers, magazines, paintings, and songs. Do not capitalize articles, conjunctions, or prepositions unless they are the first or the last words or if they have more than four letters. Capitalize all words that are part of a verb such as *call **off*** and *look **up***.

Most titles of works are either italicized or surrounded by quotation marks. (For a discussion of quotation marks and italics with titles of works, see 7.l.2 and 7.m.l.)

The Grapes of Wrath	"Mending Wall"
"To Build a Fire"	the *Los Angeles Times*
A Raisin in the Sun	*The Last Supper*
Face the Nation	"Oh, Susannah"
My Fair Lady	*Newsweek*

Capitalize an article at the beginning of a title only when it is part of the title itself. In general, do not capitalize (or italicize) articles preceding the name of a newspaper or periodical or the word *magazine* following the title of a periodical.

"The Purloined Letter"	*but*	the *Boston Globe*
A Separate Peace	*but*	an *Ebony* magazine

EXERCISE 8. Rewrite each of the following sentences, correcting all errors in capitalization of titles of works.

1. Edith Wharton's novel *the age of innocence* deals with New York society in the late 1800s. _T, A, I_

2. Henry James's novel *washington square* takes place in New York in the Greenwich Village area. _W, S_

3. In Mary Margaret McBride's novel *a long way from missouri*, the author cautions young people against the dangers of a big city like New York. _A, L, W, M_

4. "I love New York" is a quotation from Dorothy Kilgallen's novel *girl around the world*. _G, A, W_

5. New York poet Walt Whitman wrote the poem "once I pass'd through a populous city" about New Orleans, not New York. _O, I, P, T, P, C_

6. In her poem "new york" Ruth Mason Rice asks, "Where are you going, multitude of feet?" _N, Y_

7. O. Henry wrote many short stories about New York City, including "the gift of the magi." _T, G, M_

8. In Willa Cather's short story entitled "paul's case," a young boy visits New York City for the first time. _P, C_

9. The mystery play *sorry, wrong number* by Lucille Fletcher takes place in New York. _S, W, N_

10. The play *west side story*, which has music by Leonard Bernstein, also takes place in New York. _W, S, S_

11. Director Woody Allen's love for New York City is evident in his film *manhattan*. _M_

12. The television series *that girl*, which starred Marlo Thomas, was about a young actress seeking success on Broadway. _T, G_

13. The television series *i love lucy* and *the honeymooners* were about two very different kinds of people living in New York City. _I, L, L, T, H_

14. American painter John Marin painted an abstract watercolor entitled *brooklyn bridge*. _B, B_

15. Joseph Stella's painting entitled *battle of light, coney island*, captures the color and excitement of that New York beach. _B, L, C, I_

16. Georgia O'Keeffe's painting *new york night* has dark colors and sharp shapes. _N, Y, N_

17. One of the most respected newspapers in the world is the *new york times*. _N, Y, T_

18. The *new yorker* magazine publishes the latest fiction and poetry. _N, Y_

19. "the 59th street bridge song" by folk singers Simon and Garfunkel takes its title from New York's Queensboro Bridge. _T, S, B, S_

20. The song "i happen to like new york," by Cole Porter, is a tribute to New York City. _I, H, L, N, Y_

7.a.8 **Capitalization of abbreviations**

Capitalize abbreviations of proper nouns and proper adjectives. Also capitalize the abbreviations A.M., P.M., A.D., and B.C. (See 7.b for a complete discussion of abbreviations.)

A.M.	**VISTA**	**Mr.**	**U.S.S.R.**
P.M.	**FBI**	**Sr.**	**Tenn.**
A.D.	**IBM**	**Ave.**	**Oct.**
B.C.	**B.A.**	**Inc.**	**Tues.**

REVIEW EXERCISE A. Rewrite each of the following items, correcting the capitalization.

1. the Transbay bridge _B_
2. dr. Robin Wu _D_
3. democratic vote _D_
4. a *People* Magazine _m_
5. the film *oklahoma!* _O_
6. a city in the north _N_
7. the Moon _m_
8. Texas Industries, inc. _I_
9. at 8 a.m. _A, M_
10. Yosemite park _P_

11. a Sioux Chief _c_
12. "yesterday" _Y_
13. the Vietnam war _W_
14. the Ship *Maine* _s_
15. the french people _F_
16. Bayer Aspirin _a_
17. afro-American _A_
18. thanksgiving day _T, D_
19. in the year 54 b.c. _B, C_
20. "o, say can you see" _O_

REVIEW EXERCISE B. Rewrite each of the following phrases, correcting all errors in capitalization.

1. the editor of the ¢hicago ţribune *C, T*
2. a şhakespearean play *S*
3. a jewish rabbi and a ɼoman ¢atholic priest *J, R, C*
4. a current issue of ţime magazine *T*
5. ɥnited ştates citizens *U, S*
6. in ą.d. 1066 *A, D*
7. the winner of the ŋobel peace prize *N, P, P*
8. the corner of ţhompson and ƒranklin streets in ɦarris-burg, ɖennsylvania *T, F, H, P* *Accept capitalization of* streets.
9. a vice president of ɡeneral ƒoods ¢orp. *G, F, C*
10. japanese-ąmerican citizens *J, A*
11. a college in the ŋorthwest of the country *N*
12. johnson's baby powder *J*
13. the members of ¢ongress *C*
14. from 7 ą.ɱ. to 2 ɖ.ɱ. *A, M, P, M*
15. şouth ¢arolina *S, C*
16. the universities in ţexas and ąlabama *T, A*
17. the ąmerican and ƒrench flags *A, F*
18. the ştatue of ɬiberty *S, L*
19. the ŋorth ɖole *N, P*
20. the şupreme ¢ourt *S, C*

REVIEW EXERCISE C. Rewrite each of the following sentences, correcting all errors in capitalization. The number of capitalization errors in each sentence is indicated in parentheses.

1. The ąmerican poet Marianne Moore was born in 1887 in şt. ḷouis, ɱissouri. (4) *A, S, L, M*
2. ɦer family moved to the ŋortheast when she was seven. (2) *H, N*
3. Moore attended the ɱetzger ịnstitute and ɓryn ɱawr ¢ollege. (5) *M, I, B, M, C*

4. She lived in greenwich village from 1921 to 1929 and later in brooklyn, new york. (5) *G, V, B, N, Y*

5. besides being a poet, Moore was a fan of the brooklyn dodgers baseball team. (3) *B, B, D*

6. Moore's earliest poems were published in *poetry* magazine. (1) _P_

7. from 1926 to 1929 Moore was editor of dial, a famous american literary magazine. (3) *F, D̲, A*

8. Moore won the dial magazine's award for her poetry collection entitled *observations.* (2) *D̲, O̲*

9. moore once wrote that she disliked poetry. (1) *M*

10. according to moore, things are important "because they are useful." (2) *A, M*

11. moore once admitted that her poems were usually inspired by "just a word or two." (1) *M*

12. Concerning the art of poetry Marianne Moore said, "there are things that are important beyond all this fiddle." (1) *T*

13. the poem "the mind is an enchanting thing" was written after Moore's mother spoke that sentence to her. (6) *T, T, M, I, E, T̄*

14. One favorite poem of many readers is titled "in distrust of merits." (3) *I, D, M*

15. moore said that one poem of hers was simply a burst of feeling. (1) *M*

16. many critics think that moore is one of the finest twentieth-century poets. (2) *M, M*

17. Mark schorer wrote that Moore's poems read like "splendid verse essays." (1) *S*

18. The poet and critic t. s. eliot wrote, "I can only think of five contemporary poets — english, irish, french, and german — whose works excite me as much as Miss Moore's." (8) *T, S, E, I, E, I, F, G*

19. Marianne Moore won the helen haire levinson prize for her poetry in 1935. (4) *H, H, L, P*

20. Marianne Moore also won a pulitzer prize for her poetry. (2) *P, P*

7.b ABBREVIATIONS

Abbreviations are shortened forms of words. They save space and time and prevent unnecessary wordiness. For example, *3 P.M.* is more concise and easier to write than *three o'clock in the afternoon.*

Many abbreviations are more familiar than the words they represent. Some of them, however, should not be used in your regular prose writing. Abbreviations are most commonly used in scientific and statistical writing.

7.b.1 Abbreviations of titles of people

Use abbreviations for some personal titles.

Titles such as *Mr., Mrs., Jr.,* and *Sr.* and those indicating professions and academic degrees (*Dr., M.D., M.A.*) are almost always abbreviated when used with a person's name. *Ms.* and *Miss* are not abbreviations, although *Ms.* is followed by a period. Titles of government and military officials and members of the clergy are often abbreviated when used before a name.

Mrs. Truman	**Gov.** Dixy Lee Ray
Mr. Horowitz	**Sen.** Russell Long
Desi Arnaz, **Jr.**	**Brig. Gen.** Dunlap
Dr. Rosalyn Yalow	**Rev.** Jesse Jackson
Ann Sinkoski, **D.D.S.**	**Fr.** Manuel Garcia

7.b.2 Abbreviations of businesses, organizations, government agencies

Use abbreviations for names of business firms, organizations, and government agencies.

Most of these abbreviations do not take periods.

CBS	NAACP	CIA
TWA	OPEC	NATO

In regular prose writing you should spell out such names the first time they are used and give the abbreviation in parentheses after the name. In later references you may use the abbreviation alone.

> The Tennessee Valley Authority (**TVA**) supplies electricity to several states in the Southeast. The **TVA** was organized in 1933.

7.b.3 Abbreviations of places

Spell out the names of countries, states, and streets in regular prose writing.

Places may be abbreviated in addresses in informal letters, but do not use abbreviations in business letters.

U.S.A.	Shreveport, **La.**	866 Third **Ave.**
U.S.S.R.	Providence, **R.I.**	1018 Canal **St.**

The names of most states may be abbreviated in two ways. For example, both *La.* and *LA* are abbreviations for *Louisiana.* The second kind of abbreviation should be used only with the ZIP code.

EXERCISE 9. Match the abbreviations in the left column with the words they stand for in the right column.

1. St. Anne *j*
2. NBC *e*
3. Dr. Shang *h*
4. IRS *f*
5. Trent, Inc. *i*
6. Sen. Long *b*
7. NASA *c*
8. Tibbett & Co. *g*
9. Fifth Ave. *d*
10. Y.M.H.A. *a*

a. Young Men's Hebrew Association
b. Senator Long
c. National Aeronautics and Space Administration
d. Fifth Avenue
e. National Broadcasting Company
f. Internal Revenue Service
g. Tibbett and Company
h. Doctor Shang
i. Trent, Incorporated
j. Saint Anne

EXERCISE 10. Match the abbreviations in the left column with the words they stand for in the right column.

1. B.A. *f*
2. Lever Bros. *j*
3. Ph.D. *d*
4. B.S. *a*
5. USN *i*
6. S. Cedar La. *b*
7. Fr. Barbieri *g*
8. R.I. *h*
9. Prof. Nadar *c*
10. P.T.A. *e*

a. Bachelor of Science
b. South Cedar Lane
c. Professor Nadar
d. Doctor of Philosophy
e. Parent-Teacher Association
f. Bachelor of Arts
g. Father Barbieri
h. Rhode Island
i. United States Navy
j. Lever Brothers

7.b.4 Abbreviations of dates and times

Do not abbreviate the names of months and days of the week in regular prose writing.

The abbreviations listed below are used in writing dates and times. They can be used in all kinds of writing.

A.D. (*anno Domini*), "in the year of the Lord"; placed before the date — *A.D. 27*

B.C. (before Christ); placed after the date — *44 B.C.*

A.M. (*ante meridiem*), "before noon"

P.M. (*post meridiem*), "after noon"

NOT The San Francisco earthquake occurred on ~~Wed., Apr.~~ 18, 1906.

BUT The San Francisco earthquake occurred on **Wednesday, April** 18, 1906.

EXERCISE 11. Rewrite the following passage, spelling out in words all of the misused abbreviations. (You will find twenty misused abbreviations.)

[1]Wilbur Wright was born on ~~Apr.~~ *April* 16, 1867, and his brother Orville was born on ~~Aug.~~ *August* 19, 1871. [2]The two

brothers
bros. were interested in designing, building, and math at an early age. [3]O̶r̶v̶. *Orville* made kites, and W̶i̶l̶b̶. *Wilbur* built a wooden lathe by hand. [4]The Wright bros. *brothers* built their own printing press and published the *West Side News.* [5]In later years Orville and Wilbur invented a machine that changed how people traveled — not only in the U̶.̶S̶. *United States* but throughout the world. [6]Using models of a toy glider, O̶. *Orville* and W̶. *Wilbur* built the first successful aircraft that was heavier than air. [7]On D̶e̶c̶. *December* 17, 1903, the bros. *brothers* tested their Wright Flyer at Kill Devil Hill, four miles south of Kitty Hawk, a town in N̶.̶C̶. *North Carolina* [8]O̶. *Orville* made the first flight on that cold D̶e̶c̶. *December* morn. [9]He amazed everyone by staying in the air for 12 s̶e̶c̶. *seconds* and traveling 120 f̶t̶. *feet* [10]When W̶. *Wilbur* took off he flew 852 f̶t̶. *feet* in 59 s̶e̶c̶. *seconds* [11]For these and other achievements the bros. *brothers* have been included in the Aviation Hall of Fame. [12]There is also a national memorial to them in Kitty Hawk.

7.c NUMBERS AND NUMERALS

In regular prose writing some numbers should be expressed in words, while others should be expressed in figures. Numbers expressed in figures are called **numerals.**

7.c.1 Numbers expressed in words

In general, in prose spell out numbers that can be written in one or two words and numbers that occur at the beginning of a sentence.

New Hampshire is one of the original **thirteen** states.
There are **twenty-seven** students in the class.
Sixteen hundred delegates attended the convention.
I played basketball in the **ninth** and **tenth** grades.
Alaska was the **forty-ninth** state to join the Union.
She is in the **ninth** grade.

7.c.2 Numerals (numbers expressed in figures)

Use figures to express numbers of more than two words.

In addition, use figures in the following situations:

1. dates, times, addresses
2. money, decimals, percentages
3. measurements (length, area, weight)

Mount Mitchell, the highest mountain in the eastern United States, is **6,684** feet tall.

The **1964** earthquake in Alaska killed **115** people.

In **1970** the population of Los Angeles was **2,811,801.**

Henry Aaron retired after hitting his **762nd** major-league home run.

The address of the White House is **1600** Pennsylvania Avenue.

Ms. Waitz regularly runs the marathon distance of **26** miles, **385** yards.

If a sentence (or a paragraph) contains more than one number, express all the numbers in either words or numerals. Do not mix words and numerals in the same sentence. (You may, however, use a date or time expressed in numerals and a number expressed in words in the same sentence.)

The United Nations has grown from **51** members to more than **150.**

Bob ranked **65th** in the class; his brother ranked **119th.** [If *65th* were the only number in the sentence, it would appear as *sixty-fifth.*]

Their **sixtieth** wedding anniversary was celebrated at **7:00** P.M. on September **26, 1979.** [You may use words and numerals in the same sentence if you are expressing dates or times.]

There is more than one correct way to express an amount of money, a fraction, or a percentage. Be sure, however, to use the *same* form throughout your sentence, paragraph, or paper. For example, do not use *59 cents* in one sentence and *59¢* in another.

EXERCISE 12. Rewrite the following sentences, correcting all errors in the use of numbers and numerals.

1. In the 1870s "~~2~~ bits" (twenty-five cents) would buy ~~5~~ dead passenger pigeons. *two, five*
2. Live pigeons were worth ~~2~~ or ~~3~~ times as much. *two, three*
3. The greatest killing of passenger pigeons occurred in ~~eighteen seventy-eight~~ near Petoskey, Michigan. *1878*
4. ~~50~~ barrels of pigeons left Petoskey by railroad every day. *Fifty*
5. Each barrel contained from ~~400~~ to ~~500~~ birds. *four hundred, five hundred*
6. ~~1~~ blast of buckshot could kill ~~50~~ birds. *One, fifty*
7. The last ~~2~~ passenger pigeons in existence were housed in Cincinnati's Zoological Gardens. *two*
8. The ~~1~~ egg they produced in 1909 failed to hatch. *one*
9. In 1910 only one survivor remained of a species that ~~40~~ years earlier had blackened the skies. *forty*
10. In less than ~~80~~ years the entire population of passenger pigeons had been wiped out. *eighty*

EXERCISE 13. From each pair of sentences below select the one sentence that uses numbers and numerals according to preferred usage.

1. a) A bill can become law unless the President vetoes it within 10 days.
   b) A bill can become law unless the President vetoes it within ten days. √

2. a) Many workers can retire early — on their 65th birthday.
   b) Many workers can retire early — on their sixty-fifth birthday. √

3. a) The House of Representatives has 435 members. √
   b) The House of Representatives has four hundred and thirty-five members.

4. a) The average American consumes 3,300 calories per day. √
   b) The average American consumes three thousand and three hundred calories per day.
5. a) In the United States only 3 people in 100,000 live past the age of 100. √
   b) In the United States only three people in 100,000 live past the age of one hundred.

FORMING THE PLURALS OF NUMBERS AND NUMERALS

Numbers that are spelled out form their plurals like other nouns (see 5.b.4).

> They are always at **sixes** and **sevens.**
> Disco music became popular in the late **seventies.**

Numbers that are expressed in figures form their plurals by adding an apostrophe and *s.*

> Your **7's** look like **1's.**

NOTE: Do not use an apostrophe between the numeral and the *s* in showing a span of time.

> In the **1850s** tensions between the North and the South increased.

EXERCISE 14. Rewrite the following sentences, correcting all errors in the use of numbers and numerals.

1. Millions of Americans in the ~~1980's~~ have taken up jogging. *1980s*
2. In the ~~19th~~ century, however, walking was a popular sport. *nineteenth*   *Accept 19th.*
3. In 1861 Edward Payson Weston tried to walk from Boston to Washington in just ~~10~~ days. *ten*

4. Weston, who wanted to see Lincoln's inauguration in Washington, was ~~12~~ hours late. *twelve*

5. ~~6~~ years later Weston won a prize of $10,000 for walking from Portland, Maine, to Chicago, Illinois. *Six*

6. Weston had covered more than ~~1,000~~ miles in ~~30~~ days. *one thousand* *thirty*

7. Weston was able to walk approximately ~~1~~ mile in one fifth of an hour. *one*

8. When he was ~~67~~, Weston completed a walk from Philadelphia to New York. *sixty-seven*

9. In the ~~1920's~~ the hale and hearty Weston was able to fight off some intruders in his home. *1920s*

10. ~~3~~ years later Weston survived being dragged many feet by a taxicab. *Three*

7.d PERIODS

Use a period at the end of a sentence, in initials and abbreviations, and as a decimal point in writing numerals.

Eudora Welty wrote *The Golden Apples.* [declarative sentence]

Describe the heroine of *The Golden Apples.* [polite command]

He asked her who had written *The Golden Apples.* [indirect question]

Use periods with initials and with most other abbreviations (see 7.b).

John F. Kennedy   A.M.
Dr. Mark Barbieri, Jr.   Aug.
Ariz.   lb.

Do not use periods with the abbreviations of some businesses, organizations, and government agencies. Also do not use periods with the two-letter abbreviations of states that are used with ZIP codes, with abbreviations of metric measurements, or with acronyms (abbreviations that are pronounced as words). If you are unsure whether to use periods with a particular abbreviation, check your dictionary.

IBM	VT
NAACP	km
FBI	NOW

EXERCISE 15. Rewrite each of the following sentences, correcting all errors in the use of periods.

1. Martin Luther King, Jr., was born in 1929 .
2. King's parents taught him to think of his responsibilities to other people .
3. Dr.King received a degree from Boston University.
4. King asked himself whether his true calling was to be a minister.It was.
5. The Rev.Martin Luther King, Jr, was not well known outside his community until 1955.
6. After 1955 King's name became known throughout the world .
7. When Mrs.Rosa Parks was sent to jail for refusing to give up her seat on a bus, Mr.King demonstrated in Montgomery, Alabama.
8. As a result of King's demonstrations the Supreme Court ruled that segregation on public buses was unconstitutional .
9. King asked Americans whether it was only a dream that one day the nation would live out the true meaning of its creed .
10. Before his assassination in 1968, King had commanded all Americans to hold fast to their dreams .

7.e QUESTION MARKS

Use a question mark to indicate a direct question.

Who was the greatest President?
Amy Lowell's poem "Patterns" asks, "What are patterns for?"

NOTE: Use a period rather than a question mark after an indirect question. (An indirect question does not quote the person's exact words.)

She asked who the greatest President was.
I wondered why she wanted to know.

EXERCISE 16. Rewrite each of the following items, adding either a question mark or a period at the end of the sentence.

1. One of the great mysteries about birds is how they find their way home .
2. I have often asked myself how they do so .
3. Once my science teacher asked me if I knew how birds navigate the skies .
4. She wanted to know why some birds start off in a northeasterly direction .
5. How do birds know which direction is northeast ?
6. My teacher asked me if I knew what kind of maps birds used .
7. I guessed that she was asking a silly question to make a point .
8. Can you guess what her point was ?
9. Did you know that birds have a kind of built-in compass ?
10. Can you tell which direction is northeast without looking at a map ?

7.f EXCLAMATION POINTS

Use exclamation points to show strong feeling and to indicate a forceful command.

I have never seen such a mess!
What a beautiful day!
Forward, march!
Stop bothering me!

NOTE: Use a period, not an exclamation point, after a polite command.

Please open the window.

AVOIDING ERRORS WITH EXCLAMATION POINTS

Remember that it is usually better to use a period rather than an exclamation point in regular prose writing.

NOT   Astronauts landed on the moon only eight years after the first American went into space✗

BUT   Astronauts landed on the moon only eight years after the first American went into space.

REVIEW EXERCISE D. Rewrite each of the following sentences, adding periods, question marks, and exclamation points where necessary.

1. Don't you think that it is a good idea to learn something about first aid ?
2. First aid is the immediate medical care of an ill or injured person .
3. Oh, if only everyone were taught first aid !
4. An instruction manual by John S. Kelley published by the U S. Bureau of Mines has good information about first aid .
5. The primary goals of first aid are to treat serious injuries, to prevent infection, and to make the injured person as comfortable as possible .
6. Above all, do not panic .
7. If you come upon an injured person, stay calm, and take immediate action .
8. If people are crowding the injured person, make them stand at a distance .

9. Ask someone to send for medical help right away .

10. Examine the patient to determine what the injury is .

11. If the patient is conscious, ask where the pain is .

12. Comfort the patient by saying that everything will be all right .

13. Make sure the patient lies still .

14. Once you have sent for help and the patient is lying still, ask yourself which injuries require immediate attention .

15. Do not touch an open wound with your fingers .

16. You do not want to cause an infection, do you ?

17. Use sterile pads or a clean cloth to remove any dirt near a wound .

18. Because an injured person may have broken bones or internal injuries, never move the person unless it is absolutely necessary .

19. Remember to keep the injured person warm, still, and — above all — calm .

20. Don't you think that everyone should learn these basic rules about first aid ?

7.g COMMAS

Commas are one of the most common marks of punctuation. In fact, they have so many uses that you may be confused by them at first. Therefore, it will help you to realize that most comma rules follow logical patterns. Once you understand these patterns, the "mystery" of commas will be solved, and you will find commas quite simple to use.

A word or group of words that is separated from the rest of the sentence by commas is said to be *set off* by commas. As you study the rules for comma usage, keep in mind that to set off an element with commas means to put commas both *before* it and *after* it. Of course, if the element occurs at the beginning of a sentence, you need only use a comma after that element. If the element occurs at the end of a sentence, you need only use a comma before that element.

CONVENTIONAL USES

7.g.1 **Commas for personal titles**

Use commas to set off titles when they follow a person's name.

In a complete sentence the title should be set off with commas *before* and *after* it.

Alan Chin, M.D.
Nellie Tayloe Ross, Governor of Wyoming
Martin Luther King, Jr.
Nellie Tayloe Ross, Governor of Wyoming, was formerly
    director of the U.S. Mint.

7.g.2 **Commas in addresses**

Use commas to set off the various parts of an address or of a geographical term.

Little Rock, Arkansas
St. Louis, Missouri
Montgomery County, Maryland
At 7315 Wisconsin Avenue, Washington, D.C., is the
    American Institute of Chemists.

Do not use a comma between the street number and the name of the street or between the state and the ZIP code. Do use a comma after the ZIP code in a complete sentence.

Information about the Girls Clubs of America is available from their headquarters at 133 East 62nd Street, New York, New York 10021, and from local clubs throughout the nation.

7.g.3 Commas in dates

Use commas to separate the parts of a date.

Place a comma between the day of the week and the month and between the day of the month and the year. In a complete sentence always use a comma after the last part of the date.

December 28, 1856
Thursday, January 20, 1977
Woodrow Wilson was born on December 28, 1856, in Virginia.
On Thursday, January 20, 1977, Jimmy Carter was inaugurated as President.

Do not use the comma with dates in military form (as in *18 July 1982*). Do not use the comma if only the month and the numeral are given. Do not use the comma if only the month and the year are given.

7 July 1964   November 26
16 January 1952   May 1983

Thanksgiving is on November 26 this year and will be on November 24 next year.
In December 1941 the United States entered World War II.

7.g.4 Commas in letter writing

Place a comma after the salutation of an informal letter and after the closing of all letters.

Dear Maria,   Dear Uncle Jack,
Sincerely yours,   Love,
Yours truly,   Very truly yours,

NOTE: Use a colon, not a comma, after the greeting of a business letter (see 15.c).

Dear Sir or Madam: Members of the Committee:

EXERCISE 17. Rewrite the following letter, inserting the ten commas that are missing.

940 Crescent Street
Toledo, Ohio 43620
August 19, 1982

Ms. Lydia Antonini, Editor
West End News
1612 Parkhurst Drive
Toledo, Ohio 43620

Dear Ms. Antonini:

I learned a great deal from the article on health foods in the August 16, 1982, issue of *West End News.* Now I am eager to learn more about nutrition. Can you recommend several useful books on the subject?

Thank you for your fine reports. I want you to know that I also enjoyed your recent articles about health food restaurants in Washington, D.C., and in the Toledo area. I look forward to more of your interesting articles.

Sincerely,

Daniel Laurents, Jr.

Daniel Laurents, Jr.

ITEMS IN SERIES

7.g.5 Commas and words in series

Use commas with nouns, verbs, adjectives, and adverbs in a series.

Notice that a series can appear in three basic forms:

A, B, and C [This is the most common form.]
A, B, C
A and B and C [Notice that commas are not used.]

Although newspapers and some books omit the comma before the *and,* it is always better to use the comma because it helps to avoid confusion. For example, in the sentence *She sold her couch, bookcases, table and chairs* it is not clear whether the person sold a set of table and chairs together or a table and some chairs separately. If they were sold separately, a comma after the word *table* would make the meaning clear.

> We visited San Francisco, Portland, and Seattle on our vacation.
> Boston is known for its historic buildings, famous universities, and distinctive foods.
> She looked, sounded, and acted like a successful leader.
> Do not fold, tear, or crumple this card.
> It was a sunny, hot, humid day in July.

Do not use a comma between adjectives in a series if they sound unnatural with their order changed or with *and* between them. Adjectives that do not need commas between them usually describe different aspects, such as size and color, of the word they refer to.

> He grew up in a small white frame house.

EXERCISE 18. Rewrite the following sentences, adding commas where necessary. Two of the sentences are correct as written.

1. Early American colonists farmed mined and explored their new territory.
2. Many explorers lived in square brown wooden cabins.
3. New York ,Pennsylvania ,New Jersey, and Delaware produced much of the food and livestock for the colonies.
4. Many farmers in the North lived in small grey stone houses.
5. Farmers in Maryland, Virginia, and South Carolina grew mostly tobacco and rice.

6. A good crop depended upon hard work good weather and luck.

7. German Swedish and Native American farming methods were better than English methods.

8. The early settlers brought the land under control by working quickly consistently and courageously.

9. Because New England soil was poor in essential nutrients, many settlers there traded fished and industrialized.

10. The colonists helped strengthen the American economy by working diligently intelligently and competitively.

7.g.6 Commas and phrases in series

In general, use a comma after every phrase (except the last) in a series of prepositional, participial, gerund, or infinitive phrases.

The cat ran out of the door, across the lawn, and down the street. [prepositional phrases]

I found her lying in a hammock, dozing peacefully, and ignoring the lawnmower. [participial phrases]

Reading carefully, taking good notes, and outlining chapters will help you perform better on tests. [gerund phrases]

My brother promised to pay for the damage, to apologize to the neighbors, and to drive more carefully in the future. [infinitive phrases]

Do not confuse a *series* of prepositional phrases with a *succession* of *connected* prepositional phrases, which do not need commas between them (see 7.g.12).

The scissors are either in the desk drawer, on the kitchen counter, or in your bedroom. [Phrases are in a series; use commas.]

I found the scissors in a box in the closet under the stairs. [Phrases are connected; do not use commas.]

7.g.7 Commas and main clauses in series

Place a comma after every main clause (except the last) used in a series.

The band struck up a march, the door opened, and the President stepped out.

AVOIDING ERRORS WITH COMMAS AND ITEMS IN A SERIES

1. Do not place a comma after the conjunction in a series.

   NOT The mechanic repaired our car quickly, skill-fully, and cheaply.

   BUT The mechanic repaired our car quickly, skill-fully, and cheaply.

2. Do not use commas between items in a series if all the items are joined by *and, or,* or *nor.*

   NOT Everyone should bring a salad or a dessert or a beverage to the picnic.

   BUT Everyone should bring a salad or a dessert or a beverage to the picnic.

EXERCISE 19. Rewrite the following sentences, adding commas where necessary. Two of the sentences are correct as written.

1. Many people think that hypnosis is a fakery or a danger or a waste of time.
2. Some people claim, however, that hypnosis can help you to quit smoking to stop overeating or to build confidence.
3. Hypnosis may enable you to tolerate unhappiness, to lessen fears or to ignore pain.

4. Hypnosis can be done in a doctor's office, in a patient's home, or in any quiet setting.

5. Sitting on a chair in the office of a hypnotist is very relaxing.

6. Many people imagine themselves on the beach, in a forest, or on a mountaintop.

7. Trusting the hypnotist, relaxing fully, and following instructions are keys to successful hypnosis.

8. The hypnotist will tell you to take a deep breath, you will inhale slowly, and your body will relax.

9. After hypnosis you may feel peaceful, your life may be improved, and your confidence may be increased.

10. Feeling comfortable, tolerating pain, and being at peace may be worth the price of a good hypnotist.

CLAUSES AND PHRASES

7.g.8 Commas and main clauses (compound sentences)

Use commas between the main clauses in a compound sentence.

Place the comma before the coordinating conjunction (*and, but, or,* or *for*).

I am not going to the concert, for I am too tired.
Many of the prospectors searched for years, but others struck gold immediately, and some became quite rich.

The comma may be omitted if the main clauses are very short, but it is always a good idea to use the comma.

We heard a crash and Sarah gasped.
We heard a crash, and Sarah gasped.

Always use a comma if the sentence might be confusing without it.

NOT He is visiting Miami and the Everglades are
next.

BUT He is visiting Miami, and the Everglades are
next.

Long main clauses may be separated by a semicolon
instead of a comma and a coordinating conjunction. Always use a semicolon when conjunctive adverbs (see
1.h.3) are used.

Early settlers had to find new names for unfamiliar
things; thus, a distinctive form of American English developed.

EXERCISE 20. Rewrite the following sentences, adding
commas where necessary. Two of the sentences are correct
as written.

1. John Wayne worked in the film industry for almost
fifty years and made more than two hundred films.

2. Wayne's first film was *The Big Trail* (1930) and his last
film was *The Shootist* (1976).

3. John Wayne played many different roles but he starred
in more westerns than any other actor.

4. *Stagecoach* and *Red River* are two of John Wayne's
most popular films but he won an Oscar for *True Grit.*

5. The film *Rooster Cogburn* was based upon *True Grit*
for the earlier film had been very successful.

6. In 1968 Wayne starred in and also helped direct the
war film *The Green Berets.*

7. Wayne's personality was similar to his film image and
he was known for his sincere patriotism off the screen.

8. John Wayne was famous as a man of action but he also
played roles that demanded gentleness.

9. John Wayne has become a symbol of American hero-
ism and his films are appreciated by critics.

10. Wayne's last public appearance was an act of courage
for he had battled cancer since 1964.

AVOIDING ERRORS WITH COMMAS AND MAIN CLAUSES

1. In a sentence with two main clauses, remember to use a coordinating conjunction or a semicolon between the clauses. If you use only a comma between main clauses, you will create a **run-on sentence.** (A run-on sentence is sometimes called a comma splice or comma fault.)

   NOT   My grandmother is lonely︀she enjoys our visit each Sunday.
   BUT   My grandmother is lonely**, and** she enjoys our visit each Sunday.
   OR   My grandmother is lonely**;** she enjoys our visit each Sunday.
   OR   My grandmother is lonely**; therefore,** she enjoys our visit each Sunday.

2. Do not confuse a sentence that has a compound verb (see 2.h) with a sentence that has two main clauses. A compound verb with two parts does not need a comma between the parts. Remember that a sentence with two main clauses needs a comma between the clauses.

   NOT   The lawyer raised her voice︀but remained perfectly calm. [compound verb]
   BUT   The lawyer raised her voice but remained perfectly calm.

   NOT   The lawyer raised her voice︀but she remained perfectly calm. [compound sentence]
   BUT   The lawyer raised her voice**,** but she remained perfectly calm.

7.g.9 Commas and adjective clauses

Use commas to set off a nonessential adjective clause.

A nonessential adjective clause is not necessary to the meaning of the sentence. A nonessential (or nonrestrictive) adjective clause is also called an *extra* clause. It gives *extra* information about a noun or pronoun. An extra clause adds to the basic meaning of the sentence but does not change the meaning of the sentence. Remember that an *extra* adjective clause calls for *extra* commas.

> Atlanta, which is the capital of Georgia, is the transportation center of the Southeast. [nonessential clause: *which is the capital of Georgia*]
> My father, who enjoys woodworking, built a grandfather clock for our living room. [nonessential clause: *who enjoys woodworking*]

Do not use commas with a clause that is essential to the meaning of the sentence. An essential (or restrictive) adjective clause gives necessary information about a noun or pronoun.

> People who are afraid of heights do not like climbing trees. [essential clause: *who are afraid of heights*]
> The skirt that I liked the most was too expensive. [essential clause: *that I liked the most*]

EXERCISE 21. Rewrite correctly each of the following sentences that has errors in comma usage. Some sentences are correct as written.

1. Charles Willson Peale who was born in 1741 is best known for his portraits of American people.
2. Peale painted more than one thousand portraits of Americans who lived during the Revolutionary War.
3. Peale who was married and widowed three times had seventeen children.
4. Peale believed that a child should have an education that is well-rounded and thorough.

5. Peale gave his children an education that was both scientific and artistic.

6. The Peale family often played games that were designed to educate the children.

7. Peale taught French,which was the universal language at the time,to all of his children.

8. Fines were paid by those who mistakenly spoke English.

9. Even the parents paid these fines,which were used to buy sweets for the entire family.

10. Peale himself taught his children drawing and painting in watercolors and in oils,which drew the family closer together.

11. Peale's second son,who was named after the painter Rembrandt,was a talented artist.

12. The son who remained his father's favorite was Rembrandt Peale.

13. Rembrandt Peale painted a portrait of the man who later became the first American President.

14. Sophonisba,who was one of Peale's daughters,was also a gifted artist.

15. Sophonisba Peale sewed the exquisite "Star of Bethlehem" quilt that hangs in the Philadelphia Museum of Art.

16. Peale's niece Sarah,who was influenced by Peale,was a highly successful portrait painter.

17. One of the most important contributions that Peale made was the founding of the Philadelphia Museum of Art.

18. Peale entrusted the Philadelphia Museum of Art to his son Rubens,who was also named after the great Flemish painter.

19. Peale's oldest son perfected a method of still-life painting that is much admired today.

20. The family that had produced so many talented children is a model for all American families in this century to follow.

7.g.10 Commas and adverb clauses

Use commas to set off introductory adverb clauses.

Until you arrived, I thought that no one was coming.

Although I like country music, I did not want to hear her entire record collection.

If he reads the directions, he will have no trouble with the assignment.

Use commas to set off adverb clauses in an internal position that interrupt the flow of the sentence.

She behaved, when she did not get her way, like a spoiled child.

Carlos, after he thought about it a while, agreed with our idea.

In general, do not use a comma before an adverb clause at the end of a sentence unless the clause is parenthetical (or extra) or unless the sentence would be misread without the comma.

He will have no trouble with the assignment if he reads the directions.

She refuses to go, if I understand her correctly. [comma because clause is parenthetical]

I thought that no one was coming, until you arrived. [comma to avoid misreading]

Use a comma if the clause begins with *although* or *though*.

I did not say anything, although she was an hour late for the concert. [comma because clause begins with *although*]

Use a comma if the clause begins with *while* meaning "whereas."

Some people like fruit-flavored yogurt, while others prefer it plain. [comma because *while* means "whereas"]

Use a comma before *as* or *since* if the clause tells "why."

> I did not mention the accident, as she was upset enough already. [comma because *as* clause tells "why"]

Do not use a comma before *while, as,* or *since* if the clause tells "when."

> The shop repairs your shoes while you wait. [no comma because *while* clause tells "when"]

EXERCISE 22. Rewrite each of the following sentences, correcting all errors in comma usage. Some sentences are correct as written.

1. People who work during the day may not be aware of what happens while they sleep.
2. Although most people work during the day, some thirteen million Americans work at night.
3. Night workers,because they need to do their errands, have encouraged businesses to expand their hours.
4. It is now possible for both daytime and nighttime workers to do their errands as they commute.
5. Many stores stay open twenty-four hours a day because their customers shop at all hours.
6. All-night restaurants, laundries, and banks are common,as many people are active at night.
7. Now night workers can bank at night,while day workers can bank during the usual hours.
8. There has been a 50 percent increase in night telephone calls since the time when most people worked during the day.
9. Nighttime business hours are very convenient, although not all stores are open at night.
10. In the future even more businesses will offer flexible hours,since there is a growing number of people who are active at night.

7.g.11 Commas and participial phrases and infinitive phrases

Use commas to set off participles, infinitives, participial phrases, and infinitive phrases that are not essential to the meaning of the sentence.

Remember that an *extra* (nonessential) participle, infinitive, or phrase requires *extra* commas.

NOTE: Always use a comma after an introductory participle or participial phrase.

Thinking about something else, I did not answer her question. [introductory participial phrase]

His old car, abandoned, rusted away in a junkyard. [participle]

A customer stepped up to the counter, complaining loudly. [participial phrase]

To raise the money, they are planning a bake sale. [infinitive phrase]

I have no idea, to be frank, what you would like for your birthday. [infinitive phrase]

We are still undecided, to answer your question. [infinitive phrase]

Do not set off participles, infinitives, participial phrases, or infinitive phrases if they are essential to the meaning of the sentence.

A person caught in a raging thunderstorm should not stand under an isolated tree. [essential participial phrase]

The man standing by the door is my father. [essential participial phrase]

To become a doctor had been her goal for years. [essential infinitive phrase]

She wanted to become a doctor. [essential infinitive phrase]

He claimed he had nothing to regret. [essential infinitive]

7.g.12 Commas and introductory prepositional phrases

Use a comma to set off a single short introductory prepositional phrase only if the sentence would be misread without the comma.

Use a comma after the final phrase in a succession of connected introductory prepositional phrases unless it is immediately followed by the verb. Do not use commas *between* introductory prepositional phrases unless the phrases are a series (see 7.g.6).

At the last moment we decided not to go.
On the table was a bag of groceries.
To those outside, the house appeared dark and deserted. [comma to avoid confusion in reading]
During the afternoon of the day of the game, we made a big banner. [comma after a succession of connected prepositional phrases]
On the stone above the front door of the building was the date *1892.* [no comma after a succession of connected prepositional phrases immediately followed by the verb]

EXERCISE 23. Rewrite correctly each of the following sentences that has errors in comma usage. Some sentences are correct as written.

1. Running a huge office,architect I. M. Pei still finds time to design timeless buildings.
2. To most people the name I. M. Pei means good taste and quality of design.
3. To be truthful,Pei's name is one of the most respected in the field of architecture.
4. To combine a beautiful design with a practical budget is one of Pei's rare gifts.
5. Among Pei's most successful designs is the East Building of the National Gallery of Art in Washington, D.C.

6. Pei spent years trying to succeed.

7. Pei has had problems with buildings, to be honest.

8. Located in Boston, the John Hancock Tower had windows that fell out.

9. After the series of problems with the John Hancock Tower in Boston, Pei's firm lost some business.

10. Pei, attempting to solve the problems of the John Hancock Tower, replaced the windows.

11. Replacing the windows, Pei regained his reputation.

12. Architects must seek to harmonize a building's appearance with its purpose.

13. An architect should not only try to design a building that looks spectacular.

14. Knowing how a building will be used, an architect sets to work.

15. Pei also tries to limit the budget of a building.

16. For a resort hotel in mainland China, Pei created a design that pleased everyone.

17. Having been born in China, Pei used traditional Chinese elements in the modern hotel.

18. Pei wanted the Peking hotel to be approved by the government of mainland China.

19. Pei's continuing success is understandable, to be sure.

20. Becoming successful, I. M. Pei continues to work hard.

EXTRA EXPRESSIONS

7.g.13 Commas and appositives

Use commas to set off an appositive unless it is essential to the meaning of the sentence.

An **appositive** is a noun or pronoun (sometimes with modifiers) that is placed next to another noun or pronoun to identify it or to give additional information about it. A nonessential (or nonrestrictive) appositive can be considered an *extra* appositive that needs *extra* commas.

NONESSENTIAL APPOSITIVES

Margaret Mead, the famous anthropologist, studied primitive cultures on Pacific islands.

His car, a Rolls Royce, is hand made.

She has one fault, a tendency to lose her temper.

A nonessential appositive is sometimes placed before the word to which it refers.

An insurance executive, Charles Ives wrote music in his spare time.

Do not use commas for an appositive that is essential to the meaning of the sentence.

ESSENTIAL APPOSITIVES

The word *fiesta* came into English from Spanish.

Mark Twain's novel *The Innocents Abroad* is a comic story of Americans traveling in Europe. [If commas were placed around the essential appositive *The Innocents Abroad*, the sentence would seem to mean that this was Twain's *only* novel.]

President Kennedy appointed his brother Robert as Attorney General. [no commas around *Robert* because President Kennedy had more than one brother]

EXERCISE 24. Rewrite correctly each of the following sentences that has errors in comma usage. Some sentences are correct as written.

1. The American poet Emily Dickinson was born in 1830 and died in 1886.

2. Dickinson attended Amherst Academy and Mount Holyoke,a women's college.

3. One of her father's law students,Benjamin Newton, urged Dickinson to write poetry.

4. At the age of thirty-two Dickinson sent four of her poems to the *Atlantic Monthly*,a magazine of poetry and fiction.

5. A critic for the *Atlantic Monthly*, T. W. Higginson, did not appreciate Dickinson's unique style of meter and rhyme.
6. The writer Higginson never considered Dickinson's works poetry.
7. One of Dickinson's favorite writers was George Eliot, a nineteenth-century female novelist.
8. Only seven poems of the poetic genius Emily Dickinson were published during her short but productive lifetime.
9. Some of these were secretly published by Susan Dickinson, Emily's sister-in-law.
10. Lavinia Dickinson, Emily Dickinson's sister, found Emily's poems in a large box after Emily's death.

7.g.14 Commas and parenthetical expressions

Use commas to set off conjunctive adverbs, interjections, and other parenthetical expressions.

The term *parenthetical expression* does not mean that the words are surrounded by parentheses. A parenthetical expression is simply a term used to refer to an extra expression.

Nevertheless, the government intends to continue research in the area.

We were left, therefore, with only two choices.

She had not studied for the test; however, she was able to answer most of the questions.

I do not know his name, incidentally.

We left early, unfortunately.

Well, I hope you have a good excuse.

Last summer, on the other hand, the town was crowded with tourists.

Franklin and Eleanor Roosevelt were distant cousins, in fact.

7.g.15 Commas and direct address

Use commas to set off words or names used in direct address.

Tony, do you know where Maureen is?
I can order the book for you, sir, if you like.
Thank you for the ride, Mrs. Sullivan.

EXERCISE 25. Rewrite the following sentences, adding commas where necessary.

1. Unfortunately, before the eighteenth century most Native American languages were not written down.
2. It was, in fact, difficult for people to learn the languages without a writing system.
3. Well, in the eighteenth century a Cherokee named Sequoyah saw the need for a written Cherokee language.
4. Actually, most Cherokees thought that writing was the privilege of only certain people.
5. Sequoyah, however, saw how valuable a written language would be to his tribe.
6. The Cherokees had a spoken language; however, they had no system of writing.
7. The Cherokees, moreover, communicated with other tribes with smoke and drum signals.
8. Sequoyah had been hurt in a hunting accident; consequently, he had leisure to think about a writing system.
9. At this time Sequoyah was a grown man and a silversmith; nevertheless, he began to draw marks on twigs and stones in the forest.
10. No one took Sequoyah seriously after that, however.
11. For twelve years everyone laughed at Sequoyah's dream, sad to say.
12. Do you think it unusual, students, that Sequoyah spent his time making marks in the forest?
13. At first Sequoyah wanted to give every word a different symbol, incidentally.

14. After all of his struggles, however, Sequoyah was rewarded.
15. He produced, in fact, the first Cherokee alphabet.
16. Moreover, he made it possible for his tribe to write messages and record their history.
17. Therefore Sequoyah had courage and foresight.
18. It is no surprise, therefore that the Cherokees changed their minds about him.
19. Finally, in 1828 the Cherokees sent Sequoyah to be their representative in Washington.
20. Always remember, budding pioneers, that Sequoyah was successful despite the doubts of others.

AVOIDING ERRORS WITH COMMAS (GENERAL)

1. When you use commas to set off an expression in the middle of a sentence, do not forget to place a comma both *before* and *after* the expression.

   NOT   We were left, therefore with only two choices.
   BUT   We were left, therefore, with only two choices.

2. Do not place a comma between the parts of a compound subject or a compound object if all the parts are separated by *and* or *or* (see 2.e and 2.k).

   NOT   The adults playing softball and the children playing soccer argued in the field. [compound subject]
   BUT   The adults playing softball and the children playing soccer argued in the field.

   NOT   She watched the tennis match and the football game. [compound object]
   BUT   She watched the tennis match and the football game.

REVIEW EXERCISE E. Rewrite the following sentences, adding commas where necessary.

1. Literature lovers, although you may have heard of Mark Twain, you may not know that his real name is Samuel Langhorne Clemens.

2. Clemens, who was born in 1835 and died in 1910, began life in the town of Florida, Missouri.

3. When Samuel Clemens was four years old, his family moved to Hannibal, a town on the Mississippi River in Missouri.

4. Living in Hannibal, the young Clemens watched, enjoyed, and met many kinds of people.

5. The sights, sounds, and movements of Hannibal became material that Clemens used in his stories, novels, and lectures.

6. When Clemens was eleven, his father died, leaving the family without financial support.

7. After wandering in St. Louis, Cincinnati, New York, Philadelphia, and New Orleans, Clemens finally headed west.

8. In Nevada Clemens became a reporter for a newspaper, the *Territorial Enterprise.*

9. In his years of travel in the country of his birth, Clemens learned trades that helped his career as a writer.

10. To earn his living while he traveled, Clemens worked as a printer, a riverboat pilot, and a miner.

11. Clemens' profession as a riverboat pilot on the Mississippi River gave him his pen name, Mark Twain, which was a phrase that indicated how deep the water was.

12. Early books that made Twain famous include one called *Roughing It,* one called *The Gilded Age,* and one called *The Adventures of Tom Sawyer.*

13. Twain's book *The Innocents Abroad* presented a view of Europe that was critical, humorous, and mildly shocking.

14. Twain stopped traveling, Olivia Langdon married him, and they moved to Hartford, Connecticut.

15. Twain's books, because they were humorous and exciting, appealed to children.

16. Adults were the readers Twain had in mind when he wrote his books, however.

17. *The Adventures of Huckleberry Finn* is a popular children's book, but it is also read by adults who study great literature.

18. Twain was so popular, in fact, that he earned a fortune by giving lectures that were humorous, novel, and educational.

19. Unfortunately, Twain was unable to manage his money, which he often lost through bad investments.

20. The millions of people who read Mark Twain's books are rewarded with humor, wit, and insight.

REVIEW EXERCISE F. Correct all errors in comma usage in the following sentences. Rewrite each sentence, adding commas that are needed and deleting those that are incorrect.

1. Although everyone knows something about nutrition, there are, in fact, many false ideas about food.

2. Facts are the basis of nutrition, good spirits, and health.

3. Some people say that calories, the amount of energy in food, are not important; however, most scientists, doctors, and nutrition experts disagree.

4. Eating too many sweets, starches, and fats is a good way to gain weight.

5. On the other hand, if you burn off more calories than you have eaten, you will lose weight, and your energy level will decrease.

6. Because calories are important, it is wise to learn about them.

7. When you know all the facts, you will be able to decide what foods to eat.

8. Calories are found in three of the basic food groups: proteins/ and carbohydrates/ and fats.

9. Consequently, eating any food will provide you with calories,but remember that fatty foods have the most calories.

10. Proteins,which are needed to build/ and repair/ and feed body tissues,have four calories per gram.

11. Carbohydrates contain sugar and starch/ and have four calories per gram.

12. Fats have nine calories per gram,a unit of weight.

13. Since fats help you to store energy for later use,do not avoid them entirely.

14. You need calories from proteins ,carbohydrates ,and fats to survive.

15. Experts give advice about maintaining a balanced diet, and you should listen to them.

16. If you eat all three food groups,you will be sure to get the vitamins/ that you need.

17. Remember that too many or too few calories can make you tired,unhealthy,and irritable.

18. To lose weight, you must eat moderately, wisely, and practically.

19. To stay healthy,however,you must eat,drink,and sleep enough.

20. Eating a balanced diet will keep you healthy,give you energy,and make you feel confident.

7.h SEMICOLONS

A semicolon is a punctuation mark halfway between a comma and a period. (Notice that the top part of the mark is a period, and the bottom part of the mark is a comma.) Semicolons are used to mark sentence breaks that are too strong for a comma but not strong enough for a period.

7.h.1 Semicolons to separate main clauses

Use a semicolon to separate main clauses that are not joined by the coordinating conjunctions *and, but,* and *for.*

It is sometimes difficult to decide whether to use a semicolon to separate main clauses or to make the clauses into separate sentences. If the clauses are closely related, keep them in the same sentence and use a semicolon to separate them. If the clauses are not very closely related, make them into separate sentences by adding periods.

> Mildred (Babe) Didrikson Zaharias was one of the greatest golfers in history; the Babe Zaharias Trophy is named for her. [The clauses are closely related; use a semicolon.]
>
> Babe Zaharias died in 1956. Championship golfer Nancy Lopez is Babe's successor on the links. [Both sentences deal with golfers, but each sentence is about a different person. Therefore, use a period and a capital letter for each sentence.]

Use a semicolon to separate main clauses joined by conjunctive adverbs, such as *however, therefore, nevertheless, moreover, furthermore,* and *consequently,* or by such expressions as *for example* and *that is.*

In general, a conjunctive adverb or an expression like *for example* is followed by a comma.

> Babe Zaharias was a champion javelin thrower and golfer; in addition, she was a basketball star.

EXERCISE 26. Rewrite the following sentences, inserting semicolons where necessary. In some sentences you will have to replace a comma with a semicolon.

1. You may think of visual art as a painting or a sculpture in a museum; however, art can take many shapes and sizes.

2. Many artists in the past created artworks that could be displayed in a home or place of worship/; today, these works of art are found in museums.

3. Art forms have changed over the years/; in fact, many modern artists do not create small paintings or sculptures for museums.

4. Many artists wish to free art from the four walls of a museum ;these artists have turned to "earth art."

5. Earth artists create huge artworks in vast open spaces/; the entire landscape is considered part of the artwork.

6. The artwork is placed in a desert or a plain or on a mountain/; the artwork and the landscape harmonize with each other.

7. Earth artists include James Turrell, Charles Ross, and Nancy Holt/; Nancy Holt is the creator of *Sun Tunnels*.

8. *Sun Tunnels* lies in the Great Salt Lake Desert ;it is made up of two large concrete tubes in the form of an *X*.

9. Earth art changes continually/; the weather and light can change the artwork's appearance.

10. Earth art is not the final stage of art ;artists in the future may create works under the ocean or in deep space.

7.h.2 Semicolons to separate expressions containing commas

Use a semicolon to separate clauses or items in a series that themselves contain commas.

Three recent U.S. Open golf champions are Hollis Stacy, who won in 1978; Sandra Palmer, who won in 1975; and Donna Caponi, who won in 1970.

Three noteworthy American athletes are Patricia McCormick, a diver; Helen Wills Moody, a tennis player; and Wilma Rudolph, a track star.

EXERCISE 27. Rewrite the following sentences, inserting semicolons where necessary. In some sentences you will have to replace a comma with a semicolon. Two of the sentences contain no errors.

1. The American sculptor Louise Nevelson has lived in Kiev, U.S.S.R.; Rockland, Maine; Munich, Germany; and New York City.
2. Nevelson's family name was Berliawsky; she married Charles Nevelson in 1920.
3. Nevelson studied art in Munich, Germany; in fact, in that city she began her career.
4. Many artists are not willing to struggle, but Louise Nevelson worked for years without money or fame.
5. Nevelson's first sculpture show was in 1940; after that she became world renowned.
6. Nevelson makes sculptures with "found objects"; her artworks are large and intricate.
7. Nevelson uses wood, metal, and plastic for her sculptures, but her works with wood are the most popular and the most well known.
8. Nevelson was honored by the townspeople of Rockland, Maine; they gave her a party and purchased a sculpture.
9. Nevelson appeared at the party in layers of silk and velvet; moreover, she wore thick fur false eyelashes.
10. Nevelson once said, "I didn't know that I could do anything else; I felt art and I were one."

7.i COLONS

Use a colon to introduce a list, especially after such expressions as *the following* or *as follows.*

Colons are a formal mark of punctuation. They are used to introduce lists and quotations. Colons also have certain conventional uses. For instance, they are used in writing the time, in referring to sections of the Bible, and in writing business letters. Capitalize the first word of a complete sentence after a colon.

> The following suits are found in the game of mah-jongg: bamboos, circles, characters, winds, and dragons.
>
> Perform the following procedure before playing a round of mah-jongg: 1) Place all of the tiles with their backs up, 2) build a four-sided wall with all of the tiles, and 3) take thirteen tiles from the wall to make your hand.
>
> Robert Frost refers to the darkness of ignorance in the following lines: "He moves in darkness as it seems to me,/Not of woods only and the shade of trees."

> 6:30 A.M.   3:00 P.M.
> Genesis 7:24   Exodus 2:13
> Dear Sir: Dear Madam:

EXERCISE 28. Rewrite the following sentences, adding colons where necessary.

1. Many people enjoy playing board games: chess, checkers, and pachisi.
2. Chess may have spread from area to area in the following order: India, Persia, Spain, and then Europe.
3. There are several board games related to chess: checkers, the Japanese game *go*, and Chinese checkers.
4. In chess each player has the following playing pieces: one king, one queen, two bishops, two knights, two rooks, and eight pawns.
5. The following qualities are essential to a good chess player: a good memory, a quick mind, and foresight.

7.j HYPHENS

There are two basic uses for hyphens in English words. Some words require hyphens as an essential part of their spelling (for example, *sister-in-law*). Some words require hyphens in order to keep your right-hand margin lined up when you write or type a composition.

Use hyphens in compound numbers.

sixty-four	sixty-fourth
eighty-seven	eighty-seventh
thirty-five	thirty-fifth

In order to keep the right-hand margins of your paper fairly even, you may want to use a hyphen to divide a word at the end of a line.

Do not divide one-syllable words or a single syllable within a word.

NOT	str̸ing	pas̸sed	delici̸ous
BUT	string	passed	deli-cious

In general, divide a word with double consonants between the two consonants.

siz-zled	scis-sors	smal-lest
run-ning	clip-per	gig-gled

If a suffix such as *-ing* or *-est* has been added to a complete word ending in two consonants, divide the word after the two consonants.

sand-ing	crack-ing	fill-ing
dress-ing	black-est	full-est

If a word contains two consonants standing between two vowels, ordinarily divide it between the consonants.

foun-tain	fin-ger
profes-sor	struc-ture

Divide a word with a prefix or a suffix after the prefix (such as *un-*, *pre-*, and *dis-*) or before the suffix (such as *-ment*, *-able*, and *-ible*).

un-likely	align-ment
pre-packaged	laugh-able
dis-pleasure	convert-ible

To divide a compound noun or a compound adjective that is generally written as one word, place the hyphen between the two base words.

base-ball   stop-watch
head-ache   book-shop

Divide a hyphenated compound word at the hyphen.

actor-director   sister-in-law
ex-President   Chinese-American

Do not divide proper nouns, proper adjectives, or abbreviations.

NOT   Johnny Car/son
BUT   Johnny Carson

NOT   ap/prox.
BUT   approx.

NOT   Transcen/dental
BUT   Transcendental

NOT   UN/ESCO
BUT   UNESCO

EXERCISE 29. For each of the words below decide whether or not it could be divided if it appeared at the end of a line. Rewrite the words that can be divided, adding hyphens at the point of division.

1. smartest *smart-est*
2. Chinese
3. disabled *dis-abled*
4. Chaplin
5. swimming *swim-ming*
6. alone *a-lone*
7. antitrust *anti-trust*
8. someone *some-one*
9. stood
10. clapping *clap-ping*
11. ex-mayor *ex-mayor*
12. kissing *kiss-ing*
13. timetable *time-table*
14. apart *a-part*
15. singer *sing-er*
16. reachable *reach-able*
17. combed
18. blackest *black-est*
19. mountain *moun-tain*
20. football *foot-ball*

7.k APOSTROPHES

It is important to learn the proper use of apostrophes because the meaning of certain words depends upon whether or not they have an apostrophe. Consider the following examples:

three *mornings* in a row
this *morning's* newspaper
I hope *she'll* arrive tomorrow.
This *shell* is orange and red.

7.k.1 Apostrophes for the possessive

1. nouns not ending in *s*

Use the apostrophe and *s* to form the possessive of singular and plural nouns not ending in *s*. This rule applies to both common and proper nouns.

Clemente**'s** batting average
Mexico**'s** landscape
the performer**'s** costume

women**'s** rights
children**'s** activities
my feet**'s** appearance

NOTE: Do not italicize the *'s* in the possessive of italicized titles of works.

Newsweek's cover story
West Side Story's dance sequences
Moby Dick's ending

2. plural nouns ending in *s*

Use the apostrophe alone to form the possessive of plural nouns ending in *s*. This rule applies to both common and proper nouns.

the Campfire Girls**'** activities
the Allies**'** promises
the Boy Scouts**'** code of honor

the books' arrangement
the countries' treaty
the French students' final exam

3. singular nouns ending in *s*

When forming the possessive of a singular noun ending in *s* (or an *s* sound), count the number of syllables in the word. If the noun has only one syllable, use the apostrophe and an *s* to form the possessive. If the noun has more than one syllable, usually add the apostrophe alone.

the class**'s** election
Gwendolyn Brooks**'s** poetry
Harpo Marx**'s** music

Adele Davis' speech
the princess' power
Grandma Moses' paintings

NOTE: Some books do not follow the preceding rule. Although the rule states the preferred usage, it is not incorrect to use both an apostrophe and an *s* after a singular noun of more than one syllable ending in *s*.

Adele Davis**'s** speech
Grandma Moses**'s** paintings

4. indefinite pronouns

Use the apostrophe and an *s* to form the possessive of indefinite pronouns such as *someone, one, anybody, everybody, somebody else,* and *each other.*

one**'s** ideas   no one**'s** intention
everybody**'s** support   someone else**'s** fault
each other**'s** suitcase   anybody**'s** paper

5. compound words

Use the apostrophe and an *s* (or the apostrophe alone) after the last part of a hyphenated or nonhyphenated compound.

my mother-in-law**'s** office   Cape Hatteras' beauty
the court-martial**'s** effect   the Chief of Staff**'s** order

6. joint possession

If two or more persons possess something jointly, use the possessive form of the name of only the last person mentioned. The names of businesses and organizations should also be treated in this way.

> Larry and Louise**'s** children
> Abbott and Costello**'s** antics
> Strawbridge and Clothier**'s** clothing
> Johnson and Johnson**'s** baby care products

7. individual possession by more than one person

If two or more persons (or things) each possess something individually, put each name in the possessive form.

> Bob Dylan**'s** and the Beatles**'** songs
> Beethoven**'s** and Mozart**'s** music
> Denise**'s** and Judith**'s** daughters

8. units of time and money

Use the apostrophe and an *s* (or the apostrophe alone) to form the possessive of units of time (*second, minute, hour, day, week, month, year*) and money (*cent, nickel, dime, dollar*). Use a hyphen if the unit is not in the possessive form.

> five minutes**'** drive   *but*   a five-minute drive
> one dollar**'s** worth   *but*   a one-dollar increase
> ten days**'** wait   *but*   a ten-day visit

EXERCISE 30. Write the possessive form of each of the following items.

1. baby   *baby's*
2. telephone   *telephone's*
3. Henry James   *Henry James's*
4. Texas   *Texas'*
5. Procter and Gamble   *Procter and Gamble's*
6. parents   *parents'*
7. ten seconds time   *ten seconds' time*

8. nobody   *nobody's*
9. Bob and Jim hands   *Bob's and Jim's hands*
10. women   *women's*
11. prince   *prince's*
12. teacher   *teacher's*
13. Mom and Dad son   *Mom and Dad's son*
14. Barbara Walters   *Barbara Walters'*

Accept 's for Items 4 and 14.

15. *Time*   *Time's*

16. another   *another's*

17. brother-in-law *brother-in-law's*

Diane's and Tim's grades
18. Diane and Tim grades

19. one   *one's*

20. cousins   *cousins'*

AVOIDING ERRORS WITH APOSTROPHES IN POSSESSIVES

1. Do not forget to use th e apostrophe to form the possessive.

   NOT   That is ~~Elise~~ secret.
   NOT   That is ~~Elises~~ secret.
   BUT   That is Elise**'s** secret.

   NOT   He complained about the shoes defects.
   BUT   He complained about the shoes**'** defects.

2. Do not misplace the apostrophe in the possessive of a noun that ends in *s*.

   NOT   I like Judy ~~Collin's~~ music. [The singer's name is Judy Collins with an *s* at the end.]
   BUT   I like Judy Collins**'** music.
   OR   I like Judy Collins**'s** music.

3. Do not use an apostrophe with the possessive personal pronouns that end in *s* (*his, hers, its, ours, yours, theirs*). These pronouns are already possessive in form.

   NOT   That car is ~~our's~~.
   NOT   That car is ~~ours'~~.
   BUT   That car is **ours.**

EXERCISE 31. Write the possessive form of each of the following items. Two of the items are correct as written.

1. men   *men's*

2. five cents worth
   five cents' worth

the Smiths' house
3. the Smiths house

4. ours

5. ships *ships'*

6. people *people's*

7. Jim and Lee hand
   Jim's and Lee's hand

8. brothers-in-law
   brothers-in-law's

9. nephews *nephews'*

10. companies *companies'*

11. players salaries
    players' salaries

12. boys
    boys'

13. tomatoes *tomatoes'*

14. women *women's*

15. trees *trees'*

16. two years study *two years'* *study*

17. theirs

18. schoolchildren *schoolchildren's*

19. everyone *everyone's*

20. great-grandmothers
    great-grandmothers'

EXERCISE 32. From each pair of items below select the one item that correctly expresses the possessive.

1. a) boys shoes
   b) boys' shoes √

2. a) my aunt's plants √
   b) my aunts plants

3. a) The pen is her's.
   b) The pen is hers. √

4. a) anybodys books
   b) anybody's books √

5. a) the dog's paw √
   b) the dogs' paw

6. a) Illinois' cities √
   b) Illinoiss cities

7. a) my uncles books
   b) my uncle's books √

8. a) forty-five minutes'
      time √
   b) forty-five minute's
      time

9. a) the princess' hand √
   b) the princess hand

10. a) Yankee's batting
       average [team]
    b) Yankees' batting
       average [team] √

11. a) Lord and Taylor's
       branch stores √
    b) Lord's and Taylor's
       branch stores

12. a) childrens' stories
    b) children's stories √

13. a) the hen's egg √
    b) the hens' egg

14. a) teamsters strike
    b) teamsters' strike √

15. a) no one's business √
    b) no ones' business

16. a) womens' rights
    b) women's rights √

17. a) a quarter worth
    b) a quarter's worth √

18. a) Molly and Greg's
       eyeglasses
    b) Molly's and Greg's
       eyeglasses √

19. a) Is this your's?
    b) Is this yours? √

20. a) apostrophes uses
    b) apostrophes' uses √

7.k.2 Apostrophes in contractions

Use the apostrophe in place of letters omitted in contractions.

A **contraction** is a single word made up of two words that have been combined by omitting letters. Some familiar contractions are listed below:

Contraction	Original words
I'm	I am
you're	you are
she's	she is
it's	it is
there's	there is
who's	who is
I've	I have
you've	you have
he'd	he had (or he would)
you'd	you had (or you would)
don't	do not
doesn't	does not
won't	will not
we'll	we will
she'll	she will

Use the apostrophe in place of omitted numerals in such expressions as *the class of '85*.

EXERCISE 33. Write the contraction for each of the following expressions.

1. will not *won't*
2. there is *there's*
3. would have *would've*
4. does not *doesn't*
5. I am *I'm*
6. she will *she'll*
7. you are *you're*
8. we will *we'll*
9. could have *could've*
10. do not *don't*
11. who is *who's*
12. they will *they'll*
13. I have *I've*
14. should have *should've*
15. you have *you've*
16. it is *it's*
17. he would *he'd*
18. she is *she's*
19. you had *you'd*
20. he had *he'd*

AVOIDING ERRORS WITH CONTRACTIONS

1. Do not forget to use the apostrophe in contractions.

   NOT   I ~~wont~~ go to the game with you.
   BUT   I won't go to the game with you.

2. Do not confuse the contraction *it's* (it is) with the possessive pronoun *its*. Use the apostrophe only when you mean *it is*. (See 5.c for a discussion of other homonyms commonly confused.)

   NOT   ~~Its~~ going to be a pretty room when I paint ~~it's~~ walls blue.
   BUT   **It's** going to be a pretty room when I paint **its** walls blue.

3. Do not misplace the apostrophe when writing contractions.

   NOT   I ~~would'nt~~ go if I were you.
   BUT   I wouldn't go if I were you.

7.k.3 Apostrophes for special plurals

Use the apostrophe and an *s* to form the plural of letters, numbers, signs, and words used as words.

Italicize (underline) the letter, number, sign, or word, but do not italicize the *'s*.

Remember that all gerunds have *ing*'s at the end.
Your *e*'s look like *l*'s.
The *5*'s were read as *50*'s.
Please replace your *&*'s with *and*'s.
My teacher told me to replace my *henceforth*'s with *therefore*'s in my paper.

AVOIDING ERRORS WITH APOSTROPHES TO FORM THE PLURAL

1. Do not use the apostrophe to form the plural of an ordinary noun or the form of a verb that agrees with a third-person singular subject.

   NOT   There are only eight baseball ~~player's~~ on the field!

   BUT   There are only eight baseball **players** on the field!

   NOT   Mike Schmidt usually ~~hit's~~ the ball over the fence.

   BUT   Mike Schmidt usually **hits** the ball over the fence.

2. Use an *s* or an *es* without an apostrophe to form the plural of a proper name.

   My parents invited the Wong**s**, the DiGiovanna**s**, and the Jones**es** to dinner.

   There are three Maria**s** and two Bill**s** in our class.

EXERCISE 34. Write the plural form of each of the following items.

1. *100* *100's*
2. *perhaps* *perhaps's*
3. Smith and Torres *Smiths and Torreses*
4. *p* and *q* *p's and q's*
5. & *&'s*
6. Theresa *Theresas*
7. *ABC* *ABC's*
8. *6* and *7* *6's and 7's*
9. % *%'s*
10. *and* *and's*

REVIEW EXERCISE G. Rewrite the following sentences, adding apostrophes where necessary.

1. Many writers' names are familiar to lovers of poetry and fiction.

2. Under the *A*'s, for example, you'd list Louisa May Alcott, who's best known for *Little Women*.

3. No list of *The New Yorker*'s poets would be complete without the name of Elizabeth Bishop.

4. The *B*'s would also include the names of Pearl S. Buck and Gwendolyn Brooks.

5. Pearl S. Buck's novels focus on the Chinese people's culture.

6. Gwendolyn Brooks's poems deal with Afro-Americans' lives.

7. Other writers who've received attention include Agatha Christie, whose play *The Mousetrap* was famous in a theater's history.

8. Emily Dickinson, who's one of the finest American poets, didn't have her works published during her lifetime.

9. Nikki Giovanni is a poet who'd be listed under the *G*'s.

10. Giovanni's works include *Black Feeling, Black Talk* and *My House*.

11. Under the *L*'s we'd find the names Denise Levertov, Doris Lessing, and Anita Loos.

12. Levertov's poetry is complex and often sad.

13. Lessing's novels often deal with the problems of love and marriage.

14. One of Loos's screenplays was made into a film starring Marilyn Monroe.

15. At least four writers' names would be listed under the *M*'s: Carson McCullers, Edna St. Vincent Millay, Margaret Mitchell, and Marianne Moore.

16. Millay's and Moore's names would be found on anyone's list of talented poets.

17. Mitchell's and McCullers' names are familiar to lovers of excellent prose.

18. McCullers' novel *The Member of the Wedding* was adapted for the stage.

19. Most people don't know that Margaret Mitchell's *Gone With the Wind* took ten years' time to write.

20. A list of writers would include at least three *P*s: Dorothy Parker, Sylvia Plath, and Katherine Anne Porter.

21. You'd list both Parker and Plath as poets.

22. Parker's subjects are usually humorous, and Plath's are tragic.

23. The novelist Katherine Anne Porter's great-great-great-grandfather's name is also well known: Daniel Boone.

24. Adrienne Rich and Muriel Rukeyser are poets you'd list.

25. Who'd call a list complete if it didn't include Gertrude Stein and Sara Teasdale?

26. One of Stein's most famous lines deals with the word *rose*'s definition: "A rose is a rose is a rose."

27. One of Sara Teasdale's honors was a Pulitzer Prize for *Love Song*.

28. Under the *W*'s you'd list Edith Wharton and Virginia Woolf.

29. Wharton's novels take place in America during the nineteenth century.

30. Woolf's novels influenced many other writers' works.

7.1 QUOTATION MARKS

Quotation marks are most often used to point out other people's words used in a sentence. Use double quotation marks to enclose direct quotations as well as titles of short works. Place quotation marks at the beginning *and* at the end of the material you wish to enclose.

7.1.1 Quotation marks for direct quotations

Use quotation marks to enclose a direct quotation.

Capitalize the first word of a quotation that is a complete sentence. Do not capitalize a quotation that is only a partial sentence.

A famous poster questions, "What if they gave a war and nobody came?"

A Pawnee poem advises us to always remember "the sacredness of things."

Set off a quotation with a comma (or a colon) only if the quotation is a complete sentence. Do not set off a quotation that is a partial sentence.

William James wisely said, "Wherever you are, it is your own friends who make your world."

A character in a play by Edna St. Vincent Millay speaks the following lines: "Is it Tuesday, Columbine? I'll kiss you if it's Tuesday."

According to Lydia Liliuokalani, the Hawaiian people are "lovers of poetry and music."

When a quotation is interrupted by such words as *she wrote* or *he said,* enclose both parts of the separated quotation in quotation marks. Set off each part with some kind of punctuation. If the second part of the quotation is a complete sentence, be sure to begin it with a capital letter.

"You know, when you're young and curious," says Dede Allen, "people love to teach you."

"People who fight fire with fire," wrote Abigail Van Buren, "usually end up with ashes."

"It took me seventeen years to get three thousand hits in baseball," said Hank Aaron. "I did it in one afternoon on the golf course."

In writing you may want to use someone else's words without quoting them exactly. This is called using an indirect quotation (or, if you are phrasing a question, an indirect question). An indirect quotation is often preceded by *that.* Do not use quotation marks in an indirect quotation (or in an indirect question).

Exact words: "When you're as great as I am, it's hard to be humble."
—Muhammad Ali

Indirect quotation: Muhammad Ali claimed that when one is as great as he is, it is hard to be humble.

Use single quotation marks to enclose a quotation within a quotation.

President Kennedy once said, "I am one person who can truthfully say, 'I got my job through the *New York Times*.'"

In writing dialogue, begin a new paragraph and use a new set of quotation marks every time the speaker changes.

I put the brooch on the table in front of Papa.

He looked at me proudly. "Was it so hard to do, Daughter?"

"Not so hard as I thought." I pinned the brooch on my dress. "I'll wear it always," I said. "I'll keep it forever."

"Mama will be glad, Katrin."

Papa dipped a lump of sugar and held it out to me. I shook my head. "Somehow," I said, "I just don't feel like it, Papa."

"So?" Papa said. "So?"

And he stood up and poured out a cup of coffee and handed it to me.

"For me?" I asked wonderingly.

Papa smiled and nodded. "For my grown-up daughter," he said.

I sat up straight in my chair. And felt very proud as I drank my first cup of coffee.
                                                        —Kathryn Forbes

EXERCISE 35. Rewrite the following sentences, changing each direct quotation into an indirect quotation.

EXAMPLE Yantz said, "I enjoy my work."

ANSWER *Yantz said that she enjoyed her work.*

1. Robin Yantz told a reporter from the *New York Times*, "This year I became a baseball umpire, and I loved it."
   . . . that this year she became . . . and she . . .

2. "Some coaches gave me the feeling they didn't want me umpiring their games," said Yantz. *Yantz said that some coache gave her the feeling that they didn't want her umpiring .*
3. After her first game was over, Yantz complained, "I was ready to collapse.". *. . . that she was ready to collapse after her first game .*
4. Yantz said, however, "I talked over my mistakes with my fellow umpire.". *. . . that she talked over her mistakes with her fellow .*
5. Yantz claimed, "I had to prove myself on the field." *Yantz claimed that she had to prove herself on the field.*

7.I.2 Quotation marks for titles of short works

Use quotation marks to enclose titles of short works, such as stories, poems, essays, newspaper and periodical articles, chapters, songs, and television episodes.

"The Legend of Sleepy Hollow" [short story]
"The Raven" [poem]
"Jabberwocky" [poem]
"On the Duty of Civil Disobedience" [essay]
"Woody Allen's Newest Film" [newspaper article]
"The 1960s in America" [chapter]
"If I Had a Hammer" [song]
"Yesterday" [song]

NOTE: Italicize (underline) titles of long works, such as books, films, long poems, and plays and the names of periodicals, newspapers, television series, and paintings (see 7.m.1).

EXERCISE 36. Rewrite the following sentences, adding quotation marks where necessary.

1. *The Indian Heritage of America* is divided into chapters with such broad titles as "The Indians of the Southwest."
2. If you are interested in Native Americans, read the article entitled "The Origins of New World Civilization" in *Scientific American.*

3. "North American Indians" is an essay that describes the social behavior of Native Americans.

4. "The Indian Burial Ground" is a poem written by Philip Freneau.

5. Freneau also wrote a poem entitled "The Indian Student," which tells of a Native American's experiences at Harvard University.

6. Emerson Hough's short story "The Bird Woman" is about Sacajawea, a Shoshone woman.

7. Native American folk singer Buffy Sainte-Marie wrote the song "Until It's Time for You to Go."

8. In his essay "Traits of Indian Character" Washington Irving presented a romantic view of Native Americans.

9. J. G. Neihardts's *Epic Cycle of the West* includes a poem entitled "The Song of the Indian Wars."

10. "American Indians and American Life" is a recent essay about Native Americans.

AVOIDING ERRORS WITH QUOTATION MARKS

Do not forget to place quotation marks (single or double) both *before* and *after* the quoted material. Leaving out closing quotation marks is a frequent error.

| NOT | My teacher said, "Hand your papers in. |
| BUT | My teacher said, "Hand your papers in." |

| NOT | We read "The Night the Bed Fell by James Thurber. |
| BUT | We read "The Night the Bed Fell" by James Thurber. |

| NOT | Did you like Robert Frost's poem "Mending Wall? |
| BUT | Did you like Robert Frost's poem "Mending Wall"? |

QUOTATION MARKS WITH OTHER MARKS OF PUNCTUATION

1. Always place a comma or a period *inside* closing quotation marks.

   > "The frog does not drink up the pond in which it lives," states a Native American proverb.
   > Henry David Thoreau humorously advises, "Beware of all enterprises that require new clothes."

2. Always place a semicolon or a colon *outside* closing quotation marks.

   > Her father said "yes"; her mother said "no"; her brother said that he did not know.
   > There are two Spanish verbs that mean "to be": *ser* and *estar.*

3. Place the question mark or exclamation point *inside* closing quotation marks when the question mark or exclamation point is part of the quotation.

   > A famous sonnet by Shakespeare begins with these words: "Shall I compare thee to a summer's day?"
   > We recited Whitman's poem "Beat! Beat! Drums!"

   Place the question mark or exclamation point *outside* quotation marks when the question mark or exclamation point is part of the entire sentence.

   > What Shakespearean character said, "To be or not to be: That is the question"?
   > How rude of her to say "No, I cannot be there before seven"!

continued

NOTE: If both your sentence and the quotation at the end of your sentence need a question mark or exclamation point, use only *one* question mark or exclamation point placed *inside* the quotation marks.

> Is it Sonnet 18 that begins with these words: "Shall I compare thee to a summer's day?"
> I was so surprised when he yelled, "Fire!"

EXERCISE 37. Rewrite the following sentences, adding quotation marks where necessary. Three of the sentences are correct as written.

1. In 1978 *Quest* magazine published an article called "History the Hard Way," by William P. Urschel, Jr.

2. "History the Hard Way" was written from Urschel's notes of a trip he made in the Southwest.

3. Urschel said that he made the trip to find out how the American Southwest was explored.

4. Urschel said of his trip: "My only companions will be my horse and a pack mule. "

5. "My only equipment," he said, "will be what they can carry. "

6. "This is not going to be a pleasure trip," Urschel noted.

7. At the start of his trip Urschel wrote, "I suddenly realized that I don't really know what I'm up against."

8. He admitted an even greater problem: "I've never actually ridden a horse before. "

9. A Native American taught Urschel to ride and also gave him a dog, after which Urschel wrote, "Man, mule, horse, and dog finally rode out toward the Rio Grande. "

10. Urschel's animals ran home, however, and he reflected, "Homesickness takes time to cure."

11. Urschel finally caught up with his horse and mule and wrote, "I only hope I learn how to pack and handle a mule before I lose everything I own. "

12. "Even the worst days have their compensations," Urschel noted after two days of travel.

13. "It's hard to believe it's been 131 years since my predecessors first followed this river," he noted.

14. The loneliness of traveling alone outdoors is expressed in the song "Home on the Range."

15. Urschel experienced bad weather and wrote, "Within minutes we were hit by an exploding wall of wind and water."

16. Urschel noted, "The climatic change from very hot to very, very hot was more sudden and pronounced than I expected."

17. "A dust storm took me by surprise," he said, "and left me blind and choking."

18. Urschel complained that he was very fatigued.

19. Two months after setting out, Urschel wrote, "Tonight I am on foot . . . because my horse is dead."

20. "This seems an appropriate finale to the last 1,200 miles," Urschel said to himself.

21. When he reached San Diego, Urschel wrote, "I'm hardly noticed by the tourists."

22. Urschel asked himself where he should sleep.

23. The question "Where can I sleep tonight?" was suddenly very important.

24. "The most powerful influence . . . — society — was powerful only in its absence," Urschel observed.

25. Urschel asked himself, "What have I learned?"

26. "I've learned to ride fairly well," said Urschel, "shoot down a rabbit on the run, and cook it to near perfection."

27. "This is a hollow sort of education," he went on to say.

28. "What is important," wrote Urschel, "I could not have learned in any number of shorter, weekend trips."

29. He then added, "I eventually became aware of myself as a part of the environment."

30. Urschel concluded, "What I conquered was fear and fatigue."

7.m ITALICS (UNDERLINING)

Italic type is a special slanted type that is used in printing. (*This is printed in italics.*) Indicate italics on the typewriter or in handwriting by underlining. (This is underlined.)

7.m.1 Italics for titles of long works

Italicize (underline) titles of long artistic works, including books, films, plays, long poems, long musical compositions, and paintings. Also italicize (underline) the names of newspapers, periodicals, and television series.

The Scarlet Letter [book]
2001: A Space Odyssey [film]
A Midsummer Night's Dream [play]
The Song of Hiawatha [long poem]
Grand Canyon Suite [long musical composition]
Christina's World [painting]
the *Evening Phoenix* [newspaper]
Tennis World [periodical]
Nova [television series]

NOTE: Use quotation marks, not italics, to enclose titles of short works, such as stories, poems, essays, newspaper and periodical articles, chapters, songs, and television episodes (see 7.l.2).

Italicize (underline) and capitalize articles (*a, an, the*) written at the beginning of a title only when they are part of the title itself. It is preferred usage not to italicize (underline) or capitalize articles preceding the title of a newspaper or periodical. In general, do not italicize (or capitalize) the word *magazine* following the title of a periodical.

The Seventh Seal	but	the *Chicago Tribune*
An American in Paris	but	an *Orient Times*

7.m.2 Italics for names of spacecraft, airplanes, ships, trains

Italicize (underline) names of spacecraft, airplanes, ships, and trains.

Apollo 12 [spacecraft]
the *Spirit of St. Louis* [airplane]
U.S.S. *Constitution*[1] [ship]
the *Sunset Limited* [train]

EXERCISE 38. Rewrite the following sentences, underlining those elements that should be italicized.

1. Time magazine decided to call 1979 the Year of Women.

2. In the reference book Who's Who in America you will find the names Dr. Jocelyn R. Gill and Dr. Nancy G. Roman.

3. Dr. Gill worked with NASA in launching the spacecrafts Apollo 12 and Echo 2.

4. Dr. Roman's work with satellites made it possible for spacecraft to land on the moon, as Surveyor 1 did in 1966.

5. An Agatha Christie novel was made into a film entitled Murder on the Orient Express.

6. The Orient Express was a real train.

7. John Berryman's long poem Homage to Mistress Bradstreet is about Anne Bradstreet.

8. Anne Bradstreet sailed from England to America on the ship Arabella.

9. Bradstreet's poetry was published in a very popular book entitled The Tenth Muse Lately Sprung Up in America.

10. To find more information about famous women, check articles in the New York Times and Ms.

---

[1]Do not italicize the *U.S.S.* in the names of ships.

7.m.3 Italics for words and letters used to represent themselves

Italicize (underline) words, letters, numbers, and signs used to represent themselves.

Remember that you should not use the word *and* to begin a sentence.

Her typewriter did not have the numeral *1*, so she used a small *L* in its place.

He was too superstitious a person to write down the number *13*.

My English teacher asked me to replace all of the *#*'s with the word *number*.

NOTE: Use an *'s* to indicate the plural of words, letters, numbers, and signs used to represent themselves. This *'s* is not italicized.

I remembered that *ing*'s are used in present participles, and *ed*'s are used in past participles.

I changed all of the *good*'s to *fine*'s in my English composition.

EXERCISE 39. Rewrite the following items, underlining those elements that should be italicized and adding quotation marks where necessary.

1. Carlos Baker's book <u>Ernest Hemingway: A Life Story</u>
2. Hemingway's short story "Big Two-Hearted River"
3. Hemingway's novel <u>For Whom the Bell Tolls</u>
4. the film <u>For Whom the Bell Tolls</u>
5. Hemingway's play <u>The Fifth Column</u>
6. Hemingway's short story "The Killers"
7. the film <u>The Killers</u>
8. the essay "Hemingway in Hollywood"
9. Hemingway's short story "The Short Happy Life of Francis Macomber"
10. the film <u>The Macomber Affair</u>

7.n PARENTHESES

Use parentheses to set off extra material.

Commas are also used to set off extra material. The difference between parentheses and commas is one of degree. Set off with commas extra material that is fairly closely related to the rest of the sentence. Use parentheses for material that is not part of the main statement but is important enough to include.

> Johannes Kepler (German astronomer, 1571–1630) first published the laws of planetary motion.
> Satellites (moons) revolve around many of the planets.
> Planets give off a steady beam of light (reflected light from the sun).

Parentheses are used in footnotes and in citations within the text of a paper (see 14.j).

EXERCISE 40. Rewrite the following sentences, adding parentheses where necessary.

1. Gabrielle "Coco" Chanel (1883–1971) was a leading force in women's fashion.
2. It was in Paris during World War I (1914–1918) that Chanel became internationally known.
3. In the 1920s Chanel stunned the fashion world with "The Look" (short skirts and loose jackets)
4. Chanel introduced the world's most famous perfume, Chanel Number 5. (This scent is still in great demand.)
5. Many of today's fashion classics (sweaters, costume jewelry, fake pearls) were first introduced by Chanel.
6. The unisex trend (like it or not) was started by Chanel, who wore a man's trench coat.
7. Fashionable women wore what Chanel wore (not hoop skirts and stays).
8. During World War II (1941–1945) Chanel's influence on fashion lessened slightly.

Section Review Exercises can be used as diagnostic tests at the beginning of the course or as mastery tests at the end of the course.

7.n

9. Nevertheless, at age seventy-one (the year was 1954) Chanel reopened her fashion house.

10. Many contemporary women's fashions (business suits and low heels) show the influence of Chanel.

SECTION REVIEW EXERCISE I. Copy the following paragraph, correcting all capitalization and punctuation errors. You should find twenty errors.

[1]Annie Oakley, a famous american markswoman, *A* was known as "Little Sure Shot." [2]She was born in Patterson Township, Ohio, on august 13, 1860. [3]When *A* Annie was a young girl, her father died and she helped to feed her family by shooting small game. [4]She became an expert shot with a pistol, rifle and shotgun. [5]Oakley married Frank E. Butler, whom she had beaten in a shooting match and became the star of his vaudeville act. [6]In 1885 she joined Buffalo Bill's Wild West Show. [7]Touring the United states and Europe, *S* she drew large crowds with her exciting tricks. [8]At the invitation of prince Wilhelm of Germany (later *P* Emperor Wilhelm II) she shot a cigarette from between his lips.

SECTION REVIEW EXERCISE II. Copy the following paragraph, correcting all errors in capitalization and punctuation. You should find twenty-five errors.

[1]Did you know that the Morgan Library, which is located at 36th Street and Madison avenue in New *A* York City, is one of the worlds greatest collections of rare books and manuscripts.? [2]In fact, the collection is *Its* really a museum. [3]It's treasures include the following: the earliest dated Mesopotamian tablet (1714 B.C.), the only known manuscript of part of paradise lost, and *P, L* two and a half Gutenberg bibles. [4]Also in the collection *B* are such works as a thirty-five-page manuscript of Einstein's theory of relativity.

[5]The man/ who began this collection/ was J.

Pierpont Morgan ,the famous financier and industrialist. **6**Morgan spent huge sums on his collection/;at his death it contained almost half the value of his _T, A_ estate. **7**Ironically ,*The triumph of avarice* (*avarice* means "greed")is the subject of one of the greatest tapestries in the collection.

8Many stories (some of them are probably not true) are told about Morgan. **9**He was once visited at his _K_ London mansion by King Edward VII, who asked him why he had hung a certain picture so low?. **10**The American replied;"Because I like it there."

8

GLOSSARY
OF USAGE
PROBLEMS

8 Glossary of Usage Problems

See summary of section in Teacher's Manual.

Because people and their circumstances change, the language they use also changes. To give you an idea of what *change* means, in Shakespeare's time the word *deer* was used to refer to any kind of animal. Today, of course, *deer* refers to a specific kind of animal. Similarly, some words that were once considered slang — for instance, *skyscraper, jazz, hairdo* — have now become acceptable in all kinds of writing.

You know that people today are concerned about their language — and your language. They are concerned for the very reason that language and feelings about language change. There are certain areas of language, in particular, that cause concern, and you will find these discussed in the following pages. You will find advice on which words to choose and which to avoid as you write in today's world.

You may ask who decides what is acceptable usage. Who decides, for example, when to use *sit* and when to use *set*? Keep in mind that the term *usage* means just what it says. English usage is determined by the kind of language that educated people *use* when they write and speak for readers of a large newspaper, readers of a general magazine, or viewers of a television news program. The list, or glossary, that follows gives the usages preferred by these educated people.

a, an   Use *a* when the word that follows begins with a consonant sound, including a sounded *h* and the

sound *yū: a song, a poem, a hill, a history, a union.*
Use *an* when the word that follows begins with a vowel
sound or an unsounded *h: an apple, an umbrella, an
hour, an heir.*

affect, effect   See 5.c.

ain't   Do not use *ain't* in writing unless you are quoting
the exact words of a character using dialect. *Ain't* in
speaking is incorrect. Use *I am not, he is not, she is
not,* and so on.

"People just **ain't** the same anymore," the old man said.

all right   This expression is always two words. Never
write *alright.*

She said that she felt **all right** today.

all the farther, all the faster   These are highly informal
ways of saying *as far as* and *as fast as.* In speaking
and writing always use *as far as* and *as fast as.*

Many jets can travel **as fast as** the speed of sound.
We drove **as far as** western Illinois.

amount, number   Use *amount* when referring to nouns
that cannot be counted. Use *number* when referring to
nouns that can be counted.

Fort Knox contains a vast **amount** of gold.
Fort Knox contains a large **number** of gold bars.

bad, badly   See 1.f.6.

being as, being that   These expressions are sometimes
used instead of *because* or *since* in informal conversation. In speaking and writing always use *because* or
since.

Because hamsters are nocturnal, they sleep during the day.

EXERCISE 1. In each of the sentences below, select from the choices in parentheses the word or phrase that represents preferred usage.

1. The name *San Francisco* is (<u>a</u>/an) Hispanic phrase meaning "Saint Francis."
2. San Francisco, California, was claimed as a part of (<u>a</u>/an) United States territory in 1846.
3. Western explorers had traveled (all the farther/<u>as far as</u>) they were able.
4. It is not necessary to mention that San Francisco overlooks (a/<u>an</u>) ocean.
5. There is a great (<u>amount</u>/number) of Spanish and Mexican culture in San Francisco.
6. San Francisco has a large (amount/<u>number</u>) of wonderful restaurants.
7. A large (amount/<u>number</u>) of old military buildings stand in San Francisco.
8. In the late 1800s gold seekers poured into San Francisco (all the faster/<u>as fast as</u>) they could.
9. Few tents and shanties of the first gold boom remained (alright/<u>all right</u>) after four years of fires in San Francisco.
10. (Being that/<u>Since</u>) San Francisco is a popular city, tourism contributes greatly to its income.

beside, besides   Do not confuse these two different words. *Beside* means "located at the side of." *Besides* means "in addition to."

Philadelphia is located **beside** the Delaware River.
Besides anthracite coal, Pennsylvania produces mushrooms and steel.

between, among   Use *between* with two things or persons. Use *among* with groups of three or more.

What is the difference **between** Philadelphia and Chicago?
The tax money was divided **among** the five countries.

bring, take *Bring* means to move something toward the speaker or writer. *Take* means to move something away from the speaker or writer.

> Foreign visitors are not allowed to **bring** certain plants into this country.
>
> Foreign visitors sometimes **take** American money home as a souvenir.

cannot help but This expression is a double negative — therefore incorrect — because *but* is used in a negative sense. Use *cannot help* or *could not help*.

> She **cannot help** crying at graduations.

could of, might of, would of These incorrect expressions may result from the incorrect pronunciation of *could have, might have,* and *would have.* Speak clearly, and write these expressions correctly.

> Some historians say that the United States **could have** prevented the stock market crash of 1929.

different from, different than Be sure to use *different from* before a noun or pronoun. You may use *different than* before clauses and some phrases.

> Cross-country skiing is very **different from** downhill skiing.
> The scenery is **different than** I remember it.

doesn't, don't *Doesn't* is a contraction of *does not;* it is used with *he, she, it,* and singular nouns. *Don't* is a contraction of *do not;* it is used with *I, you, we, they,* and plural nouns.

> The United States **doesn't** allow people to leave school before age sixteen.
>
> Some foreign countries **don't** require that their citizens attend school.

done Use *done* only with a form of *be* or *have.*

> She **has done** all of her homework.

EXERCISE 2. In each of the sentences below, select from the choices in parentheses the word or phrase that represents preferred usage.

1. The Missouri River flows (<u>between</u>/among) Kansas City, Missouri, and Kansas City, Kansas.

2. The cities of Leavenworth and Atchison (doesn't/<u>don't</u>) lie too far away from Kansas City, Kansas.

3. You (cannot help but learn/<u>cannot help learning</u>) about Native American culture in Kansas City, Kansas.

4. (Beside/<u>Besides</u>) being the second largest city in Kansas, Kansas City has within its city limits an old Native American town called Shawnee.

5. The fascinating Shawnee and its inhabitants (<u>bring</u>/take) many tourists to Kansas City.

6. Pioneers (<u>might have</u>/might of) started down the Oregon Trail or the Santa Fe Trail at Shawnee.

7. Kansas City artist Charles Goslin's paintings of Old Shawnee are not much (<u>different from</u>/different than) the real place.

8. When you (done/<u>have done</u>) enough browsing through the Wyandotte Historical Museum, visit the Huron Indian Cemetery.

9. Manual arts, writing, and agriculture are (between/<u>among</u>) the subjects taught to children in Shawnee.

10. Life in Shawnee is (<u>different from</u>/different than) life on a real Native American reservation, however.

each other, one another Use *each other* when talking or writing about two people (or animals). Use *one another* when talking or writing about three or more.

The United States and West Germany trade with **each other.** England, Scotland, and Wales trade with **one another.**

emigrate, immigrate *Emigrate* means "migrate from" a country; *immigrate* means "migrate to" a country. Use *from* with *emigrate*, and use *to* with *immigrate*.

I. M. Pei **immigrated** to the United States.
He **emigrated** from mainland China.

farther, further   Use *farther* when referring to physical distance. Use *further* when referring to degree or time.

San Antonio is **farther** south than Dallas.
She did not question him **further.**

fewer, less   Use *fewer* when referring to nouns that can be counted. Use *less* when referring to nouns that cannot be counted. Notice that *less* can also be used with figures that are seen as a single amount or quantity.

less ice cream
fewer cookies
We traveled **less** than three hours from Philadelphia to New York City. [*Three hours* is treated as a single period of time, not as individual hours.]
It cost **less** than $30 to go by train. [The money is treated as a single sum, not as individual dollars.]

frightened   Do not write *frightened of.* Use *frightened by* or *afraid of.*

Robert was **frightened by** the bee that flew in his face.
Is Iris **afraid of** insects, too?

good, well   See 1.f.6.

had of   See *could of, might of, would of.*

had ought   Do not use *had* with *ought.*

They **ought** to close their windows to keep out the rain.

in, into, in to   Use *in* when indicating location. Use *into* when indicating direction to a place. *In to* indicates direction to something other than a place.

The car was **in** the garage.
The driver walked **into** the garage.
The guests went **in to** lunch.

EXERCISE 3. In each of the sentences below, select from the choices in parentheses the word or phrase that represents preferred usage.

1. Many people who settled in San Antonio, Texas, had (emigrated/immigrated) from Spain.

2. Two hundred miles (farther/further) south is the Mexican border.

3. Many groups of Franciscan monks helped (each other/one another) set up missions in San Antonio.

4. In 1836 Texas and Mexico fought with (each other/one another) in the Battle of the Alamo.

5. After San Antonio was taken from the Mexican people, the Texans were (frightened by/frightened of) the invasion of the Mexican army.

6. The Texas garrison had (fewer/less) men than the Mexican army.

7. The Texas garrison was annihilated, but the battle continued no (farther/further) because Sam Houston finally defeated the Mexican army.

8. Tourists (had ought/ought) to see the parchment-colored walls of the Alamo.

9. Tourists go (in/into/in to) a museum managed by the Daughters of the Texas Republic to see relics from the battle.

10. You (had ought/ought) to visit San Antonio, Texas, if you get the opportunity.

this kind, these kinds   *This* and *that* are singular and should be used with *kind, sort,* and *type. These* and *those* are plural and should be used with *kind**s**, sort**s**,* and *type**s**.*

   this sort of weather   **those kinds** of sentences

kind of a   Use *kind of* without the *a.* The rule also applies to *sort of* and *type of.*

   What **kind of** dog is that?

later, latter   *Later* can be an adjective meaning "more late" (*she was later than he*) or an adverb meaning "after some time" (*we will eat later*). *Latter* usually refers to the second of two people (or things) mentioned.

lay, lie   People often confuse these two words. *Lay* means "put" or "place" something. *Lie* means to "recline" or "be positioned"; it never takes an object.

Lay the dish on the counter.
I am going to **lie** in the sun now.
Learn all the principal parts of these verbs.

BASIC VERB	lay	lie
PRESENT PARTICIPLE	laying	lying
PAST TENSE	laid	lay
PAST PARTICIPLE	laid	lain

leave, let   *Leave* means to "go away." *Let* means "allow" or "permit." *Leave alone* means "go away from" and *let alone* means "permit to be alone."

We will **leave** if you will **let** us.
Do not **leave** your sister **alone** at the zoo.

like, as   To introduce a prepositional phrase, use *like*. To introduce a subordinate clause, use *as* or *as if*.

Phil plays baseball **like** Reggie Jackson.
Phil plays baseball **as** Reggie Jackson plays.

me, myself   See 1.d.3.

off of   Use *off* without *of*.

Take the cat **off** the sofa.

or, nor   Use *or* after *either*; use *nor* after *neither*.

Australia can be called **either** a country **or** a continent.
Neither Switzerland **nor** Austria is bordered by an ocean.

EXERCISE 4. In each of the sentences below, select from the choices in parentheses the word or phrase that represents preferred usage.

1. What (<u>kind of</u>/kind of a) city is Charleston, South Carolina?
2. Charleston, the second largest city in the state, (lays/<u>lies</u>) on the Charleston Harbor.
3. Either Charleston's mild climate (<u>or</u>/nor) its picturesque charm attracts visitors.
4. You can (lay/<u>lie</u>) down on the beaches near Charleston.
5. Visit the churches in Charleston; (these kind/<u>these kinds</u>) of sites make history come alive. -
6. Do not (<u>leave</u>/let) Charleston without a visit to the docks.
7. Charleston's Dock Street Theatre is designed (<u>like</u>/as) an old-fashioned playhouse.
8. Many bales of cotton are taken (<u>off</u>/off of) the docks of Charleston and put on ships.
9. These ships (<u>later</u>/latter) carry the cotton all over the world.
10. Some say that Savannah is as pretty as Charleston, but others prefer the (later/<u>latter</u>) city.

raise, rise   Both of these words mean "move upward." *Raise* is a transitive verb. It always takes an object (*raise your hand*). *Rise* is an intransitive verb. It does not take an object (*heat rises*).

reason is because   *Because* means "for the reason that"; therefore, the expression *the reason is because* is repetitive and incorrect. Use either *the reason is that* or *because.*

The **reason** prices rise **is that** production and shipping costs increase.

Prices rise **because** production and the costs of shipping increase.

respectfully, respectively Use *respectfully* to mean "with respect." Use *respectively* to mean "in the order named."

The President **respectfully** addressed Queen Elizabeth and her family.

Phoenix and Phoenixville are, **respectively,** in Arizona and Pennsylvania.

seeing as how This expression is incorrect. The correct expression is *since*.

Since Australia is surrounded by water, it can be considered a large island.

sit, set *Sit* means "place oneself in a sitting position"; *sit* rarely takes an object. *Set* means "place" or "put"; *set* usually takes an object.

Grandpa likes to **sit** on the porch.

Judy **set** the pots on the stove.

than, then *Than* is a conjunction used to introduce the second element in a comparison and to show exception.

Kay is taller **than** Louise.

It is none other **than** Uncle Al!

Then is an adverb or adjective used to mean "at that time," "soon afterward," "next in order," and "therefore."

She was hungry **then**.

She ate breakfast and **then** brushed her teeth.

First comes Monday; **then** comes Tuesday.

If it rains, **then** we cannot go.

try and, try to Do not use the phrase *try and* in speaking or writing. Use *try to*.

Try to remember that Salem is the capital of Oregon and not the capital of Massachusetts.

way, ways   Such expressions as *a long ways* and *a long ways off* are incorrect. Use *a long way* or *a long way off*.

Argentina is **a long way** off.

where at   Use *where* without *at*.

Where is Valley Forge?

who, whom   See 1.d.6. and 2.v.

EXERCISE 5. In each of the sentences below, select from the choices in parentheses the word or phrase that represents preferred usage.

1. You should try to (<u>raise</u>/rise) money and visit Santa Fe, New Mexico.
2. (Seeing as how/<u>Since</u>) the tourist office offers a free city map, many tourists visit this office first.
3. Santa Fe is a city for pedestrians; the (reason is because/<u>reason is that</u>) the streets are too narrow for driving.
4. A beautiful spiral staircase (raises/<u>rises</u>) up from the first floor of Santa Fe's Loretto Chapel.
5. Santa Fe residents (respectfully/<u>respectively</u>) carry a statue of the Virgin Mary during the fiesta.
6. Santa Fe is more of a historical site (<u>than</u>/then) a modern New Mexican metropolis.
7. New hotels (set/<u>sit</u>) among buildings from the 1800s.
8. The old and new hotels blend in so well that it is sometimes difficult to tell the difference between those built recently and those built (than/<u>then</u>).
9. Experts will (try and/<u>try to</u>) determine whether the adobe house on Santa Fe's De Vargas Street is the oldest house in the United States.
10. A short (<u>way</u>/ways) south of Santa Fe is the historic city of Albuquerque, New Mexico.

REVIEW EXERCISE A. In each of the sentences below, select from the choices in parentheses the word or phrase that represents preferred usage.

1. New Orleans, Louisiana, has (a/<u>an</u>) average elevation of one foot above sea level.

2. (Seeing as how/<u>Since</u>) part of New Orleans is below sea level, levees were constructed along river banks to prevent flooding.

3. The Mississippi River flows through both Baton Rouge and New Orleans, but the (later/<u>latter</u>) city is more of a tourist spot.

4. New Orleans (<u>doesn't</u>/don't) experience freezing weather very often.

5. (Being that/<u>Because</u>) it has a large port, New Orleans is a leading shipping center.

6. Many Italian people (emigrated/<u>immigrated</u>) to New Orleans after 1900.

7. Lovers of French cooking can choose (between/<u>among</u>) many restaurants in New Orleans.

8. A visitor to New Orleans (<u>cannot help admiring</u>/cannot help but admire) the lavish courtyard gardens.

9. Some of the buildings in the French Quarter date all the (<u>way</u>/ways) back to the eighteenth century.

10. No skyscrapers (raise/<u>rise</u>) above the low skyline of the French Quarter.

11. In the French Quarter shoppers wander (<u>among</u>/between) stalls where fruits, meats, fish, and vegetables are sold.

12. Visitors need go no (<u>farther</u>/further) than the French Quarter to hear jazz music.

13. There is a large (amount/<u>number</u>) of music halls in New Orleans.

14. Remember to go (in/<u>into</u>/in to) a music hall on Basin Street or Bourbon Street.

15. Since most music halls serve no food, you will simply (<u>sit</u>/set) and listen.

16. Although it is no (<u>different from</u>/different than) any other cornet, Louis Armstrong's first cornet, displayed in a New Orleans jazz museum, seems special.

17. If you (try and/<u>try to</u>) master the cornet, you will realize how difficult it is to play well.

18. Probably the most popular (kind of a/<u>kind of</u>) tourist attraction is the Mardi Gras celebration.

19. You will have to pay a great (<u>amount</u>/number) of money for a hotel room in New Orleans during Mardi Gras.

20. If you feel (<u>all right</u>/alright) after a night of celebration, you can take a steamboat ride on the Mississippi River.

REVIEW EXERCISE B. In each of the items below, select from the choices in parentheses the word or phrase that represents preferred usage.

1. Boston, Massachusetts, is a special (kind of a/<u>kind of</u>) city.

2. Boston is neither too far from ski slopes (or/<u>nor</u>) too far from ocean resorts.

3. The city of Boston (lays/<u>lies</u>) on Boston Harbor.

4. Boston (<u>might have</u>/might of) been the nation's capital if it had been more centrally located.

5. New York City and Philadelphia were, (<u>respectively</u>/respectfully), the first and second capitals of the United States.

6. Bostonians who were not (frightened of/<u>frightened by</u>) King George III's restrictions dumped many pounds of tea into Boston Harbor.

7. The first rapid transit subway (<u>in</u>/into/in to) the United States was built in Boston.

8. Boston is a very accessible city. The (reason is because/<u>reason is that</u>) it has efficient train stations and plane terminals.

9. You can enter and depart from Boston (all the faster/<u>as fast as</u>) a train or plane can take you.

10. Boston Common is just (off of/<u>off</u>) the Charles River.

11. The Charles River (<u>brings</u>/takes) water to Boston from the surrounding hills.

12. Do you know where Bunker Hill (<u>is</u>/is at)?

13. Beacon Hill is better known for beauty and historic importance (<u>than</u>/then) any other Boston area.

14. (Beside/<u>Besides</u>) being extremely narrow, Boston's Washington Street is clogged with traffic.

15. A visitor can spend an entire day at either the Boston Museum of Fine Arts (<u>or</u>/nor) the Metropolitan Boston Arts Center.

16. Visitors (<u>sit</u>/set) for hours examining the rare collections of books in the Boston Public Library.

17. Boston abounds in (these kind/<u>these kinds</u>) of historic and cultural centers.

18. Do not (<u>leave</u>/let) Boston without having a lobster dinner.

19. You (had ought/<u>ought</u>) to try Boston scrod and Boston baked beans while you are visiting.

20. Boston's New England clam chowder does not look or taste (<u>like</u>/as) Manhattan clam chowder.

REVIEW EXERCISE C. In each of the sentences below, select from the choices in parentheses the word or phrase that represents preferred usage.

1. Seattle, Washington, with its snow-capped mountains and luxuriant forests, is a city that every traveler (had ought/<u>ought</u>) to visit.

2. (<u>Let</u>/Leave) me tell you that the name *Seattle* is derived from *Sealth*, the name of a Native American chief.

3. Seattle is (<u>like</u>/as) a gateway to the state of Alaska.

4. In fact, the Alaska pipeline will (<u>bring</u>/take) more people and income into the city.

5. Southern Canada is only a short (<u>way</u>/ways) off.

6. Seattle is located midway (<u>between</u>/among) Mount Rainier and Mount Olympus.

7. Seattle is closer to Japan (<u>than</u>/then) any other major American city.

8. Many people in Seattle have (<u>emigrated</u>/immigrated) from China and Japan.

9. Few cities have grown in population (<u>as fast as</u>/all the faster) Seattle did between 1880 and 1900.

10. (Between/<u>Among</u>) Seattle's many talented artists are many Americans of Japanese and Chinese ancestry.

11. Seattle has (fewer/<u>less</u>) acreage than most major American cities.

12. The winters in Seattle will be (<u>all right</u>/alright) for people who like mild weather.

13. Seattle has (fewer/<u>less</u>) cold weather than most Washington cities.

14. The (reason is because/<u>reason is that</u>) Seattle is bordered by two large bodies of water.

15. A body of water (<u>beside</u>/besides) a city often helps to make the weather milder.

16. Lake Washington is connected by locks to Puget Sound; the (reason is because/<u>reason is that</u>) there is an eight-yard difference in water level between the two bodies of water.

17. Many pilots (<u>have done</u>/done) hydroplane racing during the SeaFair in Seattle.

18. Many Seattle residents can walk (<u>off</u>/off of) the street into their houseboats on Lake Union.

19. Henry Yesler, (a/<u>an</u>) experienced sawmill operator, built Puget Sound's first steam-powered mill.

20. The Seattle-Tacoma International Airport (<u>brings</u>/takes) millions of passengers into Seattle every year.

REVIEW EXERCISE D. Look again at the answers that you chose for Review Exercise C. Write twenty original sentences, each of which uses one correct answer from that exercise. *Answers will vary.*

9

CATCHING, CLASSIFYING, AND CORRECTING ERRORS

Catching, Classifying, and Correcting Errors

See summary of section in Teacher's Manual.

To get the most out of this section, you must understand three terms: *error, classify,* and *edit.* Then you will be a better writer. Your writing will not be spoiled by errors.

An *error,* of course, is "something incorrectly done." The important thing about making an error is to understand why it is considered an error and how you can avoid it in the future. In this section you will find a list of the common errors that people make in writing individual sentences. An error that involves only one sentence is actually easy to fix. (Sections 10–15 of this book take up writing that involves more than individual sentences.)

To classify means "to group according to certain characteristics." In this section you will see that errors can be classified. Although writers can make many errors in their sentences, there are really only seven kinds (or classifications) of grammar errors:

> errors in subject-verb agreement
> errors in case
> errors in pronoun reference
> errors with the negative
> errors with parts of speech
> errors in joining and completing clauses
> errors in clarity and style

If you realize how few *kinds* of grammar errors there are, you will probably make fewer errors.

Mary and ~~him~~ ^he^ have tickets for the ballet.

~~Her~~ ^She^ and Tom had lunch together last week.

It was ~~them~~ ^they^ who began the argument.

Could it be ~~her~~ ^she^ on the phone right now?

The audience knew ~~whom~~ ^who^ was best.

2.ʋ

case 4. Pronouns must be in the appropriate case after *than* or *as*.

1.d.1; 2.S

Jane knows Wilma better than ~~he.~~ ^him^ [The

writer means to say that Jane knows Wilma

and knows *him*.]

Jane knows Wilma better than ~~him.~~ ^he^ [The

writer means to say that Jane and *he* know

Wilma.]

REFERENCE ERRORS WITH PRONOUNS

Incorrect Reference

ref 5. A personal pronoun must agree with its antecedent in number.

1.d.1

A person can look all over, and ~~they~~ ^he^ will never

find a greater quarterback than Joe

Namath.

One can always dream, can't ~~they~~ ^one^?

ref 6. In writing, *that* and *which* should not be used to refer to people.

1.d.6

The person ~~that~~ ^who^ taught Helen Keller was

Annie Sullivan.

Weak Reference

ref

7. A pronoun must always have a clear antecedent and should not refer to an unstated idea.

p. 67

    She worked hard, ~~which~~ made her rich and ^*and her hard work*

    happy.

ref

8. A pronoun must not have two possible antecedents.

p. 58

    The director ~~told~~ the actor ~~that he~~ was going ^*knew that*

    to be very busy. ^*and told him so*

ERRORS WITH THE NEGATIVE

neg

9. In general, two negatives should not be used in the same clause.

p. 83

    There is not ~~no~~ better place to live than Los ^*any*

    Angeles.

    Most people will ~~not~~ scarcely know the

    difference between the two cars.

    King was a man who didn't like ~~no~~ kind of ^*any*

    violence.

ERRORS WITH PARTS OF SPEECH

Nouns

pl

10. The plural form of the noun must be used to show the plural even if a number word makes the meaning clear.

1.a.3; 5.b.4

    He had many hardship. ^*s*

    The house had four broken window. ^*s*

poss | 11. The possessive form of a noun must include an apostrophe. | 1.a.5;
5.b.5;
7.k.1

We can now foresee the series' end.

Are those John's red socks?

Do you remember Ted Williams' number?

Verbs

tense | 12. Past-time verbs must have the appropriate word endings. | 1.b.15 –
1.b.18

He like*d* all people whether they were rich or

poor.

It has work*ed* for me before.

Michelle use*d* to live in Pennsylvania, but now

she lives in New York.

Have you ever stud*ied* another language?

She did ~~tried~~ *try* her best!

tense | 13. The present tense should not be used if another tense is more logical. | 1.b.15

She ~~is~~ *was* said to be very pretty as a young girl.

tense | 14. The past perfect must be used to describe the earlier of two past actions. | 1.b.18

By the time I told him the news, he *had* already

heard.

tense | 15. A sentence should not shift verb tenses unnecessarily between clauses. | p. 36

He ~~is~~ *was* faithful to his team and stood by them

through thick and thin.

Adjectives

adj 16. A comparative adjective must be used when comparing two items, and a superlative adjective must be used when comparing more than two.

> Between Maui and Kauai, Kauai is ~~the most~~ more beautiful.
>
> Of Maui, Kauai, and Hawaii, Kauai is ~~more~~ the most beautiful.

l.c. 3; l.c. 4

adj 17. A double comparison must be avoided.

> I admire Winston Churchill because I think he was one of the ~~most~~ fittest men during World War II.

p. 48

adj 18. An incomplete comparison must be avoided by adding *other* or *else*.

> Henry Kissinger spent more time overseas than any other Secretary of State.

p. 48

adj 19. Some adjectives do not logically have comparative or superlative forms — for example, *perfect, unique, round.*

> Some would say that the Beatles' music is more ~~perfect~~ interesting than the Rolling Stones' is in terms of lyrics and arrangement.

Pronouns

pro 20. *Hisself* and *theirselves* are not words; *himself* and *themselves* should be used instead.

> He did the problem ~~hisself~~ himself.

p. 61

pro 21. In writing, *this* should not be used to mean
simply *a* or *an*. p. 63

There is this building in San Francisco that is

shaped like a pyramid.

a (above "this")

pro 22. *This here* should not be used to mean *this*. p. 63

Is this ~~here~~ book yours?

pro 23. *Them* should not be used to mean *those*. p. 63

For three hours we studied ~~them~~ *those* verbs.

Adverbs

adv 24. The *-ly* ending must not be omitted from
adverbs of manner. 1.f.1

The Panovs seem to dance effortless*ly* on the

stage.

ERRORS IN COMPLETING AND JOINING CLAUSES

run-on 25. A comma alone should not be used to join main
clauses. (The error results in a *run-on
sentence*.) p. 155

I admired John F. Kennedy, *H*he was an honest

man.

frag 26. A sentence must have both a subject and a
linking verb or an action verb; without both
elements a group of words is a *sentence
fragment*. 2.b

Martin Luther King, Jr., was a
A man who liked to help others.

were
The two girls jogging through Tilden Park.

p. 92

conj | **27.** Main clauses should not be joined with *so* or *yet*, but rather with *and so* and *and yet*.

Robert Kennedy knew that going out into big

crowds was like playing Russian roulette,

and
∧ yet he continued to go out.

Katherine Anne Porter grew up in the South,

and
∧ so she often writes about life in the South.

1. b. 20;
3. k

voice | **28.** A sentence should not shift unnecessarily from the active voice to the passive voice, or vice versa, between clauses.

Although she had a lot of talent, the poet was

~~known to be~~ undisciplined.

ERRORS IN CLARITY AND STYLE

Dangling or Misplaced Words, Phrases, and Clauses

p. 102

dangling | **29.** A phrase or clause should clearly modify just one word in the sentence; if there is any confusion, the phrase or clause is said to be *dangling*.

When I was young,
~~At an early age,~~ my parents taught me the
∧

difference between right and wrong.

mis-placed | **30.** A phrase or clause should be placed as close as possible to the word it is modifying.

Adlai Stevenson discussed peace and

A
prosperity at the Democratic Convention.
∧

p. 83

mis-placed | **31.** An adverb of degree should be placed as close as possible to the word it refers to.

We had only completed four of the six games.
∧

Sagging Subjects

sag | 32. If a subject and a verb are not clearly connected —both logically and grammatically—the sentence *sags*. The performer that is logically the most important performer in that particular sentence should be the subject of the main clause. | 3.i

A sagging sentence can be improved in one of the ways listed below. Some rewriting is usually required.

(1) Make the word or words that are most important the subject of the main clause.

(2) Select a new, and more logical, word as the subject of the main clause.

(3) Substitute a logical word or words for a weak pronoun as the subject of the main clause.

~~The camera can fool the human eye, and in conjunction with makeup and costuming makes for an enjoyable film.~~

[This sentence sags because the most important performer is not the subject of the main clause. What makes a film enjoyable? The camera? No. More likely, *clever photography* makes for an enjoyable film. These words should be the subject.]

Clever photography in conjunction with makeup and costumes makes for an enjoyable film.

[Now the subject *clever photography* has the main role.]

~~Plays don't have the advantages of camera angles and editing techniques that film directors have.~~

[This sentence sags because the subject

plays does not serve as the logical subject
of *don't have advantages.* The logical
subject of the sentence should be *stage
directors.*]

Stage directors don't have the advantages of

camera angles and editing techniques that

film directors have.

sag 33. The subject should not be lost in a prepositional
phrase.

In the job that I really want, I need to know

Spanish.

[This sentence sags because it places the
most important word or words —*the job* —
in an introductory prepositional phrase.
The job should be the subject of the main
clause.]

The job that I really want requires a

knowledge of Spanish.

[In this rewrite the subject is indeed *job*,
which is connected to the verb *requires.*]

As to the energy crisis and the recent gasoline

shortage, it is upsetting for all Americans.

The energy crisis and the recent gasoline

shortage are upsetting for all Americans.

By limiting gasoline sales may not completely

solve the problem.

Limiting gasoline sales may not completely

solve the problem.

sag | 34. The subject should not be lost in a subordinate clause. | 3.i

> Although soccer has for many years been
> popular in South America, ^it^ is still fairly
> new in North America.

> If Brazilians were asked to choose between
> the San Francisco Giants and the Los
> Angeles Dodgers, ^they^ would first have to find
> out what baseball is.

Wordiness

wordy | 35. A sentence should contain no unnecessary words and no redundancies. | 3.j

> Willa Cather still ~~continues to~~ live^s^ on in the
> words and actions of ~~the people in her~~ ^her characters.^
> ~~stories and novels.~~

■ Other editing signals

Here are other editing signals that you can use when looking over sentences. Make sure that you understand what each signal indicates. The column on the right also tells where in this book you can learn more about how to improve your abilities as a writer and editor.

SIGNAL	ERROR
vocab	Vocabulary: word choice (see Section 4)
sp	Spelling (see Section 5)
cap	Capitalization (see Section 7)
p	Punctuation (see Section 7)
use	Usage: commonly confused words and common misused forms (see Section 8)
∧	Missing word or punctuation

When you edit paragraphs and compositions, you will need at least one more editing signal:

SIGNAL	ERROR
⊬	Problem in paragraphing (see Section 10)

USING EDITING SIGNALS

You will see here two sample compositions written by students who were asked to write about a person whom they admired. Another person then edited the compositions. You will see in the margins the editing signals from the Editing Chart. In the body of the composition, you will notice circles and carets (∧). These point out exactly which words — or missing words — are causing trouble. The students can easily see what errors they have made and, by using the Editing Chart with its cross references, they can make the necessary corrections.

When you edit someone else's work or someone edits your paper, the system is sometimes known as student editing or peer editing. Often, though, you will be asked to edit your own paper. This system is known as self-editing. Whether your teacher edits your paper, a classmate edits your paper, or you edit your own paper, the secret is to look slowly and carefully at each individual sentence.

<u>Sample Composition 1</u>

I admire Barbra Streisand. She is the only

ref person (that) can keep a crowd of about 29,000

people quiet and settled for over an hour and a

half, as she did when she kept all the people from

yelling and screaming in the park.

People say that when she acts in movies
or ~~dramas'~~ [dramas] she looks like a goddess and when _pl; p_
~~she act~~ [she acts,] she acts with feeling and dignity and _agree; p_
pride. The main reasons that I admire her are
her voice and her beauty, [. Her] her voice is like _run-on_
~~angels~~ [angels'] singing, and she stuns people. _poss_
~~As to the~~ [The] first songs that started her off _sag_
are still best sellers today. One of her [most] famous _adj_
songs of all times was "Second-Hand Rose." Even
today people still want to hear it.

Sample Composition 2

Lou Gehrig was a member of the New York
Yankees. He inspired his team to keep on fight—
ing and led the team to many World Series. He
outhit Babe Ruth in many seasons.

There was one thing his wife, team, and
fans didn't know, [. He] he would play baseball even if _run-on_
he was ill. He once played with every bone in his
finger broken. Yet, miraculously, the bone
healed perfect [ly] _adv_

As years passed, Lou began to wear down.
He would still push his body to torture ~~on and on~~ [on and on]. _misplaced_
~~It~~ [His decline] was becoming noticeable. In spring _ref_
training Lou wasn't hitting the ball. Once he

fell over at the plate. In batting practice a
pitch came extremely close to him. From that
point on, he moved farther and farther from the
plate. After spring training the fans began to
notice. He was not hitting the ball, and he was
making many errors. Soon Lou Gehrig resigned.

mis-
placed
once
He said that ~~once~~ if he could not help the team, ∧ *p*

he would resign.

tense
resigned
After he ~~resign~~ he went to a hospital and
found that he had an incurable disease.

EXERCISE 1. Rewrite the Sample Compositions, correcting all the errors that the editor found. *See corrections
within compositions.*

EXERCISE 2. Each of the following sentences has an error
in subject-verb agreement. (Note the editing signals.) Rewrite each sentence correctly. You may use the Editing
Chart to help you in the following ways:

- Find on the chart a sentence that has the same kind of
  error.
- Correct the sentence here in the same way it is cor-
  rected on the Editing Chart.
- Use the cross reference in the right column of the
  Editing Chart to review the grammar rules.

1. The reporter write∧about interesting tourist spots. *agree*
   s
2. Therefore, the reporter get∧ to travel a great deal
   himself. *agree*
   s
3. He remember∧fondly his visit to the Albermarle region
   of North Carolina. *agree*
   were
4. Some other tourists ~~was~~ visiting the area at the same
   time. *agree*

5. The reporter don't know why more Northerners don't stop here on the way to Florida. *agree* [*doesn't*]

6. Each of the towns in the area seem like a good place to slow down and explore history. *agree*

7. Halifax and Murfreesboro makes American history come alive. *agree*

8. Eighteenth-century homes, plantations, and legends gives a tourist a taste of the past. *agree*

9. British style or West Indian architecture are obvious throughout the area. *agree* [*is*]

10. The reporter thinks that the pride of Edenton are the building and the grounds of the Chowan County Courthouse. *agree* [*is*]

EXERCISE 3. Each of the following sentences has an error in case. (Note the editing signals.) Rewrite each sentence correctly. Use the Editing Chart to help you in the ways specified in Exercise 2 (page 456).

1. Who does the sportswriter favor? *case* [*m*]

2. The Super Bowl usually brings her friends and she together. *case* [*her*]

3. The announcer hinted who he favored. *case* [*m*]

4. He brought the game to millions of viewers and we. *case* [*us*]

5. Us fans prepare for the game days in advance, but some viewers are truly fanatic. *case* [*We*]

6. Fanatics and them will watch only on a twenty-five-foot screen. *case* [*they*]

7. Him and others insist that the big screen is "the only way to go." *case* [*He*]

8. Those who do not even care for football tolerate whomever insists on watching the big game. *case*

9. The people whom are not fans cannot watch their own favorite programs on Super Sunday. *case*

10. It is them, the people who are not fans, who deserve the trophy! *case* [*they*]

EXERCISE 4. Each of the following sentences has an error in pronoun reference. (Note the editing signals.) Rewrite each sentence correctly. Use the Editing Chart to help you in the ways specified in Exercise 2 (page 456).

1. A teen-ager may travel far and wide, but ~~they~~ *(he or she)* may never have a real adventure until traveling through India by train. *ref*
2. One student took trains through India for many weeks and then wrote about it, didn't ~~they~~? *ref*
3. The student ~~that~~ *(who)* reported his amazing experiences was a high school junior from Massachusetts. *ref*
4. He traveled *(on a discount ticket)* in third-class compartments, ~~on a discount ticket~~, which gave him a chance to meet many people. *ref*
5. The student knew that Mark Twain had traveled by train in India also, and ~~he~~ *(Twain)* wrote about it. *ref*

EXERCISE 5. Each of the following sentences has a double negative. (Note the editing signals.) Rewrite each sentence correctly. Use the Editing Chart to help you in the ways specified in Exercise 2 (page 456). *Alternative answers are given for Items 2, 3, and 5.*

1. Most people will ~~not~~ scarcely recognize television in the future. *neg*
2. Television of the future ~~won't~~ *(will)* have no resemblance to television of today. *neg . . won't have any . . .*
3. Some viewers don't imagine ~~none~~ *(any)* of the break-throughs that are around the corner. *neg . . . viewers imagine none . . .*
4. Viewers who don't like ~~no~~ *(any)* kind of novelty will still have ordinary TV. *neg*
5. Many viewers, though, don't want to miss ~~nothing~~ *(anything)*: cable, videotapes, videodiscs. *neg . . though, want to miss nothing . . .*

EXERCISE 6. Each of the following sentences has an error with one part of speech. (Note the editing signals.) Rewrite each sentence correctly. Use the Editing Chart to help you in the ways specified in Exercise 2 (page 456).

1. There are many kind*(s)* of onions. *pl*

2. The onions' ability to produce tears is well known to many chefs. *onion's (alternate)*

3. People use to believe that wearing garlic, a member of the onion family, kept away evil spirits and also prevented colds. *tense*

4. If you compare regular onions with shallots, you will find the onions strongest. *adj*

5. Chives are more milder than regular onions, which can be very strong smelling. *adj*

6. An onion can indeed be more trouble to slice than any vegetable can. *adj*

7. There is this variety of onions called scallion, which is often eaten raw. *pro*

8. You must be careful when eating them onions or similar vegetables. *pro*

9. Good cooks know that they must blend garlic completely, or dishes will taste strange. *adv*

10. If you chew parsley thoroughly after eating garlic, your breath will be fresh again. *adv*

EXERCISE 7. Each of the following numbered items contains an error in the way two clauses were put together. (Note the editing signals.) Rewrite each sentence correctly. Use the Editing Chart to help you in the ways specified in Exercise 2 (page 456). *Alternative answers are given for Items 1 and 4.*

1. *Breaking Away* was one of the great movies of the late 1970s; it was about young men in a town near Bloomington, Indiana. *run-on; it was...*

2. The young men were deciding what to do after graduation from high school. *frag*

3. One of them wants to be a champion cyclist, and so he plans to race against the visiting Italian team. *conj*

4. The movie is about breaking away from the pack in a race, it is also about breaking away to start a new life in a job or at college. *run-on ..It...*

5. *Breaking Away* is a modern film like the best films of the past. *frag*

EXERCISE 8. Each of the following sentences has an error in clarity or style. (Note the editing signals.) Rewrite each sentence correctly. Use the Editing Chart to help you in the ways specified in Exercise 2 (page 456). *See answers at bottom of page.*

1. Being aware of the energy crisis, bicycles have become quite popular in the United States. *dangling*
2. Relying on bicycles, the streets of Amsterdam have long been crowded with commuters. *dangling*
3. Japanese and Italian bicycles are imported by stores for sale to Americans. *misplaced*
4. Bicycling requires human energy but provides exercise for muscles to get up steep hills. *misplaced*
5. Beginners should only learn how to get their balance on flat surfaces. *misplaced*
6. Bicycles have fewer parts and don't have the repair bills that car owners do. *sag*
7. By using bicycles will give Americans a chance to get back to nature. *sag*
8. As to fifteen-speed bicycles, it is not necessary to have one. *sag*
9. A bicycle is necessary in some countries of the world for the daily chores of the day. *wordy*
10. Here, tourists on vacation and commuters to and from work can save money by using bicycles. *wordy*

1. For people aware of the energy crisis, . . .
2. The streets of Amsterdam . . . commuters relying on bicycles.
3. . . . Italian bicycles for sale to Americans are imported by stores.
4. . . . human energy to get up steep hills but provides . . . muscles.
5. . . . learn only on flat surfaces how to get their balance.
6. . . . and don't require the repair bills that cars do.
7. Using bicycles will give . . .
8. It is not necessary to have a fifteen-speed bicycle.
9. . . . in some countries for the daily chores.
10. . . . tourists and commuters can save money . . .

10

THE PARAGRAPH

10 The Paragraph

See summary of section in Teacher's Manual.

A **paragraph** is a group of sentences that relate to one main idea or incident.

How many paragraphs are there on this and the following page? You have no trouble deciding, do you? Obviously, therefore, you know what a paragraph is. At least you can recognize one when you see it.

Although paragraphs exist to be seen and recognized by readers, they also help you as a writer. Writing your thoughts in paragraphs forces you to organize your thoughts because all the sentences in a paragraph should be related to one another in some way. Look at the individual sentences in the following paragraph, for example.

The Egyptians have taught us many things. They were excellent farmers. They knew all about irrigation. They built temples which were afterwards copied by the Greeks and which served as the earliest models for the churches in which we worship nowadays. They invented a calendar which proved such a useful instrument for the purpose of measuring time that it has survived with a few changes until today. But most important of all, the Egyptians learned how to preserve speech for the benefit of future generations. They invented the art of writing.

— Hendrik Van Loon, *The Story of Mankind*

In the above paragraph all the sentences are clearly related to one main idea.

As you work with paragraphs in this section, you should be aware that paragraphs do not usually appear alone but rather are combined with other paragraphs. Just as each sentence plays a role in a paragraph, so each paragraph plays a role in a composition. In this section you will be studying ways of building strong paragraphs. Once you can write a strong paragraph, you can then begin to link paragraphs together to form clear, logical compositions.

THE TOPIC SENTENCE

10.a THE TOPIC SENTENCE: GUIDE TO THE PARAGRAPH

The **topic sentence** of the paragraph states the main idea of the paragraph.

The topic sentence guides readers by telling them what the paragraph is about. When you write a strong topic sentence, you are helping your readers to see where they are and where they will be going. You are also helping yourself to think about what you want to say and how you will say it. If you write a topic sentence first, you are well along the way to expressing what you want to say in your paragraph.

For example, suppose you are working on a composition about writing instruments. You want to say something about pens. You start a new paragraph and begin by writing a sentence that you can use as a topic sentence.

TOPIC SENTENCE:
Through the ages people have used many different kinds of pens.

The above topic sentence is a generalization (a general statement) about pens. In the sentence following this first sentence and in the rest of the paragraph, you will go on to explain why your generalization is true. You give specific examples of different kinds of pens, from feather quills to felt-tip markers. You are on your way to building a paragraph.

Here is another example of how to build a paragraph: Suppose that you want to tell your readers about last Saturday. You make specific statements about Saturday: *The air was warm and springlike. Everyone on the street seemed to be smiling. Some early spring flowers were blooming.* Your reader may find your message clearer, though, if you begin with a topic sentence that generalizes about Saturday: *Saturday was a beautiful day.*

A topic sentence will not always be the first sentence in a paragraph. It can come in the middle or at the end of a paragraph instead. As a student writer, however, you will find it easier to put a topic sentence first.

EXERCISE 1. Identify the topic sentence in each of the following paragraphs.

1. The nautilus is an animal that never stops building its home. Like a clam, a nautilus secretes material that hardens into a shell. Unlike a clam, as the nautilus grows, it creates larger chambers and moves into them. It then seals off the old chamber with a thin wall. The result is a tightly coiled spiral of chambers, each larger than the one behind it. The nautilus always lives in the largest chamber. When the shell of a nautilus is cut open, the spiral pattern revealed is one of the most beautiful patterns in nature.

2. It is a stringed musical instrument with a body shaped like a half pear. It was played in the Middle East and Spain at least a thousand years ago. An enormous amount of music has been written for it. From the fifteenth to the seventeenth century, it was Europe's most popular instrument. The lute, once tremendously popular, has all but vanished from the musical scene. If it is played at all now, it is as an antique instrument. In its place we have the guitar, a direct descendant of the lute.

3. The glider — an airplane without an engine — is the ancestor of all modern aircraft. A glider was first flown successfully in 1891. Launched from a high place, it was guided to a safe, controlled landing by its pilot. Control was the great problem faced by inventors interested in flight. In the beginning of the twentieth century, the Wright brothers solved the problems of flight control through experiments with gliders. Glider research, plus a lightweight engine invented by the Wrights, made possible, in 1903, the world's first airplane flight.

EXERCISE 2. Below you will find six sentences followed by three paragraphs. Three of the six sentences are the topic sentences of the paragraphs. Match the topic sentences to the paragraphs to which they belong.

a. Potatoes are an excellent source of nutrition and are grown around the world.

b. Hypothermia is a subnormal body temperature.

c. Getting lost never fails to be a frightening experience.

d. *Hypothermia* means "very cold."

e. The common potato has an interesting history.

f. Anyone who spends a lot of time in a big forest will sooner or later get lost.

1. When a person is immersed in cold water, the skin and nearby tissues may cool very quickly. It may take ten to fifteen minutes before the temperature of the heart and brain starts to drop, however. When the core temperature reaches 90°F, unconsciousness may occur. When the core temperature drops to 85°F, heart failure usually occurs. *b*

2. The first things to do when you suddenly realize that you do not know which way to go are to sit down, think, and compose yourself. By studying your map, you should be able to figure out where you are. Then you can simply use your compass to find your way home. Of course, if you did not bring a map or compass, this plan would not be very helpful. *c*

3. The potato was probably first cultivated by the Incas of ancient Peru. Spanish explorers are believed to have brought it to Spain. From Spain it spread across Europe. It was then brought to North America by European settlers. *e*

EXERCISE 3. There are three lists of sentences below, labeled List *A*, List *B*, and List *C*. The sentences in each list could be used to make up Paragraphs *A*, *B*, and *C*. Decide which sentence in each list could best be used as the topic sentence of the paragraph. Be prepared to explain why you selected that sentence as the topic sentence.

LIST *A*

√ 1. The equator passes through extremes ranging from the Andes mountains (16,000 feet high and covered with snow and ice) to the Mussau Trough (21,000 feet beneath the surface of the sea).

2. Actually, 79 percent of the equator passes through oceans.

3. In between oceans lie South America and Africa, huge land masses with great contrasts.

4. In some places, like the arid desert of Kenya and the frigid peaks of the Andes, life is sparse.

5. In contrast are Brazil and Indonesia's tropical rain forests, where both plant and animal life are abundant.

LIST *B*

1. In almost every city in which Harry Houdini performed, his act included putting himself in the city jail behind locked bars and then escaping.

2. He once removed himself from a straitjacket while hanging upside down from a tall building.

3. While handcuffed, he dived from bridges into the Mississippi River and the Seine River and came up waving.

4. He was roped to a chair, chained to a ladder, and locked up in a cabinet; he always escaped.

√ 5. Harry Houdini was a master at freeing himself from difficult positions.

6. A sealed milk can filled with water, a nailed-up barrel, a giant football, an iron boiler, a roll-top desk, and a sausage skin could not contain him.

LIST C

√ 1. Radio broadcasts are beginning to attract the attention they held before television became popular in the early 1950s.

2. In Chicago recently a half-million listeners tuned in to the National Radio Theater's production of *Dracula*.

3. In New York, Theaterspace aired a production of the Greek drama *Oedipus*.

4. In Los Angeles, Sears Radio Theater has started to broadcast radio plays.

5. For those who like to hear how radio drama sounded in the old days, WNYC-AM rebroadcasts vintage serials like *Sherlock Holmes, The Shadow, Dragnet, The Green Hornet*, and *The Lone Ranger*.

6. Comedy buffs, on the other hand, can still chuckle along with Burns and Allen, Fibber McGee and Molly, Phil Harris, and Jack Benny and Rochester on *The Masters of Comedy* on WMCA-AM.

7. Even Groucho Marx came back to present his old variety shows again.

10.b WRITING THE TOPIC SENTENCE

If you know what you want to say, you can compose a topic sentence. Sometimes you have no problem deciding what you want to say and how to say it. At other times, you will have to think about it and even experiment with topic sentences. You may see some facts, figures, or other information about which you want to generalize. For example, after reading the table on page 468, write a general statement about the facts on the table.

RECENT INTERSCHOOL RACE RESULTS

Race	1	2	3	4	5	6
Team A	won	won	lost	won	won	lost
Team B	lost	lost	won	lost	lost	won

Is one of the following sentences similar to the one that you have written?

1. In recent interschool races, Team A proved superior to Team B.
2. The recent interschool races were the most exciting ever held.
3. Weather conditions played a major part in the recent interschool races.

Sentence 1 is the best general statement about the race information. The other sentences say something that you could not tell from the results.

EXERCISE 4. Read the information on the following Flight Table. Then select from the three sentences below the table the most appropriate topic sentence for a paragraph based on the table. Be ready to explain your choice.

FLIGHT TABLE

Leave New York	Arrive Miami	Arrive Ft. Lauderdale
9:00a	11:32a Nonstop	—
10:00a	—	12:23p Nonstop
10:00a	—	12:29p Nonstop
1:10p	—	3:39p Nonstop
1:15p	3:48p Nonstop	—
5:30p	—	7:59p Nonstop

Leave New York	Arrive Miami	Arrive Ft. Lauderdale
9:05p	—	11:27p Nonstop
9:05p	—	11:30p Nonstop
9:0͗p	—	11:34p Nonstop
9:10p	11:42p Nonstop	—

1. It is difficult to get to Miami from the New York area.

√ 2. New Yorkers have a number of flights to choose from when traveling to Ft. Lauderdale.

3. As train service becomes more and more unpredictable, travelers are turning to airlines for even fairly short trips.

EXERCISE 5. Look at the following table. Write a sentence that could be used as the topic sentence of a paragraph about the information in the table. Your topic sentence should begin as follows: *Answers will vary; an example follows.*

The highest mountains in the world are found . . .
                                              in Nepal, Tibet, and India.

MOUNTAIN PEAKS OF THE WORLD

Mountain Peak	Location	Height	
		feet	*meters*
Everest	Nepal-Tibet	29,028	8,848
Manaslu	Nepal	26,760	8,156
Broad Peak	India	26,400	8,047
Himal Chuli	Nepal	25,895	7,893
Gurla Mandhata	Tibet	25,355	7,728
Victory Peak	U.S.S.R.	24,406	7,439
Muztagh	China	23,891	7,282
Aconcagua	Argentina-Chile	23,034	7,021
Veladero	Argentina	22,244	6,780
Tocorpuri	Bolivia-Chile	22,162	6,755
Cuzco	Peru	20,995	6,399
McKinley	U.S.A.	20,320	6,194

Information Please Almanac, 1979

EXERCISE 6. Look carefully at the following table. Write a sentence that could be used as a topic sentence of a paragraph about the information in the table. Your topic sentence could begin as follows: *Answers will vary; an example follows.*

As people grow older, their chances of marrying . . .

OR   *diminish.*

After the age of thirty, most people . . .

MARRIAGE PROSPECTS OF SINGLE MEN AND WOMEN[1]

Age	percent of population who are single		percent of population who ever marry	
	Male	Female	Male	Female
15	99.4	97.6	95.8	97.4
17	98.1	87.9	96.0	97.3
19	87.3	59.6	95.9	96.4
21	63.3	35.1	95.0	94.2
25	27.8	13.1	89.1	82.5
30	14.2	7.9	73.8	61.2
35	9.9	6.4	57.2	42.9
40	7.6	6.1	42.3	29.9
45	7.1	6.1	30.6	20.0
50	7.6	7.4	21.6	12.8
55	7.9	7.9	13.9	7.7
60	8.0	7.8	8.2	4.4

Information Please Almanac, 1979

EXERCISE 7. There are three lists below. The items in each list could be used to write a paragraph. For each list, write a sentence that could be the topic sentence of a paragraph about that list. *Answers will vary; possibilities are given in the exercise.*

1. the latest movies *Going to a film theater can*
   popcorn   *be an exciting experience.*
   the excitement of a live audience
   the big screen
   comfortable seats

---

[1]This table shows the percentage of people at different ages who are single and the percentage of these single people who will marry someday. Note: The figures for single people do not include people who have been widowed or divorced.

2. books on almost every subject
current magazines and newspapers
mysteries, science fiction, romances, poems, plays
encyclopedias and other reference books
microfilm *A library is a treasure house*
records, tapes, and films *of general knowledge and culture.*

3. Fasten the seatbelt.
Adjust side and rear-view mirrors.
Depress the clutch.
Pump the accelerator pedal once.
Switch on the ignition. *The most difficult part of driving a*
Shift into first gear. *stick-shift car is getting it started.*
Release the parking brake.

EXERCISE 8. Examine Paragraphs *A, B, C,* and *D* below, which do not now have topic sentences. Read each paragraph over carefully, and then write a topic sentence of your own that could be used to begin the paragraph.
Answers will vary; possibilities are given in the exercise.

PARAGRAPH A

Our grandparents danced to the fox trot and the peabody, but people today dance to a different beat. In the old days men wore suits, and women wore dresses, while now both men and women wear jeans and T-shirts. The big swing bands of Glenn Miller and Harry James have been replaced by smaller rock combos. In the late 1950s, big tail fins and long, sleek cars were the rage. Today compact, economical cars are in style.

Popular fashions certainly change from
PARAGRAPH B *generation to generation.*

It has a flattened, slippery body covered with a smooth casing. It has strong legs permitting it to run quickly. The periplaneta lives in crevices and areas around sinks and water pipes in bakeries, groceries, restaurants, apartment buildings, and houses. Nocturnal in habit and ravenous in appetite, the periplaneta comes out at night in search of food. It feeds on other insects, clothing, garbage, and bookbindings. Each periplaneta leaves an unpleasant scent on the food it is unable to devour. The creature is dirty and contaminates everything it touches. It thrives where there is dirt, grease, and moisture. It is more commonly called the cockroach. *The periplaneta is a common and troublesome pest to city dwellers.*

PARAGRAPH C

Mountain climbing is now a televised sport, and enthusiasts have started mountain climbing magazines. Already there are four mountain climbing schools in Boulder, Colorado. In the 1950s there were a few isolated climbers in the area, but today there are climbers in great numbers all year long. In fact, the bulletin boards at the Boulder Mountaineer Club are filled with requests for climbing partners! Soon there may even be speed competitions. *In the past twenty years mountain climbing has become a very popular activity.*

PARAGRAPH D

A flashbulb is best used for shots four to eight feet from the camera. Remember that the flash will not light up the Astrodome nor anything else much farther than ten feet away. To avoid shadows, keep your subject a good distance from the background. You might also experiment with bouncing the flash by detaching the flash unit from the camera and aiming it at the ceiling. If the bulb snaps onto the camera itself, try holding a small white sheet at an angle to the flashbulb. *In poorly lighted areas the flash bulb is an essential piece of equipment.*

10.c STRONG VS. WEAK TOPIC SENTENCES

A strong topic sentence is neither too broad nor too limited. For example, look again at the Interschool Race Results in 10.b. Neither of the following sentences would be a strong topic sentence for a paragraph about that information.

Too broad: Interschool racing took place recently.
Too limited: Team B won the third and sixth races.

Look again at the Flight Table in Exercise 4. Would either of the following sentences be a strong topic sentence for a paragraph based on that Flight Table?

too narrow

Sentence 1: One plane landed at Miami at 12:23 P.M.

√ *Sentence 2:* Commercial air services exist between New York and Miami.

What comments do you have about these sentences as topic sentences?

The following paragraph illustrates how a topic sentence can be used effectively to introduce the reader to the paragraph's subject. Notice how the topic sentence makes you want to read the whole paragraph to find out the original meanings of people's names.

> *If Indian names such as Sitting Bull, War Eagle, and Bird Woman sound strange to us, it is because we have forgotten the original meanings of many of our own names.* Adolph, for example, means Noble Wolf. Bernard is Bold Bear, and Ursula means Little Bear Woman. Philip is Horse Lover, Agnes and Inez are Lambs, and Esther and Aster are Stars. Lewis, Louis, and Ludwig are all Bold Warriors. Peter is a Rock, Arthur is Noble, and Stephen is a Wreath of Victory. Some of our names are not very flattering. Calvin, for instance, means Bald, and Claude is Lame. Priscilla is Old, Barbara means Foreign, Lana means Wool, and Gretta is Mean.

In other cases, the topic sentence can be used effectively to sum up the ideas in a paragraph. Look at the following example.

> Before I turned eighteen, circuses delighted me, especially the animal acts. I loved to watch the bears who danced on their hind legs and the tigers who jumped through hoops. I was astounded by the lions who refused to bite off their trainers' heads when given

the chance. I couldn't believe that animals could be so clever, so much like people. Then came my eighteenth year. I visited a circus for the first time in years, and I looked forward to seeing the animals do their stuff. I was in for a surprise. Instead of being enchanted, I was revolted by the sight of the bears, tigers, and lions — magnificent, terrifying creatures — doing tricks that a child could do better. After all, the animals were *not* children; they were beasts. I grew sad watching them, as though I watched proud royalty made slaves. *The circus had not changed, you see, but I had: I saw that teaching animals tricks did not make them people, it merely ruined what made them wonderful as animals.*

It is often hard to write a topic sentence that is not too broad and not too narrow. In the following example, a student has tried to write a topic sentence for a paragraph about the American Revolution. The student's first attempt is too broad to be an effective topic sentence. Why is the third example much better than the first?

~~The American Revolution was caused by England.~~

~~The American Revolution was caused partly by England.~~

The American Revolution was caused partly by England's interference in the American economy.

EXERCISE 9. Read the paragraph on page 475, and then choose from among the three topic sentences the one that best fits the paragraph.

√ 1. The solar system is mostly space.

2. There is no conceivable way for anyone to get a "bird's-eye view" of our solar system.

3. The distance from the sun to Pluto is over 3.5 billion miles.

Only one star (the sun) and a mere nine planets occupy the empty space bordered by Pluto, the outermost planet. Each of the solar planets is separated from the others by great gulfs of space. If you backed far away from our system (as in a spaceship) until you could get all the planets into one eyeful, there wouldn't be much to see. They would all, except the sun, have shrunk to tiny points smaller and dimmer than stars.

EXERCISE 10. After you have read Paragraphs *A*, *B*, and *C*, below, decide how each italicized topic sentence could be improved. Then improve the given topic sentence either by selecting one of the alternate topic sentences listed below each paragraph or by writing a topic sentence of your own. Be ready to explain why you rejected the other sentences.

PARAGRAPH *A*

Marsupials are a group of animals. The kangaroo, the marsupial most familiar to many of us, is distinguished by its long hind legs, small fore legs, huge tail, small head, and large ears. The female kangaroo has a pouch that serves to protect her young. Baby kangaroos stay in the pouch for about eight months. The kangaroo is native to Australia as is another marsupial, the popular koala. Surprisingly, the koala is not a bear as most people think, but a marsupial. Characterized by a leathery nose and furry ears, the adult koala is about the size of a large poodle. Shortly after birth, the baby crawls inside its mother's pouch and remains there for about six months.

Alternate topic sentences   *too broad*
a. The kangaroo has some interesting physical features.
√ b. Marsupials are a group of animals that carry their young in pouches.
c. The two most popular marsupials are the kangaroo and the koala. *too narrow*

PARAGRAPH *B*

Clouds are masses of vapors. Cirrus clouds consist of feathery ice crystals that float in the higher regions of the atmosphere. Cumulus clouds are denser than cirrus and are formed by water droplets in the lower regions of the air. Stratus clouds consist of long horizontal sheets and are the lowest in the atmosphere, often found near the surface of the earth. Nimbus clouds are usually seen as a formless, dense mass. They are often called thunderstorm clouds, and they bring snow as well as rain. Nimbus are the least attractive among the clouds, but, on the other hand, they are the only clouds ever attended by the splendor of a rainbow.

Alternate topic sentences

√a. Clouds are generally classified into four kinds.

b. Thunderstorm clouds are called nimbus clouds and are very dense. *too narrow*

c. Clouds have different effects on the weather. *too broad*

PARAGRAPH C

Thurmon Munson was the first New York Yankee captain since Lou Gehrig. He won the American League's Rookie of the Year Award in 1970 and the League's Most Valuable Player Award in 1976. Munson was the only Yankee ever to win both awards. In 1977 he became the first player since Bill White (1962 – 1964) to bat .300 and drive in one hundred runs for three consecutive years. Munson never stopped working to improve his game. His Yankee teammates paid him the highest compliment when they called him "a player's player." Tragically, Munson was killed in 1979 in the crash of a small plane that he was piloting.

Alternate topic sentences

a. Thurmon Munson was unquestionably one of the finest ballplayers in baseball history to have played in the major leagues. *too narrow*

√b. Thurmon Munson was a man of great pride, dedication, and ability as a baseball player.

c. The New York Yankees have had some fine players. *too broad*

DEVELOPING THE TOPIC SENTENCE WITH SPECIFICS

10.d WAYS TO DEVELOP THE TOPIC SENTENCE

There are at least four ways to develop a topic sentence into a complete paragraph: Use (1) concrete details, (2) examples, (3) facts or statistics, or (4) incidents.

A topic sentence gives you a plan for a paragraph. Once you have written a topic sentence, you must try to show that what you said is true. You must try to support and develop the topic sentence. As you know, a topic sentence is a *general* statement. You develop the general statement, therefore, with *specific* statements — that is, statements that give details.

General Statement: In Haiti, it is hot in July.

Specific Developing Statement: On July Fourth of this year, the temperature reached 109°F and remained there most of the day.

General Statement: TV "newsmagazines" like *60 Minutes* are becoming more popular.

Specific Developing Statement: For many years *60 Minutes* was the only TV "newsmagazine" on the air, but today each network has several similar programs.

In both examples above the general statement is supported by a statement containing a fact. Facts are only one kind of specific that you can use to develop a general statement. The other kinds of specifics include concrete details, examples, statistics, and incidents, all of which are explained in greater detail on the following pages.

EXERCISE 11. Read the topic sentence and the two specific developing sentences below. Then write at least two more sentences of your own that support the topic sentence and could complete a paragraph. *Answers will vary; a possibility is given below.*

Topic sentence: My favorite article of clothing is jeans.

Specific Developing Statements: (1) I have several pairs, ranging in condition from "practically new" to "well broken-in." (2) Jeans are great clothes because they not only fit comfortably but also look and feel casual. *Jeans are also fashionable and very durable.*

10.e DEVELOPING THE TOPIC SENTENCE WITH CONCRETE DETAILS

To develop some topic sentences, you must describe the appearance, sound, smell, taste, or feel of something. To create an impression or "picture" of an object, place, person, or event, you should include concrete sensory details, as indicated in the selection below. Notice how the concrete details in the paragraph below support the topic sentence by creating an impression of fishing at the ocean's edge.

Surf casting is one of the pure pleasures of life. Standing at the ocean's edge and waiting for the fish to bite, you feel the fine and shifting sand pleasantly surrounding your feet. When the waves break on shore, a sudden chill of cold, foaming water swirls around your knees. Balancing the chill of the water is the warmth of the sunshine that slowly and silently stretches around you. Small boats with bright sails now and then bounce on the far-off horizon. Just when called for, the smell of salt air blows in on a sea-born breeze. The breeze touches and refreshes you for a moment. It tangles your

| topic sentence
| details of touch
| details of sight
| details of smell and touch

hair a bit and then wanders off across the beach. All the time, of course, you feel the tug of hope at the end of your fishing line.

EXERCISE 12. Using concrete details to make your reader see, hear, taste, feel, or smell what you describe, write a paragraph to support each of the topic sentences below. The "questions to ask yourself" after each topic sentence will help you to get ideas for the paragraph.

1. *Topic sentence:* The garden had overnight turned into a rainbow of color.

   Questions to ask yourself: What does the garden look like? What flowers have bloomed? Is there anything special about the coloring of individual flowers? Are there any unusual patterns of color in the garden? How does the variety of size and shape among the flowers contribute to the overall visual impression? How do the flowers smell?

2. *Topic sentence:* The roller coaster ride left me feeling upside down, but I would do it again.

   Questions to ask yourself: What made the ride exciting enough to "do it again"? What did it feel like? What did the world look like from the top? What sounds did you hear as the cars climbed up and then swooped down?

10.f DEVELOPING THE TOPIC SENTENCE WITH EXAMPLES

One of the most common ways to develop a topic sentence is with examples. If you were writing about how colors affect our moods, you might tell how blue is calming and yellow is cheerful, for example. If you were writing about the difficulties of living in an arctic climate, you might give as examples the special problems of keeping a home warm, of dressing for the cold, of getting a car started, and so on. This paragraph itself is an example of a paragraph developed by examples. The following paragraph about the telephone is also developed by examples. Read it carefully, paying particular attention to the linking expressions (such as *for example*) that help the writer structure the paragraph.

PARAGRAPH DEVELOPED BY EXAMPLES

Of today's modern conveniences, the telephone is among the most important to health and safety. For example, if someone has had a heart attack or been injured, a telephone can quickly summon the emergency help of paramedics or an ambulance. Even for less serious medical problems, the telephone provides a rapid link to the advice of a doctor or a pharmacist. For another example, a telephone call to the police can bring immediate help to prevent a crime or to catch a criminal. In addition, the telephone can help to reduce the damage from fire if it is used to summon the fire department at the first sign of smoke. A final example of the phone's role in safety is the way it links you with services that report the weather and storm warnings. This information is especially important if your radio is not working.

topic sentence

one example

another example

another example

last example

EXERCISE 13. Each of the topic sentences below is followed by a list of examples that may be used to develop the topic sentence. Using the given examples, or supplying some of your own, write a paragraph that develops each topic sentence. *Answers will vary.*

1. *Topic sentence:* Many convenience foods can be found in any market today.
   Examples: frozen pizza; vegetables with special sauces; frozen dinners of all sorts; frozen pancakes, french toast, waffles and other breakfast foods; frozen desserts

2. *Topic sentence:* Homeowners can supply many good reasons for growing their own vegetables.
   Examples: cheaper than store bought; guaranteed fresh; no unknown chemicals used; satisfaction of making something grow; learning more about nature, the weather, and the soil
3. *Topic sentence:* Summer is, without question, the best season of the year.
   Examples: no school; family vacation time; days at the beach; outdoor sports, backyard barbecues; staying up until late at night

10.g DEVELOPING THE TOPIC SENTENCE WITH FACTS OR STATISTICS

Supplying facts or statistics is another way to develop a topic sentence. For example, if you were to find out what kinds of telephone calls came into police stations, hospitals, emergency units, and doctors' offices, you would be able to use facts to support the topic sentence about the telephone. Also, that people call the police about runaway animals is a fact. That infants swallow poison is a fact. Dates are facts. Measurements are facts. Historical events are facts.

Statistics are numbers that have been collected with care, recorded accurately, and classified into groups. That over a period of a year a certain kind of airplane carried 146,000 people is a statistic because the passengers of every flight had been recorded for a given period.

When you use facts or statistics, your writing has an air of authority and accuracy. Look at the paragraph on page 482, which begins with the same topic sentence about the telephone that you have just seen developed by examples. This time, though, the topic sentence is followed by facts and statistics. How does the development by facts and statistics make this paragraph different from the paragraph developed by examples?

PARAGRAPH DEVELOPED BY FACTS AND STATISTICS

<u>Of today's modern conveniences, the telephone is among the most important to health and safety.</u> Recent talks with Elmsfield's chiefs of police, fire, and health administration give full support to this claim. According to Police Chief Okira, an average of 150 calls a week are received on the police emergency line. Over 95 percent of these calls result in the immediate dispatch of police to the scene of the trouble. Furthermore, since the phone alerts allow the police to arrive on the scene within minutes, 70 percent of emergency calls result in the arrest of suspected felons. The emergency fire department number also helps to save lives and to prevent property damage. Fire Chief Landers confirms that last year the department received 250 emergency calls, each of which enabled fire personnel to arrive on the scene before serious damage was done.	topic sentence fact statistic statistic statistic fact statistic

EXERCISE 14. Write a complete paragraph for the topic sentence below by using the facts provided for you. Not all of the facts provided are necessary or important to a paragraph about the Liberty Bell's role in American history. Be sure to use only those facts that relate to the topic sentence. *Answers will vary.*

Topic sentence: The Liberty Bell has played an important role in more than two hundred years of American history.

Facts:
— was made in England in 1752 for the Pennsylvania statehouse
— was of the same basic design as bells originating over two thousand years earlier in Asia

- inscribed with the words "Proclaim Liberty throughout all the Land unto all the Inhabitants Thereof"
- rung on July 8, 1776, for the first public reading of the Declaration of Independence
- was smaller than the largest bell in the world, which was the Great Bell of Moscow, cast in 1734
- was hidden by Americans during the British occupation of Philadelphia
- cracked on July 8, 1835, while tolling the death of Chief Justice John Marshall
- moved to special exhibition building near Independence Hall in 1976 for the Bicentennial

10.h DEVELOPING THE TOPIC SENTENCE WITH INCIDENTS

An incident is somewhat like a story. It tells about something that happened. If you were to complete your paragraph about the telephone by telling one or two true stories about how the telephone prevented a disaster, you would be supporting the topic sentence with incidents. The same paragraph below about the telephone is developed in this way with an incident.

PARAGRAPH DEVELOPED BY INCIDENTS

Of today's modern conveniences, the telephone is among the most important to health and safety. Sara, a friend of mine, once woke up in the middle of the night because she smelled smoke. She got out of bed and followed the smell to the door of her family's apartment. When she opened the door, she found the hallway filled with smoke. Before looking any further, she ran to the telephone and called the fire department. When the firefighters arrived, they

topic sentence

single incident developed throughout paragraph

found that Sara had led an evacuation of her building. They also found the fire in an empty apartment, and they told Sara that her prompt use of the telephone had kept the fire from spreading throughout the building.

EXERCISE 15. Use the topic sentences below to write complete paragraphs. If you know any real incidents that relate to the topic sentences, you can use these real incidents in your paragraphs. You can also use your imagination to invent incidents. (You can be as imaginative as you like.) *Answers will vary.*

1. *Topic sentence:* One night in an old, abandoned house is enough to make anyone believe in ghosts.
   Questions to ask yourself to develop an incident: What happened to you or someone you know during a night in an old, abandoned house? Why did you or someone you know spend the night in the house? What did the house look (smell, sound, feel, taste) like?

2. *Topic sentence:* Accidents, whether in traffic or at home, are usually caused by carelessness.
   Questions to ask yourself to develop an incident: How have you or someone you know been involved in an accident through carelessness? What happened in the accident(s)? What caused the accident(s)? How might the accident(s) have been prevented?

10.i DEVELOPING THE TOPIC SENTENCE WITH A COMBINATION OF SPECIFICS

In your reading, you will find that many paragraphs are developed with several different kinds of specifics. If written well, a paragraph that combines different specifics can provide variety and hold the reader's interest. If written poorly, however, such a paragraph could merely confuse the reader. Look at the paragraph on the next page for an example of effective development by a combination of incidents, facts, and statistics.

PARAGRAPH DEVELOPED BY A
COMBINATION OF SPECIFICS

Of today's modern conveniences, the telephone is among the most important to health and safety. I was reminded of this fact the other night when my father phoned the police because he thought that he had heard a prowler. The police officer who came and set our minds at rest told us that such a call is not unusual. I found out the next day in a visit to the police department that twenty emergency calls of one kind or another is a normal daily average in our small town. Many such telephone calls require additional phone calls by the police department to hospitals, ambulance units, or fire departments, I was told. My sister, who is a doctor and from time to time rides with an ambulance, told me that just last week a timely telephone call made it possible for her to save a little girl from choking to death.

topic sentence

incident

fact

statistic

fact

incident

EXERCISE 16. Choose one of the following topic sentences, and write a paragraph that makes use of at least two of the four kinds of specifics: concrete details, examples, facts or statistics, or incidents. *Answers will vary.*

1. Science fiction books (or mysteries or sports stories) are my favorite kind of reading.
2. People are healthier than they used to be.
3. Food fads change as often as clothing fads.
4. Mosquitoes can make life miserable.

REVIEW EXERCISE. Choose three of the following five topic sentences, and write paragraphs that make use of the indicated kind of specifics. *Answers will vary.*

1. The bicycle is, in many ways, a better form of transportation than the automobile. (EXAMPLES)

2. A short, ordinary trip to school or a store or home again can be full of interesting sights and sounds. (CONCRETE DETAILS)

3. People have wondered for hundreds of years what rainbows are and how they form. (FACTS AND STATISTICS: Use the facts and statistics listed below.)

350 B.C.	Aristotle, a Greek philosopher, suggested that rainbows are made of light reflected from raindrops.
1600 A.D.	Francis Bacon, an English philosopher, declared that rainbows were caused by meteors.
1637	René Descartes, a French mathematician, proved Aristotle right through experiments. He found that drops of water bend light rays and break them into colors.
1650s	Sir Isaac Newton, an English mathematician, explained the colors by proving that white light is made up of the many colors of the spectrum.

4. It is important for everyone to know something about first aid. (INCIDENTS)

5. The latest thing in games are the flashing, chirping, beeping electronic games. (EXAMPLES)

UNIFYING AND ORGANIZING THE PARAGRAPH

10.j UNITY IN THE PARAGRAPH

A good paragraph has **unity:** All the sentences have a relationship to one another and to the main idea.

All of the sentences in a single paragraph should be related in some way. If, in writing a paragraph, you start to wander away from the topic sentence or the main idea of the paragraph, you are destroying the unity of the paragraph.

To see how lack of unity can affect a paragraph, compare Paragraphs *A* and *B* below.

PARAGRAPH *A*

If properly cared for, Roquefort cheese has a matchless taste. The cheese should be protected from the open air by keeping it covered in its original wrapping or in aluminum foil. Proper wrapping preserves the natural flavor of the cheese and prevents dehydration. Roquefort should be kept in the lower part of a refrigerator or as far away from the freezer as possible. Sudden temperature changes should be avoided. Removing it one hour before eating will enhance its flavor.

PARAGRAPH *B*

If properly cared for, Roquefort cheese has a matchless taste. The cheese should be protected from the open air by keeping it covered in its original wrapping or in aluminum foil. Proper wrapping preserves the natural flavor of the cheese and prevents dehydration. Roquefort should be kept in the lower part of a refrigerator or as far away from the freezer as possible. Sudden temperature changes should be avoided. Removing it one hour before eating will enhance its flavor. All cheeses need time to thaw out, but some like Chilton, for example, can stand changes better than others.

What effect does the final sentence have on Paragraph *B*? It starts a new idea and spoils the unity of the paragraph by straying from the topic.

EXERCISE 17. In each of the following paragraphs, find the sentence that spoils the unity of the paragraph.

PARAGRAPH *A*

City governments face difficult decisions about controlling air pollution. <u>Pollution is also a concern of ecologists who worry about the increasing contamination of lakes and rivers in rural areas.</u> City governments must consider the economic and social consequences of enacting laws to reduce air pollution. Prohibiting automobiles in the downtown area of a city can destroy the business and cultural life of the city. Closing incinerators is no easier, especially if the city does not agree to provide and pay for increased garbage collection and disposal. Forcing factories to clean stack emissions raises the cost of keeping the plant in the city and causes many industries to move to the suburbs, leaving city dwellers without jobs.

PARAGRAPH *B*

Acupuncture is a medical practice of Chinese origin traditionally used as a treatment for chronic ailments such as arthritis, rheumatism, and migraine headaches. Recently, the technique has been used worldwide as an anesthetic in hundreds of thousands of operations, including open-heart surgery. Some treatments require the insertion through the skin of several thin needles at depths of several inches, sometimes for a few minutes, sometimes for many days. Such treatment has been found to restore health by controlling the flow of "universal energy" in the body. Acupuncture is thought to have been discovered when soldiers wounded by arrows found that some other ailment they had mysteriously improved.

PARAGRAPH *C*

No modern fascination with roller skating will ever replace my memories of skating as a youth. What I loved most of all then was the new-found sense of freedom that gliding down the street gave me. Tennis, which I learned later, was just as exciting but in a different way. All around our neighborhood, in autumn and spring, I could hear the clatter of metal wheels on neighboring streets. I remember the fears of hitting a bump in the pavement, of falling during a fast turn, and of not being able to stop when I wanted to. Sometimes those fears led to panic and to a fall. I had a continual badge of courage in those days, in the form of scabs on my knees and elbows. No injuries ever stopped me from skating, though.

10.k COHERENCE IN THE PARAGRAPH

A good paragraph has **coherence:** The sentences are sequenced according to a clear, logical plan of development.

Coherence simply means that the sentences in a paragraph are logically arranged. Coherence is important because you do not want your reader to feel that you are wandering around without plan or direction as you write one sentence after another. Your reader will become lost if you have become lost in the writing of the paragraph.

To understand coherence better, compare the following two paragraphs:

PARAGRAPH *A*

Yesterday was a strange day, according to the weather bureau. At sunrise, the sky was as clear as a bell. By noon, a mist had drifted in from the sea. At sunset, thick clouds hung across the sky.

PARAGRAPH *B*

Yesterday was a strange day, according to the weather bureau. At sunrise, the sky was as clear as a bell. At sunset, thick clouds hung across the sky. At noon, a mist had drifted in from the sea.

In Paragraph *A*, the writer follows the natural order of the sun during a day, moving from sunrise to noon to sunset. In Paragraph *B*, however, the writer jumps from sunrise to sunset and then back to noon. The writer of Paragraph *B* seems confused; the reader will probably also feel confused. The confusion arises because the sentences in Paragraph *B* do not follow a logical time order. We say that Paragraph *B* lacks coherence.

You can give coherence to paragraphs by following any one of several kinds of order:

1. **chronological, or time, order** — for instance, following the natural progression of a day, as in Paragraph *A* on page 489
2. **spatial order, or order in space** — for example, describing a fish from mouth to tail fins
3. **order of importance,** in which the most important item is explained first and the least important item last, or vice versa. Read the paragraph below for an example of development by order of importance.

**PARAGRAPH DEVELOPED BY
ORDER OF IMPORTANCE**

Planning a class picnic requires top-most executive ability. Decisions and details of immense variety face the organizer of such a project. These decisions include everything from what to do if it rains to how many varieties of pickles to serve. The selection of a day may be the most important order of business. Exact hours of departure and return are settled after the next two items, selecting a location and the means of transportation. Following these highly discussable issues is the crucial detail of whether hot or cold food should be served. After that, the decisions tumble down into a happy array of details, all of which can be eaten, except, of course, the pots, pans, baskets, pickle jars, and any ants that show up.

topic
sentence

most
important

next most
important

next most
important

least
important

▓ Using logical connectives to aid coherence

Logical connectives are important in organizing a paragraph. For example, notice the underlined words in the following paragraph.

PARAGRAPH DEVELOPED IN SEQUENTIAL ORDER

Fast becoming a popular sport, roller skating can be mastered in a few simple steps. First, sit down to put on your skates. Then, lace your skates only tight enough to give your ankles the support they need. Next, stand up. It will take time and practice to be able to stand still. Place your feet in a T-position by wedging the heel of one foot between the wheels of the other foot. This position will stop you from rolling when you do not want to roll. Fourth, try to balance yourself now that you are standing still. If you lean forward on your toes or backward on your heels, you will fall. Try to distribute your weight evenly. Now, get ready to fall the right way. If you fall properly, you will not get hurt. When you feel yourself falling, relax your body and go with the fall. Do not try to break it. A relaxed body will absorb the impact without injury. To get up, move into a kneeling position. Place one foot underneath you with your weight on the toe stop. Pick yourself up and immediately place your feet in a T-position. Now you are ready to skate, a feat that is not as easy as it looks. Place one foot behind the other, and you are ready to roll. This positioning provides the push for movement and the weight for balance. There is only one more step to master: stopping. Do not use the toe stop. It is meant to be used when getting up after a fall. Rather, place your back leg perpendicular to your front leg. Be sure the wheels of your back skate are on the ground. Finally, at the end of your stop, put your feet in a T-position so that you don't roll!

logical connectives: indicate first steps

indicates next step

indicates next step

indicates next step

indicates next step

indicates last step

The underlined words in the preceding paragraph, *first, then, next, fourth, now,* and *finally,* are logical connectives. They help to relate the sentences to each other in an orderly or logical way. The paragraph explains a process. The writer takes the reader through the process step by step in the order in which each step should occur. It is this step-by-step ordering that gives the paragraph its coherence. The logical connectives help to link the different steps. These logical connectives make the ordering clearer and make the paragraph more coherent.

EXERCISE 18. Read the following paragraph and the list of logical connectives on page 493. Then reread the paragraph, inserting the proper logical connectives at the points indicated by the raised numbers.

Although acrylic paints are relatively new to the art world, they are gaining in popularity rapidly for numerous reasons. [1]Acrylics require only odorless water as a mixing medium, while the older oil paints require turpentine, which gives off unhealthful fumes and offensive odors. [2]Oils take long to dry, but acrylics dry rapidly. [3]Cleanliness and ease of cleanup is a distinct advantage of using acrylics. A small container of water is all that is needed while painting. Soap and water will clean both the artist and the brushes. Although oils have been around longer and offer an unlimited choice of colors, you will find a growing selection of colors in acrylics. If you use the available colors and mix them in your own combinations, you can create almost any color desired. [4]It is thought that acrylic paintings may be more durable than oils. Acrylics seal themselves after thirty days and develop a surface that resists moisture. As a result the paintings are easier to keep in good condition. This makes them easier to maintain. In fact, art made from acrylic paint may even be cleaned using a damp cloth and a mild detergent!

LOGICAL CONNECTIVES

Furthermore *3*
Finally *4*
First and foremost *1*
In addition *2*

EXERCISE 19.   Read the following paragraph and the list of logical connectives below it. Then reread the paragraph, inserting the most appropriate logical connective at the points indicated by the raised numbers.

When the archaeologists cleared the passageway to the Burial Chamber in King Tutankhamun's Tomb, they were astonished at their discovery. There lay the mummified body of the Boy King, just as it was when he was put to rest 3,400 years ago. [1]Covering Tut's head, neck, and shoulders was one of the greatest of the world's art treasures — a polished gold funeral mask. Attached to the uppermost part of the mask was a blue-and-gold striped headdress. Positioned between the eyebrows were a vulture's head and a cobra that symbolized the Pharaoh's rule over Egypt. A faded wreath of olive leaves was still resting on Tut's brow. [2]The heavily painted black eyebrows and eyelids extended sideways toward the ears, the lobes of which had been pierced for earrings. The narrow eyes, the slender nose, the fleshy lips, and the shape of the chin were similar to Tut's features, which could be seen in the mummy. [3]On the mummy's chest, spreading from shoulder to shoulder, was a broad collar made of colored glass and intended to provide magical protection. [4]A crook and a flail were placed in the artificial gold hands that crossed over Tut's chest. The rest of the body was covered with an ornate shroud and adorned with amulets and other jewelry.

LOGICAL CONNECTIVES

Just below *2*   Slightly lower *3*
At the top of the mummy *1*   Farther down *4*

NARRATIVE, DESCRIPTIVE, AND EXPOSITORY PARAGRAPHS

10.I WRITING DIFFERENT KINDS OF PARAGRAPHS

When you begin to organize your thoughts into paragraphs, you will discover that there are various kinds of paragraphs that you can write because there are different ways, called *patterns*, of thinking. These patterns of thinking and writing are explained in greater detail in the following section, Section 11. You will now look at three basic kinds of paragraphs:

1. **narrative paragraphs** (which tell a story, real or imaginary)
2. **descriptive paragraphs** (which create an impression of something)
3. **expository paragraphs** (which explain or clarify something)

10.m NARRATIVE PARAGRAPHS

Narrative is the kind of writing that tells a story, real or imagined.

The story in a narrative paragraph may be true, like a newspaper account, or it may be made up or imagined, like a short story. Because narrative writing tells about what happened, a narrative paragraph usually follows a time order: First this happened, and then this happened, and so on. We call this chronological, or time, order (see also 10.k).

Read the following narrative paragraph. Notice the underlined logical connectives. Notice also the order in which events are described.

NARRATIVE PARAGRAPH

I appeared on television for the first and only time when I was eight years old. My mother and I were walking down a street in New York City, which we were visiting, when a young woman stopped us. The woman asked my mother if I could appear on TV. My mother agreed. A couple of hours later, I was ushered into the TV studio and told to sit on a sofa with two little blond-haired girls. I was an eight-year-old boy; we didn't have much to say to each other. Eventually, somebody brought a plate of cookies and set it nearby. Then bright lights went on and cameras pointed at us and at a man on a stool in front of us. His back was towards us, and so I didn't pay attention to what he said or did. I just ate cookies. When the cookies were gone, I waited for someone to bring more, but nobody did. I heard the man on the stool mention cartoons, but I didn't see any. Finally the bright lights went off, the man on the stool left, and we were ushered out again. My mother, who was waiting for me, said that she'd seen the show. She said I had looked cute. I wasn't interested; all I wanted was another cookie.

topic sentence

Notice the underlined logical connectives, which help to tell the time.

EXERCISE 20. For each of the following topic sentences, write a narrative paragraph. For the first topic sentence, fill in the blank with an activity you remember doing for the first time, and tell about the experience. The second topic sentence calls for you to write a story, either real or imaginary. *Answers will vary.*

1. I'll never forget the first time I _____ . (rode a horse, went to a party, flew in an airplane, saw a movie, hit a home run, etc.)

2. Though night was falling, I had to cross the mountains, and none of the tales I had heard in the village were going to keep me from following the mountain road.

10.n DESCRIPTIVE PARAGRAPHS

Description is the kind of writing that creates an impression of a person, place, or thing.

A descriptive paragraph tries to make a reader see, hear, smell, taste, or feel something. In writing a descriptive paragraph, you must use concrete details that are understandable to the senses. To show, for example, what something looks like, you would include concrete details of color, size, and shape (see 10.e).

It is usually helpful to organize a descriptive paragraph spatially — that is, in terms of space. For example, you might describe a building from its top to its bottom, or you might describe a room from its right side to its left side (see also 10.k).

Look carefully at the descriptive paragraph below. Notice the underlined concrete details. Notice, also, that the jockey is described spatially, from his shirt up to his head.

DESCRIPTIVE PARAGRAPH

He was wearing a suit of green Chinese silk that evening, tailored precisely and the size of a costume outfit for a child. The shirt was yellow, the tie striped with pastel colors. | concrete details of color

He had no hat with him and wore his hair brushed down in a stiff, wet bang on his forehead. His face was drawn, ageless, and gray. | concrete details of touch

There were shadowed hollows at his temples and his mouth was set in a wiry smile. . . . | concrete details of sight and touch

— Carson McCullers, "The Jockey"

EXERCISE 21. For each of the following topic sentences, write a descriptive paragraph. For the first topic sentence, describe the appearance of someone you know well. The second topic sentence asks you to describe a scene from your imagination. *Answers will vary.*

1. My ____ (father, mother, sister, brother, friend, uncle, aunt, etc.) is ____ .
2. I stared from the window of the train at the strange landscape of a new country.

10.0 EXPOSITORY PARAGRAPHS

Exposition is the kind of writing that explains or clarifies.

In an expository paragraph you explain something, perhaps an idea, a plan, a process, an opinion. Paragraphs that are not strictly narrative or descriptive are usually expository.

Throughout this section you have had a chance to examine a number of examples of paragraphs. You have also seen that a good way to write a paragraph is to begin with a strong topic sentence that you then support. The kinds of paragraphs best suited to strong topic sentences are expository paragraphs. You should know that there are several specific kinds of expository paragraphs that you will learn about as you progress in school.[1]

Here, however, one type of expository paragraph, called comparison/contrast, will be emphasized.

You will study comparison/contrast writing in greater detail in Section 11. For now, read carefully the following sample paragraphs. Note the topic sentences and the logical connectives (like *both, each,* and *on the other hand*) that help to structure the writing. Notice also the differences between a paragraph of comparison and a paragraph of contrast.

---

[1]The types include *comparison/contrast, definition, argument, explanation of process,* and *cause and effect.*

PARAGRAPH OF COMPARISON

The assassinations of Abraham Lincoln and John F. Kennedy are similar in many uncanny ways. Abraham Lincoln was elected in 1860; John F. Kennedy in 1960. Both Presidents were in the middle years of their lives when slain. Both wanted to bring about peace at home and abroad; neither lived to achieve it. Lincoln and Kennedy both had four children, two of whom had died. Each was slain on a Friday in the presence of his wife. Each was succeeded by a Southern Democratic senator named Johnson. Andrew Johnson was born in 1808; Lyndon Johnson was born in 1908. Lincoln's assassin, John Wilkes Booth, shot Lincoln through the back of the head in a theater and ran to a warehouse. Lee Harvey Oswald shot Kennedy through the back of the head from a warehouse and ran to a theater. The names Lincoln and Kennedy both contain seven letters; Andrew Johnson and Lyndon Johnson contain thirteen letters; John Wilkes Booth and Lee Harvey Oswald contain fifteen letters. Students of history continue to be intrigued by these many similarities.

topic sentence

logical connectives

logical connectives

logical connective

PARAGRAPH OF CONTRAST

Professional sports in the United States find their new talent in different ways. Pro baseball has a farm system that provides young potential athletes with playing experience and necessary training. It also gives the team managers the opportunity to spot those with promising skills. These lucky few are then prepared for playing in the major leagues. Pro football and basketball, on the

topic sentence

logical connective

other hand, depend on colleges to develop the skills of talented young players. As a result, football and basketball college coaching is perhaps the best in the world. In finding and developing new players, professional soccer differs radically from all other pro sports. In soccer talented players learn "on the job." Scouts look for players as young as ten and twelve and then upon their graduation from high school sign them for youth leagues. In these youth leagues players work out daily and, when they are considered ready, play other professional teams under scrimmage conditions to test their mettle. Although each professional sport finds its talent in different ways, each method has given the athletic world many superstar athletes.

| logical connective

In Section 11, examples of various ways of organizing comparison and contrast are presented. In the paragraph below, notice that both similarities and differences are included.

PARAGRAPH OF COMPARISON AND CONTRAST

Like the nightly news of the three major networks, *The MacNeil/Lehrer Report* runs for thirty minutes; similarities with traditional television newscasts go no further. Network newscasts trumpet headlines; flash closeups and serial views of disasters; broadcast reporter "stand ups" from the steps of the Capitol, the lawn of the White House, and from the base of a smokestack spewing pollution. Rat-a-tat-tat. Quick takes. A piecemeal approach to the news. Robert ("Robin") MacNeil and Jim Lehrer, editors and anchors of the report that bears

| topic sentence

their names, prefer to feast on the news —
one subject at a time, in a carefully chosen,
finely tuned format.

John Grossmann, "The MacNeil/Lehrer Approach"

EXERCISE 22. For each of the following topic sentences, write a comparison/contrast paragraph. The first sentence asks you to compare and contrast two different brands of jeans. The second sentence asks you only to compare two different situations. *Answers will vary.*

1. There are some interesting similarities and differences between designer jeans and inexpensive jeans.
2. Looking for a job is like playing hide-and-seek.

10.p WRITING DIFFERENT KINDS OF PARAGRAPHS BASED ON THE SAME INFORMATION

You decide what kind of paragraph to write when you know what you want to say about something. A trip to the moon or to a movie can provide you with information as a writer that you use in many different ways. It can lead you to want to say a variety of things and thus to write a variety of different kinds of paragraphs, for example:

Paragraph	Trip to Moon	Trip to Movie
Narrative	step-by-step account of walking on moon	(a) trip to and back (b) summary of story of movie
Description	(a) description of moon	(a) description of a character
	(b) description of spaceship	(b) description of setting
Comparison	moon vs. star	two movies

EXERCISE 23. The map below shows how Main Street in Anytown looked in 1850. Write three paragraphs, using the map as data: a narrative paragraph, a descriptive paragraph, and a paragraph of comparison/contrast.

Answers will vary.

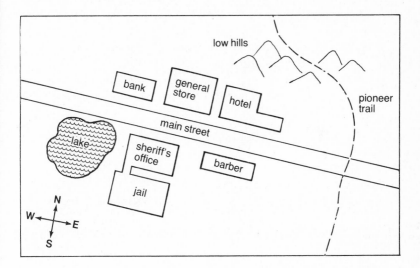

10.q REVISING YOUR PARAGRAPHS

You should not consider a paragraph or any piece of writing finished until you have read it over and revised it. Even professional writers find it extremely difficult to write a polished paragraph the first time around. The last sentence that they have written may make them want to go back and change the first sentence, for example. Writers know that revising is a very important step in the writing process.

It is at the revision stage that you can clarify ideas, add details, and improve the flow of your sentences. As you read over your paragraph, ask yourself the questions on the checklist on the following page. If you find problems with any of the items on the list, go back to your paragraph and rewrite as necessary.

■ Checklist for revising a paragraph

1. Does the topic sentence clearly state one main idea and give strong direction to the paragraph? (See 10.a – 10.c.)
2. Does each sentence relate to the main topic of the paragraph but add more rather than just repeat? (See 10.d – 10.i.)
3. Is there a logical order to the arrangement of the sentences in the paragraph? (See 10.k.)
4. Are logical connectives and other transitional devices used effectively to connect sentences and ideas? (See 10.k.)

10.r EDITING AND PROOFREADING

Once you have revised your paragraph, you should carefully edit and proofread it for matters of grammar and usage, capitalization and punctuation, and spelling. Use the questions on the following Editing and Proofreading Checklist as a guide. The cross references in parentheses indicate other sections of this book to check for review.

As you edit and proofread, you may use Editing Signals, such as those below, from Section 9.

■ Editing and proofreading checklist

1. Are all sentences complete? (See 2.a.) *frag*
2. Are varied sentence structures used? (See Section 3.)
3. Have you used the voice (active or passive) that is most effective in each sentence? (See 1.b.20.) *voice*
4. Are verb tenses consistent? (See 1.b.12.) *tense*
5. Do subjects and verbs agree? (See 2.d and 2.f–g.) *agree*
6. Do pronouns agree with antecedents? (See 1.d.1 and 1.d.7.) *ref*
7. Is vocabulary precise but varied? (See Section 4.) *vocab*
8. Are words spelled correctly? (See Section 5.) *sp*
9. Is punctuation correct? (See Section 7.) *p*

11

PATTERNS
OF THINKING
AND WRITING

11 Patterns of Thinking and Writing

See summary of section in Teacher's Manual.

You have probably found that you cannot always express everything that you want to say in a single paragraph. As you become a more skillful writer, you will find to an even greater extent that you need more than one paragraph to express your thoughts. In this section you will learn how to develop ideas that call for two paragraphs or more.

By now you should realize that the job of writing is largely a matter of combining thinking and language. The two are so much a part of each other that it is impossible to separate them. You must think before you decide what to write and how to write it. As you write, you must continue to think to be sure you express your ideas logically and clearly.

There are certain *patterns of thinking* that we all use every day in dialogue with ourselves and others. *Patterns*, here, simply means "methods used over and over." You will become more conscious of these common patterns as you do the assignments in this section. The goal is to master these patterns not only in thinking but also in *writing* as you move from sentence to sentence and from paragraph to paragraph.

You will find help in this section with three of the most common patterns of thinking:

PATTERN 1: "This is what happened."

As you know, life is full of events of all kinds. One thing really does happen right after another. You are constantly thinking about and talking about "what happened." You can use this pattern of thinking in your writing, too. It leads to *narrative* writing. Narrative writing can be made up of a series of narrative paragraphs that tell about something that happened.

PATTERN 2: "This is what it looks, sounds, smells, tastes, feels, or acts like."

Life is full not only of events but also of objects, people, and places. All around you are houses, cars, clothes, faces, gardens, food. You notice these things and talk about them, and you can write about them as well. You can use words to show what they look like, how they sound, what they smell like, and so on. This kind of writing is called *descriptive* writing. Descriptive writing can consist of a series of paragraphs that create an impression of something.

PATTERN 3: "This is like (or unlike) that."

Sometimes you want to explain how one thing is similar to or different from another thing. To do so you use a particular pattern of thinking and writing that says "this is like (or unlike) that." This kind of writing is called *comparison/contrast.* It can consist of several paragraphs in which the similarities and differences between things are discussed.

NARRATIVE WRITING

11.a NARRATION: "This is what happened."

Narration is the kind of writing that tells a story, real or imagined.

All day long people talk about what happened a few minutes ago, earlier in the day, last evening, yesterday, last month, last year, or years ago. By remembering and telling one another what happened, you give meaning and add interest to life. Every news report on TV or radio and every newspaper headline says, in effect, "This is what happened." So does every history book. You can give order to your world by telling what happened.

As a writer, you will be using this "what happened" pattern, called *narration*, frequently. In Section 10 you can study and write single paragraphs of narration. You will often want to write a narrative of more than one paragraph, however, and the examples, ideas, and exercises in 11.b – 11.d will help you to do so.

11.b A NARRATIVE MODEL

James Herriot, author of the model on the next page, wanted to write about what happened to him in a bad snowstorm. There were a number of events during the storm that he wanted to be sure to mention. If Herriot had made a brief list of these events, it would have looked like the following:

1. saw farm in the distance in the snow
2. sudden gust of wind
3. could not see a thing
4. finally wind died down
5. kept walking in deep snow
6. got to within a few hundred yards of farm
7. new blizzard hit
8. noted position of farm
9. hit by the new blizzard; realized now lost
10. turned and plodded toward right
11. felt wrong again
12. fell into holes
13. tried to believe farm must be near
14. realized could be lost and near death
15. tried to put down panic

Read the following selection and notice how, with different wording, these fifteen events form the backbone of the passage. (The number of each event in the sequence is indicated beside it in red type.)

Notice also that these events appear in the order in which they occurred in time. The words underlined in red help to relate the events to each other and to their order in time. These words are called *logical connectives*. For a further explanation of logical connectives, see 11.c.

■ Model 1: "This is what happened."

I could see the road only in places — the walls were covered over most of their length, but the farm was visible all the way. I had | event #1
gone about half a mile toward it when a | event #2
sudden gust of wind blew up the surface snow into a cloud of fine particles. Just for a | event #3
few seconds I found myself completely alone. The farm, the surrounding moor, everything disappeared, and I had an eerie sense of | event #4
isolation till the veil cleared.

It was hard going in the deep snow, and | event #5
in the drifts I sank over the tops of my wellingtons. I kept at it, head down, to | event #6
within a few hundred yards of the stone buildings. I was just thinking that it had all been pretty easy, really, when I looked up and | event #7
saw a waving curtain of a million black dots bearing down on me. I quickened my steps | event #8
and just before the blizzard hit me I marked the position of the farm. But after ten minutes' stumbling and slithering I realized I had missed the place. I was heading for a | event #9
shape that didn't exist; it was etched only in my mind.

I stood for a few moments feeling again the chilling sense of isolation. I was convinced I had gone too far to the left and, after a few gasping breaths, struck off to the right. It was not long before I knew I had gone in the wrong direction again. I began to fall into deep holes, up to the armpits in the snow, reminding me that the ground was not really flat on these high moors but pitted by countless peat haggs.

| event #10
| event #11
| event #12

As I struggled on, I told myself that the whole thing was ridiculous. I couldn't be far from the warm fireside at Pike House — this wasn't the North Pole. But my mind went back to the great empty stretch of moor beyond the farm, and I had to stifle a feeling of panic.

| event #13
| event #14
| event #15

—James Herriot, *All Creatures Great and Small*

11.c SKILLS FOR WRITING NARRATION

When you set out to tell "this is what happened," you will find two skills very helpful: (1) sequencing events or actions accurately and (2) using logical connectives and other key words effectively. You will have a chance to read about each of these skills and then to work on each by doing the Warm-up exercises that follow.

■ Sequencing events in narration

There are actually two steps involved in the sequencing of events for narrative. Following both of these steps will help you to structure your writing:

1. **List the actions or events that you wish to include. Be sure to include all necessary events. Eliminate unnecessary events.**

   I awake with my alarm at 6:00 A.M.
   I pack last-minute items into my suitcase.

Still bleary-eyed, I eat breakfast.

I go into the bathroom to wash up and get dressed.

Mom and Dad are already waiting for me in the car.

Because we have lost time, we are now in a rush to catch the plane.

After we get a few blocks away, I realize I have forgotten my plane tickets.

We return home, and I look frantically for the tickets before finding them.

Fortunately, we get to the airport just in time.

I quickly say goodbye to Mom and Dad.

The flight is smooth and restful.

As soon as I get off the plane, I find Aunt Ann, Uncle Frank, and Sally waiting for me.

2. **Sequence the events in chronological, or time, order. You may find it helpful to put the events on a time line.**

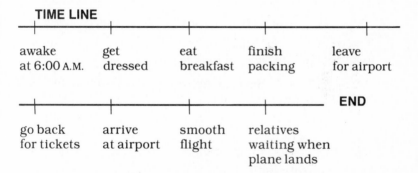

TIME LINE

| awake at 6:00 A.M. | get dressed | eat breakfast | finish packing | leave for airport |

| go back for tickets | arrive at airport | smooth flight | relatives waiting when plane lands |

END

■ Using logical connectives in narration

Logical connectives are words and phrases that connect one sentence to the next. By showing the relationship between sentences, they make clear the order and meaning of your thinking and writing. Each of the patterns of thinking and writing has its own set of logical connectives.

In narrative sequences, logical connectives serve as "timers"; that is, they indicate the relationship in time of the events. Notice, for example, the phrases *just before* and *after ten minutes,* which clearly indicate *when* events happened. Try to get into the habit of thinking of these time connectives as you write a narrative. You do not need one in every sentence, as you can see from the model, but use one if there is a reason to tell your reader *when* an event occurred.

The list below contains some common logical connectives for narrative writing:

after	finally
as soon as	just before
at the same time	next
before	soon
during	then
earlier	while

WARM-UP 1: Sequencing events.   Put the events listed below into chronological, or time, sequence.

4   a. Thursday, July 8: Governor declares emergency.

3   b. Tuesday, July 6: Small brush fires spread two miles.

2   c. Monday, July 5: Small brush fires started.

5   d. Friday, July 9: Several abandoned factories are destroyed by fire.

1   e. Sunday, July 4: High winds arise.

WARM-UP 2: Sequencing events.   Put the events listed below into chronological, or time, sequence.

4   a. first swimming training session

1   b. arrived at camp

5   c. first swim meet

2   d. first camp meeting

3   e. swim teams are chosen

WARM-UP 3: Sequencing events.   Look back at the narrative model in 11.b. Decide whether any of the numbered actions in the third paragraph of the selection can be moved to a different point in that paragraph without spoiling it. Be prepared to discuss the effects of such a change. *Answers will vary.*

WARM-UP 4: Using logical connectives in narration. Rewrite the second paragraph of the narrative model in 11.b, leaving out all of the underlined logical connectives. Be prepared to discuss the differences that the logical connectives make in the writing. *Answers will vary.*

WARM-UP 5: Using logical connectives and key words in narration. Rewrite the following paragraph, filling in the blanks with logical connectives that will help the reader understand the timing of the action. You may use the logical connectives listed after the passage or your own.

_As_ she came out of the house, Sheila walked slowly toward the big car, as if thinking of something else. _After_ reaching the car, she held her right hand hesitantly on the front door handle. _Then_ she opened the door and got in. _Now,_ suddenly alert, she felt ready to tackle the day. _Before_ putting the key in the ignition, though, Sheila adjusted the side and rear view mirrors. _Then_ she put the key in the ignition and turned it. The engine caught. _A few seconds later_ ____ , however, it sputtered and died. Frustrated, Sheila got out.

LOGICAL CONNECTIVES

As	Next	Then
After	Now	A few seconds later
Before		

11.d DECIDING WHEN TO START A NEW PARAGRAPH OF NARRATION

As you write a long narrative, you have to decide when to end one paragraph and start a new paragraph. Here are four rules that will help you:

1. **Start a new paragraph when you introduce conversation or when the conversation switches from speaker to speaker.** You can help your reader keep track of which character is speaking by beginning a new paragraph each time a speaker changes.

2. **Start a new paragraph when you change the setting.** Setting can be either place or time. If the sequence of events that you are writing about shifts to a new place, start a new paragraph. If there is a break in time, start a new paragraph. For example, you might begin a new paragraph at the following phrase: "The next day, the ship was..."

3. **Start a new paragraph if a new person enters the scene.** For example, you might begin a new paragraph with the following sentence: "At this point, there was a roll of drums, and the President stepped out on the balcony."

4. **Start a new paragraph if you switch from reporting the actions of one person to reporting the actions of another person.** Although not essential, it is usually a good idea to start a new paragraph when you begin talking about a different character.

WARM-UP 6: Paragraphing in narrative writing. Look back at the narrative model in 11.b. That passage has four paragraphs, but there is no conversation and only one character is involved. The writer, therefore, had an unusually difficult task in determining the best points at which to break for new paragraphs. Herriot must have decided that there were shifts in place, or at least changes in his sense of place. At these points, then, he began a new paragraph. Notice that the first paragraph ends with the snow settling. The setting in which the writer finds himself is then different, almost a new world, one in which he can see. Explain in terms of a shift in setting the reasons for beginning the third and fourth paragraphs.

Answers will vary.

DESCRIPTIVE WRITING

11.e DESCRIPTION: "This is what it looks, sounds, smells, tastes, feels, or acts like."

Description is the kind of writing that creates an impression of a person, place, or thing.

You use the pattern called *description* for all sorts of reasons — for example, to describe a person whom you want someone else to meet, to describe a place that you have visited, or to describe an object that you want to sell. Some things that you want to describe are made up of parts, shapes, or colors that can be seen. Other things that you describe involve your sense of hearing, smell, taste, or touch. The job of writing description, therefore, demands noticing and pointing out *sensory details,* as they are sometimes called. Sometimes you will concentrate on one sense; sometimes, on many.

You will use the "this is what it looks...like" pattern, called description, frequently in your writing. In Section 10 you can write single paragraphs of description. You will often want to write an expanded description of more than one paragraph, though, and the examples, ideas, and exercises in 11.f – 11.h will help you to improve your skills in writing description. You may want to work through Warm-ups 7 – 13.

11.f A DESCRIPTIVE MODEL

As you read the following model, notice the sensory details and the way in which the writer has ordered them. Since the writer is describing a painting, he understandably concentrates on details of sight. Can you find details describing other senses?

■ Model 2: "This is what it looks...like."

When you look at Peter Bruegel the Elder's painting *Huntsmen in the Snow*, you see in the foreground three dark-clad hunters. They are leading a dozen grey-hound hunting dogs across ankle-deep snow to the edge of a cliff. The line of the cliff toward which the hunters plod cuts diagonally across the painting, splitting it into triangles with the dividing line sloping from the left of the painting down across to the bottom right of the picture. A line of leafless trees marches out from the front of the picture across a snow-packed country-side. A few birds sit stiffly as if frozen to their branches, while one flies darkly up against the sky. The only touch of color in this part of the picture is a tan dog and yellow flicker of flame where a small fire struggles to survive. The rest is white snow.

As you look beyond the cliff into the uppermost triangle, the cliff drops off abruptly into a valley where you see a fascinating scene of ice skaters. A narrow river, frozen an eggshell blue, runs between slope-roofed buildings under a stone bridge and opens up into a lake beyond. On the left side of the lake, the same line of trees goes out beyond a few houses and grows fainter and fainter against the snow-covered low-lands. Beyond, rising up to the top right corner of the picture, is a mountain range, criss-crossed with furrows and with gloomy peaks jutting up into a sky that matches the color of the lake and river. The only touch of any other color in this part of the picture is the red apron of a woman by the lake.

Notice the logical connectives, which help to order the details spatially.

11.g SKILLS FOR WRITING DESCRIPTION

When you want to tell "this is what it looks, sounds, smells, tastes, feels, or acts like," you will find two skills very helpful: (1) noticing and ordering sensory details and (2) using logical connectives and other key words.

■ Noticing and ordering sensory details

There are several steps involved in the observation and ordering of sensory details.

1. **Determine the dominant impression you want to convey.**

   Last Saturday's football game was noisy and exciting.

2. **Observe carefully with all your senses in order to list sensory details.**

   spirited yells of cheerleaders   cheers from crowd
   school band at half time   referees' whistles
   fans waving pennants in air   brisk fall air
   smell of franks and sauerkraut   colorful pom-poms
   people jumping up and down in grandstand
   many students wearing school colors
   many huddles during the game
   smell of burning leaves from nearby yard

3. **Classify each detail by sense, using an observation table, perhaps.**

OBSERVATION TABLE

look	sound	smell	feel, touch, movements
colorful pom-poms school colors	yells of cheer- leaders cheers from crowd referees' whistles school band at halftime	franks and sauerkraut burning leaves	brisk fall air pennants waving in air people jumping in grandstand huddles on field

4. Put the details in the order in which you wish to discuss them.

a. sound
b. feel, touch, movement
c. look
d. smell

■ Using logical connectives and key words in description

The following list of logical connectives and other key vocabulary will help you in descriptive writing. Notice that these connectives and other words are most helpful for telling what something looks like.

TO HELP YOU ESTABLISH DIRECTIONS

to the right	above
to the left	below
ahead	beneath
under	on the outside
over	on the inside
horizontally	opposite to
vertically	parallel to
diagonally	overlapping with

TO HELP YOU DESCRIBE SHAPES

rectangular	semicircular
circular	square

WARM-UP 7: Noticing sensory details. Look back at the descriptive model in 11.f. What kinds of concrete details in both paragraphs appeal to the sense of sight? If the scene were a scene in real life, what senses might the fire involve? The dogs? The birds? Make a list of concrete details involving sound, smell, and touch based only on what you have read in the selection. *Examples: sound of dogs barking, smell of smoke, touch of cold air on face*

WARM-UP 8: Noticing sensory details. On a sheet of paper make five columns headed Sight, Sound, Smell,

Taste, and Movement/Touch. Then list ten sounds and at least three sights, three smells, three tastes, and three movements that you can use to describe each of the following: *Answers will vary; examples for Item a are given below.*

a. an amusement park *sight of ferris wheel, smell of popcorn, taste of cotton candy*

b. a busy corner in a village, town, or city

c. a school basketball game

WARM-UP 9: Ordering spatial details. Put the figures below into a different spatial order, trying to focus the items in a pattern. *Group circles together, triangles together, and rectangles together.*

WARM-UP 10: Ordering sensory details. Below are listed some sights, sounds, smells, and tastes that you might come across on a walk through a school cafeteria line. Decide how you can divide these concrete details into two or more paragraphs. Make your own lists of these items, one for each paragraph. *Example: 1 = sights 2 = smells 3 = things to touch*

shiny, round metal containers *1*
glass shelves *1*
steamy soup *2*
bowls of chili *2*
frosty glasses *3*
thin, white straws *1*
cheese slowly melting *1*
pink, quivering squares of jello *3*
long-handled spoons *1*
golden-brown crusts *2*
tightly wrapped saltines *3*
frothy meringues *1*
streams of cola *1*

WARM-UP 11: Using logical connectives in description. Make a list of the logical connectives in the following passage.

After wishing goodnight to my last party guest, I turned and faced a very dirty, very cluttered room. Letting my eyes slowly scan the room, I noticed first, <u>to the right</u>, the Happy Birthday sign hanging from one piece of tape. <u>On either side and beneath,</u> crepe paper streamers lay in disarray. <u>Across</u> the room and <u>in front of</u> me was the table holding the remains of the party refreshments. The table was littered with peanut shells, potato chip and pretzel crumbs, and a now-watery onion dip. <u>On the table and beneath,</u> I saw used paper cups scattered every which way. <u>On the left side</u> of the room, dozens of burst balloons added a new color pattern to the floor tiles. <u>Above,</u> a few inflated balloons still clung precariously to the ceiling. I jumped up and pulled one down, promising myself to get up early the next morning to begin the cleanup.

11.h DECIDING WHEN TO START A NEW PARAGRAPH OF DESCRIPTION

It is difficult to read a paragraph that continues for too long. As a writer, therefore, you should decide in advance how best to divide your description logically into paragraphs. Notice that in the selection about Bruegel's painting (in 11.f), the writer described the foreground of the picture in the first paragraph and the background in the second paragraph. You will usually find some logical way to divide your descriptions into paragraphs, and the following guidelines should help you.

1. **Start a new paragraph when you talk about a different sense.** For example, after describing what the different foods in a Thanksgiving dinner look like, you can begin a new paragraph to tell what they smell like, and then another new paragraph to describe what they taste like.

2. **When writing a visual description, start a new paragraph to describe a different spatial area.** For example, you may discuss in separate paragraphs the foreground and the background of a painting, the right side and the left side of a room, the top and the bottom of a building, the outside and the inside of a car, and so on.

WARM-UP 12: Paragraphing in descriptive writing. Look back at the observation table in 11.g. Assume that you will need two paragraphs to write the description of the football game. How can you divide the description into paragraphs? What will you discuss in each paragraph?

Example: first paragraph = sights and sounds   second paragraph = smells

WARM-UP 13: Paragraphing in descriptive writing. Assume that you will need more than one paragraph in which to describe each of the following items. How can you divide the description into paragraphs? What will you discuss in each paragraph? *Answers will vary; an example for Item 1 is given below.*

1. a newly designed airplane   *first paragraph = front of plane*
2. a country area or park   *second paragraph = back of plane*
3. a county fair or circus

COMPARISON/CONTRAST WRITING

11.i COMPARISON/CONTRAST: "This is like (or unlike) that."

Comparison is the kind of writing that tells about similarities. **Contrast** is the kind of writing that tells about differences.

This pattern is just one form of *expository writing*, the kind of writing that explains or clarifies. Writing that is not strictly narrative or descriptive is usually expository (see 10.o). There are several specific kinds of expository writing. In this book you will concentrate on *comparison/ contrast.*[1]

You have probably found that scarcely a day goes by without your thinking about how one thing is like or unlike something else. In fact, many of your ideas are best explained by making a comparison of some kind. You may want to explain how this weekend compares with last weekend, how the milkshakes at one restaurant compare with those at another, or how two actors in a television show compare with each other. Technically, when you talk about how things are similar, you are comparing, and when you talk about how things are different, you are contrasting. Sometimes you will do only one or the other in a piece of writing; sometimes you will do both.

In Section 10, you can write a single paragraph of comparison/contrast. Here you will see how comparison/ contrast can be expanded into two or more paragraphs. The examples, ideas, and exercises in 11.j – 11.l will help you to write longer pieces of comparison/contrast.

11.j A COMPARISON/CONTRAST MODEL

In 10.o you can read a single paragraph that contrasts the ways professional sports find new players. If the writer had had more to say, however, he could have developed the idea in three paragraphs, as the following writer did.

■ Model 3: "This is like (or unlike) that."

In the United States professional athletes in the major sports are developed in three different ways that nevertheless have some similarities. Each method has certain advantages. One of the most highly developed methods is the so-called farm

| Notice the italicized topic sentence.

| Notice the underlined logical connectives.

---

[1]The other kinds of expository writing include *definition, argument, explanation of process* and *cause and effect.*

system of professional baseball. All the major league clubs have their own farm system, which includes both a chain of minor league teams in cities and towns around the country and also a scouting system. Scouts for a major league farm system will keep an eye on promising young ballplayers in high schools, in colleges, and in sandlot teams. Finally, of course, young ballplayers must be persuaded to join one farm system or another. A farm system that is willing to provide a secure and financially expanding future for a young player has to compete with other farm systems willing to do the same.

Unlike college baseball, college basketball and football are moneymaking sports in themselves. Colleges are thus able to attract superior high school players by offering them a scholarship. In college, basketball and football players are able to develop their talents and receive good training just as young baseball players do in a farm system. Like the scouts for the baseball farm system, scouts from professional football and basketball teams can follow the progress of college players. Here, too, the competition for highly talented players is intense, so intense, in fact, that the professional football and basketball organizations have agreed upon rules for hiring college athletes. A whole system of "drafting" is followed in an effort to spread the young talent evenly among professional teams. No similar system is followed in major league baseball.

In soccer talented players learn "on the job." Scouts look for players as young as ten

| Notice the italicized topic sentence.

| Notice the italicized topic sentence.

and twelve and then upon their graduation from high school sign them for youth leagues. In these youth leagues players work out daily and, when they are considered ready, play other professional teams under scrimmage conditions to test their mettle. Although each professional sport finds its talent in different ways, each method has given the athletic world many super-star athletes.

If you compare the preceding selection with the single paragraph in 10.o, you will notice that more information is given here about baseball's farm system and about the basketball and football system. The third paragraph above, however, is exactly the same as the final sentences on soccer in the single paragraph. Whether you develop a comparison/contrast pattern into a single paragraph or into two or more paragraphs depends on how much you want to say about each item being compared.

11.k SKILLS FOR WRITING COMPARISON/CONTRAST

The job of telling how "this is like (or unlike) that" is somewhat more difficult than writing narration or description. There are two skills that will make this kind of writing easier for you: (1) selecting and ordering points of comparison/contrast and (2) using logical connectives.

■ Selecting and ordering points of comparison/contrast

Because writing comparison/contrast is a rather sophisticated task, follow the steps below.

1. **Decide whether you want to compare the items, contrast the items, or both compare and contrast.**

   compare *and* contrast a newspaper and a news magazine

2. Pick a few specific points that you wish to compare or contrast.

frequency of issue
cost per issue
amount of advertising
kind of news covered
average length of articles
coverage of human interest features

3. Group the points of similarity together, and give examples. Group the points of difference together, and give examples. You may use a comparison frame.

COMPARISON FRAME

points of comparison (+) points of contrast (−)	newspaper	news magazine
amount of advertising (+)	fair amount	fair amount
coverage of human interest features (+)	some articles	some articles
frequency of issue (−)	daily	weekly
cost per issue (−)	inexpensive	about five times as much
average length of articles (−)	short	fairly long
kind of news covered (−)	mostly local (some national and world)	national and world

4. Put the points of similarity or difference in the order that you wish to discuss them.

Differences followed by similarities:
kind of news covered (−)
cost per issue (−)
frequency of issue (−)
average length of articles (−)
coverage of human interest features (+)
amount of advertising (+)

■ Using logical connectives and key words in comparison/contrast

In comparison/contrast writing, logical connectives are essential for making clear which points are similar and which points are different. You should study the following list carefully.

TO HELP YOU POINT OUT SIMILARITIES

correspond to	resemble
in the same manner	similar to
just as	similarly
like	so to

TO HELP YOU POINT OUT DIFFERENCES

although	in spite of
but	less than
differ from	more than
different from	on the contrary
however	on the other hand
in contrast to	unlike
in opposition to	whereas

WARM-UP 14: Finding similarities and differences. Look back at the comparison/contrast model in 11.j. Make a list of the similarities that the author notes among the three systems of recruiting professional athletes. Then make a list of the differences. *Example: College basketball and football are moneymaking sports; college baseball is not.*

WARM-UP 15: Selecting points to compare or contrast. For each pair of items below, select some points of comparison or contrast. Be clear about when you will use comparison and when you will use contrast. *Answers will vary; an example for Item 1 is given below.*

1. Field hockey and ice hockey   *Field hockey is played on the ground with a ball; ice hockey is played on the ice with a puck.*
2. A short story and a novel
3. A summer vacation and a winter vacation

WARM-UP 16: Finding similarities and differences. Look at the two illustrations below. Make a list of the ways in which the two illustrations are similar. Then make a list of the ways in which the two illustrations differ. *Answers will vary.* *Example: Focus on position of furniture.*

A   B

WARM-UP 17: Using logical connectives for comparison/contrast. Look back at the comparison/contrast model in 11.j. Reread the selection, leaving out the logical connectives. Be prepared to discuss how the omission of logical connectives affects your understanding of the piece. *Answers will vary.*

WARM-UP 18: Using logical connectives for comparison/contrast. Read the following passage, filling in a logical connective for each blank. You may use those listed at the end of the passage, or you may supply your own logical connectives.

Microwave ovens and conventional gas and electric ovens are _different_ in more ways than they are _similar_. _Unlike_ conventional ovens, microwave ovens cook food in a very short period of time. Microwave ovens are, therefore, a great deal more convenient. The two kinds of ovens also _differ_ in cost. Microwave ovens are more costly than conventional ovens. _Although_ the initial cost of a microwave oven is high, that cost is partially offset by the cost to run it. _In contrast to_ a conventional oven that uses energy for an entire hour to cook a potato, a microwave oven uses energy for just a few minutes to do the same job.

LOGICAL CONNECTIVES

although	in contrast to
differ	similar
different	unlike

11.1 DECIDING WHEN TO START A NEW COMPARISON/CONTRAST PARAGRAPH

How do you divide a piece of comparison/contrast writing into paragraphs? The answer will depend to a large extent on whether you are just comparing, just contrasting, or both comparing and contrasting. It will also depend on the number of items that you are treating — two, three, or more. There is no single "correct" method for paragraph division. Just be sure that the method you use is a logical one. Also, remember that each paragraph of expository writing should have a strong topic sentence. The following guidelines should help you.

1. **Start a new paragraph when you switch from comparing to contrasting.** It is logical to break for a new paragraph at the place where you switch from talking about similar points to talking about different points. For example, in your first paragraph you may explain that your two dogs are similar because they are both terriers, both the same shade of brown, and both exceptionally frisky. Then, in a second paragraph you may explain that the dogs are different because one favors you while the other favors your sister and because one loves to play outdoors while the other is most happy indoors.

2. **Start a new paragraph when you discuss a new item.** For example, in the comparison/contrast model in 11.j, a new paragraph was begun to discuss each of the three items.

WARM-UP 19: Paragraphing in comparison/contrast writing. Look back at the comparison frame in 11.k. Assume that you will need two paragraphs to write a piece of comparison/contrast based on that information. List two different methods for dividing the information into paragraphs. Then, for each method, specify what you will discuss in each paragraph. *Answers will vary.*

WARM-UP 20: Paragraphing in comparison/contrast writing. Assume that you will need more than one paragraph to discuss each pair of items in Warm-up 15. How can you divide each piece of comparison/contrast writing into paragraphs? What will you discuss in each paragraph? *Answers will vary.*

WRITING ASSIGNMENTS: PATTERN PRACTICE

11.m USING PATTERNS TO DEVELOP DATA INTO WRITING

The following writing assignments will give you practice in using three patterns of thinking and writing: narration, description, comparison/contrast. Each assignment includes a separate writing task — or "Pattern Practice" — for each of the three patterns.

The assignments are set up to give you information that you will then write about. The information will be in the form of figures, dates, times, and amounts and will be presented in charts or tables. One of the jobs of a writer is to convert this kind of information into sentences and paragraphs by using the patterns of thinking and writing.

■ Assignment A: *Daily Time Chart*

Look at the following time chart of a school day. Prepare a similar chart for a school day of your own and a chart for a Saturday or holiday. Then, using this information, complete the following Pattern Practices. As you learned in 10.o, each paragraph of expository writing should have a strong topic sentence. Be sure to revise and edit your writing. See the checklists in 10.q and 10.r.

DAILY TIME CHART

Day: Tuesday

6:00 AM	
7:00	
7:15	wake up
8:00	breakfast
8:30	go to school
9:00	
10:00	
11:00	
	school
12:00	
1:00 PM	
2:00	
3:00	
	club meeting
4:00	
	soccer practice
5:00	

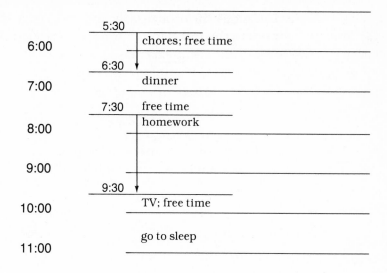

6:00	5:30
	chores; free time
	6:30 ↓
7:00	dinner
	7:30 free time
8:00	homework
9:00	
	9:30 ↓
10:00	TV; free time
	go to sleep
11:00	

PATTERN PRACTICE 1: "This is what happened." Using one of your daily charts, write two or more paragraphs of narration about what happened on a recent day. *Answers will vary.*

PATTERN PRACTICE 2: "This is what it looks ... like." Select a person, an object, or a building that was part of a recent typical day. Write two or more descriptive paragraphs telling what it looked like. *Answers will vary.*

PATTERN PRACTICE 3: "This is like (or unlike) that." In two or more paragraphs compare (a) your school day and your holiday or (b) your school day and the day on the above chart. You may want to point out similarities in the first paragraph and differences in the second paragraph. *Answers will vary.*

■ Assignment B: *Space Science*

Use the following information in Data Set I and Data Set II to complete the following Pattern Practices. As you learned in 10.o, each paragraph of expository writing should have a strong topic sentence. Be sure to revise and edit your writing. See the checklists in 10.q and 10.r.

DATA SET I: Probes to Mars

Mission #; Country	Spacecraft	Launch date	Remarks
1, U.S.	Mariner 3	11/5/64	Malfunctioned.
2, U.S.	Mariner 4	11/28/64	After midcourse correction, passed behind Mars on 7/14/65, taking 22 pictures.
3, U.S.S.R.	Zond 2	11/30/64	Power supply failed.
4, U.S.	Mariner 6	2/24/69	Came within 2,000 mi. of Mars on 7/31/69. Sent data and pictures.
5, U.S.	Mariner 7	3/27/69	Came within 2,000 mi. of Mars on 8/5/69. Sent data and pictures.
6, U.S.	Mariner 8	5/8/71	Designed to orbit Mars. Lost.
7, U.S.S.R.	Mars 2	5/19/71	Reached Mars, 11/27/71. Dropped landing capsule on surface.
8, U.S.S.R.	Mars 3	5/28/71	Like Mars 2. Capsule landed 12/2/71. TV transmission cut short.
9, U.S.	Mariner 9	5/30/71	First craft to orbit Mars; 11/13/71. 7,300 pictures: 1st close-up of Mars's moon. Transmission ended 10/27/72.
10, U.S.S.R.	Mars 4	7/2/73	Arrived 2/74; sent back photos.
11, U.S.S.R.	Mars 5	7/25/73	Sister craft of Mars 4.
12, U.S.S.R.	Mars 6	8/5/73	Scheduled to arrive 3/74. Missed.
13, U.S.S.R.	Mars 7	8/9/73	Scheduled to arrive 1974. Missed.
14, U.S.	Viking 1	8/20/75	Carrying life-detection labs. Landed 7/20/76. Sent back photographs.
15, U.S.	Viking 2	9/9/75	Like Viking 1, landed 9/3/76. Sent back photographs.

DATA SET II: A Comparison of Earth and Mars

	Earth	Mars
1. Average distance from sun:		
kilometers	150 million	230 million
miles	93 million	140 million
2. Orbital period in Earth days	365	687
3. Diameter:		
kilometers	12,700	6,800
miles	7,900	4,200
4. Surface gravity (Earth = 1)	1.00	0.38
5. Average atmospheric pressure (pounds per square inch)	14.7	0.09
6. Atmospheric composition (most abundant gases)	nitrogen and oxygen	carbon dioxide
7. Average nighttime temperature near equator	15°C 60°F	−73°C −100°F

PATTERN PRACTICE 4: "This is what happened." Write three paragraphs in which you tell about the history of exploring Mars. In your first paragraph you can discuss the early missions (missions 1–5). In your second paragraph you can take up the 1971 and 1973 probes (missions 6–13). In your last paragraph you can discuss the 1975 launchings (missions 14–15). *Answers will vary.*

PATTERN PRACTICE 5: This is what it looks . . . like." Describe Mars in two paragraphs. You may write either a factual description (based in part on photographs in old newspapers or science books) or a fantasy description (based on your imagination).

In your first paragraph describe what the planet *looks* like when you are actually standing on it. For example, de-

Pattern Practices on page 532 go with the data given on pages 530 and 531.

scribe its color, its light, or its landscape. In your second paragraph describe what it *feels* like to be on the planet. You can, for example, write about the atmospheric pressure or the gravity. *Answers will vary.*

PATTERN PRACTICE 6: "This is like (or unlike) that." Write two paragraphs in which you compare and contrast the U.S. missions and the U.S.S.R. missions to Mars.

In your first paragraph point out the similarities. For example, Were spacecraft launched in the same years by both countries? Did the spacecraft perform similar tasks? What else was the same about the missions of both countries?

In your second paragraph point out the differences. For example, Which country achieved successful missions? Which country received photographs sooner? Which country landed a capsule on Mars sooner? In what other ways did the missions of the two countries differ? *Answers will vary.*

PATTERN PRACTICE 7: "This is unlike that." Use the information in Data Set II to write two paragraphs about how Earth and Mars are different. In your first paragraph tell how the two planets are different in size and location (see 1–3). In your second paragraph tell how the two planets differ in how they affect human beings (see 4–7). *Answers will vary.*

■ Assignment C: *TV Programing*

Use the program chart on page 533, or make a similar chart for a recent night of TV programs. Then, pretending that you are a TV reviewer, complete the Pattern Practices that follow. As you learned in 10.o, each paragraph of expository writing should have a strong topic sentence. Be sure to revise and edit your writing. See the checklists in 10.q and 10.r.

TV PROGRAM CHART

	CBS	NBC	ABC	PBS
7:00	National News	National News	National News	*Over Easy* (talk show) with Isaac Stern, violinist, as guest)
7:30	*The Gong Show* (game show)	*Newlywed Game* (game show)	*Match Game* (game show)	*The MacNeil/ Lehrer Report* (news analysis)
8:00	*California Fever* (comedy-drama)	*The Misadventures of Sheriff Lobo* (comedy-drama)	*Happy Days* (situation comedy)	*Dick Cavett* (talk show with Rex Harrison, actor, as guest)
8:30			*Angie* (situation comedy)	
9:00	*Death Car on the Highway* (TV movie)	*The Last Convertible* (second installment of made-for-TV movie)	*Three's Company* (situation comedy)	*Reflections on the Third Reich* (documentary about Adolph Hitler)
9:30			*Taxi* (situation comedy)	
10:00			*The Lazarus Syndrome* (medical drama)	
10:30				
11:00	Local News	Local News	Local News	*Young and Innocent* (film)

Pattern Practices on page 534 go with the data given on page 533.

PATTERN PRACTICE 8: "This is what happened."
Assume that you are trying to review all the programs at one time using one TV set. You switch channels often, with some confusing, perhaps amusing, results. Tell about this experience, using the "what happened" pattern of writing. In the first paragraph, you may want to tell what happened in the first two hours of the evening's viewing. In the second paragraph, you may cover the next two hours. Finally, in the third paragraph, you may tell what it was like switching from one news program to another. *Answers will vary.*

PATTERN PRACTICE 9: "This is what it looks . . . like."
As a reviewer, you are especially interested in reporting on one or two particular programs (real or imaginary) that you saw during the evening. Either describe one program in two or more paragraphs, or describe two programs (or more), giving a paragraph to each. Concentrate on what the programs look like (their settings, their colors, their costumes, their characters) and sound like (music, sound effects). *Answers will vary.*

PATTERN PRACTICE 10: "This is like (or unlike) that." It is your job as a reviewer to inform the public about what they can expect to find on TV. To that end, do *one* of the following: *Answers will vary.*

1. Compare and contrast two programs (real or imaginary) that you like. You might want to talk about similarities in one paragraph and differences in another paragraph.
2. Compare and contrast what you consider to be the best program and the worst program.
3. Contrast two networks' overall programing, showing that one network offers more varied and interesting programs than the other. You can show the weaknesses of the inferior network in one paragraph and the strengths of the superior network in the second paragraph.

11.n COMBINING PATTERNS IN ONE PIECE OF WRITING

Sometimes you may want to use in the same piece of writing all three of the patterns that you have studied in this section: narration, description, and comparison/contrast. If you are writing about a trip through space, for example, you can use narration to tell what happened from day to day on your trip. You can use description to tell what the planets that you visited looked like. Then you can compare and contrast one planet with another. For a specific example of how all three patterns can be combined, read the model below.

■ Model 4: Combining Patterns

Only moments after blast-off, or so it seemed, we saw the first of the two newly discovered planets, the planet Nabob. At once the captain gave the command to orbit the planet. Within seconds, our spaceship began its slow circles, looping the planet methodically time after time as you would a ball of string. All photographic devices and testing instruments were put into operation, and radio signals in all known codes and languages scanned the planet seeking some response. After fifty-six hours of this work, our science team decided that there was no more to be tested, no voice to be heard. The captain, therefore, decided that we should continue our journey.

Narrative Pattern: "This is what happened."

That decision had scarcely been made when our huge ship was speeding out of Nabob's orbit field directed toward Sydron. That planet, more than twice the size of Nabob, lay still far off in the blackness of space, or so we thought.

Almost before the ship had settled down into routine for the journey to Sydron, an amazing thing happened. The darkness surrounding us somehow appeared less dark. From the dead of night we seemed to have moved into the hours before dawn. Obviously, our instruments, especially our long-range detection systems, were reacting, for we were slowing down, almost coming to a halt. Members of the science team were being summoned to the bridge for an unscheduled conference, and the darkness grew lighter. It was some time before our new plans were announced by the captain. The decision was to proceed, but very slowly. No one seemed to know what to expect.

(to be continued)

As we continued our journey to Sydron, we had time to discuss our reactions to Nabob. What we had seen had taken us completely by surprise. The planet was a perfect globe, like Earth, and it was neatly marked into segments like the inside of an orange, each segment narrowing at the very top and bottom, at what on Earth are called the North and South poles. The terrain inside each segment was different from the terrain in any other segment. There was no repetition and no spilling over from segment to segment. At the dividing lines, the total character of the land changed suddenly and completely. In one segment rivers wound through flat lowlands, green and willow-shaded. In the next segment, towering mountains reached up to the sky. A hot and smouldering desert lay in the sun in the segment on the other side. Other segments

Descriptive Pattern: "This is what it looks . . . like."

were composed of woodland, island group-
ings, farmland, prairies, jungles, and icy
waters, each existing side by side in its own
special climate. The unusualness of Nabob
made us especially curious about what
Sydron might be like.

(to be continued)

Once back on Earth, the wonder of our
journey into space began to dawn on us.
What we had expected to find on each of the
two new planets no one could have said.
*What we did find on both planets was very
surprising, and there was a fascinating difference between the two.* The first planet,
Nabob, was most familiar to Earth dwellers.
It was composed of nine vertical segments,
each of which resembled a different part of
Earth. Although there was no life on Nabob,
every person on Earth could have found a
segment of Nabob that spoke of home. Eskimos could have found an Artic homeland,
and tropical dwellers, a rain forest. Every
region of the United States was represented
in one segment or another, almost as if each
segment had been carved out of planet Earth
or from some still unknown planet that is
identical to Earth.

Comparison/
Contrast
Pattern: "This
is like (or
unlike) that."

Notice the
italicized
topic sentence.

Sydron, the next planet we encountered,
was completely different from Nabob, but
equally amazing.

(to be continued)

■ Assignment D: *Science Fiction*

Add a paragraph, as will be stated, to continue each
of the patterns in the preceding science fiction selection.

Pattern Practices on page 538 go with the data given on pages 535-537.

Use your own imagination to come up with ideas. As you learned in 10.o, each paragraph of expository writing should have a strong topic sentence. Be sure to revise and edit your writing. See the checklists in 12.1 and 12.m.

PATTERN PRACTICE 11: "This is what happened." Add a paragraph that will continue the narrative portion of the selection. For example, tell what happened as the spaceship grew even closer to Sydron. What happened when the ship reached the planet? Did the crew stay aboard the ship, or did they land on Sydron and explore the planet? Create any story that you choose. *Answers will vary.*

PATTERN PRACTICE 12: "This is what it looks . . . like." Add a paragraph continuing the descriptive portion of the selection. Explain what Sydron was like. Try to include sensory details for at least one sense other than sight. Perhaps your space crew was able to explore the surface of the planet and got information about what it sounded, smelled, or felt like. Be as imaginative as you can in your description. *Answers will vary.*

PATTERN PRACTICE 13: "This is like (or unlike) that." Add a paragraph continuing the comparison/contrast portion of the selection. Explain how Sydron was different from Nabob. *Answers will vary.*

12

THE COMPOSITION

12 The Composition

See summary of section in Teacher's Manual.

A **composition** is a short paper composed of several paragraphs with a clear introduction, a body, and a conclusion.

A composition can communicate your thoughts, your ideas, or your experiences. Unlike a single paragraph, a multiparagraph composition deals with several different aspects of a topic in some detail. Usually, you treat each aspect of the topic in a separate paragraph. You may often be asked to write a composition of three to five paragraphs (250–500 words).

When you write a composition, you may want to combine the various patterns of thinking and writing discussed in Section 11. For example, you may want to develop three different points, one by narration, one by description, and one by comparison and contrast.

12.a SELECTING AND LIMITING A TOPIC

The first step in writing a composition is to decide upon a topic. Sometimes the topic will be assigned to you, but usually you will have to choose your own. Selecting a topic is not as easy as it may seem, but there are definite steps to follow. First of all, you should choose a topic that interests you and that you know something about (or can learn about). Second, you must be careful that the topic is neither too broad nor too narrow. Most often, you will find that your first idea for a topic is too broad and will require narrowing down. The dangers of trying to write about too broad a topic are that you will not have room to give the details, and your reader will be dissatisfied.

■ Select a topic that interests you.

To choose a composition topic, begin by thinking about your personal interests and experience. Selecting a topic that interests you is important for two reasons. First, it is easier and more enjoyable to write about something that you have firsthand knowledge of or that you genuinely want to know more about. Second, your reader's attention will more likely be captured if you are writing about something in which you yourself are interested.

Therefore, begin by thinking about the things you like to do. Perhaps you collect old comic books or follow a particular baseball team. Maybe you sew your own clothes or go to many movies. Comic books, sports, sewing, and movies are all broad topics that you can limit further.

■ Limit the topic.

After you have chosen a general topic, you must narrow the topic so that you can comfortably write about it. There are general questions that you can ask in your effort to limit the topic.

QUESTIONS TO LIMIT A TOPIC
1. Is there a particular time period I can focus on?
2. Is there a particular person (or group) I can focus on?
3. Is there a particular event I can focus on?
4. Is there a particular object I can focus on?
5. Is there a particular type or category I can focus on?

Remember that narrowing a topic is a gradual process. Before you find a workable topic, you may have to ask several of the above questions, one after another.

For example, suppose that you choose *movies* as your broad topic. Obviously, it will be impossible to cover the entire subject of movies in a short composition — or even a short book. You must find one aspect of movies that you are interested in and that you can cover in a few paragraphs. Try asking one of the above questions — say, Question 5: *Is there a particular type of movie that you enjoy?* Perhaps *musicals* are your favorite, but *musicals* is still too broad a topic. Try asking another question, then, perhaps Question 1 or 2. You may then choose the *musicals of the 1930s* or the *musicals of Rodgers and Hammerstein.* The musicals of a certain composer or of a certain decade are subjects that are still too broad for a brief composition, however. You must narrow your topic even further. Try Question 3 or 4. Think of one specific musical of the 1930s that you enjoy — for example, *The Wizard of Oz.* You have seen it many times on television, and it has remained one of your favorite films.

Still, you cannot cover in only a few paragraphs everything you know about the movie — Judy Garland and the other actors, the ever-popular fantasy of Oz, the characters, songs, settings, photography, the production of the film, its reception by the public, and so on. For a workable composition topic you have to choose one aspect of *The Wizard of Oz* that can be treated in several paragraphs. You may wish to examine the different ways that the film creates a fantasy world. Now you have an appropriate topic for a composition, as stated below.

TOPIC
the fantasy world in *The Wizard of Oz*

EXERCISE 1. Narrow five of the following broad topics so that each will be suitable for a composition of several paragraphs. Use the questions on page 541 to help you limit the topics. *Answers will vary; an example is given below.*

1. landmarks in a town
2. soccer *"Why Pelé Is Soccer's Greatest Star"*
3. rock music
4. cats
5. skiing

6. sports cars
7. folk music
8. air pollution
9. the American Revolution
10. mystery novels

12.b DETERMINING YOUR AUDIENCE AND STATING YOUR PURPOSE

Once you decide on a topic, you must express the topic as a statement of purpose. Your **statement of purpose** will remind you of exactly what you wish to say about your topic.

A major factor to consider before arriving at your statement of purpose, though, is the audience you are writing for and the effect you wish to have on that audience. The audience for most of the writing that you do in school will be your teacher and classmates. At times, however, you will have to write for other audiences, so you must understand how audience will affect your writing.

For example, the topic this section will develop —"the fantasy world in *The Wizard of Oz*"— could be treated in a variety of ways. If you were writing for an audience of knowledgeable film students, you would include specific details of film technique that help to create the fantasy, including a discussion of the types of shots and cuts between shots, information on how the sets were made and filmed, and so on. You would use the specific vocabulary of film-makers and other mature vocabulary and sentence structures. On the other hand, if your audience were a group of young children, you would keep your explanations, vocabulary, and sentence structure very simple. You would probably focus on explaining how the story is a fairy tale. Thus, the choice of audience will affect your treatment of content, your choice of words, your type of sentence structures, and so on.

Assume that you decide that your audience for the *Wizard of Oz* paper will be your classmates. Your statement of purpose can then be expressed in a sentence such as the following:

STATEMENT OF PURPOSE

I want to explain to my classmates the ways that a fantasy world is created in *The Wizard of Oz*.

EXERCISE 2. Select a topic for a composition. (You may use one of the topics you arrived at in Exercise 1.) Write a statement of purpose for the topic. *Answers will vary.*

12.c USING PATTERNS OF THINKING AND WRITING TO DEVELOP A TOPIC

Once you have a statement of purpose, try to see how the patterns of thinking and writing (from Section 11) will help you to write your composition. Think about your topic in terms of narration, description, and comparison/contrast. At least one or two of these patterns can probably be used in your composition. Ask yourself the following questions:

QUESTIONS TO DEVELOP A TOPIC BY PATTERNS OF THINKING AND WRITING

1. Is there a story (a *narrative*) related to my topic that I can tell about?
2. Is there something important to my topic that I can clearly *describe* for my reader?
3. Are there important points that I can *compare or contrast* to emphasize my stated purpose?

You are now ready to write a list of notes that relate to your topic. Sit down with your statement of purpose in front of you and with the patterns of thinking and writing in mind. Jot down ideas, thoughts, and details as they occur to you. You may use both phrases and sentences in your notes if you wish. At this point, you need not worry about arranging these notes in any particular order. Be sure to refer to your statement of purpose from time to time to help you keep your ideas focused on your topic. When you actually begin to write your composition, you may find that some of the notes you listed are not suited to your topic and may be discarded.

The following list of notes relates to the fantasy world in *The Wizard of Oz.*

NOTES

Statement of purpose: I want to explain to my classmates the ways that a fantasy world is created in *The Wizard of Oz.*

—Dorothy and Toto fantastically transported to the strange world of Oz
—Dorothy meets a Scarecrow, a Tin Man, and a Cowardly Lion who walk, talk, and act like people.
—The friends journey to meet the Wizard of Oz.
—Munchkins, good witches, and wicked witches
—Dorothy returns to Kansas and realizes she has been dreaming.
—The story in Frank Baum's series of Oz books differs from the story in the film.
—The Emerald City, where everything is green
—Color photography for Oz versus black-and-white photography for Kansas
—The sets in *The Wiz* versus those in *The Wizard of Oz*
—Dark castle of wicked witch
—Wicked witch dissolves.
—Good witch appears in a bubble.
—Trees talk; monkeys have wings.
—The bright Yellow Brick Road
—Kansas is dry and bare, but Oz is full of trees.

EXERCISE 3. Using the patterns of thinking and writing and the three questions on page 544, make a list of thoughts and ideas about the topic you chose in Exercise 2. *Answers will vary.*

12.d WRITING THE WORKING OUTLINE

A **working outline** will guide you as you think, plan, and gather any additional information that you may need.

Once you have a statement of purpose and a list of notes about your topic, organize the notes into a working outline. Look over your list, and group together any notes that seem to fit together. You may want to organize your composition in terms of the patterns of thinking and writing.

For example, in the notes for the fantasy world in *The Wizard of Oz*, the details about the story of *The Wizard of Oz* can be grouped together. The notes describing what Oz looks like can also be grouped together. Finally, the ideas about the differences between Kansas and Oz can be grouped together. Upon reflection, if any of the notes do not relate closely enough to your topic, you may eliminate them. For instance, the ideas about Frank Baum's Oz books and about the movie *The Wiz* do not relate to the topic closely enough. A discussion of these items will not help your reader understand how a fantasy world is created in the film *The Wizard of Oz*.

After you group related thoughts and ideas, decide in which order to write about them. For example, you may want to discuss the story line of *The Wizard of Oz* first, then describe the visual impact of the film, and then talk about how Kansas and Oz differ.

To prepare a working outline, write down each of your ideas in words or phrases. List your ideas in groups, each of which will have a Roman numeral and a heading. Write your statement of purpose and thesis statement at the top of the page. Study the following working outline.

WORKING OUTLINE

Statement of purpose: I want to explain the ways that a fantasy world is created in the film *The Wizard of Oz*.

I. The fantasy of the story
   A. Whirled by cyclone to Oz
   B. Adventures along Yellow Brick Road
   C. Meeting Scarecrow, Tin Man, Cowardly Lion
   D. The Wizard
   E. Return to Kansas
II. The visual fantasy
   A. Munchkinland

B. Emerald City
C. Wicked witch's castle
D. Talking tree
E. Witch dissolving
III. The differences between Kansas and Oz
   A. Dreary Kansas vs. lush Oz
   B. Kansas in black and white vs. Oz in color

At this point you should check your working outline for completeness. Do any of the sections of the outline need further development or additional details? The following sample shows new items (in bold type) that might be added to the second section of the working outline.

II. The visual fantasy
   A. Munchkinland
   B. **Good witch's bubble**
   C. **Yellow Brick Road**
   D. Emerald City
   E. Wicked witch's castle
   F. Talking tree
   G. **Winged monkeys**
   H. Witch dissolving

EXERCISE 4. Compose a working outline from the statement of purpose and the list of ideas that you prepared in Exercises 2 and 3. *Answers will vary.*

12.e WRITING THE FORMAL OUTLINE

A **formal outline** will guide you in writing your first draft.

After you write the working outline, begin to compose your formal outline. Preparing a formal outline will help you to organize your composition because it will force you to put your ideas in a clear and logical order. Also, in the formal outline you flesh out the main ideas in the working outline by adding specifics that develop them. A formal outline can be written in either complete sentences or words and phrases. The following guidelines will help you.

■ Guidelines for formal outlines

1. *Numbering:* Use Roman numerals for each main topic, capital letters for each subtopic, Arabic numerals for the next level of subtopic, and small letters for the next lower level of subtopic. (If you have subtopics at even lower levels, use Arabic numerals in parentheses, and then use small letters in parentheses.)

   You must always have at least two subtopics in any one category. Remember that subtopics are divisions of the topic above them. Since it is impossible to divide anything into fewer than two parts, there must be at least two subtopics under any one topic.

   Do not number the title of the composition or use the terms *introduction, body,* or *conclusion* on the outline itself.

2. *Indenting:* Line up all Roman numerals under one another; line up all capital letters under one another; line up all Arabic numerals under one another; and so on as shown in the sample below.

   I. (Main topic)
      A. (Subtopic of I)
      B. (Subtopic of I)
         1. (Subtopic of I. B)
         2. (Subtopic of I. B)
         3. (Subtopic of I. B)
   II. (Second main topic)
      A. (Subtopic of II)
      B. (Subtopic of II)

3. *Capitalization and punctuation:* Begin each entry with a capital letter. Use a period at the end of items on a sentence outline but not at the end of items consisting of words and phrases.

4. *Parallelism:* Always use the same kind of phrasing at the same levels of heads. For example, if you use a noun in I, you must use nouns in II, III, and so on. If you use a prepositional phrase in A. 1, use prepositional phrases in A. 2, A. 3, and so on. The following sample shows an outline written in parallel form.

FORMAL OUTLINE

I. The fantasy world of a young girl's dream

II. The fantasy of the story
    A. From Kansas to Oz
        1. Cyclone
        2. Munchkins
        3. Witches
    B. Toward the Emerald City
        1. Yellow Brick Road
        2. Scarecrow, Tin Man, Cowardly Lion
    C. At the Emerald City
        1. Wizard of Oz
        2. Awards
    D. From Oz to Kansas

(prepositional phrases — brackets A through D)

III. The visual fantasy of sets and photography
    A. Unusual sets
        1. Munchkinland
        2. Yellow Brick Road
        3. Emerald City
        4. Castle
    B. Photographic effects
        1. Amazing bubble
        2. Talking tree
        3. Winged monkeys
        4. Dissolving witch

(participles and nouns — bracket B.1 through B.4)

IV. The contrast between Kansas and Oz
    A. Appearance
        1. Dry, bare Kansas
        2. Lush Oz
    B. Photography
        1. Black-and-white Kansas
        2. Technicolor Oz
    C. People and animals

(nouns — bracket A through C)

V. A land of dreams come true

EXERCISE 5. Correct any mistakes in the following formal outline. Change any sentences to words and phrases. Make sure that parallel items have parallel phrasing. Add or take out items. If you have difficulties, check the Guidelines for Formal Outlines on page 548. *Answer is given at the back of the Teacher's Manual.*

I. The geography
    A. Walk up and down the steep streets.
    B. Wandering through the evening fog
    C. San Francisco Bay

II. Ride the cable cars up the famous hills
    A. See Nob Hill.
    (1) Victorian mansions.
    (2) There are many famous hotels.
    B. Russian Hill
    a. Walk down the Crookedest Street in the World
    C. See Telegraph Hill.
        1. Bohemian area of San Francisco
        2. View of city from Coit Tower
        3. Stop in at one of the many cafés.

III. Visit Chinatown.
    1. Vegetable stands and fish markets
    2. Have lunch at a tearoom.

IV. The Golden Gate Bridge
    1. connects San Francisco with Marin County
    2. offers a spectacular view of San Francisco

V. Conclusion

EXERCISE 6. Write a formal outline (using words and phrases) from the working outline that you prepared for Exercise 4. You may want to change around sections of the working outline, add items, or delete items.   *Answers will vary.*

12.f WRITING THE THESIS STATEMENT

After you write your formal outline, begin work on the thesis statement. The **thesis statement** is vital to your composition because it performs three important functions: (1) It states the main point of your paper; (2) it indicates your attitude toward the topic; and (3) it suggests the organization that the paper will follow. The thesis statement will actually be part of your composition — usually the last sentence of the introduction. It will serve as a guide for you in writing and for your audience in reading.

Therefore, composing a strong thesis statement at the beginning of your composition will be one of your most important tasks.

You cannot write your thesis statement until you have your formal outline because only then are both the content and the structure of the paper clear. To write the thesis statement, go back over your statement of purpose and your outline. Your statement of purpose will keep you focused on your main topic and chosen audience. Try to compose a single sentence that suggests most of the main topics on your outline. Look, for example, at the following thesis statement for the *Wizard of Oz* paper. Notice how it encompasses main topics I, II, III, and V from the outline. Notice also that the thesis statement indicates the order in which the ideas will be developed.

THESIS STATEMENT

Through story line, sets, and photographic effects, the film creates a fantasy world about a young girl's dream, a dream that you can relive as many times as you watch the film.

EXERCISE 7. Write a thesis statement based on the formal outline that you prepared for Exercise 6. *Answers will vary.*

12.g WRITING THE COMPOSITION

After you write your formal outline and your thesis statement, you begin writing the first draft of your composition. Write freely, and do not be overly concerned with matters such as the choice of specific words or sentence structures. You can pay attention to those kinds of details when you revise your first draft (see 12.1).

In writing the first draft your major aim should be to set down your ideas according to their order in the formal outline. Each main topic in the outline (numbered with Roman numerals) will need its own paragraph (or possibly two paragraphs). Remember all that you have learned about paragraph writing, and be sure that each paragraph treats a single idea. You may add or take away ideas from your outline as you write your first draft.

Try to sketch in a short introduction and conclusion to your composition, but wait until you have written the first draft before you expand and revise them (see 12.i and 12.j).

12.h USING TRANSITIONS BETWEEN PARAGRAPHS

Transitional devices make the movement from one paragraph to another clear, smooth, and easy to follow.

In a multiparagraph composition individual paragraphs must connect smoothly to each other. To move smoothly between paragraphs, use transitional devices. The three most important transitional devices are determiners, repeated key terms, and logical connectives.

■ Determiners

Connect the first sentence of a new paragraph to the paragraph before by using the determiners *this*, *that*, and *those*. Look at the following sentences from the sample composition to see how the determiner *this* relates the second paragraph to the first.

EXAMPLE
... a dream that you can relive as many times as you watch the film.

This film presents the fantasy story of Dorothy's adventures in a magical land called Oz....

■ Repeated key terms

Relate two paragraphs to each other by repeating in the first sentence of the new paragraph an important word or expression from the paragraph before it.

EXAMPLE

...Oz is only a **fantasy world.**

The sets and photographic effects in the film create a visual **fantasy world....**

■ Logical connectives

Connect two paragraphs by using logical connectives. (See Section 11 for an explanation and lists of logical connectives.) In the following example, notice how the logical connective *furthermore* helps to connect the two paragraphs.

EXAMPLE

...These are not sights that we see in real life.

Furthermore, the image of Oz as a fantasy world is made more powerful because it is contrasted with Dorothy's life in Kansas.

EXERCISE 8. Write the first draft of a composition, using the formal outline that you prepared in Exercise 6. Do not worry about writing a perfect introduction or conclusion at this point. *Answers will vary.*

12.i WRITING THE INTRODUCTION

Once you complete the first draft of your composition, pay special attention to the introduction. A good introduction will catch the reader's attention and state the main topic of the composition. Study the following suggestions for writing introductions. The examples are for a composition about the fantasy world of *The Wizard of Oz.*

1. *Give background information on your topic.* For example, explain that *The Wizard of Oz* has attracted millions of fans since it was released by MGM in 1939.
2. *State the topic.* For example, say something about the different ways that the fantasy world is represented in *The Wizard of Oz.*

3. *Use a quotation from a poem or song.* For example, begin by quoting, "We're off to see the Wizard, the wonderful Wizard of Oz!"
4. *Ask a question.* For example, begin by saying, "Can monkeys fly and scarecrows wink? In Oz they can."
5. *Directly address the reader.* For example, begin by asking, "How many times have you wished that you could relive a happy dream over and over again?"
6. *State an interesting fact or statistic.* For example, tell about the International Wizard of Oz Club, which publishes a magazine called *Oziana*.
7. *Tell an anecdote.* For example, tell about the annual Munchkin Convention sponsored by the International Wizard of Oz Club.

EXERCISE 9. Write two different introductions to the composition you began in Exercise 8, using two of the above methods for writing introductions. *Answers will vary.*

12.j WRITING THE CONCLUSION

A concluding paragraph closes and completes your composition. A well-written conclusion also adds to the force and appeal of your writing. The list below includes methods that you may use in your conclusion. Remember that to make a smooth transition to your conclusion, you may want to use logical connectives such as *finally* or *to conclude.*

1. Write a statement that sums up all of your ideas.
2. Restate the central topic of the composition.
3. Relate the topic directly to the readers' experience.
4. Relate an anecdote.
5. Ask a question.

EXERCISE 10. Write a conclusion to the composition that you began in Exercise 8. *Answers will vary.*

12.k SELECTING THE TITLE

Once you complete the first draft of the entire composition, select a title. Remember that your title should express some aspect of the central topic of the composition as well as attract the readers' interest. For the sample composition on pages 557–558, the title "Why I Like *The Wizard of Oz*" is too dull. On the other hand, the title "A Wonderful Movie" is too general; it could refer to almost any movie. Moreover, neither title expresses the central topic of the composition. The title "A Dream Come True" is appropriate. It refers to the idea of fantasy and creates interest.

EXERCISE 11. Select a title for the composition that you began in Exercise 8. *Answers will vary.*

12.l REVISING THE FIRST DRAFT

After you complete the first draft of your composition, put it aside for a time and think about something else. After several hours or a day you will be able to look more objectively at what you have written. Then, read over your first draft to examine it for any problems. You will find it helpful to look it over with the following questions in mind. *Point out to students that revision of the first draft is not a sign of failure but a necessary part of the writing process.*

■ Checklist for revising a composition

1. Does this composition carry out my stated purpose?
2. Are the ideas presented in a clear and logical order?
3. Does each main topic on the formal outline (numbered with Roman numerals) have its own paragraph (or paragraphs)?
4. Do all of the ideas discussed relate to the thesis statement?
5. Are the transitions between paragraphs clear and smooth?

EXERCISE 12. Using the Checklist for Revising a Composition, improve the first draft of the composition that you began in Exercise 8. *Answers will vary.*

12.m EDITING AND PROOFREADING THE COMPOSITION

Once you revise the first draft of your composition, check the paper for correct punctuation, grammar, vocabulary, and spelling. No paper is complete until it has been edited and proofread. Check over each point on the following Editing and Proofreading Checklist. If you do not understand any of these points, refer to the sections indicated in parentheses.

As you edit and proofread your own or someone else's essay, you may use Editing Signals, such as those below, from Section 9.

■ Editing and proofreading checklist

1. Are all sentences complete? (See 2.a.) *frag*
2. Are varied sentence structures used? (See Section 3.)
3. Have you used the voice (active or passive) that is most effective in each sentence? (See 1.b.20.) *voice*
4. Are verb tenses consistent? (See 1.b.12.) *tense*
5. Do subjects and verbs agree? (See 2.d and 2.f -g.) *agree*
6. Do pronouns agree with antecedents? (See 1.d.1 and 1.d.7.) *ref*
7. Is the vocabulary precise but varied and interesting? (See Section 4.) *vocab*
8. Are words spelled correctly? (See Section 5.) *sp*
9. Is punctuation correct? (See Section 7.) *p*

EXERCISE 13. Edit and proofread your revised composition. Use the Editing and Proofreading Checklist for guidance, and check the appropriate sections of this book if you have any questions. *Answers will vary.*

12.n A SAMPLE COMPOSITION

Read the completed composition below about *The Wizard of Oz*, which you have seen gradually developing throughout this section.

A DREAM COME TRUE

How many times have you wished that you could relive your special dreams? Maybe you have thought that if you could only film your pleasant dreams, you might experience them many times. The people responsible for making *The Wizard of Oz* must have had a similar thought in mind. Through story line, sets, and photographic effects, the film creates a fantasy world about a young girl's dream, a dream that you can relive as many times as you watch the film.

> Notice that the composition begins with a question to the reader.

> Notice the underlined thesis statement.

This film presents the fantasy story of Dorothy's adventures in a magical land called Oz. The film begins in Kansas, where Dorothy and her dog Toto live. Soon, they are whirled by a cyclone to the land of Oz. There Dorothy meets funny little people called Munchkins as well as wicked witches and good witches. Then she begins a journey along the Yellow Brick Road to the Emerald City to meet the Wizard of Oz who she hopes can help her return to Kansas. Before long, Dorothy meets three unusual characters — a Scarecrow, a Tin Man, and a Cowardly Lion. They each decide to ask the Wizard for what they want most in the world — a brain for the Scarecrow, a heart for the Tin Man, and courage for the Cowardly Lion.

> Notice that this paragraph is developed as *narration*. Pay special attention to the underlined logical connectives that tell *when* events occur.

After many adventures, the four friends reach the Emerald City and meet the Wizard of Oz. The great Oz gives the Scarecrow a de-

> Notice this second paragraph of *narration*.

gree in "thinkology," the Tin Man a heart, and the Cowardly Lion a medal for "conspicuous courage." Then, Dorothy clicks her ruby slippers together three times and returns to Kansas. At the end of the movie, we realize she has dreamed the whole story. Oz is only a fantasy world.

The sets and photographic effects in the film create a visual fantasy world. These fairy-tale sets include colorful Munchkinland; a spiraling yellow brick road; the unusual Emerald City, where everything is green; and the sinister castle belonging to the wicked witch. The numerous special photographic effects contribute to our enjoyment of the fantasy. They include a witch appearing in a bubble, another witch dissolving, and a tree coming alive.

Furthermore, the image of Oz as a fantasy world is made more powerful because it is contrasted with Dorothy's life in Kansas. In the film, Kansas has dry flat plains, few trees, and simple houses. Unlike Kansas, the land of Oz has lush forests, sparkling streams, and a castle in the Emerald City. This fact is emphasized by filming the Kansas portions in black and white but the Oz portions in color. Moreover, the people and animals in Oz are different from those in Kansas. For example, witches in Oz can disappear in a puff of smoke, and horses can change into all the colors of the rainbow.

If you have ever dreamed of a magical land like Oz, you can relive it again and again by watching *The Wizard of Oz*. A land where the good witch always defeats the bad witch and every story has a happy ending, Oz is surely a dream come true.

Notice that this paragraph is developed as *description*.

Notice that this paragraph is developed as *contrast*. Pay special attention to the underlined logical connectives, which help point out differences.

LIBRARIES AND INFORMATION

13 Libraries and Information

See summary of section in Teacher's Manual.

The library can be a very important part of your education and entertainment. The library is a huge storehouse of information, and information is one of the most important tools you will need to succeed in school or in your job, no matter what your courses or interests are or what career you choose.

You will find not only a vast amount of information for school in your library, but also many ways to entertain yourself in your spare time. On the bookshelves you will find novels, poetry, plays, and art books. In other parts of the library you will be able to examine records, artwork, and tapes. Many libraries show films and schedule lecture series. Your library may even have a special area containing books and other materials that are appropriate for students alone. Modern libraries are busy, exciting places that serve their communities in many ways that you may not know about. Because libraries contain many books and other sources of information for work, for school, and for leisure, they are sometimes called learning resource centers.

The library is a remarkable place. It can also be a very frustrating place if you do not know how to find the information and other services that you want. Therefore, you must learn your way around the library. First, you should get an idea of the resources that most libraries have to offer. This section will introduce you to the information and many services that most libraries provide. Then, you

13.c.4 Atlases

Atlases are collections of maps.

You should turn to an atlas when you want to learn more about an area of land — whether it be your city block or the continent of Asia. The most useful atlases include the *Hammond Contemporary World Atlas*, the *Historical Atlas of the United States*, the *National Geographic World Atlas*, and *The New York Times Atlas of the World*.

EXERCISE 7. Use an encyclopedia to answer the following questions.

1. In what year did Alaska become the forty-ninth state? *1958*
2. What was Doris Lessing's first novel? *The Grass Is Singing*
3. Who invented the telephone? *Alexander Graham Bell*
4. Who discovered the element radium? *Marie and Pierre Curie*
5. Who were the first people to reach the top of Mount Everest? *Sir Edmund Hillary and Tenzing Norgay*

EXERCISE 8. Use an almanac to answer the following questions.

1. Who won the Nobel Prize for Peace in 1976? *Mairead Corrigan and Betty Williams*
2. What is the warmest place on earth? *Al Aziziyah, Libya*
3. What is the capital city of Australia? *Canberra*
4. Who was the seventeenth President? *Andrew Johnson*
5. Who won the Academy Award for Best Actor in 1977? *Richard Dreyfuss*

EXERCISE 9. Use an atlas to answer the following questions.

1. What is the elevation of Mount Whitney in California? *14,495 feet*
2. What states border California? *Oregon, Nevada, Arizona*
3. How many countries are there in South America? *14*
4. What is the tallest mountain in the United States? *Mt. McKinley*
5. Name three national parks in Washington state. *Olympic; Fort Vancouver; Mount Rainier*

13.c.5 Special reference works

A number of other reference works are useful for doing in-depth research. The most useful reference works are listed here.

1. Biographical reference works, such as *Who's Who* or *Current Biography,* contain short life stories of noteworthy men and women.
2. *Roget's Thesaurus* and *Webster's Dictionary of Synonyms* give lists of synonyms for many English words.
3. Books of quotations, such as *Bartlett's Familiar Quotations* or the *Oxford Dictionary of Quotations,* list quotations arranged by subject or key word.

EXTRA: Ask students to compare the method of listing quotations in Bartlett's Familiar Quotations with the listing in Stevenson's Home Book of Verse.

GOVERNMENT INFORMATION SERVICES

State and federal governments publish pamphlets and reports with useful information on a wide variety of topics, such as nutrition, health, education, and handicrafts. Your library will probably have some of these publications, or you may write directly to government offices for information. Here are addresses of a few:

Council on Environmental Quality
722 Jackson Place NW
Washington, D.C. 20006

Department of Justice
Constitution Avenue and Tenth Street NW
Washington, D.C. 20530

Food and Drug Administration
5600 Fishers Lane
Rockville, MD 20852

Education Department
400 Maryland Avenue SW
Washington, D.C. 20202

EXERCISE 10. Use *Bartlett's Familiar Quotations* or another source to find out who said the following:

1. "Give me liberty, or give me death." *Patrick Henry*
2. "Beauty is in the eye of the beholder." *Margaret W. Hungerford*
3. "Men are what their mothers made them." *Ralph Waldo Emerson*
4. "The only thing we have to fear is fear itself." *F. D. Roosevelt*
5. "All is fair in love and war." *Shakespeare*
6. "All I know is what I see in the papers." *Will Rogers*
7. "Mine eyes have seen the glory of the coming of the Lord." *Julia Ward Howe*
8. "To thine own self be true." *Shakespeare*
9. "To be or not to be; that is the question." *Shakespeare*
10. "Hitch your wagon to a star." *Ralph Waldo Emerson*

13.d OBTAINING LIBRARY MATERIALS

Most of the materials in the library are in **circulation**. You can check out and take home circulating materials for periods that usually range from seven days to a month. These materials include books, records, and tapes. You will need a library card in order to borrow materials from the library.

Most libraries have a collection of noncirculating materials that must remain in the library for everyone to use. Noncirculating materials include current newspapers, periodicals, microforms, and reference materials.

■ Obtaining newspapers and periodicals

Most libraries keep newspapers and periodicals together in a special area or room. Back issues of newspapers are usually now stored as microforms (see below). Some large newspapers, like the *New York Times*, print an index to back issues. A newspaper index is similar to the *Reader's Guide to Periodical Literature* and is used in the same way.

Back issues of periodicals are either put on micro-forms or bound in books and placed on bookshelves. Once you have used the *Reader's Guide* to find a list of articles that may help you, ask your librarian where back issues of periodicals are kept.

◼ Using microforms

Microforms are photographs of the printed page reduced to a very small size. Microforms make it possible to store a great deal of information — many volumes of books or periodicals — in a very small space. The most common microforms are microfilm and microfiche. (Notice that all these words contain *micro-*, which means "small.")

Microfilm consists of reels of plastic film that resembles movie film. A microfiche is a plastic card, usually four by six inches (*fiche* is the French word for "small card"). A microfiche holds between sixty and ninety-eight printed pages. Microfilm and microfiche must be viewed with special projectors. The projectors are easy to operate, but you will probably need a demon-stration before you use them.

◼ Records, tapes, and the vertical file

Many libraries offer records and tapes of music, plays, and poetry readings. In some libraries these materials are part of the reference collection and cannot be checked out. In other libraries, however, you may borrow records and tapes.

Your library most likely keeps a **vertical file** for materials of current interest. The vertical file, a special cabinet or desk, contains pamphlets, clippings, photo-graphs, government bulletins, and cartoons. The contents of the vertical file are not listed in the card catalogue, but the librarian will tell you whether it contains the material you need.

13.e THE PARTS OF A BOOK

Once you have located a book in the library, you can quickly determine whether or not it will be useful to you. If you look carefully through a book, you will see that it has a number of different parts. Each part serves a purpose. All books contain at least some of the following parts, and many books contain all of them.

1. **Frontispiece.** The frontispiece is a photograph, painting, or drawing that relates to the author or the subject of the book.

2. **Title page.** Here you will find the complete title, the full name of the author or editor, the edition number, the name of the publisher, the place of publication, and sometimes the date of publication.

3. **Copyright page.** The copyright page, usually on the back of the title page, lists the date of copyright and the name of the copyright holder. A copyright is issued by the United States government in order to protect the work of an author or publisher. It can be a crime to reprint or reproduce copyrighted material without the permission of the copyright holder.

4. **Preface, foreword, introduction.** The preface, foreword, and introduction contain material that explains the nature and purpose of the book.

5. **Acknowledgments.** The acknowledgments list books or people from whom the author has borrowed ideas or copyrighted material.

6. **Table of contents.** The table of contents lists the page numbers where the contents are found.

7. **List of illustrations, list of tables, list of special features.** If a book contains illustrations or tables, they will usually be listed in one place with their page numbers.

8. **Appendix.** The appendixes of a book contain material that the author does not include in the text itself, such as diagrams, documents, laws, charts, tables, and long quotations.

9. **Glossary.** The glossary is an alphabetical list of words and their definitions that you will need to know when reading the book.

10. **Bibliography.** The bibliography is a list of sources used by the author or recommended by the author for additional reading.

11. **Index.** An index is an alphabetical list of the subjects, names, and terms used in the book and their page numbers. Use the index to see if the book has the information you need.

EXERCISE 11. Use this textbook to answer the following questions.

1. Who published this textbook? *Macmillan Publishing Co., Inc.*

2. When was this textbook published? *1981*

3. Use the table of contents. On what page does Section 9 begin? *441*

4. Use the table of contents. How many sections are there in this book? *16 (plus Additional Exercises)*

5. How long is the index to this book? *17 pages*

6. On which pages does the book deal with subordinate clauses? *156-158; 159-170*

7. Does this book have a list of illustrations? *No*

8. How long is the table of contents in this book? *3 pages*

9. On what page does the index begin? *661*

10. Where in this book can you find information about dictionaries? How did you get the answer? *Section 6; index or table of contents*

14

THE RESEARCH REPORT

14 The Research Report

See summary of section in Teacher's Manual.

Most likely, much of the writing you have done up to now has come out of your own knowledge and opinions. The more that you read and study, however, the more you will uncover about the knowledge and opinions of others. You will then be asked to do the kind of writing that involves finding out what other people know and think. The kind of writing that involves doing library research is called a **research report** or a **library paper.**

A research report deals with a limited topic, uses three to five outside sources, and is based upon information gained from your reading or from talking to experts in a particular field. When you write the paper, though, you should make an effort to do more than simply tell what experts know. You should try to analyze what you find out. Make generalizations. Help your readers understand the meaning of what you are reporting on. You will see how a student made generalizations and gave focus to her research paper on pages 596– 602.

A research report may be 500–1,000 words long (2– 4 typed pages) or whatever length your teacher suggests.

In writing a research report you will make use of many different skills: using the library, writing an outline, writing topic sentences, and writing coherent paragraphs. You will also make use of the different patterns of writing described in Section 11: narration, description, and comparison/contrast.

Besides being a challenge, the job of writing a research report can also be fun because it gives you the chance to become an expert on a subject that you are really interested in. As you track down details and find answers to your questions, you will satisfy your curiosity and experience a sense of real accomplishment.

14.a SELECTING A TOPIC

Sometimes your teacher will assign a specific topic for your research report. If you are assigned a topic, make sure that you think about it deeply and research it carefully. Make it your *own.* More often, you will be free to choose your own topic or to choose a particular aspect of a broad topic.

The most common mistake that students make is choosing a topic that is too broad. For example, suppose that you have just had your eyes checked and want to write a research report on how the eye sees images. You will not be able to cover that huge topic in a brief research report. You will have to narrow down the topic to a workable size, perhaps in the following way:

BROAD: Vision
LESS BROAD: Faulty vision
LESS BROAD: Ways of correcting faulty vision
NARROW: How contact lenses work

Do not choose a topic that is *too* limited. For example, suppose that you select to write about your community's annual rainfall. After you give the statistics and describe how the rainfall is measured, what else is there to say? All the research in the world will not help you to write about a too-limited topic.

Before you make a final decision on a topic, see if there are enough research materials on the topic in your library. If your library has little or no information on your topic, you will have to choose another topic. Then, ask yourself the questions that will help you to choose a topic for a research report.

QUESTIONS FOR CHOOSING A TOPIC

1. Am I sufficiently interested in the topic?
2. Is the topic too broad to be covered adequately in the length specified?
3. Is the topic too limited?
4. Are there enough books or articles on the topic in the libraries that I will use?

EXAMPLE

Betsy Thomassen had to write a research paper. The only requirement was to write about something that interested her. At first Betsy Thomassen decided to write about sewing machines because she sews many of her own clothes. On her first trip to the library, however, she could not find any information that interested her about the history or the workings of sewing machines. Since Betsy had recently been fitted with contact lenses, her friend suggested that Betsy write about them. A preliminary check of the library proved that she could find adequate source material on this topic, and she chose "Breakthroughs in Contact Lenses" as the subject of her paper.

EXERCISE 1. For each of the following ten broad topics, suggest three limited topics that can be handled in a brief research report. When you have completed the exercise, choose one of the limited topics — or another limited topic — for a research report of your own. Indicate at the bottom of your paper the topic that you have chosen.

Answers will vary; an example is given below.

EXAMPLE The Women's Suffrage Movement

ANSWER *Limited topics*

The First States and Territories to Grant Women the Right to Vote

The Trial of Susan B. Anthony

How the Nineteenth Amendment Was Passed

Three Men Who Supported Women's Suffrage

1. Soccer in the United States
   "A Comparison of Designer Jeans"
2. Fashion Designers
3. Organic Gardening
4. Horror Movies
5. Thoroughbred Horses
6. Ecology
7. Stereo Equipment
8. The Olympic Games
9. Photography
10. Children's Books

14.b BEGINNING YOUR RESEARCH

After you have limited your topic, you still have to decide which aspects of it you want to learn about and write about. An encyclopedia article is a good place to begin (see 13.c.2). An encyclopedia article gives an overview of a topic and often includes a list of useful books to read. You may find your topic listed in the appropriate encyclopedia volume, or you may have to look up your topic in the general index in the last volume. (If you do not find an article on your specific topic, you may find information about it in a more general article. For example, you may not find an article on the Battle of Bunker Hill, but you will find the battle discussed in an article about the Revolutionary War.)

Write down the important aspects of your topic that are discussed in an encyclopedia article. This list will help you when it is time to prepare your working outline and to take notes from other books and magazines.

EXAMPLE

Betsy Thomassen consulted two encyclopedias. One encyclopedia contained a brief but detailed article that discussed the history of contact lenses and the different kinds now in use. The second encyclopedia article covered these same topics and also devoted a paragraph to how contact lenses are fitted.

EXERCISE 2. Read one or two encyclopedia articles for general information on the topic that you have chosen for your research report. Write down the important aspects of the topic discussed in the encyclopedia. *Answers will vary.*

14.c FINDING INFORMATION

After you read one or two encyclopedia articles for an overview of your topic, the next step is to prepare a list of other possible sources for your research report. *Source* is the term used to refer to someone or something that provides information. Try to make a list of six to eight books and articles that may help you.

FINDING SOURCES

- You will find lists of books at the ends of encyclopedia articles.
- You will find books classified in the Subject Index of the library's card catalogue.
- You will find periodical articles listed in the *Reader's Guide to Periodical Literature.*
- You may also ask your librarian if there is any information about your topic in the vertical file.

For complete information about doing research in the library, see Section 13, "Libraries and Information."

Once you have made a list of six to eight sources, locate the books and articles in your library. Some of the books and articles may not be available. Books may be checked out. Also, most libraries subscribe to only a small percentage of the magazines indexed in the *Reader's Guide.* Find out which magazines your library carries.

Remember that in order to obtain enough information about your subject you must have at least three sources. No research report can be written from a single source. If you cannot find three sources, you must change your topic to one on which you can find more information.

EXAMPLE

When Betsy Thomassen looked up the subject heading "Contact lenses" in the Subject Index of the card catalogue, she found no sources listed. She did, however, find sources listed under the related subject heading "Corrective lenses: contact lenses." Thomassen found three books listed under this subject heading. Then she used recent issues of the *Reader's Guide to Periodical Literature* and the *New York Times Index,* where she found six recent articles on contact lenses. When Thomassen looked through the library, however, she located only two of the books and four of the periodical articles. This was enough material for the time being.

EXERCISE 3. Locate and obtain at least three sources on the research report topic that you chose in Exercise 1. Use book lists at the end of encyclopedia articles, the Subject Index in the library's card catalogue, the *Reader's Guide to Periodical Literature,* and the vertical file. *Answers will vary.*

14.d PREPARING A WORKING OUTLINE

A **working outline** will guide you in your reading and note taking.

Before you begin reading your source material and taking notes, decide which aspects of your topic you want to cover in your paper and how you want to organize them. Prepare a working outline. A working outline is not as detailed as the formal outline that you will prepare before writing your report (see 14.g).

To prepare a working outline, write down three or four aspects of your topic that you want to treat in your paper and arrange them in logical order. Use the list that you wrote when you read the encyclopedia articles, and ask yourself some more questions:

QUESTIONS FOR A WORKING OUTLINE
1. Is there a story that I can tell about this topic?
2. Can I describe one particular aspect of this topic?
3. Can I write about how two aspects of the topic are like or unlike each other? Can I write about how the topic itself is like or unlike another?

Keep your working outline in front of you as you read and take notes. It will help you to concentrate and focus your attention.

EXAMPLE

After reading the encyclopedia articles on contact lenses and preparing her list of sources, Betsy Thomassen prepared the following working outline:

Breakthroughs in Contact Lenses

I. History of contact lenses

II. Kinds of contact lenses

    A. Hard lenses

    B. Soft lenses

III. Recent developments in contact lenses

Betsy Thomassen decided to tell a story in the first section of her paper. In the second section she planned to tell how hard contact lenses are like or unlike soft contact lenses. She expected to use description throughout her paper.

Examine Betsy Thomassen's final outline on page 589 to see how she eventually changed the working outline before she began to write her paper.

EXERCISE 4. Prepare a working outline for the topic you have chosen for your research report. Your outline should have three or four main headings arranged in logical order. You need not include subheadings at this point. Use your working outline to direct your reading and note taking. *Answers will vary.*

14.e KEEPING A WORKING BIBLIOGRAPHY

A **working bibliography** is a list of books and other source materials that you will consult.

Quickly look over each source, and decide whether it will be helpful to you. If so, add the source to your working bibliography. Put the following information on each card:

- the name of the author
- the title of the source
- where the source was published
- when the source was published

Use a 3 x 5– inch index card for each source. Number each card in the upper left corner. As you take notes from each source, number each note card (see 14.f) with its corresponding bibliography card number. With your note cards keyed in this way, you will be able to tell at a glance the source of your information.

You will find all the information you need to prepare bibliography cards on the title page and copyright page of the book (see 13.e). You should follow a certain style in arranging information on bibliography cards. This style is explained in detail in 14.k. Notice how Betsy Thomassen followed the style in the following sample bibliography card.

number to identify
this source

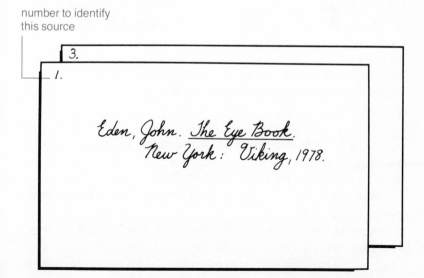

EXERCISE 5. Write bibliography cards for the sources that you plan to use in your research report. Follow the bibliographic style shown on the preceding pages. Be sure that you use at least one book and one encyclopedia article. *Answers will vary.*

14.f TAKING NOTES

Once you have collected your source material — three to five sources — and prepared a working outline, you must begin the real work of research: reading and taking notes. Arranging, rearranging, and organizing your notes will be easier if you take notes on index cards instead of on sheets of notebook paper. Most students prefer to take notes on 4 x 6–inch index cards. In the upper left corner of each note card write the corresponding heading from your working outline as well as the number of the bibliography card for the source (see 14.d and 14.e). Using the number saves having to write the author's name on each note card.

You have probably already had experience in taking notes. In taking notes you should scan the materials, looking carefully for information that is relevant to your topic. Then write down important facts and ideas in your own words. Some students take notes by rephrasing the author's ideas as complete sentences. Other students prefer to write in phrases. (See 16.b for more ideas on note taking.)

Suppose that you find a particularly good sentence or passage that you want to quote word for word in your paper. Copy it carefully, making sure that you enclose the entire quotation in quotation marks.

Whether you are rephrasing or copying a quotation, write down the page number on which the material appears in the source. Whether you borrow an idea or exact words, you must credit the author in a footnote and in the final bibliography. Remember that a research paper, or any other piece of writing, must be written using only your own ideas and words — except for passages for which you use quotation marks. Copying words or borrowing ideas without giving credit is called *plagiarism* and is to be avoided at all costs. Plagiarism can be a criminal offense, and teachers can detect when students have used another's words or ideas in a paper.

EXAMPLE

Here is a sample note card that Betsy Thomassen wrote during her research on contact lenses.

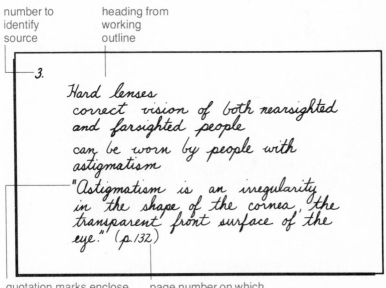

number to
identify
source

heading from
working
outline

3.

Hard lenses
correct vision of both nearsighted
and farsighted people
can be worn by people with
astigmatism
"Astigmatism is an irregularity
in the shape of the cornea, the
transparent front surface of the
eye." (p. 132)

quotation marks enclose
definition copied word
for word from source

page number on which
information appears

EXERCISE 6. Take notes from one of the sources for your paper. Bring to class note cards covering two or three pages from the source. *Answers will vary.*

EXERCISE 7. Take notes from all of the sources that you have assembled for your own research report. Remember to identify the source by number and to write a heading from your working outline on each note card. Use your own words when you take notes. If you find a sentence or passage that you want to quote in your paper, copy it carefully and enclose it in quotation marks. Always write the source's page number on the note card. *Answers will vary.*

14.g WRITING A FORMAL OUTLINE

A **formal outline** will guide you in writing your first draft.

When you decide that you have enough material for your research report, it is time to prepare a final outline. Because you have been reading and taking notes, you now know much more about your topic and can convert your working outline (see 14.d) into a more detailed formal outline. You can add, drop, or change the order of headings in your working outline.

To prepare a formal outline, read carefully through your note cards. Sort them into separate piles, one for each important aspect of your topic. You may find that some of your note cards no longer seem to fit into your topic. Set these cards aside. Compare your working outline with your piles of note cards, and ask yourself some questions.

QUESTIONS FOR A FORMAL OUTLINE

1. Do the headings on the piles of note cards correspond to the main headings in my working outline? Have I discovered in my research other main headings that should be added to the outline?
2. Do I have enough information to write about all of the main headings in my working outline? If not, should I try to find more information, or should I eliminate headings?
3. Can I find logical subdivisions for any or all of the main headings?
4. What is the best order for presenting my ideas?

Once you have considered these four questions, you may make changes in and add details to your working outline. Your formal outline should contain all the headings on your note cards and present your ideas in a logical order. See 12.e for details on setting up a formal outline.

EXAMPLE

During her reading Betsy Thomassen found information about bifocal contact lenses, a subject she had not even known about when she wrote her working outline. She decided to add "bifocal lenses" as well as several other details to her working outline. Thomassen's formal outline is shown here.

Breakthroughs in Contact Lenses

  I. Definition and history of contact lenses

 II. Kinds of lenses

    A. Hard lenses

       1. Advantages

       2. Disadvantages

    B. Soft lenses

       1. Advantages

       2. Disadvantages

III. Kinds of bifocal lenses

    A. Nonrotational lenses

    B. Rotational lenses

 IV. Recent developments in contact lenses

EXERCISE 8. Prepare a formal outline for your research report, following the outline style shown in 12.e. Use your note cards, your working outline, and the questions on page 588. The outline should have three or four main headings and one or two levels of subheadings. *Answers will vary.*

14.h **WRITING THE FIRST DRAFT**

You should begin writing the first draft of your research report with your formal outline and note cards in front of you. Set aside two or three hours of uninterrupted time; you will need to concentrate fully. Use your note cards to refresh your memory while writing, but avoid copying from them unless you are quoting directly from a source. Present your ideas in the order of your outline. Try to make the sequence of your ideas clear and easy to follow.

Do not spend too much time now in finding the exact words or the greatest variety of sentences to express your ideas. You will polish this rough draft at a later time. Now you should concentrate on getting your ideas in sequence on the paper. Keep moving from one part of the outline to the next until you have finished.

The introduction and conclusion are not listed as such on your outline, but they are a necessary part of all research papers. Write a paragraph to introduce the topic and to present your main ideas. (See the discussion of *thesis statement* in 12.f.) Write a concluding paragraph to summarize the major ideas and opinions in your paper.

When you have finished writing your first draft, put it aside for several hours or a whole day, and think about something else. You need a break before you can look at what you have written with a fresh mind.

EXAMPLE

Read the following introduction from the first draft of Betsy Thomassen's research report. Compare it with the final revised version on page 596. The first draft has the basic information even though it needs changes in words, removal of repeated phrases, smoother sentences, and more accurate punctuation and spelling.

People have always tried to make life easier for themselves. They worked to find reasons and cures for natural defects in the human body. As people leanred more about optical techmology over the centuries they made improvements in the devices to aid the visually handicapped. From the first crude lenses created by medieval scientists, scienoe has elaborated on them over the centuries, resulting in today's various types of spectacles and optical techniques. Scientists have created one type of optical aide which unlike glasses is placed directly on the eye. This most recent and interesting invention is the small contac lens.

EXERCISE 9. Using your note cards and formal outline, write the first draft of your research report. *Answers will vary.*

14.i EDITING A FIRST DRAFT

After setting aside your rough draft for a time, you should read through it carefully, correcting awkward sentences and errors in grammar, usage, and punctuation. As you read through your research report ask yourself the following questions:

1. Does my paper have a clear beginning, middle, and end? Does the introduction state the topic, and does the conclusion effectively tie together the main ideas and opinions?
2. Does my paper follow the order of my outline? Are my ideas clearly and logically presented?
3. Are the sentences clear and easy to understand?
4. Have I included enough details and specific examples?
5. Is my writing completely free from errors in spelling, punctuation, and usage?

Follow these steps as you change and correct your rough draft:

1. Reword awkward sentences. (Review 3.i– 3.k.)
2. Rewrite each paragraph so that every sentence is essential to the meaning of the paragraph. Your ideas should flow clearly from one sentence to the next. Re-arrange sentences wherever necessary. (Review 10.k.)
3. Insert transitional phrases to link ideas as well as paragraphs. (Review 12.h.)
4. Eliminate unnecessary words, and avoid monotony. (Review 3.j.)
5. If ideas are not developed enough, cut out paragraphs, or develop the ideas further. Do not be afraid to rear-range sections of your paper.

When you are satisfied with the wording and punctua-tion of your paper, add the footnotes. You must write a footnote for every direct quotation in your paper and for ideas that you have taken from other sources.

14.j FOOTNOTES

A **footnote** gives additional information, including source information, about a statement in your paper.

Use footnotes to give credit to every author you have directly quoted or from whom you have borrowed ideas. In addition to giving credit to the original author, footnotes will help your readers to locate your sources in case they want to read the original material. In a footnote you must give the important information about a source in a certain order and follow certain punctuation.

There are two parts to every footnote. The first part is a superscript, or raised number, placed in the text of your paper at the end of the quotation or borrowed idea. Usu-ally, this superscript appears at the end of a full sentence. The second part of the footnote is the note itself, which has the same number as the one given in the text.

You may place footnotes either at the bottom of the page or listed together at the end of your paper under the heading *Notes*. Follow your teacher's instructions for the placement of footnotes.

The first line of your footnote is indented a half inch from the left margin of your paper, and the second line should be even with the left margin. Here are sample footnotes for a book, a periodical article, and an encyclopedia article.

FOOTNOTE FOR A BOOK
   ¹John Eden, The Eye Book (New York: Viking, 1978), p. 55.

FOOTNOTE FOR A PERIODICAL ARTICLE
   ²Alexandra Penney, "Getting the Right Contacts," The New York Times Magazine, 22 Apr. 1979, p. 112.

FOOTNOTE FOR AN ENCYCLOPEDIA ARTICLE
   ³Louis J. Girard and Joseph Soper, "Contact Lens," Encyclopedia Americana, 1979 ed.

If you want to write another footnote for a source already noted, you may choose one of two ways. The first and most useful way is to use just the author's last name and the page number. If you are using two books by the same author, you must also give the title (or a shortened form of the title) after the author's name. The second way is to use Latin abbreviations: *Ibid.*, followed by the page number, refers to the source that has come just before. *Op. cit.* refers to some earlier source, which you must make clear in your sentence.

FOOTNOTE FOR A SOURCE ALREADY NOTED
⁴Eden, p.56.
        or
⁴*Ibid.*, p. 56.

EXERCISE 10. Add the footnotes to the edited version of your research report, following the footnote styles given on page 593. *Answers will vary.*

14.k BIBLIOGRAPHIES

A **bibliography** lists all your sources.

The bibliography is an alphabetical list of the sources that you have used in your research. To prepare your final bibliography, use your working bibliography cards, which are written in the proper bibliography style (see 14.e). Alphabetize your working bibliography cards by the last name of the author (if a source does not list an author, alphabetize it by the first important word of the title). Bibliography entries are listed on the last page of your paper. Notice that the style for bibliography entries differs from the style of footnotes in important ways. For instance, in a bibliography entry the author's last name is written first, and punctuation is used differently. The first line of a bibliography entry is even with the left margin of your paper, and the second line is indented a half inch from the left margin. Here are sample bibliography entries for a book, a periodical article, and an encyclopedia article.

BIBLIOGRAPHY ENTRY FOR A BOOK
Eden, John. The Eye Book. New York: Viking, 1978.

BIBLIOGRAPHY ENTRY FOR A PERIODICAL ARTICLE
Penney, Alexandra. "Getting the Right Contacts." The New York Times Magazine, 22 Apr. 1979, pp. 112–114.

BIBLIOGRAPHY ENTRY FOR AN ENCYCLOPEDIA ARTICLE
Girard, Louis J., and Joseph Soper. "Contact Lens." Encyclopedia Americana. 1979 ed.

EXERCISE 11. Prepare a final bibliography, using your working bibliography cards. *Answers will vary.*

14.I WRITING A FINAL DRAFT

When you have finished revising and editing your paper, you are ready to write the final draft. You may either type your research report or write it neatly in ink. Be sure to follow the style that your teacher specifies.

The first page of your report is the title page, which contains the title of your report, your name, your teacher's name, the name (or number) of your course, and the date. The title and your name should be centered, and the other information should be listed in the lower right corner. If you type, your report should be double-spaced with a one-inch margin on all sides. If your teacher asks you to place your footnotes at the bottom of each page, make sure to leave room for them.

Allow yourself enough time to proofread your paper at least twice. Correct all errors in capitalization and punctuation (See Section 7, "Capitalization and Punctuation," pages 343– 424). Make your corrections neatly in ink. (See Betsy Thomassen's finished research report, pages 596– 602.)

EXERCISE 12. Using your revised first draft, write or type the final draft of your research report. After adding the footnotes and the final bibliography, proofread the entire paper and make the necessary corrections. *Answers will vary.*

EXTRA: Divide the class into groups, and ask them to share their research reports with other members of their group.

14.m THE FINISHED RESEARCH REPORT

You have followed Betsy Thomassen's steps in writing her research report on contact lenses. Her finished report follows on pages 596– 602. (Notice that Betsy's footnotes appear at the end of the paper.)

Human beings are always trying to better themselves. Through science, they constantly work to find causes and cures for defects in the human body. As scientists have learned more about optical technology, they have made improvements in the devices and methods used to aid the visually handicapped and to combat the diseases that affect them. Since the first crude lenses, science has elaborated on spectacles over the centuries, resulting in today's various kinds of lenses and optical techniques.

One of the more recent and fascinating developments is the small contact lens, which, unlike glasses, is placed directly on the transparent front part of the eye. "Many people consider contact lenses as a vain person's substitute for spectacles, but actually they are for diseases which cannot be helped much by spectacles. Contact lenses are thin shells of glass or plastic which fit over the cornea inside the lids. They are separated from the cornea by a thin layer of fluid (tears or salt solution), and their action is pretty much that of fishes' eyes seeing under water."[1]

Real development of the contact lens began in the late 1800s, although the first one was made in 1801. Zeiss, a German maker of optics, handmade the first regular series of contact lenses around 1911. Two decades later the development of a molding technique enabled today's production of contact lenses in quantity.[2]

Many kinds of contact lenses are on the market, and many more are still in development. The two kinds used most frequently are hard contact lenses and soft contact lenses.

The next four paragraphs tell how soft lenses and hard lenses are like and unlike each other.

Hard lenses, which have been worn since the 1950s, are made of clear, hard plastic. Both nearsighted and farsighted persons can wear hard lenses because they provide good all-around clarity. Even those with astigmatism, "an irregularity in the shape of the cornea, the transparent front surface of the eye,"[3] can wear hard contact lenses because the hard surface of the lens compensates for the condition. Hard lenses are more durable and less expensive than soft contact lenses.

Notice the transitional device in the next sentence (see 12.h).

There are, however, certain disadvantages to hard contact lenses. They are a little more difficult to center on the eye and occasionally slip off the iris onto the white of the eye. It takes anywhere from eleven days to four weeks for most wearers to adjust to hard contact lenses. If people should stop wearing the hard contacts for several days, they must once again gradually build up tolerance to the lenses.

Notice the transitional device in the next sentence (see 12.h).

Soft contact lenses, on the other hand, are much easier to get used to. Usually a person wearing soft contacts needs only about a week to build tolerance to maximum daily wear.[4] Soft contacts are made of a pliable, water-absorbing plastic. They are flexible and easy to center on the iris. Soft lenses are very unlikely to pop off the eye, which makes them good for people who engage in sports.

One serious drawback to soft lenses is that they correct fewer vision problems than hard lenses do. "Because the soft lens is malleable, a slight bending tends to occur every time you blink. This results in waves in the surface of the soft lens that can create an optical distortion that does not occur with hard lenses, which retain their shape at all times."[5] Persons with astigmatism generally cannot wear soft contacts. Soft lenses are, furthermore, about twice as expensive as hard contacts.

Besides developing both hard and soft contact lenses, scientists have made breakthroughs with

<u>bifocal</u> contact lenses. Benjamin Franklin made a brilliant contribution to the world of optics when, in 1784, he invented bifocal eyeglasses. These double spectacles contain two powers of lenses in the same pair of eyeglasses, enabling wearers to see at a distance and close up without changing glasses. There are two kinds of bifocal contact lenses: nonrotational and rotational contacts.

> The student writer now will tell how nonrotational and rotational lenses are like and unlike each other.

Normally, as the eye blinks, the contact lens rotates upon the cornea. A nonrotational contact lens, however, does not rotate because it is weighted to keep it in place. Nonrotational contacts have the distance lens power on the upper half, and the near lens power on the lower half, as in bifocal spectacles.

On the contrary, a rotational lens is made with the distance lens power in the center and the near lens power completely surrounding it. As the eye blinks and the lens rotates, the near prescription is always on the bottom, enabling the wearer to read with ease.[6]

An even newer kind of bifocal lens called a rotational bifocal aspheric eliminates the "jump" that occurs when shifting from distance power to near power in regular bifocal contacts. This new lens is specially ground so that the switch is gradual, from central (distance) power to the outer (near) power.[7]

5

Dr. John Eden, an ophthalmologist in New York City, says that in his experience bifocal contacts "do not work terribly well."[8] Dr. Eden has a unique solution: He fits one eye with a lens for seeing close up and fits the other eye with a lens for seeing far away. Dr. Eden says that this system "allows one eye to see well at the distance but not sharply close up, while the other eye sees well near but not sharply in the distance."[9] The brain uses both images to create a clear view, and the wearer can see clearly close up and far away.

A new development presently being tested is a soft membrane lens that is as thin as a piece of plastic sandwich wrap. Membrane lenses can be worn without removal for as long as three months—even during sleep.[10] Other new developments include lenses made of silicone and other kinds of plastic. A unique kind of lens available today allows oxygen to flow through the plastic to the surface of the cornea.[11]

conclusion

In the past thirty years, contact lenses have developed from a revolutionary new optical aid to one that is increasingly commonplace. New kinds of lenses are constantly being researched and developed. Perhaps the day will come when contact lenses are worn by everyone, and eyeglasses are prized only as curiosities and antiques.

Notes

[1]S. Sutton-Vane, The Story of Eyes (New York: Viking, 1958), p. 193.

[2]Ray O. Scholz, Sight: A Handbook for Laymen (Garden City, N.Y.: Doubleday, 1960), pp. 62–63.

[3]Michael P. Scott, "An Update on Contact Lenses," Better Homes and Gardens, Nov. 1978, p. 132.

[4]Scott, p. 132.

[5]John Eden, The Eye Book (New York: Viking, 1978), pp. 55–56.

[6]Scott, p. 132.

[7]Scott, p. 132.

[8]Eden, p. 61.

[9]Eden, p. 61.

[10]Alexandra Penney, "Getting the Right Contacts," The New York Times Magazine, 22 Apr. 1979, p. 112.

[11]Eden, pp. 57–58.

Bibliography

Eden, John. The Eye Book. New York: Viking, 1978.

Girard, Louis J., and Joseph Soper. "Contact Lens."
    Encyclopedia Americana. 1979 ed.

Penney, Alexandra. "Getting the Right Contacts." The New
    York Times Magazine, 22 Apr. 1979, pp. 112–114.

Scholz, Ray O. Sight: A Handbook for Laymen. Garden City,
    N.Y.: Doubleday, 1960.

Scott, Michael P. "An Update on Contact Lenses." Better
    Homes and Gardens, Nov. 1978, pp. 132–136.

Sutton-Vane, S. The Story of Eyes. New York: Viking, 1958.

14.n A RESEARCH REPORT CHECKLIST

When you have finished the final draft of your research
report, check to see that it includes the following:

- a limited topic
- your own ideas supported with three to five outside
  sources
- a clear and logical organization
- ideas and quotations from outside sources credited in
  footnotes
- a title page and a bibliography following the proper
  form

15

THE LETTER

15 The Letter

See summary of section in Teacher's Manual.

Everyone writes letters from time to time. You write social letters to friends and relatives. Social letters are personal and informal. Business letters are more formal than social letters and have a different purpose. As the name implies, you write a business letter in order to do business with someone. In business, people expect a letter to have a certain style and form so that they can understand and reply to the letter quickly and accurately. The following four hints will help you write an effective business letter.

- Be clear. Plan in advance what you are going to say in the letter. This early planning will help you avoid mistakes and save time.
- Be sure to use correct grammar, punctuation, and spelling. Use a dictionary if necessary to check spellings.
- After you finish the letter, read it through carefully to check for mistakes.
- Write on one side of a sheet. If you need a second page, use a second sheet of stationery. Do not write on the back of the first sheet.

A standard business letter is divided into six distinct parts that are discussed in the following pages.

- the heading
- the inside address
- the salutation
- the body
- the closing
- the signature

15.a THE HEADING

The heading of a business letter gives your return address and the date on which the letter is written. The heading goes at the top of the page, to the right of center, and consists of three lines. Do not use abbreviations unless space is a problem.

EXAMPLE

> 52 Lakeview Road
> Lansing, Michigan 48906
> January 2, 19—

15.b THE INSIDE ADDRESS

The inside address is included in a business letter to make sure that the letter reaches the right person even if it is separated from its envelope. The inside address is single-spaced and is placed a few lines below the heading and even with the left margin. It should include the full name and address of the person (and the organization) to whom you are writing.

■ Titles of respect

The person's full name is preceded by a title of respect. The titles *Mr.*, *Ms.*, *Mrs.*, and *Dr.* may be abbreviated. Others, like *Professor* and *Rabbi*, must be spelled out.

A business title may follow the person's name. It is generally written or typed next to the name and is separated from the name by a comma. If the title is too long to fit attractively after the name, it may be placed on a second line.

Sometimes you need to write a letter to a company or an organization rather than to a person. Write the name of the company or organization as it appears in the company letterhead or advertisement, including the same punctuation and abbreviations.

EXAMPLES

Dr. Walter Johnson, Principal
East Harrington High School
Harrington, Delaware 19952

Ms. Loretta Spalding
Director of Marketing
Pyramid Productions, Inc.
310 West Central Avenue
Toledo, Ohio 43610

W. H. Cambell Co.
1066 Queens Chapel Road
Washington, D. C. 20018

Simone Okaido
McCann Advertising Agency
14 West Detroit Avenue
Great Falls, Michigan 80311

15.c THE SALUTATION

The salutation of a business letter is placed two lines below the inside address, even with the left margin. It is followed by a colon. As the following examples show, there are several different kinds of salutations to use in different situations.

1. When writing to a man whose name you know, use *Mr., Dr.,* or other appropriate title.

   EXAMPLE
   When writing to:
   Lionel Black, Editor
   Salutation:
   Dear Mr. Black:

2. When writing to a woman whose name you know, use *Ms., Miss, Mrs., Dr.,* or other appropriate title.

   EXAMPLE
   When writing to:
   Miss Alma Jiminez
   Salutation:
   Dear Miss Jiminez:

3. When writing to a woman whose title of respect you do not know, use *Ms.*

EXAMPLE
When writing to:
Barbara Shaw
Salutation:
Dear Ms. Shaw:

4. If for some reason you do not want to use a formal title of respect, you may address people by both their first and last names.

EXAMPLE
When writing to:
Ms. Karen Reilly
Salutation:
Dear Karen Reilly:

5. When writing to a specific person whose name is unknown, generally use *Sir* or *Madam.*

EXAMPLE
When writing to:
Town Clerk
Salutation:
Dear Sir or Madam:

6. When writing to a company, organization, or box number, generally use *Sir or Madam.*

EXAMPLE
When writing to:
Shop-Rite Supermarkets
Salutation:
Dear Sir or Madam:

EXERCISE 1. Write the correct heading, inside address, and salutation for letters to the following parties. Use your home address and today's date in the heading.

Salutations will vary. Answers are given at the back of the Teacher's Manual.

1. The Buyer's Guide, 1500 Manin Street, Manin, Illinois 61224

2. James Morrison, Five Star Music Company, 101 Tremont Avenue, Jasper, Missouri 64755

3. The president of Daygrow Seed Company, 659 Grand Street, Wilmington, Vermont 05360

4. Ms. Louise Hilton, Editor-in-Chief, Grand Publishing Company, 82 East 40th Street, New York, New York 10043

5. Professor R. Mark Mizner, English Department, Colby College, Waterville, Maine 04890

15.d THE BODY OF THE LETTER

The body of a business letter begins two lines below the salutation. It should be single-spaced, with double spaces between paragraphs. The body may be written in either *block style* or *semiblock style*. In semiblock style, the first line of each paragraph is indented. In block style, the paragraphs are not indented. If your letter is very short, you may double-space the entire body. (To see some sample letters, turn to pages 612-613.)

The body of every business letter has three parts:

- a beginning that makes clear your reason for writing
- a middle that communicates your information
- an ending that makes a request for action or expresses appreciation or regard

A business letter should be written in simple language that is clear and direct but not stiff or artificial. There is no need to "dress up" your language by using flowery phrases that you would never use in conversation. In general, the faster you get to the point, the better the letter will be.

15.e THE CLOSING OF THE LETTER

The closing of a business letter appears a space or two below the body and to the right of the center of the page. The first word of the closing is capitalized, and the entire closing is followed by a comma. You have a choice of several closings, ranging from very formal to personal. Choose a closing that is appropriate to the tone of your letter.

EXAMPLES

VERY FORMAL:	Respectfully yours,
FORMAL:	Very truly yours,
LESS FORMAL:	Sincerely,
PERSONAL:	Cordially,

15.f THE SIGNATURE

In a business letter you should sign your full name below the closing. You should also type or print your name below the signature, so that the spelling of your name is clear even if the signature is hard to read.

If you have a title, you may put it below your typed or printed name. A woman may also indicate how she wishes to be addressed by writing a title of respect in parentheses before her typed or printed name.

EXAMPLES

Sincerely,

Allen Davies

Allen Davies

Very truly yours,

Elena Suarez

(Miss) Elena Suarez

President

EXERCISE 2. Write the correct heading, inside address, salutation, closing, and signature for letters to the following parties. Use your own name and address for the heading and signature. Draw lines to indicate the placement of the body of the letter.

Salutations and closings will vary. Answers are given at the back of the Teacher's Manual.

1. Joyce Keating, Director, Hillcrest Photo Studios, 162 Del Paso Boulevard, Sacramento, California 95815

2. The Seacraft Company, 8500 Long Beach Road, Darien, Connecticut 06845

3. Patrick Larch, Director, All-Stars Soccer Camp, P. O. Box 660, Manchester, New Hampshire 03106

4. Manager, Cheyenne Sports Arena, Cheyenne, Wyoming 82002

5. The principal of your school

15.g THE ENVELOPE

The envelope of a business letter must be addressed in a certain style. The return address goes in the upper left-hand corner of the envelope. It should indicate your name as well as your address.

The name and address of the person to whom you are writing are placed just below and to the right of center on the envelope. The address on the envelope should be the same as the inside address of the letter, including any titles. Always include the ZIP code in the address. You can find the ZIP code for local areas in your telephone directory. ZIP codes for the entire country are listed in a ZIP code directory that you can find at your local post office or library.

```
Jeffrey Wong
8 Circle Court
Glenrio, New Mexico 88423



                    Mr. Theo Kanecke, Director
                    Trilogy Films
                    301 East 79th Street
                    New York, New York 10021
```

15.h KINDS OF BUSINESS LETTERS

Business letters can serve a number of purposes. Among the most common purposes are to request information or services and to order something from a company.

■ The letter requesting information or services

You may need to write a business letter that asks someone for information or asks someone to do something for you. You might, for example, be assigned to write a paper on education for disabled people. If library research showed you that you could get information from the National March of Dimes Foundation, you might write them. In an election year you might write to invite a local politician to speak at your school.

When you write a letter that asks for information or services, you should do the following:

- Identify yourself: "I am a student at ..." or "I am president of my class at..."
- Explain why you need assistance from the person to whom you are writing, and state a specific request.
- Tell why you have chosen to make your request to this particular person or organization.
- Close courteously with a request for action.

■ The order letter

Although printed forms are used for most mail orders today, sometimes you may need to write an order letter. In an order letter be sure to do the following:

- Give necessary information about quantity, size, color, and so forth.
- If you are enclosing payment, state how much.
- If necessary, provide a smaller envelope addressed to yourself for the reply.

EXERCISE 3. Write a letter requesting information on swimming lessons for teen-agers. Write the letter to: John Sullivan, Director, Silton Swim School, 1755 Atlantic Avenue, Manasquan, New Jersey 07232. Use your home or school address and today's date in the heading. *Answers will vary.*

EXERCISE 4. Write to the chief of your local fire department. Request that someone from the department speak at a ninth-grade assembly program on fire safety. Request that the speaker talk about ways to prevent fires in the home. Use your school address and today's date in the heading. *Answers will vary. EXTRA: Ask students to write a letter thanking the speaker from the fire department for attending their ninth-grade assembly.*

A Letter Requesting Services (*semiblock style*)

Brookdale High School | Heading
Brookdale High School | Heading
Kaysville, Utah 84037
January 18, 19–

Ms. Shirley Kanner | Inside
Kaysville Town Council | address
Kaysville, Utah 84037

Dear Ms. Kanner: | Salutation

On Monday, March 15, our history class is having a | Body
special assembly on the role of local government. The
program will begin at 1:00 P.M. Our teacher, Mr. Roger
Tindall, has suggested that we ask you to be our speaker.

We have been studying governmental responsibility
at a local, state, and national level. We would like
you to speak to us about the responsibility of local
government to the town and to the state.

Please let me know if you can speak at our assembly
program. If you need more information, I will be glad
to supply it.

Very truly yours, | Closing

David Smith | Signature

David Smith | Typewritten name
Secretary | Title

An Order Letter (*block style*)

88 Main Avenue
Kenilworth, Illinois 60043
May 1, 19—

Athletic Center
Pleasantville High School
Pleasantville, Illinois 60048

Dear Sir or Madam:

Please send me four student tickets at $2.00 each
for the Annual All-Star High School Football Game
on June 23.

Give information
about the order.

I am enclosing a money order for $8.00 and a return
envelope. Thank you very much.

State that pay-
ment is enclosed.

Sincerely,

Irene Droziok

Irene Droziok

EXERCISE 5. Write a letter asking for information on the conservation activities and responsibilities of the Forest Service for a social studies class project. Write the letter to: United States Forest Service, Department of the Interior, Washington, D. C. 20242. Use your home address and to-day's date in the heading.   *Answers will vary.*

EXERCISE 6. Write a letter ordering a seed catalogue from Miracle Grow Seed Company, P. O. Box 800, Weiser, Idaho 83672. Use your home address and today's date in the heading.   *Answers will vary.*

EXERCISE 7. Write a letter ordering a sleeping bag, catalogue number 4325, price $45.00, from Sports World, Inc., 92 Baldwin Avenue, Oakridge, Arizona 80508. Use your home address and today's date in the heading.   *Answers will vary.*

EXERCISE 8. Clip an advertisement from a magazine or newspaper, and order the item you select. Use your home address and today's date in the heading.   *Answers will vary.*

16

STUDY SKILLS AND TEST TAKING

16 Study Skills and Test Taking

See summary of section in Teacher's Manual.

Two of the skills that you use most frequently in school are studying (that is, reading, listening, and note taking) and test taking. In this section you will receive some clear guidelines to help you with your studying, whether you are taking notes on a teacher's lecture, reading a textbook, or outlining information. You will also be shown most of the different kinds of test questions that appear on classroom tests and standardized tests. For each kind of question, you will be given strategies for how to answer.

STUDY SKILLS

One of the most valuable skills you can learn in school is how to study effectively. Studying involves more than simply reading textbooks or getting ready for tests. It includes all the other methods by which you learn, such as listening to your teachers' lectures, taking notes on what you hear and read, and organizing your notes into a useful form, such as an outline or a map of the main ideas.

Unfortunately, many students seldom think about what their study habits are or whether some other methods might be better. This section, therefore, gives you some practical guidelines in listening, reading, note taking, and other skills for making the studying process easier and more effective.

16.a LISTENING AND READING SKILLS

Most of what you learn in school comes from both listening to your teachers and classmates and from reading textbooks. You are presented with a great many facts and ideas to remember, a task that is difficult for anyone. The following suggestions will help you to learn and remember more from what you hear and read, whether you are studying at home or in school.

■ Listening skills

Most students have no trouble *hearing* what their teachers say, but almost everyone has problems with *listening.* To be a good listener, you must not only pay attention to the speaker, but, you must also think about what the speaker is saying. To become a better listener, try the following techniques:

1. From time to time, think about the main points of what the speaker has already said.
2. Try to think about what the speaker is leading up to and what the speaker will say next.
3. Be alert for what the speaker may be hinting at or saying indirectly.
4. Try to listen to everything the speaker has to say before you react to it with your personal feelings. Otherwise, your reaction may cause you to miss part of what is being said.
5. Take notes if you need to remember what is being said (see 16.b).

■ Skills for reading textbooks

Textbooks are designed so that you can learn the information in them as easily as possible. The chapters and sections usually have titles or headings. Main points are often summarized in introductions and conclusions. You will learn much more from your textbook reading if you use these aids rather than simply read your textbooks as if they were stories or novels. Try to include the following steps when you read:

1. Before you begin reading, preview your assignment by looking at the titles and headings, the introduction and conclusion, and any review questions at the end of the chapter.
2. Then, as you read the assignment, pay particular attention to the points mentioned in the headings, the introduction and conclusion, and the review questions.
3. Take notes on what you read (see 16.b).

16.b NOTE – TAKING METHODS

The process of taking notes from your listening and reading is an important skill because it can help you learn in two ways. First, it forces you to decide what the important points are. Second, it helps to fix these points in your mind. In addition, of course, you can use your notes to study for tests. Two methods of note taking, outlining and mapping, are discussed in the following pages. The following general suggestions will also be helpful to you in taking notes:

1. Use your own words. You learn better if you put ideas and information into your own language.
2. Concentrate on the main ideas and important facts. Do not try to write every word or worry so much about details that you miss the main points.
3. Do not spend more than 20 percent of your time taking notes. Most of your time should be spent listening or reading.
4. Use words and phrases rather than complete sentences. The most important thing is that your notes make sense to you when you read them later. Use as many abbreviations and symbols as you can, but be sure that you will understand them a month later when you have to study for a test.

■ Outlining notes

Outlining is the most common method of organizing information into note form. In an outline the relationships between main ideas and details are shown by numbers and letters. Follow the steps and the outline form below in outlining your reading from textbooks.

1. Read the whole section or paragraph, applying the skills for reading textbooks discussed in 16.a.
2. Decide upon the first main idea, and write it down after the Roman numeral *I*.
3. List important ideas or details below the main idea, writing them after capital letters – A, B, C.
4. If you want to give further details in the outline, use numbers below the capital letters – 1, 2, 3.
5. If the passage has more than one main idea, list the second main idea after Roman numeral *II*.
6. Repeat the steps above until you have outlined the whole passage.

OUTLINE FORM
I. First main idea
   A. Idea
   B. Idea
      1. Detail
      2. Detail
II. Second main idea

For more information about outlining and a sample outline, see 12.e.

EXERCISE 1. Read and outline the following paragraph, using the form illustrated above. Notice that the paragraph contains two main ideas. *Answers are given at the back of the Teacher's Manual.*

The weaknesses of our system of electing a President are not too difficult to see. There are at least three: (1) A candidate who wins many more votes of the citizens than his opponent may fail to be elected; (2) the electors in the electoral college are legally free to vote for anyone they care to; and (3) there is always a chance that a President will have to be elected by the House of Representatives. . . . Some political groups see advantages for themselves in the electoral-college system. For example, the less populated states have as many senators as the heavily populated states. This gives the less populated states a better ratio of votes in the electoral college than they have in the popular votes. Also, the large states realize that under the electoral system, they have great power to swing an election.

— Madden, *Practical Politics and Government in the United States*

■ Mapping notes

Mapping is a method of note taking that is especially useful for class discussions and other oral presentations that are not highly organized. You can also use mapping, however, for taking notes from a textbook or lecture. Mapping is like outlining in that the information is organized on the basis of main ideas, supporting ideas or facts, and lesser details. The relationships between these pieces of information are shown by a *map,* or diagram, rather than by numbers and letters. Follow the steps and the form below in taking mapping notes:

1. Write the main idea in the center of the page, and draw a circle around it.
2. When you hear or read an important idea or fact, write it on a line connected to the circle.
3. Write subordinate details on lines connected to the first lines.

Read the following paragraph, and think about how you would take mapping notes on it. Then look at the map.

EXAMPLE

Some of the new means of mass communication came from the speeding up and simplifying of old methods. For example, a new kind of newspaper known as the *tabloid* appeared on the scene. The tabloid was a paper with pages smaller than the usual size. It contained many pictures and presented the news briefly in large type under huge headlines. The tabloids gave far more space to sports, crime, and the personal lives of famous people than to national and world affairs. The first newspaper of this kind was the New York *Daily News*, which began publication in 1919. It became so popular that within five years it had the largest circulation of any American newspaper, a position it still holds.

— Forcey and Posner, *A Strong and Free Nation*

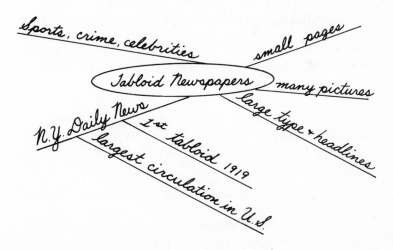

EXERCISE 2. Read and map the following paragraph, using the form illustrated above. *Answers are given at the back of the Teacher's Manual.*

Improved education continued to be a chief goal of reformers in all sections of the country. During the

1850s, the legislatures of North Carolina and Kentucky passed laws providing for free public schooling. Several southern cities set up free public libraries for the first time. The legislature of Massachusetts in 1851 passed a law that allowed state money to be used for libraries. Several of the states of the South and Middle West set up state universities that provided college educations either free or at a very low cost. Colleges, both public and private, became especially numerous in the South. With a population less than half that of the North's to draw from, southern colleges had almost as many students each year. But schooling in the "three R's" continued to be neglected in the South. About one in five Southerners in 1850 could neither read nor write. This was true of only about one in fifty Northerners.

— Forcey and Posner, *A Strong and Free Nation*

16.c GENERAL STUDY SKILLS

If you develop good listening, reading, and note taking skills, you will have taken important steps toward learning how to study effectively. Another important step for effective studying is to find a quiet place to do your school assignments. In addition, you should look honestly at what you actually do when you sit down with your assignments. The following questions will help you think about your study methods:

1. *How do I begin to study?* Rather than "easing" into the assignment that you think will offer the least resistance, take a minute to ask yourself what you want to accomplish in this study session. Set realistic goals for how long each assignment will take you. You should also plan to do your hardest assignments first, when you are most alert.

2. *How do I start an assignment that contains new material?* Remind yourself of what you may already

know about the subject of the assignment. Then ask yourself what you are trying to learn by doing it. If you have questions in mind that you are trying to answer, you will be able to concentrate better.

3. *What do I do when I finish an assignment?* When you finish studying something, summarize for yourself what you have learned. This process will help you remember the material.

4. *Should I study alone or with others?* For reading and writing assignments, other people are usually just a distraction. You may find, however, that it is helpful to work on problems and study for tests with others.

5. *When is the best time for me to study?* Try to study whenever you are most awake and alert. If you have a regular time for studying each day, you will find it much easier to get started.

6. *How long should I study before taking a break?* Most people cannot keep up their concentration for long periods without stopping. After you have studied for half an hour or forty-five minutes, take a short break and rest or do something you enjoy. Do not stretch out the break too long, however. Plan to go back to studying within ten to fifteen minutes.

CLASSROOM TESTS

Most of the tests that you take in school are prepared by your teachers to measure your understanding of the specific material you have covered in class. They thus differ from standardized tests, which measure your general knowledge and abilities.

There are two main kinds of questions on classroom tests: (1) short-answer questions, usually called "objective" questions, and (2) essay questions. You are no doubt already familiar with both kinds.

Objective questions require you to supply a short answer or to choose the correct answer from two or more possibilities. They measure your ability to recall specific facts or knowledge. Four common kinds of objective questions — true-false, matching, fill-in-the-blank, and multiple-choice — are discussed in this section. The first three kinds of questions are used primarily in classroom tests. Multiple-choice questions are often used on standardized tests as well.

As the name suggests, *essay questions* ask you to write answers of several paragraphs or longer. They test your ability to think clearly and to organize facts and knowledge in coherent language.

16.d TRUE – FALSE QUESTIONS

As the name suggests, true-false questions ask you to tell whether statements are true or false. In one way, true-false questions are the easiest kind of objective questions because you are given only two possible answers from which to choose. They are often subtle, however, and you must analyze each question carefully.

STRATEGIES FOR TRUE-FALSE QUESTIONS

1. The most important thing to remember in answering true-false questions is that for a statement to be true, it must be completely true. If any part of the statement is false, the answer to the question is "false."

2. Be on the lookout for key words like *always, none,* and *only,* which sometimes make a statement false.

Try the sample below, and then read the explanation.

SAMPLE QUESTION

Every rectangle has four equal sides and four right angles. True or False?

The answer to sample question is *false.* Every rectangle has four sides and four right angles, but only *some* rectangles have four equal sides — squares. Therefore, the inclusion of the word *every* makes the statement false.

EXERCISE 3. Tell whether each of the statements below is true or false.

1. The only verb form that can act as a noun in a sentence is a gerund. *True*

2. A semicolon may be used as the final punctuation mark in a sentence. *False*

3. The complete predicate of a sentence contains the main verbs and their objects and modifiers. *True*

16.e MATCHING QUESTIONS

Matching questions ask you to match items from two columns. For example, you may have to match terms with their definitions, countries with their capitals, or characters with the books in which they appear. Usually the two columns have the same number of items. Sometimes, however, the second column contains some items that are not supposed to be used or several items to be matched with each of the items in the first column.

STRATEGIES FOR MATCHING QUESTIONS

Match first all the items you are sure of, skipping the others. The more possibilities you eliminate in a matching exercise, the easier it will be to match the remaining items correctly.

Try the sample questions below, and then read the explanation following.

SAMPLE QUESTIONS

1. __ a famous playwright and poet

2. __ a famous novel by Mark Twain about life on the Mississippi

3. __ the site of the writing and signing of the United States Constitution

a. Philadelphia

b. *The Adventures of Huckleberry Finn*

c. William Shakespeare

If you read the previous items, you can see that Item 1 is a person, Item 2 is a novel, and Item 3 is a place. It should then be obvious that the answers are: 1.—c. (William Shakespeare); 2. —b. (*The Adventures of Huckleberry Finn*) and 3. —a. (Philadelphia).

EXERCISE 4. Match each term on the left with its definition on the right.

1. _b_ foreshadowing
2. _c_ plot
3. _a_ episode

a. one of many parts of the action that make up a story

b. an early indication that a particular event will occur

c. the arrangement of the action in a story

16.f FILL–IN–THE– BLANK QUESTIONS

Fill-in-the-blank questions are often the easiest to answer. Sometimes they take the form of a direct question to which you must supply an answer in a word or phrase. They may also consist of definitions of terms or descriptions of events with a key word or phrase left blank. The chief difference between fill-in-the-blank questions and other kinds of objective questions is that you have to supply the missing answer rather than merely select one of several possible answers.

STRATEGIES FOR FILL-IN-THE-BLANK QUESTIONS

1. Read the entire sentence carefully to be sure you understand it.

2. Then, look for a key word or phrase in the sentence that gives a clue to the missing word.

Try the sample question below.

SAMPLE QUESTION

The main idea of a paragraph is expressed in what is called the _____ sentence.

The key word in the sample question is *paragraph*. As you know, the main idea of a paragraph is expressed in the *topic sentence* (see 10.a). Do not confuse it with the thesis statement (see 12.f), which expresses the main idea of a *composition*.

EXERCISE 5. Supply the correct word or phrase for the blank in each of the following sentences.

1. *Narration* _____ is the kind of writing that tells a story, real or imagined.
2. *Description* _____ is the kind of writing that creates an impression of a person, place, or thing.
3. The direct words of a speaker are enclosed in punctuation called _____ marks. *quotation*
4. The mark of punctuation that can indicate the possessive of a noun is called an _____ . *apostrophe*
5. A *capital* , not a lower-case, letter begins a sentence.

16.g MULTIPLE–CHOICE QUESTIONS

In general, multiple-choice questions are more complicated than the kinds of objective questions discussed so far. They are also the chief kind of question used on standardized tests, such as basic skills tests and the Scholastic Aptitude Test that many high school students take in their junior and senior years. Many of the questions discussed in 16.i—16.o are multiple-choice questions.

STRATEGIES FOR MULTIPLE-CHOICE QUESTIONS

1. Be sure to read all of the choices or possible answers to the question. Many multiple-choice questions are designed so that at first glance more than one choice seems correct.
2. Once you have read all the choices, look carefully for the choice that *best* fits the question.

Try the sample question on the next page, and then read the explanation following it.

SAMPLE QUESTION

In a research paper, a specific quotation from a reference source must be credited in a(n)
(a) bibliography,   (b) appendix,   (c) subtitle,
(d) footnote

If you were reading the above question quickly, you might stop at bibliography, thinking that reference sources in a research paper are credited in a bibliography. A bibliography, however, does not credit *specific quotations* from a source. That is done in a footnote. Therefore, the answer is (d).

EXERCISE 6. Read the following questions carefully, and select the choice that best answers the question.

1. The kind of writing that tells about similarities is
   (a) narration,   (b) comparison,   (c) exposition,
   (d) contrast

2. The punctuation mark that cannot end a sentence is
   (a) a period,   (b) a comma,   (c) a question mark,
   (d) an exclamation point

3. The kind of word naming a person, place, or thing is
   (a) a verb, (b) a pronoun, (c) an adjective, (d) a noun

16.h ESSAY QUESTIONS

The essay questions on your classroom tests may ask you to show your knowledge in a variety of ways. For example, you may be asked to compare and contrast two items, to argue for or against a statement, or to analyze a poem or other work of literature. The following general suggestions, however, should be helpful to you in answering any kind of essay question.

STRATEGIES FOR ESSAY QUESTIONS

1. Read the question very carefully, noticing what facts you are asked to identify and what knowledge you are asked to demonstrate.

2. Often the question will suggest a way to begin your essay or will give an example of the point you are to prove or explain. Be sure to use these helps in your answer.

3. Organize your answer. A good essay answer will have a strong introduction, a middle section that supports the introduction, and a forceful ending that ties the whole essay together.

4. Be sure to edit and proofread your work. Reread your essay, making whatever changes in words and sentences that are necessary to make it read more smoothly. Correct only spelling and grammar errors.

Look at the following sample questions.

SAMPLE QUESTIONS

1. Shakespeare's play *Julius Caesar* is based on actual events in history. Explain in several paragraphs the events of the play as they unfold. You may devote a separate paragraph to discussing each act of the play.

2. Explain three reasons for the outbreak of World War II, devoting one paragraph to each reason.

The above questions are typical of those you may find on an English test and a history test. They both give you clear instructions for what you are to write. Furthermore, they give you an indication of how your answer should be organized and how much you are to write.

STANDARDIZED READING AND VOCABULARY TESTS

You are probably already familiar with standardized reading tests, for they are the most frequently given standardized tests in elementary schools. These tests are also given by high schools, colleges, and vocational schools.

Standardized reading tests measure your comprehension of reading passages. They also measure the extent of your vocabulary, which is an important indication of your reading skill. There are four main kinds of questions found on standardized reading tests: (1) reading-comprehension questions, (2) synonym questions, (3) antonym questions, and (4) sentence-completion questions. These questions are discussed in the following sections.

16.i READING–COMPREHENSION QUESTIONS

The passages used on reading-comprehension tests vary widely in subject and level of difficulty. The questions about them, however, are designed to test students' comprehension in just four specific ways. They will usually ask you to do the following:

1. Understand the main idea of the passage.
2. Recall or identify facts and ideas.
3. Make appropriate inferences, or conclusions, from the facts or ideas given.
4. Evaluate the author's tone or attitude.

STRATEGIES FOR READING-COMPREHENSION QUESTIONS

1. Before you read the passage, skim through the questions at the end to get an idea of what you should look for — for example, the main idea, supporting facts, style, and tone.
2. When reading the passage, concentrate on *what* is being said and *how* it is being said.
3. Underline important passages or points.

Read the sample passage below, and answer the questions that follow it.

SAMPLE QUESTION

There are three kinds of lettuce. Loose-leaf lettuce is the most popular in home gardens and greenhouses. Almost all lettuce grown to be marketed in large quantities is head lettuce. The leaves in head lettuce fold tightly over one another to make a round ball, or head. A third type, called cos lettuce, or romaine, is popular in Europe. Its leaves curl inside one another to form a long roll.

Lettuce was first grown in Asia several thousand years ago. It was served to the kings of Persia five hundred years before Christ. It spread over Europe and was grown in England in 1345. Americans have raised lettuce since colonial days. All this lettuce was loose-leaf or cos lettuce.

Head lettuce was developed fairly recently. It became popular after the railroads built refrigerated cars for shipping. Then lettuce could be sent from California and Texas to the eastern markets. Today head lettuce can be eaten during every month of the year.

Leaf lettuce is easy to grow. The seeds are simply planted in shallow rows in the garden. When they sprout, the seedlings are thinned out so that the plants are about an inch apart. They grow very rapidly. Loose-leaf lettuce can stand frost very well, but not summer heat. Seeds are sown at intervals of two weeks in order to provide a constant supply of lettuce for the table.

Recall of Fact

1. Which of the following kinds of lettuce is the most recently developed?
(A) Cos lettuce
(B) Romaine
(C) Head lettuce
(D) Loose-leaf lettuce

2. Which of the following best explains the widespread sale of head lettuce?
(A) Fertile California soil
(B) The refrigerated railroad car
(C) Resistance to frost damage
(D) Availability of a constant supply

Questions of factual detail are the easiest reading-comprehension questions; you simply find the correct answer in the passage. For example, the passage says that loose-leaf and cos (romaine) lettuce have been raised for hundreds of years, whereas head lettuce is a fairly recent development. For Question 1, therefore, the correct answer is (C). As for Question 2, the third paragraph of the passage clearly states that Choice (B), the refrigerated railroad car, is the reason that head lettuce became popular.

Making the Right Inferences

3. The most likely reason for the spread of cos lettuce from Asia to Europe in the fourteenth century is that
   (A) people learned to enjoy eating it
   (B) there were no other vegetables to eat
   (C) refrigerated railroad cars were used to ship it
   (D) improving weather conditions aided its growth

Inference questions are more difficult than ones about factual detail because they require you to use your reasoning power. Notice that the question asks you to choose the *most likely* reason for the spread of lettuce. You can eliminate Choice (C) because there were no refrigerated railroad cars in the fourteenth century. Choice (B) is very unlikely. Choice (D) may sound reasonable, but there is no mention of weather conditions in the passage. The best answer, therefore, is Choice (A). It is unlikely that lettuce would have been shipped or even grown if people had not come to enjoy eating it.

Understanding the Main Idea

4. Which of the following best describes the main subject of the passage?
   (A) The popularity of head lettuce
   (B) The superiority of head lettuce over cos lettuce
   (C) Various nations' cultivation of lettuce
   (D) Varieties of lettuce and their development

This kind of question requires you to look at the passage as a whole. Choice (B) is not even suggested in the passage. Choices (A) and (C) are discussed, but neither is the main subject. The choice that best describes the passage as a whole is (D).

Author's Tone or Attitude

5. The author's attitude towards the subject of lettuce is best described as
   (A) humorous
   (B) sarcastic
   (C) objective
   (D) personal

For this kind of question, you must look in the passage for clues to how the author feels about the subject. In this case there is no suggestion that the author regards lettuce with humor, sarcasm, or any other personal feeling. Therefore, the correct answer is (C), *objective.*

16.j SYNONYM QUESTIONS

A *synonym* is a word that has the same or almost the same meaning as another word. For example, the word *amiable* is a synonym of *friendly.* Multiple-choice synonym questions are widely used on standardized reading tests because they are a good measure of students' vocabulary. From four or five choices, you are asked to choose the word whose meaning is closest to that of a given word. The following suggestions will be helpful to you in answering synonym questions:

STRATEGIES FOR SYNONYM QUESTIONS

1. Read *all* of the choices given. Do not stop at the second or third choice just because it seems to be a synonym of the given word. One of the later choices may be a closer synonym.

2. Do not be concerned if none of the choices seems to be an exact synonym of the given word. Few words have exact synonyms. You are to find the choice that is *closest* in meaning to the original word.

3. Try different ways of thinking about the given word.

Many words can be used as more than one part of speech—as both a noun and a verb, for example. Look at the answer choices; if they are all verbs, you know that you have to consider the given word as a verb and not a noun, as you may have thought when you first looked at it. Remember, too, that some words have more than one meaning even as the same part of speech. Think about all the different possible meanings of the given word. Making up a sentence using the given word may also help you to choose the closest synonym.

Look at the following sample synonym question, and study the explanation below it.

SAMPLE QUESTION
BELLIGERENT: (A) aggressive   (B) annoyed
                    (C) nervous   (D) repugnant

This question illustrates the importance of making careful distinctions among several possible choices. A person who is *annoyed* may become belligerent, but *belligerent* suggests a much stronger and more threatening attitude than annoyance. Choice (D), *repugnant,* may refer to fighting; however, it suggests resistance, whereas *belligerent* suggests an attack. If you study all the choices carefully, you can see that Choice (A), *aggressive,* is *closest* in meaning to the given word.

EXERCISE 7. Choose the word or phrase that means the same or most nearly the same as the word in capital letters.

1. STALE: (A) pleasant   (B) old
                  (C) cold   (D) rough

2. RIVALRY: (A) friendliness   (B) sympathy
                  (C) competition   (D) rigidity

3. ANTICIPATE: (A) expect   (B) oppose
                  (C) dismiss   (D) procrastinate

4. ABRIDGED: (A) connected   (B) undercut
                  (C) cleansed   (D) shortened

5. INSCRUTABLE: (A) discerned (B) rhetorical
(C) enigmatic (D) chaotic

16.k ANTONYM QUESTIONS

An *antonym* is a word that means the opposite of another word. For example, *hostile* is an antonym of *friendly.* Standardized reading tests often include multiple-choice antonym questions that are similar to the synonym questions discussed in 16.j. They ask you to choose the word or phrase that is most nearly opposite in meaning to a given word.

STRATEGIES FOR ANTONYM QUESTIONS

In answering antonym questions, use the same strategies suggested for synonym questions in 16.j.

Try to answer the following sample question, and then study the explanation following it.

SAMPLE QUESTION
SUPPRESS: (A) ignore (B) understate
(C) make haste (D) make known

This question illustrates the importance of thinking about all the possible meanings of the given word. If you know, for example, that *suppress* can mean "subdue" or "crush," you might think at first that (A), *ignore,* is the correct choice. Ignoring something, however, is not really the opposite of subduing it; what is called for is a word like *support* or *encourage.* Since none of the choices has this meaning, you should realize that you are not thinking about the right meaning of *suppress.* Think about other things that can be *suppressed,* such as anger or evidence of a crime, and you can see that the word can also mean "restrain" or "prevent from becoming known." Choice (D), therefore, is the correct answer, because it is opposite in meaning to the phrase "prevent from becoming known."

EXERCISE 8. Choose the word or phrase that means the opposite or most nearly the opposite to the word in capital letters.

1. CURIOUS:
   (A) happy
   (B) with energy
   (C) uninterested
   (D) lacking hope

2. TACTFUL:
   (A) insincere
   (B) with style
   (C) uncertain
   (D) indiscreet

3. FLOURISH:
   (A) displease
   (B) stabilize
   (C) lighten
   (D) decline

4. PLENITUDE:
   (A) scarcity
   (B) danger
   (C) supposition
   (D) vagueness

5. COSMOPOLITAN:
   (A) mendacity
   (B) lout
   (C) pauper
   (D) morass

16.1 SENTENCE–COMPLETION QUESTIONS

Sentence-completion questions measure your skill in both reading and vocabulary. You are given a sentence with one or two words left out and indicated by a blank. From the four or five choices offered, you must choose the word or words that best complete the meaning of the sentence.

STRATEGIES FOR SENTENCE-COMPLETION QUESTIONS

1. Be alert to the clues contained in the sentence. The given parts of the sentence will always give you the hints necessary for choosing the correct answer to the question.

2. If there are two blanks in the sentence, try to understand how they are related to each other. For example, are they similar in meaning? Are they opposite in meaning?

Try to answer the following sample question by filling in the blank with a phrase, and then study the explanation following it.

SAMPLE QUESTION

The _____ price controls on gasoline could mean a bonanza for the owners of service stations.

(A) strengthening in   (B) lifting of
(C) certainty about   (D) adoption of

The part of the sentence that gives you the clue to the correct answer is the phrase "a bonanza for the owners." You should ask yourself, "Doing *what* to price controls would bring more money to the owners?" *Adoption of* or *strengthening in* price controls would have the opposite effect on the owners' income while *certainty about* is too vague to indicate the effect it would have. The only choice that makes sense in the blank is (B), *lifting of.*

EXERCISE 9. Choose the word or set of words that best completes the meaning of the sentence.

1. Many predatory animals are remarkably ____ ; they can stalk their prey for hours, waiting for the right moment to strike.

    (A) agile
    (B) vigorous
    (C) patient
    (D) fierce

2. ____ , the captain of the girls' gymnastics team performed well on the balance beam ____ her sprained wrist.

    (A) Discouraged—because of
    (B) Undaunted—in spite of
    (C) Courageously—resulting in
    (D) Regrettably—with the help of

3. Some of the telescopes in the observatories of the Southwest are slowly being ____ by the lights of the ____ expanding cities around them.

    (A) closed—gradually
    (B) enlarged—efficiently
    (C) blinded—relentlessly
    (D) enhanced—ever

STANDARDIZED TESTS OF WRITING ABILITY

There are two kinds of standardized writing tests, direct and indirect. A direct writing test contains essay questions. An indirect writing test is a multiple-choice test, for which you do not have to do any actual writing. Its questions are designed to test specific writing skills, such as mastery of capitalization and punctuation, control of grammar and usage, and skill at organizing sentences into paragraphs. The following pages discuss several kinds of multiple-choice writing ability questions that you should recognize.

16.m CAPITALIZATION AND PUNCTUATION QUESTIONS

Many questions on standardized objective writing tests are designed to test your knowledge of capitalization and punctuation rules (see Section 7). These questions take the form of sentences with three underlined parts. You are to decide if there is an error in capitalization or punctuation at any of the underlines or if the sentence has no error. You do not have to make any actual corrections in the sentence; you need only recognize the error if there is one. You can assume that capitalization and punctuation are correct in the parts of the sentence that are not underlined.

STRATEGIES FOR CAPITALIZATION AND PUNCTUATION QUESTIONS

1. Read the question slowly and carefully because you will be looking for fine details of capitalization and punctuation.
2. Remember that all elements that are not underlined are correct. Very often, the elements that are correct in

other parts of the sentence will provide good clues to the answer.

Try to answer the sample questions below.

SAMPLE QUESTION A

Francis Scott Key wrote the words of "The Star-
$\overline{\textbf{A}}$ $\overline{\textbf{B}}$

Spangled Banner" during the war of 1812.
$\overline{\textbf{C}}$

No Error.
$\overline{\textbf{D}}$

Choice A is correctly capitalized because it is a person's name (see 7.a.5); and Choice B, because it is the first word of a title (see 7.a.7). The word *war* should also be capitalized, however, because it is part of the name of a historical event (see 7.a.5). Therefore, the correct answer is C.

SAMPLE QUESTION B

Before the British burned the White House,
$\overline{\textbf{A}}$

Dolley Madison escaped with Gilbert Stuarts
$\overline{\textbf{B}}$

well-known portrait of George Washington.
$\overline{\textbf{C}}$

No Error.
$\overline{\textbf{D}}$

At Choice A the comma is correct because it follows an introductory adverb clause (see 7.g.10). At Choice C the hyphen is correct because *well-known* is a compound adjective that precedes the noun it describes (see 7.j). At Choice B, however, an apostrophe is required to make the noun possessive.

EXERCISE 10. Each of the following sentences has three underlined parts. If you think there is an error in capitalization or punctuation at any of the underlines, select the letter of that underline. If you think there is no error, choose Choice D.

1. Lester Short has observed birds in every state except
$\overline{\text{A}}$

Hawaii and has done ornithological studies in Europe,
$\overline{\text{B}}$

south America, Africa, and the Cameroons. No Error. *C*
$\overline{\text{C}}$ _____
$\quad\quad\quad\quad\quad\quad\quad\quad\quad\quad\quad\quad\quad\quad\quad\quad\quad$ **D**

2. The coauthor with Ernest Mayr of "Species Taxa of
$\quad\overline{\text{A}}$ $\quad\quad\quad\quad\quad\quad\quad\quad\quad\quad\quad\quad\quad\quad\overline{\text{B}}$

North American Birds," Mr. Short has written scien-

tific articles on the evolution and behavior of birds,

particularly woodpeckers. No Error. *D*
$\quad\quad\quad\quad\quad\overline{\text{C}}$ _____
$\quad\quad\quad\quad\quad\quad\text{C}\quad\quad\quad\quad\text{D}$

3. Mr. Short's plans for field work include a study of
$\quad\quad\quad\quad\overline{\text{A}}$ $\quad\quad\quad\quad\quad\quad\quad\quad\quad\quad\overline{\text{B}}$

Parrots in Australia. No Error. *C*
$\overline{\text{C}}$ _____
$\quad\quad\quad\quad\quad\quad\quad\text{D}$

4. James Wilson Marshall discovered gold in 1848, in
$\quad\quad\quad\quad\quad\quad\quad\quad\quad\quad\quad\quad\quad\quad\quad\quad\quad\overline{\text{A}}$

the American River at Sutter's Mill, an event that led
$\quad\quad\quad\quad\quad\quad\quad\quad\overline{\text{B}}\quad\overline{\text{C}}$

to the famous Gold Rush of 1849. No Error. *A*
_____
$\quad\quad\quad\quad\quad\quad\quad\quad\quad\quad\quad\text{D}$

5. The Central Valley Water Project, with Shasta Dam

as its key unit, cost more than $400,000,000; it was
$\quad\quad\quad\quad\quad\overline{\text{A}}$ $\quad\quad\quad\quad\quad\quad\quad\quad\quad\quad\overline{\text{B}}$

built to control floods to supply fresh water for irri-
$\quad\quad\quad\quad\quad\quad\quad\overline{\text{C}}$

gation, and to generate power. No Error. *C*
_____
$\quad\quad\quad\quad\quad\quad\quad\quad\quad\quad\text{D}$

16.n GRAMMAR AND USAGE QUESTIONS

Like capitalization and punctuation questions, grammar and usage questions take the form of sentences in which you are asked to recognize errors. Either the error will be in one of the three or four underlined parts of the sentence, or the sentence will contain no error.

STRATEGIES FOR GRAMMAR AND USAGE QUESTIONS

1. Read the question slowly and carefully. Many times the error will be a subtle one that you may miss if you read quickly.

2. Remember that anything in the sentence that is not underlined is correct.

3. Be particularly alert to such matters as agreement of subject and verb, agreement of pronoun and antecedent, and choice of words.

Try to answer the sample question below, and then study the explanation that follows it.

SAMPLE QUESTION

<u>Although</u> Ellen is a better tennis player than
  A

<u>him</u>, Henry <u>has</u> occasionally beaten her.
  B   **C**

<u>No Error.</u>
  D

As with capitalization and punctuation questions, you should look at each underlined item to try to determine what might be wrong with it. For Choice A you have to decide if *although* correctly expresses the relationship in meaning between the subordinate clause and the main clause. In Choice B you are being tested on your knowledge of pronoun case (see 1.d.1). For Choice C you must decide if the auxiliary verb *has* agrees with its subject, *Henry* (see 1.b.6).

The error is in Choice B. The beginning of the sentence contains an elliptical adverb clause that omits the word *is*. With the verb the clause should read *Although Ellen is a better player than he* [*is*]. The pronoun is the subject of the implied linking verb *is*; therefore, it must be in the subjective case (*he*). *Him* is incorrect because it is in the objective case.

EXERCISE 11. Some of the following sentences contain problems in grammar, usage, diction (choice of words), and idiom. Some of the sentences are correct. No sentence contains more than one error. Select the letter of the underlined part that must be changed to make the sentence correct. If there is no error, select Choice D. In choosing answers, follow the requirements of standard written English.

1. Caribbean monk seals <u>have not been</u> officially sighted
    **A**

   <u>since</u> 1952, and their survival remains <u>an</u> open ques-
   B **C**

   tion. <u>No Error.</u> *D*
    **D**

2. Monk seals once <u>live</u> in large herds <u>along</u> the shores
    **A** **B**

   and islands of the Caribbean Sea and the Gulf of

   Mexico, but they <u>have steadily</u> dwindled in number.
    **C**

   <u>No Error.</u> *A*
   D

3. No recent <u>photograph</u> of the monk seals exist,
    **A**

   <u>although</u> local fishers periodically claim <u>to have seen</u>
   B **C**

   the missing animals. <u>No Error.</u> *A*
    **D**

16.0 PARAGRAPH–ORGANIZATION QUESTIONS

Another writing skill that is often tested on standardized tests is your ability to organize sentences into a coherent and effective paragraph. Some of these questions ask you to select the best way of ordering a group of sentences into a paragraph. You may also be given a paragraph and asked about elements such as the topic sentence, logical connectives, and unity of thought. Each of these kinds of paragraph organization questions is illustrated in the exercises that follow. If you have trouble in doing these exercises, review the material in Section 10.

EXERCISE 12. The four numbered sentences below are followed by four choices of ways to order the sentences into a paragraph. Choose the answer that orders the sentences into the most effective paragraph.

1. The age that produced Andrew Jackson produced many great leaders in American public life.
2. Andrew Jackson stood out as the most striking personality of his time, however, even among these famous leaders.
3. The years during which he was prominent in national political life are known as the Jacksonian Era.
4. The distinguished government leaders of that time included Daniel Webster, Henry Clay, and John Calhoun.

    (A) 4, 2, 3, 1
    (B) 1, 4, 2, 3
    (C) 3, 1, 4, 2
    (D) 2, 3, 1, 4

EXERCISE 13. Read the following paragraph, and answer the questions that follow it.

(1) The polar regions of our planet are known for their barren, windswept ice fields, which bring a feeling of desolation to a traveler in those parts. (2) When

darkness falls, the same traveler is often compensated by a dazzling display that can fill the entire sky. (3) This multihued light show is known as the aurora borealis, or northern lights, in the Northern Hemisphere and the aurora australis, or southern lights, in the Southern Hemisphere. (4) They are an awesome sight to those who witness their largest manifestations. (5) In polar regions the aurora is a nightly event. (6) At lower latitudes it is less frequent. (7) In most of the United States, these light spectacles can be seen only during geomagnetic storms, when the aurora moves from its normal polar position toward the lower latitudes. (8) Observations show that not all of the solar wind energy entering the magnetosphere is steadily released into the earth's atmosphere.

1. Which of the following would be the best transitional word to begin Sentence 2?
   (A) Nevertheless,
   (B) Because
   (C) So,
   (D) Otherwise

2. Which of the following would be the best way to join Sentences 5 and 6?
   (A) ... event even though...
   (B) ... event, but at...
   (C) ... event; even so at...
   (D) ... event except at...

3. Which of the following sentences should be left out of the paragraph because it upsets the unity of the paragraph?
   (A) 3   (B) 5   (C) 6   (D) 8

4. Which of the following phrases in Sentence 2 most strongly links Sentence 2 to Sentence 1?
   (A) "darkness falls"
   (B) "the same traveler"
   (C) "a dazzling display"
   (D) "the entire sky"

ADDITIONAL EXERCISES

Additional Exercises

1. Nouns

PART A: Identify the common nouns in each of the following sentences. A sentence may include more than one common noun. (Review 1.a.1.) *Common nouns have single underlines.*

1. A nine-year-old <u>child</u> who could not speak inspired a <u>woman</u> to start a <u>school</u> for handicapped <u>students</u>. *children, women, schools, student*
2. <u>Virginia Matson</u>, a <u>teacher</u>, wrote a <u>book</u> about the early <u>days</u> of <u>Grove School</u>. *teachers, books, day*
3. On <u>Saturdays</u> during the first <u>term</u>, <u>Matson</u> tutored a <u>boy</u> and a small <u>girl</u>. *terms, boys, girls*
4. The following <u>year</u> <u>Matson</u> used some of the <u>rooms</u> of her own <u>house</u> as <u>classrooms</u>. *years, room houses, classroom*
5. She visited other <u>schools</u> and <u>clinics</u> to learn new <u>ways</u> of helping handicapped <u>people</u>, both <u>youngsters</u> and <u>teen-agers</u>. *school, clinic, way, person, youngster, teen-ager*
6. <u>Courses</u> and <u>textbooks</u> at <u>Northwestern University</u> gave <u>Matson</u> new <u>insights</u>. *course, textbook, insight*
7. <u>Grove School</u> had many <u>volunteers</u>, including a <u>group</u> of <u>men</u> from the <u>United States Navy</u>. *volunteer groups man*
8. Early on, the <u>pupils</u> attended a red brick <u>schoolhouse</u>, provided by the <u>school board</u> of <u>Milburn</u>, <u>Illinois</u>. *pupil, schoolhouses, school boards*
9. <u>Matson</u> now has a <u>facility</u> for a hundred handicapped <u>children</u> at a <u>place</u> called <u>Ridge Farm</u>. *facilities, child places*
10. Now, many public <u>schools</u> in the <u>United States</u> have special <u>teachers</u> for handicapped <u>learners</u>. *school, teacher, learner*

PART B: Now identify the proper nouns in the preceding sentences. Not every sentence has a proper noun. Some sentences have more than one. (Review 1.a.1.)

Proper nouns have double underlines.

PART C: Look at the common nouns that you identified in Part A. Now identify the five that are compound nouns. (Review 1.a.2.) *classrooms, teen-agers, textbooks, schoolhouse, school board*

PART D: Look at the common nouns that you identified in Part A. Give the plural form of each singular noun. Then give the singular form of each plural noun. (Review 1.a.3.) *See page 646.*

2. Verbs

PART A: Select the correct form of the verb or verb phrase from the parentheses. (Review 1.b.6–1.b.19.)

1. Nick Lyons and his son <u>fished</u> for three days and (catched/<u>caught</u>) nothing. *a.v., a.v.*
2. They (was spending/<u>were spending</u>) a week at a lake on the Continental Divide, and Nick's son <u>was</u> bored. *a.v., l.v.*
3. The fourth morning Nick Lyons <u>went</u> fishing alone because his son (sleeped/<u>slept</u>) late. *a.v., a.v.*
4. Alone on the lake, Nick Lyons (hook/<u>hooked</u>) six fish. *a.v.*
5. He <u>had thrown</u> five small trout back before a big one (slips/<u>slipped</u>) his hook among the weeds. *a.v., a.v.*
6. When Nick Lyons (had telled/<u>had told</u>) his son about the good luck, the boy <u>appeared</u> interested. *a.v., l.v.*
7. Nick Lyons (is using/<u>was using</u>) a fly rod, while his son <u>was fishing</u> with a shiny metal lure. *a.v., a.v.*
8. Nick Lyons (demonstrates/<u>demonstrated</u>) the proper use of a lure. *a.v.*
9. He <u>caught</u> a cutthroat trout, but still his son (did not got/<u>did not get</u>) a nibble. *a.v., a.v.*
10. The father (suggest/<u>suggested</u>) twenty more casts. *a.v.*
11. The boy (throwed/<u>threw</u>) out his line and <u>counted</u>. *a.v., a.v.*
12. He (was bringing/<u>were bringing</u>) the lure in much too fast because he <u>was being</u> impatient. *a.v., l.v.*
13. At last, on the seventeenth cast, the little glass rod on the line (diped/<u>dipped</u>) down sharply. *a.v.*

14. Nick Lyons <u>could tell</u> by the way the line <u>behaved</u>
that his son (<u>had hooked</u>/has hooked) a big fish.

15. Father and son both <u>saw</u> the big male brook trout
as it (swimmed/<u>swam</u>) around the front of the boat.

16. The fish (circle/<u>circled</u>) the anchor chain but now
<u>seemed</u> subdued. *a.v., l.v.*

17. Father and son <u>leaned</u> over the side of the boat
while Nick Lyons (tries/<u>tried</u>) to net the fish. *a.v., a.v.*

18. Both still (<u>remember</u>/remembers) the picture of
their reflected faces above the big fish, which
<u>looked</u> like a winner. *a.v., l.v.*

19. A minute later the bright dappled fish <u>was</u> in the
boat and both father and son (<u>were laughing</u>/was
laughing). *l.v., a.v.*

20. This true fish story and twenty-one others (<u>appear</u>/
appears) in the book *Fishing Moments of Truth*,
which <u>was edited</u> by Eric Peper and Jim Rickhoff.
l.v., a.v.

PART B: Reread the sentences in Part A. Now identify
any other verbs or verb phrases that you find in each
sentence. Not every sentence will have another verb.

PART C: Tell whether each verb phrase from Part A and
Part B is an action verb or a linking verb. (1.b.5)

3. Adjectives

PART A: Identify all of the adjectives (except proper adjectives) in each of the following sentences. (Do not
identify articles as adjectives.) (Review 1.c–1.c.5.)

1. <u>Great</u> geniuses have the <u>shortest</u> biographies.
—Ralph Waldo Emerson *greater, greatest*

2. Only <u>solitary</u> men know the <u>full</u> joys of friendship.—Willa Cather *more/most solitary, fuller/fullest*

3. The <u>most beautiful</u> thing we can experience is the
mysterious.—Albert Einstein

4. A <u>skywide</u> stretch of <u>cottony</u> cloud came up and
spread itself, or so it appeared, under the moon,
<u>palletlike</u>.—Eudora Welty
more/most cottony

5. A servant in waiting took my horse, and I entered the Gothic archway of the hall.—Edgar Allan Poe

PART B: Identify the *proper* adjective in the preceding sentences. (Review 1.c.6.) *Gothic*

PART C: For each adjective (except the proper adjective), indicate if it is in its *basic form* or in its *comparative form* or in its *superlative form*. For each adjective in the basic form, show the comparative and superlative forms. (Review 1.c.3–1.c.4.) *b = basic   c = comparative*
s = superlative

4. Pronouns

PART A: Select the appropriate pronoun from the parentheses within each of the following sentences. (Review 1.d.)

1. My sister, (who/whom) I am living with, is an occupational therapist.
2. An occupational therapist, like a doctor, needs to be officially registered to practice (her/their) profession.
3. If your sister becomes an occupational therapist, (they/she) will take special college courses.
4. Occupational therapists work with handicapped people (who/that) need help in learning to take care of themselves.
5. Did you ever try tying (them/your) shoelaces with one hand?
6. My sister taught (me/myself) how to do it.
7. (Whatever/Whichever) you decide to do as an adult, working with handicapped children will teach you a great deal.
8. Usually, you can learn new skills faster than (they/them).
9. (You're/Your) patience is required.
10. Therapists (theirselves/themselves) need considerable patience.

11. Physical therapists also work with people (whom/ who) have handicaps.

12. If you or your brother broke a leg, a physical thera- pist could help (you or he/you or him) learn to use crutches.

13. (What/Which) can a physical therapist do to help you or him?

14. When I broke my wrist, a physical therapist gave (myself/me) exercises for the muscles.

15. (Them/Those) also made my wrist flexible again.

16. A speech therapist helps (their/his) pupils control a stutter or lisp.

17. Which of (these/them) three professions sounds most interesting to you?

18. Occupational therapists help (they're/their) patients to do things for themselves.

19. Physical therapists use heat, whirlpools, and mas- sages on patients to help (these/them) get well quickly.

20. Speech therapists help patients speak almost as clearly as (they/them).

PART B: Reread the sentences in Part A. Now identify any other pronouns that you find in each sentence. Not every sentence will have additional pronouns.

5. Adverbs

PART A: Indicate which of the following sentences have adverbs. Identify each adverb. (Review 1.f.)

1. Approximately 25,000 Lapps live in Norway. *4*

2. Ten percent of these own herds of reindeer.

3. A Lapp herder depended heavily on his reindeer for food and clothing and tools. *4*

4. Today spring and fall roundups bring the reindeer in to be sold as meat. *1, 2*

5. Lapps can herd more easily with snowmobiles. *3*

6. During migration, runaway reindeer are carted <u>back</u> to the herd on sleds behind snowmobiles. *2*

7. When pastures become crowded, reindeer are ferried to new grazing lands.

8. Some Lapps <u>still</u> continue the nomadic tradition of migrating with the reindeer herds. *1*

9. Many continue to wear traditional deerskin shoes <u>warmly</u> insulated with sedge grass. *3*

10. Youngsters clothed <u>colorfully</u> attend schools equipped with educational television. *3*

PART B: Decide in which category each adverb belongs: (1) time, (2) place, (3) manner, (4) degree. (Review 1.f.1.)

6. Prepositions and Conjunctions

PART A: Identify each of the underlined words in the following sentences as either a preposition or a conjunction. (Review 1.g. and 1.h.) *c = conjunction   p = preposition*

1. Janice Holt was four years old <u>when</u> her family *c, 3* moved <u>to</u> [Kinta, Oklahoma.]   *p*

2. During the six [years] that the Holts lived there, *p* Janice <u>and</u> Corinne Moore became close friends.   *c, 1*

3. *Kinta* is a Choctaw word meaning "beaver," <u>and</u> *c, 1* Corinne Moore was part Choctaw.

4. Corinne's grandfather was the last principal chief <u>of</u> the [Choctaw Nation]; <u>moreover</u>, he looked the *p; c, 4* part <u>on</u> his big black [horse.]   *p*

5. <u>Neither</u> Corinne <u>nor</u> Janice had many toys; *c, 2* <u>however</u>, they used catalogue pictures for dolls.   *c, 4*

6. They played <u>outside</u> the [house] <u>whenever</u> the *p; c, 3* weather permitted.

7. Their doll house was made <u>from</u> a piano [crate], <u>for</u> *p; c, 1* Mrs. Holt had won a piano and had left the crate <u>outside</u> the [house.]   *p*

8. <u>Even though</u> Janice was still a child when the *c, 3* Holts left Kinta, she wrote many novels <u>about</u> the *p* American [frontier.]

9. Corinne helped Janice recall their childhood years, <u>for</u> the two women remained friends. *c, 1*

10. <u>After</u> her [marriage] to Henry Giles, Janice <u>and</u> he
p; c, 1 wrote two books based <u>on</u> their [life] <u>in</u> a log [cabin].
p; p

PART B: Look at the prepositions in Part A. Identify the object of each preposition. (Review 1.g.1.) *Objects of prepositions are enclosed in backets.*

PART C: Look at the conjunctions that you identified in Part A. Decide in which category each conjunction belongs: (1) coordinating conjunction, (2) correlative conjunction, (3) subordinating conjunction, (4) conjunctive adverb. (Review 1.h.1.–1.h.4.)

7. Verbals and Verbal Phrases

Identify the verbal or verbal phrase in each of the following sentences. Indicate whether it is a gerund, a participle, or an infinitive. (Review 1.j–1.p.)

1. Thomas Jefferson is justly famous for <u>designing</u> *ger* both Monticello and the University of Virginia.

2. <u>To appreciate Jefferson's wide talents</u>, you might *inf* consider his smaller achievements.

3. He designed a bell-clock that not only struck the hours but also permitted a bell-ringer <u>to ring it</u> at any time. *inf*

4. <u>Seeking out his own clay</u>, Jefferson designed molds *part* that allowed for shrinkage.

5. His mortar mix hardened in water, <u>providing</u> *part* <u>damp-proof cellar walls</u>.

6. He discovered that <u>splintering</u> was common when *ger* lumber dried in a kiln.

7. He had glue for his home made from fresh hide, <u>cooked in a huge double boiler</u>. *part*

8. <u>Landscaping</u> was another talent of Thomas Jeffer-*ger* son's.

9. <u>Appreciating formal gardens</u>, Jefferson designed *part* some for the grounds of Monticello, his home.

10. The University of Virginia today includes a fine school of architecture, originally <u>planned by Thomas Jefferson.</u> *part*

8. Verbal Phrases

Identify each verbal phrase in the following sentences. Indicate whether it is a gerund phrase, a participial phrase, or an infinitive phrase. Some sentences have more than one verbal phrase. (Review 1.j–1.p.)

1. <u>Exploring Utah's Red Rock country in winter</u> takes a hardy nature. *ger*
2. Southwestern Utah is not easy <u>to get through</u> in winter. *inf*
3. With altitudes <u>ranging from 4,000 feet to 10,000 feet,</u> the countryside is awesome in snow season. *part*
4. The pink sandstone castles of Bryce Canyon are frosted with a <u>whipped-cream topping of snow.</u> *ger*
5. The ski resort of Brian Head offers snowmobile fans a chance <u>to have a dizzying climb.</u> *inf*
6. <u>Skiing</u> in Utah is wonderful. *ger*
7. Zion National Park promises warmer temperatures amid vistas of rocks <u>weathered by age.</u> *part*
8. The <u>filming of *Planet of the Apes* near Kanab</u> makes the tiny town's surroundings seem familiar. *ger*
9. <u>Traveling southwest into Nevada,</u> the explorer will find Lake Mead <u>nestled among rounded hills</u> <u>covered with sagebrush.</u> *part* *part* *part*
10. Not far away in the Valley of Fire sunset transforms craggy rockpiles, <u>coloring the walls red.</u> *part*

9. Complete Sentences vs. Sentence Fragments

PART A: Identify each of the following items as a *complete sentence* or a *sentence fragment.* (All of these familiar sayings were written by one man, Miguel de Cervantes, in *Don Quixote de la Mancha.*)(Review 2.b.)

frag 1. The proof of the pudding/*is in the eating.*

sent 2. There is no sauce in the world like hunger.

sent 3. Let every man mind his own business.

frag 4. ~~Catches~~ no flies. *Vinegar catches*

sent 5. I begin to smell a rat.

frag 6. I'll turn over a/*new leaf.*

sent 7. I can see with half an eye.

frag 8. ~~Calls~~ the kettle black. *The pot calls*

frag 9. ~~An~~ honest man's word. *Never doubt an*

frag 10. ~~Able~~ to do great kindnesses. *The humblest person is able*

PART B: Look again at each sentence fragment that you identified in Part A. Make each fragment into a complete sentence. (You can complete each fragment by quoting the famous saying or by adding words of your own.) *Answers will vary. Possibilities are given in the exercise.*

10. Subjects and Predicates; Subject-Verb Agreement

PART A: Identify the complete subject and the simple subject in each of the following sentences. Ignore the choices in parentheses at this time. (Review 2.a–2.c.)
Complete subjects have single underlines. Simple subjects have double underlines.

1. <u>All <u>snakes</u></u> (has/<u>have</u>) the remarkable habit of shedding their skin.

2. "<u><u>Sloughing</u></u>" (is/are) another word for this habit.

3. There (is/<u>are</u>) <u>several <u>signs</u> of sloughing.</u>.

4. <u>One of these <u>signs</u></u> (is/<u>are</u>) dull colors and markings.

5. <u>Cloudy, opaque <u>eyes</u></u> also (signals/<u>signal</u>) shedding.

6. <u><u>Three</u> or <u>four</u> sheddings each year</u> (is/<u>are</u>) the average for an adult snake.

7. <u><u>Shedding</u> more often</u> (is/<u>are</u>) not unusual.

8. <u>A good <u>appetite</u></u> (<u>has</u>/have) been found to cause more frequent shedding.

9. <u><u>Hibernation</u> in cold temperatures</u> (<u>prevents</u>/prevent) a snake from shedding.

10. *Snakes of the World* (<u>contains</u>/contain) some fascinating facts about snakes and their habits.
11. <u>Removing the old skin</u> (<u>is</u>/are) not difficult.
12. <u>The nose</u> (and) <u>the jaw</u> (is/<u>are</u>) simply rubbed against rough surfaces.
13. <u>Some snakes</u> (yawns/<u>yawn</u>), causing the skin to break.
14. <u>The loose skin</u> then (<u>catches</u>/catch) on twigs and branches.
15. <u>A bush</u> (or) <u>rock cleft</u> also (<u>offers</u>/offer) an opportunity to remove old skin.
16. <u>The snake's color</u>, as well as its markings, (<u>becomes</u>/become) brighter after the old skin is shed.
17. <u>It</u> (<u>seems</u>/seem) to have the appearance of paint.
18. <u>The Brazilian rainbow boa</u> (<u>turns</u>/turn) silvery white before shedding.
19. <u>Many a hiker</u> (<u>has</u>/have) found an old snakeskin on a tree branch.
20. <u>Every kind of snake</u> (<u>uses</u>/use) this method of replacing worn or wounded skin.

PART B: Select the appropriate form of the action verb, linking verb, or auxiliary from the parentheses in each of the preceding sentences. Your choice must agree in number with the simple subject of the sentence. (Review 2.d–2.g.)

11. Direct Objects, Indirect Objects, Predicate Nominatives, Predicate Adjectives, Predicate Adverbs

Identify the direct object, indirect object, predicate nominative, predicate adjective, or predicate adverb in each of the following sentences. (Review 2.k–2.m.3.)

1. Project Mercury was America's first major space <u>program</u>. *p.n.*
2. In 1959 NASA selected the original seven <u>astronauts</u>. *d.o.*

3. These seven men were quite courageous. *p. adj.*

4. First, the astronauts underwent strenuous tests. *d.o.*

5. After two years of preparation, the Mercury spacecraft was ready. *p. adj.*

6. The NASA officials gave Alan Shepard the honor of the first flight. *i.o.* *d.o.*

7. The launching sight was Cape Canaveral, Florida. *p.n.*

8. Television cameras gave millions of Americans a *d.o.* view of the launch. *i.o.*

9. Commander Shepard experienced space travel for only fifteen minutes. *d.o.*

10. John Glenn became the first American in earth orbit. *p.n.*

11. On February 20, 1962, Glenn circled the earth three times. *d.o.*

12. Glenn was weightless during most of the flight. *p. adj.*

13. His view of the earth was magnificent. *p. adj.*

14. Because of his speed, Glenn saw three sunsets (and) three sunrises in five hours. *d.o.*

15. Returning the capsule to earth required complicated maneuvering. *d.o.*

16. The job of the recovery ship was to retrieve Glenn's capsule from the Atlantic Ocean. *p.n.*

17. For many people, space flight had seemed only science fiction. *p.n.*

18. Many admiring Americans wrote Glenn letters of congratulation. *i.o.* *d.o.*

19. President John F. Kennedy awarded each astronaut the Distinguished Service Medal. *d.o.* *i.o.*

20. The Mercury astronauts had become heroes. *p.n.*

12. Subordinate Clauses

PART A: Identify each subordinate clause in the following sentences. (Review 2.n and 2.p.)

1. The old-fashioned country store, which has almost disappeared, was more than just a store. *adj. cl.*

2. A farmer could leave the children there <u>while he went to see the blacksmith.</u> *adv. cl.*

3. It was a place <u>where friends and neighbors could meet.</u> *adj. cl.*

4. People came from miles around to buy <u>whatever they needed.</u> *n. cl.*

5. The store usually had one wall <u>that served as a bulletin board.</u> *adj. cl.*

6. <u>As soon as the winter cold had set in,</u> folks would sit around the glowing stove. *adv. cl.*

7. Farmers talked about <u>what they would plant in the spring.</u> *n. cl.*

8. The farmers' wives could ask <u>when the new shipment of drygoods was due.</u> *n. cl.*

9. Children especially loved the store <u>because it was full of exciting sights and smells.</u> *adv. cl.*

10. The storekeeper, <u>who was also the postmaster,</u> was an important person in the community. *adj. cl.*

PART B: Identify each subordinator (subordinating conjunction, relative pronoun, or other subordinator) in the preceding sentences. (Review 2.r.) *Subordinators have double underlines.*

PART C: Tell whether each subordinate clause in the preceding sentences is a noun clause, an adjective clause, or an adverb clause. (Review 2.s–2.u.)

13. Subordinate Clauses and Main Clauses; Kinds of Sentences

PART A: Identify each main clause in the following sentences. (Review 2.n. and 2.o.) *Main clauses have single underlines.*

1. <u>Experience is a teacher indeed;</u> yet did <u>Billy's years make his experience small.</u>—Herman Melville *compound*

2. <u>She wrapped herself well in her quilt,</u> <u>which her mother had made before dying young</u>.—Maxine Hong Kingston *complex*

3. <u>At first its weak flame made no impression on the shadows;</u> then Zeena's face stood grimly out

against the uncurtained <u><u>pane</u></u>, <u><u>which had turned</u></u>
<u><u>from grey to black.</u></u>—Edith Wharton *c - c*

4. <u><u>The door was thrust open</u></u>, <u><u>although no human
form was perceptible on the other side of the half-
window.</u></u>—Nathaniel Hawthorne *complex*

5. <u><u>There was a terrible grace in the move of the waves,</u></u>
(and) <u><u>they came in silence, save for the snarling of
the crests.</u></u>—Stephen Crane *compound*

PART B: Identify each subordinate clause in the preceding sentences. (Review 2.n and 2.p.)

Subordinate clauses have double underlines.

PART C: Determine whether each sentence is a simple sentence, compound sentence, complex sentence, or compound-complex sentence. (Review 2.w.)

14. Capitalization, Semicolons, Colons, Apostrophes, Quotation Marks, Italics, and Parentheses

Rewrite the following paragraphs, correcting all errors in capitalization and the use of semicolons, colons, apostrophes, quotation marks, italics, and parentheses. You should find twenty errors. (Review 7.a, 7.h, 7.i, and 7.k–7.n.)

1 Norman Rockwell was probably America's best-
2 known illustrator. His most famous pictures ap-
3 peared in the <u>Saturday Evening Post</u>. Rockwell cre-
4 ated more than three hundred of this magazines
5 covers. His pictures were often amusing/; however,
6 some people considered them corny. They fre-
7 quently were nostalgic portrayals of small-town
8 American life."I do ordinary people in everyday sit-
9 uations,"he once said. His subjects were very famil-
10 iar:families, children, pets, apple pie, the flag. His
11 most popular illustrations (depicting, for example,
12 Boy Scouts and a returning soldier)reminded Amer-

13 icans of values they cherished. One of his most
14 famous pictures is entitled <u>Freedom from Want</u>. It
15 shows a cheerful grandmother serving a large
T 16 ⟨thanksgiving turkey to her family.
17   Rockwell grew up in New York City. In 1916 he
18 sold his first cover to the *Saturday Evening Post*
19 (he was 22). The *Post's* circulation was two million
20 copies a week/; consequently, Rockwell soon became
21 nationally known. He did not consider himself a
22 true artist, however. His own words show his mod-
23 esty: "I am a storyteller. Id love to have been a
24 Picasso, but I just havent got it." Nevertheless, many
25 Americans found Rockwells work more appealing
26 than Picasso's paintings. Rockwell died in the old-
27 fashioned town of Stockbridge, Massachusetts. He
28 left several decades' worth of pictures. Only one
29 other artist became as familiar to Americans: Walt
30 Disney.

15. Commas, Periods, Exclamation Points, Question Marks, Hyphens, Numbers, and Abbreviations

Rewrite the following paragraphs, correcting all errors in the use of commas, periods, exclamation points, question marks, hyphens, numbers and numerals, and abbreviations. You should find twenty-five errors. (Review 7.b–7.g and 7.j.)

1   The year is 1980. The television image of a twenty-
2 five-year-old man is fed into a computer. *Twenty* 20 seconds
3 later another image appears on the screen. It shows
4 the same man, but now he is sixty years old. This
5 invention is called the Age Machine, and/ its inven-
6 tor is Nancy Burson.
7   You may ask how this machine works?. Assume
8 that you want to see how you will look at the age of

9 fifty. A television camera takes your picture/ and
10 stores it in a specially programmed computer. The
11 computer's memory bank also stores general infor-
12 mation,/ about the aging process. For example, fat
13 people tend to get fatter as they grow older, while
14 thin ones become thinner. Men's faces tend to age
15 less quickly,/ than women's/ because their beards
16 help hold up the skin. After the Age Machine classi-
17 fies your face by type, it takes the difference between
18 a standard face of that type at age 5̶0̶ *fifty* and one at
19 your own age. That difference is applied to your
20 photograph, along with the aging information. The
21 result is a television picture of the future you.

22   What is the use of such a machine/? In fact there
23 are many possible uses/ that may not have occurred
24 to you. Mug shots of criminals could be brought up
25 to date, although they might be many years old. D̶r̶s̶. *Doctors*
26 could use the Age Machine in reverse to show pa-
27 tients how they might look after a face lift. Film-
28 makers might even be able to use the machine to
29 show the same actor playing a character in youth, in
30 the prime of life, and in old age.

Index

respectfully, respectively, 435
Restrictive (essential) clauses
   and phrases, 162–164, 382,
   386
Return address, 610
Revising
   compositions, 555
   paragraphs, 592
   sagging sentences, 451–453.
     See also Editing
rise, raise, 434
Roget's Thesaurus, 572
Roman numerals, 548–549, 619
Roots, word, 254–270
Run-on sentences, 92, 155, 381,
   449

Sagging subjects, 451–453
Salutation, 606–607
Schwa (ə), 297, 333
Scientific information, 332,
   336
Secondary accent mark, 334
See also cards, 564
See cards, 564
seeing as how, 435
Self-editing, 454
Semiblock style, 608, 612
Semicolons, 395–397
   to join main clauses, 92,
     153–154, 396
   and quotation marks, 416
   to separate expressions
     containing commas, 397
Sensory details, 515–516
Sentence adverbs, 77
Sentence-completion questions,
   636–637
Sentence fragments, 114, 449
Sentences, 183–238
   capitalization of, 345
   clarity in, 232–235
   complex, 157–158, 172, 202–
     224
     with adjective clauses,
       216–217 (*see also* Adjective
       clauses)
     with adverb clauses, 202–212

(*see also* Adverb clauses)
   with noun clauses, 224 (*see*
     also Noun clauses)
   compound, 153–154, 194–200
     (*see also* Compound sentences)
   compound-complex, 157–158,
     172, 226–227
   declarative, 127
   defined, 112
   diagraming, 172–181
   imperative, 113, 127, 371
   improving, 232–238
   interrogative, 127–128
   with participial phrases,
     229–230 (*see also* Participial
     phrases)
   positions of adjectives in, 43
   run-on, 92, 155, 381, 449
   sagging, 451–453
   simple, 153–154, 171, 184–185
Sequential order, 502, 508–510
Series entry, 563
set, sit, 435
shall, will, 23
Short-answer questions, 623–624
should, ought to, 23
Signature, 609
Signs
   italics for, 421
   plurals of, 309, 408
Silent consonants, 295–296
Simple sentences, 171
   and compound sentences,
     153–154
   defined, 184
   expanding, 185–186
   kinds of, 184–185
since, 427
Sir or Madam, 607
sit, set, 435
so, and so, 450
Social letters, 604
Sources, 582.
   See also Bibliography; Foot-
     notes
Spatial order, 490
Speech
   dictionary guidance on,
     332–334

List of
Reference Keys

LIST OF REFERENCE KEYS

There are several ways for you to become familiar with the content of each section of this book. First, there is the Table of Contents. Second, there is the title page of each section, listing all the main divisions of the section. Third, there is the following list of reference keys.

Each main head within a section is marked by a reference key. Each subhead is marked by another key. The main keys are also used as tabs on the top of right-hand pages to help you locate material.

SAMPLE FROM SECTION 1, "PARTS OF SPEECH"

main head
marked by
reference key

tab at top of
right-hand page

1.f

1.f ADVERBS

An **adverb** is a word that tells more about a verb, an adjective, or another adverb.

Adverbs are words that tell *when, where, how,* or *to what degree.* In the examples below, the arrows show you which words the adverbs modify.

EXAMPLES

Bright red trucks **quickly** drove **there yesterday.**
degree   how   where   when

My **very** dirty sneakers **now** are drying **slowly outside.**
degree   when   how   where

subhead marked
by another
reference key

1.f.1 Kinds of adverbs

There are five basic kinds of adverbs: adverbs of time, adverbs of place, adverbs of degree, adverbs of manner, and sentence adverbs.

PARTS OF SPEECH

PARTS OF A SENTENCE

WRITING SENTENCES

VOCABULARY

SPELLING

THE DICTIONARY

CAPITALIZATION AND PUNCTUATION

─── **GLOSSARY OF USAGE PROBLEMS** ──────

── **CATCHING, CLASSIFYING, AND** ──────────
CORRECTING ERRORS

── **THE PARAGRAPH** ───────────────

PATTERNS OF THINKING AND WRITING

THE COMPOSITION

LIBRARIES AND INFORMATION

THE RESEARCH REPORT

THE LETTER

STUDY SKILLS AND TEST TAKING

EDITING SIGNALS AND REFERENCE KEYS

Editing for grammar and clarity	Editing signal	See Editing Chart
Error in subject-verb agreement	*agree*	pp. 443–444
Error in case	*case*	pp. 444–445
Error with pronoun reference	*ref*	pp. 445–446
Error with the negative	*neg*	p. 446
Error in noun plurals	*pl*	p. 446
Error in possessive	*poss*	p. 447
Error in verb tense	*tense*	p. 447
Error in comparative, superlative	*adj*	p. 448
Error in reflexive pronoun	*pro*	p. 448
Error with *this* or *them*	*pro*	p. 449
Error with *-ly* adverb	*adv*	p. 449
Using commas instead of end marks	*run-on*	p. 449
Incomplete sentences	*frag*	p. 449
Misusing conjunctions	*conj*	p. 450
Shift in voice	*voice*	pp. 447, 450
Dangling elements	*dangling*	p. 450
Misplaced elements	*misplaced*	p. 450
Sagging sentences	*sag*	pp. 451–453
Wordiness	*wordy*	p. 453

	Editing signal	See reference key
Editing for spelling	*sp*	5.a–5.d
Editing for capitalization	*cap*	7.a.1–7.a.8
Editing for punctuation	*p*	7.b–7.n
Editing paragraphs and compositions		
Weak topic sentence	*t.s.*	10.c
Topic sentence poorly supported	*support*	10.d–10.i
Lack of unity	*unity*	10.j
Lack of coherence	*cohere*	10.k
New paragraph		11.d, 11.h, 11.l
Weak introduction	*intro*	12.i
Weak sequencing of details	*seq*	11.c, 11.g, 11.k
Weak transitions	*trans*	11.c, 11.g, 11.k, 12.h
Weak conclusion	*conclusion*	12.j